ESSAYS ON DESCARTES' *MEDITATIONS*

PHILOSOPHICAL TRADITIONS
(formerly the MAJOR THINKERS series)

General Editor
Amélie Oksenberg Rorty

ESSAYS ON DESCARTES'
Meditations

Edited by Amélie Oksenberg Rorty

UNIVERSITY OF CALIFORNIA PRESS

BERKELEY   LOS ANGELES   LONDON

University of California Press
Berkeley and Los Angeles, California

University of California Press, Ltd.
London, England

Library of Congress Cataloging in Publication Data

Main entry under title:

Essays on Descartes' Meditations.

  (Major thinkers series ; 4)
  Bibliography: p.
  1. Descartes, René, 1596–1650. Meditationes de prima
philosophia—Addresses, essays, lectures. 2. First
philosophy—Addresses, essays, lectures. I. Rorty,
Amélie. II. Series.
B1854.E88   1986   194   85–8643
ISBN 0–520–05509–8 (alk. paper)

Printed in the United States of America

The paper used in this publication meets the minimum
requirements of American National Standard for Information
Sciences—Permanence of Paper for Printed Library Materials,
ANSI Z39.48–1984. ∞

Contents

Preface

Descartes urges his readers not to interpret the *Meditations* as a work composed of a set of separate and disjoined theses, but rather to follow him in his meditational exercises. He means to bring his readers to a realization of their essential natures: the exercises are to reveal the meditator's capacities, his power to avoid error and to discover truth. Descartes has weighty reasons for writing this book, and writing it in this way, not as a treatise in epistemology, or even as a treatise on the metaphysical foundation of science.

The bold confidence of Cartesian science is a manifesto of the Enlightenment as well as an assurance of the truth of a deductive theoretical physics. The method that founds this science, and that rules all its demonstrations, is simple and elementary. The reflective analysis by which the mind can discover its essence and demonstrate its own existence can also prove the existence of God and the truths of nature. Any attentive mind, capable of the kind of critical reflection required by the application of the law of noncontradiction in indirect proofs, can acquire scientific knowledge of the essence of Extension, the basic laws of nature. No authority, no revelation, no classical learning is necessary; only clarity, reflection, and carefulness are required. Not even Galileo made a claim as revolutionary as this. Like the Enlightenment programs that followed his epistemological revolution, Descartes' scientific projects might well be thought to have had profound political and theological consequences.

Whether Descartes saw these consequences and disguised his wel-
come, or whether he was not fully in a position to see what followed
from his epistemological revolution, is a matter for speculation. This
much is clear: he wrote the *Discourse on Method* to assure the enlightened that common sense is not undermined by the revision of
beliefs required by Cartesian science. Even if the analytic method has
a skeptical moment, it reconstructs rather than destroys ordinary beliefs about the physical world. Nor need it disrupt the order of daily
life or the order of political authority. Properly understood, the method
does not substitute one set of dogmas for another: because it provides
a test for the truth of its claims, it is both self-critical and constructive.

Having in mind Galileo's fate, Descartes is also eager to assure the
religious authorities that the central tenets of theology are not
threatened by the metaphysical system on which his revisionary anti-
Scholastic science rests. Indeed he wants to show that the very method
which establishes the validity of a deductive mathematical science of
the system of Extension is the method that can prove the existence
of God and the immortality of the soul—or, as he puts it in a somewhat
more modest passage, the distinctness of the soul from the body—on
the basis of natural reason alone. He has come, as he intimates in his
dedication of the *Meditations*, to "the most wise and illustrious Deans
and Doctors of the sacred Faculty of Theology in Paris," to fulfill the
Scholastic promise of unifying science and theology. But Descartes
did not cast his assurances in the form of classical meditations solely
to assure the theologians of his orthodoxy: he follows the authors of
the traditional meditations in wanting to transform his readers. It is
for this reason that he insists that the reader meditate with him,
bearing in mind the movement of the work as a whole. Like the
authors of traditional meditations, Descartes intends to free the reader
from illusion and falsity, and to bring him to a true understanding of
his place in God's creation. Certainly Descartes revises as well as uses
the meditational form. The reader comes to identify himself with his
capacities for rational thought rather than with his faith: the mind is
not part of the soul, but the whole of the soul which thinks. The God
to which the Cartesian meditator is brought is the guarantor of the
validity of rational argument. The structure of the *Meditations* is meant
simultaneously to reassure the Deans and Doctors of the Faculty of
Theology, and to assure the meditator that he can discover all the
necessary truths of nature by the simplest use of his own intellectual
powers, powers available to any mind capable of reflection.

The essays in this book are organized to follow the sequence of
Descartes' *Meditations* as closely as possible. The authors were asked

to focus on a set of specific texts in the *Meditations*, to analyze their functions in the meditational development of the work, bearing in mind the traditional form of the genre of such writing, as well as Descartes' rational revision of the meditational mode. Both Aryeh Kosman and Amélie Rorty discuss the structure of the work as a whole, focusing on the ways in which the reader is meant to be transformed by following the exercises and regimen presented in the text. They examine the role of the author as a director of a meditational exercise in effecting that transformation.

The next set of essays—those by Hatfield, Garber, Williams, and Matthews—focus on the first, or cathartic, stage of Descartes' Meditations. Gary Hatfield discusses Descartes' theory of perception, as it is developed in the catharsis of sensation in the First Meditation. He compares Platonic views on the relation between sensation and cognition with those Descartes presupposes in the *skepsis* of the First Meditation and those he explicitly develops in the *Optics* and the physiological works.

Daniel Garber analyzes the effect of the skeptical catharsis in Descartes' account of the relation between commonsense ideas of physical objects, clear and distinct philosophic ideas about the essence of Extension, and scientific theories about the nature of bodies. Michael Williams locates Descartes' use of skeptical arguments within the skeptical tradition; Gareth Matthews compares Descartes' treatment of the problem of other minds with that of Augustine.

E. M. Curley and Vere Chappell prepare the way for the movement from cathartic despair to analytic reconstruction. They analyze Descartes' theory of ideas, and the role that the criteria for clarity and distinctness play in the transition from the method of doubt to the method of analysis.

The essays by Carriero and Normore trace some of the influences on Descartes' arguments. John Carriero argues that the *cogito* argument shows Thomistic influence: its importance is not so much in its being a proof for the existence of the self as in its being a demonstration of the essence of the self, derived from its primary activities. Calvin Normore locates the medieval sources of Descartes' principles concerning formal and objective reality.

The papers by Loeb, Rodis-Lewis, Marion, Wilson, and Baier present analyses of the central sections of the *Meditations:* they examine the pivotal proofs for the existence of God. Louis Loeb argues that the proofs of the existence of God are not necessary to the foundation of a secure, demonstrative, mathematical science. Geneviève Rodis-Lewis discusses the relations among the various proofs for the existence of God offered in Meditations III and V. Jean-Luc Marion analyzes the meanings of the various "names" of God presented in the proofs, showing how Descartes used, but revised, medieval terms. Margaret Wilson examines the argument from infinity, and gives an account of Descartes' views on the indefinite and the infinite. Annette Baier evaluates the role of the idea of God in the transition from the cathartic to the reconstructive enterprises of the *Meditations.*

The papers by Bolton and Rosenthal focus on the moments of critical reflection: having assured himself of a God who certifies the truth of science, the meditator must explain the possibility of human fallibility. Martha Bolton analyzes the theory of error, and the role of the will in affirming confused and obscure ideas of sense. David Rosenthal examines the function Descartes assigns to the will in forming judgments: the conditions that assure the possibility of valid demonstration also explain the possibility of error.

The last set of essays—those by Lachterman, Ishiguro, Mattern, Schmitt, and Rorty—turn to the final task of the meditations, the reinterpretation and reconstruction of the physical world and the compound unity of mind and body. Lachterman gives an account the place of mathematics in Descartes' analysis of the essence of Extension and the proof of its existence. Hide Ishiguro compares the role of the laws of logic in Cartesian and Leibnizian proofs, and discusses their respective views on the role of mathematics in theoretical physics.

Ruth Mattern analyzes the account of physical objects presented in the Sixth Meditation, giving close attention to the relation between Descartes' reinstatement of the commonsensical ideas of physical objects and his characterization of the scientific idea of Extension. Frederick Schmitt gives an account of Descartes' foundationalism, distinguishing the principles of science presented in the Sixth Meditation from the substantive assumptions of theoretical physics. Amélie Rorty examines the role that the passions play in Descartes' account of the union of the mind and the body.

A. O. R.

Chronology

1596:   Descartes born in La Huaye, Touraine.
1606–1614:   Studied at the College de la Flèche.
1616:   Studied law at Poitiers.
1618–1619:   Volunteer in the Dutch and Bavarian armies.
1619:   The dream of a scientific philosophy.
1628:   Wrote *Regulae ad directionem ingenii* (published posthumously).
1633:   Galileo condemned.
1634:   *Le Monde et le Traité de l'Homme* (published posthumously).
1637:   *Discours de la Méthode; Optics, Geometry, Metereology.*
1641:   *Meditationes de Prima Philosophia in qua Dei existentia et animae immortalitas demonstratur.* This edition, containing the first six Objections gathered at Descartes' request by Father Pierre Mersenne, was published, along with Descartes' Replies, in Paris. A set of Seventh Objections and Replies was added to the second edition, published in 1642 by Louis Elzevir in Amsterdam. The French translation of the *Meditations* by the Duc de Luynes and that of the Objections and Replies by Clerselier, which appeared in 1647, were (with the exception of the Fifth Objections and Replies) revised by Descartes himself.
1644:   *Principia Philosophiae.*
1649:   Resident at the court of Queen Christina in Stockholm; *Les Passions de l'Âme.*
1650:   Died of pneumonia in Stockholm.

General Bibliography

The standard edition of Descartes' works is *Oeuvres de Descartes*, publies par Ch[arles] Adam et P[aul] Tannery (Vrin, 1957–1974). Vrin prints both the Latin and the French texts of the *Meditations*, Vols. VII and IX. References to this edition are abbreviated as AT. The edition and translation of Elizabeth S. Haldane and G. R. T. Ross, *The Philosophical Works of Descartes* (Cambridge: Cambridge University Press; reprinted 1969), is cited as HR. References to *Descartes: Philosophical Letters*, translated and edited by Anthony Kenny (Oxford: Clarendon Press, 1970) are standardly abbreviated as K. The *Discourse on Method; Optics, Geometry and Meteorology* was translated with an introduction by Paul J. Olscamp (Indianapolis: Bobbs-Merrill, 1965). The comprehensive bibliography of works on Descartes is Gregor Sebba's *Bibliographia Cartesiana* (The Hague: Nijhoff, 1964). For a sound and selective bibliography on Descartes after 1964, consult the bibliography in Margaret Dauler Wilson's *Descartes* (London: Routledge & Kegan Paul, 1978), pp. 245–250. See also the excellent bibliography gathered by Willis Doney, published in Michael Hooker's *Descartes: Critical and Interpretive Essays* (Baltimore: Johns Hopkins University Press, 1978). Another useful source is Stephen Gaukroger's collection, *Descartes: Philosophy, Mathematics and Physics* (Sussex, N.J.: Barnes and Noble, 1980).

1

The Structure of Descartes' *Meditations*

Amélie Oksenberg Rorty

"I . . . treat the whole of First Philosophy. . . . I would never advise anyone to read it excepting those who desire to meditate seriously with me, and who can detach their minds from affairs of sense and deliver themselves entirely from every sort of prejudice, I know too well that such men exist only in small number. But for those who, without caring to comprehend the order and connections of my reasonings, form their criticisms on detached portions arbitrarily selected, as is the custom with many, these I say, will not obtain much profit from reading this Treatise." (AT VII, 9–10)

"I rightly demand special attention on the part of my readers and have purposely chosen a special style of writing which I considered most suitable for this aim. . . . I think it quite fair to ignore altogether and despise as of no weight the criticisms of people who are unwilling to meditate with me and instead persist in holding their preconceived views. I know how difficult it is for anyone—even someone who gives it his full attention and who is really seriously trying to discover the truth—to keep before his mind the whole compass of my *Meditations* and at the same time grasp each part, both of which must, in my opinion, be achieved if the full point of my work is to be comprehended." (AT VII, 158–159)

The details of Descartes' directions and warnings to the reader indicate his sensitivity to issues of style and genre. His preoccupation with methodological issues, his attempts to formulate the rules governing stages of inquiry and demonstration, extend to a concern for issues of philosophical rhetoric. He is sensitive to the difficulties of addressing readers who are not yet convinced of the propriety of his methods of inquiry and demonstration. It is no accident that Descartes wrote in a remarkable variety of genres. We have *Regulae ad directionem in-genii* (1628), *Le Monde* (written in 1634, published in 1664), *Discours de la Méthode* (1637), *Meditationes de Prima Philosophia* (1641; the author-ized French translation was published in 1647); a posthumously pub-lished dialogue entitled *La recherche de la Vérité par la lumière naturelle*, *Les Principes de la Philosophie* (1644), *Traité des Passions de l'Âme* (written in 1645–1646; published in 1649). This variety attests to his experimen-tation with modes of philosophical exposition, with a series of distinc-tive voices and positions. Sometimes—as in the *Discours*—he writes in French for a more popular audience; sometimes—as in the *Regulae*—in Latin for learned scholars. Sometimes he writes in the first person to present an intellectual autobiography; sometimes—as in the *Traité des Passions*—he presents an impersonal analytic treatise. Sometimes he straightforwardly formulates rules for scientific thought. Some-times he carries the reader through a meditation designed to clear the mind of superstition and prejudice in order to bring it to a realization of its scientific powers. In such works, he is preparing the reader to follow the rules for scientific investigation, in the conviction that doing so ensures truth.

The *Meditations* is an artfully constructed work, following the struc-ture of the traditional meditational genre. That tradition is both ancient and varied. Descartes might well have had several quite different reasons for borrowing, conjoining, and transforming its diverse strands. The full title of his book intimates his intention to synthesize: *Meditations on First Philosophy*, not "Meditations on God's Creation" or "A Treatise on First Philosophy." Following Descartes' suggestion, I propose to read the *Meditations* as a work within the traditional meditational form, rather than as a treatise composed of a series of arguments. While some of the familiar objections to the "arguments" of the *Meditations*—particularly the various charges of circularity—lose their sting under such a reading of the *Meditations*, other, analogous problems arise, problems that are more central to Descartes' concerns and directions.

Although various species of meditations all bear the mark of their Stoic origins, Marcus Aurelius's book was originally called *Ton Eis Heauton Biblion*, "his book to himself." The tradition is reflexive as well as reflective: the author transforms himself by following a staged reflection, a self-reform through self-examination.[1] Though he writes for himself, the author intends to be read as a guide, if not also as a director. His reforming and reformed self are not uniquely his: they represent any and every mind capable of reflexive transformation. Along with set forms, meditational manuals feature set topics: the ego's relation to sense, imagination, its own body, and the physical world; the search for what is trustworthy, stable, and structured; the relation between the meditator's ideas of divinity and divinity itself, as well as the relation between divinity and cosmic order; the proper place of the essential self in that order. When these topics are treated attentively in a proper sequence with an appropriate regimen, true understanding has existential consequences: the self comes into its proper inheritance, its proper mode of existence.

The traditional meditational mode offers Descartes a number of distinct attractions. Because the reader must enact his own transformation, the meditational mode serves Descartes' antiauthoritarian purposes. Since that transformation involves a series of catharses of sensation, common opinion, and superstitious prejudice, it supports Descartes' provisional use of skepticism as a scourge of falsity. The introspective and reflective aspects of meditational exercises suit Descartes' program of examining confused ideas to discover the mind's clear and distinct innate ideas. And because such exercises are intended to strengthen the will and purify the understanding, they serve Descartes' constructive program of laying the foundations of proper science, the true understanding of the world.

But there are distinctive varieties of the meditational mode, differing in outcome, structure, and in the author's relation to the reader. A philosopher's choice among the varieties of meditations signals his conception of the nature of his philosophic enterprise. Some meditations are intended to effect a radical transformation in the meditator and his world. Everything in his world is meant to be affected by his transformation: his embodiment, his friendships, his practical and political life, his relation to divinity. In contrast to such revolutionary meditations, interpretive meditations bring the meditator to a new understanding of himself, the significance of his practices and convictions, but they leave everything—particularly practical and political matters—essentially unchanged. If seeing the world in a different light transforms a person, the meditator is changed; but the change is a change in his understanding of the significance of what he does rather than a change in what he does.

The Stoics were divided among themselves, and most were also divided in mind about whether meditational reflection could transform sensations and passions, practical and political life, or whether everything would—and should—be left unchanged save that it is understood anew. The inheritors of the Stoic tradition retain this ambivalence. Spinoza's *Emendation of the Human Understanding* is evasive on this issue, as is Freud's presentation of psychoanalysis as a form of the classical meditational exercise. Wittgenstein is singularly ambiguous on the issue of whether philosophical understanding transforms everything or leaves it exactly as it was. And Descartes, too, inherits this Stoic uncertainty: Does he leave his starting pont behind, or is it reinterpreted, transformed but not transcended? Or does he attempt to effect a compromise by transforming scientific understanding while leaving practical life intact? Scholastic science is demolished, replaced by an entirely new edifice constructed with new materials, on a new foundation. But practical matters, and moral and political life are to remain within the domain of common sense and common understanding. Yet this alternative also has its ambiguities. Descartes does not provide the theoretical structure for a distinction between scientific and practical understanding. His position is thoroughly evasive. On the one hand, practical matters are not to be disturbed by the method of doubt; on the other hand, common opinion represents confused ideas, just the sorts of ideas to which a scientific mind should give no credence.

There are other varieties of meditational writing: Both revolutionary and interpretive meditations can be ascensional, and both can be penitential. Ascensional meditations move the reader relatively smoothly, without reversals or turmoil, to a new mode of existence or to a new mode of understanding. Both revolutionary and interpretive ascensional meditations can be—as Stoic meditations tend to be—primarily intellectual. Others—those of neo-Platonic Christians like Saint Bonaventure and Cardinal Bellarmine—border on the celebratory and ecstatic.[2] The author of an ascensional meditation moves to self-realization through exhortation and admonition, celebration and prayer, but he does not suffer the dark night of the soul. Metaphors of light and illumination, clarity and precision of vision, are used with strongly heuristic intent. An intellectual ascensional meditation stresses the primacy of cognitive understanding in the gradual clarification of ideas, the individual mind's movement to innate truths reflecting the cosmic mind. Because the emphasis is on a step-by-step movement from confused to clear ideas, the will's rejection of falsity is relatively muted. Since falsity is regarded as stemming from confusion rather than from illicit assertion, the author-guide can illuminate the reader-meditator without demolishing his previous beliefs. Standardly, an ascensional meditation moves upward through a series of reflections: the meditator follows a practice or develops a train of thought that embeds a series of presuppositions. Reflection on his meditation—for instance, that the stages in the regimen of doubt presuppose that sensory and mathematical knowledge are distinguishable or that the capacity for reflection presupposes that remembering and perceiving are distinguishable—reveals a set of presuppositions that are (so to say) dramatically, or phenomenologically, demonstrated.

Though speaking to himself, the author of an ascensional meditation speaks to be overheard; his soliloquy and his conversation have the same voice and language. He is Everyman, marking the signposts of his journey for others to follow. Guide rather than director, he does not manipulate the stages of the reader's self-realization. The reflective reader will find the light of nature within himself; it is in him already, awaiting the turn of his attention. Parables, masks and unmaskings, indirections, ambiguities are unnecessary—all minds are implicitly united in *nous,* the cosmic mind. As we are all of one mind, the distinctions between reader and author, between the order of self-discovery and that of guidance, need not be rigidly enforced.

The intellectual ascensional mode has enormous attractions for Descartes. Its neo-Platonic echoes underwrite his conviction that mind contains the formulae of Extension. Since individual minds have these formulae among their innate ideas, they can turn to their real selves and return to their proper immortality in *nous* by scientific inquiry, following the light of nature. The lure of this mode is that it supports Descartes' claim that a meditator reflecting on the logical order of clear and distinct ideas must rationally believe that those ideas truthfully represent the ontological order that causes them. Reflective introspection and scientific investigation are one and the same enterprise. It is no incidental benefit of the ascensional mode that it is meant to assure the meditator of the immortality of his soul, even if it does not assure him of the immortality of his individuality. Nor is it an incidental benefit of the ascensional mode that it gives an account of an order of degrees of reality in a hierarchy that culminates in perfection.

In contrast to the ascensional meditational mode, the penitential mode places the author in a much more complex relation to his reader.[3] Because the penitent reader's condition is not merely confused but fallen, not merely mistaken but perverse, self-transformation requires more than the detached stance of an ascensional guide. It requires a director to manipulate a penitent's catharsis. When the reader-penitent is unaware of his fallen condition, he must first be brought to a state of despair. Saint Ignatius of Loyola instructs spiritual directors in the techniques of evoking penitential self-lacerating guilt and anguish.[4] The author of such a meditation is not just slightly further along the same path as the reader: he stands in a different place altogether, staging and directing as well as guiding. Because the director-author's understanding of what he says is radically different from that of the penitent, he must speak in parables, images, darkly with double meaning. The penitent undergoes ritual exercises, sensory deprivations, trials. Often there are three distinct positions and voices in such works: the author's training advice to the spiritual directors, speaking as a teacher; the spiritual director's commands to the penitent, speaking as a guarded authority; and the penitent's inner dialogue, speaking to himself with reproach and encouragement.

Like the ascensional mode, the penitential mode can be either revolutionary or interpretive; it can change the meditator's life or his understanding of his life. In the revolutionary mode, all the stages leading to the true self are transcended, the ladder is kicked away at the end. The new person bears no continuous relation to the old, not even to the self who undertook the penitential quest: everything about the past self, even his motives for seeking the Way, is suspect and must be abandoned. Even when such a penitential meditation is intellectual rather than passionate or spiritual, skeptical cleansing is only provisional. In the ascensional mode, skepticism can be abandoned once it has revealed itself to be self-destructive. But in the interpretive penitential mode, all stages of the penitential quest are preserved, perpetually reenacted. The mediating skeptical asepsis, the cleansing of error, is continuously required, even after the self is transformed, fully realized. Both ascensional and penitential meditations require complexity, if not actual division of mind. But there is an important difference between the two modes. An ascensional meditation requires only that the capacity for reflection includes the ability to discover the presuppositions implicit within the meditational movement, whereas a penitentional meditation also requires the capacity to disassociate from, and even to deny, beliefs that may persist even after the mediator realizes their falsity. (Someone who understands the laws of optics still experiences perceptual illusions, and so, too, someone who understands the epistemological status of confused ideas still finds herself inclined to assert them.)

Descartes is attracted to the penitential mode because it streses the activity of the will in rejecting error: the penitent detaches himself from his false beliefs by a series of exercises that reveal and strengthen the will. Ironically enough, this view is used to support the Enlightenment rationalism that emphasizes the autonomy of the individual inquiring mind. Descartes' critique of authoritarian and dogmatic establishments attracts him to those aspects of Augustinian theory which centralize the autonomy of the will as the condition for self-improvement and transformation. The mind's ability to free itself from error depends on the will's capacity to suspend judgments it had once affirmed. The movement from error to truth is discontinuous. The distance separating the author-guide from the reader-meditator, which is so distinctive of penitential meditations, reflects this discontinuity: the movement to truth requires a clearing of old rubbish to prepare the ground for a new foundation.

In addition to the ascensional and penitential meditational modes, Descartes also adopts a mode of analytic reconstruction, a logical analysis that begins by testing complex beliefs and dissolving them into their basic constitutive elements.[5] "I have used only analysis in my Meditations, which is the best and truest method of teaching. . . . Analysis shows the true way by which a thing is methodically discovered and deduced. . . . If the reader cares to follow . . . and pays attention to every point, he understands the matter no less perfectly and makes it his own as if he had discovered it himself" (AT VII, 155–156). The sequence of stages moves analytically to locate structural elements rather than to effect an ascension or a catharsis. The probing, testing movement from sensation to perception and perceptual memory, to commonsense beliefs, to physics, then to mathematics and on to theology ends in a self-certifying reflection. When the analysis reaches this indubitable and unanalyzable Archimedean pivotal point, the method becomes reconstructive and architectonic: the world is reconstructed from that point.

In an analytic meditation, skeptical arguments are probative and probationary rather than penitentially destructive. They do not lead to a cathartic expulsion of fallible beliefs. They are used to locate those irreducible and self-certifying beliefs that serve as the foundational basis for the reconstruction of scientific knowledge. Reflections on the ways that such truths are self-certifying—methodological analyses of the presuppositions and the logical structure of self-certifying arguments—do not add further premises to such arguments. Rather they explicate and articulate the implicit criteria that validate them. The presuppositions uncovered by analytic reflection on self-certifying truths reveal the criterion by which such truths are validated. Analysis discovers a self-evident truth; reflection on that truth uncovers the measure of its truthfulness. It is as if the analytic method could—by riding on the skepticism of a penitential meditation and the reflective unfolding of an ascensional meditation—find the standard meter, which then certifies itself as the appropriate unit of measure. Descartes' hope is that introspective analysis reveals the foundations of a deductive mathematics, which turns out to provide the foundations for an ontologically significant science that reveals the structure of the world.

Like the traditional meditation, the analytic-architectonic mode is meant to turn the soul and reconstitute the mind, freeing it from falsity and confusion. This turn of thought, that the analytic-architectonic mode is not only scientifically productive but also metaphysically validated, may well have struck Descartes with something of the force of divine revelation. It seemed natural to suppose that the analytic method could be combined—and indeed fused—with a traditional meditation, whose stages appear loosely isomorphic with those of an analytic inquiry. The analytic search for the elements of thought requires just the sort of probing, skeptical cleansing that traditional religious meditations require. Once the analytic elements of thought are discovered, more radical skeptical doubts appear: doubts that reproduce the moments of nihilistic despair in religious meditations. Analysis can discover the elements of thought; but, once they are discovered, there is a question about whether the elements of psychological thought are the elements of proper science, and whether the elements of a properly rigorous science are the elements of ontology. An analytic discovery of self-validating truths is parallel to the meditator's discovery that his despair is itself a sign of God's truth within him. Analytic reflection on the method that validates self-certifying truths reproduces the meditator's reflection that the stages of his meditation reveal both his finitude and his creator's benevolence. And, finally, in both the traditional meditation and in its analytic counterpart, the assurance of divine veracity is followed by a return of the world, a recovery of the reliability of knowledge. Of course the divinity that Descartes' analytic mode discovers is the God of the rationalists—to some no divinity at all—and the knowledge that is reaffirmed is scientific knowledge of the mathematical properties of Extension rather than the claims of faith. But still, Descartes speaks in his boldest and most confident tone in the analytic-architectonic mode. Yet that mode could not have stood on its own, validating itself: it rests on the practices of ascensional and penitential meditations and on the presuppositions embedded in the actual exercise of such meditations.

One of the attractions of combining the analytic-architectonic mode with traditional meditations is that it could provide Descartes with a way of transposing and using the sequence of a traditional meditation as a method for discovering the elements of thought. Once the foundational elements are identified, the traditional meditational mode provides an ontological ground that validates the use of an analytic method in mathematical physics. Descartes might well have hoped that grafting the analytic with the traditional meditations would enable him to use the advantages of each to provide needed support for the other. Descartes already knew he had a working deductive mathematical physics. He wanted a metaphysics and a theory of cognition that would support his physics: he wanted to legitimize introspective analysis as a method for discovering the epistemological elements—basic analytic self-certifying truths—that express and define ontologically basic elements. The reflective self-reformer engaged in intellectual catharsis is the ancestor of the author of *Der Logische Aufbau der Welt*, itself the first volume of a complete new science of the world, a science that is in principle available to Everyman.

The enlightenment resulting from an analytic-architectonic meditation offers further hidden practical and political benefits. Because its metaphysical elements and the rules for their combination are quite simple, the analytic-architectonic meditation is openly accessible. Only care, clarity, and reflection are required from the reader-meditator in order to reach truth. Despite Descartes' suspicion that very few will be able to read the *Meditations* with the care it requires, the confluence of the ascensional, the penitential, and the analytic modes of meditation promises equality of minds and the freedom of individual minds from mystification, established authority, and worldly power. Descartes wants the road to truth to be straightforward: because the directions are simple, they can in principle be followed even by the simple.

But wishing, even bold confident wishing, doesn't make it so. Descartes' stance to us, his readers, is most devious and controlling when he appears to speak with artless candor. His attempts to fuse the varieties of meditational modes, his use of a traditional religious form to transform his reader into a rational inquirer are hidden under the surface of what appears to be a straightforward expository argument. This indirection—his use of the associations and impetus of meditational writing—undermines his enlightenment enterprise. Descartes speaks with forked tongue. On the one hand, he assures us that there is no danger in following the method of doubt: it is a purely intellectual exercise that need not endanger practical, moral, or political life. On the other hand, in the preface of the French edition of the *Principles*, written six years after the *Meditations*, Descartes speaks of philosophy as a tree whose branches are medicine, morality, and mechanics: the fruits of his philosophy are, it seems, in action and in practical life. Does Descartes speak with forked tongue merely to assure his safety from the authority of the Church, while urging the reader to follow no authority but reason itself? Or does he really intend his enlightenment to remain purely intellectual, leaving authority and practice untouched?

If so, what would be the point of having a new mind in an old self? Descartes' new analytic mathematical physics can of course remain purely intellectual. But can the psychology and ontology that support it remain within the bounds of a purely intellectual enlightenment? How can his new metaphysics fail to challenge Scholastic doctrines, and consequently the power of Scholastic institutions? The crucial question is: What is to be taught in the Schools, the old authority or the new science? Because the old and the new are not compatible, Cartesian enlightenment cannot possibly remain purely intellectual: it must move to a reforming practice, if only of the curriculum of the Schools. It is not surprising that Descartes, writing in the shadow of Bruno and Galileo, could not write frankly. He may not himself have been fully aware of the extended ramifications of his intellectual revolution. Perhaps he had been so devious with his readers that he became devious with himself. Or perhaps his thoughts were not, after all, as transparent to his investigations as he believed.

I

The six staged days of the *Meditations* can be read as moments in an ascensional meditation, or as moments in a penitential meditation, or as stages in an analytic investigation. Each of these suggests a distinctive interpretation of the import of the stage, its function in the work of transforming the mind.

First, there is Descartes' embarrassing, presumptuous echo of the six days of Creation in the six stages of the *Meditations*. The new creation is the new science of the world: Meditation I begins by Descartes' separating the light of certainty from the darkness of confusion, and Meditation VI ends with an account of the composition of a man, a being composed of mind and body, a fallible but rational being. Although the stages of classical meditations vary depending on the significance of the writer's favorite mystical number (6, 7, 9, 10, or 12) they generally follow a standard form:

Stage 1:   *Catharsis*, detachment, or analysis: a movement from sensation to imagination and memory, to science and mathematics, to theology.

Stage 2:   *Skepsis*, despair, or nihilism.

Stage 3:   Reflection (*peripeteia*), a reflection that performs a revolutionary change.

Stage 4:   Recognition (*anagnorisis*) of the reflexive, corrective power of the will; the discovery of the law of noncontradiction as a methodological principle validating *reductio* arguments.

Stage 5:   Ascension from the psychological to the ontological order; proofs for the existence of God.

Stage 6:   Reconstruction of the world and the self.

The sequence of Descartes' *Meditations* clearly conforms to this traditional structure.[6] But since all the varieties of meditational modes follow the same stages, the structure of the *Meditations* does not by itself reveal Descartes' rationale for attempting to use, fuse, and transform the three varieties of meditational modes. While each stage can be read ascensionally, penitentially, and analytically, some stages are more hospitable to one mode of interpretation than to the others. Sometimes the modes pull in different directions, resisting Descartes' attempts to yoke them together.

Stage 1 most happily combines the three meditational modes in a mutually supportive reading. In an ascensional reading, the movement from sensations and perceptions to common beliefs about the physical world, to physics, to mathematics, then to logic and, finally, to theology is a movement from confusion to greater precision and clarity. Here Descartes is, of course, following a familiar Platonic movement of abstraction from the confusions of sensation to increasingly more powerful and more stable levels of explanation. Since the movement also presents skeptical arguments designed to perform a series of catharses of confused, dubitable ideas, it is crucial for Descartes to combine his adaptation of the Platonic movement with a penitential reading. He wants to set the stage for the realization that an ascension through a skeptical catharsis has been effected by the power of a free will, whose operations are independent of those of the understanding. The carefully staged sequence of skeptical doubts that moves from sensations through ordinary belief to mathematics also introduces distinctions central to an analytic reading of Stage 1. On the principle that whatever is distinguishable is distinct, the sequence of catharses shows that intellectual memory is independent of perceptual memory, that theoretical physics and mathematics are independent of common sense, that the law of noncontradiction is a formal principle independent of the particular contexts of its application, and that it is possible to affirm, deny, or refrain from judging the truth of the same idea. These basic distinctions and principles of analysis are introduced and embedded in the ordered sequence of an ascensional reflection and a penitential cleansing. Once such distinctions and principles are used in the meditational movement, the presuppositions implicit in their application can be uncovered by further ascensional reflection.

While this confluence of influence works very well for Stage 1, the varieties of meditational modes pull in different directions in Stage 2. In an ascensional reading, the moment of nihilistic despair can—for good reasons—only be a rhetorical trope. If skepticism really ends in nihilism, then even the reflection that skepticism and nihilism are self-destructive cannot be trusted. A fully despairing self cannot trust its Augustinian reflections that guilt and anguish presuppose and reveal a sound conscience and that the realization of error evinces an implicit criterion of truth. A fallen self that recognizes its condition may speak comfortingly to itself: but can it believe its own words of comfort? If the moment of reflection really does overcome the anguish of nihilism, then the moment of despair must have been superficial. If the idea of righteousness (and thus the possibility of righteousness) is implicit in the sense of guilt, and a criterion of truth is implicit in the recognition of error, then the stage of despair is only notional. Descartes must be evasive: he needs ascensional trust to support the reflections that move the soul out of despair. But if that ascensional trust is in working order, the tears of anguish were histrionic. Descartes trusts the force of ascensional reflection to reveal the presuppositions of the meditational exercises in order to overcome the complete despair of a strict penitential nihilism.

Stage 3, the stage of reflection, again nicely combines the three meditational modes. On an ascensional reading, reflection reveals the presuppositions of the lower levels, presuppositions which, when made explicit, bring the mind to a clearer and more powerful understanding. On a penitential reading, reflection is the moment of turning: the point at which the erring soul recognizes that its capacity to be aware of its errors reveals that it is using a criterion of truth, even if that criterion is not self-certifying. On an analytic reading, the stage of reflection articulates the criterion with which the meditator identifies self-certifying elements from which complex experience is constructed. The conclusion of this stage is, on all of the meditational modes, a modest one: there is no presumption that the criterion which reflection discovers is itself self-validating.

The fusion of the three meditational modes again becomes problematic in Stage 4. Combining the penitential and the ascensional modes introduces an assumption that would be illicit within an analytic-architectonic framework. Reflection on the structure of self-certifying truths and of the presuppositions embedded in the cathartic movements of Stages 1 and 2 reveals two working principles. One is a criterion of error: self-contradictory judgments are false. The other legitimizes constructive *reductio* arguments: a proposition can be proven true by showing that its negation leads to a contradiction. The penitential reading of this stage emphasizes the will's capacity to free itself from error, whereas the ascensional reading emphasizes the discovery of premises presupposed by the meditational exercises. (For instance, if it is possible to doubt the validity of sensory knowledge while not yet doubting that of mathematical truths, then the truths of mathematics are independent of those of sensation.) Fusing the ascensional and the penitential modes allows Descartes to think that he has legitimized *reductio* proofs by reflecting on the presuppositions embedded in his applying a criterion of error. Within a strictly penitential meditation, such a reflection at best reveals the structure and the psychology of a finite and untrustworthy mind. No validation of ontologically informative epistemological principles can follow solely from such phenomenologically bracketed reflections.

From the point of view of an analytic-architectonic, Stage 4 illicitly introduces a set of question begging assumptions. The will's capacity to suspend dubitable judgments is identified with its capacity to construct valid arguments. But in principle, at any rate, it might be possible for the will to recognize dubitable judgments and refrain from affirming them, without necessarily also having the capacity to preserve truth through valid arguments. It is one thing to recognize that the will has, and uses, the principle of noncontradiction as a criterion of error to identify dubitable judgments, and another to enlarge on the principle of noncontradiction to support constructive *reductio* arguments. The principle of noncontradiction does not by itself permit the detachment of a valid conclusion, affirming the truth of a proposition whose denial has proved contradictory. That the will can avoid error assures us that we need not be deceived by a malignant demon. But defeating the hypothesis of a malignant demon only establishes that we need not live in error. It does not yet establish that we can live in truth: what ensures freedom from error does not necessarily also ensure the validity of constructive proofs in science.

Superficially, the sequence of Meditation III and Meditation IV violates the stages of a classical meditation. On an analytic reading of Meditation III, Descartes seems to present proofs for the existence of God before he has validated the modes of demonstration used in the proofs. He seems to move from the psychological order of ideas arranged in a hierarchy according to degrees of perfection (measured by an ascensional criterion of explanatory independence and perfection) to ontological conclusions about the existence of the causes of those ideas. On such an analytic reading, the proofs for the existence of God illicitly introduce new, ungrounded principles and premises required to warrant detaching existential conclusions from psychological premises. The principles that would, if anything does, legitimize such inferences are not introduced or established until Meditations IV and V.

The charitable reading of Meditation III is ascensional and penitential. On this reading, Meditation III does not offer any ontologically significant proofs that detach existential conclusions from the psychological or even the logical order of ideas. On such a reading Meditation III presents a phenomenological explication of the presuppositions and the structures of the meditator's system of ideas. Ontological conclusions are bracketed: they are conclusions about what the meditator must *posit* as existing.

At the beginning of Meditation III, Descartes has three tasks before him. First, he must show that the hypothesis of a deceptive demon is incoherent. Second, he must show that a meditator who has followed the argument to this stage does in fact implicitly have the idea of a being more perfect than himself; if he can rank ideas by their degrees of perfection, he also has an idea of a most perfect being. Third, he must show that such a meditator cannot conceive himself to be the cause of his idea of a perfect being. Without having established the propriety of *reductio* arguments, Descartes cannot, and does not, attempt to provide any ontological proofs for the existence of this most perfect being.

In order to move to the ratification of *reductio* proofs, two further steps are required. Descartes must overcome the penitential hypothesis of a malignant deceiver, and he must discover the principle that expresses the causal order implicit in the hierarchical ordering of ideas according to their degree of explanatory independence and perfection. Any meditator who supposes that there might be a malignant deceiver has a criterion by which he identifies dubitable ideas. Since he is also manifestly capable of refusing to affirm such dubitable ideas, he is not a plaything of a deceptive demon . . . or, at any rate, he need not be. Such a meditator may have been deceived into thinking that he *had*, as he supposes, followed the meditational regimen. But if he is *really* capable of considering that doubt, then he is indeed capable of identifying dubitable ideas. So the hypothesis of a malignant deceiver is self-defeating as a *hypothesis:* it is incoherent. Might there nevertheless *be* such a malignant demon, even though no meditator can coherently conceive his existence? Perhaps; but even that hypothesis—that what is inconceivable may nevertheless exist—is incoherent. On an ascensional reading of Meditation III and IV, the idea of *truth* operates *within* the system of ideas. The refutation of a malignant demon is—in the terminology of phenomenological interpreters of Descartes—ontologically bracketed.

By Meditation III, then, the meditator has been shown to be fallible, finite, and imperfect. He could not therefore himself have produced a principle by which the rationality of inferences is tested. A fallible being could not have invented or created a criterion for identifying confused or dubitable ideas. But since the meditational exercises dramatically show that the meditator does in fact have, and can appropriately apply, such a principle—the principle that self-contradictory ideas are, at the very least, dubitable—the meditator manifestly has and uses a principle of which he could not have been the adequate cause. He may be fallible, but if he is able to recognize his fallibility, he is also rational. The penitential reading of Meditation III is negative: it shows the fallibility of the meditator. An ascensional reading unfolds a constructive premise: reflection on the success of the meditational exercise reveals that a meditator who successfully applies a criterion of error is rational, at least in the minimal and negative sense that he need not be deceived and make false judgments.

Still, since the meditator is fallible, he cannot have been the cause—the adequate explanation—of his rational powers to identify dubitable ideas. Reflecting on capacities that he could not have granted to himself, he must at least have the idea of a being more perfect than himself, upon whom his rational capacity to identify error depends.

With this argument, Descartes has fulfilled the task set by Stage 3. The argument that overcomes the hypothesis of a malignant demon also establishes that the fallible but rational meditator must have an idea of a perfect being; furthermore, he must also know that he cannot be the cause of his idea of a perfect being. Such a penitential and ascensional reading of Meditation III frees it from the charge of drawing illicit conclusions, conclusions affirming the necessary existence of entities beyond the system of ideas. Even the principle of adequate causation only establishes a hierarchical ordering of ideas. On such a reading then, Meditation III is not an interpolation of Stage 5 before Stage 4: rather it is a preparation for Stage 4, which articulates the conditions that legitimate constructive, as well as *reductio* arguments.

The three modes of meditation again support each other in Stage 4, Meditation IV. On an ascensional reading, the reflective meditator articulates the presuppositions of his rationality, his ability to avoid error. His ability to suspend his judgment, to detach assent from dubitable ideas that he continues to entertain, reveals that he has at least two independent intellectual faculties, neither fallible in itself. The understanding is not fallacious: it merely entertains ideas without affirming their truth; and the will need not assent to unclear, confused, or incoherent ideas. It can refrain from affirming what is dubitable. On a penitential reading, Stage 4 establishes that the will can suspend judgment from error and falsity. On an analytic reading, this stage establishes the independence of propositional contents from propositional attitudes: it assures the identity of propositional content through changes in propositional attitudes. On all three readings, the rationality of the meditator is shown to be secure. Not only is he capable of successfully applying the criterion of error, but, more significantly, there is nothing within his psychological structure that makes him prone to error. He is indeed fallible, and thus imperfect; but he is not necessarily prone to fallacious reasoning, and thus doomed to imperfectibility. Stage 4 implicitly establishes another principle. It is not ideas as such, but only affirmative or negative judgments that are true or false. Truth and falsity are attributed to judgments rather than to ideas or to the referents of ideas.

Stage 5 again presents difficulties in determining the order of dominance among the various meditational modes. In Stage 5, Descartes attempts to move from the psychological to the ontological order, from the idea of perfection to a demonstration that such a perfect being exists. Having moved from a purely psychological order to a logical and rational order, the meditator is now meant to move outside the order of ideas. Phenomenology is meant to establish the propriety of a realistic ontology. As it stands, the principle of adequate causation only establishes that a meditator must have an idea of a perfect being. From Meditation IV, he also knows that, imperfect as he may be, he is not so constructed that he must be mistaken. In principle, then, he ought to be able to trust his use of the criterion of error. Stage 4 was meant to prepare the way for the transition from a purely negative use of *reductio* arguments in identifying dubitable ideas to their constructive use in establishing valid conclusions. But it is one thing to doubt the truth of a self-contradictory proposition, and another to affirm the truth of a proposition whose denial is self-contradictory.

Even though the three meditational modes coincide in Meditation IV, Meditation III does not support an analytic reading. The premises it provides for Meditation V remain within the system of the meditator's ideas. Nothing in an ascensional or a penitential reading establishes the propriety of moving from a negative to a positive use of *reductio* arguments using the principle of adequate causation ontologically (to demonstrate the existence of a perfect being) rather than psychologically (to show that a finite meditator cannot consistently deny the existence of a perfect being). As many commentators have argued, using constructive *reductio* arguments to detach the conclusion of an ontological proof presupposes the existence of just the perfect being that it is meant to establish.

These criticisms only affect Descartes' attempt to fuse the analytic with ascensional and penitential meditational modes. They do not, by themselves, invalidate reading the analytic mode as contained within ascensional and penitential meditations. On such a reading, the ontological proof is itself bracketed. It does not move the meditator from the system of his ideas to a wholly independent realm. Rather it explicates the consequences of the meditational exercise. Not only does the meditator necessarily have an idea of a perfect being, but his idea of that being is necessarily an idea of a being whose existence must be conceived by him as necessary. Nor can the meditator conceive the possibility that the world might be otherwise. He cannot suppose that a perfect being may not exist.

If the fusing of analytic with ascensional and penitential modes was meant to establish the validity of a realistic ontology that starts entirely within a psychological and a logical order, the meditations have failed. This would be a reading that places ascensional and penitential meditations within the structure of an analytic-architectonic. If the Meditations are read as a sequence of logical arguments, they do not establish a detachable conclusion. On another interpretation—an interpretation that places the analytic modes within the framework of ascensional and penitential meditations—the Meditations do not form a sequence of arguments validating a detachable ontological conclusion. On such an interpretation, the meditations have succeeded in bringing the meditator to a new place. Starting from a set of dogmatic confusions, he has gradually been brought, step by step, to realize the power and structure of his mind. In a way, Descartes has after all fulfilled his promise to the Doctors of Divinity at the University of Paris. He has shown that someone who has followed his meditation must acknowledge that there are rational arguments for the separability of the soul from the body. Such a meditator must also acknowledge that he exists as a rational being, and that such a rational being must, in accordance with his rationality, think that God necessarily exists. On this interpretation, the task of the meditational exercises has succeeded.

It would be pretty to think that the *Meditations* is itself a structured transformation of the meditational mode, starting with the dominance of intellectual ascensional mode, moving through the penitential form, and ending with the analytic mode. Unfortunately, the text does not sustain such an easy resolution to our problems. Instead we see that different modes seem dominant at different stages: their subterranean connections and relations remain unclear.

We could try a nesting of mask, face, and skeleton in Descartes' use of these traditions. He may have unself-consciously inherited an ascensional skeletal structure, fleshed it with the musculature of an analytic meditation, and masked it with a penitential meditation for the sake of safety in orthodoxy. But the penitential mode cannot be unmasked: it provides essential skeletal support. And, as we have seen, the analytic flesh does not always conform to the articulation of an ascensional skeletal structure.

The problem is that the various readings subtly undermine one another. There are solid clues for reading the composition of the work: there are in fact too many. The work we see when we use some of these clues is quite different from the work we see when we follow others. Did Descartes do this deliberately? An extremely charitable reading would turn him into a new sort of Socrates, constructing puzzles to force us to examine the truth of his dialectical arguments. But whatever else Descartes may be, he is not Socrates. He is defensive as well as devious, proud as well as prickly. And he is not funny.

II

But the six days of the *Meditations* does not really end Descartes' work. We might ask: What is the beginning, middle, and end of the book? Is *Meditations on First Philosophy* really just the core six days? Or does it include the prefatory dedication and the synopsis as essential parts? And, crucially, what about the objections gathered and presented to Descartes by his friend Mersenne? At Descartes' suggestion, six of these objections were printed, together with Descartes' replies, in the first edition of the work. Does the *Meditations* properly contain the Objections and Replies?[7]

I think it does. The core six days of the *Meditations* can profitably be read as providing a transition from Descartes' arrogant, courtly obeisance to the Doctors of Theology at the University of Paris, to whom the work is addressed, to Descartes' real audience, his correspondents—opponents and friends alike—engaged in argument and debate. To be sure, Descartes grants himself the last word, at least in his published work.

Like the core days of the meditation, the preface, and the postscript Objections and Replies, are themselves transformations of traditional genres. The preface combines a religious with a secular dedication. It acknowledges authority but promises, with breathtaking presumption, to provide the rational proofs that had eluded the theologians, proofs for the existence of God and for the immortality of the soul (or, at any rate, its separability from the body), to be given without assumptions borrowed from faith, authority, or tradition, and without any metaphysical devices. But, as we have seen, Descartes did, after all, rely on tradition, and not only on a literary tradition but on the pre-suppositions embedded in that tradition. However self-conscious he may have been about manipulating those traditions, he was not prepared to admit what he had done. How could the confident Enlightenment architect consider himself a manipulative spiritual director?

The Objections and Replies are themselves transformations of a tradition. His interlocutors are not invented to present roles in a fixed intellectual drama. Unlike Plato, he does not put words in the mouths of well-known historical figures. Descartes invites his opponents to speak for themselves, in their own words, for as long as they like: not a constructed dialogue but a genuine correspondence. Nor does he edit his interlocutors—not a Thommistic snippet *Sed Contra* followed quickly by a *Responsio*. Nor does he present a showy dialectical *Disputatio*, with a *defendens* and *impugnans*. Rather he asks respected fellow scholars to present him with their criticisms. Their objections and his replies are published together; readers can weigh and consider the merits of the arguments in privacy and at their leisure rather than immediately, at a public event. That Descartes is sometimes testy, often evasive, and certainly defensive shows the voice of the individual person, not of the mind. It may be a defect of character, but it is not a defect of the genre.

Read in this way, the *Meditations* has a surprise ending. Descartes intended to construct science from the refined, tested, proved truths that survived skeptical dissolution. But examining the Objections and Replies gives us quite a different picture of that science. It is not an isolated meditator's reflective analytic and foundational architectonic but the published correspondence of a group of debaters animated by mutual respect. In truth, then, the *Meditations* in its final printed form moves us from a world of prefaces addressed to doctors of divinity to a world defined as a community of philosophers and scholars. The meditator's reflective self-transformation from a confused believer to a rational scientific inquirer provides the transition between those two worlds.[8]

NOTES

1. See Louis L. Martz, *The Poetry of Meditation: A Study in English Religious Literature* (New Haven, Conn., 1969) and Pierre Pourrat, *Christian Spirituality*, trans. W. H. Mitchell and S. P. Jacques (London, 1928–1936); Lewis Beck, *The Metaphysics of Descartes* (Oxford, 1965).

2. Bonaventure, *Itinerarium Mentis in Deum*, trans. P. Boehner (New York, 1956) and Robert Bellarmine, *The Ascent of the Mind to God by a Ladder of Things Created*, trans. TB (London, 1928).

3. See Saint Bernard of Clairvaux, *Saint Bernard, His Meditations; or: Sighes, Sobbes and Teares . . . Also His Motives to Mortification*, trans. W. P.; and *The Twelve Degrees of Humility and Pride*, trans. Barton R. V. Mills (London, 1929).

4. See St. Ignatius of Loyola, *The Spiritual Exercises of Loyola*, trans. W. H. Longridge (London and Oxford, 1950).

5. Cf. E. M. Curley, "Analysis in the *Meditations*," this volume.

6. These six stages do not exactly correspond to the six meditations. For instance, Stage 2 begins towards the end of Meditation I, roughly at AT IX, 17, and stops a few paragraphs after the beginning of Meditation II, roughly at AT IX, 19. Although Stages 4, 5, and 6 correspond roughly to Meditations IV, V, and VI, Stage 3 begins in Meditation II, at roughly AT IX, 19, and extends to the end of Meditation III, AT, IX, 42. I know of no explanation of the rationale for the breaks in the meditational days, no explanation of why they do not always correspond to what might seem to be the natural standard psychological stages. Descartes certainly meant his reader to pause between each meditational day. Understanding the rationale of the form of each day would require an extended comparative study of the variations among the traditional meditations. I suspect that spreading Stage 2 between Meditations I and II is a way of diminishing its importance, indicating that there cannot be a moment, or stage, of "pure" skeptical despair. The large scope of Stage 3 indicates the far-reaching character of the reflective revolution: besides locating the pivotal point in the demonstration of the existence of the thinking substance, Stage 3 requires an investigation into the real character and significance of the meditator's ideas of himself, his body, his world.

7. The author of the First Objections is Caterus, a theologian from Alkmaar; the Second Objections were probably written by Mersenne and by Gibieuf, the Third by Hobbes, the Fourth by Arnauld, the Fifth by Gassendi, the Sixth by de la Barde and some mathematician friends of Mersenne, the Seventh, called the *Sixth* after Gassendi's objections were withdrawn, were by the Jesuit Bourdin. Because Gassendi had complained at the publication of a private communication, Descartes omitted the Fifth Objection from the first French edition of the *Meditations*. He was careful to make public his reasons for doing so. He remarks that Gassendi had expanded his objections "into a book of great size" containing further objections responding to his replies.

8. An earlier draft of some sections of this essay appeared as "Experiments in Philosophic Genre: Descartes' *Meditations*" in *Critical Inquiry*, Autumn, 1983. I am grateful to Rüdiger Bittner, John Etchemendy, Victor Gourevitch, and Robert Wengert for discussions and comments. Reading Gary Hatfield's essay (in this volume) further clarified some ideas.

2

The Naive Narrator: Meditation in Descartes' *Meditations*

L. Aryeh Kosman

We sometimes remember, though perhaps not often enough, that Descartes' *Meditations* is not merely a treatise or a discourse but a set of meditations or, as I shall here suggest, the narrative account of a set of meditations. But what are we to make of this formal and stylistic fact about the *Meditations*? In this essay, I will begin by outlining very briefly some thematic respects in which the fact that the *Meditations* consists of meditations may be of interest. Then I will consider what might seem a more purely stylistic feature of the work, and what, if anything, we might learn from it.

THE *MEDITATIONS* AS MEDITATIONS

To begin, then, let us consider some obvious respects in which the fact that a work is entitled *Meditations* should affect the ways in which we think about it. In the first place, a meditation is a spiritual or mental exercise that must be gone through by anyone who wishes to benefit from it; there is no detachable product in which a meditation results that could be acquired by someone who has not been through the meditation's actual praxis. For a meditation just is a praxis, and not the making of some alienable product.

The *Meditations*, then, if it consists of meditations, consists of a series of philosophical exercises to be gone through, and not merely a series of philosophical arguments and conclusions that can be appropriated by any simple theoretical understanding. This is the very reason that Descartes gave, in his reply to Mersenne, for having written meditations in the first place.[1] The reader is carefully advised of this fact in the *Meditations'* prefatory remarks; the author doesn't expect that there will be many readers of his book; "on the contrary," he writes, "I counsel no one to read this work, except those who are willing to meditate seriously with me."[2] This is merely to generalize what Étienne Gilson and others have recognized about the First Meditation—that it is "not so much a theory to be understood as an exercise to be practiced."[3]

Second, we need to remember that Descartes was not the first person to write a work consisting of, or in some other way intimately involved with, meditations. There was by the time of the appearance of the *Meditations* an established and rich genre of meditational writing.[4] The location of a work like the *Meditations* within such a stylistic genre emphasizes the ways in which, and the degree to which, the work concerns itself with the themes characteristic of that genre.

One of the characteristics of the genre of meditational literature is that it is about reflexive awareness, about self-consciousness and self-examination.[5] The *Meditations* therefore announces itself as a work within that reflexive tradition, as a work about self-discovery and self-knowledge. That it is within the tradition of meditational literature keeps this fact focused for us, in case we should ever be tempted to suppose that it is simply a work about skepticism or foundationalism or any other epistemological (or ontological) issue cast solely in "impersonal" terms. Here the central issues must remain self-knowledge, self-consciousness, subjectivity: those issues traditionally central in so much of meditational literature.

Equally important is the fact that the tradition of meditational literature concerns itself with exercises designed to effect the purification and eventual salvation of the meditator. One should expect that Descartes' *Meditations* will somehow concern the same theme. Of course the salvation at work here is in some sense more "philosophical" than that of the standard meditational treatise; one might think of the *Meditations* as an essay on epistemological salvation.

The *Meditations,* of course, is not in any simple sense "about" the themes prominent in the tradition of meditational literature; for it is in an important sense a revisionary essay, an essay in which the author appropriates a genre by taking over elements of its style and traditional concerns, but reforms that style and reshapes those concerns. Here, as I've suggested, Descartes replaces traditional themes with, for example, the theme of epistemic salvation. The hero of our meditations is cleansed of error and doubt, not (simply) of sin, and, on one reading at least, "logodicy" replaces theodicy as a central issue: the justification of reason to man, in the face of dubitability.

The revisionary nature of the *Meditations* is evident in the way in which Descartes begins by undoing the hold that the tradition exercises over the thinker.[6] This undoing takes place both at the level of the internal argument of the *Meditations*—in the story, so to speak, that it tells—and at the stylistic or discursive level of the work. So the philosopher begins by emptying himself of all belief, but really so as to empty the demon deceiver of his power. He accomplishes this by withholding from the objects of his consciousness the judgment that pronounces them true or false, thereby reducing them simply to representations. The demon is thus robbed of his power by the exercise of *epokhe*, by the deceptively simple act of refusing to believe that of which one is aware; this holding in consciousness that from which at the same time one withholds assent is central to what's going on in the *Meditations*.

At the same time an analogue of this process is at work at the discursive level: for as the first act of the narrator is to empty himself of all prior belief, so the first act of the writer is to empty himself of the prior philosophical and meditational tradition. But just as the narrator empties himself, not by struggling against his beliefs, but by holding them without assent, so the mode in which Descartes refuses the power of the prior tradition is not in an act of radical (that is, mere) repudiation, but in the more truly liberating act of transformative repetition.

In any case, even revisionary appropriation is, after all, an act of appropriation. Rejection itself is a form of stylistic and conceptual *praeteritio*, for it is impossible to reject a tradition without in some sense invoking it. And this is especially true when the movement of rejection is, as it were, double, that is, when the rejection takes the form of imitation. There is, in short, no way to escape a tradition, only ways to create new and descendant traditions. And, in this case, the recognition of the fact that traditional meditative literature and Cartesian meditative literature are "isomorphic," and the understanding that religious salvation and epistemic salvation are versions of a deeper structure of salvation, are important and of interest. Equally important, when we begin to think of the *Meditations* in the context of a traditional meditative literature, is the fact that we might be led thereby to think anew about what the central philosophical claim of the *Meditations* is.

THE *MEDITATIONS* AS FICTIONAL MEDITATIONS

These are among the themes that I hope will be further illuminated, if somewhat obliquely, by the consideration of what may be thought of as a more literary point about the *Meditations*. A meditation, in the primary sense, is the action of a human being, an instance of a person meditating. Written works within the meditative tradition are thus standardly treatises on meditation, or instructions on how to meditate. "Every meditation is a thought," as one important early meditative treatise put it.[7] There is, of course, a secondary sense in which a piece of discourse—a written work or a speech—which is "of a meditative character" might be said to be a meditation.[8] But this sense is clearly derivative; a written work is called a meditation because it recounts or records or projects an act (real or imaginary) of meditation. So James Hervey opens his *Meditations Among the Tombs* by describing to the Lady to whom he addresses the work how, while traveling one evening through a Cornwall village, he "could not avoid falling into a train of meditations," which he hopes will be of interest "now they are recollected and committed to writing."[9]

A work entitled *"Meditations . . . "* (for example on hobbyhorses or first philosophy) is thus like a work entitled "Conversations . . . " (on country paths or the good life) or like a work entitled "Dialogues . . . " (on natural religion or two new sciences). A work is called a dialogue because it recounts or represents or reproduces a dialogue that took place, or is imagined as taking place, among the work's characters. So a written work called a meditation is only called so derivatively; it is a representational account or description of that which is a meditation in the strict and primary sense.

Indeed, meditational works are even more clearly representational in this sense than are works that are styled "Dialogues" or "Conversations." For a dialogue may be mimetic in the sense that what it reproduces is a piece of discourse like itself, and so it may imitate that of which it tells. But a piece of discourse cannot imitate a meditation any more than it can imitate a landscape or an action; here it can only describe or narrate.[10] We may think of a written work capable of being mimetic in this sense as an inscription, and a work that is not as a description. A written dialogue inscribes a spoken dialogue through an act of mimesis; the one discourse imitates the other. But since a meditation is an act of thought or contemplation, it cannot be inscribed in a written meditation, but only described by it.

Descartes' *Meditations* is thus a descriptive or, we might even say, a narrative work; for it provides us with a narrative account of a series of meditations undertaken by someone identified only as "I." It is the referent of this "I" (whom we might call the meditator) who meditates throughout the *Meditations,* and who at the same time graciously provides us with a running, simultaneous narrative of his meditations. We ought, as I shall argue in a moment, to identify the narrator-meditator with Descartes the author only in a limited and most carefully thought-out sense. And in the same way, we ought not to assume that there are before us when we read the *Meditations* any real meditations in the primary sense; what we have is a representational account of the meditator-narrator's meditations. In this sense, the meditations within Descartes' *Meditations* are "fictional," where "fictional" does not mean untrue, but merely represented.

THE *MEDITATIONS* AS A BOOK OF MEDITATIONS

Consider, however, this argument, which suggests that although the distinction between inscription and description may be an interesting one, it does not really apply in the case of the *Meditations.* A difference is marked, in the meditative tradition itself, between contemplation and meditation; meditation is a discursive activity, like argument or analytic reasoning, which results in a contemplative state.[11] It is the contemplative state that we might think cannot be reproduced in a system of signs, and so cannot be imitated purely but only represented; but a meditation, as a discursive act, can be represented in much the same way that a speech can. So it is that the contemplation that occurs at the end of the Third Meditation is not recounted in the text of the *Meditations,* precisely because it is not discursive and therefore cannot be imitated in a work, but must happen as it were, offstage. The meditations of the *Meditations,* however, can be imitated, and so they are like a dialogue that can be inscribed, rather than merely described.

The fact that a meditation may be discursive is related to a further consideration. The term *meditation* can refer not only to an act of meditating but also to the internal object of such an act, or to a written account of such an object. *Meditation,* in other words, is like *prayer;* a book of prayer is after all a book of prayers, and not a narrative account of people praying. It may be a manual for prayer, or an instruction on how to effect prayer, but it is such because it consists of a series of individual, written prayers. Just so a book called *Meditations* may consist of individual, written meditations.

What this means is that *prayer* and *meditation* have complex senses, like the words *narrative* and *narration;* a considerable literature in narratology has made familiar to us the fact that *narrative* may refer (a) to the act of narrating or (b) to what is narrated in the course of such an act or (c) to the narrative statement, that is, the oral or written discourse in which or with which the act is performed. Let us call these, respectively, following some theorists, (a) *narration,* (b) *story,* and (c) *discourse.*[12] The distinction marked by these terms is not limited to narration, but may be applied generally to a range of actions that we perform in or with language. So a prayer may be (a) an act of praying or (b) what is prayed or (c) the piece of discourse with which one prays; and similarly a meditation may be (a) an act of meditating or (b) what is, so to speak, meditated—the internal object of the act of meditation—or (c) the discourse in which the meditation is performed.

This distinction between story and discourse will prove interesting in what follows for other reasons, and it shows how misleading is the picture given in the previous section. But it does so merely in that it makes sense of the fact that a written work itself might be called "meditations," and shows why a work called by that title is more like one titled "Dialogues on Doubt" than like one titled "The Epistemic Adventures of R. D." It shows, in other words, that a meditation may be thought of as a written work, and not simply what a written work describes. It does not show, however, that a meditation might be, in the sense I've suggested, purely mimetic. When, in the Book of Samuel, Hannah prays, the section is sometimes called "Hannah's prayer." But it's not the book that's praying, it's Hannah, and so her prayer is still "fictional" in the special sense I have here introduced, even if the object prayer can be inscribed and not merely described. The meditations of Descartes' *Meditations,* then, are, in this special sense, the fictional meditations of the person who is described as meditating in the course of the work.

So a meditation—that is, a written work that is entitled "Meditation"—is not purely mimetic, but is representational. As a result, we are not presented with the actual, primary meditation, but with a written account of it. But I have now suggested an alternative way to read the notion of a meditation and, historically, there appeared early on a literary form called a "meditation," as though there were a desire to purify the form of its representational quality, and return it to mimesis, constituting the meditation as itself a literary form.

Where in all this is Descartes' work? Notice how the answer to this question is unclear, and how the *Meditations* straddles, as it were, the two forms of being a meditation. On the one hand, the *Meditations* is clearly descriptive: it is addressed to the reader, as though relating to the reader prior and independent meditative acts. The reference at the beginning of the Second Meditation to "yesterday's meditation [*hesterna meditatione*],"[13] like the talk in general of the particular days of meditation, indicates that reference throughout the work is to such meditations of which the written work is an account. And in general, we feel as readers as though something is being described to us, as though we were reading the narrative account of a series of meditations. In that sense, the work is a representational description of a series of fictional meditations.

But at the same time, the *Meditations* itself insists in a number of ways on its own autonomy and meditative priority; the text demands to be read not simply as an account of Cartesian meditation but as in some sense the locus of that meditation and its vehicle. So the descriptive account, just as it is a first-person account, is strikingly in the present tense, as though to effect in these ways an identity between narrative and narrated; we are made to feel constantly in the presence of the meditation, as though the meditation actually were the narrative account being given of it.

STORY AND DISCOURSE IN THE *MEDITATIONS*

So the distinction between the senses of "meditation," which I have associated with the distinction between story and discourse, signals a complexity in the literary structure of the *Meditations*, a complexity that has so far seemed to be about the relation between the reported meditation and, as it were, the meditative reporting.

This distinction between story and discourse, between the narrated and the narrative in which it is narrated, may strike us as an inappropriate, or at least an evasive, distinction to draw in "nonliterary" texts, in texts of philosophy for example, or theology. We might be tempted to think that it is precisely a difference between literary and nonliterary texts that the distinction can be made in the former but not in the latter. But this may be wrong; the truth may be that the distinction in fact can be made in "nonliterary" texts, but that we have not yet understood how to make it. We may need still to understand what is the analogue of the story in such cases, and what is the relation in these cases between discourse and story.

In some philosophical texts, the writings of Plato for example, the task is made relatively easy by the dramatic or narrative form that the work takes. The *Republic*, for example, lends itself easily to the question: How is the political constitution in the story amplified, qualified, undermined, or whatever, by what goes on in the political development at the dramatic surface of the dialogue? But even in this case, since it is discourse that is being narrated, there is another layer that has to be understood, a nested narrative within a narrative. And the last "narrative" is not a standard narrative, for the story it tells is not of historical events, but of the eternal structures of being, understanding, the good, and so forth.

In the same way, we may uncover several levels in the *Meditations*: the deepest story is that purely theoretical story of self, idea, world, and God, which the first level of meditation tells; that discourse, in turn, is itself related in the meditative telling that is the narrative text of our *Meditations*. It would be an interesting exercise in the analysis of philosophical discourse to spell out the relationships among these levels. We might consider, for example, the complex relationships between the times of the narrative and the times of the story it tells. Such an analysis is often fruitful in narratology;[14] for in narratives, and particularly in novels, which have been a central subject of much of the sort of analysis I'm speaking of, time is of central importance. In philosophical texts, however, this may be a less significant feature, and other relations between story and discourse will prove more interesting. These will remain, however, relations in language—in mood, point of view, and so on—which signal the fundamental relationship, built directly into the very structure of language itself, between, on the one hand, the speaker and the speaker's speaking and, on the other, that of which the speaker speaks.

THE STORY OF THE *MEDITATIONS*

One story we might tell ourselves about what happens in the *Meditations* is the following: for many years a man has been troubled by how much of what he believed to be true has turned out to be false, and by the consequent uncertainty and doubt that have resulted as a consequence. One day, therefore, he sets about to restructure completely his system of beliefs in such a way that he will be able to believe only what he knows with certainty to be true. This feat he accomplishes by doubting everything that he has once believed, in the hope that he will encounter something that cannot be doubted, something that is indubitable. His own existence proves to be such a truth; from it he is able to discover the existence of God as an equally certain truth, and he is furthermore made to realize that the certainty he has with respect to the existence and perfection of God is prior to, and the source of, the certainty of any other of his beliefs. Finally, on the basis of all this, he is able to emerge with a certain, and nonskeptical, set of beliefs concerning God, himself, and the world.

In one sense, this is a reasonable story to tell about the *Meditations*, and it is, furthermore, a story that can be made to go well with taking seriously the fact that the *Meditations* consists of meditations.[15] But there are at least two respects in which it seems to me a misleading story, and it is these respects with which I will here be concerned, and which will lead me to suggest a quite different reading of the story and of the central philosophical point of Descartes' *Meditations*.

1. While it is true that the narrator opens the account of his meditations with the clear goal of establishing grounds for absolute certainty and for the foundations of a sure and indubitable body of knowledge—a true "strenge Wissenschaft," as a later "Cartesian" voice will put it—and while it may be true that the narrator never explicitly rejects this goal, the central and important fact about the *Meditations* is other. It is not that God provides the certainty for which the narrator has been searching; it is rather that God releases him—and thus releases us—from the feeling that this certainty is lacking, and that it can be secured only through his being freed from the very possibility of error and doubt. The central fact is that meditation—and finally the discursive activity of narrative meditation—provides the narrator, and thus consciousness in general, with a perspective that makes that goal of unimpeachable certainty, like the doubts so earnestly entertained in its behalf, silly—worthy of our laughter and finally of our rejection.[16]

2. The path by which this release from the need for certainty and consequent escape from the snares of skepticism is achieved is not a uniform, day-by-day progression through a series of truths beginning with the existence of the self, proceeding to the existence of God, and thence to the existence of the so-called external world. The self and God are not entities given as objects to consciousness in the way in which ordinary entities are, and belief in their existence is consequently not part of the content of the meditator's belief in the same way that belief in the existence of other objects is. There cannot therefore be any simple deductive argument by which we are entitled to proceed from self to God to world. Finally, belief in the real, "formal" being of the world, I shall suggest, is restored by meditation on the basic trustworthiness of God and therefore of our consciousness. Skepticism is thus disarmed not by the power of philosophical reason to defeat its arguments but by the power of philosophical meditation to restore a rational (and reasonable) faith which will reveal the unreasonableness of those arguments.

AUTHOR AND NARRATOR IN THE *MEDITATIONS*

One version of the relation between story and discourse, discussed at some length in the Anglo-American tradition of literary theory, is the relation between the narrator and the author, and the relation between the narrator's and the author's visions of what the story is.[17] What I have now suggested is the fact—in one sense simple and unassailable—that the author of the *Meditations* knows more than the central narrative voice knows, and it is this fact, uncovering another level of complexity in the discursive structure of the *Meditations*, on which, together with its ramifications, I now wish to concentrate.

The presence of an author who knows more than the narrating voice, who stands at one narrative level above the voice, qualifies the earlier remarks about the nature of meditation as self-discovery. For in fact there are two controlling "I"s—two selves we might say—in the *Meditations*; the outspoken "I" of the narrative account, and the silent, ordering, auctorial presence, which never announces itself as "I" within the narrative account, and which indeed cannot do so without becoming the narrating "I." It would be fruitful to consider the narrating "I" as an analogue of the conscious "I" whose existence is discovered in the course of the *Meditations*, and the ordering, outward "I" as an analogue of the narrating "I" that achieves and recounts the discovery, that is, to see them respectively as reflecting and reflected consciousness. But here I want to consider simply the claim that it is not the central narrative voice that determines the main philosophical thrust of the *Meditations*.

This view will not even appear initially plausible unless we are able to accept the possibility of something like an "unreliable narrator" or, more appropriately, a naive narrator, at the heart of the *Meditations*. We must, in other words, envision the possibility that the narrative voice does not understand exactly what is going to happen or indeed what is happening in the course of the *Meditations*. Even in our most casual readings of the *Meditations*, we do allow this possibility; for we allow the genuineness of the narrator's doubts in the First Meditation, even though we are fully aware, as is the author, that these doubts are soon to be resolved. But if we allow that the narrator is here genuinely doubting, that is, is genuinely uncertain of the outcome of his quest for the certain, why not allow the limited perspective of the narrator in a more radical sense; why not, that is, allow that the narrator does not understand the nature of the project itself, and that the project changes in the course of the *Meditations*?

It might be objected that there is no question in the *Meditations* of anyone really not knowing; it's only a case of pretending not to know. But who is it that's pretending not to know? It certainly is not the narrative voice, or the entire project is called into question (and the common cries of students who are annoyed at Descartes because "he's not really doubting" or because "he knows all along how it's going to come out" will prove justified). It must then be the author. The author, however, is not pretending uncertainty in any simple or straightforward sense; the Preface to the Reader and the synopsis of the six meditations make perfectly clear what will be the outcome of this dubious enterprise. The only sense in which we might say that the author is simulating doubt or ignorance of the outcome of the exercise is this: he creates a narrative voice and this voice is doubtful and ignorant. This, after all, is what it means for him to be an author; for the very heart and essential act of literary composition is the creation of a speaking voice.

It is the narrator then, that voice which I have been calling the narrative voice, which is genuinely in doubt. The genuineness of this doubt and the complexity of the relation between the author and the narrator of the *Meditations* may be gauged by the curious opening of the Second Meditation:

I have been plunged by yesterday's meditation into such doubts that I neither can any longer forget them nor see in what way they might be resolved.[18]

No one, of course, supposes that there necessarily passed twenty-four hours between the time of Descartes' writing one meditation and his writing the next; we wouldn't be in the least surprised to discover that the Second Meditation had been written immediately upon the heels of the First, or that five weeks had passed between the times of their writing. "Yesterday" is not deictic with reference to any time of writing, but to a fictional time of meditating, a time that is a dimension of the fictional world of the narrator and not the real world of the writer. It is no more a dimension of Descartes' world than it is of the reader's world. Is anyone—no matter how zealous a follower of Descartes' advice to accompany him in the meditative exercise—ever led by the opening sentence to question her conviction that it was actually the day before yesterday that she read the First Meditation?

This may be too obvious or too nice a point. What is curious about the opening of the Second Meditation, however, is the sense the narrator conveys with his "conjectus sum" (I have been plunged), of his having the day before been overtaken by doubt, of his having been passively cast into a condition of doubt.[19] But what bad faith! Being so severely in doubt was yesterday's very project. He didn't fall into doubt; he worked hard and carefully to get there. The doubt of the First Meditation was sought after and cultivated with great care, and was achieved over the subtle objections and maneuvers of a strong second voice in the First Meditation, the voice of someone we might call the antidoubter. That voice is a calm, conservative voice, which attempts to lull our meditator back into comparative certainty and attempts to break his resolve to doubt everything, or at least to provide arguments that will convince him that assurance is reasonable, arguments that our meditator is able to unmask as themselves merely reasonable, and helpless therefore before the strategy of radical doubt.

There is a point (an auctorial point, and thus Descartes' point) to these maneuvers. For one might imagine a narrator who introduced to us the malign genius at the very beginning of his exercise; since the supposition of such a genius is the most powerful and general of the skeptical arguments, why not introduce it from the first? Or, since each of the succeeding fantasies is more general and more powerful in its skeptical force than the preceding one, why not introduce at least one of them? Why does the narrator, for instance, not begin with the supposition that he is dreaming, a supposition that would make merely local doubts about the reliability of the senses seem weak and trivial by comparison?

Surely the point must be cultivation: the seed of skepticism will grow only in properly prepared soil; otherwise the robust common sense of the antidoubter will simply find ridiculous and dismiss out of hand the neurotic fantasies on which skepticism is based. One would have to be a lunatic, one's brain weakened by persistent melancholy vapors, to entertain just like that the notion that one is being globally deceived by a malign and most ingenious genius; one might as well believe that all one's friends and neighbors are with the CIA, or that the police are all Venusians. People who think this way are out of their minds; "amentes sunt isti."[20]

This point about the cultivation of doubt in the First Meditation highlights the apparent passivity of the meditator at the beginning of the Second; the narrator's simulated doubt has become real and threatens to overpower him. But surely the author experiences no such forgetfulness, and is not himself overwhelmed by the doubt he simulates through the narrator's simulation. Descartes knows what he's doing, even if his narrator has the sense of "having unexpectedly fallen into a deep raging sea."

Alternatively to being a lunatic, one might be a philosopher, engaged seriously in thoughts that are, under one description (and so described at the beginning and at the end of our meditations), ridiculous, but which under another constitute the exercise that makes possible at its end our finding doubts ridiculous, not in the fearful and thoughtless way of the antidoubter but in the wise and accepting certainty of one who has looked doubt in the face and has returned unharmed. It's all in how you laugh at the doubt.

It is clear that the doubt of the First Meditation, cultivated and worked for so assiduously by the narrator, comes, by the end of the *Meditations*, to seem to be ridiculous in just this way, so that the designs of the narrator are once again seen to be subsumed in the larger patterns and strategies of the *Meditations* itself. And more globally, the project with which the narrator has begun, the project that promises either mathematical certainty or resigned acquiescence to skepticism, is subtly replaced by the different project—a project of far greater sanity, at once more urgent and less ambitious—of restoring a basic trust in the reliability of our experience, or, as it might differently be put by those of us accustomed to talking that way, faith in the trustworthiness of God. It is thus that the *Meditations* ends with the meditator's ability to recognize, that is, to acknowledge, our nature—its limitations and its fallibility. But because it is the nature given us by God (that is, the nature we have), the mediator is also able to recognize its basic reliability.[21]

It is the existence of these two different projects, that of the narrator and that of the *Meditations* itself, that I mainly wish to draw attention to. The ultimate end of the *Meditations* is not the certainty which the narrator sets out to accomplish, but rather his discovery of faith in God's trustworthiness, which releases him from an undue desire for certainty.

GOD AND SELF IN THE *MEDITATIONS:* SELF

I turn now to the second respect in which the standard version of the *Meditations'* story is misleading. The question concerning any idea of the narrator's experience, say the idea of X, is this: is the existence of an ideal X (that is, the idea of X) matched by the existence of a real X; that is, does there correspond to the objective being of X—the being X has insofar as it exists objectively for my consciousness, insofar, that is, as it is the object of that consciousness in that I have an idea of it—does there correspond to this a formal being that is not merely the ideal X but the real and actual X itself, which exists not merely as an object of my consciousness? The ideal X, the X that has objective existence, may or may not correspond to a real X, an X, as Descartes says, that has formal existence. The *Meditations* may be read as an account of the unsettling realization, through an analysis of consciousness, that the world may exist only for consciousness, may have only objective being, and then of the subsequent rediscovery of the necessity, in order to make sense of the very consciousness for which alone we feared the world existed, of the formal being of the world. In this sense, it is less correct to say that the *Meditations* is an apology for or a defense of reason, and more correct to say that it is an apology for or a defense of consciousness, a vindication of the ability of consciousness to reveal (formal) and not merely to create (objective) being.

But no considerations of this sort enter into the account of the discovery of the self's existence. For there is in the *cogito* no idea of the self that is an object of consciousness and on the basis of which the meditator is able to infer the existence of the real self. This is the reason why in the Second Meditation it proves so difficult to surrender the notion that the "I" is less well known. The meditator finds himself unable to stop thinking that the "I" is less well known to him, not out of some penchant for the corporeal but because the corporeal is the object of consciousness, and the claim that the mind is better known than the body or, as we might say, that consciousness is better known than its objects, is not based on an argument that consciousness can become one of its objects, an object as it were that one can get a good view of, but rather on the claim that it is the source of the objectivity of objects, that for which they are objects. What is discovered in the Second Meditation, in other words, is the existence of the subject for which the world is an object, but which is itself no object. And the argument concerning the knowability of the subject is based clearly and explicitly on this fact:

> . . . *si judico ceram existere, ex eo quod hanc videam, certe multo evidentius efficitur me ipsum etiam existere, ex eo ipso quod hanc videam.*[22]

If, the meditator argues, I judge that the wax exists from the fact that I see it, it certainly follows much more clearly that I exist, from the fact *that I see it.* Not, note, from the fact that I see myself; there is no mention here of objective or reflective consciousness of the self. The "I" then is not an object in my experience; it is a condition (one of the conditions, as I shall suggest) for there being experience. It is not, therefore, at the end of the Second Meditation, another thing in my experienced world. This fact is at the heart of the denial in the Second Meditation that I know myself to be anything other than a consciousness. The "I" that is known is nothing other than a subject that is conscious, a *res cogitans*.

The "existence" of the "I" is therefore not like the existence of other beings in the world capable of becoming objects for consciousness. This fact is at the heart of the "mind-body problem"; that problem concerns not simply the difficulty of understanding the relationship between corporeal entities and "spiritual" entities, whatever they may be, but the difficulty of seeing how an entity that is an object of consciousness and in the world can be related to an entity that is the subjective center of consciousness and therefore not in the world. (It is for this reason that the subsequent critique/elaboration of the Cartesian view proceeds by showing both the respects in which consciousness is in the world and the respect in which the body is not.)

But what of God? On the one hand, the case with respect to God is the same as with any object in the world; the argument of the Third Meditation is precisely that, from the ideal God, one can infer the existence of the real God. And the same argument, which argues for the necessity of there being a cause sufficient to explain the objective reality of the idea, is used in the Sixth Meditation to infer the existence of material things. So here it looks as though the case of God is quite different from the case of the "I"; the one is not an object in my experiential field, and therefore not another thing among the things of the world; the other precisely is.

In a sense this must be true; for the tale is told from the point of view of the subject "I," so that even God, who has difficulty being an object of awareness is, relative to this "I," objective. But in another sense, God is more like the subjective "I" than at first might appear. To see this, we need to consider the structure of the *Meditations* in slightly more detail.

GOD AND SELF IN THE *MEDITATIONS:* GOD

We may think about the progress of the first several meditations in the following way:

1. In the First Meditation, the narrator actively courts and cultivates, through the systematic practice of doubting, a condition of skeptical doubt. This condition consists of a state of detachment in which the world disclosed in experience is revealed to be, as far as he knows, merely objective, that is, real only insofar as it is disclosed for experience, insofar as it exists for consciousness.

2. In the Second Meditation, the narrator is made certain of the existence of his subjective self in the sense I've suggested, as correlative to the objective world. What is disclosed to the narrator (and reader) in these first two meditations is thus the minimal structure of experience: on the one hand a world, which is revealed to be only a-world-for-me and thus to collapse into objectivity, and on the other hand the pole of subjectivity, in which is revealed the existence of the subject as the principle of the for-me aspect of the world-for-me.

At the end of the Second Meditation, then, the narrator has not transcended the phenomenal limits of "objective," that is, ideal, experience, but has merely begun to articulate the structure of that experience. The use of radical doubt to reveal everything as objective means not that the world disappears, but that it exists only as an ideal representation; I no longer know whether it is real in any sense other than as represented. And this fact remains unchanged; what is discovered is merely that aspect of representational experience that is its condition on the subjective side. In discovering itself in this way, consciousness in a sense escapes the polar structure of subject/object by becoming aware of it; but this is not the same as discovering the real, as opposed to the merely objective, existence of some item within experience.

In the Second Meditation, then, the narrator has not proved the existence of himself, but merely the existence of the "I" *qua res cogitans,* the conscious subject. It is for this reason, as a number of people have correctly argued, that in the Second Meditation the narrator does not claim that thinking is his essence, nor that what he is cannot be corporeal. For the claims made in that meditation are with respect only to what the narrator is able to know at that point in the course of his meditations. At the end of the Second Meditation, he does not know for certain what he is; he knows only that the essence of what he is insofar as he knows himself to exist is to be a thinking thing. But this is not what he is; what he is is a human being, which, as he learns in the Sixth Meditation, and not until the Sixth Meditation, is a particularly perplexing union of body and soul.

3. But the same is true with respect to God in the Third Meditation; what emerges from this meditation is knowledge of the existence of God insofar as he can be known by the narrator there and in that context. Thus we read at the end of the Third Meditation:

The whole force of the argument is this: I recognize that it would not be possible that I exist being of such a nature as I am, that is, having in me the idea of God, unless God indeed also exists, that very God, I mean, of which the idea is in me, that is, having all those perfections which in any way I'm able to think of even if I don't understand them, and subject to no defects.[23]

These summary remarks make clear the qualifications that attach to God's being in that meditation; what has been shown to exist is not God *tout court* (and not, as Pascal found so distressing, the God of Abraham, Isaac, or Jacob) but God qua that being whose nature is carefully delineated in the argument of the Third Meditation, and whose being is relative to that argument; the being whose existence is proved in the Third Meditation is the being that explains my ability to recognize my imperfections, that is, the being that explains my ability to recognize that there is a difference between the being of my ideas and the being of what my ideas are ideas of. In the Third Meditation, in other words, the narrator shows the existence of a being whose nature is analogous to that "I" the existence of which he knows at the end of the Second Meditation.

The argument of the first three meditations is relative to a concept of God under that very description. The narrator argues: (1) I am conscious of a world. (2) This consciousness carries with it awareness of the possibility of error; I am aware, that is, of the possibility that things may not be as they appear to me to be. (3) This awareness is in turn, then, an awareness that I am imperfect, in that I cannot guarantee the reality of the objects of my consciousness. If, after all, I were not imperfect, I would be God and would then make things be what I am conscious of them as being.

But if I were the source of my being, I would neither doubt, nor desire, nor in any way at all be lacking. For I would have given to myself all the perfections of which I have any idea, and so I myself would be God.[24]

Consciousness then involves an awareness of being imperfect which is, at the same time, an awareness of the distinction between the self that has ideas and the objects of its ideas. (4) A condition of this awareness is the idea of perfection, in the light of which the awareness of myself as imperfect is alone possible. Where does that idea of perfection come from by virtue of which I'm able to recognize myself as in error, and thus able to recognize my experience as objective? (Here is one of those moments when the shift from the early to the modern sense of "objective" can perhaps be glimpsed.)

The answer to this question is: "Not from myself, but from the perfect itself, that is from God." Whatever we think about the legitimacy of this conclusion, it's important that we be able to recognize how functionally determined by the course of the argument it is. What is shown to "exist" is the principle by which consciousness is able to recognize itself as subject over and against the objectivity of its experience. The earlier meditations had led to the discovery of the I or, more accurately, to the focusing of consciousness on its very self as a condition of (though not an objective element in) all its experience. This discovery, or focusing, reveals the respect in which the world is for me: that is, the respect in which experience is not possible except from a point of view that is radically defined by my subjectivity. But to see this as a point of view, that is, to discover subjectivity rather than just hold the world in a naive acceptance, is to discover the respect in which the world is given to me. Here then consciousness discovers itself and in the same moment discovers that it cannot be the source of itself, discovers that subjectivity immediately leads dialectically to objectivity, and that objectivity leads directly to God (or, alternatively, to madness).

God then is simply the source of the recognition that although one is the center of one's experience, one is not the center of the universe, and therefore not the source of one's experience. This recognition that although I am the center of my world I am not the center of the world may be thought of as a mark of sanity; or it may be thought of as the recognition that I am not God, which is, I would say, a central component in the belief in God. These facts may explain the connection made in the *Meditations* between God and sanity, how it is God that helps me see the difference between recognizing that our stuff is of flesh and blood and thinking that our heads are thrown from clay, or our bodies blown from glass, or that we are, like some mad emperor, altogether pumpkins.[25]

It is with some weight then that at the end of the Third Meditation the narrator announces that before going on it seems right to stay for a while in contemplation of this very God (*in ipsius Dei contemplatione immorari*).[26]

MEDITATION IN THE *MEDITATIONS*

What follows the argument of the Third Meditation is in a sense the geographic center (or the graphic center) of the *Meditations*: the end of the Third Meditation and the short Fourth. These sections, it seems to me, constitute a pivotal moment in the progression of the meditations, a moment around which the entire argument is centered—or rather around which the meditator's attitude and whole mode of thinking are centered. The end of the Third Meditation is devoted to the contemplation envisioned in the passage I've quoted above. Here is continued the practice of ending each meditation with a shift into an actual "meditative," that is, a contemplative, mode. Thus at the end of the First Meditation when the malign genius has been successfully summoned into the world of credibility, the narrator resolves to remain "obstinate in hac meditatione defixus";[27] and at the end of the Second he pauses so that by "diuturnitate meditationis" the new thought of his subjective being may be firmly infixed in his memory.[28] As in these two meditations, so now in the Third, the contemplative and meditative activities continue beyond the written meditation; the meditation takes place, as it were, offstage, outside all but the briefest narrative view of the written work. But this offstage meditation is of critical importance, for it is the source of the ability of the narrator to discover, in the Fourth Meditation, how to temper his will and to come to trust consciousness at one with a will thus tempered.

At the center of the meditative progression is not the discovery of reason but, in the Fourth Meditation, this tempering of the will, a tempering that has been made possible by the growing vision of the prior three days of meditation and by the contemplation, on the third afternoon, of God's trustworthiness. And it is in general this trustworthiness which is the central object of the narrator's meditation and which is finally the central theme and "discovery" of the *Meditations*, that which allows the narrator in the second half of the *Meditations* the restoration of the world lost to him through doubt.

In that second half, the existence of God and self are again established, but now with a difference. For what is shown to exist in the Sixth Meditation is the self as possible object of consciousness, the objective, embodied "me" whose relation to the subject-self of the Second Meditation is problematic but undeniable. Similarly, the God of the Fifth Meditation is a being whose nature, rather than relative to the context of doubt, is "genuine and immutable," "a determinate nature or form or essence, which is not fashioned by me, and does not depend on my mind."[29] In each half of the *Meditations*, then, are revealed God and self, but differently: in the first half as nothing more than necessary aspects of the structure of experience, in the second as beings whose existence transcends that experience.

The structure of the *Meditations* is thus the structure of one classical form of meditation. The meditator detaches himself from his world; experience is stripped of its content in order that there may be revealed the formal structure of experience and, as a consequence, self and God. But when the self has been quieted and its true nature and rhythms comprehended, the meditator is free to reappropriate and reintegrate effortlessly God, body, and world.

If we attend simply to the logic of progression in the *Meditations*, we will want to say that it is meditation that bridges the two halves of the *Meditations*; it is the contemplation of God and self that allows, in the second half, the restoration of the being of God, self, and, ultimately, the world that was bracketed in the first half. That this restoration should be accomplished by meditation, rather than by any simple philosophical demonstration or subsequent recognition of the conclusions of such demonstration, will be surprising to us only insofar as we forget that that *Meditations* lives in the tradition of religious meditative writing. One major moment in that tradition is made up of those works whose purpose is, as Louis Martz puts it, that "sin lose its fearsomeness in the realization of God's overwhelming love."[30]

So Descartes' meditator, beginning with a sense of his sin as error, doubt, and deficiency, is led to a vision of the perfect order of nature, with its vestiges of God[31] in which that deficiency loses its fearsomeness. If we are not gods, we are part of God's divine order, subject as mere parts of that order to occasional error but not doomed thereby to the despair of skepticism. Thus we ought not to fear that what the senses daily reveal to us may be false, but ought to laugh off the stage the exaggerated doubts of skepticism concerning the reality of things (*hyperbolicae dubitationes, ut risu dignae, sunt explodendae*).[32] Here the narrator has not performed a volte-face, but has been restored through his meditations to a calm acceptance of his fallibility, to an acceptance of his nature. "So I need not in the least doubt the truth of things if, having summoned all my senses, memory and intellect, no testimony is brought forth by any of them which contradicts that brought forth by the others. For since God is no deceiver, it follows that in these things I am not deceived. But since practical necessities do not always afford us the leisure for such accurate examination, we must acknowledge that human life is always liable to error concerning particulars, and we must recognize the infirmity of our nature."[33]

The infirmity, which must here be recognized ("agnoscenda est"), is not a fatal infirmity, but the necessary finitude of our nature, which must be acknowledged as ours. I quote Martz again in his description of Bonaventure's *Journey of the Mind to God*, a description which I think may be equally applied to Descartes' journey:

Thus the process of self-scrutiny does not end in self-contempt, but moves beyond this to a recovery of self-esteem; self-contempt is only a half-knowledge: full self-knowledge demands a recognition of the incalculable value of the Image which lies beyond and beneath all deformity.[34]

THE *MEDITATIONS* AS MEDITATION

I have argued that the central project of the *Meditations* is not a quest for apodeictic certainty, but a project of release from that quest and a consequent release from that pathological form of skepticism which is but the other face of that quest. But this is not initially the project of the narrator, who early announces his intention to effect "a general destruction [*eversio*] of all his opinions."[35] It is the *Meditations* itself which, almost in spite of its central voice, carries out this deeper project, and carries the narrator along with it. We may think of this as a triumph of discourse over story or, more accurately, as an instance of that narrative logic by which story, rather than being an independently determinate structure merely reported by discourse, is itself shaped by the very play of discursive forces.

But equally, and perhaps less fancifully, we may think of the project as that of Descartes, who gives us an account of meditations which, if read properly, provides for its reader, as for its central character, the occasion for a meditation which, through the contemplation of God, transcends doubt in that calm certainty which can accept doubt. We should note, then, how thoroughly we have retreated from our original claim that a narrative can be a meditation only in a secondary and derivative sense. For in fact Descartes' *Meditations* turns out to be Descartes' meditation: not just a description of meditation, but the actual meditation itself, the very exercise in which the project I have described is carried out. The written word, which as philosophers we spend so much of our time creating and studying, here becomes the actual vehicle of epistemic salvation, of the release from that fearful and strangling hold which the myth of certainty has on us.

But if the text is in this sense a meditation, it has a meditative life only because it is there to be read, only because it invites us, as Descartes makes explicit, to join in the exercise of meditation it presents. "I counsel no one to read this work, except those who are willing to meditate seriously with me [*nullis author sum ut haec legant, nisi tantum iis qui serio mecum meditari . . . volent*]."[36] Without that joining of the reader, Descartes has written no meditation, but merely a narrative account of meditations. We may then, in a playful and midrashic moment, hear in this, as a motto of meditative writing, "*nullis author sum nisi tantum iis qui serio mecum legere volent*: I am the author for no one who is not willing to read seriously with me."

NOTES

1. Reply to the second set of Objections (AT VII, 158; HR II, 51). For an explanation of abbreviations AT and HR, see the General Bibliography at the beginning of this volume.

2. Preface to the Reader (AT VII, 9.25; HR I, 139).

3. Étienne Gilson, *Études sur le rôle de la pensée médiévale dans la formation du système cartésien* (Paris, 1951), 186. See Harry G. Frankfurt, *Demons, Dreamers, and Madmen: The defense of reason in Descartes's Meditations* (Indianapolis, 1970), 15.

4. See Louis L. Martz, *The Poetry of Meditation* (New Haven, 1954), and Amélie O. Rorty, "The Structure of Descartes' *Meditations*," this vol., chap. 1.

5. Ibid.

6. I have here in mind an instance of what Harold Bloom calls *kenosis*. See his *The Anxiety of Influence* (New York, 1973), 77 ff.

7. Frances de Sales, *Treatise on the Love of God* (1616), quoted in Martz, *The Poetry of Meditation*, 14.

8. Thus the Oxford English Dictionary gives as one meaning of *meditation*: "A discourse, written or spoken, in which a subject (usually religious) is treated in a meditative manner, or which is designed to guide the reader or hearer in meditation."

9. James Hervey, *Meditations Among the Tombs* (Philadelphia, 1857), 3.

10. See Gérard Genette, "Frontières du récit" in *L'analyse structural du récit, Communications* 8 (Paris, 1966): 158 ff., and *Narrative Discourse*, trans. Jane Lewin (Ithaca, 1980), 162 ff.

11. Martz, *The Poetry of Meditation*, 16–20, 248.

12. See Tzvetan Todorov, "Les catégories du récit littéraire" in *L'analyse structurale du récit*, 131–157; Gerard Genette, *Narrative Discourse*, 25–32; Jonathan Culler, "Story and Discourse in the Analysis of Narrative" in *The Pursuit of Signs* (Ithaca, 1981), 169–188; Seymour Chatman, *Story and Discourse* (Ithaca, 1978).

13. Second Meditation (AT VII, 23.28; HR I, 149).

14. See Genette, *Narrative Discourse*, for a general and extended prototype of such an analysis.

15. See, for example, Frankfurt, *Demons, Dreamers, and Madmen*, 3 ff.

16. Sixth Meditation (AT VII, 89.20; HR I, 199).

17. See Wayne Booth, *The Rhetoric of Fiction* (Chicago, 1961); Chatman, *Story and Discourse*.

18. Second Meditation (AT VII, 23.25; HR I, 149). The French version unfortunately separates this sentence into two parts and alters its sense.

19. The French again blunts this point by turning the passive into an active verb, and treating *meditation* as the sentence's subject.

20. First Meditation (AT VII, 19.5; HR I, 145).

21. Sixth Meditation (AT VII, 90.15; HR I, 199).

22. Second Meditation (AT VII, 33.6; HR I, 156).

23. Third Meditation (AT VII, 51.29; HR I, 171).

24. Third Meditation (AT VII, 48.69; HR I, 168).

25. First Meditation (AT VII, 19.4; HR I, 145). I may be wrong to suppose that Descartes wants to link kings and pumpkins (or, more properly, gourds); but there is a tradition that does, for which see Dio Cassius's account in *Historica* 60.35 of Seneca's fancied *apopumpkinosis* of the Emperor Claudius.

26. Third Meditation (AT VII, 52.13; HR I, 171).
27. First Meditation (AT VII, 23.4; HR I, 148).
28. Second Meditation (AT VII, 34.9; HR I, 157).
29. Fifth Meditation (AT VII, 64.15; HR I, 180).
30. Martz, *The Poetry of Meditation*, 149.
31. See Bonaventure, *The Mind's Road to God*, trans. George Boas (Indianapolis: Bobbs-Merrill, 1953); Martz, *The Poetry of Meditation*, 151.
32. Sixth Meditation (AT VII, 89.20; HR I, 199).
33. Sixth Meditation (AT VII, 90.7; HR I, 199).
34. Martz, *The Poetry of Meditation*, 152.
35. First Meditation (AT VII, 18.2; HR I, 144).
36. Preface to the Reader (AT VII, 9.25; HR I, 139).

3

The Senses and the Fleshless Eye: The *Meditations* as Cognitive Exercises

GARY HATFIELD

. . . so I do not see how it would make sense to say God is not deceitful, if in fact they [sensory ideas] proceed from elsewhere, not from corporeal objects. Therefore corporeal objects must exist. It may be that not all bodies are such as my senses apprehend them, for this sensory apprehension is in many ways obscure and confused; but at any rate their nature must comprise whatever I clearly and distinctly understand—that is, whatever, generally considered, falls within the subject-matter of pure mathematics. There remain some highly doubtful and uncertain points; either mere details, like the sun's having a certain size or shape, or things unclearly understood, like light, sound, pain, and so on. But since God is not deceitful, there cannot possibly ocur any error in my opinions but I can correct by means of some faculty God has given me to that end; and this gives me some hope of arriving at the truth even on such matters. (AG, 116)[1]

This passage from the Sixth Meditation marks an ending and a beginning. It brings to fruition that portion of the metaphysical project of Descartes' *Meditations on First Philosophy* which pertains to the material world. The meditator regains knowledge of corporeal objects, knowledge of which had been undermined by the doubts of the First Meditation. The meditator now has a clear conception of both the existence and the essence of material things—their essence being extension, "the subject-matter of pure mathematics." As the passage implies, however, the completion of this metaphysical project allows the beginning of two further projects: (1) that of developing a precise theory of the senses, partially in order to give an account of "things unclearly understood," and (2) that of filling in "details" about the structure of nature, which constitutes the project of "natural philosophy" (or natural science).

This passage does not reveal that the world regained is different from the one that was earlier lost. Consonant with Descartes' revolutionary aims, the "clean sweep" achieved by the doubt at the beginning of the *Meditations* has cleared the ground of previous cognitive constructions—especially the dominant Scholastic Aristotelianism of his time—to make room for Descartes' new conception of the mind and the corporeal world. The two projects mentioned above constitute new construction, to replace a discarded theory of the senses and conception of nature.

Descartes' doctrine of the senses lay at the heart of his revolution, for it was by shifting the status of the senses as sources of knowledge that Descartes effected his attack on Scholastic Aristotelianism. He did not confront the old metaphysics directly, but indirectly by undercutting and replacing the model of the knower woven into Aristotelian philosophy. At the core of the Aristotelian conception of the knower lay a sense-based epistemology, which was distilled into the slogan, "Nothing is in the intellect that was not first in the senses." As elaborated by Thomas Aquinas and subsequent Aristotelians, this implied that all knowledge, including knowledge of God, the soul, and the truths of mathematics, is attained by the intellectual abstraction of universals from sensory particulars.[2] In the course of the *Meditations,* Descartes reaches the opposite conclusion, that the things known first and known best are not known by or through the senses, but through the independent operation of the intellect. Descartes' replacement dictum might be phrased, "Nothing is accepted from the senses that was not first in the intellect." In the reformed hierarchy of knowing faculties the intellect stands autonomous and supreme. The radical upshot is that the metaphysical picture provided by the intellect will guide the formation of a new theory of the senses and the construction of a new science of nature (with the aid of sensory observation and experiment). Just as the intellect rules the senses, metaphysics frames the theory of sense perception and of all physics proper.

This construal of Descartes' strategy in the *Meditations* brings into prominence an aspect of the use of skeptical doubt in that work which has previously been obscured. Usually, Descartes' "method of doubt" is placed in the context of two intellectual currents against which Descartes was reacting: skepticism and Scholastic Aristotelianism. The doubt of the First Meditation serves as a way to undermine (Aristotelian) orthodoxy by overturning the applecart.[3] Further, the well-worn arguments of the skeptics are raised in order to show that they can be refuted (in subsequent Meditations), and to underscore the high degree of certainty of Descartes' own doctrines, which will be established in the face of stringent skepticism.[4] But these functions of the doubt do not reveal its special use in the *Meditations*, which derives from a peculiar characteristic of that work: that it is cast in the form of meditations. As Descartes maintained in response to Hobbes' complaint that the First Meditation vends stale goods, an essential function of the doubt is "to accustom the reader's mind to consider intelligible objects and distinguish them from corporeal things—and to this end such doubts are indispensable" (HR II, 61). The doubt itself does not "accustom" the mind to consider intelligible objects, but it provides a means for suspending judgment about corporeal things and drives one to a last refuge of certainty in the direct apprehension of one's own thought. It serves as a kind of exercise for the mind. It is, I shall argue, indispensable in this regard because it provides the means for freeing one's attention from sensory ideas in order to attend to an independent source of knowledge: the pure deliverances of the intellect. It thus serves a function in Descartes' *Meditations* similar to that of doubt and other "purgings" of the senses in the tradition of spiritual meditation stemming from St. Augustine.

According to the reading I shall offer, Descartes' use of the meditative mode of writing was not a mere rhetorical device to win an audience accustomed to the spiritual retreat. His choice of the literary form of the spiritual exercise was consonant with, if not determined by, his theory of the mind and of the basis of human knowledge. Since Descartes' conception of knowledge implied the priority of the intellect over the senses, and indeed the priority of an intellect operating independently of the senses, and since, in Descartes' view, the untutored individual was likely to be nearly wholly immersed in the senses, a procedure was needed for freeing the intellect from sensory domination so that the truth might be seen. Hence, the cognitive exercises of the *Meditations*.

This reading entails a distinctive attitude toward the role of argument in the *Meditations*. Although works of religious meditation may make use of argument, their purpose is not to present a continuous argument that compels by force of logic; they serve as guidebooks to prepare the soul for illumination from above or within. Similarly, Descartes' *Meditations* are not so much a continuous argument as a set of instructions for uncovering the truths that lie immanent in the intellect. Not that there are *no* arguments in the *Meditations;* the language of argument is interspersed throughout the work. But some

conclusions seem to arrive out of nowhere, without discursive argument—such as the conclusion that the essence of matter is extension,
or that one can discover in one's thought the idea of an infinite,
benevolent being. I want to suggest that Descartes' work is constructed
in such a way that the force of such conclusions depends on the ability
of the meditative exercises to evoke in the reader certain experiences
that bring their own content and carry their own conviction. The
Meditations must evoke the appropriate cognitive experiences in the
meditator.

I

My argument depends upon establishing with some exactness the
relationship between Descartes' *Meditations* and the types of spiritual
exercises available to him in the Roman Catholic tradition. Although
virtually all devotional literature in the early seventeenth century
shows the influence of Augustine, a division can be made into two
groups, which I will call Ignatian and Augustinian. This division reflects differing accounts of the cognitive basis of meditative experience
implicit or explicit in various writers. Ignatius assumes an Aristotelian
account of cognition; writers in the Augustinian tradition, such as
Eustace of St. Paul, reveal the influence of Augustine's neo-Platonic
bent.[5] Descartes would have been familiar with both traditions, the
Ignatian from his Jesuit school days, the Augustinian from his contact
with the Parisian oratory during the 1620s.[6]

By the early seventeenth century a generalized structure had insinu-
ated itself into meditative writing, the essentials of which were expressed in Ignatius's *Exercises* (1548) and the attendant *Directory* (1591),
and had been implicit in Augustine's *Confessions*. This generalized
structure may be summarized according to two trinitarian doctrines:
the three powers and the three ways. The "three powers" refers to
three powers of the soul—memory, understanding, and will—and
enjoins that meditation should engage each of these.[7] The memory,
including imagination, is used to contemplate various subject matters,
such as original sin, hell, or the passion of Christ. Where possible, the
meditative text will aid in calling forth vivid images of the fires of perdi-
tion or the suffering of the Savior. The understanding then draws
implications from the object lesson (e.g., hell should be avoided),
with the end of raising affections in the will (e.g., the desire to follow
steadfastly the example of Christ) and strengthening its resolve (e.g.,
to avoid the evil of sin). The guidance of the will is the ultimate
objective of meditation.

The second doctrine parallels the first by introducing three "ways" or stages through which the meditator should pass. In the first of these, the purgative, the body is mortified, so that one may turn away from sin, the senses, and sensuality. This prepares the soul for the illuminative way, in which one endeavors to achieve a positive exercise of the Christian virtues by becoming aware of the moral power of the soul through the example of Christ or by other divine illumination. Souls that have achieved illumination may then enter the unitive way, seeking union with God through the joining of their own wills with the divine will.[8]

Parallels between these formal doctrines and the structure of Descartes' *Meditations* are striking. The three ways, leading away from the world to God, are paralleled by Descartes' meditator, who "purges" the senses and even the perception of simple mathematical truths (First Meditation), is illuminated by the *cogito* and by the knowledge of God (Second and Third Meditations), and seeks to direct his will in the manner intended by God (Fourth Meditation). Moreover, one sees in various meditations the use of the three faculties—memory, understanding (or intellect), and will. Hence, at various places in the First Meditation the meditator recalls (a) that what he has accepted as true to this time was known by means of the senses and that the senses have deceived him, (b) instances of being deceived by dreams, and (c) "the old opinion that there is a God who can do everything." From these remembered notions together with other considerations the understanding draws various conclusions about the deceptiveness of the senses and the possibility of delusion even about mathematics. The Meditation ends with the meditator focusing on the grounds for doubt, and even positing the evil deceiver, as means for strengthening his will so that he can withhold assent from his old, possibly erring, opinions (see also the "resolutions" of the will at the end of the Second and Fourth Meditations).

A second type of parallel is not revealed by the formalized doctrines just discussed. Meditations carried their force in at least two ways. First, they brought forward "considerations" that could appeal to the understanding; these were cast in the form of discursive arguments.[9] Second, they called for the exemplification of various matters directly before the mind, as in a direct vision of God, or as Christian virtue is exemplified in a contemplation of the life of Christ. Here one was not supposed to be persuaded by argument, but rather to become immediately acquainted with God or to gain practice in directing the will toward virtue (through following the example of Christ).[10] Especially in the Augustinian tradition, exemplification involved illumination of the intellect and will by divine light, yielding direct apprehension of eternal truth (or of the supreme good) akin to Platonic contemplation of the forms.[11]

Similarly, Descartes' Meditations contain both argument and exemplification. Sometimes argument is used in the service of exemplification, as when the skeptical arguments of the First Meditation are used, not to achieve a positive conclusion, but to suspend judgment in order to uncover something that is immediately and indubitably known. Much of the rest of the *Meditations*, which comes out looking rather odd when treated as argument, is quite naturally seen as exemplification.[12] Thus, the briefly sketched argument to the conclusion "that the proposition 'I am,' 'I exist,' whenever I utter it or conceive it in my mind, is necessarily true" (AG, 67) is ultimately presented as resting on the direct apprehension of the meditator's own thinking (HR II, 207). This direct apprehension requires that the mind "must be abstracted from the senses," an achievement that is prepared for by the doubt of the First Meditation (cf. HR II, 60–61), and realized in the Second Meditation's meditation on the human mind (cf. HR II, 32). the conclusion of *sum* from *cogito* is regarded as established not by argument, but by "recognising it as something self-evident, in a simple mental intuition" (AG, 299; cf. AG, 300–301), and is recalled as such at the beginning of the Third Meditation. This intuition is not attained by the *cogito* argument itself, but by the succeeding investigation of "this 'I' that necessarily exists" (AG, 67–71).

Exemplification in intuition is at work at other key points in the text. Thus, at various places before Descartes' meditator draws the mind-body distinction, he gives the reader practice at conceiving the mind as thinking and nonextended (Second Meditation, AG, 68–76; Third Meditation, AG, 84; Fourth Meditation, AG, 92). When he asserts at the opening of the Fifth Meditation that extension is what is clearly known in body, he neither gives an argument there nor relies on a previous one; however, he can rely on previous instances of exercising the mind in the perception of particular bodies as extended, as in the thought experiment with the piece of wax in the Second Meditation (AG, 72–73), which is recalled and generalized in the Third Meditation (AG, 83). Hence, exemplification provides both the immediate apprehension that extension constitutes the essence of material things, and the apprehension that thought is completely distinct from extension, thereby providing the crucial premises for the argument to the distinctness of mind and body (AG, 114–115). Similarly, the immediate apprehension of the idea of God serves as a basis for the argument to God's existence (Third and Fifth Meditations). And so exemplification in intuition importantly underlies the chief metaphysical conclusions of the *Meditations*, regarding mind, matter, and God.

The appeal to exemplification and illumination reveals the extent to which meditative literature depends on the evocation of experiences in the reader. By carefully arranged settings and preparatory exercises, the reader is brought into the proper state to receive the light of grace (in spiritual meditations) or to perceive the unvarnished truth by the light of nature (in Descartes' cognitive exercises). In consonance with the experiential thrust of the practice of meditation, the meditative text itself often contained an explicit theory of cognitive function—as in the doctrine of the three powers—which explained the role of the various cognitive faculties in the reception of illumination. Descartes' *Meditations* were no exception.

In his account of the cognitive base of meditation, Descartes radically broke with the mainstream Ignatian tradition and turned to the tradition stemming from Augustine.[13] The mainstream reflected in a broad way the teaching of Thomas Aquinas, and laid heavy stress on the use of the faculties of memory and imagination. Aquinas himself, with his Aristotelian, sense-based epistemology, contended that (revelation aside) God can be known only by means of our sensory contact with His creation. Correspondingly, Aquinas stressed the role of sensible objects in meditation, and especially recommended applying the imagination to the passion of Christ.[14] In the tradition of formal meditation, this emphasis on imagination was heightened—Ignatius invites one to see, feel, hear, taste, and smell the horrors of hell[15]—and the role of the understanding was limited to drawing conclusions from imagined material. In this tradition, the meditator turns away from mundane sensory and sensual distractions for a period, the better to focus the mind on spiritually uplifting sensory materials constructed by the imagination.

Augustine, in contrast, searches memory (and imagination) through and through, and does not find God. God cannot be found in memory, because He is not known by way of image, as are corporeal things.[16] Indeed, in the *Confessions* Augustine returns again and again to the theme that it was his attempt to conceive God as extended in space, and therefore as able to be portrayed in the imagination, that had prevented him from knowing the deity.[17] In order to see God, he needed "to brush away the swarm of unclean flies that swarmed around the eyes of my mind."[18] The clearing of an intellectual vista to the deity was achieved by sweeping away his earlier (Manichean) opinions through the clever ploy of adopting a skeptical doubt.[19] The skeptical doubt then dissolves in the face of a direct vision of God, which itself was achieved through contemplating the immateriality of his own mind.

And thus by degrees I was led upward from bodies to the soul which perceives them by means of the bodily senses, and from there on to the soul's inward faculty, to which the bodily senses report outward things—and this belongs even to the capacities of the beasts—and thence on up to the reasoning power, to whose judgment is referred the experience received from the bodily sense. And when this power of reason within me also found that it was changeable, it raised itself up to its own intellectual principle, and withdrew its thoughts from experience, abstracting itself from the contradictory throng of fantasms in order to seek for that light in which it was bathed. Then, without any doubting, it cried out that the unchangeable was better than the changeable. From this it follows that the mind somehow knew the unchangeable, for unless it had known it in some fashion, it could have had no sure ground for preferring it to the changeable. And thus with the flash of a trembling glance, it arrived at *that which is*. And I saw thy invisibility understood by means of the things that are made.[20]

By turning away from the senses and discovering his own intellect as an invisible, immaterial, and yet mutable power, he was led to see with the fleshless eye of the mind the invisible, immaterial, immutable deity. For one who wished to follow Augustine in his process of contemplation, the doubt and subsequent turning away from the senses ("the contradictory throng of fantasms") would not be undertaken in order to provide the proper frame of mind for examining new sensory and imaginal materials; rather, the senses and imagination would be neglected because they cannot possibly afford a knowledge of God or the soul. Only the intellect turning inward can know the immaterial.

Here then is a model for the *Meditations* of Descartes, in which the meditator uses skepticism and contemplation of his own thought to withdraw the mind from the senses, and then, having fought off the "images of sensible objects" that blind the "mind's eye" (AG, 87), achieves contemplation of God ("the beauty of this immeasurable light" [AG, 91]). Consistent with the Augustinian character of the *Meditations*, Descartes repeatedly stresses the importance of the skeptical doubt, and of the *cogito*, as means for bringing the appropriate cognitive resources to bear in his search for first truths. The clear and distinct perception of his own existence yields a "great illumination of the understanding," which prompts a "great inclination of the will" to judge what is so understood to be true, thereby nullifying the force of skeptical doubt and hesitation (AG, 97). A will momentarily unfettered by prejudice and habit can seek truth in an autonomous faculty of understanding. Descartes reviews the progress of the first three Meditations in just these terms:

In the last few days I have accustomed myself to withdraw my mind from the senses; I have been careful to observe how little truth there is in our perceptions of corporeal objects; how much more is known about the human mind, and how much more again about God. I thus have now no difficulty at all in turning my thoughts from imaginable objects to objects that are purely intelligible and wholly separate from matter. (AG, 92)

As he remarks in the Objections and Replies, he has chosen the meditative mode of writing because of the great difficulty in arriving at a clear and distinct perception of the primary notions of metaphysics: "For, though in their own nature they are as intelligible as, or even more intelligible than those the geometricians study, yet being contradicted by many preconceptions of our senses to which we have since our earliest years been accustomed, they cannot be perfectly apprehended except by those who give strenuous attention and study to them, and withdraw their minds as far as possible from matters corporeal."[21] Descartes repeatedly emphasizes the need to spend days and weeks in the study of each Meditation, not merely because the subject matter is difficult and full attention is required, but because he is asking the reader literally to think in a new way.[22] Descartes' meditator does not forsake things sensory merely to avoid interruption, but to discover a new manner and object of thought. The meditative mode of writing is chosen because it invites one to turn inward, and that is where Descartes believed his metaphysical first principles were to be discovered, lying immanent in the intellectual faculty of the meditator.

The Augustinian character of Descartes' *Meditations* can be consolidated by reflection on its differing uses of the faculty of memory. We have seen that meditations in the tradition of Aquinas and Ignatius employ the memory as a source of materials for contemplation. Augustine could not find God in memory, but at first could remember only his mistaken search for God among corporeal things; later he uses memory as a repository for knowledge of the deity achieved through illumination.[23] Descartes uses memory as a source of materials for contemplation primarily in the First Meditation, where he recalls various "old opinions"—such as that the senses are the chief source of knowledge—as well as recalling various reasons for doubting these old opinions—such as the possibility of a deceiving God (since this idea is *recalled*, not perceived directly by the intellect, a deceiving God is a possibility). Prior to the illumination of the *cogito* and the actual contemplation of God, the meditator is reasoning within the domain of common experience and belief; memory is a repository of commonly accepted errors. As the meditator initiates his search for an Archimedean point, he forsakes memory (and thereby tradition, except as a source of old, erroneous opinions),[24] and searches his own immediate experience. Memory then becomes a means for retaining the knowledge gained through the *inspectio* of the *cogito* and the idea of God (AG, 75, 100, 107).

Despite the numerous parallels between Descartes' work and Christian meditation, a wide gulf separates the two. In each case the purpose of meditation is constructive: the meditator is to be transformed, through achieving a new understanding and through the reformation of the will. But the types of understanding and reformation are distinct. The Christian seeks new understanding and acquaintance with God in order to guide the will in attaining Christian virtue. Descartes' meditator achieves knowledge of God, but does so in the service of gaining a better acquaintance with his own cognitive faculties, ultimately in order to recognize the strengths and limitations of human understanding and to curb the source of its errors in the impetuous will. The Christian returns from meditation with a firmer resolve to avoid sin (or moral error) and to embrace virtue. Descartes' meditator returns from contemplation with a firmer resolve to avoid epistemic error and to seek the truth, in the hope of establishing "some secure and lasting result in science" (AG, 61).[25]

When Descartes was in school the Jesuit practice was to hold an extended spiritual retreat once each year. The Augustinians of the Oratory also were fond of the retreat. Descartes, however, counseled a *cognitive* retreat only once in a lifetime. He wrote to Elizabeth in June of 1643:

> I think it is very necessary to have understood, once in a lifetime, the principles of metaphysics, since it is by them that we come to the knowledge of God and of our soul. But I think also that it would be very harmful to occupy one's intellect frequently in meditating upon them, since this would impede it from devoting itself to the functions of the imagination and senses. I think the best thing is to content oneself with keeping in one's memory and one's belief the conclusions which one has once drawn from them, and then employ the rest of one's study time to thoughts in which the intellect cooperates with the imagination and the senses. (K, 143)

Descartes seems to be saying that once one has, through metaphysical meditation, achieved a knowledge of the principles of metaphysics, one should then return to the affairs of the world (just as Augustine used the memory of God as a source of strength for confronting worldly affairs). Descartes' meditator returns to the world not only with a fresh knowledge of God and the soul but also with a fresh understanding of the nature of corporeal things. With the metaphysical knowledge that extension is the essence of matter firmly implanted in memory, the meditator is prepared to employ the senses and imagination in the investigation of nature.[26]

A final, fundamental point of comparison underscores the autonomy of the meditator. Mystical and meditative writings stress the experience of the meditator himself. Although spiritual exercises may be guided by a director, the individual seeks his own experience of God. The instructions of the director and the guidance of the text itself become secondary to the individual's personal illumination. Yet this illumination is not held out as something the individual can achieve on his own. No human aid may be required, but meditators from Augustine to Eustace of St. Paul recognized the dependence of the exercitant on the assistance of faith granted through divine grace. In Eustace's *Exercises spirituels* (1630), the meditator purges not only the senses and imagination but the intellect as well, thereby abandoning the human faculty of judgment in the hope of illumination from on high.[27] The success of meditation in achieving union with God ultimately depends on the inscrutable dispensation of grace.

For his pursuit of permanent results in science, Descartes makes the autonomy of the meditator absolute. This autonomy emerges parenthetically in the synopsis of the *Meditations:* "I do not intend to speak of matters pertaining to Faith or the conduct of life, but only of those which concern speculative truths, and which may be known by the sole aid of the light of nature" (HR I, 142). Descartes' meditator never forsakes his own faculty of judgment, or "natural light"; early in the Third Meditation, he explicitly puts its deliverances absolutely beyond doubt.[28] Moreover, the autonomy of the meditator is not diminished by his conclusion that the trustworthiness of the natural light derives from its source in God (and therefore that a knowledge of God is necessary to avoid skepticism and achieve lasting science), for that conclusion itself is derived under the aegis of the natural light.[29] Furthermore, this divine gift is dispensed equally to all, so no one can claim special illumination regarding matters that fall within the purview of human reason (as opposed to matters of faith). As befits one whose aim was to secure an independent stance for natural science, Descartes never makes the search after truth dependent upo. the grace of God.[30] The investigation of nature may proceed independently of revealed doctrine.

II

Descartes' elaboration of a meditative mode of arriving at metaphysical first truths reflected his doctrine that the intellect constitutes a source of knowledge distinct from the senses. This non-Aristotelian doctrine of the autonomy of the intellect required a reconception of the relationship between the intellect and the senses. Although the senses no longer could play the exalted role of providing the only content for thought, Descartes' intellectualism did not allow him to ignore their role in cognition. Aristotelian philosophy had provided a unified account of sense perception and cognition; rejecting a part of it required replacing it all. Moreover, Descartes' abiding concern with natural science demanded an investigation into the possibility and reliability of sensory knowledge of natural things; for, no matter to what extent the intellect dominates the senses, the object of study in the investigation of nature—the corporeal, "visible" world—can be known in its details only by means of the senses.

In the *Meditations* proper Descartes gave only a very general picture of his theory of the senses. The senses are demoted from chief stewards of knowledge (AG, 111–114) to a more mundane, pragmatic function as navigational guides and arbiters of immediate bodily benefits and harms (AG, 117–119). By edict of First Philosophy, the deliverances of the senses are subject to evaluation and correction by the intellect. The meditator reaches the verdict that when sensory ideas are regarded as representations of material objects, the ideas of geometric (or "primary") properties more clearly represent reality than do the ideas of sensory qualities (or "secondary qualities") such as color, odor, and sound. Hence, the conclusion: "It may be that not all bodies are such as my senses apprehend them, for this sensory apprehension is in many ways obscure and confused; but at any rate their nature must comprise whatever I clearly and distinctly understand—that is, whatever, generally considered, falls within the subject-matter of pure mathematics" (AG, 116).

The authors of the sixth set of Objections challenged Descartes' doctrine that "the certitude of the understanding far exceeds that of the senses"; they asked whether instead the certitude of the understanding does not depend on "a good disposition of the senses," and whether the correction of sensory errors does not result from a comparison among the reports of several senses, rather than from a direct judgment of the understanding (HR II, 238). In response to this challenge to the epistemic independence and priority of the intellect, Descartes provided a sketch of his physiology and psychology of sense perception (a sketch that can be filled in from several of Descartes' other writings).[31] This discussion of the physiological and psychological aspects of sense perception allowed Descartes to distinguish those portions of the sensory process to which certitude and error can properly be attributed from those portions that occur in accordance with nature and hence are not properly said to err or not to err. Descartes' response therefore provides a detailed guide to his conception of the line between the sensory and the intellectual aspects of sense perception.

Descartes distinguished three stages or "grades" of sense perception: (1) "the immediate affection of the bodily organ by external objects," that is, the pattern of motion in the sense organ and brain caused by sensory stimulation; (2) "the immediate mental result, due to the mind's union with the corporeal organ affected"—Descartes lists the ideas of secondary qualities to exemplify this level, but in the case of vision also includes visual form; and (3) "those judgments which, on the occasion of motions occurring in the corporeal organ, we have from our earliest years been accustomed to pass about things external to us" (HR II, 251). These levels might be denoted "physiology," "sensation," and "perception"; the first comprises merely corporeal activity, the second implicates mind-body interaction, and the third involves the distinctively mental operation of judging.

The significance of Descartes' account of sense perception can best be grasped against the background of the standard Aristotelian account. The most radical contrast pertains to sensory physiology and the physics of light. For purposes of comparison, an Aristotelian account may be characterized in terms of the doctrines of form and matter and of the sensitive soul. In this connection, a thing's *form* may be understood as that which, in infusing a material substrate, makes a thing what it is. Any given substance has its essential form (as the form *man* informs a human, having the essence "rational animal"), as well as various accidental (nonessential) forms that determine its properties: a thing is red by virtue of instantiating the form of redness, and so on for roundness, coolness, and so forth. In the process of vision by which we perceive an object's redness or roundness, the forms of redness and roundness are transmitted through the optical medium (without the matter of the thing) to the sense organ and through the optic nerves to the seat of judgment (the Aristotelian "common sense"). The sentient soul receives and senses the very form of redness that exists in the red thing.[32] Color as experienced by the percipient is a "species" of the color in the object. As Descartes put it, the Aristotelian conceives experienced color as "resembling" color in objects (AC, 79, 194–196); color, like shape, is a "real property" of corporeal things.

In contrast, Descartes developed a wholly mechanistic account of light and visual physiology. The properties of objects, including both color and shape, are accounted for by appeal to geometrical properties alone (size, shape, position, and motion); the transmission of light from objects to the eye, and the attendant physiological processes in the optic nerve and brain are explained wholly in mechanical terms. Properties of objects such as size, shape, and motion are perspectivally projected onto the retina by the rectilinear propagation and refraction of light (a motion in the aether) through various media; the retinal pattern is then transmitted to the surface of the pineal gland (the seat of mind-body interaction) via the fibers of the optic nerves, the motions of which cause a set of pores lining the interior of the brain to open, which allows "animal spirits" (very fine particles filtered out of the blood at the base of the pineal gland) to flow (rectilinearly) from the gland into the pores, all the while preserving the relative ordering of the parts of the retinal image. Diverse colors in objects are actually diverse surface textures (micro-variations in the shape of the surface), which impart spins of various velocities to particles of light, causing distinctive jigglings of the optic nerve fibers, leading to corresponding variations in the openings of the internal pores and hence in the character of the flow of animal spirits from the surface of the gland.[33] In sum, in the first stage of sensory activity—the pineal flow pattern— shape and size are represented in perspective projection, and color is represented by variations in the (amplitude of the?) flow of animal spirits. The processes involved are conceived in a purely mechanistic manner, contrary to the contemporary Aristotelian account, which attributes sentience and discriminative ability to the eye itself, owing to the presence there of the sensitive soul. For Descartes, there is nothing of the mental in the first grade of sense perception.

To the second stage of sensory activity belongs "the perception of the color or light" reflected from an object, resulting from the mind's being affected by the motions in the brain. This first properly mental component of sense perception comprises a sensation of a pattern of color and light corresponding to the pineal image.[34] This sensory image typically goes unnoticed, for it provides the immediate basis for the third grade of sense perception, which includes perception of the size, shape, and distance of seen objects. These properties are perceived as a result of rapid, habitual judgments based on the sensory image. Just as the first and second grades straddle the dividing line between the corporeal and the mental, the second and third grades mark a distinction between what is properly sensory and what pertains to the intellect. For, as Descartes insisted, "that magnitude, distance and figure can be perceived by reasoning alone, which deduces them one from another, I have proved in the Dioptrics."[35] These judgments are so rapid that they go unnoticed, and we seem to apprehend directly the sizes and shapes of objects at a distance, unaware that our perception of those objects is mediated by the sensory image and the activity of the judging intellect.[36]

Although the second and third grades of sensory activity constitute the boundary between the purely sensory and the properly intellectual, a comparison between the two does not underlie Descartes' doctrine of the greater certitude of the intellect over the senses. Descartes accepts the traditional Aristotelian teaching that the senses do not err, but that we err only insofar as we judge.[37] In his application, this implies that error (and hence certainty or uncertainty) does not reside in the first and second stages of sensory activity, but only in the third, which does not properly belong to the faculty of sense, but is "vulgarly" assigned there because the intellectual activity involved is habitual and unnoticed. Descartes accepts the common appellation of these unnoticed judgments as "sensory." His doctrine then draws a distinction between the third grade of "sense" and the greater certainty of yet a fourth level of considerations regarding sense perception, the mature judgments of the understanding. To use his example, the visual perception of a stick half-submerged in water as bent results from the habitual judgment of visual localization, which goes awry owing to the refractive properties of the interface between water and air. This faulty judgment is not corrected by simply trusting the implicit judgment of the tactual sense that the stick is straight, but rather by the mature judgment of the understanding that, under these conditions, touch is to be trusted over sight (HR II, 252–253).

If the notion that the intellect must certify sensory reports were all that Descartes' claim of the greater certitude of the intellect over the senses amounted to, it would be a rather unexceptional doctrine that surely would have been assented to by the more Aristotelian of the Aristotelians. But Descartes affirmed a deeper sense in which the mature judgments of the intellect frame the deliverances and correct the errors of the senses (or of the implicit judgments of ordinary sense perception). For Descartes maintained that, although the senses themselves do not deceive, they provide material for error in the obscure sensations of color, sound, heat, and so forth. These sensations are obscure in that they do not in themselves afford a knowledge of what color, sound, heat, and so forth, *are* (when considered as properties of objects): that is, they do not reveal that these properties are dispositions of the size, shape, and motion of the minute corpuscles of objects (and their surrounding media) to produce sensations in us.[38] Nonetheless, owing to the prejudices of childhood, we habitually judge that these sensations do afford us an immediate knowledge of the properties of objects and, in fact, that the external objects implant in us through the senses a "likeness" or "picture" of themselves or, indeed, that sensations "resemble" the properties of objects (AG, 79–80); for "since I had no conception of these objects from any other source than the ideas themselves, it could not but occur to me that they were like the ideas" (AG, 112). It is this habitual childhood (and Aristotelian) prejudice that must be corrected by the mature intellect.

Descartes' "no resemblance" doctrine of sensory qualities such as color constituted a second major break with the Aristotelian account of the senses, or rather constituted a second aspect of his departure from that orthodoxy. Descartes' account introduces a sharp division between color as a property of objects, together with its effect on the medium and the nervous system, and the sensation of color experienced by the mind. The mental experience of phenomenal color (resulting from pineal agitation) falls under the mystery of mind-body interaction (AG, 116–117); its physical and physiological causes may be investigated through the clear and distinct conceptions of mechanistic physics.

Descartes' new doctrine raised a new problem of explanation and justification—namely, to show why color in objects should be thought of geometrically and mechanistically rather than as a real or primary property. In the sentence quoted above, Descartes adumbrates that this justification must come from a source other than the sensory ideas themselves. What are the candidate sources? One might suppose that mechanistic physics itself does all the work that need be done here, by providing a clear and compelling account of the operation of the senses. But notice that this account appeals to microproperties of objects, sensory media, and the nervous system, which are at best inferred. Why should one accept a mechanistic rather than an Aristotelian account of the senses in the first place? This poses a general question about the sources of knowledge that frame both particular sensory judgments and the theory of the senses itself, and forces us to come to grips with the status of the intellect as an independent source of knowledge.

III

According to the reading I shall give, Descartes' new geometrico-mechanical theory of the senses received its justification as part of the larger project to "geometrize" nature as a whole. Descartes' doctrine that all sensory qualities are reducible to the (macro- or micro-) geometrical properties of objects was simply part and parcel of his doctrine that matter possesses only geometrical (including kinematic) properties *tout court*. Both were justified by the metaphysics of the *Meditations*.

In the earlier *Rules for the Direction of the Mind* Descartes had derived his account of human knowledge from reflection on his conception of the best natural-scientific account of the senses and imagination; he had worked from an account of the operation of these organs to a general conception of nature.[39] Having aborted this project and confronted skeptical challenges, Descartes reversed the direction of conceptualization and justification in his mature period (after 1629).[40] He now would work not from an account of the sensory process, but from the metaphysical conception of pure intellect. Consonant with the meditative genre, in the *Meditations* Descartes cast his account of the relation between sensory knowledge and metaphysics in terms of cognitive faculties. In considering the usefulness of the senses, the meditator concludes that he should not "draw any conclusion from sense perception as regards external objects without a previous examination by the understanding; for knowledge of the truth about them seems to belong to the mind alone, not to the composite whole" (AG, 118); it is an error to use the senses "as if they were sure criteria for a direct judgment as to the essence of external bodies" (AG, 119). The admonition of a "previous examination" by the intellect is not practical advice to think before looking; it suggests deciding by the mind alone (without looking) what properties one should expect to find in external objects. Metaphysical knowledge of the corporeal world is prior to sensory knowledge, because it is obtained by the intellect operating independently of the senses. In Descartes' mature thought, metaphysics frames physics, including the theory of sense perception, in that it allegedly provides, independently of sensory experience and of any theory of the corporeal world or the operation of the sense organs, direct insight into the fundamental nature of matter. This insight then delimits and guides the construction of an account of sensory knowledge.

The key metaphysical insight behind Descartes' geometrization of

The key metaphysical insight behind Descartes' geometrization of nature is the doctrine that the essence of matter is extension ("the subject-matter of pure mathematics" [AG, 108, 116]). In the Fifth Meditation, where he introduces the notion that pure extension constitutes the essence of material things, the meditator contends:

Before enquiring whether any such objects exist outside me, I must consider the ideas of them, precisely as occurring in my consciousness, and see which of them are distinct and which confused. I distinctly imagine, the so-called continuous quantity of the philosophers; that is to say, the extension of quantity, or rather the quantified object, in length, breadth, and depth. I can enumerate different parts of it; to these parts I can assign at will size, shape, position, and local motion; and to these motions I can assign any durations I choose. (AG, 101)

The distinct ideas of bodies comprise extension and its geometrical modifications (together with the extrinsic denominations of arithmetic enumeration and temporal duration).[41] The meditator later concludes from the notion that only extension is clearly known in body that it constitutes the essence of body. Of interest here is the fact that in establishing the distinctness with which extension is known, the meditator says that one can distinctly *imagine* quantity, which could imply that metaphysical knowledge of body ultimately depends on the faculty of imagination. Such an implication would conform to the teaching of the *Rules*, according to which the certainty of our knowledge of extension is certified by the fact that in employing the imagination to contemplate an extended area, we contemplate an actual exemplar of extension in the "really material body" of the imaginal faculty of the brain (Rule 14).[42] This justificatory strategy makes sense in the *Rules*, since Descartes could refer back to the earlier account (Rule 12) of the operation of the senses and imagination in terms of modifications of figure alone (i.e., figural modifications of an extended bodily organ). Such a strategy is not available in the *Meditations*, since in the Fifth Meditation the existence of the body, and hence of the corporeal faculty of imagination, is still in doubt. Imaginings are available as a part of the meditator's experience, and any use of imagination could appeal only to such experience, independently of a physiological account of the imagination or the senses.

Be that as it may, a reading of the *Meditations* that makes Descartes' conclusion regarding the essence of matter rely on the faculty of imagination is untenable, for it conflicts with the account of geometrical knowledge in that work, and extension is the object of geometry. Descartes' meditator contends that imagination alone would be insufficient as a faculty of geometrical knowledge, since the objects of geometry actually grasped by the mind outstrip that faculty's representational power. In the Second Meditation, the meditator is brought to realize that he can comprehend the potential of the wax for an infinity of changes in shape and size, though he cannot imagine every distinct shape and size it might take on; in the Sixth Meditation, the meditator realizes that he can understand a chiliagon, even though he cannot picture its one thousand sides to himself.[43] In taking these points as an argument for the independence of the intellectual apprehension of geometrical objects from imagination, the meditator implicitly rejects the Aristotelian notion that the role of the intellect in geometry is to abstract geometrical universals (which would apply to an infinity of particulars) from a finite number of imperfect sensory and imaginal instances.[44] The only argument for regarding the intellect as an independent source of geometrical knowledge—other than the bare assertion in the Sixth Meditation that it is—comes in the Fifth Meditation (in continuation of the passage quoted above). The meditator remarks that the truth of various details of geometry "is obvious and so much in accord with my nature that my first discovery of them appears not as the learning of something new, but as the recollection of what I already knew—as the first occasion of my noticing things that had long been present to me, although I had never previously turned my mind's eye towards them" (AG, 101). Here one is presented with a putative experiential fact about geometrical truths—that they are unlearned, or that coming to affirm them is a matter of drawing out what is latent in the mind.

It is a rather straightforward matter to show that Descartes insisted on the doctrine that the objects of geometry can be grasped autonomously by the pure intellect. It is another matter to provide an interpretation of what it means to have a mental conception of a figure such as a triangle, pentagon, or chiliagon "without the aid of imagination" (AG, 110). How can one intellectually apprehend figure, independently of picturing it to one's self or seeing it?

One attractive answer embarks from Descartes' considerable contribution to the development of mathematical thought. A distinctive feature of Descartes' mathematics after the *Rules* is that it abandons the idea that all mathematical operations should be depictable in the imagination. In his *Geometry* proper Descartes developed the notion of a pure science of proportion, expressed in terms of algebraic equations and conceived in terms of proportions among line lengths.[45] Perhaps when Descartes spoke of a nonimaginal understanding of the triangle, he had in mind the kind of understanding that is embodied in knowing the equations for expressing the relations among the sides of a triangle, deriving the area of a triangle, and so on. The "pure conceivings" of the intellect are in this manner assimilated to an algebraic understanding of continuous quantity and its proportional relations.

But what kind of understanding is that? The temptation of the twentieth-century mind to consider this as a kind of purely formal or symbolic understanding (whatever that would be) clearly will not do. Descartes scorned attempts to make words or symbols and formal rules for manipulating them primary; these are merely arbitrary sensory reminders for the content manifest in thought itself.[46] So even if we suppose the pure conceivings to be "algebraic," the question naturally arises of what it is like to contemplate a triangle algebraically, without the aid of imagination or of sensory props. Which puts us back at asking what it's like to have a pure conceiving of a triangle in the first place.

A second way of understanding this doctrine, which draws less on Descartes' actual mathematical results but which is more satisfying from an historical point of view, connects Descartes' doctrine of a nonimaginal understanding of geometry with the Platonic tradition, especially as expressed by Proclus, and thus forges a connection between this mathematical doctrine in the *Meditations* and the neo-Platonism in the Augustinian tradition of meditation.

Plato himself of course regarded mathematical studies as a means for leading the "eye of the mind" from the visible, sensible world to the invisible, intelligible world.[47] His suggestive remarks in the *Republic* regarding the division between sensibles and intelligibles, and between sensory and intellectual faculties, were elaborated at length by Proclus in his *Commentary on the First Book of Euclid's Elements* (a work well known to seventeenth-century mathematicians).[48] Proclus struggled long with the problem of how the immaterial mind can know the objects of geometry, which are extended and so apparently divisible, unless it employs the imagination (a corporeal faculty) to create an extended figure. But dependence on a corporeal substrate (even in the imagination as directed by the mind) would make geometrical objects, which are eternal and unchanging, partake of the changeable; in any case, how could there exist in the corporeal faculty of the imagination such ordinary geometrical objects as points without extension and lines without breadth? Although imagination may be the organ that presents us with palpable images of geometrical figures, the perfection of geometrical objects requires that they be knowable by the mind alone: "Plato calls geometrical forms 'understandables' and asserts that they separate us from sensible things and incite us to turn from sensation to Nous [intuitive reason]—the ideas of the understanding being, as I said, indivisible and unextended, in keeping with the peculiar character of the soul."[49] The objects of pure geometry—points, lines, and surfaces without color or any sensory quality—belong to the domain of invisible, unchanging objects. Hence they must be known by a faculty appropriately directed toward that domain, the faculty of understanding (*dianoia*), which employs unitary (indivisible) ideas to grasp objects that are "separate" from sensible things.

It is in accordance with a Platonic account of mathematical understanding that I would interpret Descartes' doctrine that geometrical objects can be known by the mind independently of the imagination and senses. Yet Descartes was not properly a Platonist, for he replaced the theory of the forms with his theory of innate ideas. The "recollection" of geometrical truths by Plato's slave boy in the *Meno* is cast as a recollection of an earlier apprehension of the transcendent realm of the Forms; the escape from the cave in the *Republc* brings one directly to face with an external light.[50] For Descartes, the light of nature is an innate light.[51] It retains a connection with the divine by virtue of its divine origin, but unlike the direct contemplation of the Forms it is not itself a grasping of the divine. Consonant with his desire to separate the contemplation and investigation of creation from the contemplation of the creator, Descartes has replaced the Platonic and neo-Platonic conceptions of the intellectual apprehension of eternal truths in terms of transcendental Forms, or *archae*, in the divine mind, with his conception of a natural light instilled in the mind by the creator. Moreover, the eternal truths embedded in this natural light are, according to Descartes, free and arbitrary creations of the divine will.[52] The deity freely decrees the laws of geometry that define the essence of matter, and implants a natural light adjusted to those decreed laws in the created minds. In this manner, Descartes could defend the notion that he had a priori insight into the very essence of matter, without setting up a world of forms coeternal with God, and without audaciously having to claim direct insight into the mind of God itself.

IV

We have, on the one hand, the autonomy and priority of the intellect over the senses as a source of knowledge of the constitution of nature. On the other hand, there remains the project, intimated in the opening quotation of this essay, of filling in various details about the natural world (such as the size of the sun). How are these details to be determined? A common answer has been that Descartes believed he could derive them in a wholly a priori manner, spinning all of natural science out of his first principles. However, the myth of Descartes as a complete a priorist with regard to natural science—a myth founded in seventeenth-century rhetorical exchanges and soberly recounted even in recent scholarship—should soon be put to rest by the increasing number of fine studies showing the systematic role assigned to experiment by Descartes in his conception of scientific method.[53] The explosion of this myth leaves the problem of precisely characterizing the relationships among experiment, sensory experience, and metaphysics in Descartes' mature thought; or between the details to be filled in empirically and the deliverances of the intellect.

One of the details to be filled in is the theory of the senses itself. In section 2 we saw that Descartes put forward a theory of the senses fully integrated with his mechanistic natural science and dualist metaphysics. The crux of this theory—and the part that makes it mesh with his natural science as a whole—is the distinction between primary and secondary qualities. At the end of section 2 the question of the justification of this account to the exclusion of an Aristotelian account was left unanswered. Let us now bring the results of section 3 to bear on this question, through an examination of the two strategies that Descartes employed in his mature works to win acceptance for a mechanistic conception of nature.

The first strategy was to reveal by concrete example the power of the mechanistic hypothesis to provide a unified and intelligible account of natural phenomena. Descartes employed this strategy in his earliest publshed writings. Thus, in the *Optics* and *Meteorology*, two of the three "essays" attached to the *Discourse on Method*, mechanistic accounts of the operation of the sense organs and of various natural phenomena near the surface of the earth are put forward under the umbrella of a few "hypotheses." The most general statement of these hypotheses, presented at the outset of the *Meteorology*, is that all natural bodies are composed of small particles of various shapes and sizes, such that even the smallest interstices are filled with very fine matter.[54] From this hypothesized corpuscularism (with plenum), Descartes proceeds to frame explanations not only of natural phenomena, such as vapors and exhalations, winds, and clouds, but also to account for the properties of objects that cause sensations in us, such as heat, color, and light, all by means of positing various motions in diversely shaped corpuscles. His justification for introducing this very general form of mechanistic explanaton, as he recounted it in various letters written in 1637 and 1638, was not a priori and metaphysical, but a posteriori and empirical. The pattern is hypothetico-deductive. Certain configurations of corpuscles—usually microscopic in size, and envisioned by analogy with macroscopic mechanisms—are posited to *explain* various phenomena, or "effects." Then, if the explanation is plausible, the causes may be "proven" by the effects. The more effects that can be explained by a given causal mechanism, the more probable that the cause is the true one: "It is true that there are many effects to which it is easy to fit many separate causes, but it is not always so easy to fit a single cause to many effects, unless it is the cause which truly produces them" (K, 58). Following this strategy, Descartes claimed his account of nature to be preferable to that of Scholastic Aristotelianism owing to its greater comprehensiveness and simplicity (K, 38–41, 43–44, 48–49, 55–59).

Any attempted a posteriori justification is limited by having to base its appeal on comparative advantages, such as intelligibility, simplicity, and comprehensiveness. But any merely comparative advantage cannot rule out the competition once and for all. Scholastic Aristotelianism provided one account of natural phenomena, which was closely integrated with an account of how these phenomena are known (via sense perception and intellectual abstraction). Descartes provided an alternative account, with an alternative theory of sense perception. According to the one, color is a real property of objects and is perceived via the transmission of a sensible species into the nervous system; according to the other, color is a sensation produced by mechanical agitation of the nervous system, which affects the mind with a sensation. Why should one accept that perceived color arises from microscopical particles agitating nerve fibers rather than from the reception of a "form" transmitted through the medium? Later natural philosophers might point to the successes of the new science as a justification for its acceptance. Descartes, however, was in the position of achieving acceptance for a view of nature which in fact had not yet produced remarkable comparative successes.

Descartes' second strategy was intended to provide the absolute justification he desired for his general conception of nature, by establishing that bodies have no other properties than modifications of extension. The success of this strategy depends upon showing that, of the various properties of objects seemingly manifest to the senses, extension and extension alone is clearly known (from which it is inferred, in accordance with the notion that God is no deceiver, that extension is the sole essence of bodies).

Prima facie, it is difficult to see why color as we experience it should be regarded as confused and obscure in comparison with shape. Phenomenally, color seems no more "out of focus"—confused and obscure—than the other dimensions of visual experience. Descartes granted as much in the *Principles:* "Pain, color, and so on are clearly and distinctly perceived when they are considered merely as sensations or thoughts" (*Principles* I, no. 68, AG, 194; cf. AG, 78–80). The difference comes when ideas are regarded as representing something external to the mind that has them; it is by comparison with the external standard of material nature itself that some sensory ideas are regarded as confused representations of their objects, whereas others are deemed clearer. But how is this comparison to be effected? If one proceeds empirically, it is difficult to see how to give a straightforward justification to the claim that ideas of shape more clearly represent the actual properties of objects than do ideas of color. Shape seems no more primitive and fundamental to our sensory experience than does color: colored things are always experienced as spatially articulated, but nothing is experienced as spatially articulated unless it varies in lightness or color. Perhaps later authors could claim that spatio-temporal properties are more thoroughly entrenched in scientific discourse, but that is partially as a result of the program that Descartes helped launch.[55]

Descartes sought to solve the problem by appealing to a criterion outside the domain of sensory ideas. The difficulty of sorting among phenomenally given sensory ideas in order to determine their representational value is circumvented by appealing to a source of knowledge from which one can directly determine the sorts of properties that material objects may possess. The greater clarity attending the perception of shape is not, in the first instance, sense-perceptual; it is intellectual. By the natural light of the intellect, the only aspect of material things that can be clearly perceived or understood is pure, continuous quantity: the attribute of extension. Color isn't even a starter, since the objects of pure geometry as perceived by the intellect do not possess any sensory qualities. When the corrective judgments of the intellect are brought to bear on sensory ideas, it can be directly intuited that color is at best an obscure and confused representation of the geometrical properties of corporeal objects. Its comparative obscurity is determined not by a direct comparison with shape as experienced through the senses, but with the intellectual apprehension of shape as a geometrical property.

This strategy for sorting out sensory ideas applies to the whole of nature. Descartes' claim is that, a priori, the only sorts of explanations that can be considered in natural science are ones that appeal only to geometrical properties such as size, shape, and motion. Metaphysics provides a way of setting aside other forms of explanation once and for all, in order to proceed with the elaboration of a mechanistic account of nature. Various particular mechanistic explanations cannot be defended on the basis of metaphysics alone, since mathematical intuition per se gives no direct insight into the particular geometrical configurations of actually existing bodies. The latter must be determined by sensory observation and experiment; by positing particular mechanistic hypotheses, and checking the empirical plausibility of the posit. Metaphysics reveals what kinds of properties can be used in constructing hypotheses; sensory observation and experiment must be used to determine which of these constructions fit the actual order of things.[56]

V

A reading of the *Meditations* as meditations brings into prominence the extent to which its arguments and conclusions depend upon its guidance of the reader to certain experiences. The indubitability of the *cogito*, the apprehension of thought as something known independently of the body, the idea of a benevolent Supreme Being, the pure conception of extension without attendant sensory qualities—these are the experiences upon which depend the success of the *Meditations* in establishing Descartes' First Philosophy.

My emphasis on the experiential thrust of Descartes' chief work may seem to yield an implausibly (or uncomfortably) psychologistic interpretation. In fact, Descartes has been ascribed "the glory of having determined the true character of the psychological method" for searching after truth, thereby setting Locke on the pathway of investigating the phenomena of human understanding in his *Essay*.[57] Although Descartes did enjoin one to turn inward and to discover the givens of one's own experience, his method cannot patly be described as introspective. For Descartes was not asking one simply to look within. He was not interested in his own or his reader's passing psychological states. (Nor was he bringing the reader to an awareness of sense-data.)[58] Rather, he was hoping to help the reader discover, through the process of meditation, a source of impersonal, objective judgments that lies hidden in the intellect. The meditator is to sift through his own experience until he arrives at that which compels assent, and thereby to discover what lies behind the possibility of universal agreement in such subject matters as mathematics and logic.[59] Descartes' "introspective" discovery of clear and distinct perception presumes to have arrived at the experiential basis behind the demonstrations of geometry.

Descartes has the meditator seek illumination for himself through the cognitive exercises of the *Meditations*. The need to experience illumination for one's self may be understood through Descartes' methodological writings. In both the *Rules* (esp. 5–7, 11) and the *Discourse* (pt. 2, AG, 20), intuition serves as the starting point for all knowledge. The Cartesian method seeks to begin with what is intuitively certain and to derive consequences by steps which themselves possess intuitive certainty. A discursive argument hence takes its life from purely mental intuition. Intuition—or, in the language of the *Meditations*, clear and distinct perception or intellectual illumination—is the starting point and the support of all progress in demonstrative knowledge, and therefore in First Philosophy.

Intuition can only be had for one's self. Whether in geometry or metaphysics, proper judgment of the truth results only when one feels one's own will compelled to give assent—compelled not by any external factor, but by one's own intellectual apprehension (AG, 96; HR I, 204). Descartes believed it more difficult to achieve self-illumination and self-guidance in metaphysics than in geometry. Geometry had achieved systematization and acceptance, presumably because its principles are among those "so clear that they may be acquired without any meditation" (HR I, 205). Metaphysics, while potentially possessing the certainty of geometry, appeared in relative disarray. Descartes explained in the dedication to the *Meditations* that, although the demonstrations contained therein

. . . are equal to, or even surpass in certainty and evidence, the demonstrations of Geometry, I yet apprehend that they cannot be adequately understood by many, both because they demand a mind wholly free from prejudices, and one which can easily be detached from affairs of sense. (HR I, 135)

Moreover, agreement was expected in geometry, and so the reader might be willing to give the benefit of the doubt. In metaphysics, Descartes was faced with the task of helping readers to achieve illumination despite prejudice or lack of faith. Hence, his requirement that one "meditate seriously" with him (HR I, 139).

Cartesian meditation is a method of discovery. Descartes explained his work in those terms in the second set of Replies. Pressed to formulate his First Philosophy in "geometrical fashion," he hesitantly complied, explaining the necessity for the meditative genre. While a geometrical exposition from definitions, postulates, and axioms has demonstrative force at each step, it does not reveal how these steps are arrived at, nor does it bring one to a direct intuition of the first principles. This may not be of great moment for the exposition of geometry, since "the primary notions that are the presuppositions of geometrical proofs harmonize with the use of our senses and are granted by all" (HR II, 49). (Presumably it would hinder geometrical *discovery* to proceed always in this fashion.) The primary notions of metaphysics are quite otherwise, Descartes lamented. Here the problem is not to carry out proofs (which might well be assented to, given the definitions and axioms), but to discover the axioms themselves (which are hopelessly obscured by the prejudices of the senses). The reader cannot feel the intuitive force of these first principles until he apprehends them. Hence, the cognitive exercises of the *Meditations* are engineered to suspend prejudice through skeptical doubt, to exercise one's intuition through the illumination of the *cogito* and the proofs of God's existence, and to prepare one for the intuitive apprehension of mind and body as having distinct essences through the exercises of the Second Meditation, which are consolidated in the arguments of the Sixth Meditation. The *Meditations* is successful when it can be laid aside in favor of direct apprehension of the clear but remote principles of First Philosophy.

But does the sincere participant in a Cartesian retreat have the experiences called for by the *Meditations?* We are likely to have no problem in admitting the indubitability of the *cogito* (although the subsequent step to the separate substantiality of the mind will not find the same acceptance). But the same success will not be forthcoming with the appeal to an innate idea of God and to a direct mental perception of pure, continuous quantity. Although both theism and mathematics persist, they do so without the cognitive foundations envisioned by Descartes.

What did Descartes have in mind in staking his claims on these experiences? He did not, I think, intend that what we might (inappropriately) call the "mere" (but nonetheless considerable) literary merits of the text should carry the day. Rather, his choice of the meditative genre reflected his serious commitment to invoking these experiences in the reader, in accordance with his methodology of intuition. That he could reasonably expect to do so for his audience, and that the expectation no longer is reasonable, reveals the extent to which this most ahistorically conceived of texts is historically conditioned. Just as those places in his writing where Descartes believed he was pointing the way to an unconditioned intuition of the truth, we find that the very intelligibility of his text requires the deepest historical analysis.

Descartes could expect to invoke the appropriate responses in (some of) his readers because the *Meditations* drew on two ongoing practices: spiritual meditation and speculative mathematics. We have seen that, in the Augustinian tradition of meditation, one sweeps away the sensory world in order to see God with the eye of the mind. Similarly, in the neo-Platonic mathematical tradition, one uses the imagination as a convenient aid to display the continuous proportions that are known to pure intellect. No matter what the practitioners of this regimen actually did experience (could this be decided?), the account they each gave of their practice included the intellectual apprehension of God on the one hand and of the objects of mathematics on the other. There existed communities of meditators and mathematicians in the time of Descartes who were used to describing their experiences in the manner of the *Meditations*.

Yet one cannot rest content with totally relativizing Descartes to this historical context, for his work continues to speak. One way in which it speaks is through its appropriation by philosophical traditions indifferent (or antipathetic) to Descartes' intellectualist metaphysics, as when the First Meditation is used as a standard statement of skepticism in the teaching of twentieth-century sense-data epistemology. Here, a more recent philosophical tradition makes of Descartes what it will. But in another sense Descartes must speak to us because he was on to something. Even if one does not find force in the reasons Descartes gave for accepting his project of natural science, his conception of the project was nonetheless efficacious. His vision of a unified celestial and terrestrial physics that emphasized spatio-temporal properties planted seeds for the development of modern physical thought that bore fruit in Newton. Moreover, Descartes stands at the beginning of modern philosophical investigation into the relation between the knower and the known. Even if we no longer are taken with his foundationalist enterprise, his epistemic individualism, or his account of cognitive faculties, the problematic of characterizing the contribution of the knower (or community of knowers) to the very constitution (or fabrication) of knowledge remains. Not only does the tradition make (what it will of) Descartes; Descartes has made the tradition.[60]

NOTES

1. AG—*Descartes: Philosophical Writings*, trans. Elizabeth Anscombe and P. T. Geach (Indianapolis: Bobbs-Merrill, 1971). For an explanation of the abbreviations AT, HR, and K, see the General Bibliography at the beginning of this volume. Op—*Discourse on Method; Optics, Geometry, and Meteorology*, trans. Paul J. Olscamp (Indianapolis: Bobbs-Merrill, 1965).

2. Thomas Aquinas, *Summa Theologica*, pt. 1, qu. 12, arts. 11–12; qu. 84, art. 7; qu. 85, art. 1. Here and below I contrast Descartes' position with an Aristotelian position, which, of course, need not have been Aristotle's position (though, as in the present case, it may have textual support in Aristotle—cf. *De Anima*, bk. 3, chap. 4, 429a18–29, and chap. 8, 432a3–14). The Aristotelian position sketched constitutes a common medieval and seventeenth-century interpretation of Aristotle, via Thomas.

3. This important function of the doubt has been emphasized by E. M. Curley in *Descartes Against the Skeptics* (Cambridge; Harvard University Press, 1978), chaps. 2–3; and by Margaret Dauler Wilson in *Descartes* (London: Routledge & Kegan Paul, 1978), chap. 1.

4. These are the second and third of three uses for the doubt given by Descartes in his reply to Hobbes (Objections and Replies III: HR II, 60–61). The antiskeptical thrust of Descartes' work has been emphasized by Richard H. Popkin in *The History of Skepticism from Erasmus to Spinoza* (Berkeley, Los Angeles, London: University of California Press, 1979), chap. 9.

5. Ignatius's *Constitutions of the Society of Jesus* (trans. George E. Gauss, based on the final Spanish text of 1594 [St. Louis: Institute of Jesuit Sources, 1970]) established Aristotelian philosophy as the official doctrine of the Jesuits in logic, natural and moral philosophy, and metaphysics; Aristotelian features of his *Spiritual Exercises* will become apparent below. Eustace of St. Paul's *Exercices Spirituels* (Paris, 1630; 2d ed., 1640) emphasized the Augustinian doctrines of continuous creation (pt. 1, Meditation 3) and the efficacy of grace above understanding and will (pt. 1, Meditation 19). Eustace was an acquaintance and correspondent of Pierre de Bérulle, and so was connected with the circle of Descartes. His *Exercices* was written in Paris during the 1620s and presumably was in use, for in 1626 Pope Paul V authorized a plenary indulgence for all who practiced *les exercices* for ten days. For a general comparison of Jesuit and Augustinian thought in seventeenth-century France, see Robert G. Remsberg, *Wisdom and Science at Port-Royal and the Oratory: A Study of Contrasting Augustinianisms* (Yellow Springs, Ohio: Antioch Press, 1940).

6. Yearly retreats were an integral part of the curriculum at Jesuit colleges such as Descartes' La Flèche; Camille de Rochemonteix, *Un College de Jésuites aux XVIIe et XVIIIe Siècles: Le College Henri IV de la Flèche*, 4 vols. (Le Mans, 1889), 2:140–142. A helpful discussion of the relations between Descartes and members of the Parisian Oratory is provided by A. Espinas in his "Pour l'Histoire du Cartésianisme," *Revue de Metaphysique et de Morale* 14 (1906):265–293. L. J. Beck, in *The Metaphysics of Descartes* (Oxford: Clarendon Press, 1965), chap. 2, sec. 2, provides an interesting discussion of the connection between the *Meditations* and Ignatius's *Spiritual Exercises*.

7. Ignatius of Loyola, *The Spiritual Exercises*, 4th ed., trans. W. H. Longridge (London: Mowbray, 1950), First Week, First Exercise, 52–57; *The Directory to the Spiritual Exercises* (ibid.), chap. 14, secs. 2–3 (the directory was prepared by Ignatius's followers). The treatment of memory, understanding, and will as the three powers of the soul stems from Augustine's *Trinity*, bk. 10, chaps. 11–12. In the *Confessions*, Augustine describes his search for Christian faith in terms of these three powers: on the memory, see bk. 10, chaps. 8–25; on

the understanding, bk. 7, chaps. 10 and 18; on the will, bk. 8, chaps. 5, 7, and 12. The doctrine became commonplace; see, for example, Francis de Sales, *An Introduction to a Devoute Life*, trans. J. Yakesley (Douai, 1613), pt. 2, 138–143. I am indebted to Katharine Park for discussion of various doctrines concerning the powers and faculties of the soul.

8. *Directory*, chap. 39. Augustine passes through parallel stages in the *Confessions:* purging the senses and turning to intellectual illumination (bk. 7, chaps. 10 and 17), and seeking to unite his will with God's (bk. 9, chap. 1). Early seventeenth-century meditative works were often divided in accordance with the three ways: de Sales, *Devoute Life*, pts. 1, 2, and 3–4; Eustace, *Exercices* (three parts).

9. De Sales labels these "considerations" for the understanding as the "meditation proper," *Devoute Life*, pt. 2, 138.

10. Adolphe Tanquerey, *The Spiritual Life*, trans. H. Brandeis (Westminster, Maryland: Newman, 1948), 300; *Directory*, chap. 14, sec. 3.

11. On Augustine's conception of illumination, see Ronald H. Nash, *The Light of the Mind: St. Augustine's Theory of Knowledge* (Lexington: University Press of Kentucky, 1969), chap. 6–8.

12. The paucity or the poorness of argument in one or another portion of the *Meditations* is frequently remarked in recent critical work; see for example Bernard Williams's treatment of the Second Meditation passage on wax, and the Fifth Meditation statement on the essence of matter, in *Descartes: The Project of Pure Enquiry* (New York: Penguin, 1978), chap. 8. Of course, much of what I maintain that Descartes put forward as known by what I have termed "exemplification"—such as that what is clearly known in body constitutes its essence (AG, 101, heading and second paragraph; cf. *Principles* I, 53–54)—depended on tacit assumptions within the context of philosophical thought that Descartes worked. We might choose to draw these assumptions out as premises in a reconstructed argument, but at present we're interested in characterizing Descartes' conception of the force of the *Meditations*. In the concluding section of this essay I will examine what remains of this force.

13. As Pierre Courcelle has shown in his very useful *Les Confessions de Saint Augustine dans la Tradition Littéraire* (Paris, 1963), Augustine's *Confessions* was used in various ways during the Middle Ages and Renaissance. In the eighth and ninth centuries it was excerpted and rearranged along thematic lines as a doctrinal work; interest in its autobiographical character increased in the tenth and eleventh centuries (pt. 2, chap. 2). By the twelfth century, it was being recommended as a means for turning inward to a direct contemplation of God, and as a guidebook to the reform of one's own conduct (chap. 3). Devotional works in the Augustinian tradition arose, including Bonaventure's *The Mind's Road to God*, trans. George Boas (Indianapolis: Bobbs-Merrill, 1953).

14. *Summa theologica*, pt. 2, 2d pt., qu. 82, art. 3.

15. Ignatius, *Exercises*, First Week, Fifth Exercise.

16. St. Augustine, *Confessions*, trans. A. C. Outler (Philadelphia: Westminster, 1955), bk. 7, chap. 25, art. 36.

17. Ibid., bk. 4, chap. 15, art. 31; bk. 5, chap. 10, art. 19, and chap. 12, art. 25; bk. 6, chap. 3, art. 4; and bk. 7, chap. 1, arts. 1–2.

18. Ibid., bk. 7, chap. 1, art. 1.

19. Ibid., bk. 5, chap. 10, art. 19, and chap. 14, art. 25. Augustine explicitly mentions Academic skepticism.

20. Ibid., bk. 7, chap. 17, art. 23. This passage just hints at the role of immediate knowledge of the self in Augustine's overcoming skeptical doubt; that role is made explicit in the *Trinity* (bk. 9, chaps. 3 and 4; bk. 10, chap. 3, art. 5, and chap. 4, arts. 14–16) and in *De Libero Arbitrio* (bk. 2, chap. 3). Arnauld pointed out the kinship of the last with Descartes' *cogito* (HR II, 80).

21. Objections and Replies II (HR II, 49–50). The passage continues further on: "This is why my writing took the form of Meditations rather than that of Philosophical disputations or the theorems and problems of a geometer." See also the prefatory material to the *Meditations* (HR I, 135, 139, 140), where the need to withdraw the mind from the senses is repeatedly emphasized.

22. Among the numerous admonitions to spend days or weeks on the First Meditation alone, many are found in the Objections and Replies II (HR II, 31). Such admonitions were a common feature of devotional meditations.

23. *Confessions*, bk. 7, chaps. 24–25, arts. 35–36.

24. Descartes uses memory to recall old opinions about the nature of the mind (Second Meditation: AG, 67–68) and about "the real" (Sixth Meditation: AG, 111–113). These remembered doctrines contain several Aristotelian shibboleths, including the definition of man as a "rational animal" (AG, 67) and the meditator's belief that "I had nothing in my intellect that I had not previously had in sensation" (AG, 112).

25. As Richard Kennington has pointed out in his interesting article, "The 'Teaching of Nature' in Descartes' Soul Doctrine" (*Review of Metaphysics* 26 [1972]:85–117), Descartes introduces his work in the letter to the Sorbonne by emphasizing its apologetic aims, but soon replaces the original faithful/infidel dichotomy with a division between the philosopher and those "who arrogantly combat the truth" (HR I, 136). In the Synopsis and the First Meditation the cognitive aims of the work are made evident.

26. Descartes explicitly states his intention that the *Meditations* should accommodate the reader's mind to the foundations of his physics (letters to Mersenne, 11 November 1640 and 28 January 1641 [K, 82, 94]).

27. Augustine attains a glimpse of the highest being by means of his own intellectual powers (*Confessions*, bk. 7, chap. 17, art. 23, quoted above). In the end, however, abiding knowledge of God is granted him only through grace (bk. 7, chap. 12, art. 29). The recurrent Augustinian slogan, "First believe, then understand," marks the dependence of understanding on faith and hence on grace (see Nash, *Light of the Mind*, chap. 3). Eustace mortifies the intellect and declares its dependence on the light of grace in the *Exercices Spirituels* (pt. 1, Meditation 19).

28. "Whatever the light of nature shows me (e.g. that if I am doubting it follows that I exist, and so on) is absolutely beyond doubt; for there can be no faculty, equally trustworthy with this light, to show me that such things are not true" (AG, 79).

29. Even if one regards this derivation as circular, it nonetheless does depend on the natural light.

30. Descartes is quite explicit about delimiting what he calls "theology proper," which treats of matters that depend on revelation, from metaphysics, which, even if it treats of God, does so within the bounds of human reason (letter to Mersenne, 15 April 1630 [K, 10]; cf. letter to Mersenne, 27 May 1630 [K, 15]). He criticizes Comenius for seemingly wanting "to combine religion and revealed truths too closely with the sciences which are acquired by natural reasoning" (letter to Hogeland, [?] August 1639 [K, 60]). In the *Discourse*, pt. 1, he characterizes theology as requiring "aid from heaven" (AG, 12). On his doctrine that we all share the same natural light, see ibid. (pp. 7–8) and a letter to Mersenne, 16 October 1639 (K, 66).

31. Descartes' chief accounts of sensory physiology and psychology occur in the *Treatise on Man*, trans. T. S. Hall (Cambridge: Harvard University Press, 1972), 35–68 and 91–100; *Optics*, esp. pts. 4–6; *Principles* IV, nos. 187–200; and *Passions of the Soul*, pt. 1, arts. 12–35 (HR I, 337–348). His chief accounts of the cognitive and metaphysical aspects of sense perception outside the *Meditations* occur in the fourth set of Objections and Replies (HR II, 105–107) and in the *Principles* I, nos. 66–74.

32. Aristotle, *De Anima*, bk. 2, chaps. 5–7, and 12, and bk. 3, chaps. 1–2; Aquinas, *Aristotle's De Anima in the Version of William of Moerbeke and the Commentary of St. Thomas Aquinas*, trans. K. Foster and S. Humphries (New Haven: Yale University Press, 1951), commentary on the passages just cited, esp. secs. 418 and 551–554. I have discussed various Aristotelian accounts of sense perception and compared them with Descartes' account in an article with William Epstein, "The Sensory Core and the Medieval Foundations of Early Modern Perceptual Theory," *Isis* 70 (1979):363–384.

33. *Optics*, pt. 5; *Passions*, pt. 1, 10–16; *Treatise on Man*, 83–86.

34. Descartes characterizes this sensation in terms of its "extension . . . , its boundaries, and its position relatively to the parts of my brain" (HR II, 252).

35. HR II, 252. Here Descartes explains distance perception solely in terms of unnoticed judgments, thereby suggesting a reading of the celebrated "natural geometry" passage in the *Optics*, pt. 6 (Op, 106) in terms of implicit reckoning. However, in the *Treatise on Man*, he explained distance perception in a nonjudgmental, psychophysical manner, as directly elicited by brain events (pp. 61–63 and 94), which is consonant with the statement in the *Optics* that the act of thought in natural geometry is "a simple act of imagination" (Op, 106). The intellectualist emphasis in the passage from the Objections and Replies may have arisen from the fact that here Descartes is speaking more as a philosopher than as a sensory physiologist, and so is seeking a close fit between his metaphysics and theory of the senses; see Nancy Maull's insightful article, "Cartesian Optics and the Geometrization of Nature," *in* Stephen Gaukroger, ed., *Descartes: Philosophy, Mathematics and Physics* (New Jersey: Barnes and Noble, 1980), 23–40.

36. Descartes' account of judgment makes both will and intellect essential (Fourth Meditation; *Principles* I, nos. 32–35). The intellect merely apprehends, whereas the will affirms and denies (being irresistibly drawn to affirm what the intellect apprehends clearly and distinctly). In the passage under discus-

sion, Descartes uses *intellectu* to refer to the operation of the will and intellect together in judging (AT VII, 436–439).

37. Aristotle, *De Anima*, bk. 3, chap. 3, 427b. Descartes, Third Meditation (AG, 78).

38. Third Meditation (AG, 83–84); Objections and Replies IV (HR II, 105–107).

39. Descartes broke off work on the *Rules* in 1628; the work was first published in 1701. In the *Rules* the doctrine that the world is best described mechanistically grows out of the claim that such a description provides the clearest account of the operation of the senses, and of the relationship between the sense organs and the things sensed (Rule 12); geometrical knowledge is founded on an account of the faculty of imagination (Rule 14; see n. 42, below). See John A. Schuster, "Descartes' *Mathesis Universalis*, 1619–1628," in Gaukroger's *Descartes*, 41–96, esp. pt. 3.

40. In a letter to Mersenne of 15 April 1630, Descartes declared that "I have found how to prove metaphysical truths in a manner which is more evident than the proofs of geometry" (K, 11); the letter suggests that this discovery derived from the use of reason to know God and the self, and that it allowed him to discover "the foundations of Physics" (K, 10). This programmatic statement fits well the strategy of the *Meditations;* Descartes may have been discussing the results of his work on an early version of the *Meditations* during the previous nine months (AT I, 17, 182; K, 19; Beck, *Metaphysics*, chap. 1, sec. 1).

41. Denumerability and temporal duration apply to both mental and material substance; geometrical modifications are proper to matter, see *Principles* I, nos. 48 and 55.

42. HR I, 56–59; see Schuster, "Mathesis Universalis," 64. Margaret Wilson (in her *Descartes*, 169–171) argues that in the *Meditations*, too, geometry is made to depend on the imagination.

43. In the Second Meditation, remarking on the ability of the piece of wax to take on an indefinitely large number of figures as it is heated, the meditator concludes that "I should mistake the nature of wax if I did not think this piece capable also of more changes, as regards extension, than my imagination has ever grasped" (AG, 73). From this he concludes that the nature of wax— specifically, the wax as an extended thing—is known "not by imagination, but by purely mental perception"; and further on: "the perception of wax is not sight, not touch, not imagination; nor was it ever so, though it formerly seemed to be; it is a purely mental contemplation" (AG, 73), effected by the "mental power of judgment" (AG, 75). In the Sixth Meditation the meditator affirms that geometrical figures such as the triangle, pentagon, and chiliagon can be known by the understanding independently of imagination, and that intellection, but not imagination, is essential to the nature of mind (AG, 109–110). See also HR II, 229 and 66.

44. Aquinas, *Commentary on the Metaphysics of Aristotle*, 2 vols., trans. John P. Rowan (Chicago: Regnery, 1961), bk. 3, lesson 7 (on *Metaphysics*, bk. 3, chaps. 2–3) and bk. 11, lesson 3, esp. sec. 2202.

45. In Rule 14 Descartes sought to ground all of mathematics in the imag-

ination of geometrical (figural) displays of arithmetic units and the operations performed on them. The project collapsed in the attempt to extend it (in Rules 18 and 19) to the extraction of roots and the solution of higher-order equations. Compare with the opening paragraphs of the First Book fo the *Geometry*. For a helpful treatment of these matters, see Schuster, "Mathesis Universalis," pt. 3, and the more extensive treatment in his doctoral dissertation, "Descartes and the Scientific Revolution, 1618–1634" (Ann Arbor: University Microfilms, 1977), chap. 6.

46. Objections and Replies III (HR II, 66 and 69).

47. *Republic*, bk. 7, 524c–531d. It is difficult to determine the degree to which Descartes was acquainted with actual texts of Plato. He mentions Plato's account of Socrates' last days in a quite offhand manner (suggesting familiarity) in two letters to Elizabeth, November 1646 (AT IV, 530) and 22 February 1649 (AT V, 281); otherwise, there is no mention of Plato in the correspondence. Plato is characterized as a skeptic in the Author's Letter to the *Principles* (HR I, 206); the same letter uses one of Plato's images in the phrase "living without philosophy is just having the eyes closed without trying to open them" (HR I, 204), cf. *Republic*, bk. 6, 506c. Platonic thought infused the Oratory (see Espinas, "l'Histoire du Cartésianisme").

48. Proclus, *Commentary*, trans. Glenn R. Morrow (Princeton: Princeton University Press, 1970), bk. 1, chaps. 5–6, bk. 2, chap. 1. The works of Proclus (fifth century A.D.) as well as other neo-Platonic mathematical writings, were widely available by the sixteenth century, and were much discussed in the prefaces to mathematical works after that time; see Edward W. Strong, *Procedures and Metaphysics: A Study in the Philosophy of Mathematical-Physical Science in the Sixteenth and Seventeenth Centuries* (Berkeley: University of California Press, 1936), chap. 8. Christopher Clavius' edition of Euclid's *Elementorum* (Rome, 1603), which was used at La Flèche in Descartes' day, contains typical mention of Proclus' teaching that mathematics sharpens the eye of the mind for considering things apart from matter, thus preparing one for contemplation of the divine (pp. 15–19). Incidentally, in the *Meditations* this process is reversed; contemplation of God and the soul are used to reveal the foundations of physics in the conception of pure extension.

49. Proclus, *Commentary*, 40.

50. *Meno*, 81b–86b; *Republic*, 514a–518d.

51. Descartes to Mersenne, 15 April 1630 and 16 June 1641 (K, 11 and 104).

52. See the letters to Mersenne from 1630 (K, 10–15). See also Emile Bréhier, "The Creation of the Eternal Truths in Descartes's System," *in* Willis Doney, ed., *Descartes: A Collection of Critical Essays* (Notre Dame: University of Notre Dame Press, 1967).

53. Such studies, too numerous to list, range from Ralph M. Blake, "The Role of Experience in Descartes' Theory of Method," *Philosophical Review* 38 (1929):125–143 and 201–218, through Alan Gewirth, "Experience and the Non-Mathematical in the Cartesian Method," *Journal of the History of Ideas* 2 (1941):183–210, to chap. 7 of Williams's *Descartes*.

54. Op, 264. A strategy similar to the one described above can be found in the opening chapters of *Le Monde* (AT, XI).

55. Boyle and Locke argued for the distinction between primary and secondary qualities, not on metaphysical grounds but on the basis of the utility and clarity of the mechanistic hypothesis; see Boyle's *About the Excellency and Grounds of the Mechanical Hypothesis* (London, 1674) and Locke's *Essay Concerning Human Understanding* (London, 1690), bk. 2, chap. 8 together with bk. 4, chap. 3, secs. 24–26 and chap. 12, secs. 10–13.

56. Descartes' most explicit published statement of the need for experiment comes in the *Discourse*, pt. 6 (HR I, 120–121).

57. Francisque Cyrille Bouillier, *Histoire et Critique de la Révolution Cartésienne* (Lyon, 1842), 380–386, quotation from p. 380. My paraphrase of Bouillier's statement about Locke is not intended as an endorsement.

58. It is not uncommon to find Descartes discussed as if he were seeking to reconstruct the world out of incorrigibly known sense-data (a venerable project from the early part of our century); e.g., Richard Rorty, *Philosophy and the Mirror of Nature* (Princeton: Princeton University Press, 1979), chap. 1, sec. 2, esp. p. 30. Descartes was seeking to go from the mind to the world, but the bridge is, in the first instance, via intellectual intuition, not sensory ideas.

59. Descartes' conception of truth as that which compels assent from any unprejudiced judge finds expression in the *Rules*, Rule 2 (HR I, 3) and the *Discourse*, pts. 1–2 (AG, 11–12, 21–23).

60. My debts are too numerous to thank all explicitly, but all are thanked. I must especially express appreciation for the helpful criticism and conversation of Wilda Anderson, John Carriero, Hannah Ginsborg, Owen Hannaway, Paul Hoffman, David Lindberg, John Rogers, Amélie Rorty, and David Sachs. I also express gratitude to the American Council of Learned Societies for financial assistance, which allowed me to work on the paper while enjoying the hospitality of the Department of Philosophy of Harvard University as a Visiting Scholar.

4

Semel in vita:
The Scientific Background to
Descartes' *Meditations*

DANIEL GARBER

Descartes opens Meditation I with his persona, the meditator, reflecting on the project to be undertaken. Descartes writes:

> I have observed for some years now how many false things I have admitted as true from my earliest age, and thus how dubious are all of those things that I built on them; and so, I observed that once in life [*semel in vita*] everything ought to be completely overturned, and ought to be completely rebuilt from the first foundations, if I want to build anything firm and lasting in the sciences. (AT VII, 17)[1]

And with this, the project has begun. Descartes' meditator quickly begins by rejecting the commonsense epistemological principles on which everything he formerly believed rested, and quickly sets about putting the world back together again. Of course, one of the central projects undertaken in this connection must be the replacement of the epistemological principles rejected with new, more trustworthy principles. Just as Descartes' meditator undermined his former beliefs by undermining the epistemology on which they were based, he will rebuild his world by rebuilding its epistemology. New epistemological principles thus seem to be the very "first foundations" on which he will build something "firm and lasting in the sciences." But an obvious question to raise about this, the opening sentence of the *Meditations*, and about the project that follows out of it, is *why*? Why does Descartes believe it necessary even *once* in life to rebuild all of our beliefs in the

way he suggests? Why does Descartes feel called to such an epistemological project? Why is any genuine knowledge, anything "firm and
lasting in the sciences" not possible without entering into such a
Herculean labor, cleaning out and rebuilding from the bottom up the
cluttered stable-stalls of the mind?

There is an answer to this question that has been put forward by
a wide variety of commentators, and has become, perhaps, the standard account of Descartes' motivation for taking up epistemology in
the *Meditations*. In that view, one sees Descartes as engaged in a
debate with radical skepticism; the claim is that the call to new foundations is primarily a call to find epistemological principles immune
to skeptical attack.[2] This is a reading for which there is a great deal
of support; both the general intellectual climate, the revival of skeptical
thought in the sixteenth and early seventeenth century, and the details
of Meditation I where Descartes presents a number of arguments
derived from the skeptical tradition for later response, point to skepticism as a major intellectual problem for Descartes in the *Meditations*.

But, I claim, this is not the whole story. In a letter Descartes wrote
to his close friend Marin Mersenne on 28 January 1641, while he was
composing the Replies to the Objections submitted to his *Meditations*,
and preparing the whole work for publication, Descartes confided:

> I may tell you, between ourselves, that these six *Meditations* contain the
> entire foundations for my physics. But it is not necessary to say so, if you
> please, since that might make it harder for those who favor Aristotle to
> approve them. I hope that those who read them will gradually accustom
> themselves to my principles and recognize the truth in them before they
> notice that they destroy those of Aristotle. (AT III, 297–298 [K, 94][3]

Descartes, thus, is absolutely clear that the program of the *Meditations*
is not an autonomous philosophical project, but the prelude to a larger
scientific program; his remarks to Mersenne suggest that the motivation for the *Meditations* cannot be merely the refutation of skepticism,
a problem that, it would seem, is of no pressing concern to the practicing scientist.[4] The *Meditations* is, as it were, a Trojan horse that
Descartes is attempting to send behind the lines of Aristotelian science.
Now, there are a number of ways in which the *Meditations* can be
seen to lay the foundations for Cartesian science. One can see, for
example, in the discussions of body, its distinction from mind and
its nature as extension and extension alone, hints of Descartes' mechanistic accounts of the human body, and the world of physics, as we
shall later see. But I think that Descartes meant something deeper
still. I shall argue that the Meditations are intended to give the *epistemological* foundations of the new science as much as its *metaphysical*

foundations;[5] the account of knowledge, of clear and distinct perception, imagination and sensation that forms the backbone of the *Meditations* is, I claim, intended to undermine the epistemology that underlies Aristotelian metaphysics, and lead directly to its replacement by a Cartesian conception of the way the world is. It is in this sense, too, that the *Meditations* contains "the entire foundations for my physics."[6]

This, then, is what I'll try to do in this essay—set the epistemological project of the *Meditations* into the broader context of the Cartesian program for science,[7] and show why Descartes thought that such an epistemological project was a necessary preliminary to scientific investigation. I shall begin in part 1 with a brief discussion of the Cartesian program in physics, and the conception of the world against which it was explicitly directed. I shall argue there that Descartes saw both the Aristotelian and common views of the world as closely connected with certain deeply held but very mistaken epistemological views. I shall then try to show how both the skeptical arguments of Meditation I and the more positive arguments of the succeeding Meditations function in the overthrow of the commonsense epistemology and the Aristotelian metaphysics it supports, and in the establishment of epistemological foundations for the Cartesian science (parts 2 and 3). In this way, I hope to show one motivation, over and above any worries about skepticism, for entering into the epistemological project of the *Meditations*.

MECHANISM, THE VULGAR PHILOSOPHY, AND THE SINS OF YOUTH

If we are to read the *Meditations* as a prelude to Cartesian science, then we must begin with a few words about just what Descartes' conception of science was. While there are complications in dealing with Cartesian medicine and psychology, complications introduced by the mind and its union with body, in physics the program is straightforward: Descartes the physicist was a mechanist, and held that all physical phenomena were ultimately explicable in terms of the shape, size, and motion of the normally insensible corpuscles that compose the gross bodies of everyday experience.[8]

A full account of Descartes' physics is far beyond the scope of this paper.[9] But the program as given in parts 2–4 of his *Principles of Philosophy*, its most careful and systematic development, can be summarized as follows.[10] Descartes begins with an account of the nature of body, which, as he says, "does not consist in weight, hardness, color, or the like, but in extension alone" (Pr II, 4; cf. Pr II, 11), and an account of the modes of body, shape, size, and motion. Of these, motion, defined as "the translation of one part of body, or of one body, from the neighborhood of those bodies which immediately touch it . . . , and into the neighborhood of others" (Pr II, 25), gets special attention. Descartes is careful to distinguish motion, a mode of extension, so he claims, from its principal cause, God, who, in continually recreating the world from moment to moment, is responsible for the changes in place bodies are observed to have.[11] And from the activity of God, "not only because he is in himself immutable, but also because he acts in as constant and immutable a way as possible" (Pr II, 36), Descartes derives the laws of motion, the laws that govern bodies as such, the conservation of quantity of motion, the persistence of size, shape, and rectilinear motion, and the laws bodies obey in impact (cf. Pr II, 36–42).[12] And with this, the mechanist program is off and running. Since all matter is of the same sort and obeys the same laws, we have no choice but to explain the special behavior that individual bodies exhibit (the heaviness of stones and the lightness of air, the color of milk and the attractive properties of lodestones) in terms of the differing size, shape, and motion of the smaller bodies (or corpuscles) that make them up, and the laws of geometry and motion that govern them (cf. Pr II, 22–23). Descartes thus wrote in his *Principles* II, 64, after this analysis of motion and just prior to the execution of his program in III and IV:

> . . . I openly acknowledge that I know of no other matter in corporeal things other than that which is divisible, shapable, and movable in every way, and which the geometers call quantity, and take as the object of their demonstrations; and that there is nothing in it to consider except those divisions, shapes, and movements; and that nothing concerning these can be accepted as true unless it is deduced from these common notions, whose truth we cannot doubt, with such certainty that it must be considered as a mathematical demonstration. And because all natural phenomena can thus be explained, as will appear in what follows, I think that no other principles of physics should be accepted, or even desired. (Pr II, 64. Cf. AT II, 542; AT III, 686)

And thus Descartes observes in his Sixth Replies that, in his physics, all of the sensible properties that bodies seem to have, all color, sound, heaviness, and lightness are to be eliminated from the physical world, leaving only geometry and the laws of motion behind:

> I observed that nothing at all belongs to the nature [*ratio*] of body except that it is a thing with length, breadth, and depth, admitting of various shapes and various motions; that its shapes and motions are only modes which no power could make to exist apart from it; that colors, odors, tastes, and the like are merely sensations existing in my thought, and differing no less from bodies than pain differs from the figure and motion of the weapon that inflicts

it; and finally that heaviness [*gravitas*], hardness, the powers [*vires*] of heating, attracting, purging, and all other qualities which we experience in bodies consist solely in motion or its absence, and in the configuration and situation of their parts. (AT VII, 440 [HR II, 253–254])

The details of Descartes' ambitious program, the imaginative accounts of light, color, magnetism, gravity, and a host of other phenomena that Descartes attempted to explain in these terms, are very interesting and well worth the study, even if they tell us more about Descartes' scientific personality than about the world. But for the moment I would like to turn away from Cartesian physics and examine an alternative conception of the physical world.

Descartes' mechanism is in explicit opposition to a different conception of the world, a combination of common sense and Scholastic-Aristotelianism. In the commonsense view of the world, at least as Descartes imagines it, everything is, for the most part, just as it appears to us. Things really are colored, they are hot or cold, bitter or sweet, and pains are, for the most part, just where you think they are.[13] Bodies, in this view, have some internal property (resistance) by which they resist motion, and something (heaviness or gravity) by virtue of which they move themselves toward the center of the earth. And, Descartes thinks, when we see no body, common sense is inclined to believe that no body is present, that is, there is vacuum.[14]

This much is common sense, what most people take the world to be. But, Descartes thinks, it is this that underlies the principal opponent to his mechanism in the learned world, the Aristotelian worldview common to the Scholastics that Descartes was taught at La Flèche, what he called the "vulgar philosophy" on occasion, in recognition of its widespread acceptance (cf. AT I, 421; AT III, 420 [K, 109]; AT IV, 30). Late Scholastic Aristotelianism, the philosophy taught in the universities and colleges in Descartes' day, was a phenomenon of great complexity, encompassing a number of different schools of thought with important differences on a number of different issues.[15] But Descartes was not interested in the fine points of the Scholastic debates. Descartes writes in a letter to Mersenne from 1640:

I do not think that the diversity of the opinions of Scholastics makes their philosophy difficult to refute. It is easy to overturn the foundations on which they all agree, and once that has been done all their disagreements over detail will seem foolish. (AT III, 231–232 [K, 82])

What he objected to in Scholasticism was something he saw as common to all schools, a common conception of the makeup of the physical world together with a closely connected pattern of explanation in physics.

Basic to that view, as Descartes understood it, was the notion of a form or a real quality, and the explanation of the behavior of bodies in these terms.[16] Forms and qualities are, as Descartes put it, "the immediate principle of action of things," introduced "so that through them we can explain the actions proper to natural things, of which the form is the principle and source" (AT III, 503, 506 [K, 128, 129]). And so, corresponding to salient qualities or characteristic kinds of behavior, the Scholastic posits a form whose function it is to explain the quality or behavior observed. Eustacius a Sancto Paulo, a seventeenth-century Scholastic whose work Descartes knew and considered representative of the tradition, thus wrote:

> There are individual and particular behaviors [*functiones*] appropriate to each individual natural thing, as reasoning is to human beings, neighing to horses, heating to fire, and so on. But these behaviors do not arise from matter. . . . Thus, they must arise from the substantial form.[17]

The extent to which forms are linked to specific behaviors is emphasized in another passage, where Descartes gives his confidant Mersenne an account of what he takes to be "the most common explanation of heaviness of all in the Schools" in preparation for giving his own mechanistic account:

> Most take it [i.e., heaviness] to be a virtue or an internal quality in every body that one calls heavy which makes it tend toward the center of the Earth; and they think that this quality depends on the form of each body, so that the same matter which is heavy, having the form of water, loses this property of heaviness and becomes light when it happens that it takes on the form of air. (AT II, 223)[18]

Here the observed behavior is so closely linked to a specific form that a change in characteristic behavior from heavy to light requires a change in form.

Insofar as the activity the Scholastic attributes to the body itself is, Descartes thinks, comprehensible only through the category of the mental, the Scholastic account of the characteristic properties of bodies amounts to the attribution of a "tiny mind," as he put it, linked with specific behavior, to inanimate bodies, in order to explain that behavior (AT III, 648 [K, 135]; cf. AT VII, 441–442 [HR II, 254–255]). And so, for example, Descartes thinks of the Scholastic notion of heaviness as something mental, a substance linked to body that "bears bodies toward the center of the earth as if it contains some thought of it [i.e., the center of the earth] within itself" (AT VII, 442 [HR II, 255]). This allows Descartes to appeal to the Scholastic account of heaviness to convince confused correspondents that insofar as they find the philosophy they learned in school comprehensible, they should have no particular trouble with Descartes' own conception of mind-body interaction; the Scholastic account of gravity is, in essence, a misapplication of a notion that "was given us for the purpose of conceiving the manner in which the soul moves the body" (AT III, 667 [K, 139]), a projection of our dual nature onto the inanimate world.[19] And thus Descartes wrote in a letter in 1641:

The first judgements that we have made since our childhood, and since then, the vulgar philosophy [i.e., Scholasticism] have accustomed us to attribute to bodies many things which only pertain to mind and to attribute to mind many things that only pertain to body. One ordinarily mixes the two ideas of body and mind, and in the compounding of these ideas, one fashions real qualities and substantial forms, which I think should be entirely rejected. (AT III, 420 [K, 109])

There are, to be sure, traces of Scholastic ontology in Descartes' own metaphysics, and ways of reconciling Descartes' own mechanical philosophy with the Scholasticism he rejects.[20] But there is, from Descartes' point of view, at least, a clear contrast between the two. Thus Descartes writes in *Le Monde*, comparing his own theory of combustion with that of the Scholastics:

When it [i.e., fire] burns wood or some other such material, we can see with our own eyes that it removes the small parts of this wood, and separates them from one another, thus transforming the more subtle parts into fire, air, and smoke, and leaving the grossest parts as cinders. Let others imagine in this wood, if they like, the form of fire, the quality of heat, and the action which burns it as separate things. But for me, afraid of deceiving myself if I assume anything more than is needed, I am content to conceive here only the movement of parts. (AT XI, 7)

And in more general terms Descartes writes in a 1638 letter:

Compare my assumptions [suppositions] with the assumptions of others. Compare all their real qualities, their substantial forms, their elements and their other countless hypotheses with my single assumption that all bodies are composed of parts. . . . All that I add to this is that the parts of certain kinds of bodies are of one shape rather than another. (AT II, 200 [K, 59])

The contrast is a basic one. For the Scholastic, there is an indefinitely large variety of distinct principles of action in the world, one corresponding to each kind of characteristic behavior that the Scholastic chooses to recognize in his physics. But for Descartes, while there are an infinite number of ways that extended matter may subdivide into smaller parts, there is only *one kind of stuff* in the physical world, and it all behaves *in the same way,* in accordance with geometry and the laws of motion; it is in terms of this matter, its laws, and the particular geometric configurations it forms in different bodies that *all* bodily phenomena are to be explained. In the Cartesian world, no body is literally heavy, or hot, or red, or tasty. All of these observed properties are a result of geometry and motion. The mechanistic explanations of such phenomena Descartes gives, their reduction to configurations of matter in motion, may in the end turn out to be every bit as ad hoc as the stage Aristotelian's dormitive virtue explanation of the behavior of opium; it is just as easy to appeal to an unknown corpuscular substructure, an occult mechanism, as it is to appeal to an occult quality. But there is no confusing the two kinds of explanation.

Given Descartes' conception of Scholastic philosophy, it is not difficult to see why he often links the errors of Scholasticism with the errors of common sense.[21] Common sense attributes to bodies the qualities and tendencies to behave in particular ways that bodies appear to have, the properties our senses tell us bodies have. The Scholastic philosopher takes this one step further, and posits in bodies forms and qualities, principles of action that are intended to explain the properties that sense tells us are in bodies. Since the qualities that sense attributes to bodies are largely mental qualities, the sensations and volitions of the mind itself, projected onto the physical world as colors, tastes, and tendencies, the forms and qualities must be "tiny minds," mental substances capable of receiving the properties that common sense attributes to them. The Scholastic world is, thus, nothing but the world of common sense, with sensible qualities transformed into mental substances—forms and real qualities—and embedded in the world of bodies.[22] Put briefly, the Scholastic world, as Descartes understood it, is simply a metaphysical elaboration of the world of common sense.[23]

This, then, is how Descartes sees the matter, his own conception of the world, the forces of light, against the dark world of common sense and the obscurities of Scholasticism. But although he thought his opponents wrong, he did not underestimate the attractiveness and virtual inevitability of their position. For, Descartes thought, the commonsense worldview and the Scholastic metaphysics it gives rise to is a consequence of one of the universal afflictions of humankind: childhood.

Though childhood is a stage through which we all must pass, Descartes finds little to recommend it. It is a time when reason and the soul are eclipsed by matters corporeal, when we are "governed by our appetites and by our teachers" (AT VI, 13), and when we acquire most of the prejudices that cloud the adult mind and make it difficult to apprehend the truth. Descartes writes in the *Principles:*

> And indeed in our earliest age the mind was so immersed in the body that it knew nothing distinctly, although it perceived much clearly; and because it even then formed many judgements, it absorbed many prejudices from which the majority of us can hardly ever hope to become free. (Pr I, 47; cf. Pr I, 71; AT IV, 114 [K, 148]; etc.)

Childhood, in Descartes' view, is the cause of a variety of prejudices. The immersion of the mind in the body, its domination by the imagination and sensation, faculties that, in Descartes' account, derive from the mind's union with the body, cause us, for example, to confuse the ideas we have of the mental with the material, if not ignore the former altogether, and make it difficult for us to comprehend the distinction between mind and body.[24] This confusion of the mental and the material is an important prop for the commonsense and vulgar philosophies, the imposition of colors, tastes, and tendencies onto a senseless and unwilling world. But underlying this largely metaphysical confusion and, in a way, leading us directly to it is a basic epistemologic confusion. The immersion of the mind in the body, the domination of the mind by the corporeal faculties of sensation and imagination, leads us to the unfounded prejudice that those faculties represent to us the way the world really is. Descartes writes in the *Principles:*

> . . . Every one of us have judged from our earliest age that everything which we sensed is a certain thing existing outside his mind, and is clearly similar to his sensations, that is, to the perceptions he has of them. (Pr I, 66; cf. AT VII, 74 f.)

Or, as Descartes develops the theme in a later section of the *Principles:*

> . . . In our earliest age, our mind was so allied with the body that it applied itself to nothing but those thoughts alone by which it sensed that which affected the body, nor were these as yet referred to anything outside itself. . . . And later, when the machine of the body, which has been so constituted by nature that it can of its own inherent power move in various ways, turned itself randomly this way and that and happened to pursue something pleasant or to flee from something disagreeable, the mind adhering to it began to notice that that which it sought or avoided exists outside of itself, and attributed to them not only magnitudes, figures, motions, and the like, which it perceived as things or modes of things, but also tastes, smells, and the

like, the sensations of which the mind noticed were produced in it by that thing. . . . And we have in this way been imbued with a thousand other such prejudices from earliest infancy, whch in later youth we quite forgot we have accepted without sufficient examination, admitting them as though they were of the greatest truth and certainty, and as if they had been known by sense or implanted by nature. (Pr I, 71; cf. Pr I, 73)

In our earliest years, then, aware of only what the bodily faculties tell us, but, through our dealings with the world, aware that there are things outside of our immediate control and thus outside of us, we came almost spontaneously to the belief in a world of external objects similar to our sensations. These judgments became so natural to us, Descartes thinks, that we confused them with the sensations themselves, and we came to believe that it is our sensory experience itself that gives us the belief in an external world of sensible properties. As Descartes wrote to the authors of the Sixth Objections:

> In these matters custom makes us reason and judge so quickly, or rather, we recall the judgements previously made about similar things, and thus we fail to distinguish the difference between these operations and a simple sense perception. (AT VII, 438 (HR II, 252])[25]

In this way, we come, in our adulthood, to put our trust in the senses as an accurate representation of the way the world is.

The prejudice in favor of the senses, the belief that the senses represent to us the way the world of bodies really is, gives rise to a multitude of prejudices, as this passage suggests. In an obvious way, it leads us to think that "seeing a color, we saw something which existed outside of us and which clearly resembled the idea of that color which we then experienced in ourselves" (Pr I, 66). Similarly, when we have a painful or pleasant sensation, this epistemological prejudice leads us to believe that it is "in the hand, or in the foot, or some other part of our body" (Pr I, 67. Cp. Pr I, 47, 68). Such prejudices also lead us to posit vacua where we sense no objects (cf. Pr II, 18; AT V, 271 [K, 240]), to think that more action is required to move a body than to bring it to rest (Pr II, 26), that bodies in motion tend to come to rest (Pr II, 37), and that bodies have an internal resistance to motion (AT II, 213–214). And with these prejudices, which make up what I earlier called the commonsense worldview, we have laid the groundwork for Scholastic physics, the metaphysicalization of this commonsense world of sensible properties and tendencies and the positing of forms and qualities.

At this point we can turn back to the *Meditations*. These prejudices, grounded in the epistemological prejudices of youth are, I think, chief among the "many false things I have admitted as true from my earliest age" that Descartes has in mind in the opening sentence of Meditation I, and one of the chief purposes of the *Meditations* is to eliminate those prejudices and replace them with a true picture of the way the world is. It is in this sense that the *Meditations* is intended to lay the foundations for Cartesian science and eliminate the foundations of the Aristotelian. But in order to overturn these prejudices, we must find a way of setting aside the prejudice for the senses that we have had since youth, and replace our dependence on the senses with an altogether different epistemological principle; Descartes' revolution in physics must begin with a revolution in epistemology. It is in this sense that Descartes holds that "once in life [*semel in vita*] everything ought to be completely overturned, and ought to be rebuilt from the first foundations," from our epistemology up, "if I want to build anything firm and lasting in the sciences," if I want to find out how the world *really* is. This project, as Descartes carries it out in the *Meditations,* involves two principal stages. We must first break the hold of the senses and of all of the prior beliefs we have held that are based on our faith in the senses; what is called for is a kind of intellectual infanticide, to use Gouhier's somewhat violent image, the elimination of the child that remains within us.[26] This, I shall argue below, is one of the important functions of Meditation I. And, second, we must carefully reexamine the epistemological foundations of knowledge, and replace our exclusive dependence on the senses and the imagination with a more sophisticated view of knowledge that puts the senses in their proper place and subordinates them to another cognitive faculty, which will allow us to establish the real nature of the world, as opposed to how it *appears* to us—extended stuff, nonextended rational souls, and God—and will allow us to set aside the prejudices of common sense and the errors of the Scholastic philosophy. This, I shall argue, is one of the important functions of the remaining Meditations.

SKEPTICAL THERAPY

So far I have concentrated on the opening sentence of the *Meditations,* and offered an interpretation of it in terms of what Descartes wrote outside of the *Meditations* itself. I have argued that the *Meditations* must be read not merely as a philosophical project to defeat skepticism but, more generally, as an epistemological preparation for science. It

is now time to turn to the Meditations themselves and work out some
of the details of the reading I propose. The first question to be taken
up must be the skeptical arguments of Meditation I. Meditation I *seems*
to announce skepticism as the problem of the *Meditations*. But, I claim,
it does more than that. Meditation I, I claim, is the first step in building
a new epistemology, the destruction of the prejudice in favor of the
senses and in favor of the closely related faculty of imagination, which
constitutes a necessary first step in the construction of an epistemology
appropriate for Cartesian science.

In the previous section, I emphasized Descartes' account of our
intellectual development, our initial trust in the senses and the conception of the world that grows out of it. These prejudices, Descartes
thinks, interfere with our perception of the way things are, and must
be removed before we can find true and certain knowledge; we must,
as Descartes puts it, withdraw our minds from the senses, from the
body, from the things we formerly believed. And so Descartes wrote
in the Second Replies that, even though the account of the foundations
of the world that he is attempting to outline in the *Meditations* is, to
the open mind, even more obvious than geometry,

> . . . yet being contradicted by the many prejudices of our senses to which
> we have since our earliest years been accustomed, they cannot be perfectly
> apprehended except by those who give strenuous attention and study to
> them, and withdraw their minds as far as possible from bodily matters. (AT
> VII, 157 [HR II, 49–50]; cf. AT I, 350–351; AT IV, 114 [K, 148]; AT VI, 37)

And thus Descartes tells a correspondent in 1638, " . . . those who
want to discover truth must distrust opinions rashly acquired in childhood" (AT II, 39 [K, 53]).[27]

It is with this in mind that we should approach the skeptical arguments that are the main business of Meditation I. Much of the content
of the *Meditations* had been made public some four years earlier, in
part 4 of the *Discourse*. But some readers had problems following the
arguments there. Part of the problem derived from the brevity of
treatment in the *Discourse*. But Descartes acknowledged another problem as well. In a letter written in 1637, Descartes sympathizes with
one such reader and confesses that "there is a great defect in that
work you have seen, and I have not expounded the arguments in a
manner that everyone can easily grasp." But, Descartes continues,

> . . . I did not dare to try to do so, since I would have had to explain at length
> the strongest arguments of the skeptics to show that there is no material
> thing of whose existence one can be certain. Thus I would have accustomed
> the reader to detach his thought from sensible things. (AT I, 353 [K, 34])

In the *Meditations* the defect is corrected, and Descartes rehearses at some length important skeptical arguments missing in the earlier work.[28] And one prominent reason he gives for doing so is the reason he suggested to his earlier correspondent. It is this motivation, the therapeutic value that skeptical arguments have in eliminating prejudice, that Descartes emphasizes in the synopsis he gives of Meditation I:

> In the First Meditation, I present the reasons why we can doubt generally of all things, and particularly of material things, at least as we have no other foundations of the sciences than those that we have had up until now. Even though the utility of such a general doubt is not apparent at first, it is, however, quite considerable, since it delivers us from all sorts of prejudices, and prepares for us a very easy way to accustom our mind to detach itself from the senses. (AT VII, 12)

Similarly, when Hobbes grumbled that he " . . . should have been glad if our author . . . had refrained from publishing these matters of ancient lore" (AT VII, 171 [HR II, 60],[29] Descartes replied that the arguments were put there quite deliberately. The skeptical arguments that open the *Meditations* set up questions answered in the course of the work, and provide a standard of certainty for later arguments, Descartes explains. But the very first reason Descartes gave Hobbes for rehearsing them at such length is that they " . . . prepare the minds of the readers to consider intellectual things and distinguish them from corporeal things, for which those arguments always seemed necessary" (AT VII, 171–172 [HR II, 60]). The separation of the intellectual from the corporeal is an obvious reference to the distinction between mind and body, which is one of the central conclusions of the *Meditations.* But it also refers to the distinction between the intellectual faculties and the corporeal, between reason and sense, whose confusion underlies the confusion between the mental and the material, as noted earlier. The skeptical arguments of Meditation I, then, are to eliminate prejudice and prepare us to see things as they are, as reason, the intellect sees them, as opposed to the way things appear to us through our corporeal faculties.

And it is clear when one reads Meditation I that the trust in our corporeal faculties, our senses, the most fundamental prejudice we have from youth, is a central focus of Descartes' attention. The task of Meditation I, as Descartes puts it, is the "general overthrow of my opinions" (AT VII, 18). This task is to be accomplished not by eliminating them one by one, as his later metaphor of the apple-basket suggests (cf. AT VII, 481 [HR II, 282]), but by eliminating the foundations on which all of those prejudices rest:

Since the destruction of the foundations by itself brings about the downfall of that which is built on it, I shall now attack only those principles on which all that I once believed rested. (AT VII, 18)

And these foundations, these principles, are epistemological, Descartes thinks—the most prominent being the faith we have had in the veracity of the senses. Descartes seems to begin by eliminating, first of all, the epistemic principle in accordance with which everything we learn from the senses is trustworthy. This epistemic principle is easily set aside with the observation that the senses sometimes deceive. (Cf. AT VII, 18.) Descartes then continues with the consideration of a second epistemic principle, again concerned with sensory knowledge:

But it may be that although the senses sometimes deceive us concerning certain things that are small or remote, there are yet many others about which we clearly cannot doubt, although we take them in by their means [i.e., by means of the senses]. (AT VII, 18)

This second principle, a guarded statement of the first, limiting the trustworthiness of the senses to middle-sized objects in our immediate vicinity, is eliminated by means of Descartes' celebrated dream argument, however precisely it is taken to work.[30]

So far we have been dealing with purported knowledge acquired directly from the senses. But at this point, the argument takes an inward turn: " . . . now let us assume that we are asleep," Descartes says, "and that all these particulars, e.g. that we open our eyes, shake our head, extend our hands, indeed that we have such hands, or such a body, are false" (AT VII, 19). Under this assumption Descartes formulates a third and a fourth epistemic principle. The third is suggested in the following passage:

At the same time we must at least confess that those things which are seen [*visus*] in sleep are like certain painted images [*imagines*] which can only have been formed as things similar to real things; and therefore these general things, eyes, head, hand, and the whole body, are not [merely] imaginary, but really exist. (AT VII, 19)

Here the suggestion is that dream images are formed of components that correspond to things that exist at some indefinite time in a real external world, even if they may not be arranged in the real world as they are in our dreams. So, one would claim on the authority of this principle, one can establish the *sorts* of things there really are in the world on the basis of our dream experience. This third epistemic principle, though, quickly gives way to a fourth:

And for the same reason, although these general things, eyes, head, hands, and the like, may be [merely] imaginary, we must however confess that certain other things, yet more simple and universal, are real, from which our images [*imagines*] of things, whether true or false are made, just as all of them are made from true colors. The nature of body in general, its extension, and also the shapes of the extension of things, quantity . . . , the place in which it exists, and the time through which it endures, and the like seem to be of this sort. (AT VII, 20)

And, Descartes continues:

That is why we will perhaps not be reasoning badly if we conclude that physics, astronomy, medicine, and all the other sciences which depend on the consideration of composite entities are, indeed, uncertain whereas arithmetic, geometry, and the other sciences of this sort, which treat only of the simplest and most general things, without sufficiently concerning themselves [*parum curant*] about whether they occur in nature or not, contain something certain and indubitable. For whether I am awake or whether I am asleep, two and three together will always make the number five, and the square will never have more than four sides; and it does not seem possible that truths so evident [*perspicuae*] can ever be suspected of any falsity. (AT VII, 20)

The epistemic principle here is somewhat tricky. The idea seems to be that even if our dream experience does not inform us about the world as it is now, or give us access to things like eyes and hands, it does display the most general features of the real world, extension, time and, perhaps, color, the elements "from which our images of things . . . are made," just as, in the third principle, eyes, hands, and the like are considered as the elements of our dream images and, for that reason, are supposed to be real. When the meditator takes this principle to underlie the certainty of geometry and arithmetic, it is not because these disciplines concern truths that are wholly independent of the real world. Rather, they can be certain in spite of the fact that they don't give sufficient consideration to the question of whether or not circles and triangles exist in nature, and they can get away with this lapse in argument because the fourth principle of evidence guarantees that such objects do exist. This is why geometry and arithmetic are on better foundations than physics, astronomy, and medicine, the existence of whose objects is doubtful under the assumption that we are dreaming.[31]

While the third and fourth principles of evidence may appear to have little to do with our faith in the senses, there is, in Descartes' mind, an intimate connection. What we are dealing with in these two principles is sensation taken in the very most general way, knowledge about the makeup of the world which we claim to derive from sensory images, considered apart from any assumptions about their immediate causal history; what we are dealing with are our mental images of bodies considered irrespective of the question as to whether they are genuine sensations, images that derive from the sense organs, or mere imaginations, mental pictures that we have from some other source.[32] In this way, then, when the final skeptical argument of this series, the deceiving-God argument, eliminates the third and fourth epistemic principles, it eliminates (among other things, perhaps) what appears to be the last hope of knowledge from the senses and, more generally, from all the corporeal faculties, both sensation and imagination, those that arise from our connection to our body.[33]

The skeptical arguments of Meditation I, then, are carefully directed at the youthful prejudice in favor of the senses that, Descartes argues, must be eliminated before we can attain real knowledge. Their function as therapy intended to withdraw the mind from the senses is underscored in the final pages of the *Meditations*. Descartes writes:

But it is not sufficient to have made these remarks; we must also be careful to keep them in mind. For these habitual opinions will still frequently recur in my thoughts, my long and familiar acquaintance with them giving them the right to occupy my mind against my will. (AT VII, 22)

It is for this reason that Descartes proposes the famous demon hypothesis, to fix the elimination of prejudice that the skeptical arguments began:

I will therefore suppose that not the best God, who is a fountain of truth, but some malignant demon, no less deceitful than powerful, has bent all his efforts to deceive me. (AT VII, 22)[34]

The role of Meditation I as skeptical therapy directed against the prejudices of youth is also underscored by the indications he gives readers as to how the arguments of Meditation I should be read. In the appendix to the Second Replies, the arguments from the *Meditations* drawn up *modo geometrico* at the request of the objectors, the following postulate (*postulata*—literally a request or demand) is what corresponds to Meditation I:

The first request I press upon my readers is a recognition of the weakness of the reasons on account of which they have hitherto trusted their senses, and the uncertainty of all the judgements that they have based on them. I beg them to turn this over in their minds so long and so frequently that they will acquire the habit of no longer reposing too much trust in them. For I deem this necessary in order to attain to a perception of the certainty of things metaphysical. (AT VII, 162 [HR II, 54])

This strongly suggests that the arguments of Meditation I are to be treated in the same way, meditations in the truest sense of the term, exercises to practice in order to free the mind from prejudice.[35] We must take very seriously the remarks Descartes made about Meditation I in the Second Replies when he wrote:

> Nothing conduces more to the obtaining of a secure knowledge of reality than a previous accustoming of ourselves to entertain doubts especially about corporeal things. . . . I should be pleased also, if my readers would expend not merely the little time which is required for reading it, in thinking over the matter of which the *Meditation* treats, but would give months or at least weeks, to this, before going on further; for in this way the rest of the work will yield them a much richer harvest. (AT VII, 130 [HR II, 31])

Descartes is also quite serious when he says in the introduction to the *Meditations* (to what must have been his publisher's dismay) that "I don't recommend reading this to anyone except those who want to meditate seriously with me, and who can detach their minds from the senses, and deliver them from all kinds of prejudices" (AT VII, 9; cf. AT IX, 1, 3 and AT VII, 157–159 [HR II, 50–51]). To fail in this way, to simply read the *Meditations* rather than meditate *with* Descartes is to miss the point of the book.

The skeptical arguments of Meditation I do, indeed, set up arguments for Descartes to answer in the course of the *Meditations*. But they are also exercises we must undertake before beginning science, a necessary prelude to constructing an epistemology that will lead us to knowledge of things, not as they appear to us, but as they really are.[36]

REASON, SENSE, AND IMAGINATION

The elimination of our infantile prejudices in favor of the senses is an essential first step toward the true science, Descartes thinks. But it is only a first step. Descartes must then replace the conception of knowledge rejected in Meditation I with a different foundation for knowledge, one that will allow us to see things for what they really are. The new foundation is, of course, clear and distinct perception, the light of reason, a light capable of illuminating the mind without the aid of the sensory organs. Reason will show us the true nature of body, extension and extension alone, offering us the means to begin rebuilding the world well lost in Meditation I, a brave new world without color or sound, taste or heaviness, form or real quality, a world not without sense and imagination, but a world in which the light perceptible to the eye is properly subordinated to the light directly

perceptible by the mind. The validation of reason must, then, be a
central project in the *Meditations* and its trustworthiness as important
to the theme I am stressing, the laying of epistemological foundations
for the sciences, as it is for the theme more often emphasized, the
refutation of skepticism. But, it is important to note, the defense of
reason against skeptical attack is not the only epistemological project
Descartes undertakes in the *Meditations*. In the body of the *Meditations*
there is, I claim, a series of arguments very carefully and systematically
directed against the commonsense prejudice for the senses; the disease
treated by skeptical therapy in Meditation I is subjected to the light
of reason in the Meditations that follow. The careful treatment of the
prejudices of the senses throughout the epistemological discussions
of the *Meditations* demonstrates, I think, that Descartes was concerned
not only with the refutation of skepticism, but with the elimination
of a false epistemology and its replacement by the true, with the
elimination of the commonsense dependence on the faculties of sensation and imagination that lead toward Aristotelianism, and their
replacement with a conception of knowledge appropriate to grounding
the new, mechanical philosophy.

Before entering into these arguments, it will be helpful to say something about how the *Meditations* is written. The authors of the Second
Objections asked Descartes to set out his principal arguments *more
geometrico*, with formal definitions, postulates, axioms, and with careful formal proofs (cf. AT VII, 128 [HR II, 29]). While Descartes complied
with their request (cf. AT VII, 160–170 [HR II, 52–59]), he was not
entirely comfortable doing so. For reasons obvious from the discussion
of the previous section, he told the objectors that, while the Euclidean
mode of exposition is fine for geometry, it is unsuited to the material
at hand, which requires, for its proper comprehension, the therapeutic
withdrawal from the senses which, I have argued, is an important
function of Meditation I. It is in this context that Descartes tells his
objectors a bit about how the *Meditations* themselves were written.
"In my *Meditations* I have followed only analysis, which is the true
and best way for teaching," Descartes wrote (AT VII, 156 [HR II, 49]).
Analysis, in contrast to the more usual mode of argument (*ratio demon-
strandi*) in geometry, what Descartes calls synthesis, is presented as
the mode of argument that shows "the true way by which a thing
was methodically and, as it were, *a priori* discovered" (AT VII, 155
[HR II, 48]).[37] Descartes' conception of analysis and its precise distinction from synthesis is obscure and has given rise to much discussion.[38]
But an examination of the six Meditations shows one clear sense in
which they can be read analytically, showing how one might actually

come to discover for oneself the conclusions reached. Actual discovery involves false steps as well as true, bad arguments considered and rejected as well as good arguments that ultimately lead to enlightenment. This, I claim, is an important aspect of the expository strategy of the *Meditations*. In the course of reestablishing the epistemic foundations of knowledge and showing the inadequacy of common sense, Descartes allows the commonsense bias for the senses to have its turn at trying to establish the way the world is. As a consequence, woven through the texture of positive arguments in the *Meditations* is a genuine dialogue between the claims of common sense and the claims of reason, between the prejudices of youth and the wisdom of Cartesian maturity, a dialogue all too easily missed by the reader who focuses too closely on the validation of clear and distinct perception and the refutation of skepticism. While the dialogue pervades much of the text, I would like to emphasize two important exchanges, the discussion of the wax example in Meditation II, and the aborted proof for the existence of body from our adventitious ideas of sensation in Meditation III, before showing in some detail how the claims of sensation and reason are finally resolved in the discussion of the existence of body that Descartes presents in Meditation VI and in the discussion of the teachings of nature that immediately follows.

The path to knowledge begins, of course, in Meditation II, with the *cogito* and the *sum res cogitans*, arguments that establish the existence of the knowing subject as a thinking thing, "the first and most certain of all that occurs to one who philosophizes in an orderly way," as Descartes puts it in the *Principles* (Pr I, 7). But as soon as that first step in the argument is taken, there is an objection from common sense: certainly bodies, things that we are acquainted with by way of the corporeal faculties of sensation and imagination, are better known to us than the mind, which can be conceived through neither of those faculties. As the meditator puts it:

> But nevertheless it still seems to me and I cannot keep myself from believing that corporeal things, images [*imagines*] of which are formed by thought, and which the senses themselves examine are much more distinctly known than that something I know not what of myself which does not fall under the imagination. (AT VII, 29)

Descartes' response to this objection, which he considers natural in the fullest sense, is to let the mind wander and consider what it is that it really knows and how it knows it. Through the consideration of the celebrated piece of wax, Descartes tries to show us that, contrary to the prejudices of youth as embodied in common sense, neither sensation nor imagination gives us access to the nature of bodies, and that whatever we are able to learn about the existence of body through the senses and imagination, our knowledge of the existence of mind is prior to that of body in a well-defined sense, despite the inaccessibility of mind to the faculties of sensation and imagination.

Descartes begins the response to common sense by pointing out that sensation cannot give us the distinct comprehension of the piece of wax under consideration, since all of its sensible properties can change, while the wax itself remains the same; put it by the fire, melt it, and "what remains of the taste evaporates, the odor vanishes, its color changes, its shape is lost, its size increases," and so on (AT VII, 30). Thus, the nature of the wax, what makes it the thing it is, what persists through change, is inaccessible to the senses. But it is also inaccessible to the imagination. "Rejecting everything which does not belong to the wax," Descartes suggests that the wax itself, what persists through the sensible changes, is just "something extended, flexible, movable" (AT VII, 31). But if so, then I conceive the wax as something able to take on an infinite number of shapes, round, square, triangular, and everything in between, an idea that goes beyond my imagination, the capacity I have for forming mental pictures (cf. AT VII, 31). Although the full consideration of the nature of body will have to await Meditation V, Descartes at this stage believes that he is entitled to conclude that it is an inspection of the mind alone (*solius mentis inspectio*) that reveals the nature of the wax (AT VII, 31), that it is the mind itself, working apart from the body-connected faculties of sensation and imagination that allows us to "distinguish the wax from its external forms, and consider it as if naked, having removed its clothing" (AT VII, 32). "It is only the prejudices of youth, and later habits derived from those prejudices, that could convince me otherwise" (AT VII, 31–32).[39]

It is thus no challenge to the priority of the *cogito* and *sum res cogitans* argument to say that the object under consideration, the mind, is not known through the senses. Neither is the body. And at this point it is easy for Descartes to establish his second claim, that the knowledge of the existence of the mind is prior to the knowledge of the existence of body. For whether or not the wax I see or imagine really exists, the sensations or imaginations themselves entail that mind exists; and however sensory experience may serve to establish the existence of body, any such sensory experience demonstrates, with certainty and immediacy, the existence of a mind (cf. AT VII, 33). It is in this precise sense that mind is "better known than the body," as Descartes puts it in the title of Meditation II.

The wax example tames the unruly prejudices of childhood, but only temporarily. Although the meditator seems to accept the priority of knowledge of mind over knowledge of body, he keeps on pressing the insistent claims of commonsense knowledge of body. Meditation III begins with a kind of introduction, where Descartes reflects on the conclusions reached so far and lays out the strategy of the argument to come. Descartes tells us that having established the existence of the knowing subject, we must establish the existence and nature of its creator before anything can be known for certain (AT VII, 34–36). But after this introduction, Descartes returns to the argument proper: "and now good order seems to demand that I should first classify all my thought into certain types and consider in which of these types there is, properly, truth or falsity" (AT VII, 36–37). That is, having established the existence of mind as a thinking thing, we must see what can be drawn from an examination of the thoughts themselves. And at this point, almost as soon as the order of argument is resumed, the claims of common sense assert themselves again. The meditator again attempts to show that the senses lead us directly to a knowledge of the external world of bodies.

The meditator begins by distinguishing ideas, properly speaking, thoughts that are like images of things (*tanquam rerum imagines*) insofar as they are representative, unlike volitions or emotions (AT VII, 37).[40] The ideas are then broken down into three categories, the innate ideas that seem inborn, the adventitious ideas that seem to come from without, and the factitious ideas that seem to have been created by me (cf. AT VII, 37–38). Of particular interest to Descartes' meditator are the adventitious ideas: "If I now hear some noise, if I see the sun, if I feel heat, I have hitherto judged that these sensations proceeded from some things which exist outside of myself . . . and resemble those objects (AT VII, 38). The reasons given for these commonsense judgments are three: (1) nature seems to teach me so; (2) the sensations I have are independent of my will; and (3) "nothing is more plausible [*obvium*]" than that the external thing imposes its own likeness (*similitudo*) on me rather than anything else (AT VII, 38; cf. AT VII, 75–76). The claim is a familiar one; it is, in essence, a reprise of the second principle of evidence from Meditation I, the claim that our senses give us access to the familiar world of middle-sized bodies around us.

And, once again, common sense is rejected. Descartes first of all distinguishes the teachings of nature from the light of nature, the faculty to which he will appeal in his own argument for the existence of God, later in that same meditation (AT VII, 40). The teachings of nature, what causes me to judge that my sensory ideas derive from body, is a mere inclination to believe (*quodam impetu . . . ad hoc creden-*

dum) rather than an irresistible impulse to belief, a faculty, like the light of nature, which is indubitable in the sense that "there can be no other faculty which could teach me that what this light of nature shows me as true is not so, and in which I could trust as much as in the light of nature itself" (AT VII, 38–39).[41] And, Descartes notes, since natural inclinations have in the past led me astray in distinguishing good from bad, I should not trust them uncritically in this case either (cf. AT VII, 39). As for the fact that sensations are involuntary, this too is insufficient reason for thinking that they derive from something external to us. Recalling the dream argument of Meditation I, Descartes suggests that, for all I know, there might be some faculty in me independent of my will that I do not, at this point, know of, which is responsible for my present sensory ideas, without the need for an external cause, just as some such faculty may cause the dream experiences I have in sleep (AT VII, 39).[42] And finally, Descartes challenges the claim that our ideas of sense resemble external things, even if it is conceded that they are caused by things external. The claim is that the idea we have of an object from our senses is different from the idea we have of the same object through reason ("certain innate ideas"), and that "reason persuades me that the idea that seems to come directly from the thing is that which least resembles it" (AT VII, 39). Although the example he uses here is different (the sun as regarded by the senses and by the astronomers), the point here is largely the same as the one he made earlier in connection with the wax example.

At this point in the argument, Descartes puts aside the ideas of sense and the question of external bodies, and initiates a train of argument that leads in a fairly direct way to the existence of God in Meditation III and to the validation of reason in Meditation IV. While the prejudices of youth are addressed on a number of occasions in the course of these arguments,[43] it isn't until Meditation V that the question of our knowledge of the external world is addressed again and, in fact, becomes the focus of Descartes' attention:

> . . . having noticed what must be avoided or done in order to arrive at the knowledge of the truth, my principal task now is to attempt to escape from the doubts into which I have fallen in these last few days, i.e., in the previous [Meditations] and to see if we can know anything certain about material things. (AT VII, 63)

Descartes begins the project in Meditation V, with an account "of the essence of material things" (AT VII, 63), an explicit statement of some ideas first introduced in the wax example of Meditation II. The "something extended, flexible, movable" that is the nature of wax, inaccessible to sensation or imagination (AT VII, 31), is identified in Meditation V with the nature of body itself: what I "imagine distinctly" in bodies and what must, therefore, constitute their nature is "extension in length, width, and depth," together with various modes that pertain to individual extended things, "sizes, shapes, positions, and motions" together with duration (AT VII, 63).[44] This settles part of the debate between reason and common sense; the argument of Meditation V is intended to give us a definitive refutation of the commonsense claim, prominent in earlier discussions, that bodies resemble our sensory ideas of them. And once this question is settled, Descartes turns to the question of the existence of material things in Meditation VI. Here, though, the treatment of common sense is more subtle. Like common sense, Descartes believes in the existence of bodies external to the mind, even though his geometrical conception of body is quite distant from the sensuous world of common sense. And, like common sense, Descartes believes that sensation and imagination and the teachings of nature have roles to play in our coming to believe in a world of bodies, even though the roles they play are importantly different from the roles assigned them by common sense. The final move in the dialogue between truth and prejudice is not so much a refutation of common sense as it is a reinterpretation, an attempt to find what is right in common sense and show how at least some of our youthful convictions can find their place in the Cartesian system. It is in this way that the dialogue is finally concluded.

The final reconciliation begins in Meditation VI with a consideration of imagination, and a discussion of the extent to which imagination can establish the existence of an external world of bodies. Imagination, Descartes points out, the faculty we have for forming mental pictures, is something quite different from pure intellection, the faculty we have for grasping the concepts of, say, geometrical objects in a nonsensuous way. This faculty, Descartes claims, "is in no way necessary to my essence" and thus "depends on something other than myself" (AT VII, 73). And, Descartes continues, appealing to a conviction, presumably from common sense, a conviction suggested earlier in Meditation II, "and I readily conceive that if some body exists with which my mind is so joined that it can consider it whenever it wishes, it could be by this means that it imagines corporeal things" (AT VII, 73; cf. AT VII, 28).[45] The passage concludes with an appeal to an argument from the best explanation: "I easily conceive, I say, that the imagination can work in this fashion, if indeed bodies exist, and because I cannot find any other way in which this can be explained equally well, I therefore conjecture that bodies probably [*probabiliter*] exist" (AT VII, 73). But, Descartes notes, "this is only probable, and although I carefully consider all aspects of the question, I nevertheless do not see that from this distinct idea of the nature of body which I find in my imagination, I can derive any argument which necessarily proves the existence of any body" (AT VII, 73).[46] The faculty of imagination can, indeed, lead us to a belief in body, Descartes seems to concede. But, the claim is, not in the way that common sense might originally have thought. The argument Descartes offers is very different from the kinds of arguments suggested in the third and fourth principles of evidence in Meditation I, where the meditator suggested that a consideration of our dream experience, a variety of Cartesian imagination, might give us access to some of the general features of an external reality. The argument Descartes offers common sense in its place is an argument from the very faculty of imagination, and Descartes suggests, somewhat dogmatically, this is the only argument we are to get from imagination. Furthermore, the consideration of imagination will give us only probability, only a belief in the plausibility of an external world, and not the real conviction that we thought we had.

For real certainty we must turn to the senses, Descartes thinks. The final argument for the existence of external bodies, the argument that Descartes finally and unambiguously endorses is an argument that appeals crucially to sensation and the teachings of nature, considerations prominent in the abortive Meditation III argument, but now used in a way that is not open to the objections raised earlier. The argument goes as follows.[47] I find in myself "a certain passive faculty of sensing, that is, of receiving and recognizing the ideas of sensible objects." From this it follows that there must be a certain "active faculty for producing or forming these ideas, either in me, or in something else." This active faculty cannot be in me, Descartes argues. While this step of the argument is obscure, it seems to depend on two doctrines assumed or established earlier. One such doctrine is the claim that the mind contains only two faculties, a cognitive faculty for the apprehension of ideas, and volition. While this doctrine is not argued for explicitly in the *Meditations* it seems to underlie the analysis of error that leads to the epistemic principle of clear and distinct perception in Meditation IV (cf. AT VII, 56 f.; Pr I, 32; PS, 17). The second assumption necessary for this step is the claim that all cognitive faculties, like imagination and sensation, are modes of pure intellection. This is suggested in the argument from imagination, earlier in Meditation VI, where Descartes distinguishes imagination from pure intellection, and argues that imagination (presumably unlike intellection) is not essential to mind. In a passage immediately preceding the argument we are now considering, Descartes extends this conclusion to sensation, and clarifies the status of both. Sensation and imagination are, he claims, distinct from pure intellection in the same way that shapes are distinct from extension, as modes from that of which they are modes: "thus in the notion that we have of these faculties . . . they contain some sort of intellection, from which I conceive that they are distinct from me as figure, motion, and other modes or accidents of body are from the bodies which sustain those modes" (AT IX, 1, 62).[48] The implication here is that *all* cognitive faculties must be modes of pure intellection.[49] From these two doctrines Descartes can establish that the active faculty that causes sensations in me is not, itself, in me. That active faculty "plainly presupposes no intellect," Descartes claims, from which it follows that it cannot, like sensation and imagination, be a mode of the cognitive faculty of intellection. And since the sensations I have "are produced without my cooperation and often against my will [*invitae*]," they cannot derive from my will.[50] Thus they must derive from something outside of me. But, Descartes argues, God would be a deceiver if they derived from Himself or from anything other than from bodies themselves:

> For since he plainly gave me no faculty to know that [i.e., that ideas of sensation come from something other than body] but on the contrary a very great propensity [*propensitas*] to believe that they come from corporeal things, I do not see how God could for any reason fail to be a deceiver if they [i.e., the ideas of sensation] come from anything but corporeal things. (AT VII, 79–80)

From which, Descartes concludes, corporeal things, bodies, exist.[51]

Descartes' argument is not altogether unproblematic or convincing, as later philosophers have been quick to remark. But rather than dwelling on the infirmities of the argument, I would like to clarify the way it fits into the debate between commonsense sensualism and reason, which we have been tracing. This argument for the existence of body makes prominent use of two of the commonsense beliefs that formed the basis of the abortive Meditation III argument. As he did in the Meditation III argument, Descartes here appeals to the involuntariness of sensation. But in contrast to the argument in Meditation III, this commonsense fact about sensation is not, by itself, taken as grounds for believing in bodies. In the Meditation VI argument the involuntariness of sensation gives us only a piece of the argument, the claim that the active faculty causing sensation is external to mind.

And even this weaker conclusion is endorsed only in the context of certain claims about mind and its faculties, claims that undermine the hidden-faculty objection Descartes raised against the appeal to the involuntariness of sensation in Meditation III. The final argument also makes use of the teachings of nature, the strong inclination we have to believe that our sensations derive from bodies, which was presented as one of the principal supports of our belief in the external world in Meditation III. In Meditation III the inclination to believe is taken as, itself, grounds for belief, grounds that are rejected because of the known untrustworthiness of inclinations in other circumstances. But in Meditation VI, the inclination to believe in bodies as the cause of my sensations is used only in the context of a careful examination of when such inclinations are reliable and when they are not. The claim is that if, in any particular case, the teachings of nature were untrustworthy, then the veracious God would have given us the means to correct it. Because, in the specific case at hand, he didn't, and *only* because he didn't give us anything to correct the belief our inclination leads us to, we can, in this *specific* instance, trust the teachings of nature and believe that our sensations proceed from bodies, in spite of the fact tht our inclinations are not always trustworthy. But when another faculty, reason, of course, gives us the means to correct the teachings of nature, then they must be rejected. Such is the case with the inclination we have to believe that objects resemble the sensations we have of them, an inclination that is explicitly noted in the abortive Meditation III argument, and is closely connected to the wax example of Meditation II. In the end, while Descartes uses sensation to establish the existence of bodies, he is very careful to claim that sensation, by itself, does not establish the *nature* of bodies. Immediately after concluding that bodies exist, he wrote:

> Nevertheless, they [i.e., bodies] are not perhaps entirely as we comprehend them through sense, since there are many ways in which the comprehension of the senses is very obscure and confused. But at least everything that I clearly and distinctly understand is in them, that is, everything, generally speaking, which is included among the objects of pure mathematics. (AT VII, 80)

That is, the bodies whose existence the argument from sensation has proved are not the objects of sensation, colored, warm or cold, salty or sweet, but the extended things of Cartesian science.

It should be clear that implicit in the argument for the existence of bodies, which Descartes finally endorses, is a general principle of evidence that pertains to all the claims of common sense, a principle of evidence that can guide the use of sensation, imagination, and the natural and habitual inclinations to belief which Descartes calls the teachings of nature. And just as Descartes draws the principle of clear and distinct perception from the example of the *cogito* argument in the beginning of Meditation III, he draws his new principle of evidence for the teachings of nature from the example of the argument for the existence of bodies in Meditation VI (cf. AT VII, 35).[52] In the paragraph following the proof, Descartes writes:

> As for the rest, there are other beliefs which are very doubtful and uncertain, as that the sun is of such a size or shape, etc., or less clearly understood, as light, sound, pain, and the like. But however dubious and uncertain they are, from the fact that God is not a deceiver, and that consequently he has not permitted any falsity in my opinions, without my having some faculty to correct them, I have a certain hope of learning the truth about these things as well. (AT VII, 80)

Common sense is not *always* wrong, Descartes claims. But before we can trust it, we must examine it carefully using reason, the faculty which, by the argument of Meditation IV, is always trustworthy if used properly, the only faculty that God (and Descartes) have given us to correct common sense. If reason concurs or is silent, then we can trust common sense, otherwise not. The convictions of youth, unceremoniously shuffled out in Meditation, I now return, properly tamed by reason.[53]

And in this we have the resolution of the debate between common sense and reason that we have been tracing throughout the *Meditations*. Common sense, sensation, imagination are not eliminated. They remain part of Cartesian epistemology, but under the watchful eye and domination of reason. Thus Descartes writes in Meditation VI:

> But I do not see that it [nature] teaches me that I should conclude anything from these sense perceptions concerning things outside of ourselves unless the intellect has previously examined them. For it seems to me that it is the business of the mind alone, and not of the being composed of mind and body [from which derives sensation and imagination] to decide the truth concerning such matters. (AT VII, 82–83; cf. AT VII, 438–439 [HR I, 252–253])

With this, the new epistemology is in place. All that remains is to work out the details of the new world that reason will show us with the assistance of the senses.[54]

In the *Meditations*, Descartes is thus interested in more than the refutation of skepticism. This is not to deny that the refutation of skepticism is important; until the skeptical challenges to knowledge are settled, we can have no genuine knowledge. But Descartes is interested in more than the possibility of knowledge. He is interested in the actual pursuit of knowledge, in formulating the true account of the way the world is. The *Meditations* is intended both to establish the possibility of knowledge, against the skeptics, and to set knowledge on its proper epistemic foundations. By delineating the proper path to knowledge, the priority of the intellect and its clear and distinct perceptions over the deliverances of the senses, Descartes is intending to lay the epistemic groundwork for his revolution in physics, and for the arguments that establish the world of mechanism and allow us to set aside the commonsense and sense-bound world that the Aristotelians have mistaken for the world we live in. It is this project, the dethroning of the senses that, from our earliest years, ruled the mind, and the elevation of reason, the rightful sovereign of the intellect, which must be undertaken, once in life, lest we remain trapped in the false world we have from our earliest years imagined ourselves to inhabit.[55]

NOTES

1. All textual citations will be given in the body of the paper. References in brackets are to English translations of the text. There are no translations cited for the *Meditations* or the *Discourse on Method*, since these works are readily available in editions keyed to AT. The abbreviations AT, HR, and K are explained in the General Bibliography at the beginning of this volume. In addition, I use the following abbreviations: PS—Descartes, *Passions of the Soul*. French text in AT XI, and English translation in HR I. References by section number. Pr—Descartes, *Principles of Philosophy*. Latin text in AT VIII; French text in AT IX-2; partially translated in HR I and E. Anscombe and P. T. Geach, *Descartes: Philosophical Writings* (Indianapolis: Bobbs-Merrill, 1971), translated in full *in* V. R. and R. P. Miller, trans., *Descartes: Principles of Philosophy* (Dordrecht: Reidel, 1983). References by part (in Roman) and section number (in Arabic). In preparing the translations for the text, I have consulted K, HR, and the English translations of Laurence J. Lafleur, *René Descartes: Discourse on Method and Meditations* (Indianapolis: Bobbs-Merrill, 1960).

2. For recent developments of this reading, see Harry G. Frankfurt, *Demons, Dreamers, and Madmen* (Indianapolis: Bobbs-Merrill, 1970), esp. pp. 174–175; Richard H. Popkin, *The History of Scepticism from Erasmus to Spinoza* (Berkeley, Los Angeles, London: University of California Press, 1979), chap. 9; and Alexandre Koyré's introductory essay *in* E. Anscombe and P. T. Geach, *Descartes: Philosophical Writings*. E. M. Curley's *Descartes Against the Skeptics* (Cambridge, Mass.: Harvard University Press, 1978, pp. 8–9) also suggests such a

view. But in private communication, Curley has emphasized that in stressing the attack on skepticism, he did not mean to deny that the *Meditations* plays other equally important roles in Descartes' philosophy, most prominently in the grounding of his physics. See his chap. 8. For a valuable discussion of Descartes' attitude towards skepticism, see Henri Gouhier, *La Pensée Métaphysique de Descartes* (Paris: Vrin, 1978), chap. 1.

3. On the importance of the *Meditations* project as the first step in building his new science, see also the introduction to the French edition of the *Principles of Philosophy* (AT IX–2, 13–17 [HR I, 210–213]). The importance of the program of the *Meditations* as a foundation for the sciences is also suggested by Descartes' critique of the apostate Henricus Regius. See, e.g., AT IX–2, 19–20 [HR I, 214] and AT IV, 625.

4. For an account that suggests that skepticism was a problem for practicing scientists, see e.g., Philip Sloan, "Descartes, the Skeptics, and the Rejection of Vitalism in Seventeenth-Century Physiology," *Studies in History and Philosophy of Science* 8 (1977):1–28. But see also my discussion of this essay in *Studia Cartesiana* 2 (1981):224–225.

5. I don't intend, in putting the matter this way, to suggest that there is a radical distinction between metaphysical and epistemological concerns. Descartes' epistemology strongly depends on issues relating to the nature of mind, its relation to the body, and its relation to the benevolent God who created it.

6. For similar readings of Descartes' project, see, e.g., Étienne Gilson, *Études sur le Rôle de la Pensée Médiévale dans la Formation du Système Cartésien* (Paris: Vrin, 1975), pt. 2, chap. 1; and Margaret D. Wilson, *Descartes* (London: Routledge & Kegan Paul, 1978), 3–4; 104. Wilson's point of view is contrasted with Curley's in Willis Doney's "Curley and Wilson on Descartes," *Philosophy Research Archives*, Jan. 1, 1980.

7. It should be noted here that I am using the term *science* in an anachronistic way here, and mean it to refer to areas of inquiry that we call scientific, physics, biology, etc. In Latin, science, *scientia*, means just knowledge. Thus Descartes wrote in Rule II of his early *Rules for the Direction of the Mind:* "All science is certain and evident cognition" (AT XI, 362).

8. For general accounts of the so-called mechanical philosophy, see, e.g., Richard Westfall, *The Construction of Modern Science* (New York: John Wiley and sons, 1971); Marie Boas, "The Establishment of the Mechanical Philosophy," *Osiris* X (1952):412–541; or E. J. Dijksterhuis, *The Mechanization of the World Picture* (Oxford: Oxford University Press, 1961), esp. pt. 4, chap. 3.

9. For some general accounts of Cartesian physics, see, e.g., Paul Mouy, *Le Développement de la physique Cartésienne* (Paris: Vrin, 1934), 1–71; J. F. Scott, *The Scientific Work of Descartes* (London: Taylor and Francis, 1952); and E. J. Aiton, *The Vortex Theory of Planetary Motions* (New York: Neale Watson, 1972).

10. The principal statements of Cartesian physics are the *Le Monde* of 1632 (in AT XI; translated by Michael Mahoney as *René Descartes: The World* [New York: Abaris Books, 1979]); the *Optics* and *Meteorology* of 1637 (in AT VI;

translated by Paul J. Olscamp in *René Descartes: Discourse on Method; Optics, Geometry, and Meteorology* [Indianapolis: Bobbs-Merrill, 1965]), and *Principles of Philosophy* of 1644. The *Principles* is the only attempt Descartes made at a complete and systematic exposition of his physics.

11. See Pr II, 36 and AT V, 403–404 [K, 257]. This latter passage suggests that God is not the only cause of motion in the world, and that mind can be a genuine cause of at least some motion. On this see my essay, "Mind, Body, and the Laws of Nature in Descartes and Leibniz," *Midwest Studies in Philosophy* 8 (1983). On the role God plays in the derivation of the laws of motion in Descartes, see, e.g., Gary Hatfield, "Force (God) in Descartes' Physics," *Studies in History and Philosophy of Science* 10 (1979):113–140; and Martial Gueroult, "The Metaphysics and Physics of Force in Descartes," *in* Stephen Gaukroger, ed., *Descartes: Philosophy, Mathematics, and Physics* (Sussex, N.J.: Barnes and Noble, 1980), 196–229.

12. For an account of the derivation of the laws of motion, see e.g., Alan Gabbey, "Force and Inertia in the Seventeenth Century: Descartes and Newton," *in* Stephen Gaukroger, *Descartes*, 230–320.

13. See, e.g., the commonsense mistakes that Descartes calls attention to in Pr I, 46, 66–68.

14. On the commonsense conception of resistance, see, e.g., Pr II, 26: AT II, 212–213. It is in this sense that Descartes denies "inertia or natural tardiness" to bodies, a tendency to come to rest or a resistance to being set in motion from rest (AT II, 466–467), although Descartes is perfectly willing to admit as a consequence of his conservation law that one body moving another will lose some of its own motion (AT II, 543 [K, 64]; AT II, 627). On commonsense conceptions of heaviness, see, e.g., AT III, 667 (K, 139); AT VII, 441–442 (HR II, 254–255). On the commonsense prejudices that lead to a belief in vacua, see, e.g., Pr II, 17–18.

15. For a survey of some aspects of late Scholasticism relevant to the foundations of physics, see William A. Wallace, "The Philosophical Setting of Medieval Science," *in* David C. Lindberg, ed., *Science in the Middle Ages* (Chicago: University of Chicago Press, 1978), 91–119. For an account of the diversity of seventeenth-century Scholasticism on some of the issues about substance relevant to Descartes, see A. Boehm, *Le "Vinculum Substantiale" chez Leibniz: ses Origines Historiques* (Paris: Vrin, 1962), 33–81. For an account of Descartes' relations with late Scholasticism, see Gilson, *Rôle*, and the extremely valuable collection of Scholastic texts that Gilson published in his *Index Scolastico-Cartésen* (Paris: Vrin, 1979).

16. It should be noted that Descartes' representation of Scholastic doctrine is not always accurate. As Gilson notes (*Rôle*, 163), Descartes' view is that the Scholastic form is a substance (AT III, 502 [K, 128]), a conception that is a matter of some controversy among Scholastics. Also, Descartes draws no distinction between the Scholastic conceptions of form and real quality. Cf., e.g., Descartes' definition of form in AT III, 502 (K, 128) with the conception of real quality expressed, e.g., in AT III, 648 (K, 135); AT III, 667 (K, 139); AT V, 222 (K, 235); AT VII, 441–442 (HR II, 254). Consequently, I shall draw no distinction between form and quality. The account of the Scholastic con-

ception of substance given in the text is not intended to be an accurate account of Scholastic doctrine. It should be read as a representation of what the Scholastic opponent looked like to Descartes.

17. Gilson, *Index*, sec. 209. See also Eustacius a Sancto Paulo, *Summa Philosophica* . . . (Cambridge: Roger Daniel, 1648), 123–124, 127, 140; and a passage from Suarez, *Disputationes Metaphysicae* . . . given in Gilson, *Index*, sec. 211. For Descartes' judgment of Eustacius, see AT III, 232 (K, 82).

18. Cf. Gilson, *Rôle*, 159–162.

19. See also the discussion of this question in sec. 2 of my essay, "Understanding Interaction: What Descartes Should Have Told Elizabeth," *Southern Journal of Philosophy*, supplement to vol. 21 (1983):15–32.

20. One trace of Scholastic ontology is the notion of tendency that is essential to Descartes' derivation of the laws of motion. On this and the closely related notion of force, see, e.g., Gueroult, "Metaphysics and Physics," and Thomas L. Prendergast, "Motion, Action, and Tendency in Descartes' Philosophy," *Journal of the History of Philosophy* 13 (1975):453–462. Another trace of Scholasticism is in his notion of the relation between mind and body. Descartes sometimes claims that mind can be regarded as the substantial form of the body, the only such form he recognizes. See, e.g., AT III, 503, 505, AT IV, 168, 346. On this see, e.g., Gilson, *Rôle*, 245–255; Geneviève [Rodis-] Lewis, *L'Individualité selon Descartes* (Paris: Vrin, 1950), 67–81. It is also possible to assimilate Aristotelian ideas to Cartesian in the other way, by interpreting Aristotle as a Cartesian. This was an idea that attracted the young Leibniz. See his letter to Jacob Thomasius, April 20/30, 1669, *in* Leroy Loemker, ed. and trans., *G. W. Leibniz: Philosophical Papers and Letters* (Dordrecht: Reidel, 1969), 93–103. In that letter, Leibniz cites a number of his lesser known contemporaries in connection with this view.

21. For example, in the quasi-autobiographical account of the origin of his views on the physical world in the *Sixth Replies* (AT VII, 441–442 [HR II, 254–255]), Descartes makes no real distinction between the commonsense world, and the Scholastic account of the behavior of body. See also AT II, 213 where the opinions of the common people are linked to those of "la mauvaise Philosophie," and AT III, 420 (K, 109) where the "vulgar philosophy" is linked to "the earliest judgements of childhood," where Descartes thinks that the commonsense faith in the senses derives, as we shall see. See also Gilson, *Rôle* (pp. 168–173), "La psychologie de la physique aristotélicienne."

22. In seeing the errors of Scholasticism as deriving from the errors of commonsense epistemology, Descartes does not mean to suggest that the Scholastic metaphysics is a completely uncritical translation of commonsense sensory beliefs into metaphysics. Unlike common sense, for example, the orthodox Scholastic would deny that there are vacua.

23. For a more explicit development of what is much the same idea, see Nicholas Malebranche, *De la Recherche de la Vérité*, Bk. 1, chap. 16, and Bk. 6, pt. 2, chap. 2, in Thomas M. Lennon and Paul J. Olscamp, trans., *Nicolas Malebranche: The Search After Truth* (Columbus: Ohio State University Press, 1980), 73–75; 440–445.

24. Descartes' account of sensation and imagination as deriving from the connection between the mind and the body, see, e.g., Pr IV, 189–197; PS, 19–26. Sensation and imagination are, for Descartes, both faculties we have by virtue of which we can have mental pictures, and differ only as to whether those pictures derive from the sense organs (sensation) or the brain (imagination). On our early confusion between mind and body, see, e.g., AT III, 420 (K, 109); AT III, 667 (K, 139); AT VII, 441–442 (HR II, 254–255).

25. The discussion of sensation in the Sixth Replies from which this passage is excerpted makes it clear that, strictly speaking, the prejudice for the senses which for Descartes is characteristic of common sense is a prejudicial judgment about the cause or content of our ideas of sensation. That is, what is wrong is the judgments we make about sensory ideas; the ideas themselves, Descartes is clear, are neither true nor false.

26. See Henri Gouhier, *Pensée Métaphysique*, 58.

27. This claim offers Descartes an interesting reply to objectors not convinced by his arguments. Descartes can claim that his objectors are still dominated by the prejudices of youth, and for that reason cannot see what is present to their mind's eye. (Cf., e.g., AT III, 267 [K, 87–88], and AT VII, 9–10.)

28. In a sense, all of part 1 of the *Discourse* can be read as a skeptical argument. But the explicit skeptical arguments that occupy a full Meditation in the later work occupy just a few lines in part 4 of the *Discourse*. Furthermore, the *Meditations* contains two arguments missing in the *Discourse*, the deceiving-God argument and the hypothesis of the evil demon.

29. It is interesting to note that when, somewhat later, Hobbes presented his own philosophy, he made use of a device similar to hyperbolic doubt, though without the full battery of skeptical arguments that Descartes used. See *De Corpore*, chap. 7, sec. 1.

30. See Margaret Wilson, *Descartes* (chap. 1, secs. 4 and 6) for an account of the main lines of interpretation in the literature and an extremely plausible proposal for reconstructing the argument.

31. Cf. Frankfurt's explication of this passage in *Demons* (pp. 74–76). While I am not certain that I can agree with everything he says about the treatment of mathematics in Meditation I (see *Demons*, chaps. 7–8), I do agree with Frankfurt that, in the particular passages under consideration, the meditator is clearly thinking of mathematics as a science that pertains to certain features of an external world. (In general, I should point out that my account of the arguments in Meditation I owes an obvious debt to part 1 of *Demons*). As strange as this account of mathematics may seem, it may well have been the way in which Descartes himself thought about mathematics in his earlier years. On this see John A. Schuster, "Descartes' *Mathesis Universalis:* 1619–28," in Stephen Gaukroger, *Descartes*, 41–96. Schuster's suggestion seems to be that in the late 1620s, Descartes thinks of the primary objects of mathematics as imaginative pictures, mental representations of physical impressions in the brain.

32. Dream images, under consideration in this context, are, for Descartes, a kind of imagination, one that derives from the activity of the brain. (See PS, 21, 26.) But this portion of the argument is intended, I think, to deal with

imagination of all varieties, both involuntary (like dreams) and voluntary, all of which derive from the union of mind with a body, and any knowledge that we may claim to have from imagination.

33. I don't mean to suggest that this is the only thing that the deceiving-God argument eliminates. It is plausible to read it, as most commentators have, as eliminating *all* of the meditator's former beliefs, both those from the senses as well as those beliefs he may have had from reason, thus setting up the problem that is ultimately resolved in Meditation IV with the validation of clear and distinct perception. But this is a question that relates to the function of Meditation I as setting skeptical questions to be answered in the later Meditations, a question that goes beyond the scope of my interest in Meditation I here.

34. In presenting the demon hypothesis in this way, as a therapeutic device, I mean to reject Martial Gueroult's celebrated reading, in accordance with which the demon hypothesis is intended as a genuine argument, distinct from the deceiving-God argument. According to Gueroult, the demon argument is answered by the causal argument for the existence of God in Meditation III, whereas the deceiving-God argument is answered by the ontological argument in Meditation V. For a clear and concise statement of Gueroult's position, together with the defense of a position much like the one I am advancing here, see Henri Gouhier, "L'Ordre des Raisons selon Descartes," in *Cahiers du Royaumont: Descartes* (Paris: Éditions de minuit, 1957), 72–87.

35. Cf. Gilson, *Rôle*, 186.

36. For similar readings of the aim of Meditation I, see Gilson, *Rôle*, 184–190; Gouhier, *Pensée Métaphysique*, chap. 2; Wilson, *Descartes*, chap. 1, sec. 3; and Mike Marlies, "Doubt, Reason, and Cartesian Therapy," in Michael Hooker, ed., *Descartes: Critical and Interpretive Essays* (Baltimore: Johns Hopkins University Press, 1978).

37. "A priori" seems meant in an epistemic rather than in the usual metaphysical sense. For a short discussion of the textual problems this sentence raises, see Daniel Garber and Lesley Cohen, "A Point of Order: Analysis, Synthesis, and Descartes' Principles," *Archiv für Geschichte der Philosophie* 64 (1982):136–147, esp. n. 5, and the references cited there.

38. For discussions of Descartes' conception of analysis and synthesis, see Garber and Cohen, "Point of Order," and E. M. Curley, "Analysis in the *Meditations*," this volume.

39. Descartes claims here that we are deceived by our ordinary ways of speaking into thinking that we literally *see* the wax, just as we are, strictly speaking, mistaken when we say that we see people in the street below the window; if we can be said to see anything at all, it is coats and hats.

40. This passage naturally enough misled Hobbes into thinking that all ideas are mental images for Descartes, i.e., that the only cognitive faculties are sensation and imagination. In his reply to Hobbes, Descartes is clear that this is not the intention in this passage. (See AT VII, 179–181 [HR II, 66–68].) Ideas are *tanquam rerum imagines* only insofar as ideas and images are representative of things other than themselves.

41. It is interesting here that Descartes says of the light of nature at this

stage, before it has been validated in Meditation IV, that it "shows me that which is true." The teachings of nature seem to be the customary judgments connected with the senses from early youth, which we have mistaken for direct deliverances of the senses. (See AT VII, 436–439 [HR II, 251–253] and the discussion above in part 1.)

42. This objection relates closely to the dream argument of Meditation I as interpreted in Wilson's *Descartes* (chap. 1, sec. 6). According to Wilson, in Meditation I Descartes is not worried about our supposed inability to tell whether or not we are awake. Rather, she claims, the question is why, since we are not tempted to think that our dream experiences represent an external reality, do we think our waking experiences are any different on this score? The objection to the commonsense reason for believing in an external world is similar. The fact that our sensations are involuntary is no indication that they proceed from something external, since our dream experience, which is also involuntary, may not require an external cause.

43. In the course of the causal argument for the existence of God in Meditation III Descartes examines the ideas of sense, attempting to persuade common sense that these ideas are obscure and confused. (See AT VII, 43–44 and Wilson, *Descartes*, chap. 3, sec. 2.) Later in that same Meditation, after concluding the first causal argument for the existence of God, Descartes raises and answers three objections (AT VII, 45–47). At least two of those objections depend on the belief that any ideas we have of infinity and perfection must derive from ideas we have of the finite and imperfect, a belief quite natural to the sensualist, for whom every idea derives from sensory experience of finite and imperfect things. And in Meditation IV, the question of the grounds of our belief in corporeal things comes up in the course of an analysis of error (AT VII, 58–59). Descartes there contrasts the spontaneous and irresistible urge to believe in the existence of the mind with the less strong inclination to believe in body, arguing that only the former is a proper use of the faculty of judgment, in a passage that recalls the distinction between the light of nature and the teachings of nature in Meditation III.

44. Duration seems new here. It is also interesting that the starting place for Descartes' analysis of the idea of body is an idea of imagination, a mental picture of body. He begins the analysis with the claim that "I imagine quantity distinctly" (AT VII, 63). When a short while later an example is considered (AT VII, 64), it is the idea of a triangle in imagination ("And when, for example, I imagine a triangle . . . ").

45. The passage from Meditation II reads: " . . . to imagine is nothing but to contemplate the shape of a body or its image." It is not clear here whether Descartes is claiming that imagination is the contemplation of a mental picture, or the contemplation of a physical picture in the brain (the pineal gland), which is the cause of the mental picture. (Cf. the account of sensation and imagination in the *Treatise of Man* [AT XI, 174–177], in Thomas Steele Hall, trans., *René Descartes: Treatise on Man* [Cambridge: Harvard University Press, 1972], 84–87. In Descartes' account there, sensation and imagination are literally the contemplation of a shape in the pineal gland, a shape that is isomorphic to an external body in the case of sensation.)

46. The conclusion here is probable, plausible rather than certain, because of the hypothetical form of argument, presumably.

47. All quotations from Descartes' statement of the argument are from AT VII, 79–80.

48. I quote here from the French edition, which in this instance is much clearer than the Latin. The significance of the difference between the two texts suggests Descartes' own hand in this passage of the French edition.

49. On this, see Wilson, *Descartes*, chap. 4, sec. 2. In this important discussion, Wilson argues for the primacy of the pure intellect in Descartes' conception of the mind, as against the view that all mental events, sensations, imaginations, and pure intellections are on the same footing. I think that Wilson goes too far, though, when she claims that "Descartes regarded his mind as *essentially* only intellect" (p. 181). While the intellect may be the only passive faculty that pertains essentially to mind, Descartes also recognizes an active faculty, volition, which is distinct from the intellect.

50. It is because the imagination is, at least sometimes, under our voluntary control, that the argument must proceed from sensation rather than from imagination.

51. It is interesting to compare this argument with the parallel argument for the existence of body in Pr II, 1. That version lacks the twist at the end, that if my inclination to believe in bodies were mistaken, the veracious God would have given me a faculty to correct it. In Pr II, 1 the claim is that we "seem to see clearly that the idea [i.e., of a material thing] comes from something outside of us." The claim is that God would be a deceiver if this clear idea were mistaken. This seems to be a direct application of the validation of clear and distinct perceptions to our inclination to believe in bodies, as opposed to the *Meditations* version of the argument, where the inclination to believe is an ingredient in a more complex reasoning, and where Descartes never makes the claim that we clearly perceive the external existence of bodies.

52. I don't mean to claim that in the *Meditations* the principle of clear and distinct perception is derived from the example of the *cogito* alone. At the beginning of Meditation III the *cogito* suggests the principle to the meditator. But in Meditation IV it is given a careful derivation from an analysis of the proper use of the faculty of judgment and the veracity of God. (See AT VII, 56–60.) In that derivation, the earlier statement of the principle plays no role whatsoever.

53. It is interesting that this principle of evidence for sensation seems missing from the *Principles*, a fact closely related to the version of the argument for the existence of body in Pr II, 1. See the discussion of this argument in note 51. It is not clear to me whether this represents a change in Descartes' position, or whether it is a consequence of the fact that Descartes intends only a simplified presentation of the contents of the *Meditations* in the *Principles*.

54. The fact that sensory knowledge is admitted, under appropriate circumstances, is crucial to reconciling Descartes' demand for certainty in science with his frequent claims to being an experimental scientist. For a discussion of this question, see my essay, "Science and Certainty in Descartes," in

Hooker, *Descartes*, 114–151. The breakdown in certainty comes, I claim, not with experiment, which can, if used properly, under the control of reason, lead to certain knowledge, but with the use of something like hypothetico-deductive method, which can never lead to certainty. For another recent attempt to deal with these questions, see Desmond M. Clarke, *Descartes' Philosophy of Science* (University Park: The Pennsylvania State University Press, 1982). Clarke, arguing from Descartes' scientific writings rather than from his philosophical writings about science (see p. 2), also emphasizes the proper use of experience in Descartes' science, under the control of reason (see chaps. 2 and 3). But Clarke argues that Descartes' actual method in science is largely hypothetico-deductive (chaps. 5 and 6).

55. I would like to thank Amélie Rorty and E. M. Curley for helpful comments on earlier drafts.

5

Descartes and the Metaphysics of Doubt

MICHAEL WILLIAMS

I

Descartes' *Meditations*[1] recounts a journey from prephilosophical common sense to metaphysical enlightenment, each step of which is taken in response to an encounter with skepticism. The first encounter induces a provisional doubt, clearing Descartes' mind of prejudices that would blind him to new truths. This allows subsequent encounters to lead him to new certainties, by which the provisional doubt is gradually overcome, though not of course in a way that simply returns him to his initial position.

According to this story, the problem of skepticism emerges within the framework of common sense, to be solved within that of Cartesian metaphysics. The First Meditation doubts must thus be "natural," in the sense of metaphysically noncommittal, or at least noncontroversial. They must be developed out of resources that common sense can recognize as its own and must not depend, either for their intelligibility or power to command attention, on prior acceptance of controversial metaphysical ideas, particularly those which seemingly emerge in response to them.

It is essential to Descartes' project that the story be told this way. The promise of a response to skeptical problems will not be a point in favor of a system of philosophical ideas if those ideas help generate the problems in the first place, especially since the problems, once grasped, tend to be more compelling than any particular solutions. But, for Descartes, there is also a question of method. If, as is surely the case, the *Meditations* is meant to exemplify inquiry conducted according to Cartesian precepts, its argument must follow the order of reasons, at each stage depending only on considerations that have been explicitly avowed and validated. This means that the metaphysics is precluded from playing a covert role in generating the initial skeptical problems.

I think, however, that Descartes' doubts are much less natural, much less metaphysically noncommittal, than they are made to seem. In this essay, I want to explain why this is so and how the illusion of naturalness is created.

We are so familiar with Cartesian skepticism that its unnaturalness may not always be easy to see. We need something to compare it with. Classical Greek skepticism comes to mind.

Descartes represents, and perhaps understood, his own skeptical arguments as deriving from the classical tradition, implying that he had discovered new solutions to commonly recognized problems. And it is true that, with the exception of the Evil Deceiver, the materials of the First Meditation are all traditional.[2] Descartes nevertheless understates his own originality. Myles Burnyeat has argued, convincingly, that the central Cartesian problem, the problem of the external world, was never posed by the ancients.[3] Somehow, in Descartes' writings, traditional skeptical topics, such as madness and dreaming, take on a new significance.

Burnyeat thinks that Descartes saw that the traditional materials sustain a more radical doubt than the classical skeptics realized. He was able to do so because, for him, the significance of skepticism is exclusively methodological. Skepticism is encountered in the course of a project of pure, theoretical inquiry, for the purposes of which all practical constraints are set aside.[4] By contrast, the classical skeptics saw skepticism as a path to happiness, a way of living in the world, whose existence can therefore hardly be the subject of skeptical doubt.

There is something to this. Descartes does insist on the theoretical and methodological character of his doubts. Part of the significance of meditating is that doing so involves withdrawal from the world. But Descartes does not *extend* traditional skepticism, he transforms it. Cartesian and classical skepticism are radically different in kind, which is why it is illuminating to compare them. Doing so will provide a way of bringing out the distinctive commitments of Cartesian skepticism, the metaphysics of Cartesian doubt.

II

In the First Meditation, Descartes induces an intense, if provisional, doubt by reflecting on a carefully arranged sequence of epistemological problems. Perhaps by now his procedure seems too familiar to deserve comment. Yet for the classical skeptics, neither this connection with doubt nor this exclusive dependence on epistemological arguments was a feature of skepticism.

As Sextus tells it, the skeptic begins as a doubter but does not end as one.[5] The skeptic's capacity for suspension of judgment (*epoche*) is his remedy for doubt, not a means of inducing it.

The skeptic-to-be is a "talented" individual who finds his peace of mind, which he prizes more than anything, disturbed by his awareness of various problems and puzzles. His response is to look into matters for himself, so as to determine the truth. This shows, I think, that his initial state can quite properly be described as one of doubt or uncertainty. Doubt is the state in which we want to know the truth but cannot decide where it lies: and, judging by his reaction to his disquiet, this is just the state the skeptic-to-be starts out in. His inquiries, however, produce an unexpected result. Instead of resolving his uncertainties, they produce a lively sense that no disputes are ever resolvable, that it is possible to argue with roughly equal plausibility (*isosthenia*) for and against anything, and thus they lead him to make a practice of suspending judgment. To his surprise, this is the point at which the skeptic achieves the tranquillity (*ataraxia*) he has sought all along.[6]

Why doesn't his failure to bring his inquiries to a definite conclusion intensify his disquiet? The answer can only be that acquiring the distinctive skeptical capacities for *isosthenia* and *epoche* attenuates or even eliminates the urge to really *know* how things are. This is confirmed by the way the accomplished skeptic lives. In large measure, he follows what Descartes calls "the teachings of nature," to distinguish them from the results of informed rational judgment. Suspending judgment does not lead, as Hume notoriously supposes, to slow suicide. Rather, having got beyond the need to justify and explain, the skeptic lives by his spontaneous observations and impulses, the customs he has grown up with or come to feel comfortable with, and the practices of his trade or profession. He lives by how things strike him, acknowledging his opinions as just his opinions. He calls this living by "appearances."[7]

Obviously, nothing could be more distant from Descartes' outlook.

Descartes starts out in something like the classical skeptic's position: dissatisfied with the current state of his knowledge and hoping to do better. But whereas skepticism creeps up on the classical skeptic, as the result of his persistent inability to bring disputes to a definite conclusion, skepticism for Descartes is a theoretical problem that he *chooses* to confront. From the outset, skepticism is under his control: it is not, as it is for the classical skeptic, something with a life of its own, which might affect his motives in unforeseen and, perhaps initially, even unwelcome ways. Since Descartes' confrontation with skepticism takes place in a context where his fundamental motive, the urge to really know, is unaffected by skeptical reflections, a context where even the teachings of nature are minimally insistent, such reflections serve to intensify the initial uncertainty rather than eliminate it. Skepticism becomes wedded to doubt.

But for the purposes of this essay, the differences between the ways Descartes and the classical skeptics reach their respective skeptical states are even more significant than the differences between the states themselves.

Though classical suspension of judgment is not doubt, it is reached by means that involve an extension of ordinary, nonphilosophical doubting, the sort of doubting that comes as a result of exposure to conflicting opinions, each plausible in its way. The classical skeptic achieves *epoche* by mastering the art of meeting any given argument or thesis with a countervailing argument or thesis of equal plausibility. Since ethical arguments and theses will be met by countervailing ethical arguments and theses, physical by physical, logico-philosophical by logico-philosophical, no special importance attaches to arguments derived from theoretical considerations in epistemology. This explains the extreme discursiveness we find in Sextus (and in Montaigne, the true heir to the classical tradition). The accomplished skeptic has to master a potentially endless number of conflicting arguments, not just a short list of epistemological problems: he cultivates a kind of learned ignorance. If there is a problem here, it is not yet that of solving a canonical list of skeptical problems, derived from theoretical considerations in epistemology, though this is what the problem of skepticism became after Descartes.

The classical skeptics are not, of course, innocent of epistemological arguments. But the arguments they use, and the way they use them, grow out of the practice of *isosthenia*, which remains the basis of classical skepticism.

These arguments are summarized by the famous "modes."[8] To make sense of the Ten Modes, the first set Sextus presents, we should begin by separating out the ninth and tenth. The tenth simply illustrates how skeptics practice *isosthenia* in ethical disputes, whereas the ninth makes the point that whether an object is counted amazing or precious seems to depend more on its scarcity than on its intrinsic character. With these modes set aside, it becomes apparent that those remaining exemplify a single pattern of argument: all are versions of the so-called "problem of the criterion."

The first step of this argument is given in general form by the eighth mode: how things are judged to be is always *pros ti*, relative to something or other: the person judging, the conditions under which the judgment is made, and so on. Since, the argument continues, we inevitably face conflicting opinions, we can avoid suspension of judgment only if we have a criterion by which to determine where the truth lies. To take an example from conflict among the senses, if sight tells us that an object is smooth and touch that it is rough, shall we believe sight or touch? The skeptic finds that attempts to answer such questions invariably fail. If we make one sense the judge of truth, we simply beg the question against the other and, in any case, reason in a circle. If we propose an independent criterion, our hypothesis will be met by a conflicting hypothesis, yielding a new dispute to be adjudicated and threatening us with either a circle or a regress. Whatever we try, all roads lead to *epoche*.

The Five Modes, given as discrepancy, regress, relativity, hypothesis and circular reasoning, present in a more abstract form the strategy illustrated diversely by the Ten. Discrepancy and/or relativity suggest the need for a criterion; but any attempt to establish one will lead either to brute assertion (hypothesis), circular reasoning, or an infinite regress, each of which in one way or another leads to *epoche*.

The Two Modes are even more abstract, presenting an entirely general form of the regress problem. Any attempt to justify anything can be made to lead either to circular reasoning or an infinite regress. This suggests that the problem of the criterion can be regarded as a special case of the regress problem: that problem as it arises in connection with epistemological standards.

The important point is that the modes are not presented as theoretical arguments for the impossibility of knowledge. They are offered as techniques for heading off attempts to escape the effects of *isosthenia* by establishing a criterion for resolving disputes. The context in which to apply them is always provided by discrepancy and conflict between opinions: if there were no disagreements, there would be no occasions to apply the modes. The marshaling of conflicting opinions, therefore, remains the basis of classical skepticism. This extension of ordinary doubting needs no basis in epistemological theory. Nor does use of the modes, which are deployed defensively against antiskeptics who themselves admit the need for a criterion. The skeptic himself need have no views one way or another.

In contrast, Cartesian skepticism is the outcome of exclusively epistemological arguments. True, there are echoes of *isosthenia* in the *Meditations*, particularly in the discussions of God and the Deceiver, where Descartes propounds competing accounts of his origin and relation to Providence which he cannot yet rule out and some of which call in question the veracity of his previous beliefs. By balancing these disturbing possibilities against his deep-rooted but unexamined convictions, he achieves a general doubt. But this is not the fully fledged classical technique. If Descartes turns to theological speculation, it is not, as it would be for Sextus, in order to suspend judgment on religious matters, but to raise the question of whether our beliefs arise in a way that makes them likely to be true. The theological trappings derive their importance from their epistemological implications. Epistemological argument remains the basis of Cartesian skepticism.

We see, then, that Descartes does not simply put the resources of traditional skepticism to new uses. He reduces and redirects them. So our first question is: why?

But we have to ask not only why Descartes makes skepticism a matter of purely epistemological argument but also whether the epistemological considerations he exploits are the same as those exploited by the classical tradition? There are reasons for suspecting that they cannot be.

In its limited use of epistemological arguments, classical skepticism makes exclusive use of what I shall call the "formal" problems of the regress and the criterion. They are formal in the sense that they represent questions that can be asked of any antiskeptic who thinks that his beliefs can be justified. They depend on no substantive theories of justification: for example, theories about what kinds of beliefs can legitimately be cited in justification of what other kinds. And they are always fully general; they are applied indifferently to beliefs of all kinds and all subject matters.

As a result, classical skepticism is "flat." It never communicates a sense that some beliefs may be more problematic than others. In contrast, Cartesian doubt is, intentionally, differentiated. Descartes wants to show that we can, in a provisional way, entertain doubts about anything, but *especially* about material things.[9] It is also *stratified:* the sequence of arguments given in the First Meditation conveys a strong sense of probing ever more deeply into the bases of our convictions. We need to investigate how this sense of differentiation and stratification is inculcated and what epistemological considerations a stratified doubt implies.

III

Like Descartes, Bacon believes that the reconstruction of scientific knowledge must be preceded by a provisional doubt. But whereas Descartes favors the use of very general epistemological problems to empty our minds, Bacon recommends we counteract the force of received opinion by filling our minds with all the new facts and theoretical possibilities we can find.[10] This straightforward adaptation of classical skepticism shows that putting skepticism to a methodological use does not by itself lead to the reduction of skepticism to a purely epistemological problem. But there are several reasons why the classical technique of *isosthenia* would not serve Descartes' purposes.

In a letter to Mersenne of 1641 Descartes writes:

> . . . I may tell you between ourselves that these six *Meditations* contain all the foundations of my *Physics*. But please do not tell people, for it might make it harder for supporters of Aristotle to approve them. I hope that readers will gradually get used to my principles, and recognise their truth, before they notice they destroy those of Aristotle.[11]

The classical skeptic would induce *epoche* by balancing the new principles against the old. But in Descartes' view the new and the old never balance. To the prejudiced mind, under the spell of the senses, the new principles will seem absurd; to the mind properly prepared they will be compelling. To get the new principles a fair hearing, then, will require tact and indirection. Too early and too definite an identification of the substantive questions at issue must be avoided. Accordingly, the provisional doubt is made to turn on general epistemological considerations alone.

But perhaps even more significant is the fact that Cartesian doubt necessarily pretends to a kind of systematicity and closure that has no place in classical *epoche*. The provisional doubt of the First Meditation is to be resolved by finding new principles, which will modify our understanding of whatever previous beliefs are eventually reinstated. Descartes' original opinions, as originally understood, have been definitively undermined, made dubious beyond recall. In contrast, classical skepticism is open-ended and represents a continuing engagement rather than a completable project. It is comprehensive, in that the skeptic will try to deal with all theses and arguments that come his way. But it is not closed: the classical skeptic is always ready to deal with new claims or attempts to revive old ones. He never claims to have dealt definitively and in advance with everything a particular kind of dogmatist might say, for this itself would be a kind of dogmatism.

Descartes' definitive doubt is the mirror image of his definitive certainty. Having raised, as he claims,[12] all *possible* doubts, he will be able subsequently to claim that whatever principles survive his skeptical scrutiny have been established with metaphysical finality. Classical skepticism, even if used as a methodological device, could support no such claim. With the emergence of a new idea, the balance, even if at present dramatically tipped, might always be restored, or even tipped the other way. Ordinary doubting, and its sophisticated extension, classical *isosthenia*, are always contingent on the current state of knowledge. They offer no test for absolute certainty.

To make plausible the idea of a definitive skeptical doubt, hence of definitive metaphysical certainty, Descartes must represent the credibility of his former opinions as resting ultimately on certain highly general epistemological principles that can be exhaustively examined for possible sources of error. But Descartes does not acknowledge the theoretical considerations that mandate this reduction of skepticism to a theoretical problem in epistemology. Rather, he represents the reduction as a condition of making his project practicable. To effect a "general upheaval" of his former opinions, he writes:

. . . it will not be requisite that I examine each in particular, which would be an endless undertaking, for owing to the fact that the destruction of the foundations of necessity brings with it the downfall of the rest of the edifice, I shall only in the first place attack those principles upon which all my former opinions rested.[13]

This is misleading. It is not simply "not requisite" to examine each opinion on its specific merits; it is requisite not to.

The epistemological systematicity implied by the metaphor of "foundations" allows beliefs to be undermined in a "topic-neutral" way; that is, independently of their particular content, the current state of collateral knowledge, and all concrete problem-situations and contexts of inquiry in which they might be examined. But the possibility of this kind of doubt is a requirement, not a discovery. There is no argument anywhere in Descartes' *Meditations* to show that common sense recognizes the conception of justification, embodied in the metaphor of foundations, on which Descartes' definitive doubt depends. For all he has shown, commonsense doubting, hence commonsense certainty, may always be to some degree context-bound. Classical skepticism, which is in a way "an endless undertaking," allows for this possibility. But Descartes excludes it by projecting into common sense a theoretical conception of justification disguised as a matter of practical convenience.

What makes this projection seem more innocent than it is is Descartes' extreme vagueness as to the nature of the "principles" on which his former opinions rested. All he tells us is that these opinions were derived by way of the senses. Though there may be some sense in which this is uncontroversially true, to generate the skeptical doubt he requires Descartes will have to interpret it in a way that is far from uncontroversial. But before we can look into how the required interpretation is introduced and how its theoretical character is disguised we must deal with the question of how Cartesian doubt, unlike classical *epoche*, conveys the sense of stratification we noted earlier.

IV

In the first four of the Ten Modes, Sextus presents and rebuts a sequence of progressively more specific responses to the problem of the criterion. The First Mode questions the least common denominator of dogmatic solutions to the problem, the assumption that men are the judges of truth. Why not other animals, who in some respects seem to have the advantage over us? The sequence of questions then continues: if men, which particular man or men, given that men disagree? If some particular man or men, by what sense or faculty, given that various senses and faculties often suggest different judgments? And if by some particular sense or faculty, under what conditions or in what circumstances, given that what is thought to be true is influenced by conditions and circumstances?

At each "stage" in the sequence the same argument is presented, the argument we are already familiar with. The first step is invariably to claim that the proposed criterion either itself produces discrepant opinions or is in conflict with other prima facie equally plausible criteria. Subsequent steps argue that any attempt to remedy the situation will lead to brute assertion, circular reasoning, or an infinite regress. Each failed attempt to resolve the problem of the criterion leads to a *comprehensive* suspension of judgment.

Now contrast this with Descartes' procedure in the First Meditation. The crucial feature of the way Descartes develops his doubt is that it is *not* complete at every stage. Rather, at each stage some beliefs are called in question but others survive, pending the deployment of more powerful skeptical considerations.

The first point Descartes makes is that he cannot trust his senses without qualification because they have often deceived him about objects that are barely perceptible or very far away. But this leaves untouched beliefs about objects close by and in plain view. To call these in question he needs the dreaming argument. But even the dreaming argument, as Descartes understands it, leaves unscathed beliefs about things that are "very simple and very general," and to undermine the credibility of these he has to raise questions about his origin, nature, and relation to Providence, a line of thought encapsulated in the conceit of the Evil Deceiver. And even this final, "hyperbolical" doubt seems implicitly to concede Descartes some knowledge. For he does not end the First Meditation in a state of complete confusion. He knows at least how things *seem* to him, even if as yet he has no idea how they really are.

This stratification of doubt imposes a corresponding stratification of knowledge. Through the progressive development of his doubt, Descartes effects a context- and subject matter-independent partitioning of his beliefs into broad epistemological classes, ordered according to how difficult it is to doubt them. First in the order come the beliefs that are never doubted, subsequently to be identified as those that involve Descartes' immediate knowledge of his own "thoughts," whose exemption will be retrospectively justified on the grounds of their supposed incorrigibility. Moreover, the order of justification, which Descartes calls "the order of reasons," must reverse the order of doubt. The progressive development of Cartesian doubt insinuates, without ever directly arguing for, a foundational conception of knowledge, the view of knowledge that sees justification as constrained by just the sort of context- and subject matter-independent order of epistemic priority that is implicit in Descartes' stratified doubt.

The skepticism that develops within a foundational conception of knowledge contrasts sharply with classical skepticism, even in its most purely epistemic form. Acceptance of the notion of a context-independent order of epistemological priority makes skepticism turn on problems about inference: the skeptic challenges us to show how beliefs of a given kind can be justified on the basis of beliefs that, in virtue of their place in the epistemic hierarchy, constitute the proper evidence for them. The classical skeptic's undifferentiated *epoche* thus gives way to a form of skepticism organized around specific skeptical problems: the external world, induction, other minds, and so forth. This transformation of skepticism is the legacy of Descartes' *Meditations*.

It is not immediately apparent that the First Meditation will issue in a radical transformation of skepticism. At the first stage of the doubt, Descartes could be taken to be following Sextus, proposing a rather vague criterion of truth (the senses) and, having found it wanting, replacing it with something more refined (the senses operating under ideal conditions).[14] But with the argument that begins by mentioning madness and modulates into a discussion of dreaming, his divergence from the classical tradition becomes increasingly evident.

Whereas dreaming is of crucial significance for Descartes, Sextus mentions it only incidentally as one of the "conditions or dispositions" that influence judgment. (The others include madness, old age, sickness.) Here is his discussion in full:

Sleeping and waking, too, give rise to different impressions, since we do not imagine when awake what we imagine in sleep, nor in sleep what we imagine when awake; so that the existence of our impressions is not absolute but relative, being in relation to our sleeping or waking condition. Probably, then, in dreams we see things which to our waking state are unreal, although not wholly unreal; for they exist in our dreams, just as waking realities exist, although nonexistent in dreams.[15]

Notice the emphasis on the *difference in content* between waking experience and dreams. Because of this difference, dreaming offers one more way into the familiar problem of the criterion, which is why Sextus attaches no *special* significance to it.

Various textual echoes suggest the second book of Cicero's *Academica* as the likely source for Descartes' discussion of dreaming. As in the First Meditation, dreaming is discussed in connection with the question of whether the senses are a source of certainty. Lucullus, the antiskeptic in the dialogue, has claimed that the delusions of dreams, drunkards, and lunatics are feebler than, hence easily distinguished from, veridical sense-experiences. Cicero replies that this need not be so, since men are sometimes fooled by dreams and hallucinations. Whatever makes normal experience convincing can be mimicked by dreams, which means that normal experience does not convince us in virtue of anything that guarantees its truthfulness. But, just as in Sextus, the argument stresses the discrepancy between the content of waking perception and that of dreams, the point being to ask why we take the one and not the other to be veridical.[16]

Like Sextus and Cicero, Descartes begins by associating dreaming with madness and pointing up the discrepancy between waking perception and dreams. Thus:

> I am a man, and . . . consequently in the habit of sleeping, and in my dreams representing the same things, or sometimes even less probable things, than do those who are insane in their waking moments.[17]

However, he promptly executes an abrupt volte-face, continuing:

> How often has it appeared to me that in the night I dreamt that I found myself lying in this particular place, that I was dressed and seated near the fire, while in reality I was lying undressed in bed?[18]

Suddenly the emphasis is on the "fact" that dreams can *reproduce the content of the most commonplace waking experiences.* This shift of emphasis allows Descartes to pose a question that never occurs to the classical skeptics: How can Descartes *ever* be sure that he is not dreaming? Might not his entire conscious life be a kind of dream?

Cicero evidently sees no such general problem, for he writes:

> As if anyone would deny that a man that has woken up thinks that he has been dreaming, or that one whose madness has subsided thinks that the things that he saw during his madness were not true.[19]

While dreaming, we may not realize it. But when we are awake we know it. Descartes, however, though awake and in possession of his senses, is "almost capable of persuading" himself that he is dreaming. Not surprisingly, since the situation he recalls having dreamt himself to be in corresponds exactly to the situation he finds himself in at the moment.

The shift of attention from the discrepancy between waking perception and dreaming to the possibility of their convergence also serves to detach dreaming from madness. This is essential to the way Descartes develops his doubt. Associating dreaming with drunkenness and lunacy suggests that the dream-state may be one of mental confusion. But Descartes holds that our capacity to judge, hence potentially to know, is unaffected by our being in a dream rather than awake. This allows him to continue his stratification of knowledge, arguing that there are still beliefs unscathed by the dreaming argument. For example:

. . . whether I am awake or asleep, two and three together always form five and the square can never have more than four sides . . . [20]

Dreaming and waking do not, therefore, involve radically different kinds of experiences. Rather, the difference between them must be entirely extrinsic, and Descartes hints more than once that it has to do with causation. As the *Meditations* progress, "dreaming" will be reinterpreted to mean "experience, apparently of objects, but without the usual corresponding external causes," and eventually, "experience without any physical causes whatsoever."

There are several steps to be taken before we confront the nightmare fantasy of a being *sans corps, sans monde*. Descartes takes the dreaming argument to leave open the possibility that our experiences, dreams though they may be, are caused by, and in some suitably abstract way correspond to, external physical objects. Only after he has questioned his relation to God, alternatively the Deceiver, is he able to ask:

. . . how do I know that he has not brought it to pass that there is no earth, no heaven, no extended body, no magnitude, no place, and that nevertheless I possess the perceptions of all these things and that they seem to exist just exactly as I now see them?[21]

Nevertheless, the materials that make it possible to raise the general skeptical problem about the external world are substantially in place by the end of the dreaming argument. The problem emerges as that of inferring, from what we know, whether we are awake or dreaming (i.e., how things seem), the existence and nature of the supposed external causes of our perceptions, which is why it is essential that the Cartesian dreamer retain intact his ability to think.

We see, then, that the progressive doubt of the *Meditations* is informed throughout by a foundational conception of knowledge. Descartes' distinctive skeptical problems, and the metaphysical framework that makes it possible to raise them, are introduced together. If they seem compelling, it is through the power of Descartes' narrative. There is no argument for accepting the foundational conception, even for the purposes of a philosophical reconstruction of knowledge, still less for projecting it into unreconstructed common sense. Cartesian skepticism is not, like classical skepticism, an extension of common-sense doubting. It is dependent from the outset on a metaphysic as essential as it is unavowed. It remains for us to explore the devices by which the theoretical character of the doubt is both clarified and disguised.

V

Gassendi dismissed the First Meditation as contrived and unnecessarily prolix. Only when he came to comment on the Third did it begin to dawn on him what Descartes had been up to:

> You seem afterwards to make it doubtful not only whether any ideas proceed from external things, but also whether there are any external objects at all. And you seem thence to infer that although there exist in you the ideas of things said to be external, those ideas nevertheless do not prove that the things exist, since they do not necessarily proceed from them, but may be due to yourself or to some other cause, I know not what. It was for this reason I fancy that you previously continued to say: That you had not previously perceived earth, sky, or stars, but the ideas of earth, sky and stars, which might possibly be a source of delusion.[22]

Here we see Gassendi interpreting the First Meditation in the light of things that have become clear to him in the course of the Second and Third, though the objection he goes on to level might make us wonder whether, even at this point, he has really grasped the structure of Descartes' problem.[23]

This belated and retrospective understanding of the First Meditation doubt is, nevertheless, entirely appropriate to the way the *Meditations* is written. The First Meditation suggests far more than it says. But in the Third Meditation Descartes finally identifies both his former certainties and the "principles" on which they rested:

> They were the earth, sky, stars, and all other objects which I apprehended by means of the senses. But what did I clearly and distinctly perceive in them? Nothing more than that the ideas or thoughts of these things were presented to my mind. And not even now do I deny that these ideas are to be met with in me. But there was yet another thing which I affirmed, and which, owing to the habit which I had formed of believing it, I thought I perceived very clearly, though in truth I did not perceive it at all, to wit, that there were objects outside of me from which these ideas proceeded, and to which they were entirely similar. And it was in this that I erred . . . [24]

This brings out very clearly what is involved in the skeptical problem about the external world. Our basic knowledge is of our own thoughts or ideas: the question is how to justify inferences from this basic knowledge to beliefs about the existence of the supposed external, physical causes of those ideas. What was only implicit in the First Meditation is finally brought into the open.

This process of clarification and interpretation is resumed in the

Sixth Meditation. Again, Descartes represents his beliefs about bodies and their qualities as depending on inferences from "the ideas of all these qualities which presented themselves to my mind, and which alone I perceived properly or immediately."[25] The grounds for such inferences, however, were the vividness of the ideas of sense and their independence of his will, reasons which seem wholly inadequate when he reminds himself that

I have never believed myself to feel anything in waking moments which I cannot also sometimes believe myself to feel when I sleep, and as I do not think that these things which I seem to feel in sleep, proceed from objects outside of me, I do not see any reason why I should have this belief regarding objects which I seem to perceive while awake.[26]

Again, the metaphysical presuppositions of the doubt are made clear in a way they never were when it was first developed. These are, to summarize:

1. The assumption that there is a universal, context- and subject matter-independent order of reasons; that knowledge conforms to a foundational structure.

2. The identification of our "thoughts," the contents of our "minds," as all that we perceive "properly or immediately."

3. The assimilation of sensations to "thoughts" as characterized above. This assimilation allows Descartes to entertain the possibility that his "sensations" might be just what they are even if he had no senses—if there were no physical world at all—while, by trading on the commonsense notion that the (physical) senses are what put us (embodied persons) in touch with external objects (i.e., objects outside our bodies), preserving the idea that "sensations" are the sine qua non of knowledge of external reality. "Sensations" thus become the ultimate, if prima facie noncommittal, evidence on which inferences to beliefs about that reality must be based.[27]

It is clear why Descartes cannot be open about these presuppositions from the start: not until later in the *Meditations* does he have the necessary theses and distinctions in hand. To take just one example, common sense does not recognize the Cartesian analysis of sensation into mental and physical components, if for no other reason than that it does not recognize the Cartesian conception of the mental. To make it appear as if the doubt about the external is generated out of resources that common sense does recognize as its own, Descartes must project back into his prephilosophical position metaphysical considerations that are properly available only after common sense has been left far behind.

This projection is accomplished, and disguised, in the Third and Sixth Meditations where, as in the passages just cited, he interprets the First Meditation doubts, which are deliberately left somewhat vague and indeterminate, under the guise of recalling them for the purpose of further examination. But this "recollection" is only a pretense.[28] Consider again Descartes' question about the bodies he used to take himself to perceive:

> . . . what did I clearly and distinctly perceive in them? Nothing more than that the ideas or thoughts of these things were presented to my mind?[29]

But the answer ought to be simply "Nothing." Descartes was in no position to perceive clearly and distinctly that the ideas of these things were presented to his mind because he had not, at that stage, thought his way through to a clear and distinct conception of either "thought" or "mind." Descartes must pretend that he always in some way recognized that only his ideas were properly and immediately known, for only in that way can he suggest that his previous beliefs rested on a dubious inference from these basic data. But his question would be more properly put, not as what *did* he clearly and distinctly perceive when he was mired in common sense, but as what *could* he have come to perceive that way if he had had the relevant distinctions already in hand? Put that way, however, the question would subvert rather than reinforce the illusion that the doubt about the external world was generated out of the resources of common sense alone.

This pretense of recollecting, while in fact interpreting, is aided considerably by Descartes' practice of playing back and forth between the commonsense understanding of "external object," "dream," and so on, and the senses that such terms take on in the light of his own metaphysical innovations. Thus consider the following passage, where Descartes is considering whether his ideas need have *any* "external" cause, even a nonphysical one:

> . . . perhaps there is in me some faculty fitted to produce these ideas without the existence of external things, even though it is not yet known by me; just as, apparently, they have hitherto always been found in me during sleep without the aid of external objects.[30]

In its first occurrence, "external" means outside the Cartesian mind; in the second, it bears the familiar meaning of spatially external to the body. In a similar way, dreams are sometimes experiences we have while asleep, a state in which an implication of embodiment exists: but when the Evil Deceiver is said to produce "illusions and dreams," dreams are the experiences of a bodiless, worldless self. Such equivocations allow Descartes to read metaphysical innovations back into his commonsense starting point without his appearing to do so.

VI

From the argument so far, one thing at least should be clear: that there is no such thing as *the* argument from dreams. So I am not claiming that any skeptical argument which appeals to the fact that we dream is metaphysically loaded in just the way Descartes' argument is. Equally, it is no objection to claim that *a* version of the dreaming argument can be developed in a more metaphysically noncommittal way. What would need to be shown is that a version could be developed that would lend itself to the same uses that Descartes puts his version to.

We can clarify the metaphysically loaded character of the Cartesian argument from dreams by returning briefly to the ancients. Doing so will allow us to determine more precisely what ancient materials Descartes makes use of and how he transforms them.

I argued above that, whereas Descartes appeals to the (alleged) fact that dreaming can mimic waking to the point of being indistinguishable from it, the ancients stress the discrepancy between what we experience in dreams and what we experience when awake. This point needs to be made with some care, however. It applies without qualification to the Pyrrhonians. But the Academics argue somewhat differently. Indeed, they argue in ways that, superficially, are more than a little reminiscent of Descartes.

Pyrrhonian skepticism exploits the "formal" epistemological problems of the criterion and the regress of justification. Central to Academic skepticism, however, is a quite different argument: that, since nonveridical perceptions can be identical to, or at least indistinguishable from, veridical perceptions, no perception guarantees its own veracity. Consequently, since all knowledge begins with perception, there is no guaranteeing the veracity of anything we accept: that is, nothing can be known.[31]

When we add to this the fact that the Academics cite dreams and hallucinations—perceptions of objects that have no real existence—as examples of false perceptions that may be indistinguishable from true ones, it may seem that we must credit them with the very argument that Descartes uses to pose the problem of our knowledge of the external world. It may further seem that, if they did not pose this problem themselves, they must simply have failed to see the implications of their own arguments, as Burnyeat has claimed about the ancient skeptics in general.

However, on closer examination, a different picture emerges. We can find in the Academic skeptics the elements of Cartesian doubt, but not in their distinctively Cartesian alignment. Properly understood, the Academics confirm, rather than create difficulties for, the argument I have been developing.

The first thing to notice is that the Academic arguments exploit two quite distinct ways in which true perceptions might be indistinguishable from false. The first, as in Descartes' version of the dreaming argument, has to do with content: or, more precisely, with the objects presented (*visa*). The second has to do, not with what is presented, but with the mode of presentation: in particular, with whether veridical perceptions have a distinctive persuasiveness, a feeling of reality or substantiality that nonveridical perceptions lack. Now, and this is the crucial point, perceptions that are indistinguishable in respect of content are always thought of as perceptions of (= caused by) indistinguishable objects: the standard examples are two eggs, and a man and his twin brother. As a result, this kind of indistinguishability is not what is at issue when the discussion turns to dreams and hallucinations, where there are no real objects causing the perceptions. When these false perceptions are brought up, it is always to make the argument that, since the dreamer can be taken in by his dreams, and the madman by his delusions, whatever makes true perceptions persuasive may be equally characteristic of false ones: in this sense, perceptions to which no real objects correspond may be indistinguishable from true perceptions. Accordingly, we find opponents of the Academics making two quite distinct replies: that no two real objects are perfectly indistinguishable; and that dreams and hallucinations are not persuasive in quite the same way as ordinary waking perception.[32]

Though there can be little doubt that the sources of Cartesian skepticism are primarily Academic, we see that Descartes' dream argument is the product of uniting considerations that the Academics keep distinct. To effect the union, Descartes must dissociate indistinguishability of perceptions with respect to content from causation by near-identical objects. His new conception of the mental, which allows him to think of "sensations" in abstraction from the senses, makes this possible. Lacking this, the Academic skeptics think of sensation in partly causal-physical terms, as an affection of the living organism.[33] Accordingly, they think of similar perceptions as perceptions of (caused by) similar objects. This precludes uniting their arguments so as to raise the question of whether there is any external world at all.

Not that they would have wished to unite them. Academic skepticism with respect to the senses seems to have developed in response to the Stoic attempt to explain a "cognitive" impression (*phantasia kataleptike*) as an impression that, in virtue of being caused in a certain standard way, is both incapable of falsity and distinctively persuasive.[34] Against this Stoic solution to the problem of the criterion, the Academics argue that the existence of indistinguishable objects shows that normal causation does not guarantee true opinions. Present successively even a Stoic sage with two eggs and he will be unable to say whether he has seen two eggs or the same egg twice. He can go wrong, even though the conditions of perception are ideal. Notice that the whole point of this argument turns on associating indistinguishability of objects presented with causally normal perception.

That we sometimes "perceive" things that do not really exist makes a different but complementary point. Where the causal background is *ex hypothesi* deviant, as in dreams and madness, there is no reason to suppose that ordinary experience will ever be exactly duplicated. Indeed, the point the Academics want to make becomes more striking given the commonsense idea that strange things are seen in madness and in dreams. For the point is that, since dreamers and madmen can be taken in by their delusions, not even the wildest experiences need differ from ordinary perceptions in respect of persuasiveness, however else they may differ. Thus, not merely does normal causation not guarantee truth, deviant causation does not guarantee unpersuasiveness. The Stoic theory of cognitive impressions fails on two counts.

So, though the elements of Cartesian skepticism are Academic, the way they are put together is Descartes' own. His tacit metaphysical presuppositions are what make possible this realignment of traditional materials.

VII

We may conclude that Descartes' doubts are not natural, not metaphysically noncommittal. On the contrary, they are informed from the outset by the metaphysical considerations that are supposed to emerge in response to them. Only Descartes' artful method of exposition—which involves developing his doubts in a way that is initially rather vague, but also reminiscent of traditional skepticism, and subsequently clarifying and interpreting them, under the guise of recollecting what has already been agreed—prevents this from being immediately apparent.

This means that the story told by the *Meditations* cannot be taken at face value. In this story, metaphysical discoveries are made in the course of exploring the limits of skepticism. But the skepticism whose limits are explored involves the special dubitability of beliefs about the external world, and the external world only emerges as a distinct problem once the important metaphysical concessions have already been made.

The unnaturalness of the Cartesian doubt is, however, perhaps not always easy for a modern reader to see. When we approach the First Meditation for the first time, most of us are either already vaguely familiar with some central Cartesan ideas, or we are taken through the Meditations by a teacher who is thoroughly familiar with them. This is why the uncomprehending reactions of intelligent contemporaries like Hobbes and Gassendi are worth pondering.[35]

In his *Dictionary* article, "Pyrrho," Bayle records a doubtless fictitious conversation between two priests, one hostile to skepticism, the other sympathetic. The hostile priest expresses surprise that there are any skeptics left. He can understand how there might have been pagan skeptics, for the pagans lacked the guidance of revelation; but he cannot understand expressions of skepticism from men of his own time, who live in the light of the Gospels. But the sympathetic priest replies that it is even easier for modern men to be skeptics than it was for the ancients. Not merely is Christian doctrine itself a fertile source of paradoxes (think of the Trinity), but arguments deriving from the new science of bodies, which tend to show that some qualities we used to ascribe to bodies, color and heat, for example, are really ideas in the mind, are readily extended to all qualities, with the result that we must wonder whether we know anything about physical reality.

If my argument in this essay is correct, and we interpret their remarks rather freely, Bayle's priests are both right. The one hostile to skepticism is pointing to the impossibility of a modern man's being a classical skeptic, and, whether he was right that this was an impossibility in religion, it was fast becoming an impossibility in science. In Sextus' time, it may have been possible to argue with roughly equal plausibility for, say, Aristotle's conception of matter on the one hand, and Democritus' on the other. Indeed, even Montaigne, writing in the second half of the sixteenth century, could still argue in the manner of Sextus, parading the endless diversity of philosophers' opinions with a view to inducing in the reader a sense of the futility and ridiculousness of ever claiming to know the truth about anything. But the time was fast approaching when no one could seriously claim to be able to argue as convincingly for Aristotle's physics as for Newton's. The classical route to skepticism through the balancing of conflicting opinions was being closed off, at least for large areas of inquiry. The persistence of irresolvable conflict was on its way to becoming an indication that the dispute was merely verbal, as it is in Hume.[36] But, by a curious irony, metaphysical reflections connected with the very scientific advances that killed classical skepticism were in the process of giving rise to a new form of skepticism, in its way far more disturbing. This is what Bayle saw: indeed, what he saw, correctly, as the legacy of Descartes.

NOTES

1. In *The Philosophical Works of Descartes*. Subsequent references to this work are cited as HR (see the General Bibliography at the beginning of this volume).

2. The Deceiver is the only feature of his development of skepticism for which Descartes claims originality. See *Descartes' Conversation with Burman*, translated with Introduction and Commentary by John Cottingham (Oxford: Clarendon Press, 1976), 4. Subsequent references to this work are cited as CB, followed by page number.

3. Myles Burnyeat, "Idealism and Greek Philosophy: What Descartes Saw and Berkeley Missed," *Philosophical Review* (January 1982):3–40. For making me think about the novelty of Descartes' skepticism, I am also grateful to Avner Cohen for letting me read some chapters from a book he is preparing on the history of skepticism.

4. In emphasizing this aspect of Descartes' project Burnyeat is influenced by Bernard Williams. See his *Descartes: The Project of Pure Enquiry* (Harmondsworth: Pelican, 1978), esp. chap. 2.

5. Sextus Empiricus, *Outlines of Pyrrhonism*, bk. 1, no. 12. Subsequent references are cited as OP, followed by book and marginal number. The edition I have used appears as *Sextus Empiricus*, vol. 1, with translation by R. G. Bury, Loeb Classical Library (London: Heinemann; Cambridge: Harvard University Press, 1933; reprinted 1967).

6. OP, 1, 25–29.

7. OP, 1, 23–24. Such "appearances" are evidently not sense-data. For an interesting discussion of the Pyrrhonian notion of "appearance," see Myles Burnyeat, "Can the Sceptic Live His Scepticism?" in *The Skeptical Tradition*, ed. Burnyeat (Berkeley, Los Angeles, London: University of California Press, 1983), 117–148.

8. OP, 1, 31 ff.

9. See the opening of the Synopsis of the *Meditations*, HR I, 140.

10. *Novum Organum*, bk. 2, aphorism 32. In *Philosophical Works*, ed. Spedding, Ellis, and Heath (London: Longmans, 1879), vol. 4.

11. Descartes, *Philosophical Letters*, translated and edited by Anthony Kenny (Oxford: Oxford University Press, 1970), 94.

12. CB, 4.

13. HR I, 145.

14. Burnyeat interprets Descartes this way in "Idealism and Greek Philosophy" (see pp. 32 ff.). A similar reading can be found in Harry G. Frankfurt, *Demons, Dreamers, and Madmen* (Indianapolis: Bobbs-Merrill, 1970), chap. 5.

15. OP, 1, 104.

16. Cicero, *Academica*, in *Cicero*, vol. 19, with translation by H. Rackham, Loeb Classical Library (London: Heinemann; Cambridge: Harvard University Press, 1933: reprinted 1979), bk. 2, sec. 27. Margaret Wilson interprets Descartes' dreaming argument in a way that has Descartes arguing along what may seem to be the same lines as Cicero, and noting Cicero as his probable source would strengthen her case. But though I think that Descartes had the *Academica* in mind when composing the *Meditations*, his version of the dreaming argument differs significantly from Cicero's, as I show in section 6, where I discuss Descartes' adaptation of Academic materials. For Wilson's interpretation, see her *Descartes* (London: Routledge & Kegan Paul, 1978), chap. 1.

17. HR I, 145.

18. HR I, 145–146.

19. *Academica*, 579.

20. HR I, 147.

21. HR I, 148.

22. HR II, 154–155.

23. For example, he asks why one born blind has no idea of color.

24. HR I, 158.

25. HR I, 187.

26. HR I, 189.

27. On the novelty of Descartes' conception of sensation, see Wallace Matson, "Why Isn't the Mind-Body Problem Ancient?" in *Mind, Matter, and Method*, ed. Paul Feyerabend and Grover Maxwell (Minneapolis: Minnesota University Press, 1966), 92–102.

Bernard Williams (*Descartes*, 57 f.) sees an important difference between the doubt based on the dreaming argument, which allows us to question any given perceptual belief, and the hyperbolical doubt based on the Deceiver, which calls in question all beliefs at once, thus raising the skeptical problem about the external world. Moreover, he notes that the latter doubt has built into it "a causal model of perception." The hyperbolical doubt thus poses a problem for Williams's attempt to defend the reasonableness and metaphysically noncommittal character of Cartesian doubt by portraying it as the natural outcome of transposing commonsense ideas about knowledge into the context of pure theoretical inquiry. Williams is inclined to cope with this difficulty by suggesting that the hyperbolical doubt is not strictly necessary for Descartes' methodological purposes.

There are two things to say about this. First, a causal model of perception does not by itself create the possibility of the hyperbolical doubt: indeed, understood a certain way, it may even block the road to the skeptical problem of the external world, as my discussion of the Academics in section 6 shows. Thus the metaphysical presuppositions of Cartesian doubt are much more extensive and have much less to do with common sense than Williams implies. They include at least epistemological foundationalism and a new conception of mind. Second, they cannot be brushed aside, for the specal dubitability of the very existence of the external world, hence the hyperbolical doubt, is essential to the purposes Descartes has in mind for his doubt. Who can doubt that the reconstruction of knowledge would proceed very differently if this special dubitability were never argued for?

28. Paul Feyerabend finds a similar rhetorical technique in Galileo. See *Against Method* (London: New Left Books, 1975), chap. 7.

29. HR I, 158.

30. HR I, 161.

31. Cicero: *Academica*, 519 f., 573 f. Sextis: *Against the Logicians* I, 409 f. in *Sextus Empiricus*, vol. 2. The first passage from Cicero, where Lucullus is expounding the Academic arguments, is especially striking for containing other ideas that will become important to Descartes: God's omnipotence and the mind's power to "move itself" (p. 527). But these ideas are not put to Cartesian uses. Lucullus's replies to the arguments he has expounded show that his remarks about false perceptions being potentially indistinguishable from true show that they are to be interpreted along the lines I indicate in the text.

32. *Academica*, 529–541.

33. *Against the Logicians* I, 162.

34. See Michael Frede, "Stoics and Skeptics on Clear and Distinct Impressions" in Burnyeat's *The Skeptical Tradition*.

35. Hobbes saw nothing new in Descartes' arguments for skepticism, which he referred to slightingly as "those matters of ancient lore." See HR II, 60.

36. Hume takes the capacity to be subverted by "a due contrast and opposition" to be the hallmark of the vacuous opinions that are produced by the "capricious" principles of the imagination. See his *Treatise on Human Nature*, ed. L. Selby-Bigge (Oxford: Clarendon Press, 1888; reprinted 1965), 225.

6

Descartes and the Problem of Other Minds

Gareth B. Matthews

Is the Problem of Other minds to be found in Descartes? And, if it is, does Descartes offer the Argument from Analogy as its solution?

The most natural place to look for an answer to those questions is in Descartes' reconstruction of knowledge just after he has established his own existence and has told us what a mind is—that is, in the last part of Meditation II. The closest thing one finds there to a statement of the Problem of Other Minds is this:

> Thus when the wax is before us we say that we see it to be the same wax as that previously seen, and not that we judge it to be the same from its retaining the same colour and shape. From this I should straightway conclude that the wax is known by ocular vision, independently of a strictly mental inspection [*visione oculi, non solius mentis inspectione*] were it not that perchance I recall how when looking from a window at beings passing by on the street below, I similarly say that it is men I am seeing, just as I say that I am seeing the wax. What do I see from the window beyond hats and cloaks, which might cover automatic machines? Yet I judge those to be men. In analogous fashion, what I have been supposing myself to see with the eyes I am comprehending solely with the faculty of judgement, a faculty proper not to my eyes but to my mind. (Kemp Smith trans.)

Is this a statement of the Problem of Other Minds? There is certainly a contrast here between what one sees to be the case and what one judges to be the case. That reminds us of the contrast that underlies the Problem of Other Minds between what can be observed directly (bodies, perhaps, and one's own mind but not other minds) and what can only be inferred. So far, so good. We have just had in the immediately preceding discussion the example of a piece of wax that has lost all the perceptible qualities it formerly had. It is not that it now has no perceptible qualities at all. Rather, each perceptible quality it formerly had has gone, but there are now other perceptible qualities instead. Descartes then makes the point that one cannot see by "ocular vision" that it is the same wax in a new state, though one can make the judgment by "mental inspection." The hats-and-cloaks analogy is meant to underline this contrast between what one can see by "ocular vision" and what must be left to judgment by "mental inspection." Thus one does not see from the window, by "ocular vision," that there are human beings under those hats and cloaks, though one may judge that there are by "mental inspection."

It's worth emphasing that Descartes does *not* say, as one might have expected him to say, that he doesn't see minds, or thoughts, within those bodies. Rather, he says one does not see, *from the window,* that there are *men* (i.e., human beings) under those hats and cloaks, rather than automatic machines. Judgment must take over because the eyes, from the window anyway, cannot rule out the following possibility:

P1.   There are not men under the hats and cloaks, but only automatic machines.

To get the Problem of Other Minds going, one would need to introduce the suggestion that, even if we went down into the street and disrobed those figures, we could not rule out, by "ocular vision," this possibility:

P2.   There are no minds to go with those human bodies.

The worry about how to rule out (P2) is, of course, not excluded by the text, but it goes well beyond it. There is no explicit suggestion in the text of a worry that could not be dispelled by taking off the hats and cloaks, or perhaps simply peeking discreetly under them. Without a worry about how I can be justified in inferring that there are other minds, when the only one I can observe directly is my own, there is no Problem of Other Minds.

I can imagine someone protesting that my reading of the hats-and-cloaks passage is very superficial. After all, Descartes has before him the case of the odorless, colorless, tasteless, inaudible liquid that is the product of melting down a piece of sweet-smelling, sweet-tasting, milky-looking, and solid-sounding wax. His point is that one cannot *see* the liquid stuff to be the same wax; one *judges* it to be so. It is no accidental, or remediable, circumstance that prevents us from making the identification by ocular vision. The persistence of a sensible substance through a change in all its sensible properties cannot be observed; *in principle* it cannot be observed. The disappearance of the first set of properties can be observed, as can the appearance of the new set, but not the persistence of the substance through this total exchange in perceptible qualities.

Now if that is Descartes' example—and it certainly is—and he moves to illuminate it by the hats-and-cloaks case—as he certainly does— surely the illuminating example shouldn't be one in which what blocks seeing that *p* is simply some accidental circumstance, such as the temporary obstruction of one's view by hats and cloaks. Surely, if the example is to be apposite to Descartes' purpose, one should be unable *in principle* to see that these are men. Therefore what is at stake must be whether these bodies have *minds* to go with them or whether, alternatively, they are only automatic machines.

No doubt it has been exegetical reasoning like this that has led people to suppose that the Problem of Other Minds must be what is at stake in the hats-and-cloaks passage in Meditation II. The fact remains that Descartes never actually states the Problem of Other Minds there or, so far as I can discover, anywhere else. No doubt he sets things up in a way that encourages us to state the problem for ourselves. But that is the most one can say.

So here is my judicious verdict on the hats-and-cloaks passage. To a reader today it may indeed suggest the Problem of Other Minds. But Descartes does not himself pose the problem here (or elsewhere). In this passage Descartes is making a point about how we may be misled by ordinary language. We are inclined to say, he tells us, that we *see* the wax to be the same wax as that we saw earlier, as though its identity through the change in all its visible (indeed, all its perceptible) qualities could be recognized by ocular vision. What we really do, he insists, is to *judge* it to be the same wax. By way of analogy he points out that we are also inclined to say that we *see* figures passing on the street to be men even when, for all we can see, they might be "automatic machines" covered by hats and cloaks. Just as in that case, what we really do is judge those figures to be men, so in the wax case, what we really do is judge the colorless liquid before us to be the same wax.

To us this passage may suggest the question, How do we get from what we really see, or directly observe (e.g., things like hats and cloaks or, perhaps more basically, bodies and their movements or, even more basically, shapes and patches of color) to what we judge or infer (e.g., that those figures are human beings, creatures with minds)? It may even suggest, as a reply to that question, a version of the Argument from Analogy. (Thus: It is by noting the similarity between [a] the movements of those bodies and [b] certain movements of my own body with whom I have previously correlated mental contents, that I may infer there are similar mental contents, and hence minds, associated with those hatted and cloaked bodies.)

Descartes, however, raises no such question. Nor does he provide any such answer. He doesn't ask how one can know there is another mind, in addition to one's own. He simply insists that one judges, rather than sees, that those are human beings, creatures with minds, and not automata.

Although the Problem of Other Minds is not raised explicitly anywhere in Descartes, it is raised, it seems, in Augustine. Not only is it raised in Augustine, Augustine, it seems, seeks to solve it with the now familiar Argument from Analogy. Here is the passage from Augustine that I have in mind:

> For we also recognize, from a likeness to us, the motions of bodies by which we perceive that others besides us live. Just as we move [our] body in living, so, we notice, those bodies are moved. For when a living body is moved there is no way open to our eyes to see the mind [*animus*], a thing which cannot be seen by the eyes. But we perceive something present in that mass such as is present in us to move our mass in a similar way; it is life and soul [*anima*]. Nor is such perception something peculiar to, as it were, human prudence and reason. For indeed beasts perceive as living, not only themselves, but also each other and one another, and us as well. Nor do they see our souls [*animas*], except from the motions of the body, and they do that immediately and very simply by a sort of natural agreement. Therefore we know the mind of anyone at all from our own; and from our own case we believe in that which we do not know [*ex nostro credimus quem non novimus*]. For not only do we perceive a mind, but we even know what one is, by considering our own; for we have a mind. (*De trinitate* 8.6.9, trans. mine)

The question of how much Descartes borrowed from Augustine in developing his own philosophy has been a subject of scholarly debate ever since Arnauld first raised it in Descartes' own lifetime.[1] Certainly a number of passages in Augustine seem, at least, to anticipate Descartes' *cogito*.[2] Then there is the very concept of mind itself. In his *Contra academicos* Augustine sketches the notion of a world of subjective experience that is directly and incorrigibly known to its subject. This notion seems to anticipate Descartes' concept of mind.[3]

Closely related to the question of what reasoning, and what concepts, Descartes may have taken over from Augustine is the question of what problems he may have inherited from him. In my paper, "On Being Immoral in a Dream,"[4] I argue that Descartes, like Augustine, has a serious problem in justifying our assumption that we are not responsible for the acts, and especially the mental acts, of our dream selves. In fact, Augustine seems better to have appreciated the seriousness of this problem for his philosophy than Descartes did for his, though Descartes is aware of the problem.

Then there is the Problem of Other Minds. The *De trinitate* passage above suggests that Augustine realizes that the Problem of Other Minds is a serious problem for anyone with his (and, as it turns out, Descartes') philosophical assumptions. If this is right, then he is already, it seems, a step ahead of Descartes. Moreover, Augustine seems to offer in this passage, as a response to the Problem of Other Minds, the very argument that recent philosophers have taken to be the natural Cartesian response, namely, the Argument from Analogy. Since the Argument from Analogy is not to be found in Descartes either, Augustine seems, again, to be far ahead of his time.

Natural as this assessment of the situation is, it is also, I think, quite wrong. To see why it is wrong let's turn again to Descartes.

The Problem of Other Minds assumes an egocentric starting point, from which one than asks how one knows that there is a mind besides one's own. The egocentric starting point is certainly Cartesian; indeed, it is from Descartes that modern philosophers have learned to begin their reconstruction of knowledge from an egocentric beginning. Though Descartes does eventually, in the last Meditation, undertake to solve the problem of the External World and break out of his egocentrism, he never focuses specifically on the Problem of Other Minds.

If, however, one uses Part V of the *Discourse on Method* to flesh out Descartes' thinking on the External World, one can easily come up with something germane to the Problem of Other Minds. There Descartes occupies himself with the question of which entities have minds. His first concern is over how we might recognize that even cleverly constructed robots are not human beings. He offers two tests. One is language, the other is a certain adaptability through reason ("reason is a universal instrument . . . [whereas] these organs [of the machines] need a particular disposition for each particular action"). By these same means, Descartes goes on to say, we can distinguish human beings from beasts. It soon becomes clear that the distinction he is interested in here is the possession of a rational mind, or soul. The two tests he offers to mark off human beings from both the most cleverly constructed robots and the most humanlike beasts are thus really tests for whether or not something has a mind.

To bring into focus just what Descartes attempts to show with respect to other minds, and what he doesn't, it is important to distinguish these claims:

A. There are minds in addition to my own.
B. That individual over there has a mind.
C. Each functional individual of the kind, K, has a mind.
C*. Some functional individuals of the kind, K, have minds.

The modern Problem of Other Minds takes its form against the background assumption that the rational reconstruction of knowledge requires that (A) be justified, if at all, as a generalization from (B)-type claims. The point of the Argument from Analogy is to establish a (B)-type claim, and, by that means, to establish (A) itself.

Descartes shows no specal interest in establishing (A). It is not that he rejects it, or even thinks it questionable. Certainly he thinks it true. What he is primarily concerned about, however, are (C)-type claims. He accepts this one:

C1. Each functional individual of the kind, human, has a mind.

Maintaining in Part V of the *Discourse* that "there are no men so dull-witted and stupid, not even imbeciles, who are incapable of arranging together different words, and of composing discourse by which to make their thoughts understood," Descartes supports (C1) by the language test.

Descartes rejects this (C)-type claim:

C2. Each functional individual of the kind, animal, has a mind.

All nonhuman animals, he supposes, fail both the language test and the adaptability test. Moreover, Descartes rejects this (C*)-type claim:

C*1. Some individuals of the kind, automaton, have minds.

Again, his basis for rejecting (C*1) is that all automata fail both tests for having a mind.

Concentrating on the language test, we have these three arguments so far:

Argument I

(1)   Each language-user has a mind (Language Test).
(2)   Each functional individual of the kind, human, is a language-user.

∴(3)   Each functional individual of the kind, human, has a mind (C1).

Argument II

(4)   Only language-users have minds (Language Test).
(5)   Not all functional individuals of the kind, animal, are language-users.

∴(6)   Not all functional individuals of the kind, animal, have minds (the denial of [C2]).

Argument III

(7)   Only language-users have minds (Language Test).
(8)   No individual of the kind, automaton, is a language-user.

∴(9)   No individual of the kind, automaton, has a mind (the denial of [C*1]).

As for (A), it is clearly available to Descartes by a valid argument from

(10)   There are several functional individuals of the kind, human,

together with the conclusion of Argument I, above, namely, (3). (To be more precise, what one gets is "There are several minds." One then needs to add the assumption, "If there are several minds, there are minds in addition to my own.")

By the time Descartes gets to Part V of the *Discourse*, he certainly thinks he has good reason to accept (10). So he has available to him, as he would suppose, a very good basis for accepting (A), that is, for thinking that there are indeed minds other than his own.

In summary, Descartes shows no special interest in establishing (A). But by the time he gets to Part V of the *Discourse* he clearly accepts premises (namely, [1], [2], and [10]) that place it comfortably beyond doubt. Moreover, that line of argumentation is independent of, and, I should have thought, quite superior to, the Argument from Analogy.

Is it not only superior, but also good? If "language-user" is interpreted strictly enough to make (1) plausible, then (2) seems false or, at least, suspect. But if we change the "all" in (2) to "several" then the result is surely acceptable; and we have an even simpler argument for (A), namely this:

Argument IV

(11) Each language-user has a mind (Language Test).
(12) Several functional individuals of the kind, human, are language-users.

∴(13) Several functional individuals of the kind, human, have minds.

∴(14) There are several minds.
(15) If there are several minds, there are minds in addition to my own.

∴(16) There are minds in addition to my own (A).

Here is surely a better way of dealing with the Problem of Other Minds than any that makes essential use of the Argument from Analogy. And it is quite honestly Cartesian, even though it is not stated in so many words by Descartes himself.

Someone might object that my reconstruction of Descartes is entirely inappropriate. After all, I explained the Problem of Other Minds as something that begins with a contrast between what one can observe directly and what must be inferred. The problem then takes shape from the thought that other minds cannot be observed directly; at most it is human bodies, perhaps only the apearances of human bodies, that can be observed directly. The question is then how one can be justified in inferring, on the basis of what one observes directly, that there exist other minds.

Now I have just maintained that Descartes' best response to the Problem of Other Minds is an argument from other language-users. But surely whether *x* is a genuine language-user is not something that can be observed directly; it must be inferred from the actions and noise-emissions of some body. So either the solution I have given Descartes is an *ignoratio elenchi* because it ignores the problem altogether, or else it is ineffective because it does not show how the existence of other minds may be inferred from properties that are directly observable.

Here is my reply. Certainly the argument I have reconstructed from Descartes does not seek to establish the existence of other minds as an inference from properties that are directly observable. But that is part of its genius. To attempt that would be rather like trying to establish that there exist noncounterfeit coins by producing some examples and defending the proposition that those particular coins, or perhaps even any coins with specified observable properties that those coins share, couldn't possibly be counterfeit. One knows that there are noncounterfeit coins, not by knowing that this one is certainly noncounterfeit, and that one is, but rather by knowing that there are governments that have set up mints that have produced authorized coins. One can know that without being able to produce a single coin that could not possibly turn out, on later inspection, or on further investigation, to be counterfeit.

So it is with other language-users. Perhaps a computer program can be written that will make it impossible for me to determine whether or not there is a human being on the other end of my telephone connection. Some day a thoroughly convincing robot may instantiate such a program. But such a possibility does nothing to impugn facts about human societies that place beyond doubt the proposition that there are other language-users. For the knowledge that there are other language-users does not rest on an induction from specific cases. The argument I have reconstructed from Descartes is thus a good response to the Problem of Other Minds. And part of the reason it is a good response is that it begins from another starting point altogether.

I can imagine someone still resisting my claim that the argument from other language-users is superior to the Argument from Analogy. It is small comfort, my objector will insist, to be told that

(12) Several functional individuals of the kind, human, are language-users

need not be established by proving that this individual is a language-user (in an appropriately strong sense of "language-user") and that one is, and so forth. Claims about large groups of people are no less open than are claims about individuals to the kind of skepticism that leads Descartes in Meditation I to suppose that "the heavens, the air, the earth, colours, shapes, sounds and all external things that we see, are only illusions and deceptions" and that he has "no hands, eyes, flesh, blood or senses" at all but only wrongly believes that he has those things.

The objection is significant, but not, I think, devastating. Perhaps one has no general knowledge of there being language-users that will stand up to the hyperbolical doubt of Meditation I. But we should remember that Descartes does not attempt to prove even the existence of the "external world" without appeal to the existence and nature of God. When he gets around to proving that there exists an external world, in Meditation VI, he argues that God, being no deceiver, "has permitted no falsity in my opinions which he has not also given me some faculty capable of correcting." Since he has no faculty for correcting his belief that there exists an external world and, indeed, a strong inclination to believe that there is one, that belief, he supposes, is true.

Similar reasoning would apply to skepticism about other language-users. The belief that I am now confronted by another language-user is something I might be mistaken about in a way that I do have a "faculty" for correcting. For example, I might question my "conversation" partner in such a way as to expose the fact that his responses are all preprogrammed. By contrast, the belief that there simply exist other language-users is of an entirely different order. How could it be the case that I alone use a language that others only parrot? The belief that there simply exist other language-users, unlike the belief that there is one at the other end of the telephone line, or across the desk from me, is a belief that I have no faculty for correcting. Since I have a strong, indeed an overwhelming, inclination to accept it, and no faculty for correcting it, it must, by Descartes' reasoning, be true.

To round out our discussion let's return briefly to Augustine. I suggested much earlier on that it seems to be Augustine, rather than Descartes, who presents the Problem of Other Minds and offers the Argument from Analogy as its solution. But that really isn't true either. The point of the passage I quoted earlier from Augustine's *De trinitate* is, in fact, rather different from anything we have considered so far. It has to do, not with the limits of what one can *know*, but rather with the limits of what one can *think about*. Augustine wants to explain how it ever occurs to us, or to beasts, to attribute minds, or souls, to other beings.

Augustine's explanation incorporates his version of the Argument from Analogy. We notice, he says, the similarity between the movements of other bodies and those of our own body. We then attribute to another body a soul that, as we suppose, moves it much as we "observe" that our own soul moves our own body. In attributing a mind or soul to another body we make up a representation, he supposes, from the direct acquaintance we have with our own mind, or soul. We know the mind of anybody else, he says, from our own (*Animum . . . cuiuslibet ex nostro novimus*). And from our own case, he adds, we postulate, or believe in, what we do not know; that is, what we are not acquainted with (*ex nostro credimus quem non novimus*). Attributing a mind to another is thus, according to Augustine, a matter of postulation, or faith, not knowledge. His version of the Argument from Analogy is meant to be an account of how we come to think, or believe, that there are other minds, not how we come to know this.

Let me now summarize the discussion.

The Problem of Other Minds is generally considered to be a problem we owe to Descartes. The standard solution to it, the Argument from Analogy, is also considered to be Cartesian. In fact, Descartes himself does not actually state the Problem of Other Minds, though there are reasons why a reader might jump to the conclusion that the hats-and-cloaks passage from Meditation II does present it. Having failed to state the Problem of Other Minds, Descartes also fails to offer the Argument from Analogy as its solution.

In Book VIII of his *De trinitate* Augustine not only presents what looks very much like the Problem of Other Minds, he also presents what looks like the Argument from Analogy as its solution. So the question arises, did Augustine outstrip Descartes by actually stating the Problem of Other Minds and by presenting what, from a Cartesian perspective, is the best solution for it, namely, the Argument from Analogy?

The answer to that complex question, I have argued, is a simple "No." What looks superficially like a solution to the Problem of Other Minds in Augustine is actually, I have suggested, an account of how we come to postulate other minds, or to think about them, not how we come to know they exist. But even if Augustine had put forward the Argument from Analogy as a solution to the Problem of Other Minds, he would not, I think, have bettered Descartes on that score. Descartes, as I have argued, had ready for himself a much more effective response to the Problem of Other Minds than the Argument from Analogy. It is the argument from other language-users—not from this or that language-user, but simply from the fact that there are other language-users. A version of that argument withstands critical examination and recommends itself to us as well.[5]

NOTES

1. See fourth set of Objections, HR II, 80, 86, 90, 94 f. (The abbreviation HR is explained in the General Bibliography at the beginning of this volume.)

2. In my paper, *"Si fallor sum,"* in *Augustine: A Collection of Critical Essays* (R. A. Markus, ed. [Garden City, N.J.: Doubleday, 1972], 151–167), I have tried to interpret Augustine's reasoning concerning his own existence and to compare it with Descartes' reasoning concerning his existence.

3. See my "Consciousness and Life," *Philosophy* 52 (1977):13–26.

4. *Philosophy* 56 (1981):47–54.

5. This essay was completed while the author was on a fellowship from the National Endowment for the Humanities.

7

Analysis in the *Meditations:* The Quest for Clear and Distinct Ideas

E. M. CURLEY

I begin with a fact about the way Descartes wrote his *Meditations:* that he conceived them as illustrating a very special way of proving things, a way peculiarly appropriate to metaphysics, a way he called the analytic manner of demonstration. This much, I think, would generally be admitted, and admitted to be important.

But what does this fact mean? What do we know about the *Meditations* when we know that they were written in the analytic mode? And why is this manner of demonstration peculiarly appropriate to metaphysics? So far as I can see, there is no general agreement on an answer to these questions.[1] And if we accept the Cartesian proposition that disagreement indicates that no party to the dispute has knowledge (AT X, 363, VI, 8), then we must say that no one knows, at this stage, what that important fact means.

We know well enough, of course, what Descartes *says* it means. Mersenne had suggested in the Second Replies (AT VII, 128) that Descartes should present his reasoning in the *Meditations more geometrico,* prefacing it with the necessary definitions, postulates, and axioms, so that each reader might be able to satisfy himself at a glance that the reasoning was sound. In his Second Replies (AT VII, 155) Descartes counters he has already been writing in the way characteristic of the geometers, that it is necessary to distinguish between the geometric order and the geometric manner of demonstrating. Order requires simply that the things first proposed be known without the aid of anything that follows, and that the rest be demonstrated solely from the things that precede them. Descartes claims that he has tried to follow this order very accurately in his *Meditations*.

But presenting things in the right order—which Descartes implies is the essence of the geometrical method—may be done in either of two ways. One can use analysis, which

shows the true way by which the thing has been discovered, methodically, and as it were, a priori. (AT VII, 155)

Or one can use synthesis, which proceeds

as it were a posteriori . . . , and, indeed, demonstrates clearly its conclusions using a long series of definitions, postulates, axioms, theorems, and problems . . . (AT VII, 156)

In general, the advantage of analysis is that, for the right reader, it yields a deeper understanding. If the reader is willing to follow it and to attend sufficiently to everything, he will understand the matter as perfectly as if he had discovered it himself. The advantage of synthesis is that it can force the assent even of a hostile or inattentive reader. If he denies any of the conclusions, we can show him immediately that it is contained in antecedent propositions which he has presumably accepted.

Because it can yield a deeper understanding, analysis is the best method for teaching even in mathematics, where everyone readily accepts the first notions, and there is no difficulty in attaining a clear and distinct perception of them. But in metaphysics, where the first notions are more remote from the sense, and may even be in conflict with prejudices encouraged by the senses, a clear and distinct perception of those notions is more difficult, and ready agreement to them cannot be presumed. So in metaphysics analysis is much the more appropriate way of presenting things than in synthesis.

That, more or less,[2] is what Descartes *says*. But what does it mean? The first thing that is apt to strike a modern reader is the claim that the analytic mode proceeds "as it were a priori," while the synthetic mode proceeds "as it were a posteriori." If synthesis is exemplified by the best known work of ancient mathematics, Euclid's *Elements of Geometry*, or by the exposition *more geometrico* which Descartes appends to the Second Replies, then it is no small surprise to see it characterized as an a posteriori method. The commentators[3] may come to our aid here, pointing out that in medieval and seventeenth-century usage, the terms *a priori* and *a posteriori* had a different sense from the one they have nowadays, that an a priori argument was one proceeding from cause to effect, whereas an a posteriori argument was one proceeding from effect to cause. But though Descartes no doubt understands these terms that way, it is hard to see that the *Meditations* exemplify a procedure that is, in that sense, a priori. The *Meditations* begin, on the face of it, with a proof of the existence of the self, proceed to proofs of the existence of God, and then move on to a proof of the existence of the world, that is, they go from effect to cause and back again to effect. And the proof of God's existence which is given the apparently privileged position, that is, the first proof, is an argument from one of God's effects, my idea of God, to his existence as its cause. So the first thing which is apt to strike us about the characterization of these two modes of proof is likely only to confuse us.[4]

We are left then with the idea that the analytic mode of presentation recapitulates a viable method of discovery,[5] whereas the synthetic mode, insofar as it begins from a series of definitions, postulates and axioms, does not. That much may be correct, and potentially illuminating. But it is also potentially misleading. In an earlier attack on this problem,[6] I argued that it seriously misled Spinoza.

Spinoza's first venture into print was an exposition *more geometrico* of Descartes' *Principles of Philosophy*. Spinoza was well aware of Descartes' distinction between analysis and synthesis, and he took himself, in his exposition of Descartes, to be putting into the synthetic mode of work Descartes had written in the analytic mode, just as Descartes himself had done at the end of the Second Replies. Whereas there Descartes had presented synthetically a fragment of the analytic Meditations, in his own work Spinoza undertook to present synthetically a large portion of the analytic Principles.

But if we may trust the *Conversation with Burman*,[7] the Principles are already written in the synthetic mode, so there is no need to recast them to make them a synthetic work. In that earlier article, trusting the *Conversation with Burman*, I inferred that Spinoza had been misled by the apparent absence of formal apparatus in the *Principles* and had not seen its essential similarity to the clearly synthetic Geometric Exposition at the end of the Second Replies.

The *Principles* does not *begin* with a long series of definitions, as the Geometric Exposition does. But it does at least regularly offer explicit formal definitions of central terms,[8] whereas the *Meditations* typically introduces central terms in a more informal way, by providing an instance of the concept being defined.[9] That's why, when we are seeking a formal definition of some concept like clarity and distinctness, or thought, or substance, we tend to go to the *Principles of Philosophy* rather than to the *Meditations*.

Similarly, the *Principles* does not *begin* with a list of axioms, as the Geometric Exposition does. But it does recognize, in a more forthright way than does the *Meditations*, the role of axioms, or common notions, or eternal truths, in the argument from the self to God to the world. That's why Burman finds a tension between the *Meditations* and the *Principles*. Citing the passage from the Second Replies in which Descartes had said that

when we perceive that we are thinking things, that is a first notion which is not inferred from any syllogism, nor does someone who says "I think, therefore, I am or exist" deduce existence from thought by a syllogism . . . (AT VII, 140)

Burman asks whether Descartes had not asserted the opposite in *Principles* I, 10, when he said that, in claiming "I think, therefore, I exist" to be the first and most certain proposition of all those that might occur to someone philosophizing in the proper order.

I did not on that account deny that before this one must know what thought is, what existence and certainty are, and also that it is impossible that what thinks should not exist . . . (AT VIII-1, 8)

The reason for this tension, I suggested, is that the analytic method requires postponement of the recognition of the role of general principles until after we have found ourselves deploying them in particular cases. For the nature of our mind is to form general propositions from the knowledge of particulars.[10] In the beginning of the *Meditations* Descartes is tracing the course of a man who is beginning to philosophize, and who attends only to what he *knows* that he knows.[11] At first, Descartes' meditator is a sensual man, a man too attached to the senses, as we all are before philosophy, and he is not aware of his innate knowledge of these eternal truths.

So far I have been stating a problem and outlining[12] a solution I had presented earlier. Although that earlier article has been subjected to some criticism,[13] I still believe that its central thesis is correct. In what follows I propose to develop the thesis more fully, to extend it to problems I had ignored before, and to modify it in certain non-essential respects.

The central thesis might be stated as follows: Descartes' argument in the *Meditations* requires him to deploy concepts and principles which are very abstract and removed from anything we might think we had learned directly from the senses, concepts, and principles which we may understand implicitly, but which we will normally not understand explicitly in a way that is clear and distinct; it requires Descartes to use principles which the ordinary man of *bon sens* will know, but will not know that he knows. So the essential task of the analytic method is to bring that knowledge to consciousness, to turn the unclear and indistinct ideas of common sense into the clear and distinct ideas Descartes needs to make his argument demonstrative.

In the earlier article I stressed Descartes' move from the particular to the general, his introduction of concepts by means of examples, and his postponement of the recognition of general principles, or eternal truths, until after we have seen those principles in operation. It now seems to me that, as far as this goes, it is right, and an important theme in Descartes' thought. But it does not go far enough. There is more to the process of acquiring clear and distinct ideas than that.

What I should now stress is Descartes' use of what I have come to call a dialectical method. By a dialectical method I mean the essentially Platonic procedure[14] of beginning with a conjecture, considering what can be said against that conjecture, and then revising the conjecture in whatever ways the objections suggest. The initial conjecture may be (typically, will be) a false start, in the sense that it will ultimately be rejected in the form in which it is first proposed. But typically it will also be a proposition which recommends itself to common sense.[15] The process of conjecture, refutation, and revision may be repeated indefinitely until the inquirer reaches a result to which he can find no further objection. If the initial conjecture was not a totally false start (and normally it will not have been), something of what it asserted will survive in the final result. Descartes explicitly recognizes what I am calling the dialectical character of his method in the Fourth Replies, when he writes that

the analytic manner of writing which I followed permits me to sometimes make suppositions which have not yet been sufficiently examined, as was evident in the First Meditation, where I had assumed many things which I subsequently refuted. (AT VII, 249)

Examples of this sort of procedure are not limited to the First Meditation, they abound throughout the whole work. I begin with two clear cases.

Descartes' argument for the real distinction between mind and body requires him to first have clear and distinct ideas of both the mind and the body (AT VII, 78). And though the work of acquiring clarity about these ideas really begins in the First Meditation, it will be most convenient for us to start with the Second. No sooner does Descartes recognize *that* he is, than he asks himself *what* he is (AT VII, 25). He begins by asking what he previously thought he was, as a way of eliciting the kind of answer a man would naturally give to this question before he began to philosophize.[16] He thought he was a man, but what is that? To answer as a scholastic philosopher would, that man is a rational animal, is not helpful, since it only raises questions more difficult than the original question: What is an animal? What is it to be rational? The Scholastic answer would be a false start which contains no usable truth in it. So Descartes resolves to "attend rather to what occurred to my thought previously, whenever I reflected spontaneously and naturally on what I was" (AT VII, 25–26). I thought of myself as a composite of body and soul. And this is not an unhelpful answer. For while my prephilosophic concepts of body and soul may have been confused, they had some truth in them.

Previously I thought of the body as

whatever is apt to be bounded by some shape, to be circumscribed by a place, to fill space in such a way that every other body is excluded from it, to be perceived by touch, sight, hearing, taste or smell, and also to move in various ways . . . (AT VII, 26)

Now some of what Descartes had previously thought body to be was wrong. For example, one of the many morals Descartes will draw from his analysis of the piece of wax is that the perception of a physical object is not an act of sight or touch, as he had previously thought, but an inspection of the mind alone (AT VII, 31). But some elements in Descartes' prephilosophic conception of body are right, and to be retained. Body *is* whatever is apt to be bounded by a shape, to be circumscribed by a place, and to fill space.

The process of rendering our idea of body clear and distinct is a very gradual one, which occupies Descartes throughout the *Meditations*. What it essentially involves is sorting out what is and what is not to be retained in our prephilosophic conception of body, and exploring the implications of those elements which are to be retained. The reason Descartes' statement about the essential nature of material things in the Fifth Meditation (AT VII, 63) can be so brief is that he has already laid a great deal of the groundwork for it in the preceding Meditations.[17]

Descartes goes through an analogous procedure with his prephilosophic concept of mind (*mens*) or soul (*anima*). Here the very choice of terminology is significant. Descartes uses both *mens* and *anima* to refer to the same thing, a thinking thing. But though both terms, in that sense, mean the same, Descartes generally prefers the

term *mens* because he feels that the term *anima* has unfortunate connotations. It suggests something corporeal.[18] So it is no accident that,
in Descartes' first self-conscious discussion of the nature of the mind
in the *Meditations*, he should choose to designate it by the term *anima*.
In this exceptional context, he wants to suggest those usually unfortunate connotations:

> It occurred to me also that I am nourished, that I walk, sense, and think,
> all of which actions I referred to the soul (*anima*). But what this soul was, I
> either did not consider, or else (FV: if I did consider it) I imagined it to be a
> something-I-know-not-what, something very subtle, like wind, or fire, or air,
> which was infused throughout the grosser parts of me. (AT VII, 26)

One of the things Descartes must do, in order to clarify this prephilosophic concept, is to recognize that not all the activities he had previously ascribed to the soul are necessarily to be ascribed to it. Nutrition
and motion clearly presuppose the existence of a body (AT VII, 27).
But Descartes is proceeding, at this point, on the assumption that he
has no body. So he cannot ascribe nutrition or motion to the soul.
The case of sensation is more difficult. At first the meditator is inclined
to say that sensation requires a body, and hence is not to be ascribed
to the soul (AT VII, 27). Later he realizes that it is possible to conceive
of sensation as not necessarily involving a body, but only a peculiar
kind of thought, the kind of thought in which we perceive corporeal
things as if through the senses (AT VII, 29). And conceived this way,
sensation is properly attributed to the soul, as are all thought processes. Thinking is a property he cannot deny to himself, since any
hypothesis he might entertain in an attempt to cast doubt on his
thinking would imply that he thinks.[19]

So the only thing that is left of his prephilosophic conception of
himself is that he is a soul conceived as a thing that thinks (AT VII,
27, line 13). And at this point he introduces the term *mens* as a synonym
for "thinking thing." Henceforth the term *mens* will displace the term
anima as the preferred prephilosophic term for referring to the thinking
things.[20] Descartes remarks that the meaning of the term *mens* was
previously unknown to him, which must mean that previously he
had no clear concept of the mind. He has, after all, frequently used
the term before in the *Meditations* in a perfectly natural and correct
way which did not seem to carry any particular theoretical load.[21]
This substitution of a term without misleading connotations for a term
which definitely does have misleading connotations is another part
of the process of clarifying our prephilosophic conception of the mind,
or soul.

After having explained once what a thinking thing is by enumerating various synonyms—*mens, animus, intellectus,* and *ratio*—Descartes returns to the topic later when he enumerates the various activities which exemplify thought: doubting, understanding, affirming, denying, willing, not willing, imagining, and sensing (AT VII, 28, line 20). This list is not arbitrary. There is a rationale for each element in it. But to discuss that rationale would carry us too far afield and involve repetition of things I have already said elsewhere.[22] Suffice it for now to say that this is part of the process of achieving clarity and distinctness in our idea of the mind or soul.

So far our examples of Descartes at work on the clarification of concepts have involved concepts expressed by terms well entrenched in ordinary language: *body, soul, mind,* and *thought.* Descartes takes the meaning each term has in ordinary language, represented by his own prephilosophic concept, as a starting point. But of course he is not interested simply in giving an analysis of ordinary language. Ordinary language reflects a metaphysic which may have some truth in it, but which should not be accepted uncritically. While it may be the first word, it is certainly not the last word.

But sometimes it is not even the first word. Some of the concepts Descartes is anxious to develop are not expressed by terms well entrenched in ordinary language. Consider the term *idea,* which is central to Descartes' proofs of the existence of God, but which also figures largely in his developing analysis of the concept of mind, since all thought, according to Descartes, involves ideation. As a Latin term, the word *idea* does not have a home in ordinary language; it is rare in classical Latin, a borrowing from the Greek, which came to be used by medieval philosophers to signify "the forms of the perceptions of the divine mind."[23] Descartes' use of it in connection with human thought was novel and the source of much confusion among his readers.

In the *Meditations* Descartes' official explanation of the meaning of this term occurs rather early in the Third Meditation:

> But now order seems to require[24] that first I distribute all thoughts into certain kinds and inquire in which of these truth or falsity properly consists. Some of my thoughts are, as it were, images of things, and it is to these alone that the term 'idea' properly applies, as when I think of a man, or a chimera, or the heavens, or an angel, or God. (AT VII, 36–37)

Note that what we have here is a combination of definition by example and definition by metaphor. Ideas are like images. In this case, as we shall see, it is the metaphor, not the examples, which carries the weight of the explanation.

Descartes' enumeration of the other kinds of thought explains why I said above that ideation is essential to all thought, and incidentally sheds a bit more light on the concept of ideation:

> Other thoughts have other forms: when I will, when I fear, when I affirm, when I deny, I always, indeed, apprehend some thing as the subject of my thought, but I also include something more than the likeness of that thing.

So ideation involves apprehending something as the subject of my thought, an apprehension which in turn involves a likeness of the thing thought of. And when I will something or judge something, I always have an idea of that thing, to which I then add something else. This theory of the nature of thought will be explored further in the Fourth Meditation, when Descartes analyzes the nature of judgment.[25] What interests me here is the way Descartes has prepared us for it in earlier passages of the *Meditations*.

Descartes' official explanation of the term *idea* does not represent his first serious use of it in the *Meditations*. That came even earlier in the Third Meditation, when Descartes asked himself what he had previously perceived clearly concerning the objects of the senses, and replied:

> That the very ideas, or (*sive*) thoughts, of such things appear to my mind. Even now I do not deny that those ideas are in me. But it was something else that I used to affirm, and that I also, because of certain habits of belief I had formed, thought I perceived clearly (though really I didn't perceive it): that there are certain things outside me, from which those ideas proceeded, and to which they were completely similar. (AT VII, 35)

From the point of view of the passage we looked at first, Descartes' official explanation of 'idea,' this informal account of ideas must be regarded as imprecise insofar as it simply equates ideas with thoughts. But it is also imprecise in another way. It incorporates a prephilosophic theory of the nature of sense perception, according to which objects external to us cause us to have thoughts exactly like the objects which cause them. And as is generally the case, that prephilosophic theory is a mixture of truth and falsity.

What is true in it will find expression later in the Third Meditation, in the doctrine that the objective reality of an idea requires a cause containing, formally or eminently, as much reality as the idea contains objectively (AT VII, 41).[26] But the qualifications with which this truth is hedged warn us that our thoughts are not exactly like their objects.

Not only may they be inaccurate in their representation of reality, as when they represent a square object as round—they may also be radically misleading, as when they represent what is merely a vibration of the air as a sound, inducing us to imagine that there is something in objects like our sensation of sound.[27] So the prephilosophic theory of perception contains a good deal of falsity.

Descartes does not spring that theory of perception on us without warning in the Third Meditation. He has already suggested it to us as early as the First Meditation. No sooner has Descartes' meditator found in dreams a ground for doubting what he perceives through the senses than his common sense reasserts itself (AT VII, 19–20). Suppose I am dreaming, suppose none of those particular things are true which I thought most evident: my eyes are not open, I am not moving my head, or extending my hand, perhaps I even have no hands, no body, still

I must confess that the things I see in my sleep are like certain painted images of things, which can only be formed according to the likeness of true things. Therefore, at least these general things are true and not imaginary: eyes, head, hands, and the whole body.

There are limits on the power of the imagination, as is shown by the attempts of painters to conjure up bizarre new creatures. They never come up with anything completely new, they only mix familiar ingredients in new ways. So even if things as general as eyes, heads, hands, and so on, could be imaginary, nevertheless

I must confess that at least other things, still more simple and universal, are true, and that all those images of things which are in our thought, whether they are true or false, are formed from these simple and universal things as if from their true colors.

At this stage of the First Meditation Descartes' meditator is an empiricist, not only in the sense that he thinks that our beliefs derive their justification from the evidence of the senses (AT VII, 18), but also in the sense that he holds the classic empiricist theory of the origin of our concepts: the simple ones must come from experience; complex ones may not answer to anything that exists, so long as they can be compounded from ones that do.

In this form, the prephilosophic theory will not last long. Before the meditator has left this Adam and Tannery page, he will have recognized that the sciences which treat of the simplest and most general things of all, like arithmetic and geometry, "care little" whether their objects exist in nature. This insight will later blossom into the theory of innate ideas touched on in the Third Meditation (AT VII, 38, 39) and be developed more fully in the Fifth (AT VII, 63–65).[28] But some elements of the theory of perception will be retained. The notion that our thoughts are *like* pictures of things persists throughout the *Meditations.* Here in the First Meditation it is expressed in terms natural to the man who has not yet begun to philosophize, who is inevitably an empiricist. Not only are our thoughts *like* certain painted images of things (AT VII, 19, line 27), they *are* mental images of things (AT VII, 20, lines 12–14).

By the time the mediator has reached the Third Meditation, he has learned, through the discussion of the wax, to distinguish between the intellect and the imagination. The wax is not perceived by the senses, nor by the faculty of imagination, but by the intellect alone (AT VII, 34). So when his prephilosophic theory of perception resurfaces at the beginning of the Third Meditation (AT VII, 35), it is expressed, not in terms of images, but in terms of ideas. And this choice of terminology is quite deliberate:

> I used this term because it was already in common use among the philosophers to signify the forms of the perceptions of the divine mind, although we do not recognize any capacity for having images in God. And I had no term more appropriate. (AT VII, 181)

Since God's thought is free of images, we use a term originally deployed in connection with his thought to express the fact that our thought can be without images. But our theory of the mental activity which this term is now used to designate is developed, by criticism, from a theory to which the man ignorant of philosophy would naturally be drawn.[29]

As with "idea," so with "substance." In classical Latin the technical use of the term *substantia* emerges rather late, as a way of representing the Greek concept of *ousia.* Descartes defines it informally about halfway through the Third Meditation (AT VII, 44) as a thing capable of existing through itself, but he has already been using the term without any kind of definition for several pages, ever since he informed us that ideas of substances contain more objective reality than ideas of modes (AT VII, 40). How can this use be justified? What has Descartes done to prepare us for it?

If Descartes' usage has any justification at all, it must lie in the analysis of the piece of wax. And indeed, it seems to me that that passage does prepare us for Descartes' definition of substance. Even though the analysis of the wax does not explicitly use the term *substantia*, it does use the correlative term *modus*, a perfectly ordinary term in Latin, whose most relevant meaning here is "manner" or "way," though it is usually translated *mode*. By insisting strongly on the distinction between the wax itself and the various ways in which it appears to me—now tasting of honey and smelling of flowers, hard and cold, and so forth, now tasteless, odorless, fluid, hot, and so forth—Descartes prepares us to regard the term *substantia*, when it appears, as simply a very general term for referring to objects conceived as things which may continue to persist in existence in spite of radical changes in the way they exist. Descartes even has another metaphor to help us understand this contrast. The modes of substance are like the hats and coats worn by people I 'see' passing in the street; the substance itself is like the people wearing those clothes. Just as I do not, strictly speaking, see the people, but only infer their existence from the clothes which I do see, so I do not, strictly speaking, see the wax, but only infer its existence from the existence of the various modes I perceive through the senses.[30]

This way of introducing the concept of substance, however, is evidently no more than a heuristic device. If we may judge from the *Synopsis of the Meditations* (AT VII, 14), Descartes does not really think the wax is a very satisfactory example of a substance. In outlining there the proof of the immortality of the soul which he confesses that he has not given in the *Meditations*, Descartes observes that the proof depends on an explanation of the whole of physics. This is necessary, first,

> . . . in order to know that, in general, all substances, or things which must be created by God to exist, are incorruptible by their nature, and can never cease to exist unless they are reduced to nothing by the same God's denying them his concurrence . . .

Descartes would infer from this that while body, taken in general, is indeed a substance, and so never ceases to exist (unless destroyed by God), particular bodies, like

> the human body, insofar as it differs from other bodies, is only composed of a certain configuration of members, and other accidents of the same kind . . .

The human body is not a substance, since it

> becomes different simply because the shape of certain of its parts is changed, from which it follows that the body very easily perishes . . .

I take this to mean, not that the body perishes as soon as *any* of its modes changes—then the body would indeed perish all too easily— but that there are certain parts of the body whose existing configura- tion is critical to the body's continued functioning as a body. So pre- sumably the human body cannot survive just any change in its modes, and neither, presumably, can the wax.

In the absence of the fuller explanation which Descartes hinted might appear in his physics, we can only speculate about what this means. But one thing seems quite clear: the human body's status as a substance is not thrown into doubt simply by its dependence on God for maintenance in existence. For that dependence is something the body shares with the mind. If it were sufficient to make the body not a substance, then the mind too would not be a substance. But Descartes is quite clear in this passage that he thinks the mind is a substance, capable of surviving *any* change in its modes. It is on this that he proposes to base a proof of its immortality. So any attempt to explain the apparent claim of the *Synopsis,* that there is only one material substance, by appeal to the definition of substance as an independent being (see *Principles* I, 51) seems premature. (Only those who are prepared to discount Descartes' claim to believe in the immor- tality of the soul are entitled to deploy that line of reasoning. No doubt there are still interpreters of Descartes who would regard that suspicion as reasonable. To such interpreters I have nothing to say.)

So far I have been explaining the way in which the Descartes of the *Meditations* explains the central concepts of his metaphysics with- out using the kind of formal definition that appears in the Geometric Exposition or the *Principles of Philosophy.* My choice of examples has not been accidental. I have been guided by the list of definitions which forms the first section of the Geometric Exposition (AT VII, 160–162). And I believe that I have shown how most of the concepts there defined, or at least most of the most important ones, are explained in the *Meditations.*

But I have saved for last the most important concept: that of God. If there is any notion not readily grasped by men mired in the senses, any notion whose introduction must be carefully prepared by dialec- tical argument, it is the notion of God as conceived by Descartes, the concept of a purely spiritual being who is infinite in every respect. And yet we must, according to Descartes, not only conceive of God, but know that he exists, if we are to have any certainty about anything (AT VII, 36).

No one will need to be reminded that the concept of God is intro- duced in the First Meditation, in the context of a doubt about the simplest propositions of mathematics. What we must attend to now is the way in which the concept is introduced. As our previous discussion might lead us to expect, God is first mentioned as a being in whom Descartes has long believed—which is to say that his belief in God is one he has held from an early age, and hence, uncritically. Later (AT VII, 36) he will refer back to this belief as a preconceived opinion. If what I have been arguing is correct, Descartes' characterization of belief in God as part of his prephilosophic theory of the world will imply not only that the belief does not rest on any firm foundations,[31] but also that it involves a mixture of truth and falsity. And it is not evident what Descartes might later think was false in this belief, given that initially he had conceived of God simply as a being who can do all things, and who had, in particular, created him.

As soon as Descartes has introduced this conception of God, he begins to raise doubts about what it implies. If God can do anything, then presumably he can cause me to be mistaken, even in my beliefs about the things that seem easiest to understand. But *perhaps* he didn't want to deceive me. For he *is said to be (dicitur)* supremely good. But *if* he is supremely good, and *if* he can do anything he wishes, why does he allow me sometimes to be deceived? There can be no doubt that sometimes I am deceived. Except for this last, the reasoning here is extremely tentative, a fact which Descartes emphasizes by suggesting that some might prefer to deny the existence of a God so powerful, rather than believe that all other things are so uncertain. And indeed, in the final paragraph of the First Meditation Descartes resolves to conduct his subsequent meditations, not on the hypothesis of a supremely good God, who is the source of truth, but on the hypothesis of an Evil Spirit (*malignus genius*), supremely powerful and cunning, who has done everything he could to deceive him.

Note that by the end of the First Meditation, the two characteristics in Descartes' original definition of God have grown to four. God is not merely an omnipotent creator, but a supremely good source of truth. His goodness is not just something others say of him, but an essential characteristic in Descartes' conception of him. This is shown by Descartes' decision to withhold the name "God" from the omnipotent deceiver he conceives in the final paragraph.[32] An omnipotent being who is not good would not be God.

But this, of course, does not solve the problem of the possibility of divine deception. Perhaps the term "God" should be reserved for a being who combines all the attributes mentioned so far: omnipotence, supreme goodness, being the creator, and being a source of truth. Perhaps what we mean by the term "God" is just a being who has all those attributes. But our possibly arbitrary definition cannot legislate such a being into existence. We cannot solve the problem of the possibility of divine deception simply by listing the various attributes contained in our concept of God. For those attributes may not all be combined in one being. Perhaps there is no God in the sense in which we understand that notion. Perhaps the closest approximation in reality to God as we conceive him is a being who has only some, but not all of the attributes contained in our concept of God. Perhaps our creator is a being who is omnipotent, but not supremely good and not a source of truth. In order not to violate the conventions of our language, we shall call him the Evil Spirit, understanding by that term a being who combines the following attributes: omnipotence, being the creator of all things other than himself, and being supremely malicious. How do I know that it is not the Evil Spirit who is my creator?[33]

As I read the *Meditations,* Descartes' answer to this is that, on reflection, we find the concept of the Evil Spirit to be incoherent. The attributes just enumerated as defining the Evil Spirit cannot be combined in one being, for the attributes involved in our concept of God are necessarily connected with one another. But seeing why this is so requires a close examination of the way Descartes develops the concept of God in the remaining meditations.

Meanwhile, we must also note that even though Descartes' conception of God has grown more complex in the space of a few paragraphs, it is still not easy to see what there is in it that is false. None of the four characteristics that define the conception of God Descartes has reached here will be rejected by the end of the *Meditations.* I suggest that, if his concept of God is confused at this stage, it is primarily because the characteristics he has so far identified, while essential to God, in the sense that God would not be God without them, do not strictly speaking state the essence of God, but only certain necessary consequences of his essence.[34] We might add that Descartes is also uncertain what these characteristics imply and how they are related to each other. More of that later.

The Second Meditation does nothing, so far as I can see, to enrich Descartes' concept of God. God is perhaps referred to once, when Descartes asks: "Is there some God, or whatever I shall call him, who sends me these very thoughts?" (AT VII, 24). But the expression "some God," combining as it does the equivalent of an indefinite article (*aliquis*) with a proper name (*Deus,* capitalized), and Descartes' uncertainty about what to call this hypothetical deceiver, only indicate the level of his confusion. In subsequent references to the deceiver in that Meditation (AT VII, 25, 26) Descartes carefully refrains from calling him God.

At the beginning of the Third Meditation, God reappears (AT VII, 36), conceived vaguely once again (*aliquis Deus*), and conceived as a potential deceiver regarding the truths of mathematics. Because of this possibility, we must consider whether God does really exist, and whether he can be a deceiver, and the examination of these questions requires us to develop more fully our initial concept of God. At first this is done in the manner of the First Meditation, by enumerating the attributes our idea of God represents him as having. There are two such lists, in fact:

(1)   . . . that [sc. idea] by which I understand a supreme God, eternal, infinite, omniscient, omnipotent, and creator of all the things there are, apart from himself . . . [35]

(2)   By the term God I understand a certain infinite substance, independent, supremely intelligent, supremely powerful, and by whom both I myself and also everything else that exists—if anything else does exist—have been created.[36]

These two lists display some interesting differences from one another,[37] but what interests me most are their differences from what preceded them and what follows them. That Descartes has added a number of attributes not mentioned in the First Meditation is evident, as is the fact that he has omitted the attribute which apparently caused trouble for the deceiving God hypothesis in the First Meditation: goodness.

I suggest that these variations reveal an inherent defect in this way of proceeding. Although Descartes will shortly say that his idea of God is most clear and distinct (*maxime clara & distincta*, AT VII, 46), I take it that he really regards the enumeration of attributes as not ultimately a satisfactory way of clarifying this concept. No sooner has he made the bold claim that he has a most clear and distinct idea of God, than he leaps from the listing of particular attributes to a general formula covering them all. He has included these several perfections in his idea of God because fundamentally this idea is the idea of a supremely perfect and infinite being (AT VII, 46).

This is a decisive moment in the dialectic. It provides a rationale for thinking of all these various attributes as attributes of one being. Descartes now has a principle which determines what should or should not appear on any list of attributes:

Whatever I perceive clearly and distinctly that is real and true and that implies some perfection, the whole of it is contained in this [FV: idea]. It does not matter that I do not comprehend the infinite, or that there are innumerable things in God which I cannot comprehend, and perhaps will not even be able to attain any conception of. (AT VII, 46)

It does not matter that Descartes' analysis of his idea of God cannot be exhaustive, because now, at least, he has a principle for deciding individual cases. Insofar as this principle entails that this or that feature will appear on the list, a list which an infinite intellect could extend to infinity, it explains why precisely those features are involved in our concept of God. And insofar as it entails other previously unsuspected characteristics,[38] it shows itself to define the idea of a true and immutable nature, not an arbitrary fiction.[39]

But its most important consequence is that it explains why these various features cannot be clearly conceived in isolation from each other:

> One of the chief perfections I understand to be in God is the unity, simplicity or (*sive*) inseparability of all those things that are in God. (AT VII, 50)

With this deduction from the concept of God as a supremely perfect being, one of the principal confusions of the earlier Meditations has been removed. If the perfections are inseparable from one another, then the concept of the Evil Spirit as a supremely powerful being is revealed to be a concept involving a contradiction.[40] The perfection of omnipotence cannot exist in isolation from the perfection of goodness. Hence Descartes will conclude, by the end of the Third Meditation, that the God he has an idea of, as a being possessing all perfections, cannot be a deceiver (AT VII, 52). For it is manifest by the natural light that all fraud and deception depend on some defect.

So far so good. It is easy enough to see that over the course of the first three Meditations Descartes has been gradually clarifying his initial concept of God. But it is also easy to imagine that by the end of the Third Meditation the process is complete. Does Descartes not claim, when he introduces the concept of God as a supremely perfect being (AT VII, 46, line 8), to have an idea of God which is most clear and distinct (*maxime clara et distincta*)?

We must, of course, answer "yes" to this last question. But doing so does not commit us to regarding the process of clarification as complete. When Descartes or, rather, his meditator, repeats his claim to possess a clear and distinct idea of God at the end of the paragraph just cited (AT VII, 46, line 28), he introduces an interesting qualification: "the idea I have of God is the " . . . clearest and most distinct of all [the ideas] that are in me." The meditator's idea of God may well be clearer and more distinct than any other idea he has and still not be as clear and distinct as it needs to be for the subsequent argument.

Having a clear and distinct idea of a thing, or of a kind of thing, I have been assuming, is a matter of seeing what is and what is not involved in being that thing or a thing of that kind. More precisely, it is a matter of recognizing that there are certain properties we cannot but ascribe to a thing of that kind (clarity) and others which we are not at all compelled to ascribe to it (distinctness).

The meditator's idea of God will not be as clear and distinct as Descartes would like it to be until he recognizes that he cannot think of God except as existing (AT VII, 66 and 67), that God is the only being to whose essence existence belongs (AT VII, 68), that there cannot be two or more Gods (ibid.). So the ontological argument of the Fifth Meditation is not, as it might appear, a kind of afterthought in which Descartes returns to a proposition already satisfactorily proven earlier. It is, rather, the culmination of Descartes' search for a clear and distinct idea of God, a culmination to which the clarifications of the preceding Meditations were a necessary preliminary.

To recognize these implications of the idea of God, the meditator must already have attained a certain level of clarity. He must, first of all, have risen from the idea of God as possessing this or that perfection to the idea of God as possessing all the perfections, whatever they may be.[41] That is what the dialectic of the Third Meditation contributes to the quest. But the meditator must also have recognized that his idea of God as a supremely perfect being is free of contradiction. That is why the dialectic of the Fourth Meditation is necessary before the ontological argument can be advanced.

To say this is to claim that Descartes anticipated a criticism of his version of the ontological argument which Leibniz pressed repeatedly: that Descartes had assumed too easily the possibility of a supremely perfect being.[42] To be sure, Descartes does not undertake, in the manner of Leibniz, an a priori proof of the compatibility of all perfections. But he does make it a criterion of a clear and distinct perception that it not involve a contradiction (cf. AT VII, 71). And he does at least attempt to remove from his idea of God what he perceives as the most dangerous threat of contradiction.

From the beginning he had conceived of God as his creator. But as he comes to see that he conceives of God also as a supremely perfect being, it becomes increasingly urgent to understand how a supremely perfect being could be the creator of a manifestly imperfect being. To achieve this understanding is the project of the Fourth Meditation. Whether or not we think Descartes is successful in that project, we must at least recognize that success there is essential to a proper presentation of the ontological argument. When Descartes is presenting his thoughts in the best of all possible orders, the ontological argument must be postponed until after the arguments of the Third

and Fourth Meditations, for the best order does not simply assume
that we possess the requisite clear and distinct ideas, it shows a process
by which someone with confused ideas can acquire clear and distinct
ones. Conversely, when Descartes allows himself to assume possession of a clear and distinct idea of God, he can begin, as he does in
his synthetic works, with the ontological argument.[43]

Ultimately, I think, Descartes' project does fail. His attempt to solve
one mystery leads only to a deeper mystery. To explain how a perfect
being can be the creator of an imperfect being, he ascribes to the imperfect being a freedom which will, in the end, be no easier to reconcile
with the perfection of his creator than error was.[44] But that is a story
for another day. *My* project here has simply been to explain what in
practice the use of the analytic method in the *Meditations* comes to.
And I think we have seen enough examples now of the kind of thing
which I claim is characteristic of this method to have a clearer and
more distinct idea of the nature of analysis in the *Meditations*.[45]

NOTES

The abbreviation AT is explained in the General Bibliography at the beginning
of this volume.

1. For a representative selection of previous treatments of this issue, see
L. J. Beck, *The Method of Descartes* (Oxford: Clarendon Press, 1952), chap. 18.
G. Buchdahl, *Metaphysics and the Philosophy of Science* (Cambridge, Mass.: MIT
Press, 1969), 118–147; J. Hintikka, "A Discourse on Descartes' Method" in M.
Hooker, *Descartes, critical and interpretive essays* (Baltimore: Johns Hopkins
Press, 1978); M. Gueroult, *Descartes selon l'ordre des raisons* (Paris: Vrin, 1953)
1:22–28, 357–360; J.-M. Beyssade, "L'ordre dans les *Principia*," *Les études philo-
sophiques* (1976):387–403.

2. "More" because decisions about what to quote, what to paraphrase,
what to omit, how to translate what is quoted, and how to paraphrase what
is paraphrased, all involve some element of interpretation; "less" because I
have deliberately omitted certain prima facie important claims, some because
I think they are apt to be misleading in the end, others because I want to
postpone them for later attention.

3. See, for example, Alquié's annotation of the French version of Descartes'
reply, in *Descartes, Oeuvres philosophiques*, ed. F. Alquié (Paris: Garnier, 1967),
2:581–585.

4. A full account of this passage would have to explain what reservations
Descartes has in mind when he says that analysis is "as it were" (*tanquam*)
an a priori procedure (and similarly, *mutatis mutandis*, for synthesis). Cf.
Beyssade, "L'ordre dans les *Principia*." It would also have to explain why

Descartes says, in a parenthesis (AT VII, 156), that often, in synthesis, the proof itself is more a priori than in analysis.

5. In fact, Descartes claims more than just that it shows a *viable* method of discovery. He claims that it shows the *true* way the thing was discovered. See the passage cited below in n. 7. But I take that claim with a grain of salt.

6. "Spinoza as an expositor of Descartes," in *Speculum Spinozanum*, ed. S. Hessing (London: Routledge & Kegan Paul, 1977), 133–142.

7. See *Descartes' Conversation with Burman*, trans J. Cottingham (Oxford: Clarendon Press, 1976), 12. Since this work is at best Burman's record of Descartes' replies to his questions, and since the text may be corrupt for a variety of reasons, it must be treated with some suspicion, particularly where it seems to contradict Descartes' own works. For an interesting discussion of the reliability of the *Conversation*, see an article forthcoming in the *Archiv für Geschichte der Philosophie*, by Roger Ariew, "Infinite and Indefinite in Descartes's *Conversation with Burman*."

In this case Burman's report of Descartes' reply contradicts Descartes' claim in the Second Replies that the analytic method is the best one for teaching. In my earlier article I suggested (without argument) that Descartes might have changed his mind about which method was best for teaching. Beyssade, in his excellent edition of the conversation (*Descartes, L'entretien avec Burman* [Paris: PUF, 1981], 42), cites a letter to Mersenne of 31 December 1640 (Alquié II, 307) in which Descartes, referring to the *Principles*, says that he is engaged in writing his philosophy in such a way that it can easily be taught. This letter evidently was written before the Second Replies were written (see the article by Garber and Cohen, cited below, pp. 143–144), so it does not show a change of mind after the Second Replies. But it does show that, even in writings which are uncontestably Cartesian, Descartes was of two minds about what method was best for teaching.

8. In the article cited above, I mentioned the definitions of thought (*Principles* I, 9) and clarity and distinctness (*Principles* I, 45). I might have added those of substance (I, 51), attribute (I, 56), mode (I, 56), and the natural light (I, 30).

9. In the article cited above, I mentioned the introduction of the concepts of clarity and distinctness via the example of the wax, and the explanation of thought at AT VII, 28. Analogously, the concept of the natural light is introduced in the *Meditations* by giving examples of things known by it (AT VII, 38–39). But clearly, not all of Descartes' central concepts will be open to that mode of explanation. Most importantly, the idea of God will not be.

10. See AT VII, 140, and cf. Descartes' Letter to Clerselier (Alquié, 2: 841–842). Since the general propositions grasped in these contexts would be eternal truths, this is not any ordinary induction. The move from the particular to the general would be like what is sometimes referred to in discussions of Aristotle as an intuitive induction, i.e., a process not of reasoning but of direct insight into first principles, "mediated psychologically by a review of particular instances" (W. D. Ross, *Aristotle* [New York: Meridian, 1959], 44, cf. 211). I make no attempt to judge whether this represents a just interpre-

tation of Aristotle. Cf. Jonathan Barnes's notes to *Posterior Analytics* B, 19, in his edition of that work (Oxford: Clarendon Press, 1975), 248–260.

11. Cf. the *Conversation with Burman*, 3.

12. But not simply summarizing. The text and the footnotes provide additional evidence in favor of that interpretation, some of which I had not noticed when I wrote the earler article.

13. By Daniel Garber and Lesley Cohen, in "A point of order: analysis, synthesis, and Descartes' *Principles*," *Archiv für Geschichte der Philosophie* 64 (1982):136–147. Garber and Cohen primarily challenge the claim that the *Principles* was written according to the synthetic method, pointing out that our only direct evidence for this comes from the (suspect) *Conversation with Burman* and that, on various occasions when Descartes might have been expected to call attention to this synthetic character, he did not do so. I am inclined to think that the explanation for this silence is that Descartes recognized that the *Principles* did not have the formal features his audience would expect in a synthetic treatise, that he did not have the patience for the kind of labor that would be involved in a full-scale treatment of the whole of philosophy *more geometrico*, and that he did not want to arouse expectations he had no intention of satisfying. For the purposes of this article, whose concern is with the *Meditations*, I have no need to defend the claim that the *Principles* is synthetic. It will be enough to compare the *Meditations* with the Geometric Exposition. But I do, in fact, still think that the *Principles* is fundamentally a synthetic work. For the purposes of my earlier article, it would be sufficient if it were, as Gueroult and Gouhier have suggested (in *Descartes* [Paris: Cahiers de Royaumont, 1957], 108–140, and *La pensée métaphysique de Descartes* [Paris: Vrin, 1968], 109), a hybrid work, combining features of both methods.

14. A procedure Plato gives examples of in nearly all the dialogues, but which he theorizes about most helpfully in the *Republic*, 531e–540. I take it that for all their respect for the axiomatic procedures of the mathematicians, neither Plato nor Descartes really finds it satisfactory simply to assume his first principles without argument. The problem is to find a way of arguing for first principles which will not permit the cry of dogmatism to be raised in turn about the principles of the argument.

15. That is, propositions which would be accepted by all or by most people, particularly those uncorrupted by the false philosophy taught in the schools. Unlike Aristotle, who also conceived of dialectic as a path to first principles (*Topics* I, i–ii), Descartes would not give special standing to "the wise."

16. So it is not only in the First Meditation that Descartes makes his meditator begin with confused ideas. The procedure is used repeatedly in the *Meditations*, in the Third (AT VII, 38), in the Fourth (AT VII, 54), in the Fifth (AT VII, 66), and in the Sixth (AT VII, 74 ff.). Part of Descartes' justification for this procedure lies in his conviction that old habits of belief are hard to break (cf. AT VII, 22, 29), and that we must, therefore, be weaned from them gradually. But partly it lies in his confidence that the perceptions of a man untutored by philosophy (and therefore uncorrupted by false philosophy) must contain some truth.

17. Beginning in the First Meditation (AT VII, 20) and continuing through-out the early meditations (e.g., in AT VII, 30–31, 43–45). I have discussed this in more detail in chap. 8 of *Descartes Against the Skeptics* (Cambridge: Harvard University Press, 1978).

18. "In good Latin *anima* signifies *air* or *breath*, from which usage I believe it has been transferred to signify the *mind* [mens]; that is why I said it is often taken for something corporeal." Letter to Mersenne, 21 April 1641 (Alquié 2:327); cf. AT VII, 161.

19. Here I assume an interpretation argued for at length in *Descartes Against the Skeptics*, chap. 4.

20. The list of synonyms given at AT VII, 27, lines 13–14, does contain the term *animus*, which translators have sometimes rendered *soul*. But while clas-sical usage of *animus* and *anima* certainly overlaps (see the entries in the *Oxford Latin Dictionary*), classical authors do sometimes make a distinction which Descartes surely intends here. Lewis & Short cite the following from Nonius Marcellus: *Animus est quo sapimus, anima, qua vivimus*. It is not easy, however, to find a good term in English with which to make the distinction.

21. Descartes frequently uses the term *mens* or its cognates (e.g., *amens, demens*) in a nonreflective way earlier in the *Meditations* (e.g., at AT VII, 17, 19, 21). Particularly interesting is AT VII, 25, since a doubt about the existence of minds had *not* been suggested in the First Meditation.

22. See *Descartes Against the Skeptics*, 187–188. It is interesting to note that when essentially the same list is repeated at the beginning of the Third Meditation (AT VII, 34), the French version adds two further activities of the mind: loving and hating (AT IX, 27). Beyssade suggests (personal correspon-dence, 4 April 1984) a reason for the addition: that between 1641 (the date of the Latin text) and 1647 (the date of the French translation) Descartes has developed his theory of intellectual love and hate (see the letter to Chanut of 1 February 1647). Beyssade, however, finds it curious that memory is omitted from the list.

23. On the history of the term *idea*, see H. A. Wolfson, "Extradeical and Intradeical Interpretations of the Platonic Ideas," in his *Religious Philosophy* (Cambridge: Harvard University Press, 1961). For Descartes' sensitivity to this history, see his reply to Hobbes (AT VII, 181) cited below. For classical usage, see the *Oxford Latin Dictionary*.

24. Here, as is often the case, the French version differs. And here, as is rarely the case, it seems virtually certain that the variation is one in which we should see Descartes' hand: "And so that I can have the opportunity to examine this without interrupting the order of meditation I have proposed for myself, which is to pass gradually from the notions I first find in my mind to those I can find there subsequently, I must first divide, etc." (AT IX, 29). This whole paper might be regarded as a commentary on that passage.

25. And in the Fifth, when Descartes develops the theory of innate ideas mentioned in the Third Meditation. I return to this below. For now the point is simply that the analysis of the concept of mind is far from complete in the Second Meditation.

26. Cf. the Geometrical Exposition, comments on Axiom 5.

27. I take my example from the first chapter of *Le monde*, where this pre-philosophic belief occupies center stage.

28. I take it that a theory of innate ideas is implied in the First Meditation when Descartes suggests (AT VII, 20–21) that the truths of mathematics are not touched by the dream argument, and so require the hypothesis of a deceiving God to render them doubtful. If mathematics cares little whether its objects exist in nature, it cannot be affected by an argument casting doubt on the evidence of the senses, which are preeminently a way of learning what exists in nature. If mathematics is a science indifferent to the exemplification of its objects in physical nature, then even its fundamental concepts are not to be thought of as having been derived from experience.

29. For more on Descartes' concept of ideas, see my article, "Descartes, Spinoza, and the Ethics of Belief," in *Spinoza, Essays in Interpretation*, ed. M. Mandelbaum and E. Freeman (La Salle, Ill.: Open Court, 1975).

30. Cf. *Principles* I, 52.

31. This does not, however, mean that it cannot serve perfectly well as a ground for doubting the truths of mathematics in the First Meditation. See *Descartes Against the Skeptics*, chaps. 3–5.

32. Some have thought that Evil Spirit is not in fact omnipotent, largely because Descartes never seems to mention doubt about mathematical truths in connection with him. For example, mathematical propositions are not included in the list of prior beliefs to be rejected in the final paragraph of the First Meditation, or in the second and third paragraphs of the Second Meditation. See R. Kennington, "The Finitude of Descartes' Evil Genius," *Journal of the History of Ideas* 32 (1971):441–446. And it appears that traditionally demons were conceived as limited in power, capable of acting on the mind only by presenting deceptive sense experiences. See Tullio Gregory, "Dio ingannatore e genio maligno," *Giornale critico della filosofia italiana* (1975):477–516. If the Evil Spirit were finite in power, this might explain why Descartes says in the Third Meditation (AT VII, 36) that the only reason he had doubted the truths of mathematics was because "some God" could have given him such a nature that he could be deceived about the most manifest things.

Nevertheless, when Descartes introduces the demon at AT VII, 22, he calls him *summe potentem*, a phrase repeated with reference to the *deceptor nescio quis* at AT VII, 25. Similarly the *deceptorem aliquem* at AT VII, 26, is *potentissimum*. Although Descartes does hold that supreme power and malignity are incompatible (see AT V, 150), it appears that his meditator does not appreciate that fact at this point of the *Meditations*.

33. Note that, in shifting from God to the deceiver, we shift from a being in whom we have long believed, though no doubt without adequate warrant for our belief, to one whose epistemic status is more dubious. No doubt belief in demons was more common in Descartes' time than in ours, but belief in omnipotent demons must have been rare even then. See Gregory, "Dio ingannatore e genio maligno." This illustrates what I think is an important fact about the *Meditations:* that a ground of doubt need not be probable on the

evidence, nor even believed; it is sufficient that it is not known to be false. For more on this, see *Descartes Against the Skeptics*.

34. This way of putting things is perhaps not one Descartes himself would choose; my reading here, and throughout this essay, owes much to Spinoza.

35. AT VII, 40. The French version adds: "immutable" (AT IX, 32).

36. AT VII, 45. The French version adds: "eternal and immutable" (AT IX, 35–36).

37. As Professor Rodis-Lewis points out, in the notes to her bilingual edition, *Meditationes de prima philosophia/Méditations métaphysiques* (Paris: Vrin, 1978), 45, *independent* replaces *eternal*; but according to the First Replies these two attributes are necessarily connected (AT VII, 119).

38. E.g., that there is nothing potential in his idea of God (AT VII, 47, 51), or that God has the power of existing per se (AT VII, 50).

39. This will be essential to the ontological argument. Cf. the First Replies (AT VII, 117) and *Descartes Against the Skeptics*, 148–152.

40. See the *Conversation with Burman*, 4.

41. Cf. AT VII, 67: "For although it is not necessary for me ever to have any thought of God, nevertheless, as often as it does please me to think of the first and supreme being, and to draw, as it were, the idea of him from the treasury of my mind, it is necessary for me to attribute all perfections to him, even if I do not then enumerate all of them or attend to them individually."

42. See, for example, Leibniz's Letter to Oldenburg of 28 December 1675, in L. Loemker, Leibniz, *Philosophical Papers and Letters* (Dordrecht: Reidel, 1969), 166.

43. In the article cited above, Garber and Cohen complained that "even if one accepts the claim that the *Principles* are synthetic, this difference between the *Meditations* and the *Principles* [viz. that the order of the arguments for the existence of God is different in the two works, the order in the *Principles* corresponding to that in the Geometric Exposition] is not easily explained. Curley's account of analysis and synthesis, for example, seems to leave this divergence between the two texts unexplained" (p. 146n). Certainly my earlier article on this topic offered no explanation of that phenomenon. But I would contend that the natural extension of it presented in this article meets the challenge.

44. Cf. *Principles* I, 40–41.

45. I leave for another day the difficult question of whether the analytic method of the *Meditations* is the same as the analytic method of the *Regulae*. But as readers of *Descartes Against the Skeptics* might expect, I think we should not be surprised if they are not the same, and should not presume that the *Regulae* can be used to interpret the *Meditations*. Some previous discussions of analysis seem to me to have assumed too easily that the two methods are essentially the same.

8
The Theory of Ideas

Vere Chappell

The preface to the *Meditations* contains, among other things, Descartes' response to two objections that critics had made to his treatment of God and the soul in the *Discourse*, which had been published three years earlier. The second of these concerns his major argument for the existence of God, the same argument he would be presenting more fully in the Third Meditation. The objection is that, "from the fact that I have in me an idea of a thing more perfect than myself, it does not follow that the idea itself is more perfect, much less that that which this idea represents exists" (preface to the *Meditations:* AT VII, 8; HR I, 138).[1] Descartes' response to this objection is that the word "idea" is ambiguous. For it can, he says, "be taken materially, for an operation of the intellect, in which sense it cannot be said to be more perfect than myself." Or it can be taken "objectively, for the thing that is represented by this operation, which thing, even if it is not supposed to exist outside the intellect, can nonetheless be more perfect than myself, because of its essence." Descartes concludes by promising to show, in the *Meditations* to come, just how it does follow, "from the fact that the idea of a thing more perfect than myself is in me, that this thing really does exist" (ibid.).

The distinction drawn in this passage, between the "material" and the "objective" senses of "idea," is the key to understanding Descartes' whole theory of ideas, which itself is the central component of his theory of knowledge. It is true that this distinction is not made explicitly anywhere else in the Cartesian corpus (though there are several passages in which a related distinction is drawn; see page 000, below). But it is implicit at many points, in the *Meditations* and in later works, as well as in the *Discourse*. That is, Descartes *uses* the word with these different meanings, and it is often crucial to the cogency or even the intelligibility of a particular passage that the right one of the two be understood.

Not only are the two meanings of "idea" distinguished in the passage before us; they are also quite fully specified. Indeed, a good deal of the Cartesian theory of ideas is packed into the definitions provided. We can thus, on this basis alone, tell the following about Cartesian ideas. An idea in the material sense of the word is a mental *act* or event, something that occurs in the mind. An idea in the objective sense, by contrast, is something upon which the mind is directed, a mental *object*. (From now on I shall abbreviate "idea in the material sense" and "idea in the objective sense" to "idea$_m$" and "idea$_o$," respectively.) Ideas$_m$ and ideas$_o$, furthermore, are related, in that the latter are things *represented* by the former. The passage does not specify the nature of this relationship, beyond calling it "representation"; it does not even indicate whether the two terms related, ideas$_m$ and ideas$_o$, are distinct entities or not. But it does suggest that the relation is necessary, at least on the side of the idea$_o$: for it suggests that every idea$_o$ is represented by an idea$_m$. Later on we shall see that the relation is necessary on the other side also, and that every idea$_m$ represents an idea$_o$. Descartes' position, indeed, is that there is, for every idea$_m$, exactly one idea$_o$ that it represents, and for every idea$_o$, exactly one idea$_m$ that represents it.

My aim in this essay is to spell out the central provisions of the Cartesian theory of ideas, or at least of that version of the theory that is encapsulated in the preface to the *Meditations*. I cannot hope, in one essay, to cover more than the central provisions; but I shall try to identify some of the further topics that a full treatment of the theory would have to pursue. I first focus on ideas$_m$, taking them by themselves, and ask what it is to be an idea in Descartes' material sense. I then address the same question with respect to ideas$_o$. In the course of both inquiries I consider the notion of representation that Descartes invokes in our passage, by which he takes ideas$_m$ and ideas$_o$ to be related to one another. It is worth noting here at the outset that this is not at all the notion that most philosophers—including, on occasion, Descartes himself—have in mind when they speak of representation in an epistemological connection. Finally, I take up a broader question about the relation between ideas in the two senses: to what extent are an idea$_m$ and its associated idea$_o$ two distinct entities? Here again it is useful to know beforehand what the answer will be. It is that these are not distinct entities at all—not one individual thing and then a second, different one—but are rather one thing on the one hand, and an aspect or component of that same thing on the other. The idea$_m$ and the idea$_o$ only differ from one another, to use Descartes' own expression, by a "distinction of reason."

The Cartesian theory of ideas—the theory that occupies a central position in the epistemology of the *Meditations*—is a theory about ideas in both the material and the objective senses of the word. But these are not the only two meanings with which the word "idea" occurs in Descartes' writings; there are in fact two others at least. (1) In some early works, while discussing imagination and sense perception, Descartes uses "idea" to mean "corporeal image."[2] An idea, in this sense of the word, is a material entity, something that exists in the brain and not in the mind. But this use is largely abandoned, and indeed is explicitly repudiated on several occasions, in later works; and it does not appear in the *Meditations* at all.[3] This does not mean that corporeal images cease to play any role in the philosophy of Descartes' maturity—on the contrary. Nor are such images irrelevant to the theory of ideas of the *Meditations*—on the contrary again, since that theory is meant to accommodate sense perception and imagination as well as pure intellectual thought. What is the case is that Descartes no longer calls these material entities "ideas."[4] (2) Descartes uses "idea" with a different meaning again in a few letters written after the *Meditations* had been completed, and even, arguably, once or twice in the *Meditations* itself.[5] This use occurs when (and only when) innate ideas are being discussed. Normally, an innate idea is an idea$_m$ for Descartes, specified as having its origin or source within the mind, yet without having been created by it. In these passages, however, the word "idea" is applied to this source or origin itself, and this is, as the surrounding discussion makes clear, not a momentary state but a standing capacity or faculty of the mind, a potentiality or disposition rather than anything actual or occurrent. The Cartesian doctrine of innate ideas is certainly a part of the theory of ideas as a whole (though not a part to be treated in this paper). But this dispositional use of the word "idea" is in no way essential to that doctrine, nor does it reflect any distinctive feature thereof. Indeed, it is likely that this use is merely inadvertent on the part of our author, considering the fact that the "idea" in "innate idea" does, in the overwhelming majority of cases, stand for a mental occurrence—that is, it has the material sense.[6]

It will be useful to have an example in mind as we proceed. Suppose that, looking out my window some morning, I see the sun. Alternatively, suppose that I think of the sun, shut up in my closet at night, without in any way sensing its presence. In either case, Descartes would say, I have an idea. The idea is *mine,* something that attaches to me in some way. The idea exists or occurs at a *time*—the time at or during which I am engaged in seeing or thinking. And it is an idea *of* something, namely the sun. The question arises: In which of Descartes' two senses of the word is it true that I have this idea, with these characteristics? The answer is: Both. I have both an idea$_m$ and an idea$_o$; each of them has me for its subject, each has a locus in time, and each is an idea of the sun. This one example, therefore, can serve us in both parts of the discussion to come: it provides an instance both of an idea$_m$ and of an idea$_o$.

IDEAS IN THE MATERIAL SENSE

Descartes defines an idea$_m$ as "an operation of the intellect." The intellect is one of the two general faculties or powers that make up the mind, the other being the will. The characteristic activity of the intellect is perception, and this, together with volition, constitutes thought. "Thinking," indeed, is Descartes' term for "mental activity" in general, and perceiving and willing are the two most general "modes" of thinking. Each of these in turn comprises a number of specific modes of thinking, "sensing, imagining, and pure understanding [*intelligere*]," for example, in the case of perceiving, "desiring, disliking, affirming, denying, [and] doubting" in that of willing (*Principles* I, 32; AT VIII–1, 17; HR I, 232). Hence, not only are sensation, sense perception, and imagination, as well as "intellection" or conception, species of thought for Descartes; all are alike intellectual activities, exercises of the intellect.

The mind, Descartes holds, belongs to the metaphysical category of substance. It follows that all the things we ascribe to the mind—its powers and faculties no less than its activities, states, and properties—are, metaphysically speaking, the attributes or modifications of a substance. Thought, indeed, is the "principal attribute" or "essence" of the mind; and what this means, Descartes tells us, is not just that the mind is necessarily endowed with the power of thought but that it is always actually engaged in cogitative activity.[7] All substances—at least all created substances, which includes all minds—are temporally persisting entities for Descartes; so to say that the mind is always thinking is to say that some thinking is occurring in it at every moment of its existence. This thinking is not, however, uniform and unvarying from moment to moment. In fact it is constantly changing, for many reasons and in many ways, and its changes mark off distinguishable stretches within it, different thinking events. These thinking events are what Descartes calls (individual) "thoughts (*cogitationes*)"; and the succession of thoughts in a mind constitutes that mind's thinking or thought (*cogitatio*) as a whole. Descartes also uses the phrase "mode of thinking," in a sense different from that remarked earlier, to refer to these individual units of the thinking process; here "mode" means something like "item" or "incident" rather than "type."[8] It is to be noted that thoughts, though typically rather short-lived, are noninstantaneous. Each of them takes some positive time to occur, and so the number of thoughts that belongs to any one mind—given a life span of finite duration—is finite.[9]

Thinking is the essence of the mind; so it is impossible, as Descartes puts it, for a mind ever to exist without thinking. Equivalently, no mind can ever be without some individual thought or other, since thinking is wholly made up of thoughts. But no single thought by itself, existing at one certain time, is essential to its possessor; none is ever such that the mind, in which it occurs as a matter of fact, necessarily has to have it, at that time or ever.[10] An individual thought, like thinking itself, is an attribute or modification of a substance, namely, the mind to which it belongs. But it is an accidental rather than an essential attribute, a "mode" of a substance in still another Cartesian sense of the word, different from both of those we have so far encountered; in this sense "mode" just means "accident."[11]

Thoughts then, for Descartes, are modes of the mind, which is to say, temporary, accidental attributes of mental substances, hence momentary mental states or mental occurrences. Descartes also uses the terms "operation" and "act (*actus*)" to convey this same feature of thoughts; that is as synonyms for "event" or "occurrence."[12] An individual thought may thus be said to be an operation or act, as well as a mode, of the mind. Descartes' position, be it noted, is not merely that all thoughts are mental operations, but also the converse, that all of the mind's operations—all of its modes in the sense of "mode" now before us—are thoughts.

We saw earlier that there are different kinds of mental activity for Descartes, different modes of thinking in the sense of different species thereof: perception and willing, and then, subdividing these, imagining and sensing, desiring and doubting, and so on. The same division applies to individual thoughts: some are perceptions and some are volitions, with these comprising, for example, sensations and images on the one hand, desires and doubts on the other. We also saw earlier that perceiving is the peculiar activity of the intellect, the specific mode of thinking that this department or portion of the mind engages in. The individual operations or acts of the intellect, therefore, are not merely thoughts but, more specifically, perceptions. Recalling now that Descartes defines an idea in the material sense of the word as an "operation of the intellect," we can conclude: ideas$_m$ are perceptions. It is also the case that ideas$_m$ are thoughts, since perceptions are thoughts; and likewise, that ideas$_m$ are modes of thinking, in the sense of temporally delimited portions of the thinking process, since that is what thoughts are. Not all thoughts, however, are ideas$_m$, whereas ideas$_m$ and perceptions are coextensive.[13]

This is not, of course, a result that any reader of the *Meditations* will find surprising. Descartes frequently and explicitly speaks, in that work and elsewhere, of ideas both as thoughts and as modes of thinking.[14] There are also passages, though not so many, in which he says that ideas are perceptions.[15] The point to be stressed, however, is that it is ideas in the material sense of the word, ideas$_m$, that Descartes relates thus to thoughts and perceptions.

If ideas$_m$ are perceptions, then the characteristic features of perceptions must belong to them also. One point that Descartes gives some weight to in discussing perceptions is that they are passions with respect to their subject, things that the mind undergoes, as opposed to actions properly so called, which are things done or produced by the mind.[16] In perceiving, in other words, the mind (or the soul) accepts or receives its thoughts, as a patient; and only in willing is it truly active, performing its thoughts as an agent. The same thing can be said, therefore, of ideas, and in one passage at least Descartes does indeed say it. "The difference," he writes in a letter to Mesland dated 2 May 1644, "between the soul and its ideas [is] exactly like that between a piece of wax and the diverse shapes that it can receive. And just as it is not properly an action but a passion in the wax to receive diverse shapes, so it [is] also a passion in the soul to receive this or that idea, and it is only its volitions that are actions" (AT IV, 113; K, 148). A question might arise as to how this point can be squared with Descartes' indiscriminate use of the word "act" for all thoughts in the mind, perceptions as well as volitions—a use we took note of a moment ago. The answer, of course, as it so often is with Descartes, is that "act" in his writings has two different senses, in this case one broader or looser, the other narrow and strict. It is, then, only in the strict sense that volitions alone, and not also perceptions, are acts of the mind.[17]

As should be apparent by now, Descartes' theory of ideas, at least in the material sense of the word, is no more than a specialized part of his metaphysical theory in general, and in particular its central component, the doctrine of substance. Ideas$_m$ are temporary modifications of Cartesian substances. In terms of the example I cited earlier, the idea$_m$ of the sun that I have is an "act" or a "mode" of the substance my mind is, and it "inheres in" or "belongs to" this substance, in the special senses given all of these terms by the Cartesian system. Once this is understood, then further features of ideas$_m$ can be inferred from other provisions of the theory of substance. It is a principle of that theory, for example, that substances generally have more "reality" or "perfection" than modes or accidents do (Second Reply: AT VII, 165; HR II, 56). This explains, then, why it is that, as Descartes says, my idea of God, in the material sense of "idea," "cannot be said to be more perfect than myself." For my idea here, which is to say my idea$_m$, is a "mode or accident," whereas I am a substance.[18]

So far, we have been discussing the nature of Cartesian ideas$_m$— what they are. We have now to consider what might be called their function—what they do. By its nature (or essence), Descartes tells us, an idea$_m$ "is only a mode existing in the human mind" (Letter to Regius, June 1642: AT III, 566; K, 134). In this respect, not only are all ideas$_m$ like one another, but ideas$_m$ as a class do not differ from thoughts of all other kinds. In addition to being mental modes, however, ideas$_m$ serve to represent things to the mind. It is this representative function, Descartes says in one prominent passage at least (Meditation III: AT VII, 37; HR I, 159), that distinguishes ideas$_m$ from thoughts generally. Furthermore, even though every idea$_m$ must represent something (Meditation III: AT VII, 44; HR I, 164; cf. the French version at AT IX–1, 34–35), different ideas$_m$ represent different things; and this difference among things represented—among things to which they bear the representative relation—serves to differentiate ideas$_m$ as well. We know from the *Meditations* preface passage that the things represented by ideas$_m$ are ideas$_o$; and we cannot reach a full understanding of representation or of the differences among represented objects until we have examined ideas in this other sense of the word. But we are in a position to see the difference between the distinction Descartes draws in that passage and the distinction we have encountered just now. The former is a distinction between ideas$_m$ and ideas$_o$. The latter is a distinction within the class of ideas$_m$ alone: it is a distinction, corresponding to that between their nature and their function, between these same entities considered either as they are in themselves or in relation to their representata—or between ideas$_m$ with respect to their intrinsic as opposed to their relational properties.

This is a distinction that Descartes calls attention to on several occasions: in the *Meditations* (AT VII, 40; HR I, 161–162), in his Reply to Arnauld (AT VII, 232; HR II, 105), and in the *Principles* (AT VIII-1, 11; HR I, 225–226). That it is related to the distinction drawn in the *Meditations* preface is clear. That it is nonetheless a different distinction should be equally clear.

There is one further feature of ideas$_m$ that needs to be mentioned before we proceed to consider ideas$_o$. Every idea$_m$ for Descartes is a *conscious* event in the mind of the person who has it. This must not be taken to mean that the event itself—the idea$_m$—is conscious or has consciousness. The property of being conscious attaches rather to the substance, that is, to the mind, of which the idea$_m$ is a mode. Minds are conscious in and through their ideas$_m$; the latter might be said to manifest consciousness, or to include it as a kind of pervasive ingredient. In any case, it is not only in its ideas$_m$ that a mind's consciousness is to be found. According to Descartes, all thoughts—all the momentary modes of the mind—are conscious occurrences or states. In some passages, indeed, he makes their relation to consciousness the defining characteristic of thoughts. Thus in the Second Reply he stipulates: "By the term 'thought' I understand everything that is in us [sc. in our minds] in such a way that we are immediately conscious [*conscii*] of it" (AT VII, 160; HR II, 52). And again in the *Principles*: "By the term 'thought' I understand all those things that happen in us, being as we are conscious [*nobis consciis*], insofar as the consciousness [*conscientia*] of them is in us" (AT VIII-1, 7; HR I, 222).

The passages just quoted reveal an additional fact about consciousness. To be conscious is to be conscious *of* something; consciousness must have an object. Both passages suggest that it is the thoughts themselves—ideas$_m$ for example—of which one is conscious. But this is not in fact Descartes' position. The precise object of consciousness, as we shall see, is not the conscious event, not the thought or idea$_m$, but rather the idea$_o$ that necessarily is associated with it. We shall have to find out about ideas$_o$, therefore, before our discussion of consciousness can be completed. But the topic had to be introduced at this point because it is thoughts, and hence ideas$_m$, by which consciousness is carried in the Cartesian mind: they are its indispensable vehicles even if not its specific targets.

IDEAS IN THE OBJECTIVE SENSE

Let us go back to the example of my seeing the sun on some occasion. For as long as my seeing continues, I have (or my mind has) an idea of the sun. Both an idea$_m$ and an idea$_o$ exist during this time; and each is mind in some way, something I have. We now know what the idea$_m$ is on this occasion, and what it is for me to have it. What then is the idea$_o$, and in what way is it related to me, while I am seeing the sun?

From Descartes' definition of "idea," taken *objective*, in the *Meditations* preface, we can conclude: the idea$_o$ is what is *represented* by the idea$_m$—in this case, its representatum. And what that is might seem obvious: it is the sun. Descartes, indeed, often uses expressions of the form "idea of x" and "idea which represents x" interchangeably (he also uses "idea which exhibits x" in the same way). This then would seem to commit him to saying that the sun itself is the idea$_o$ that I have when I see the sun. It is certainly the sun that my idea$_m$ is an idea of. It must also be the sun, therefore, that my idea$_m$ represents.

This cannot be Descartes' position, however. Apart from the oddity of calling the sun an idea of mine, in any sense of the word, the sun is supposed to be an entity distinct from myself; it is supposed to exist "outside me." In Descartes' view, there is always a question, with respect to any such entity, whether in fact it does exist, even if I have an idea of it (any sense). But every idea$_m$ that I have must represent something no matter what (Meditation III: AT VII, 44; HR I, 164). Thus I have ideas of angels, of animals, and of other men like myself, Descartes says, and I do so "even if there are no other men, nor animals, nor angels, anywhere in the world" (Meditation III: AT VII, 43; HR I, 164). And similarly with respect to the sun: there is something that my idea$_m$ of it represents whether or not there is any such thing as the sun. Some of my ideas indeed are of things that I know do not exist. My idea of the chimera is one example; another is my idea of time, or that of number, which is of something universal in nature, whereas all existing things are particulars (*Principles* I, 58–59: AT VIII–1, 27–28; HR I, 242–243; cf. *Regulae* vi: AT X, 382; HR I, 16). If there must be an idea$_o$ in these cases, as Descartes holds there does, then this cannot be identified with what the idea is of; for there is no such thing.

Now the sun, to be sure, is a particular, and it does exist. But if the possibility of its not existing does not suffice to differentiate it from what my idea$_m$ of the sun represents, Descartes provides another consideration which does suffice. There are, he observes in the Third Meditation, two different ideas of the sun that may come before me (Meditation III: AT VII, 39; HR I, 161). What he means is that either one of two dissimilar ideas$_o$ might be associated with any idea$_m$ I might have of the sun at some given time. Descartes' point is that these two ideas$_o$, since they do not resemble each other, cannot both resemble the sun, which is one heavenly body existing outside me. But it also follows that the two ideas$_o$ cannot both *be* the sun, just because they are two and it is one. This does not show that no representatum can be identified with any external object. But it does prove that representata, or ideas$_o$, are not in general identical with the things that these ideas, or their associated ideas$_m$, are said to be of.

What then is the representatum of my idea$_m$, what is the idea$_o$ that I have when I think of the sun, if it is not the sun itself? Descartes may not have had a well-developed doctrine on this matter at the time he wrote the *Meditations*. But he worked one out in responding to the First Objection, under the pressure of the questions that were put to him by Caterus. Caterus was troubled by the Cartesian principle that ideas must have causes. In his view, ideas are not actual entities; they have no real being and hence don't require causes. For an idea, he says, "*est ipsa res cogitata, quatenus objective est in intellectu*" (First Objection: AT VII, 92; HR II, 2). But this "objective being in the intellect," he goes on, is merely an "extrinsic denomination"; it doesn't make any difference to the thing that partakes of it. To be in this way is tantamount to not being at all, whence Caterus concludes that it doesn't take any being to cause it.

Descartes may or may not have understood Caterus's reasoning here. But he was in any case bound to reject his conclusion. What is striking is that he does so while accepting the formula that Caterus had used to define an idea: "the very thing thought of, insofar as it is objectively in the intellect" (First Reply: AT VII, 102; HR II, 9). Descartes even claims to have written these words himself at some time in the past (though in fact they don't appear in any work of his, earlier than the *Meditations*, that has come down to us). At any rate, having appropriated his critic's formula, Descartes proceeds to put his own construction on it. The result is a position very different from the one that Caterus had taken.

Descartes begins by claiming, in effect, that the term "*res cogitata*" is ambiguous. Caterus had taken it to stand for something outside the mind, and Descartes agrees that, with respect to that sort of thing, objective being is an extrinsic denomination. But it can also be applied to something that exists in the mind, which is how Descartes understands it. His reason is apparent: he wants to identify the *res cogitata* with an idea; and an idea, he says, "never exists outside the intellect" (First Reply: AT VII, 102; HR II, 10). It is important to notice that what Descartes is speaking of here is an idea$_o$. It is obvious that ideas$_m$ exist in the intellect, because they are operations thereof. What is not obvious—and what Descartes is explicitly proclaiming here—is that ideas$_o$ exist in the intellect also. An idea$_o$, Descartes is saying, is a thing that is thought of in the sense in which such a thing is something that exists in the mind.

The point, then, of the qualifying clause—*"quatenus est objective in intellectu"*—on Descartes' interpretation of Caterus's formula, is to specify the sense in which the term *"res cogitata"* is to be taken. Objective being, when the *res cogitata* exists in the mind, is simply being; it is just the kind of being that, by its nature, such a thing partakes of. For Descartes holds that there are different modes of being or existence, different ways in which things are. Objective being is the mode in which things in the intellect characteristically exist. This sort of being is contrasted with actual or formal being, which is the mode in which things outside the intellect exist. The acts or operations of the intellect—including all ideas$_m$—also have actual or formal being. Indeed, the only things that have objective being are ideas$_o$—the *res cogitatae* that exist in the mind. Objective being is also the only being that these things have. Descartes remarks that this objective mode of being "is far more imperfect than that by which things outside the intellect exist, but it is not therefore nothing at all" (First Reply: AT VII, 103; HR II, 10). This much at least he had already said in the Third Meditation (Meditation III: AT VII, 41; HR I, 163.

A thing that is thought of is an object of thought. Descartes' position is that, whenever anyone thinks, his thought has an object, and that this object is something in the thinker's own mind. But the phrase, "thing that is thought of," still is ambiguous. In many cases—not in all—in which someone thinks of something, there will be, in addition to the *res cogitata* that must exist in his mind, another *res cogitata* existing outside it. There will then be, in effect, two objects of thought, an external as well as an internal one. The external object will exist actually or formally, the internal only objectively. But both objects will exist in some way or other. And both objects will be *res cogitatae*, though not in the same sense of the term. Descartes says that, when I have an idea of the sun, my idea$_o$ is "the sun itself existing in the intellect, not indeed formally, as it does in the sky, but objectively, that is in the mode in which objects characteristically are in the intellect" (First Reply: AT VII, 102–103; HR II, 10). So it is an objective sun, as we might put it, that is the internal object of my thought. But in this case my thought has an external object as well, namely, the actual sun, or the sun "as it is in the sky."

Reflecting on this example, we might want to say that there are, in Descartes' view, two different suns, as well as two objects of thought, or things thought of in two different senses of the term. It could be misleading, however, to speak in this way—as if *sun* were a species of entity, with *the actual sun* and *the objective sun* as its instances. An alternative would be to refer to the sun that exists in my mind, and the external or actual sun, as *counterparts* of one another. My $idea_o$ of the sun would be an objective counterpart of that familiar body that exists in the sky; it, in turn, would be the actual counterpart of my $idea_o$. Some $ideas_o$ could then be said to have no actual counterparts— for example, the $idea_o$ of number or that of the chimera.

There is a great deal to be said, obviously, about the relationship between the two entities when an $idea_o$ does have an actual counterpart. This is a major topic in Descartes' philosophy and, though I won't be pursuing it very far in this essay, I will have one or two comments to make on it later on. In the meantime, there are things to be added to the account I have given of Descartes' $ideas_o$, the internal objects of thought that people have in their minds whether or not there are any actual things existing outside them. So far my account has been based almost entirely on Descartes' statement of his position in the First Reply. This is by far his fullest and most explicit statement of views on this subject. Even the definition of "idea" (sc. "$idea_o$") that he takes over from Caterus, "*ipse res cogitata, &c.,*" is repeated only twice in later works, both times without elaboration.[19] But there are several passages in the *Meditations*, and in works and letters subsequent to it, from which further details about Descartes' conception of $ideas_o$ can be gleaned.

We have seen that an $idea_o$ is an object of thought, a *res cogitata* existing objectively in somebody's intellect. And it is an entity that exists only in the objective mode. Now different $ideas_o$ may differ from one another by being associated with different $ideas_m$, $ideas_m$ occurring in different minds or in the same mind at different times. But the most significant differences among $ideas_o$, and perhaps the only ones capable of making them numerically distinct from one another, are differences of *content*.[20] My $idea_o$ of the sun is unlike my $idea_o$ of the moon, and would be so even if they both appeared to me at the same time and were, *per impossibile*, attached to the same $idea_m$. Of course the actual sun, the external counterpart of my $idea_o$ of the sun, has different properties from those of the actual moon: it is bigger, brighter, different in color, and farther away from me, among other things. And there is no doubt that this difference of properties is somehow reflected in the $ideas_o$ I have, at least typically. But the dissimilarity of the actual sun and moon cannot be, nor can it wholly account for, the dissimilarity of my $ideas_o$ of the sun and the moon. Not all $ideas_o$ have actual counterparts: those I have of the chimera and of Pegasus do not, yet they do differ from one another. And sometimes dissimilar $ideas_o$ have the same actual counterpart: Descartes' two ideas of the sun, for example. Nor can we say that the different $ideas_o$ themselves have the different properties in question: different size, color, and so forth. For $ideas_o$ all exist in the mind, and nothing in the mind has any size, color, and the like; besides which, these are actual properties, and it is hard to see how any but actual beings could have actual properties.

Descartes in fact suggests two ways of dealing with this problem. One is to ascribe properties to $ideas_o$, the same properties that actual beings have, but to do so in some qualified manner; for example, by saying that an $idea_o$ appears to have the property of being F or that it is as-if (*tanquam*) F. The other way is to postulate objective counterparts of the properties actual beings have; that is, objective counterparts of actual properties—objective size, color, distance, and also wingedness and monsterhood and being goat-bodied. The two ways perhaps come to the same thing in the end, for we can certainly express the fact that something has objective F-ness by saying that it is objectively F, and Descartes often does this. It is then just a short step to saying that the thing in question is as-if F. Descartes indeed states a principle linking these latter two idioms: "Whatever things we perceive as-if (*tanquam*) in the objects of ideas, are in the ideas themselves objectively" (Second Reply: AT VII, 161; HR II, 53).[21]

One property of things that is of special importance to Descartes is *reality*. This is the property the objective counterpart of which is most often discussed in the Cartesian texts. The causal principle relating objective reality to formal or actual reality is, after all, the crucial premise in Descartes' main argument for the existence of God. Objective reality is always attributed to ideas by Descartes. Since, as we have now seen, it is only objective beings that can be said to have objective properties, the precise subject to which objective reality is ascribed must always be an $idea_o$. This means not only that it is not the actual sun, as opposed to the sun in my mind, that objective reality belongs to, but also that it is not an $idea_m$, the mental act by which I think of the sun. Both the actual sun and my mental acts have formal, not objective, reality, since both have formal or actual being rather than objective being. Descartes sometimes indeed attributes formal reality to ideas. But it is clear that, when he does so, the subjects of attribution are $ideas_m$. There are also a few passages in which it appears that one and the same idea is being said to have both formal and objective reality. In the Third Meditation, for example, Descartes writes: "Such is the nature of this idea [sc. my idea of heat or of a stone], that of itself it requires no other formal reality besides that which it borrows from my thought, of which it is a mode. But for this idea to contain this or that objective reality rather than another, it must certainly get it from some cause in which there is at least as much formal reality as the idea contains of objective reality" (AT VII, 41: HR I, 162–163). A careful reading of this passage, however, reveals that objective reality is not being *ascribed* to the idea that is said to have formal reality—and which is, ipso facto, an idea$_m$. The idea here is not said to *have* objective reality—or to *be* objectively real—but rather to *contain* it. Nor should the use of this word "contain" be surprising, if indeed the precise subject of objective reality is an idea$_o$ for I have already characterized an idea$_o$ as the "content" of an idea$_m$. The same point can also be made, I believe, for the rest of the passages in question.[22]

It is evident from the preceding paragraph that objective reality must be distinguished from objective being in Descartes' philosophy. No less is reality itself (formal reality) to be distinguished from (formal or actual) being. Being belongs to a thing or it doesn't; either something is or it isn't. But reality admits of degrees; everything that is has some of it, and some things have more than others (Second Reply: AT VII, 165; HR II, 56). The same is true of objective reality and being. Few commentators seem to have noticed this difference.

Descartes maintains that we have ideas of things that have properties—for example, the sun, other men like ourselves, the chimera, God. These are the ideas$_m$ that exhibit or represent substances. We also have ideas of properties by themselves, ideas$_m$ that represent modes or accidents (Meditation III: AT VII, 40; HR I, 1620: examples are the size of the sun and the heat of the fire by which I am sitting. Size is an instance of a class of qualities (of bodies) that Locke and later philosophers called "primary"; heat is a "secondary" quality. (Descartes makes this distinction—see, e.g., Meditation III: AT VII, 43; HR I, 164; and *Principles* I, 69: AT VIII–1, 33–34; HR I, 248—but does not employ this terminology.) It is to be noted that the properties in these two cases are particulars, no less than the substances in which they inhere are particulars. Given Descartes' position that what is represented by an idea$_m$ is an idea$_o$, and that an idea$_o$ is just the thing it is said to be of, in, so to speak, its objective version, we can say that objective particular properties are among the ideas$_o$ he recognizes, as well as objective particular substances.

There are, then, objective particulars, both substances and qualities, in Descartes' philosophy. There are also objective universals, again both substance- and property-universals, though this is not a distinction Descartes takes any note of. There is, however, this difference between these two types of idea$_o$, that whereas objective particulars have actual counterparts, typically anyhow, objective universals do not.[23] In the case of universals, in other words, the qualification "objective" is otiose; for Descartes, universals *are* ideas (*Principles* I, 58–59: AT VIII-1, 27–28; HR I, 242–243; cf. Letter to Regius, 24 May 1640: AT III, 66; K, 74). The Cartesian theory of universals is never developed in any detail, and what little is said on the topic raises problems both of interpretation and of philosophical substance, problems which cannot be gone into here.[24] For our purposes, it suffices to note that the ideas with which universals are to be identified are ideas$_o$.

I think I have now said enough about what an idea$_o$ *is* for Descartes. The next question concerns what it is for a person to *have* an idea$_o$. We know that an idea$_o$ must occur in association with an idea$_m$. We know further that the idea$_o$ is represented by its associated idea$_m$. It appears, then, that for me to have a certain idea$_o$ is simply for it to be the representatum of some idea$_m$ that I have. An idea$_m$ is a mental operation or act; I have an idea$_m$ by experiencing it, or by its taking place in my mind; and it stands to me as a mode of the substance I am. An idea$_o$, therefore, bears to me the compound relation consisting of its being represented by an idea$_m$, and the latter's belonging to me as a mode. The idea$_m$, we might say, is mine directly; but I have the idea$_o$ indirectly, by way of the idea$_m$.

This is not the whole story, however. For representation, at least as Descartes conceives it in the *Meditations* preface, is not merely a two-termed relation between a mental state and an object of thought, with a thinker attached, as it were, by a different relation to the mental state.

Representation is rather a three-termed relation with the thinker as one of its terms. The thinker's (or the mind's) role in representation itself is just as essential as that of the representing state, and its link to the represented object is no less intimate and direct. The mind, or myself, Descartes says, is what the objects of my thought are represented *to*. My mental acts serve to represent things, but they represent them *to me*. The verb *"repraesentare"* occurs very often in Descartes' text with an indirect object, specified by a dative construction; ideas very often represent things to someone; and the same occurs also with the verb *"exhibere,"* which Descartes uses interchangeably with *"repraesentare"* in this connection.[25] The things that are represented (in the sense of the word under discussion) are always, it must be remembered, objective entities, internal objects of thought, ideas$_o$: it is the objective sun that my idea$_m$ of the sun represents or exhibits to me.

But there is even more to it than this. The representative entities in Descartes' view, the ideas$_m$ that, so to speak, do the representing to me, are more properly instruments or vessels than agents. My idea$_m$ of the sun is that by which the (objective) sun is brought before or rendered present to me. Descartes sometimes says that his ideas (by which he means his ideas$_o$) *appear* (*obversantur*) to him or to his mind.[26] Now for something to appear or be present to or simply be before the mind, as Descartes uses these expressions, is not merely for it to have a certain locus or status with respect to the mind. It is for the mind to grasp or apprehend it, and to do so, moreover, in a way that implies *consciousness*. From the mind's point of view, the representation relation is a matter of "perceiving" or "contemplating" or "understanding (*intelligendi*)" or "intuiting" or "cognizing (*cognoscendi*)" or "sensing" ideas$_o$, all of which terms designate conscious mental activities or attitudes on the part of the mind. For me to have an idea$_o$ of the sun, in sum, is for me to be aware of the sun, understanding by "the sun" here, of course, "the objective sun."

I noted earlier that consciousness, besides being an ingredient of all cognitive or perceptual acts (ideas$_m$), also must have an object, and that the objects of consciousness are ideas$_o$. Having seen the way in which consciousness is, so to speak, built into the representative relation, the relation that links ideas$_m$ and ideas$_o$ in and to the mind, we are now in a position to see how it is that ideas$_o$ are able to serve in this capacity. I see the sun; in doing so I have an idea of the sun; and this means, in the terms of the Cartesian theory, both that I have an idea$_m$ and—in a different sense of the phrase—that I have an idea$_o$. In addition, Descartes would say, I perceive my idea of the sun and thus am conscious of it as well. In this case, however, it is only the idea$_o$ *of which* I am conscious, and not the idea$_m$. The object of my awareness—what I perceive—is the objective sun; it is not my perceptual state or my being aware.

The foregoing effort to spell out what it means for someone to have an idea$_o$ has required us to specify the main features of the representation relation in the Cartesian theory—a task we deferred several pages ago. It is important to realize, however, that the relation we have just been describing is very different from the relation philosophers are wont to call by that name. Our relation, the relation invoked by Descartes in the *Meditations* preface, is wholly intramental. Its terms, apart from the mind itself, are ideas$_m$ and ideas$_o$, and these exist solely within the mind. The philosophers' relation, by contrast, serves to link entities inside with entities outside the mind, things that exist in the "external world." It is, furthermore, (at least quasi-) semantic in nature: representing in the philosophers' sense is akin to standing for or signifying or depicting or referring or denoting. In the Cartesian sense, *re*presentation is really *pre*sentation, in which the represented entity itself, and not merely some sign or symbol thereof, is displayed or brought before the mind.

These two relations are different; but my point here is only that they must be distinguished, and not confused with each other. I am not saying that the philosophers' relation is not to be found in the Cartesian theory. On the contrary, I have already taken note of its presence, for this is precisely the relation that holds between an idea$_o$ and its actual counterpart, in those cases in which an actual counterpart exists. And not only is this relation recognized by Descartes himself, in addition to that mentioned in the *Meditations* preface; but the same word "represents," is often used to express it.[27] Here we have another instance of the Cartesian practice of using one technical term with two or more distinct meanings. As for the importance of representation in this other sense of the word, I have remarked it as well. There is in fact no topic, of all those I have mentioned and not pursued in this paper, whose full airing is more crucial to understanding the Cartesian theory as a whole.

I come now to my final question, that concerning the relation between ideas$_m$ and ideas$_o$, in the sense of the nature of the distinction between them. That ideas in Descartes' two senses of the word are distinct in some way or other is established by his having distinguished them, and further by the fact that we have been able to consider them separately. But we have also seen that there is no idea$_m$ that is not joined to some one idea$_o$ by the representative relation, and conversely. So these are not things that are even capable of existing apart from each other. Descartes himself, in the *Principles*, recognizes three sorts of distinction, "real," "modal," and "rational" (*Principles* I, 60–62: AT VIII–1, 28–30; HR I, 243–245). Forced to choose among these, we should have to say that an idea$_m$ and its associated idea$_o$ are only distinct *ratione*; but this turns out not to be very illuminating. The trouble is that Descartes gives us very little beyond this to go on. There is perhaps a clue to be found in the Cartesian habit, already noted, of speaking of ideas as "containing" things, the specification of which makes it evident that they, the contained things, are objective entities of various types, hence ideas$_o$. This being so, the ideas that do the containing must be ideas$_m$. And what this suggests is that ideas$_m$ in general are being conceived as vessels or coffers, and ideas$_o$ as their contents. We know that an idea$_m$ is a mode for Descartes, and that a mode is a dependent entity; it must be attached to a substance—a mind—in order to exist. To consider an idea$_m$ by itself, therefore, is to abstract it from the substance to which it belongs; and the subject of consideration is then an abstraction, whereas the original substance, including this mode, is a concrete entity. In similar fashion, Descartes may be thinking of an $idea_m$ with its associated $idea_o$—container and content together—as a kind of *concretum*, like a bottle of wine; and of the $idea_o$—and the content—as an abstraction from that: the wine by itself. To be sure, the *concretum* in this case is itself an abstraction, absolutely speaking. It is only concrete by comparison with the $idea_o$—which is to say, it is more, or more nearly, concrete. But, by the same token, the $idea_o$ is abstract by comparison with it, hence more, or rather doubly, abstract. This metaphor of container and contents must not, of course, be followed too far: an $idea_m$ cannot be emptied of content, nor can an $idea_o$ be transferred to a different container. But $ideas_o$ do seem to be abstract entities for Descartes, in a way that $ideas_m$ are not; and the metaphor does suggest a means of understanding this fact. This is hardly a full answer to the question before us; but no fuller answer, as far as I have been able to tell, is to be found in the Cartesian texts.[28]

NOTES

1. In addition to the abbreviations AT, HR, and K (explained in the General Bibliography at the beginning of this volume), I use MSM for Michael Sean Mahoney's translation of *Le Monde* (New York: Abaris Books, 1979); TSH for Thomas Steele Hall's translation of the *Treatise on Man* (Cambridge: Harvard University Press, 1972); PJO for Paul J. Olscamps' translation of the *Discourse on Method* (Indianapolis: Bobbs-Merrill, 1965); and JC for John Cottingham's translation of the *Conversation with Burman* (Oxford: Clarendon Press, 1976). The English translations of the Cartesian passages I quote are usually my own, and not those of the publications cited (especially in the case of Haldane and Ross), though I have often been guided by the latter. In quoting from the *Meditations* I have used the original Latin text, unless otherwise noted.

2. The works in question are the *Regulae* and *l'Homme*; passages in which "idea" occurs with the meaning "corporeal image" are, e.g., *Regulae* xii (AT X, 414; HR I, 38); *Regulae* xiv (AT X, 441; HR I, 56); and *l'Homme* (AT XI, 174, 175, 176–177, 181, 183, 185, and 201; TSH 83, 84, 86–87, 92, 94, 97, and 113).

3. Two examples are to be found, however, in Part Five of the *Discourse* (AT VI, 55; HR I, 115), and four in Parts Two and Three of the *Passions* (AT XI, 384, 417, 429, and 444; HR I, 364, 384, 391, and 400). Passages in which Descartes repudiates the use of "idea" to mean "corporeal image" are to be found in, e.g., the Second Reply (AT VII, 160–161; HR II, 52); Third Reply (AT VII, 181; HR II, 67–68); Fifth Reply (AT VII, 363–364; HR II, 215); and in his Letter to Mersenne, July 1641 (AT III, 392–393; K, 105).

4. Nor does he even consistently so call them in his early works. In *Le Monde* and *La Dioptrique*, both of which were apparently written around the same time as *l'Homme*, and only shortly after the *Regulae*, corporeal images are called "images" or "pictures," and the word "idea" is reserved for entities that are mental in nature and exist in the soul or mind. See, e.g., *Monde* (AT XI, 3, 4, 5, and 10; MSM, 1, 3, 5, and 13); and *Dioptrique* (AT VI, 85, 112, 113, and 131; PJO, 68, 89, 90, and 101).

5. See, e.g., the Letters to Mersenne of 16 June 1641 and 22 July 1641 (AT III, 383 and 418; K, 104 and 108); to Hyperaspistes, August 1641 (AT III, 424 and 430; K, 111 and 117); and to Clerselier, 17 February 1645 (AT IV, 187). The *Meditations* passages in question are in Meditation III (AT VII, 51; HR I, 170); and in Meditation V (AT VII, 67; HR I, 182); but the former of these needs to be read in conjunction with Hobbes' Objection and Descartes' Reply at AT VII, 187189; HR II, 72–73. See also Descartes' Reply to Gassendi (Fifth Reply: AT VII, 382; HR II, 228).

6. This contention is developed and defended in my paper, "Descartes on Innate Ideas," forthcoming.

7. Letter to Hyperaspistes, August 1641 (AT III, 423; K, 111); cf. Letter to Gibieuf, 19 January 1642 (AT III, 478; K, 125); and Letter for Arnauld, 4 June 1648 (AT V, 193; K, 231).

8. See Meditation III (AT VII, 34–35; HR I, 157) for an instance of such use. Further, whenever Descartes characterizes ideas—as he frequently does—as "modes of thinking," it is this sense of the phrase that he is employing. See note 14, below, for references.

9. This might be challenged, on the ground that two or more thoughts can occur in a mind at the same time. This is indeed a possibility that Descartes admits—at least he does so if the *Conversation with Burman* is an accurate report of things that he said. But he also makes clear that the number of thoughts that a mind can entertain simultaneously is limited. See *Conversation with Burman* (AT V, 148; JC 6).

10. *Conversation with Burman* (AT V, 150; JC 8); cf. Letter for Arnauld, 29 July 1648 (AT V, 221; K, 234–235).

11. Or at least "accidental attribute," since though Descartes usually takes being an accident to entail being an attribute, in one passage he says that "some accidents, viewed in themselves, may be substances, as clothing is an accident of a man" (Letter to Regius, December 1641: AT III, 460; K, 121).

12. See Third Reply (AT VII, 175–176; HR II, 64); Fourth Reply (AT VII, 246; HR II, 115); and Letter to Mersenne, 21 April 1641 (AT III, 361; K, 100).

13. That some thoughts are not ideas is clearly indicated in Meditation III (AT VII, 37; HR I, 159); and also in a letter to Clerselier dated 23 April 1649 (AT VII, 354; K, 253). But there are one or two other passages that might seem to cast doubt on this. In a letter to Mersenne (28 January 1641: AT III, 295; K, 93), Descartes writes: "I claim that we have ideas not only of everything that is in our intellect, but even of everything that is in the will. For we are not able to will something without knowing that we will it, nor to know this otherwise than by an idea. But I do not hold that this idea is different from

the action itself." Descartes' meaning here is not altogether clear, but he could be interpreted as saying that volitions themselves *are* ideas—which directly contradicts what he says in the *Meditations* passage just cited. See also Descartes' Response to Hobbes (AT VII, 181; HR II, 68). Anthony Kenny discusses these passages, and the problems they pose for the Cartesian theory, in his *Descartes* (New York: Random House, 1968), 111–114.

14. Ideas are called "modes of thinking (*modi cogitandi*)" in, e.g., Meditation III (AT VII, 40; HR I, 161); and in *Principles* I, 17 (AT VIII–1, 11; HR I, 225). Passages in which ideas are said to be thoughts (*cogitationes*) are to be found in, e.g., Meditation III (AT VII, 35; HR I, 158, and AT VII, 37; HR I, 159). There are also a few passages in which Descartes says not that ideas are thoughts, but something slightly different, namely, that ideas are the *forms* of thoughts. See, e.g., Second Reply (AT VII, 160; HR II, 52); Third Reply (AT VII, 188; HR II, 73); and *Notae* (AT VIII–2, 358; HR I, 442). The explanation of this discrepancy, I believe, is that Descartes is speaking, in these latter passages, not of ideas$_m$ but of ideas$_o$.

15. See, e.g., Third Reply (AT VII, 185; HR I, 71); and Letter to Clerselier, 12 January 1646 (AT IX–1, 210; HR II, 129).

16. See *Passions* I (AT XI, 342; HR I, 340, and AT XI, 359; HR I, 350, et passim); cf. Letter to Regius, December 1641 (?) (AT III, 455).

17. There is some tendency on Descartes' part to use the word *"actio"* when he wants to convey the strong sense of "performance by an agent," and to reserve *"actus"* for the broader meaning. See the letters to Regius dated May 1641 (AT III, 372; K, 102) and December 1641 (?) (AT III, 454–455) for examples of *"actio,"* and the letter for Arnauld, 29 July 1648 (AT V, 221; K, 235) for one of *"actus,"* used in this way. There are a few passages, however, in which *"actio"* too seems to have the broad sense; see, e.g., Meditation II (AT VII, 26; HR I, 151).

18. What is the relation between myself and my mind for Descartes? In some passages he says that my mind *is* myself, whence it follows that I am not my body but merely have it in some way. In other passages, however, Descartes suggests a different relation: even though my mind and my body are substances, complete beings in their own right, nonetheless together they constitute something more unified, more "substantial" even, than a mere compound or composite. This situation poses an interesting problem for Cartesian scholars, but it is fortunately not one that we need to resolve.

19. It appears once in the Fourth Reply (AT VII, 233; HR II, 106), and once as a footnote to the Latin edition of the *Discourse* (AT VI, 559), both of which were written after the First Reply. Caterus' formula is also echoed, though not quite repeated, in the *Meditations* preface; this too was probably written after Descartes' exchange with Caterus.

20. Descartes is not at all clear on this question of the identity conditions for ideas$_o$. In general, his ontology makes no provision for any entity that is able to maintain its identity as one single thing while yet appearing or being instantiated at many different places or times. He is quite explicit in holding that universals are merely ideas or concepts (*Principles* I, 58–59; AT VIII–1,

27–28; HR I, 242–243). As such, they have no existence "outside our thought," and it is hard to see how they could be or occur in different minds, or even intermittently in the same mind, without so existing—especially in view of the Cartesian principle that "nothing can be in the mind, inasmuch as it is a thinking being, of which it is not conscious" (Fourth Reply: AT VII, 246; HR II, 115). It is true that Descartes appears to make an exception of mathematical objects, which are universals but which also have "true and immutable natures." In a few passages he suggests that the geometer's triangle, for example, has a mode of being that is different from both actual being and from objective being or being-in-the-mind (see Meditation V: AT VII, 64; HR I, 179–180; and the discussion of this topic by Anthony Kenny in his *Descartes*, 146–156). Even if so, however, these mathematical objects then *are* an exception, and the point holds for universals of all other kinds. There are several passages, however, in which Descartes clearly seems to be assuming that one and the same idea$_o$ can exist in different minds, or in the same mind at different times; see, e.g., Meditation III (AT VII, 44–45; HR I, 165); and Fifth Reply (AT VII, 371; HR II, 220–221). Indeed, this assumption appears to be made in the very passage in which Descartes' major account of universals is stated, at *Principles* I, 59—the passage just cited above. How, then, is this passage to be interpreted; and what *is* the Cartesian doctrine of universals? These are questions that a full account of the theory of ideas would have to resolve.

21. The context makes it clear that by "things we perceive" in this passage Descartes means properties, and I am assuming that "objects of ideas" refers to internal *res cogitatae*, e.g., to the sun existing objectively in the intellect.

22. One such is to be found in Meditations III, in the paragraph immediately preceding that in which the passage quoted occurs (AT VII, 40; HR I, 162). I know of no other place in which it appears that objective reality is being ascribed to what is clearly an idea$_m$—or formal reality to an idea$_o$, for that matter. There are of course many other passages in which objective reality is said to be "contained" in an idea. But these are passages in which the idea in question is certainly an idea$_o$. It might then be objected that ideas$_o$ are supposed, by my own profession, to *have* objective reality and not just to contain it. My response to this is that Descartes evidently does use "contain" to convey property possession, and does so frequently in this very connection. But my point was that "contain" does not *have* to be so understood, and *is* not to be where the context suggests that some other sort of relationship is being contrasted with that of containment. This condition is met in the case of the two passages cited, and is not in the others.

23. If mathematical objects do have a mode of being distinct from objective being (see note 20, above), then mathematical universals—the ideas$_o$ corresponding to these objects—could be said to have counterparts. But these still would not be actual counterparts, since they would not be actual beings.

24. Some of these problems are, however, suggested in note 20, above.

25. For *"repraesentare"* used in this way see Meditation III (AT VII, 44; HR I, 164); Second Reply (AT VII, 136; HR II, 35); Fifth Reply (AT VII, 385; HR II, 230); and Letter to [Mesland], 2 May 1644 (AT III, 12X; K, 152). For *"exhibere"*

see Meditation III (AT VII, 40; HR I, 162); Fourth Reply (AT VII, 234; HR II, 106); and *Principles* II, 1 (AT VIII–1, 40–41; HR II, 254).

26. See, e.g., Meditation III (AT VII, 35; HR I, 158); and Meditation IV (AT VII, 59; HR I, 176).

27. Passages in which "represents" is used for the philosophers' "external" relation can be found, e.g., in Meditation III (AT VII, 44; HR I, 165); Second Reply (AT VII, 161; HR II, 52–53); Fourth Reply (AT VII, 234–235; HR II, 107); and *Principles* I, 59 (AT VIII–1, 27; HR I, 243).

28. Versions of this paper were read at the 1980 meeting of the Seventeenth-Century Study Group at the Institute for Advanced Study in Princeton, and at Dartmouth College in 1983. I am grateful to my auditors on those occasions, and particularly to Robert Adams, Willis Doney, and Robert Sleigh, for helpful criticism.

9

The Second Meditation and the Essence of the Mind

JOHN P. CARRIERO

Recent interpretations of Descartes' views on the nature of the mind—
that the indubitability of mental states reveals its essence—fail to
understand the structure of the argument of the Second Meditation,
fail to see it as a single, coherent investigation. If the mind is characterized by the fact that we have a special awareness of our existence because we have a special awareness of our mental states, then the Meditation presents not a sustained argument but a series of reminders:

> . . . most of the work of changing the notion of "mind" [is] done under the
> table, not by any explicit argument but simply by verbal maneuvers which
> [reinterpret the notion] at each passage in which the mind-body distinction
> came to the fore.[1]

On this reading, Descartes' yoking his discussion of the essence of
the mind with a discussion of the real nature of a piece of wax appears
wholly fortuitous.

A chief reason for this misreading of the Second Meditation is that,
partly because of Descartes' enormous influence on subsequent philosophical thought, we have forgotten the high Scholastic tradition he
inherited, rejected, and reshaped. Since Descartes borrows a good
deal of the structure for the presentation of his account of the mind
from his predecessors, it is impossible to follow the argument of the
Second Meditation without some attention to Scholastic teaching on
intellectual self-knowledge. In the Second Meditation Descartes tries

to do exactly what Aquinas thought could not be done: he tries not only to prove his existence but also to understand the *nature* of the human mind without assuming that body exists. It is this enterprise that links the *cogito* with the rest of the Second Meditation and, in particular, with his consideration of the nature of a piece of wax, thus forming a single, sustained argument.

Like Aristotle, Aquinas thought that the senses as well as the intellect were necessary for human understanding. He held that Socrates' understanding of the universal, *doghood*, presupposes his having had sensory experience of individual dogs. When Socrates has sensory experience of a dog, his sensitive soul becomes in a way identical with a single, materially individuated, dog; his sensitive soul assumes the sensible form of the dog—the so-called *sensible species*. But sensory experience includes a great deal—the individual dog's particular color, odor, shape—that obscures the universal nature of dogs, which is the natural philosopher's primary concern. The intellect must abstract from all that belongs to the particularity of individual dogs in order to arrive at an understanding of the universal, *doghood*. When abstraction occurs, a new sort of identity emerges between cognizer and cognized; the intellectual soul assumes the intelligible form of the dog's universal nature, the so-called *intelligible species*. Aquinas gives the senses the crucial role of providing the intellect with the material that is necessary in order for the intellect to understand, but it is the intellect itself that performs the highest cognitive operation, understanding:

According to [Aristotle's] opinion, then, on the part of the phantasms, intellectual knowledge is caused by the senses. But since the phantasms cannot of themselves affect the passive intellect and require to be made actually intelligible by the active intellect, it cannot be said that sensible knowledge is the total and perfect cause of intellectual knowledge, but rather it is in a way the material cause. (ST I, Q. 84, A. 6)[2]

How does Aquinas, who believes that *nihil est in intellectu, nisi prius fuerit in sensu*, understand the role of sensory experience in our knowledge of the intellect and of God? If he cannot convincingly argue that what knowledge we do have of the divine and of the intellect can be traced back to the senses, then the scope of the principle *nihil est in intellectu, nisi prius fuerit in sensu* will be severely limited. Aquinas tries to show the relevance of sensory experience to our knowledge of God by arguing that human beings have no direct understanding of the nature of God—that is, of *what* God is—but only a knowledge of God acquired by indirect methods:

We conclude, then, that in the case of immaterial forms we know *that* they exist; and instead of knowing *what* they are we have knowledge of them by way of negation, by way of causality, and by way of transcendence. (*In Boetium de Trinitate,* Q. 6, A. 3)

And the senses clearly play a role in each of these three methods of knowledge:

Clearly, we cannot know that God causes bodies, or transcends all bodies, or is not a body, if we do not form an image of bodies. (*In Boetium de Trinitate,* Q. 6, A. 2, ad 5)

How does Aquinas show the relevance of sensory experience to intellectual self-knowledge? Here are the central elements of Aristotelian/Thomistic teaching on intellectual self-knowledge:

1. *Two kinds of knowledge.* According to Aquinas, the intellect knows itself in two ways:

Therefore the intellect knows itself not by its essence, but by its act. This happens in two ways: In the first place, singularly, as when Socrates or Plato perceives that he has an intellectual soul because he perceives that he understands. In the second place, universally, as when we consider the nature of the human mind from knowledge of the intellectual act. (ST I, Q. 87, A. 1)

Elsewhere, Aquinas expresses the difference between the two kinds of intellectual self-knowledge as the difference between the way in which the soul knows *that* it is and the way in which the soul knows *what* it is:

Just as we know, through itself, that the soul is, in so far as we perceive its act, and we seek to discover what it is, from a knowledge of its acts and objects, by means of the principles of the speculative sciences, so also we know concerning the things that are within our soul, such as powers and habits, *that* they indeed are, by virtue of our perception of their acts; but we discover *what* they are from the qualitative character of their acts. (SCG III, 46, 11)

Let's consider each kind of knowledge in turn.

The first sort of knowledge that the soul has of itself is its automatic perception of its own individual existence through its perception of its cognitive acts. "The mere presence of the mind suffices" for this sort of knowledge, since "the mind itself [is] the principle of action whereby it perceives itself."[3] The fact that the mind automatically perceives its existence upon acting explains why no one can deny that he exists:

In the other way, [to think that something does not exist] is taken to mean that assent is given to what is thus conceived. In this sense, no one can assent to the thought that he does not exist. For, in thinking something, he perceives that he exists. (*De Verit.*, Q. 10, A. 12, ad 7)[4]

The second kind of intellectual self-knowledge is the intellect's knowledge of *what* it is. Aquinas attaches much greater importance to this sort of knowledge of the soul. It involves knowing "how it [the soul] differs from other things; which is to know its essence and nature."[5] As such, this way of knowing the intellectual soul is the "mode that the intellect and the intelligible are treated in the sciences."[6] Unlike the automatic perception of its existence from its acts, the intellect's knowledge of *what* it is requires "a careful and subtle inquiry," as evidenced by the significant amount of disagreement found among philosophers concerning the nature of the soul.[7]

2. *Methodology.* According to Aristotle, the faculties or powers of the soul are understood through their acts or operations and an act or operation is understood through its object.[8] For example, understanding the faculty of nutrition requires understanding eating, which in turn requires understanding food. Aquinas nicely summarizes how this methodology bears on understanding the intellect in *De veritate:*

> For, from the fact that the human soul knows the universal natures of things, [philosophers] have perceived that the species by which we understand is immaterial. Otherwise, it would be individuated and so would not lead to knowledge of the universal. From the immateriality of the species by which we understand, philosophers have understood that the intellect is a thing independent of matter. And from this they have proceeded to a knowledge of the other properties of the intellective soul. (*De verit.*, Q. 10, A. 8)

In accordance with Aristotle's methodology, Aquinas' sketch of our knowledge of the intellect begins by characterizing the object of human understanding, the universal nature of material things. The universal nature of a thing is immaterial in that it includes only what that thing has in common with the other members of its species; it does not include any of the thing's idiosyncratic features, that is, its individuating material features. But if the *object* of understanding is immaterial, then the intelligible species by which we understand that object—that is, the intellectual form through which our intellect is brought into conformity with the universal—must also be immaterial. Finally, since the intelligible species (which brings about the *act* of understanding) is immaterial, the subject in which the species inheres, the intellect (the *power* or *faculty* in which understanding takes place), must also be "a thing independent of matter."

Aquinas' conception of intellectual self-knowledge extends in a natural way the reasonable thesis that our understanding of *body* depends on sensory experience to encompass the *intellect* as well: if we can have no acquaintance with universals without sensory experience, then we cannot learn that the universal is immaterial without such experience, a fact that governs the rest of Aquinas' account of the intellect. The human intellect, like God, is known by us only remotely, through its relation to body. Just as we know God as that which is not a body, causes bodies, and transcends bodies, so also we know the human intellect as that which understands the universal nature of bodies.

3. *Essence.* Aquinas understands the Aristotelian methodology to require that the essence of the soul be investigated through the powers for which it is responsible:

We proceed from objects to acts, from acts to faculties, and from faculties to essence. (*In II De Anima*, Lect. 6, n. 308)

St. Thomas defines the soul as that which is ultimately responsible for all of a (living) thing's vital functions:

To seek the nature of the soul, we must premise that the soul is defined as the first principle of life in those things which live: for we call living things *animate*, and those things which have no life, *inanimate*. (ST I, Q. 75, A. 1)

Thus, according to Aquinas, the soul's essence is understood through an examination of the vital powers. The standard Aristotelian list of such powers comprises the faculties of nutrition and reproduction, the faculties of sensation, imagination, and locomotion, and, finally, the faculty of understanding.

4. *Types of dependence on body.* Because Descartes makes several claims about the dependence of human properties on body in the Second Meditation, it is helpful to note that his Scholastic predecessors recognized at least three ways in which a human property might depend on body. Some properties of a human being—such as having dimension or being capable of being sensed—follow from being embodied. Others—such as eating, moving, and sensing—that depend on the human soul also depend on body in that they occur *in* corporeal organs. Finally, human understanding, although taking place *in* an

immaterial subject, depends on the *possession of* corporeal organs to provide the sensory experience necessary for abstraction.

Let's turn to the Second Meditation. The general purpose of the Second Meditation, as indicated by the heading that Descartes gives to the Meditation, "Of the Nature of the Human Mind; and that it is more easily known than the Body," is to show that the *nature* of the mind—and not simply the *existence* of the mind—is more easily known than the body. Descartes echoes this sentiment in the Fourth Replies, where he claims that he has shown in the Second Meditation that the mind can be understood "in a complete manner" or "as a complete thing" apart from body:[9]

> But mind can be perceived clearly and distinctly, or sufficiently so to let it be considered to be a complete thing without any of those forms or attribute by which we recognize that body is a substance, as I think I have sufficiently shown in the Second Meditation; and body is understood distinctly and as a complete thing apart from the attributes attaching to the mind. (HR II, 99–100; AT VII, 223)

But what does it mean to understand the mind "in a complete manner" apart from body? Is such an understanding arrived at simply by forming an idea of an incorporeal thinking subject—by picturing to oneself, as it were, thought existing by itself in a thing-like condition? But allowing Descartes' position to rest on an unarticulated intuition concerning the possibility of incorporeal thinking subjects, makes his position unnecessarily arbitrary and mysterious; it leaves the sustained treatment of the nature of the mind in the Second Meditation unanalyzed.

Fortunately, the Aristotelian teaching on intellectual self-knowledge suggests a quite sophisticated picture of what is involved in a complete understanding of the human mind. In fact, the Aristotelian methodology for understanding the soul—namely, that its essence is to be understood through its powers, its powers through their acts, and its acts through their objects—yields a working map of the Second Meditation. After establishing his existence in the *cogito* passage, Descartes begins an investigation of "what I am, I who am certain that I am," the first conclusion of which is that his essence is to think ("I am, however, a real thing and really exist; but what thing? I have answered: a thing which thinks"). Then, after pausing to consider the role of the imagination in his newly acquired knowledge of himself, Descartes resumes his investigation of his nature by considering the powers and activities associated with his essence, thought. ("What is a thing which thinks? It is a thing which doubts, understands [conceives], affirms, denies, wills, refuses, which also imagines and feels.") Finally, Descartes distinguishes, though in a decidedly non-Aristotelian fashion, the special nature of his intellectual acts from the nature of his other cognitive acts.[10]

Descartes' general strategy for showing that the nature of the mind can be understood apart from body is to offer a complete account of the nature of his (existing) mind while assuming that no bodies exist. This project leads him to move against the medieval Aristotelian tradition on two fronts. First, he must reject the doctrine of abstraction: if the correctness of intellectual ideas depends on homomorphisms between the soul and the world originating in sensation and purified through abstraction, then it is nonsense to think that one can understand *anything* if no bodies exist. Against the abstractionist account, Descartes holds that God stocks the human understanding with a certain number of innate ideas at its creation. I have argued elsewhere that when Descartes brings into question the sensory foundations "upon which all of my former opinions rested" in the First Meditation, he has the doctrine of abstraction in mind.[11] I shall assume in what follows that the meditator enters the Second Meditation having suspended belief in the doctrine of abstraction. (Of course, to the extent that it turns out that Descartes employs concepts in his account of the nature of the mind that cannot be plausibly regarded as innate, he has failed to make his case against Aquinas.) Second, Descartes rejects the Aristotelian thesis that an account of understanding begins with a characterization of the object that the intellect apprehends, and works backward (or what seems to us backward) through principles concerning the identity of knower with known to a characterization of the nature of the intellectual self. It would be impossible for Aquinas to begin his account of what an (existing) intellect is without positing the existence of material particulars that share universal features. In the Second Meditation Descartes' attempt to offer a full account of the nature of an (existing) mind under the assumption that no bodies exist is, in the main, a response to the Aristotelian claim that the intellectual self can be known only remotely.[12]

Descartes' strategy of offering a complete account of the nature of his (existing) mind while assuming that no bodies exist serves his long-range aim of showing that the mind can exist apart from body. If he can offer a full account of the *nature* of the mind, an account of *what* the mind is, while assuming that no bodies exist, then he can reasonably claim to have shown that the nature of the mind does not depend on body; for, if the mind's nature did in fact depend on body, then (granting, of course, that the mind exists) one would not be able to work out an account of its nature without positing the existence of whatever corporeal entities are involved in its nature. The argumentative strategy depicted here differs from the infamous argument from doubt, that is, the argument that I can know that my mind is really distinct from body because I can be certain that my mind *exists* while being uncertain as to whether any bodies exist.[13] Commentators have rightly felt that the latter argument is untenable: that I can be certain that my apple tree exists without being certain that any roots exist does not afford good grounds for the conclusion that God could, if he so desired, create an apple tree without roots. Notwithstanding their disenchantment with the argument from doubt, commentators have also rightly felt that the skepticism with respect to the existence of body in effect throughout the Second Meditation must be playing *some* role in the meditator's coming to realize that the mind can exist without body. The interpretation presented here has the virtue of giving the skepticism with respect to the existence of body a prominent place in Descartes' development of the nature of the mind without leaving him with an argument that runs into the difficulty just canvassed: if I could have a full understanding of the nature of my (existing) apple tree while assuming that no roots exist, then, arguably, I would be in a position to conclude that God could, if he so desired, create an apple tree without roots.

Equipped with a conception of the general structure and strategy of the Second Meditation, we now turn to the first two moments in its treatment of mind, the *cogito* argument and the determination of the mind's essence. Descartes begins the development of his conception of the mind with the establishment of his existence through the *cogito* argument:

So that after having reflected well and carefully examined all things, we must come to the definite conclusion that this proposition: I am, I exist, is necessarily true each time that I pronounce it, or that I mentally conceive it. (HR I, 150; AT VII, 25)

The *cogito* represents an argument from the immediate reflexive perception of mental acts to the perception of one's existence. That Descartes intends his argument to be based on one's immediate perception of one's mental acts is clear from his response to the objection that any human act would have served just as well in a proof of his existence:

When you say that *I could have inferred the same conclusion from any of my other actions*, you wander far from the truth, because there is none of my activities of which I am wholly certain (in the sense of having metaphysical certitude, which alone is here involved), save thinking alone. For example you have no right to make the inference: *I walk, hence I exist*, except in so far as our awareness of walking is a thought; it is of this alone that the inference holds good, not of the motion of the body, which sometimes does not exist, as in dreams, when nevertheless I appear to walk. Hence from the fact that I think that I walk I can very well infer the existence of the mind which so thinks, but not that of the body which walks. (HR II, 207; AT VII, 352)

The reason that Descartes gives for the unacceptability of nonmental human acts is that one's knowledge of their existence is undermined by the hypothesis that he is dreaming: consonant with the general strategy outlined above, none of the argument in the Second Meditation is to depend on assumptions concerning the state of the corporeal world, such as "My legs are moving" or "My senses reliably indicate that my legs are moving." The *cogito* argument, therefore, depends on the following two claims: (1) the reliability of the perception of one's own mental acts does not depend on any assumptions concerning the corporeal world, and, in particular, does not depend on the assumption that one has sensory organs that accurately inform one of the condition of the corporeal world, and (2) one can perceive one's own existence through perception of one's mental acts. Let's look at each of these claims in turn.

It is difficult to see how (1) might be reasonably disputed. Even the Aristotelian tradition, a tradition not especially sympathetic to the claims of nonsensory cognition, was prepared to concede the obvious here, namely, that human beings do not need to be told when they are having thoughts. To be sure, Aquinas insists that the intellect's perception of its intellectual acts presupposes that proper intellectual acts have already taken place, which in turn presupposes sensory experience of the material world and therefore the possession of a body. This dependence of the intellect's perception of its acts of understanding on sensory experience does not, of course, entail that one must *know* that one has had sensory experience of the material world or that one possesses a body before one can be aware of one's intellectual acts. Obviously, one can be aware that one understands something while one is ignorant of the material preconditions that must obtain in order for such understanding to take place. Even for Aquinas, then, one's awareness of one's thoughts is not undermined by Descartes' dreaming hypothesis.

It is no less difficult to see how (2) might reasonably be disputed: since human beings do not need to be told when they are having thoughts, they do not need to be told that they exist. And the Aristotelian tradition was prepared to concede the obvious here as well, namely, that we can become aware of our existence through our awareness of our cognitive acts. As we saw above, Aquinas observed:

No one can assent to the thought that he does not exist. For, in thinking something, he perceives that he exists. (*De Verit.*, Q. 10, A. 12, ad 7)

And Aristotle himself had written:

We sense that we sense and we understand that we understand and because we sense this, we understand that we exist. (*Ethica Nicomachea*, 1170a30; McGlynn's translation of Thomas' citation at *De Verit.*, Q. 10, A. 8)

Descartes can thus reasonably expect that his use of the meditator's awareness of his thoughts as a way of leading the meditator to an awareness of his existence should cause little difficulty for the Aristotelian segment of his audience, the segment of his audience that one would expect to be the least sympathetic to his nonsensory account of the nature of the mind.[14]

Although Aquinas is prepared to concede the obvious concerning one's perception of one's mental acts, he is not prepared to go any further. He does not want such a concession to damage his adherence to the principle *nihil est in intellectu, nisi prius fuerit in sensu*, so he cordons off such introspective knowledge to the soul's knowledge of its individual existence, a sort of knowledge "for which the mere presence of the mind suffices," from the more important scientific knowledge of what the soul is, a sort of knowledge that requires "a careful and subtle inquiry."[15] Thus, although Descartes' claim to be able to prove *that* he is, while in a state of uncertainty concerning the existence of body, does not mark a clear departure from the teaching of his predecessors, his announcement immediately following the *cogito* passage that he will try to discover *what* he is, while in a state of uncertainty concerning the existence of body, does constitute a striking break with the Aristotelian tradition:

But I do not yet know clearly enough what I am, I who am certain that I am; and hence I must be careful to see that I do not imprudently take some other object in place of myself, and thus that I do not go astray in respect of this knowledge that I hold to be the most certain and most evident of all that I have formerly learned. (HR I, 150; AT VII, 25)

Descartes begins his investigation of *what* he is with a consideration of his previous beliefs about himself. He is interested, in particular, in those of his beliefs that he takes to have arisen in him naturally as opposed to those beliefs that he takes to be a product of formal training in the schools:

> What then did I formerly believe myself to be? Undoubtedly I believed myself to be a man. But what is a man? Shall I say a reasonable animal? Certainly not; for then I should have to inquire what an animal is, and what is reasonable; and thus from a single question I should insensibly fall into an infinitude of others more difficult; and I should not wish to waste the little time and leisure remaining to me in trying to unravel subtleties like these. But I shall rather stop here to consider the thoughts which of themselves spring up in my mind, and which were not inspired by anything beyond my own nature alone when I applied myself to the consideration of my being. (HR I, 150–151; AT VII, 25–26)

Although Descartes is content to dismiss the technical Aristotelian definition of man as a rational animal, something very close to the Aristotelian picture of the human being emerges from those "thoughts which of themselves spring up in my mind." Descartes' asymmetrical attitude toward different facets of the Aristotelian tradition is of a piece with his general attitude toward Scholastic philosophy as the systematization of the uncritical worldview of the common man.[16] Some parts of that tradition—such as its teaching on syllogisms and its use of technical definitions in terms of genus and species—belong primarily to the construction and so are best simply ignored or dismissed. Other parts of that tradition—such as its teaching on the relationship of sensation to human understanding and its teaching concerning the nature of the soul—remain close enough to a natural, if unconsidered, worldview to provide valuable starting places for Descartes' criticism. And so the meditator's beliefs about himself turn out to involve a division of his properties into those which could even belong to a (lifeless) corpse and those (vital) properties for which the soul is responsible:

> In the first place, then, I considered myself as having a face, hands, arms, and all that system of members composed of bones and flesh as seen in a corpse which I designated by the name of body. In addition to this I considered that I was nourished, that I walked, that I felt, and that I thought, and I referred all these actions to the soul: but I did not stop to consider what the soul was, or if I did stop, I imagined that it was something extremely rare and subtle like a wind, a flame, or an ether, which was spread throughout my grosser parts. (HR I, 151; AT VII, 26)

Descartes' previous opinions about himself mark a division into body and soul according to which his nonvital properties belong to body and his vital properties to the soul; and the actions he ascribes to the soul have been chosen to represent the major divisions of faculties on an Aristotelian account of the powers of the soul: nutrition ("I was nourished"), which is characteristic of the vegetative soul; locomotion ("I walked") and sensation ("I felt"), which are characteristic of the sensitive (animal) soul; and understanding ("I thought"), which is characteristic of the human soul.[17]

The Aristotelian picture of the human being that emerges from the meditator's review of his previous opinions provides Descartes with a useful background against which to discover more clearly "what I am, I who am certain that I am."[18] He proceeds by examining which, if any, of the things he used to consider to belong to himself still seem to belong to him. He takes up, first, the corporeal properties, the properties that he used to consider to belong to himself simply insofar as he is embodied:

> But what am I, now that I suppose that there is a certain genius which is extremely powerful, and, if I may say so, malicious, who employs all his powers in deceiving me? Can I affirm that I possess the least of all those things which I have just said pertain to the nature of body? I pause to consider, I revolve all these things in my mind, and I find none of which I can say that it pertains to me. It would be tedious to stop to enumerate them. (HR I, 151; AT VII, 26–27)

Descartes' reasoning here depends on his account, presented in the previous paragraph, of his naive understanding of body (i.e., "those things which I have just said pertain to the nature of body," which it would be "tedious to stop to enumerate"):

> By the body I understand all that which can be defined by a certain figure: something which can be confined in a certain place, and which can fill a given space in such a way that every other body will be excluded from it; which can be perceived either by touch, or by sight, or by hearing, or by taste, or by smell: which can be moved in many ways not, in truth, by itself, but by something which is foreign to it, by which it is touched: for to have the power of self-movement, as also of feeling or of thinking, I did not consider to appertain to the nature of body: on the contrary, I was rather astonished to find that faculties similar to them existed in some bodies. (HR I, 151; AT VII, 26)

Descartes' naive understanding of body is, in short, that body is what can be sensed, occupies space, and can be moved (but is not self-moved). But he can see no reason to conclude that the "I who am certain that I am" can be sensed, occupies space, or can be moved;

therefore, he has no reason to think that the "I who am certain that I am" is corporeal.

Descartes' discovery that he cannot affirm that he possesses "the least of those things" that "pertain to the nature of body" deserves close attention, as it is the place in the Second Meditation where he most directly touches on incorporeity of the mind. Exactly what is Descartes claiming here? One might have expected him to have begun with the relatively weak conclusion that whatever the "I who am certain that I am" is, it does not appear to be simply a body, since there are aspects of it, such as consciousness, for which body alone cannot account. Such a conclusion would have roughly corresponded to the Aristotelian conclusion that the soul is not identical with body because the soul is responsible for vital operations for which body alone cannot account. The conclusion that Descartes actually draws is, however, a good deal stronger: he can find no reason to attribute to the "I who am certain that I am" any of the properties that characterize his conception of body—he can find no grounds to locate the "I who am certain that I am" in a sensible, spatiotemporal order. His conclusion is surprisingly close, then, to the Aristotelian conclusion that the intellect is immaterial—that is, that human understanding does not take place in a corporeal organ as does nutrition or sensation. But the way in which he arrives at his conclusion differs significantly from the way in which Aquinas arrives at the conclusion that the human intellectual faculty lacks a corporeal organ. Aquinas reasons from the immaterial nature of the object of understanding, a universal, to the immaterial nature of the form through which understanding takes place, to the immaterial nature of the subject in which such a form can inhere, that is, the immaterial nature of the intellect. This course is not open to Descartes, who does not want to begin his account of the mind with a characterization of the object of understanding and work backward, on the basis of principles concerning the identity of cognizer with cognized, to a characterization of the subject of understanding. His route to this conclusion is, therefore, a good deal more direct: he observes that none of the properties that pertain to the nature of body seem to belong to the entity whose existence was demonstrated by the *cogito* argument.

The skeptical assumption that no bodies exist, which is in effect throughout the Second Meditation, does not play a direct role in Descartes' reasoning for the conclusion that the "I who am certain that I am" is incorporeal. Indeed, it would be absurd for Descartes to argue that, since he is certain that the "I who am certain that am" exists but uncertain that body exists, he has no reason to suspect that the "I who am certain that I am" is corporeal. For, since the corporeality of the "I who am certain that I am" is precisely what is at issue here, it is an open question whether when the existence of the "I who am certain that I am" was proven, the existence of a body was also thereby demonstrated. Indeed, a chief obstacle to the meditator's acceptance of the *cogito* argument was his inability to consider the mind apart from body:

I myself, am I not at least something? But I have already denied that I had senses and body. Yet I hesitate, for what follows from that? Am I so dependent on body and senses that I cannot exist without these? But I was persuaded that there was nothing in all the world, that there was no heaven, no earth, that there were no minds, nor any bodies: was I not then likewise persuaded that I did not exist? Not at all; of a surety I myself did exist since I persuaded myself of something. (HR I, 150; AT VII, 24–25)

As the meditator's previous beliefs about the soul include "that it was something extremely rare and subtle like a wind, a flame, or an ether, which was spread throughout my grosser parts" (HR I, 151; AT VII, 26), he will not be sure what to make of his ability to know that he exists while being uncertain whether any bodies exist; he will be unsure whether, in learning of his existence, he has also been convinced of the existence of some flame or ether. The observation that there is no reason to locate the "I who am certain that I am" in a sensible, spatiotemporal order—in short, his discovery that the "I who am certain that I am" is not a body—enables him to continue his exploration of his nature while remaining agnostic concerning the existence of body.

It might seem that, if Descartes has already provisionally arrived at the conclusion that the mind is incorporeal, there is not much that remains to be accomplished in the rest of the Second Meditation. This appearance, however, is quite deceptive. His dispute with Aristotelianism has barely begun. Even if the intellect or the mind or the "I who am certain that I am" is incorporeal, it does not follow that the *nature* of an (existing) mind can be understood without positing the existence of body. It might turn out, for example, that one cannot understand how one's intellectual acts differ from sensory or imaginative acts without positing the existence of a physical world composed of material individuals sharing universal natures. Even though the meditator has already come to the preliminary—and, from an Aristotelian perspective, relatively uncontroversial—conclusion that the "I who am certain that I am" is incorporeal, Descartes' account of the nature of the mind is incomplete.

After rejecting those properties that he formerly believed he possessed which could belong to a corpse, that is, to body alone, Descartes continues his investigation of *what* he is by turning to the properties that he formerly referred to the soul. Since the "I who am certain that I am" is not a body, the meditator is still left uncertain as to whether any bodies exist. And, since the meditator does not yet have good reason to conclude that any bodies exist, he is not in a position to attribute to himself those of the soul's faculties whose activities take place in corporeal organs:

Let us pass to the attributes of soul and see if there is any one which is in me? What of nutrition or walking? But if it is so that I have no body it is also true that I can neither walk nor take nourishment. Another attribute is sensation. But one cannot feel without body, and besides I have thought I perceived many things during sleep that I recognised in my waking moments as not having been experienced at all. (HR I, 151; AT VII, 27)

If I am not in a position to attribute to myself a mouth and stomach, legs and feet, or eyes and ears, then I am not in a position to attribute to myself a faculty of nutrition, a faculty of locomotion, or a faculty of sensation.

After observing that he does not have good reason to conclude that any of the soul's faculties that take place in corporeal organs belong to the "I who am certain that I am," Descartes comes to the one faculty that he can unproblematically attribute to himself:

What of thinking? I find here that thought is an attribute that belongs to me; it alone cannot be separated from me. I am, I exist, that is certain. But how often? Just when I think; for it might possibly be the case if I ceased entirely to think, that I should likewise cease altogether to exist. I do not now admit anything which is not necessarily true: to speak accurately I am not more than a thing which thinks, that is to say a mind or a soul, or an understanding, or a reason, which are terms whose significance was formerly unknown to me. I am, however, a real thing and really exist; but what thing? I have answered: a thing which thinks. (HR I, 151–152; AT VII, 27)

In this passage, which represents the culmination of the first stage of the meditator's attempt to know more clearly what he is, the meditator makes the central discovery that the essence of the "I who am certain that I am" is thought. The meditator has been brought to this discovery through reflection on the various properties that he is in the habit of attributing to himself. The only one of these properties which the meditator finds he is still able to attribute to himself is thought. But there is more: not only does the meditator find that thought belongs to the "I who am certain that I am," but he notices that thought "*alone cannot* be separated from me," and "I am *not more than* a thing which thinks" (emphasis mine). What lies behind this last discovery, I take it, is that the meditator has come to appreciate that it is something special about the nature of thought which licenses the *cogito* argument: that is, the meditator has come to realize that *any* act of thought and *only* an act of thought can be used to show the existence of the "I who am certain that I am." At this point in the meditation, Descartes thus has the meditator reconsider the *cogito* reasoning:

I am, I exist, that is certain. But how often? Just when I think; for it might possibly be the case if I ceased entirely to think, that I should likewise cease altogether to exist.

Having recognized that it is his awareness of his acts of thought that licenses the *cogito* argument, the meditator is able to move from the fairly superficial characterization of himself as the "I who am certain that I am" to a more fundamental characterization of the entity shown to exist in the *cogito* argument—a characterization that captures what it is about that entity which makes the argument for its existence possible. And so, upon appreciating the crucial role played by thought in the *cogito* argument, the meditator concludes: "I am, however, a real thing and really exist; but what thing? I have answered: a thing which thinks."[19]

If Descartes is to convince the Aristotelian members of his audience that he can understand what the mind is without positing the existence of body, he must convince them that he can distinguish the intellect from the lower cognitive faculties of sensation and imagination without positing the existence of a physical world composed of material individuals sharing universal natures. He uses the examination of a piece of wax as the occasion to differentiate his faculty of understanding from his other faculties of knowledge. It is for this reason that he structures the consideration of the piece of wax so as to show the meditator which of the cognitive faculties supplies him with his most "evident and perfect conception" of the nature of the piece of wax (HR I, 156; AT VII, 32). First, the senses are rejected as the source of the best conception of the wax: "Nothing of all that the senses brought to my notice [counts as my most distinct knowledge of the wax], since all the things that fall under taste, smell, sight, touch, and hearing, are found to be changed, and yet the same wax remains." Then, having reflected that his most fundamental understanding of the wax comes through the conception of it as something that is flexible and mutable, he considers whether the faculty of imagination could produce this conception ("But what is the meaning of flexible and mutable? Is it not that I imagine that this piece of wax being round is capable of becoming square and of passing from a square to a triangular figure?"). But the complexity involved in the conception of mutability and extension outstrips the representational power of the imagination ("I comprehend its [the wax's] potentiality for an infinity of such changes but I cannot run through an infinite number of them in imagination").[20] Descartes thinks that the imagination is unable to provide him with his best conception of the wax because the pictures formed by that faculty are incapable of depicting the rich mathematical structure implicit in the notion of extension—a deficiency that, as we learn in the Sixth Meditation, renders the imagination useless for "discovering the properties which go to form the distinction between a chiliagon and other polygons."[21] In the face of the shortcomings of the lower cognitive faculties, Descartes concludes that the "mind alone" must be responsible for his conception of the wax as an extended thing that is mutable:

We must then grant that I could not even understand through the imagination what this piece of wax is, and that it is my mind alone which perceives it. . . . But what must particularly be observed is that [the wax's] perception is neither an act of vision, nor of touch, nor of imagination, and has never been such . . . but only an intuition [*inspectio*] of the mind. (HR I, 155; AT VII, 31)

The mathematical conception of the piece of wax that leads Descartes to an appreciation of the nature of pure understanding is, of course, bound up with his rejection of Aristotelian science in favor of the new science.[22] If a piece of wax is fundamentally an element in a kinetic/geometrical array, it is not a particular substance sharing certain characteristic powers and qualities with other substances of the same species. And if the relationships among the piece of wax and other instances of extension are essentially determined by their position in a kinetic/geometrical matrix, then one no longer has cause to think that understanding the wax is a matter of abstracting from sensory experience the universal qualities that it shares with other particular substances. To conceive the piece of wax mathematically is not somehow to conceive its "universal." As Descartes insists, his intellect comprehends the individual piece of wax—the very same thing that his faculties of sensation and imagination comprehend:

We must then grant that I could not even understand through the imagination what this piece of wax is, and that it is my mind alone which perceives it. I say this piece of wax in particular, for as to wax in general it is yet clearer. But what is this piece of wax which cannot be understood excepting by the [understanding or] mind? It is certainly the same that I see, touch, imagine, and finally it is the same which I have always believed it to be from the beginning. (HR I, 155; AT VII, 31)

As the mathematical relationships among extended beings become central in the new science, sensory and imaginative experience, incapable of clearly depicting the distinction between a chiliagon and a myriagon, play only an auxiliary role in our comprehension of the physical world.

The nature of the intellect is not understood through the special character of its objects, but rather through its ability to produce representations of mathematical complexity that cannot have their origins in sensation or imagination. Whereas Aquinas characterizes the intellect in terms of its proper object, in terms of *what* it conceives, Descartes characterizes it in terms of *how* it conceives. To be sure, as both thinkers hold that understanding involves the correspondence of knower and known, neither believes that the nature of the faculty of understanding and the character of the subject matter of understanding can be understood independently of one another. The difference is in argumentative direction: Aquinas begins with facts concerning the subject matter of physics and argues on the basis of the correspondence of knower and known to the nature of the faculty that is responsible for the comprehension of such a subject matter; Descartes begins with an appreciation of the nature of an intellectual conception of body and argues on the basis of the correspondence of knower and known, through the divine guarantee, to the nature of the subject matter of physics. This difference in direction enables him to conclude in the Second Meditation that the conception of the wax provided by his mind alone is better than that afforded by the senses or the imagination, simply on the grounds that there is nothing found in the latter two conceptions "which might not as well have been perceived by the animals":

I prefer to pass on and consider whether I had a more evident and perfect conception of what the wax was when I first perceived it, and when I believed I knew it by means of the external senses or at least by the common sense as it is called, that is to say by the imaginative faculty, or whether my present conception is clearer now that I have most carefully examined what it is, and in what way it can be known. It would certainly be absurd to doubt as to this. For what was there in this first perception which was distinct? What was there which might not as well have been perceived by any of the animals? But when I distinguish the wax from its external forms, and when, just as if I had taken it from its vestments, I consider it quite naked, it is certain that although there may still be found some error in my judgment, I can nevertheless not perceive it thus without a human mind. (HR I, 156; AT VII, 32)

The difference in direction observed here is integral to Descartes' project of laying a new and permanent foundation for the sciences in an understanding of the mind, a project that would foster the sense over the next three centuries that philosophy can and should begin with questions of mind and knowledge.

The Second Meditation marks Descartes' attempt to undo the Aristotelian doctrine that the intellectual self is known only remotely. When the Meditation is read in this light, it is seen to consist of a sustained discussion of the nature of the mind, treating of the mind's essence and powers, and how the intellectual power—the mind alone—differs from the lower cognitive powers. Understanding the Second Meditation as a whole helps us to see the burden that each part must carry. Although the immediate reflexive perception of cognitive acts is important for Descartes' conception of mind, it does not by itself constitute that conception. Moreover, we see that his account of the mind's nature would be seriously incomplete without his treatment of our different conceptions of a piece of wax.[23]

NOTES

1. Richard Rorty, *Philosophy and the Mirror of Nature* (Princeton: Princeton University Press, 1979), 57–58.

2. The following conventions have been used in citing the works of St. Thomas Aquinas: The *Summa Theologica* (ST) is cited by part, question (Q.), article (A.), and, if relevant, objection (Obj.) or response to objection (ad). Thus, "ST I, Q. 2, A. 3, ad 4" is an abbreviation for the response to the fourth objection in the third article of the second question in the first part of the *Summa Theologica*. *De Veritate (De Verit.)* and *In Boetium de Trinitate* are cited in like manner. The *Summa Contra Gentiles* (SCG) is cited by part, chapter, and paragraph of the translation. Aquinas's commentary on Aristotle's *De Anima* is cited by book (roman numeral), lectio (Lect.), and note (n.).

The following translations of Aquinas's works have been used: *Aristotle's "De Anima" in the Version of William of Moerbeke and the Commentary of St. Thomas Aquinas*, trans. Kenelm Foster and Silvester Humphries (New Haven: Yale University Press, 1951; reprinted 1959); *The Division and Methods of the*

Sciences, trans. Armand Maurer (Toronto: Pontifical Institute of Mediaeval Studies, 1963) (a translation of the fifth and sixth questions of *In Boetium de Trinitate*); *Summa Contra Gentiles*, 4 pts. in 5 vols., trans. Anton C[harles] Pegis, Vernon J. Bourke, James F. Anderson, and Charles J. O'Neil (Notre Dame: University of Notre Dame Press, 1975; first published 1955–1957); *Summa Theologica*, 4 pts. in 5 vols., trans. Fathers of the English Dominican Province (Westminster, Md.: Christian Classics, 1981; first published 1911); *Truth*, in 3 vols., trans. Robert W. Mulligan, James V. McGlynn, and Robert W. Schmidt (Chicago: Henry Regnery Co., 1952–1954).

3. ST I, Q. 87, A. 1.

4. The first interpretation that Aquinas considers of "to think that something does not exist" is "to form the thought that something does not exist":

> To think that something does not exist can be taken in two ways. In one, it is taken to mean that these two things are grasped at the same time. In this sense, there is nothing to prevent one from thinking that he does not exist, just as he thinks that at one time he did not exist. However, in this sense, we cannot at the same time conceive that something is a whole and that it is less than a part of itself, for one of these excludes the other. (*De Verit.*, Q. 10, A. 12, ad 7)

5. ST I, Q. 87, A. 1.

6. SCG II, 75, 13.

7. ST I, Q. 87, A. 1.

8. An especially clear statement of this methodology is found at *De Anima*, 415a14–23:

> But if one is to say what each of them is (namely the intellectual power or the sensitive or the vegetative) one must first say what it is to understand or perceive by sense; for actions and operations are prior to faculties in the order of thought. And if this is so, one ought first to consider the appropriate objects; which are prior even to the operations and correspond to them; and thus to determine, in the first place, what these objects are—for instance, food and the sense-object and the intelligible. (Rendered by Foster and Humphries after the Latin translation of William of Moerbeke)

9. Descartes takes the expression "to understand in a complete manner" to mean the same thing as "to understand that a thing is complete" (HR II, 98; AT VII, 221; the abbreviations HR and AT are explained in the General Bibliography at the the beginning of this volume). It is worth observing that Descartes takes the relevant spadework concerning the nature of the mind to be so complete by the end of the Second Meditation that he would have gone on to argue for the real distinction there, were it not for the doubt raised in the First Meditation concerning whether "things are in their true nature exactly as we perceive them to be":

> Consequently, if I had not been in search of a certitude greater than the vulgar, I should have been satisfied with showing in the Second Meditation that *Mind* was apprehended as a thing that subsists, although nothing belonging to body be ascribed to it, and conversely that *Body* was understood to be subsistent without anything being attributed to it that pertains to the mind. And I should have added

nothing more in order to prove that there was a real distinction between mind and body. . . . But, since one of those hyperbolical doubts adduced in the First Meditation went so far as to prevent me from being sure of this very fact (viz. that things are in their true nature exactly as we perceive them to be), so long as I suppose that I had no knowledge of the author of my being, all that I have said about God and about truth in the Third, Fourth and Fifth Meditations serves to further the conclusion as to the real distinction between *mind* and *body*, which is finally completed in Meditation VI. (HR II, 101–102; AT VII, 226)

10. See below, pp. 214–215.

11. HR I, 145; AT VII, 18. See my dissertation, "Descartes and the Autonomy of the Human Understanding" (Harvard University, 1984; Ann Arbor, Mich.: University Microfilms, 1984), 4–31.

12. I am using "remotely" here in the same sense that it was used above on p. 205.

13. A discussion of the issues surrounding the argument from doubt is found in Margaret Wilson, *Descartes* (Boston: Routledge & Kegan Paul, 1978), 186–201.

14. Despite the general agreement here between Descartes and his Scholastic predecessors, there are significant differences over the details. For example, the fact that Aristotle remarks, on the one hand, that we *sense* that we sense, but, on the other hand, that we *understand* that we understand, is significant: the understanding is not (reflexively) aware of the senses' acts and the senses are not aware of the understanding's acts. For Aquinas, the only entity capable of being aware of all human cognitive activities—and therefore the only entity capable of accounting for what might be called "the unity of consciousness"—is the entire human soul, which, as we saw above, is what is ultimately responsible for all of a human being's vital functions (see Joseph De Finance's dissertation, *Cogito cartésien et réflexion Thomiste* [Paris: Beauchesne et Ses Fils, 1946], 44). There is no specifically cognitive faculty which, like the Cartesian mind, is aware of both the operations of the understanding and the operations of the senses. In particular, Aquinas restricts the use of the term *mens* to only the soul's immaterial powers, understanding, willing, and the incorporeal aspect of memory; understood in this way, *mens* does not include sensation or imagination (see Aquinas, *De Veritate*, Q. 10; and text no. 281 of Étienne Gilson's *Index scolastico-cartésien*, 2d ed. rev. and augmented [Paris: Vrin, 1979; 2d ed. first published 1966; 1st ed. first published 1913], which is taken from Aquinas' *In quatuor libros sententiarum Petri Lombardi*, Book I, Dist. 3, Q. 3, A. 1).

15. Surely one reason why Descartes is so difficult to pin down on the nature of the inference involved in moving from "I think" to "I am" (see, for example, Margaret Wilson's discussion in *Descartes* [Boston: Routledge & Kegan Paul, 1978], 51–71) is that his predecessors treated one's ability to perceive one's existence through the perception of one's cognitive acts as a special sort of knowledge, set apart from science. From their point of view, there is no reason to expect that this inference would fall under the usual scientific demonstrative patterns.

16. Descartes offers accounts of the origin of Aristotelian philosophical conceptions in, for example, his Reply to the sixth set of Objections, HR II, 251–255; AT VII, 436–442, and *Principles* I, nos. 71–73.

17. Significantly, Descartes uses the word *cogitare* (to think) here where one would have expected *intelligere* (to understand). Descartes needs the more general term because he is moving away from an Aristotelian conception of several faculties that are cognitively independent of one another in the way outlined in note 14 above, to a conception of a single mind, capable of different modes of conceiving: thus, when the mind acts alone, an act of pure understanding occurs, and when the mind acts in conjunction with body, either an act of imagination or an act of sensation occurs. This transition, which begins in the Second Meditation (see below, pp. 00 ff.), is not complete until the Sixth Meditation, where Descartes offers his positive accounts of imagination (HR I, 185–187; AT VII, 71–73) and sensation (HR I, 191–198; AT VII, 79–89).

18. I am, of course, not denying that this starting place might lead to a conclusion that is more historically conditioned than Descartes would be willing to acknowledge.

19. What Descartes has done thus far roughly corresponds to a Scholastic philosopher's coming to define the soul as the principle of life. Establishing the aptness of a definition is not, of course, a straightforward matter. For example, Aristotle, from whom the Scholastic definition of the soul is taken, does not define the soul until the first chapter of the second book of *De Anima*, after devoting the first book to a survey of other thinkers' views on the soul and to a consideration of the sorts of things for which a theory of the soul ought to account. Similarly, Descartes does not attempt to establish that the most fundamental characterization of, the essence of, the "I who am certain that I am" is thought, by arguing according to the (synthetic) geometrical method from a set of prior premises, but rather roots that discovery in a certain amount of reflection—but now a Cartesian kind of reflection based on one's native intellectual resources rather than on a patient working-through of the experience of other thinkers.

20. I have used Anscombe and Geach's translation, because Haldane and Ross's (textually unfounded) use of "imagine" in their translation—"No, certainly it is not that, since I *imagine* it admits of an infinitude of similar changes, and I nevertheless do not know how to compass the infinite by my imagination" (emphasis mine)—is confusing.

21. Descartes' criticism of the imagination in the Sixth Meditation is as follows:

But if I desire to think of a chiliagon, I certainly conceive truly that it is a figure composed of a thousand sides, just as easily as I conceive of a triangle that it is a figure of three sides only; but I cannot in any way imagine the thousand sides of a chiliagon, nor do I, so to speak, regard them as present. And although in accordance with the habit I have formed of always employing the aid of my imagination when I think of corporeal things, it may happen that in imagining a chiliagon I confusedly represent to myself some figure, yet it is very evident that this figure is not a chiliagon, since it in no way differs from that which I represent to myself when I think of a myriagon or any other many-sided figure; nor does it serve my purpose in discovering the properties which go to form the distinction between a chiliagon and other polygons. (HR I, 185–186; AT VII, 72)

22. A fuller discussion of Descartes' justification of the geometrization of nature is found in Part III of Gary Hatfield's "The Senses and the Fleshless Eye: The *Meditations* as Cognitive Exercises," included in this volume.

23. This essay develops material from my dissertation. I am grateful to my dissertation adviser, Paul Hoffman, for his helpful criticism of both the earlier work and the present essay; I am also grateful to the Mrs. Giles Whiting Foundation for financial support during my final year of dissertation work. Many friends and colleagues have read and criticized earlier versions of this paper; the substantive and detailed comments of Joshua Cohen, Gary Hatfield, and Amélie Rorty were especially instrumental in shaping the current draft.

10

Meaning and Objective Being: Descartes and His Sources

CALVIN NORMORE

I

The view that concepts are mental words and that thinking them is the forming of mental sentences was a commonplace within late Scholasticism. Though Descartes never explicitly adopts such a picture of thought, what he says about thinking can be explored with such a picture as a guide and many of the problems that arise for an account of the functioning of Cartesian ideas are also problems that arise for theories of the meaning and the reference of linguistic expressions. This suggests that some of the more striking features of Descartes' account of ideas may be features designed to provide an account of those aspects of thinking whose analogues for language are explored within theories of meaning and of reference. This essay is a partial exploration of that suggestion.

Descartes' doctrine of ideas is out of fashion. We do not think meaning is in our heads or that reference requires (something like) causal contact with the referent. Add these worries to the more traditional ones about the way ideas stand between us and the world and one has a strong case, at least prima facie, for consigning to the scrap heap a view that makes peculiar mental quasi entities, which are both private and innate, central to cognition. But this judgment of Descartes' view may be both unfair and wrong. Descartes develops a surprisingly powerful and sophisticated attempt to explain why thinking is informative and why it is informative about objects. Any adequate theory must deal both with issues of meaning and issues of references. When it is considered as an attempt to do both of these tasks, Descartes' view is not only ambitious but also attractive.

Thoughts, like words, refer and mean. A theory of reference is a theory of what expressions are about—a theory about how, in general, expressions connect with the world and, in particular, with which features or parts of the world an expression connects. It can crudely be distinguished from a theory of meaning, a theory about what a speaker or hearer who is proficient in the language understands. In the light of this distinction, we can further distinguish two extreme theories.

The "purely referential" theory is inspired by the view advanced in William Ockham's *Summa Logicae,* but has affinities with a number of twentieth-century accounts as well. This theory divides expressions into syncategorematic terms like *and, not, on,* and *all* and categorematic expressions like *man, moon,* and *man on the moon.* Categorematic expressions in turn divide into absolute and connotative. Connotative terms are made up of absolute terms and syncategoremata. If *man* and *moon* are absolute terms, *man on the moon* would be an example of a connotative term. Absolute terms are rigid designators. They pick out certain objects, the ones to which they are first applied, and if they are proper absolute terms that is all they do. If they are general terms, absolute terms pick out the objects to which they are first applied and all others of the same kind. Absolute terms have no a priori criteria of application; they are like labels.

The second extreme theory concentrates on the holism of meaning. With this second theory, picture language becomes like a map without a legend. Expressions mean what they do in virtue of their relations to other expressions and refer as they refer in virtue of what they mean. The bigger and more detailed the map, the fewer bits of the world it could plausibly be a map of. One might dream of a map so rich that only one way of assigning referents to its symbols would preserve accuracy, a map so rich it could only map one terrain. Similarly, one might hope that perhaps only one way of assigning meaning to words would give us a language whose analytic sentences are all true.

The hope associated with the second theory of language is almost surely vain. If the only constraint on meaning is that it determine reference in such a way that all the analytic sentences (or for that matter any consistent set of sentences) of the language come out true, then if the language is first-order or can be modeled in set theory, there will be many adequate models of any consistent set of its sentences. There will therefore be many ways of assigning referents (and, if that is what determines reference, meanings) to its terms that will meet the constraint.

But the first, purely referential picture of language suffers a difficulty akin to the one we've just seen, namely that, even if the references of rigid terms are fixed, one could be completely deceived about how they are fixed. Since absolute terms have no a priori criteria of application, I may be completely wrong about which interpretation of the terms is picked out and still accept exactly the same sentences. I believe that Jonah was a man. If "Jonah" in fact referred to a dog and "man" referred to dogs, there would be a (peculiar sense) in which my belief would be true. And yet surely I would be deeply deceived.

The lesson suggested by these difficulties is that, if it is to justify our confidence that we know what we are talking about, our account of meaning must be richer than either the quantificational holist or the pure referentialist will allow. We need to get at least some meaning back inside our heads so that what determines reference can both connect firmly to the world and be grasped a priori. It is this Janus-like role that Descartes intended his ideas to play.

II

Although the Third Meditation is subtitled "of God, that he exists," by far the greater part of it is devoted to the nature and behavior of ideas. The proof of God's existence emerges as an application of a general account of ideas.

Having turned his attention to himself at the very beginning of the Third Meditation Descartes discovers that he is certain that he is a *res cogitans* and that "those modes of thinking which I call sensings and imagining insofar as they are only some modes of thinking are in me." He then adduces his rule of certainty "that everything is true which I clearly and distinctly perceive."

Truth and falsity, then as now, are ordinarily properties of judgments or sentences and it would be natural to suppose the scope of the clarity and distinctness rule to be judgments. Strictly speaking that is true, but Descartes also admits

. . . some other material falsity in ideas when they represent a nothing as a thing [*cum non rem tanquam rem repraesentant*]: so for example the ideas which I have of heat and cold are so little clear and distinct that from them I am unable to learn whether cold may be a privation of heat or heat a privation of cold or both may be real qualities or neither. And because there can be no ideas which are not as if to be of things [*Et quia nullae ideae nisi tanquam rerum esse passunt*] if it is indeed true that cold is nothing other than the privation of heat the idea which represents that to me as something real and positive would not be called false without merit and so of the others. (AT VII, 43–44)[1]

Descartes' claim that "there can be no ideas which are not as if to be of things" is, as Margaret Wilson noted, the claim that ideas as such have what she calls "representational character." They "are received by the mind *as if exhibiting to it* various things or as if making things *cognitively accessible.*"[2] For Descartes, ideas are not *merely modi cogitandi* ready to be reflected upon. They purport to be about things, and it is this purporting that makes material falsity possible.

In the *Conversation with Burman* Descartes indicates that an idea is not materially false because it represents a nonexistent as an existent, but rather that an idea is materially false when what it represents (that is, what it purports to be an idea of) does not have the *reality* it seems to have.

For example: I may consider the idea of colour, and say that it is a thing or a quality; or I may say that the colour itself, which is represented by this idea, is something of the kind. For example, I may say that whiteness is a colour; and even if I do not refer this idea to anything outside myself—even if I do not say or suppose that there is any white thing—I may still make a mistake in the abstract, with regard to whiteness itself and its nature or the idea I have of it. (JC, 11)[3]

Ideas that are not clear and distinct may be materially false. They will be materially false if what they represent is not as represented. Whiteness, for example, is represented by our usual idea of it as a color—which is a quality—but it is Descartes' view that the only real qualities of matter are size, shape, and motion. Hence our usual idea of whiteness is materially false.

This discussion raises two questions. The first concerns the notion of reality at work here and the second concerns the ontology which Descartes supposes in his examples.

The notion that there are degrees of reality is an ancient one which is enshrined in medieval speculation through Anselm of Canterbury's discussion in his *Monologion*, of the pure perfections, and is developed by John Duns Scotus and his followers. It is, I believe, closely related to the notion of ontological dependence and it applies in the first instance not to objects but to natures. A nature A has a higher degree of reality than a nature B if when we analyze B we discover that it depends on A, that is, if an adequate account of what B is requires a reference to its dependence on A.

For Descartes God has the highest degree of reality. That is because God is absolutely independent. God could exist without anything else. Below God in the ontological hierarchy come finite mind(s) and extension. What each of these *is* cannot be adequately described without mentioning each one's relation to God. Next in turn come the modes of minds and the modes of extension. The natures of these in turn canot be adequately described without mentioning that they are modes of minds and extension, respectively. They have, thus, less reality than minds and extension themselves.

It is not the case that to have reality is to exist. Descartes, for example, thinks the chimera has reality but doesn't exist. But ideas that represent what has reality are ideas that could represent things. While having reality does not entail existing it does entail possibly existing. I will return to this connection further on.

The discussion of material falsity in Meditation III is part of Descartes' program for getting us to reject the "commonsense" ontology of things and their accidents in favor of an ontology in which the only real properties are "mathematicized": If this is so then we have reason to think that our ideas will have a surface structure and a deep structure. On the surface we will find ideas of whatever the commonsense ontology posits, but these ideas will be of two kinds. One kind, those ideas which are clear and distinct, will be ideas of the ingredients of the new ontology. The others, those ideas which are obscure or indistinct, will be so because they reduce structure—they represent a privation (which is a complex of a positive idea and a negation) as something positive, or a sensation (which is a complex motion) as something simple.

The possibility that ideas may represent without there being anything that is represented raises the question of the nature of the property of representing which ideas are said to have. What is it about an idea that makes it as if to be of things [*tamquam rerum esse*].

The key to answering this question lies in Descartes' remark that "some of these [thoughts] are as if images of things, to which ones alone the name of idea applies properly" (AT VII, 37). In making this claim Descartes is availing himself of a rich Scholastic tradition of discussion of the character of images. One prominent position within late Scholasticism requires that an image be causally dependent on the thing imaged and appropriately similar to it. These are jointly necessary and sufficient for one object to be an image of another. In this view, there is nothing intentional about the image relation: if the causal and similarity conditions are met, one thing is just an image of another.

The view that ideas are like images leads Descartes in what may seem to us a curious direction—namely, to distinguish between the formal and the objective realities of ideas. He is attempting to determine whether "some of those things the ideas of which are in me exist outside me" (AT VII, 40). If ideas are modifications of thinking, Descartes claims there is no hierarchy among them. But when we consider them as representations, they can be hierarchically arranged according to their degrees of objective reality.

> For without doubt those which exhibit substances to me are something more and, so I may say contain more reality objectively in themselves than those which represent only modes or accidents; and again that through which I understand some highest God, eternal, infinite, omniscient, omnipotent, and the creator of all things which there are besides himself certainly has more objective reality in itself than those through which finite substances are exhibited. (AT VII, 40)

The next step in the argument is to claim a principle connecting causes and their effects:

> For it is manifest to the natural light that there should be at least as much being [*esse*] in an efficient and total cause as in the effect of that cause. (Ibid.)

and to extend it to the objective reality of ideas and the causes of that:

> And this not only is clearly true of those effects of which the reality is actual and formal but also of ideas in which only objective reality is considered. (Ibid., 41)

Moreover just as the cause of something that is actual must be something actual so, surprisingly, must the cause of the objective reality of an idea be something actual.

> Nor ought I to suspect that since the reality which I consider in my ideas may be only objective, it is not necessary that the same reality may be formally in the causes of those ideas but suffices if it is in them also objectively. For inasmuch as this objective mode of being applies to ideas from their nature so the formal mode of being applies to the causes of the ideas, at least the first and principal one from their nature. (Ibid.)

This passage contains the core of Descartes' argument. It is because it is of the nature of the first and principal cause of an idea (or perhaps more accurately of the objective being of an idea) to be real formally that he can conclude that the cause of an idea of infinite perfection must be infinitely perfect, that is, must be God.

A superficial reading of this crucial passage might suggest that all ideas have objective reality, indeed that it is of the nature of an idea to have objective reality. But in his reply to Arnauld, Descartes clearly says something that entails the denial of this. Arnauld objects to Descartes' doctrine of material falsity with this argument:

> For what is the idea of cold? Cold itself inasmuch as it is objectively in the intellect. But if cold is a privation it cannot be in the intellect through an idea whose objective being is a positive being. Therefore if cold is only a privation there will never be a positive idea of it and so none which is materially false. (AT VII, 206)

Descartes' reply is that the idea of cold is not cold itself objectively in the intellect

> . . . for it often happens in obscure and confused ideas among which those of heat and cold are to be numbered that they are referred [*referantur*] to another thing [*quid*] rather than to that of which they are in truth the idea. Thus if cold is only a privation, the idea of cold is not cold itself as it is objectively in the intellect but another thing [*quid*] which is wrongly taken for that privation; certainly it is some sensation [*sensus*] having no being outside the intellect. (Ibid., 233)

The idea of cold then does not contain objectively the privation that is cold, but contains (is referred to) a sensation, which is the sort of thing for which the distinction between being objectively and being formally does not arise.

Riverside Park has formal reality (that of a mode of extension) and it exists. If I think about it, that is, form the idea of Riverside Park, then it has objective reality as my idea. In Descartes' view my sensation is an *ens positivum*, a positive being, but it has no being outside the intellect. Suppose then that I feel warm (that there is a sensation of warmth in me). Suppose that I think about it—think, for example, that this sensation of warmth is pleasant. Do I now form an idea in which the sensation of warmth is present objectively? If that were what happened then the epistemological transparency so crucial to getting the Cartesian program going would be undermined. On the assumption that it is not what would happen, my idea of this sensation of warmth is just the sensation itself. Descartes does not, of course, hold that thinking about feeling warm is feeling faintly warm. There may be all sorts of ideas of a sensation other than the sensation itself. But it seems a sensation is an idea of itself. While Descartes never actually says this, he claims that in some cases ideas are not distinct from their objects. He writes

I claim that we have ideas not only of all that is in our intellect, but also of all that is in the will. For we cannot will anything without knowing that we will it, nor could we know this without an idea; but I do not claim that the idea is different from the action itself. (K, 93; Letter to Mersenne, 28 January 1641)

It is a good thing that Descartes does not believe that the distinction between objective and formal reality extends to all ideas. In Meditation III Descartes claims of ideas that

. . . if indeed they are false, that is, represent no things, it is known to me by the natural light that they proceed from nothing, that is they are not in me from any cause other than something lacking in my nature. (AT VII, 44)

But from this and the principle that there is no more reality objectively in the effect than formally in the cause we can conclude at once that there is no more than zero reality objectively in false ideas. It follows, as Margaret Wilson has shown, that we must distinguish the representative character of Cartesian ideas from their objective reality. All ideas represent, or purport to be about, something. Some ideas really represent something and it is those which have objective reality.

If the Cartesian dream of an a priori science can be realized, there must in principle be a way of telling whether an idea has objective reality or not. Descartes thinks he has such a method but what he says leaves it unclear just what it is. Of his idea of God in Meditation III he says

. . . since it is maximally clear and distinct and contains more of objective reality than any other there is none more true in itself nor in which less suspicion of falsity arises. (AT VII, 46)

This makes it sound as though both clarity and distinctness and fullness of objective reality are grounds for thinking an idea true; but one needs to have grounds for thinking an idea true to be justified in thinking it has objective reality. This is not devastating. The problem with materially false ideas is that they are so obscure there is no telling what they contain objectively. But Descartes thinks that his idea of God is clear enough for him to see that it is certainly about an infinite being of the greatest perfection. But since the content of that idea specifies its object uniquely, in seeing that its objective content is the infinite being, one sees that it has the maximum objective reality. When an idea is clear and distinct, we can see how it represents— whether it represents by presenting us with an object objectively, or simply by itself being an object of a certain kind. Because this distinction is manifest we can tell when we require an explanation for the objective reality of an idea.

III

Almost all of the research on Scholastic background of this aspect of Cartesianism has focused on Descartes' debt to Thomas or to Francesco Suarez. There is reason for this. Descartes was educated in a Jesuit College (La Flèche) and the Jesuits were heavily influenced by the intellectual climate of the Spanish universities. In Spain, Aquinas' *Summa Theologiae* had largely replaced the *Sentences* of Peter Lombard as the keystone of theological training: Aquinas's thought had indeed moved to the center of Scholasticism. Suarez and Aquinas are among the few Scholastics whom Descartes mentions by name. But Thomism was not the only current within sixteenth-century Scholasticism and Suarez was far from the dominant intellectual figure. Because Descartes was concerned not to appear learned in Scholastic philosophy, and because we now know little about late Scholasticism, it is difficult to know where to turn. Rather than working back from Descartes I propose to begin in the fourteenth century and work forward.

The problem of objective being and its relation to being simpliciter arises within medieval philosophy within two contexts. The first is a context in debt to the *Timaeus*. In the *Timaeus* the Demiurgus looks to the *eidoi* to fashion the universe. The Forms have whatever ontological status they have independent of any mind. Philo of Alexandria in his *De Opificio Mundi* moves the Forms into the Divine Mind and there through the influence of Clement of Alexandria and others they are firmly lodged by the time of Augustine. They lodge uneasily, though, because the multiplicity of forms troubles the simplicity of the divine mind.

The second context within which objective being appears is that of accounting for informative thought. Alexander of Aphrodisias' *Commentary on Aristotle's De Anima* develops the doctrine that to understand something is literally to have its form in the intellect. Now of course the form cannot be in the intellect in the way in which it is in matter or we would literally become what we thought about. So it must be there in some unusual way. This problem and the related problem of how we can understand general terms if everything is particular seems to have inspired Avicenna's doctrine that a nature is in and of itself neither general nor particular. (Cf. *Sufficientiae*, pt. 1.) When it exists *in rebus* it is a particular, when it is *in intellectu* it is general.

But that is all prehistory and is assumed by the actors in the story I want now to tell. That story begins with Book I, Distinction 35, of Duns Scotus' *Commentary on the Sentences* where he asks the question "Whether in God there are eternal relations to everything knowable as quidditatively known."

Scotus' answer is that God is related to the knowable things in the third mode of relation (*Opera Omnia*, vol. 6, 258, para. 31).[4] This sort of relation is one which can be created or destroyed without change in at least one of the relata. Scotus claims that God does not change when He creates and when He determines what can be created (in an instant of nature). It is this last claim—that what *can be* created is dependent on God—which makes Scotus' position striking. He writes:

> . . . it can be conceded that there are eternal relations in God to things known [*cognita*] but not prior naturally to those things known as objects [*in ratione obiectorum*]. This can be maintained thus: God in the first instant [of nature] understands his essence under a simply absolute [non-relational] concept [*ratione*]; in a second instant he produces a stone in esse intelligibili and understands the stone so that there is a relation in the stone understood to the divine understanding but still no relation in the divine understanding to the stone but the divine understanding terminates the relation of the stone as understood to it. (Ibid., vol. 6, 258, para. 32)

A little later Scotus adds, speaking of "idea" in a sense he attributes to Augustine, "it seems that the stone understood can be called an idea" (ibid., vol. 6, 261, para. 40).

Scotus employs an account of knowledge in terms of objects with some sort of *esse cognitum* for the human intellect as well. For example in his *Lectura* I (Distinction 36, Question 1) he writes:

> . . . if it were supposed that I had been from eternity and that from eternity I had understood a rose then from eternity I understood a rose according to its *esse essentiae* and according to *esse existentiae* and however it had no *esse* except [*esse*] *cognitum*. . . . Hence the terminus of understanding is *esse essentiae* or *esse existentiae*—and however that which is the object of the understanding has only *esse diminutum* in the understanding. (Ibid., vol. 6, 469, para. 26)

A little later in the text he replies to the objection that if something is produced it must have *esse reale*. He replies:

> . . . it should be said that such is the being of something produced according as such a producing *esse* produces itself; here however a thing has *esse entitatem* in a respect [*secundum quid*] as it founds a relation of reason and therefore there is produced intelligibly [*intelligibiliter*] that whose *esse* is in a respect [*secundum quid*]. (Ibid.)

Scotus' doctrine requires that intentional objects, objects with *esse cognitum* or *esse diminutum*, be caused. The consequence being that objects of thought are in some sense distinct from the mind thinking them, which provoked a reaction. His close student and admirer William of Alnwick devotes five careful *Questiones Disputatae* to the subject. The burden of these questions is to show that the divine ideas are just the divine essence in so complete a way that it makes no sense to speak of them as produced by God. Alnwick is noteworthy not only because he focuses his criticism on the most striking similarity between the Cartesian and Scotist views but because he is, so far as I have been able to discover, among the first and perhaps the first to use the formal and objective terminology in this connection. In asking how the same thought can be a thought of many distinct things, if cognition and *esse cognitum* are the same, Alnwick replies:

I answer that for some things to be distinguished in being known [*esse cognito*] or being represented [*esse repraesentato*] may happen in two ways: in one way formally . . . [while] . . . in another way some things can be understood to be distinguished in being known [*esse cognito*] objectively because the cognition of them terminates at those distinct things or at the distinction between them. (Alnwick 26)[5]

So far the debate centered on objects of intentional intellectual acts like thinking. But it was soon extended to the status of hallucinations, apparent motion, and other sensory phenomena, and to the status of the objects of statues and paintings. Alnwick himself took the second step—persistently conflating the *esse cognitum* of Scotus's stone with the *esse repraesentatum* of a statue of Caesar. The first step was taken by Peter Aureoli who used the full panoply of illusions and hallucinations to argue for an *esse apparens*.[6] Among the examples Aureoli employed are virtual mirror images (examples he borrowed from Al-Hazen's *Perspectiva*). Objects of thought were in the mind, Aureoli argued, as images are in a mirror. The mirror account of mind is here employed in a precise and technical way.

The next step in the dialectic is the fourteenth-century debate between William Ockham and Walter Chatton, which led to Ockham's conversion away from a Scotist position to one quite different.

Ockham's interest in the queston of objective reality seems to have been motivated both by theological concerns about how God could know particulars and by epistemological worries.

Ockham begins (Primum Sentenitiarum, Distinction 2, Question 8) by considering how we could think about nonexistents including universals.[7] He concludes that such nonexistents must have *esse cognitum* or *esse objectivum*. Once he has this device available he then extends it (ibid., D. 25 Q. 5) to an account of how God knows each thing, existent or not, and from there to his account of how *we* know particulars. In this early view, for me to be aware of you or of a particular whiteness (note the extension to sensory qualities) is for you or that whiteness to be objectively in my mind.

Walter Chatton objected to objective-existence theories on three grounds. First he charged that they compromised direct realism by making the object of awareness the thing with *esse objectivum* (*Lectura* I, Distinction 3, Question 2).[8] Second, he claimed that objectively existent entities could neither be created nor destroyed (Prol., Q. 2). And, third, he claimed that they are redundant. This last claim is based on the following argument.

If *a* is distinct from *b*, then *a* can exist without *b*. Therefore, if an act of thought were distinct from its intentional object it can exist without it.

But if an act of thought existed without its intentional object it wouldn't be a thought of anything.

This is absurd.

Therefore the intentional object of an act of thought is not distinct from the act of thinking and need not be posited in addition to it.

But Chatton's ultimate argument against the objective-existence theory is to put forward an alternative. He claims that acts of thought are acts-of-thinking-of-a-golden-mountain and are directed to their real objects by their properties, not by being connected to intentional objects.

Ockham accepts Chatton's view in his *Quodlibets* (IV, Question 19) but never quite gets around to explaining how it might work for God, and so even for Ockham's followers the doctrine that there is an ontological status that is the being-of-being-an-object-of-thought remained attractive.

It seems then that as early as 1340 all the ingredients of the Cartesian theory of formal and objective reality—including at least some anticipation of a causal principle connecting the two modes—were in place. It remains only to connect them up with "idea" in the wide Cartesian, rather than in the narrow Augustinian, sense.

Although the conventional wisdom is that Descartes' use of "idea" marks a sharp break with tradition, there is reason to think that there was already a move in that direction much earlier. Francis Mayronnis used "idea," and (in I *Sent.*, D. 36, Q. 3) the enormously influential Durandus of St. Pourcain claims:

It remains therefore that an idea in us is only the object of our intellect on account of which it is necessary to say proportionately that in God an idea . . . is only the object of the divine intellect.[9]

This is not yet the single inner world in which "bodily and perceptual sensations, mathematical truths, moral rules, the idea of God, moods of depression and all the rest of what we now call 'mental' were objects of quasi-observation."[10] It is however a step towards that view, and a step away from the view that individual ideas are exemplars.

There remains the question of spelling out the medieval theory of imagery which underlies Descartes' conception of idea, and the problem of clarifying the notion of eminent containment employed in Descartes' claim that it is only in the case of God that one can argue from the objective reality of the idea to the existence (as contrasted with the formal reality) of its object.

IV

Descartes claims that ideas are "as if images of things" (AT VII, 37). He frequently denies that ideas are similar in nature to images in the imagination (HR II, 37, 52; K, 105). But how can an idea be both like an image and different in kind from anything in the imagination?

The term *image* is used in a rather technical sense within Scholasticism. It enters philosophical discussion by two avenues—commentaries on Genesis (1, 27): "And God created man to his image," and commentaries on Augustine's claim that the human mind is an image of the Trinity (e.g., in Peter Lombard's *Sentences*; I, Distinction 3). The text from Genesis is usually glossed in the light of the sentence that precedes it, which speaks of making man in God's image and likeness and so encourages a distinction between image [*imago*] and likeness [*similitudo*]. Because it presupposes that one immaterial thing can be an image of another, Lombard's discussion of Augustine encourages severing the link between images and perception.

How the distinction between an image and a mere likeness is to be drawn was a matter of controversy during the Middle Ages. Some (William Ockham, for example) held that an image was a likeness produced intentionally by an artisan, or at least used by an agent to call the thing imaged to mind. Others, like Francesco Suarez, insist that "an image involves two relations, one of similarity and one of being produced with that similarity" (*De Mysterio Trinitatis*, bk. 9, chap. 9, p. 5; *Opera Omnia*, 25:747).[11]

Descartes is in the second of the Scholastic traditions. Cartesian images are both similar to and causally connected with what they image, and Cartesian ideas, which are "as if" images, both resemble and are causally connected with what they are ideas of. It is this double relation that enables ideas to play their Janus-like role. Because ideas are connected causally with their objects, they are *about them,* and so there is a nonholistic constraint on "reference." Because ideas resemble their objects, having the idea is having information about the object, and so there is a nonreferential aspect to "meaning."

But just how are the relevant relations of causality and similarity to be spelled out and what role does the concept of objective reality play?

In the Third Meditation Descartes divides ideas into fictitious, adventitious, and innate (HR, 160). Fictitious ideas are always constructed from others by operations of the mind and so their properties should be determined by the powers of the mind and the properties of the ideas out of which they are constructed. Adventitious and innate ideas are thus fundamental. Of adventitious ideas Descartes remarks in the Third Meditation that "even if they proceed from things distinct from me it does not follow that they should be similar to those things" (AT VII, 329). And, as he points out in the *Principles* and in the *Notes Against a Certain Programme,* strictly speaking "nothing reaches our mind from external objects through the organs of sense besides certain corporeal movements" and "even these movements and the figures which arise from them are not conceived by us in the shape they assume in the organs of sense" (HR I, 443). Even the resemblance or similarity of adventitious ideas to the objects conceived is thus not produced by those objects operating on our senses. How then is it produced?

The traditional Scholastic use of the term *idea* is to refer to the exemplars in the mind of God, the divine ideas God creates by looking to these exemplars. But how is it that when God looks to the (a?) horse-exemplar and creates, the creature is a horse and not, say, a goat? Part of the answer should be the conceptual point that, if looking to an exemplar is the way God produces a goat, then that exemplar is a goat-exemplar and not a horse-exemplar. That is just what it is to be an exemplar of a particular sort. Another part of the answer might be had from a story about the nature of the causal connection. Within the scholastic philosophies, the paradigm of causal activity is reproduction. In reproduction among plants and animals, it was believed, it is only if the cause is defective or if something obstructs its activity that an effect not of the same kind as the cause is produced.

In artistic reproduction the prototype or model from which the artist works plays the role of one of the parents in organic reproduction. If the activity is not random but rational, then the effect produced will be of the same kind as the prototype, and only when the skill employed is defective or obstructed will something not of that kind be produced. When an artist works not from a model but from an idea nothing crucial to the account changes. An artist working from an idea may behave just like one working from a model. God is an artist whose skill is neither defective nor capable of being obstructed. Therefore God's products are of the same kind as the divine ideas from which God works. This story and the earlier conceptual point converge to suggest that God's creations and the divine ideas are of the same kind.

Our ideas of things do not usually function as exemplars. If they are causally related to things it is usually as effects rather than as causes. Yet our innate ideas are furnished us by the creator of the objects themselves. Since these ideas are not part of our nature, God does not create them in us simply by creating us. It is plausible to suppose that God furnishes us with an idea of something by looking to the divine idea of that thing and creating a mode of our minds. But if that is so then our ideas are just as much effects of the divine ideas as are the things themselves. In whatever sense the causal relation preserves resemblance our ideas resemble the divine ideas and so, where the divine ideas have been used as exemplars, resemble the objects themselves.

In what does the similarity of idea and object consist? Within the Scholastic tradition, for two things to be similar is for them to have properties in common. But what properties could an idea, a mode of mind, have in common with, say, a mode of extended substance?

One approach to this problem is to focus on the relational properties of the idea and the object and to attempt to locate the idea among other ideas in a way isomorphic to the way the object is located among other objects. But this approach requires taking relations as real, and there is strong pressure within Scholasticism to resist the reification of relations. A very different approach would be to claim baldly that objects and properties can have more than one ontological status and to identify the divine ideas with the objects themselves. On this approach the divine idea of a particular just is that particular with *esse objectivum*, and the divine idea of a nature just is that nature with *esse objectivum*.

There is a close connection between *esse objectivum* and possible existence for Descartes. In the *Rationes* appended to the Replies to the second set of Objections to the *Meditations*, he lays it down as an axiom that possible or contingent existence is contained in every idea or concept of a thing other than God and that necessary and perfect existence is contained in the idea of God (AT VII, 166). Thus if an idea has objective reality, and is thus *of* a thing, that thing possibly exists. This suggests the equation of the objective reality of an idea with the objective existence (the *esse objectivum*) of its object and the objective existence of an object with the possible existence of that object. The objective reality of an idea of something is then just the possible existence of that thing.

One advantage of this approach is that it connects Descartes' views on objective reality with his views about modality, and so explains why he thinks that objective reality of an idea requires a formally real cause. Descartes believes that not only all that is actual but also all that is possible depend on the divine will. If there were no God nothing would be possible and, had God decided other than as He did, what is possible would be other than as it is. If possible existence requires an actual cause and the objective reality of an idea is just the possible existence of its object, then the objective reality of an idea will require an actual cause that was formally a real cause. And that is Descartes' view.

The equation of the objective reality of an idea of something with the possible existence of that thing invites one to wonder how the criterion of clarity and distinctness could work for ideas. How, on the basis of having a certain mental mode, could one tell that some object is possible? Perhaps the simplest (and perhaps the most naive) way of connecting a mode of mind with an object in such a fashion that the existence of the mode guarantees the possibility of the object is to suppose that the mode just is a contact with the (possible) object. This move was available within the tradition. Indeed it is just this approach which Ockham and his followers take to the problem of how there can be many divine ideas and one utterly simple divine mind. Ockham (in I *Sent.*, D. 35) equates the divine idea of a thing with the thing itself as a possible object, and supposes God to be acquainted with it. To suppose Descartes to have taken this option might be to underestimate the force of the claim that ideas are *modes* of mind, but it was an available option.

Not all of the problems for "Suarezian" theories of imagery arise from puzzles about similarity. It is a central feature of late Scholastic accounts of causation that whatever can be produced through secondary causes can be produced by God acting alone. One consequence of this is that, if ideas are effects, it cannot be both that they are of whatever produced them and that there is an infallible phenomenological mark of what they are about. This would pose a serious problem for a theory that hoped to show a general connection between ideas and the existence of the causes of their objective reality. It could be, for all that the objective reality of ideas shows, that there exists only God and the mind having the ideas, and that all the ideas are produced by God directly.

But this is not a problem for Descartes. He is concerned to argue that from the objective reality of our ideas we can infer the existence of God and not the existence of anything else. We can infer to the reality of other things but that, if the argument above is sound, is just their possible existence. For something to be possible only God's power need be actual. Only in the special case of God, Descartes argues in the Fifth Meditation, does possible existence entail actual existence.

It is to deal with the case of an idea of something that does not actually exist but which would, if it did exist, have properties which God does not have, that Descartes distinguishes between having a property formally and having it eminently. If God had not created extended substance, the idea of extended substance would still have objective reality. Moreover we could still have such an idea even though there would be no actual extended thing to cause it. Extended substance would exist eminently, but not formally, in God. The notion of eminence at work here is closely connected with that of degrees of perfection. Central to it is an analogy with someone who has the power to lift, say, one hundred pounds. This person also has the power to lift fifty pounds. The power to lift fifty pounds is not, in this case, really distinct from the power to lift one hundred pounds; if it were, God could conserve the power to lift one hundred pounds while destroying the power to lift fifty, and that is impossible. The power to lift fifty pounds is contained eminently in the power to lift one hundred just because in lifting one hundred one lifts fifty and then some. To apply the analogy one must conceive of an object as a collection of characteristics which, like ontological independence, come in degrees. Something that possesses one of these characteristics to a degree thereby possesses it to all lesser degrees, and something that possesses each of a set of characteristics to degrees greater than n thereby contains eminently anything which has essentially only those characteristics and each of them to a degree less than or equal to n. God gives to each creature every characteristic it has. Since nothing can give what it does not have, every characteristic a creature has must be either a characteristic which God has or must be in some sense reducible to (supervenient on ?) characteristics which God has and has to at least the same degree as the creature. Thus God contains every creature formally or eminently.

V

In the Third Meditation Descartes is conjuring with the stock-in-trade of late medieval metaphysicians: God, univocal causality, formal and objective reality, and formal and eminent containment. These items are employed in the deconstruction of the ontology of Scholastic common sense. They are also employed in the construction of an account of thought which makes its operation out to be piecemeal rather than holistic and which centers on the notion that an idea is a presentation of the very object represented. This suggests a Descartes firmly rooted in a Scholastic tradition which is deeply in debt to Duns Scotus and closely allied with fourteenth-century developments in epistemology and in the theory of meaning. This makes the problem of Descartes' immediate sources and the question of his originality even more puzzling.

NOTES

1. References to AT, HR, and K are explained in the General Bibliography at the beginning of this volume.

2. Margaret Dauler Wilson's *Descartes* (London: Routledge & Kegan Paul, 1978), 102.

3. References to *Descartes' Conversation with Burman*, trans. with intro. and comm. by John Cottingham (Oxford: Clarendon, 1976) are cited as JC.

4. References to Scotus are to Iohannis Duns Scoti, *Opera Omnia* (Vaticana, 1950). References give volume, page, and paragraph number in that order.

5. References to Alnwick are to the page in Fr. Guillelmi Alnwick, *Quaestiones Disputatae De Esse Intelligibili et de Quodlibet*, ed. P. Athenasius Ledoux, O.F.M. (Quaracchi, 1937).

6. Petrus Aureoli discusses these matters in *In Sent.* I, proem. See Petrus Aureoli, *Scriptum super primum Sententiarum*, ed. E. M. Buytaert (Franciscan Institute, St. Bonaventure, N.Y., 1955).

7. References to Ockham are to his Commentary on Lombard's *Sentences* in *Opera Philosophica et Theologica* (Franciscan Institute, St. Bonaventure, N.Y., 1974).

8. For Walter Chatton's discussion, see *Lecturae Chaton Anglici in Sententias*, Prol., Q. 2, ed. J. J. O'Callaghan in J. R. O'Donnell, ed., *Nine Mediaeval Thinkers* (Pontifical Institute of Medaeval Studies, Toronto, 1955) and Gedeon Gal, "Gualteri de Chatton et Guillelmi de Ockham Controversia de Natura Conceptus Universalis," *Franciscan Studies* 27 (1967):191–212.

9. Cf. Durandus a St. Porciano, *I Sent.*, D. 36, Q. 3 (Louvain, 1587), p. 222 sqq., quoted in Alnwick (see n. 5), 120.

10. Richard Rorty, *Philosophy and the Mirror of Nature* (New Jersey: Princeton University Press, 1979), 50.

11. References to Suarez are to the *Opera Omnia* (Paris: Vives, 1856–).
*Special thanks to Ann Getson, Sidney Morgenbesser, and Amélie Rorty for helpful discussion and ideas. Earlier versions of this paper were read to the members of the Philosophy Colloquia at Columbia University and the Graduate Center of the City University of New York. Their discussion helped enormously.

11

Is There Radical Dissimulation in Descartes' *Meditations*?

Louis E. Loeb

INTRODUCTION

According to dissimulation hypotheses, Descartes, in the *Meditations,* intentionally misrepresented important aspects of his philosophy. There are a number of versions of such dissimulation hypotheses, depending on where the points of misrepresentation are located.[1] For the purposes of this essay, I am interested in the thesis that Descartes was not sincere either about his proofs of the existence of God in Meditation III, or about his appeal to Divine veracity in order to validate clear and distinct perception in Meditation IV, and in order to prove the existence of the material world in Meditation VI.[2] I will call this thesis "the dissimulation hypothesis." I believe there is a serious possibility that the dissimulation hypothesis is correct, and hence that a number of claims at the core of the *Meditations* do not represent Descartes' considered philosophical views. My purpose in this essay is to explore this possibility.

I will sketch quite briefly, two considerations that are strongly suggestive of dissimulation with respect to the epistemological role assigned to God in the *Meditations.* The first consideration relates to the problem of the Cartesian circle. The texts that serve as the initial stimulus for dissimulation hypotheses are precisely those which evidence circularity in the argument of Meditations III and IV.[3] Commentators have found the procedure of Meditations III and IV question-begging on the ground that Descartes must prove the existence of a nondeceiving God in order to validate clear and distinct perception; however, he must rely on clear and distinct perception in conducting these proofs. That there is the strong appearance of circularity is not controversial. In the fourth set of Objections, Arnauld accused Descartes of "circular reasoning" (HR II, 92; AT VII, 214).[4] Gassendi objected repeatedly that there was a circular argument beginning in Meditation III.[5] A closely related objection is raised in the second set of Objections (HR II, 26; AT VII, 124–125). The circularity has seemed so obvious that one wonders whether Descartes could have failed to be aware of it.

The second consideration relates to the substance of the arguments for the existence of God in Meditation III.[6] The two arguments are notoriously weak.[7] Both rely on the principle that there must be at least as much formal (actual) perfection in the efficient and total cause of an idea as objective perfection in the idea itself. Unfortunately, it is difficult to see what there is to recommend this principle other than its suitability for Descartes' argumentative purposes.[8] One wonders how a figure of Descartes' intelligence, who has undertaken "to withhold . . . assent from matters which are not entirely certain and indubitable" (HR I, 145; AT VII, 18), and who includes beliefs about mathematics within the scope of the doubt (HR II, 158–159; AT VII, 35–36), could nevertheless unhesitatingly embrace the principle about causation as a deliverance of the light of nature.[9]

In sum, Descartes' argument in Meditations III and IV seems so obviously question-begging as to suggest the possibility that Descartes was himself aware of the circularity, and hence not sincere in his appeal to the existence of a nondeceiving God in order to validate clear and distinct perception. The considerations relating to the problem of the Cartesian circle are reinforced by those relating to the substance of the arguments for the existence of God in Meditation III. Such glaring deficiencies as the appeal to the intrinsically implausible causal principle suggest the possibility that Descartes was not sincere in proposing them. This is one way to sketch a prima facie case for dissimulation, with respect to both the arguments for the existence of God in Meditation III, and the appeal to Divine veracity in order to validate clear and distinct perception in Meditation IV.[10]

While I believe that this prima facie case can be considerably strengthened, my goal in this essay is neither to elaborate on the considerations I have sketched, nor even to argue directly for the truth of the dissimulation hypothesis. My objective is to remove certain objections to the acceptance of a dissimulation hypothesis of the sort

I have introduced. Two obstacles are frequently discussed. The first is the methodological problem of developing general criteria for interpretation under the assumption of dissimulation.[11] The second is a reluctance to attribute to Descartes the defects of character—dishonorableness, cowardice, and so forth—which the dissimulation hypothesis might seem to entail.[12] The obstacles I have in mind are more purely interpretive and philosophical. The arguments for the existence of a nondeceiving God are prompted by the doubt "concerning things which seemed to me most manifest" (HR I, 158; AT VII, 36) raised at the fourth paragraph of Meditation III. The obstacle is simply this: what are we to make of this doubt on the hypothesis that Descartes was not sincere in his response to it, was not sincere in his claims about God's epistemological role in Meditations III and IV?

In part 2, I argue that there is textual evidence that Descartes in fact minimizes the importance of the doubt of Meditation III. In part 3, I locate in Descartes a rationale for not taking the doubt of Meditation III seriously. The outcome is to identify in Descartes a nontheological epistemological position compatible with the dissimulation hypothesis. In part 4, I provide a brief account of the motives Descartes possessed for engaging in dissimulation.

THE SLIGHT AND METAPHYSICAL DOUBT OF MEDITATION III

In the second paragraph of Meditation II, Descartes states: " . . . it *seems* to me that already I can establish as a general rule" (HR I, 158, italics added; AT VII, 35) that whatever is clearly and distinctly perceived is true. It would, however, be premature to take this general rule as established. In the fourth paragraph, Descartes introduces the following ground for doubt:

> But when I took anything very simple and easy in the sphere of arithmetic or geometry into consideration, e.g. that two and three together made five, and other things of the sort, were not these present to my mind so clearly as to enable me to affirm that they were true? Certainly if I judged that since such matters could be doubted, this would not have been so for any other reason than that it came into my mind that perhaps a God might have endowed me with such a nature that I may have been deceived even concerning things which seemed to me most manifest. But every time that this preconceived opinion of the sovereign power of a God presents itself to my thought, I am constrained to confess that it is easy to Him, if He wishes it, to cause me to err, even in matters in which I believe myself to have the best evidence. (HR I, 158; AT VII, 35–36)

In the context, it is natural to take the doubt about "things which seemed to me most manifest," or "matters in which I believe myself to have the best evidence," as relating to clear and distinct perception.[13]

No comparable doubt is introduced in the *Rules for the Direction of the Mind*. This is an early, and unfinished, work; however it contains Descartes' most extended account of doctrines relating to clear and distinct perception. In the *Rules*, Descartes employs the technical term *intuition* (*mental vision*) to refer to an act or operation of the mind in which a proposition is perceived all at once or in a moment, and so clearly and distinctly as to be certain or indubitable (cf. Rules III, VII, XI). Deduction does not rely on any second basic cognitive faculty distinct from intuition; a deduction consists of a sequence of connected intuitions.

In the *Rules*, Descartes writes that "deduction, or the pure illation of one thing from another . . . *cannot be erroneous* when performed by an understanding that is in the least degree rational" (HR I, 4–5, italics added; AT X, 365). As for intuition, "it is *more certain than deduction itself*, in that it is simpler, though deduction, as we have noted above, *cannot by us be erroneously conducted*" (HR I, 7, italics added; AT X, 368). Descartes thus introduces the discussion of intuition and deduction at Rule III as follows: "we shall here take note of all those mental operations by which we are able, *wholly without fear of illusion*, to arrive at the knowledge of things" (HR I, 7, italics added; AT X, 368). In the *Rules*, there is no hint of skepticism about intuition, the mental act involving clear and distinct perception. Descartes treats intuition as unproblematic, and exhibits nothing but confidence in it.

Against this background, the introduction of the skeptical hypothesis of Meditation III constitutes a surprising about-face.[14] The question that arises is how to explain the discrepancy between Descartes' treatment of clear and distinct perception in the *Rules* and in the *Meditations*. There are at least three possible lines of interpretation. The first is that the discrepancy reflects a significant change in Descartes' view about the epistemological status of intuition or clear and distinct perception. Both the second and third interpretations deny this, holding that any change in view is more apparent than real; these interpretations differ as to how the (merely) apparent change in view is to be explained. On the second interpretation, the *Rules* and the *Meditations* simply address different problems; the *Rules* is concerned with the method proper, whereas the *Meditations* is concerned with the metaphysical foundations of the method. On the third interpretation, Descartes was not sincere in raising the doubt about clear and distinct perception in Meditation III. It is this third interpretation that is congenial to the dissimulation hypothesis. It is easier to believe that Descartes was not sincere in his claims for God's epistemological role if he was not sincere about the doubt that prompts the proofs of the existence of a nondeceiving God.

There are a number of features of the way in which Descartes raises the doubt in the fourth paragraph of Meditation III which suggest that he may not have taken the doubt seriously. These features emerge most clearly if one compares the hypotheses that generate radical doubt in Meditations I and III, respectively. The doubts raised in these two Meditations differ in scope, that is, in the classes of beliefs to which they apply. In Meditation I, Descartes introduces the hypothesis of an omnipotent deceiver who causes him to have sensory experiences as if material objects existed; this hypothesis generates a doubt about beliefs based on sensory experience.[15] In Meditation III, Descartes introduces the hypothesis of an omnipotent deceiver who causes him to have false beliefs about matters that seem most certain; this hypothesis generates a doubt about beliefs based on clear and distinct perception or intuitive apprehension.

Whereas Descartes describes the grounds for the doubt of Meditation I as "very powerful and maturely considered" (HR I, 148; AT VII, 21), he describes the grounds for the doubt of Meditation III as "very slight, and so to speak metaphysical" (HR I, 159; AT VII, 36).[16] This marked contrast in tone cries out for explanation.[17] The two hypotheses of a deceiver seem relevantly parallel. Both hypotheses are offered as representing epistemic possibilities: for all Descartes knows, at the points in the *Meditations* where the respective hypotheses are advanced, it is possible that they are true. For all Descartes knows, at the close of Meditation I, there might exist an omnipotent being who causes him to have false beliefs based on sensory experience; for all Descartes knows, early in Meditation III, there might exist an omnipotent being who causes him to have false beliefs based on clear and distinct perception. In neither case does Descartes make any claim about the likelihood or probability that the hypothesis is true.[18] In these circumstances, it is difficult to find a rationale for the description of one doubt as "very slight, and so to speak metaphysical," and the other doubt as "very powerful and maturely considered." Descartes states that the ground for doubt in Meditation III is slight and metaphysical "since I have no reason to believe that there is a God who is a deceiver, and as I have not yet satisfied myself that there is a God at all" (HR I, 159; AT VII, 36). But it is equally true, in the context of Meditation I, that he has no reason to believe in the existence of a deceiving God, and that he has not yet proved that

God exists. The two hypotheses seem to share the same epistemological status, and hence the doubts they generate should be equally slight, or equally powerful.[19] Why, then, does Descartes employ language that minimizes the doubt introduced in Meditation III as compared to that introduced in Meditation I?

There are two respects in which the hypothesis of Meditation III is disanalogous to the hypothesis of Meditation I.[20] Consider the latter. How could it be the case that one's belief in the existence of a material world, where that belief is based on the sensory evidence in fact available to one, is false? Descartes is quite explicit: perhaps God "has . . . brought it to pass that there is . . . no extended body, and that nevertheless [I possess the perceptions of all these things and that] they seem to me to exist just exactly as I now see them (HR I, 147; AT VII, 21). The hypothesis has two components: first, an explanation of how it could be the case that no material objects exist (an omnipotent being has caused it to be the case that none exists); and second, an explanation of how one could nevertheless have sensory experiences as if material objects existed (an omnipotent being has caused one to have those sensory experiences). Descartes' hypothesis explains how the belief in a material world could be false, and how one could have the evidence one does have for that belief in the circumstances that it is false.

The hypothesis of Meditation III seems entirely to lack any analogue to the first component of the hypothesis of Meditation I. The belief in the existence of a material world would be false if an omnipotent being "brought it to pass that there is . . . no extended body." In Meditation III, Descartes offers no explanation as to how one's most certain beliefs, such that two and three together make five, could be false. It is tempting to suppose that we have located an explanation of why Descartes treats the doubt raised in Meditation III as slight and metaphysical in contrast to the powerful and mature reasons for the doubt raised in Meditation I. The hypothesis of Meditation I, unlike that of Meditation III, includes an explanation of how the beliefs in question could be false. Descartes describes circumstances in which the belief in a material world would be false; he does not describe circumstances in which his most certain beliefs would be false. The doubt of Meditation III then appears slight in the sense that Descartes at best *asserts* that it *is possible* that it is false that, for example, two plus three equals five, without describing how this is possible.

Unfortunately, this attempt to explain why Descartes treats the doubt of Meditation III as slight is not satisfactory. It is true that in Meditation III Descartes does not provide an explanation of how it could be false that two plus three make five. However, he could have provided such an explanation by invoking his body of doctrine about the "eternal truths" (see K, 11, 13–15, 150–151, 236–237; HR II, 226, 248; CB 33; AT I, 145–146, 149–153, IV, 118–119, V, 223–224, VII, 380, 431–432, V, 159–160]. The eternal truths approximately coincide in content with what might be called presumptively necessary truths. According to Descartes' doctrine, the eternal truths are in fact contingent or dependent upon God's will. Descartes' ground for this is simply that God would not be omnipotent were He bound by any truths that were strictly necessary in the sense of being independent of His will. Further, Descartes holds that God established the eternal truths "by *the same kind of causality* as he created all things" (K 14; AT I, 151–152). Descartes states his doctrine of eternal truths as early as 1630, as late as 1648, and in his replies to the fifth and sixth sets of Objections. In light of this body of doctrine, Descartes could have hypothesized in Meditation III that an omnipotent deceiver "brought it to pass" that it is false that two plus three make five, much as in Meditation I he hypothesized that an omnipotent deceiver "brought it to pass" that there exists no extended body. The doctrine of the eternal truths, however, is not mentioned in the *Meditations*.[21] Thus, we have not succeeded in explaining why Descartes treats the doubt of Meditation III as slight.

An interesting question is why Descartes does not avail himself of this doctrine in order to establish a greater parity between the hypotheses of Meditations I and III.[22] Suppose Descartes did take the doubt of Meditation II as seriously as that of Meditation I, and that he was committed to his doctrine about the eternal truths. Under these circumstances, we would expect him to invoke this doctrine in order to provide an explanation of how our beliefs in presumptively necessary truths could be false.[23] But Descartes does not do so. This suggests that either Descartes did not take the doubt of Meditation III seriously, or that he did not take his doctrine about the eternal truths seriously, or both. It should be noted that the position that he was serious about the doubt of Meditation III, but not about the doctrine of the eternal truths, concedes that outside of the *Meditations* Descartes was involved in dissimulation with respect to his views about Divine omnipotence.

Consider the second component of the skeptical hypothesis of Meditation I. This component provides an explanation of how one could have sensory experiences as if material objects existed in the circumstances that they do not exist. On the hypothesis of Meditation I, God "brought it to pass that there is no earth, no heaven, no extended body, no magnitude, no place, and that nevertheless [I possess the perceptions of all these things and that] they seem to me to exist just exactly as I now see them" (HR I, 147; AT VII, 21). How does God bring it to pass that one has such sensory experiences? Perhaps God endows the mind with a faculty or capacity which itself generates the sensory experiences. It is clear from the passage in Meditation VI where Descartes reconsiders the hypothesis of Meditation I that this is not the mechanism he envisions. Descartes writes: " . . . since God is no deceiver, it is very manifest that He does not communicate to me these ideas [of sensible things] immediately and by Himself, nor yet by the intervention of some creature in which their reality is not formally, but only eminently, contained" (HR I, 191; AT VII, 79). In other words, the hypothesis of Meditation I involves an omnipotent being who causes one's sensory experiences directly in the sense that he induces them one by one.[24]

In offering this particular explanation, Descartes commits himself to a definite argumentative strategy. To see what I have in mind, let us distinguish between beliefs about the material world, and the mechanisms that might cause those beliefs. For example, beliefs about the material world might be based on sensory experiences that are caused by mechanisms involving causal interactions between extended bodies and the sense organs and the brain, that is, by mechanisms of the sort which we take to be operative in connection with everyday beliefs about the material world. I will refer to such mechanisms as "sense-perception." Alternatively, beliefs about the material world might be based on sensory experiences that are caused directly by the volitions of an immaterial omnipotent deceiver.

Two strategies are available to challenge beliefs about the material world. The first is to suggest that sense-perception might be intrinsically defective in the sense that it is an unreliable belief-forming mechanism (or set of belief-forming mechanisms). (An unreliable belief-forming mechanism is one that leads to false beliefs more often than not—either in actual or in relevant possible circumstances.) The second strategy is to suggest that beliefs about the material world might be caused by some unreliable mechanisms distinct from sense-perception, such as the direct volitional activity of an omnipotent deceiver. The second strategy leaves open the question of whether sense-perception itself is reliable. It is this second strategy that Descartes employs.

Descartes never uses the first strategy; he never raises the possibility that sense-perception is intrinsically defective. He merely notes that "it is sometimes proved to me that these senses are deceptive, and it is wiser not to trust entirely to any thing by which we have once been deceived" (HR I, 145; AT VII, 18). Here, Descartes calls attention to the *fallibility* of sense-perception, making the point that beliefs based on sense-perception are *sometimes* false. He does not question the *reliability* of sense-perception by suggesting that beliefs based on sense-perception might be false more often than not.[25] Descartes abstains from directly challenging the reliability of his perceptual faculties, that is, of the faculty of sense-perception.

I believe Descartes considers the possibility of such a challenge, and consciously declines to employ it. This is the significance, at least in part, of the cryptic discussion of madness in the fourth paragraph of Meditation I. Descartes asks:

And how could I deny that these hands and this body are mine, were it not perhaps that I compare myself to certain persons, devoid of sense, whose cerebella are so troubled and clouded by the violent vapours of black bile, that they constantly assure us that they think they are kings when they are really quite poor, or that they are clothed in purple when they are really without covering, or who imagine that they have an earthenware head or are nothing but pumpkins or are made of glass. (HR I, 145; AT VII, 18–19)

Two of the three examples are beliefs about perceptible features of the world. This suggests that Descartes is raising the possibilty that he has unreliable perceptual faculties.[26] His response is to dismiss the hypothesis: such persons "are made, and I should not be any the less insane were I to follow examples so extravagant" (HR I, 145; AT VII, 19). Descartes is not rejecting the hypothesis of defective perceptual faculties as an epistemic possibility. For all he knows, the hypothesis could be true. He is declining to invoke the possibility that sense-perception might itself be defective as a ground for doubt about beliefs based on sensory experience. Thus, in Meditation I, the possibility of defective or unreliable perceptual faculties is raised, and dismissed, in paragraph four. Descartes chooses to use the second strategy I have described, hypothesizing that sensory experiences are caused directly by an omnipotent deceiver.

Consider the second component of the hypothesis of Meditation III. It falls to this component to explain how one could have false beliefs in presumptively necessary truths. It is the role of the omnipotent being "to cause me to err, even in matters in which I believe myself to have the best evidence." This hypothesis has a superficial parity to that of an omnipotent being who causes me to have false beliefs about the material world. The apparent parity vanishes, however, if one asks how the omnipotent being of Meditation III causes false beliefs. There are two possibilities. The first is that the omnipotent being causes one to have a cognitive faculty—"intuition," "reason," "the light of nature," whatever—which is intrinsically defective, unreliable in the sense that its normal operation leads one to misapprehend falsehoods as truths. This would be analogous to the hypothesis that our perceptual faculties are defective. The second possibility is that the omnipotent being directly causes one to have the clear and distinct perceptions or intuitive apprehensions on which the false beliefs are based. This would be analogous to the mechanism embodied in the hypothesis of Meditation I, where the omnipotent being directly causes our sensory experiences.

The hypothesis of Meditation III seems to rely on the first mechanism, on which the false beliefs issue from a defective cognitive faculty. Descartes writes: " . . . it came into my mind that perhaps a God might have endowed me with such a *nature* that I may have been deceived even concerning things which seemed to me most manifest" (HR I, 158, italics added; AT VII, 36). This strongly suggests that Descartes is envisioning a being who endows him with some stable faculty, the operation of which is the proximate cause of his misapprehending falsehoods as truths. Suppose Descartes was envisioning a being who directly causes his misperception or misapprehension of falsehoods as truths. If so, it would be misleading to write of the being's endowing him with a *nature* such that he is deceived, for by hypothesis there would be nothing in Descartes' nature, nothing about his faculties, to account for the false beliefs. The development of the hypothesis of Meditation III, unlike that of Meditation I, depends upon the possibility that a cognitive faculty is unreliable.[27]

Once again, it is tempting to suppose that we have located an explanation of why Descartes treats the doubt of Meditation III as slight in contrast to the powerful doubt of Meditation I. Descartes' explanation of how one could have false beliefs about the material world does not rely on the supposition that one's perceptual faculties themselves are unreliable; Descartes' explanation of how one could have false beliefs about necessary truths does rely on the supposition that one's rational faculties are unreliable.[28] Descartes could have maintained parity, however, between the second components of the hypotheses of Meditations I and III; he could have supposed that the omnipotent being causes false mathematical beliefs by causing clear and distinct perceptions directly, rather than by endowing us with a defective faculty of reason.

The situation is similar to that in connection with the first component of the two hypotheses. Descartes explains how our beliefs about the material world could be false; he does not explain how our beliefs about necessary truths could be false. He could have maintained parity, however, between the first components of the hypotheses of Meditations I and III; he could have appealed to his doctrine of the eternal truths in order to explain how our beliefs about putatively necessary truths could be false. There are thus two disanalogies between the omnipotent deceiver hypotheses of Meditations I and III *as these hypotheses are presented* by Descartes. However, Descartes could have constructed the two hypotheses in such a way as to remove these disanalogies. Apparently, Descartes preferred to build disanalogies into the two hypotheses, thereby enabling him to minimize the doubt of Meditation III.

In part 1, I presented a prima facie case for the following claims: that at the time he wrote the *Meditations*, Descartes was aware of the circularity in his argument in Meditations III and IV; and that he did not himself accept the arguments for the existence of God in Meditation III. If so, Descartes was not sincere about the epistemological role assigned to God in Meditations III and IV. This seems implausible if Descartes was sincere about the doubt of Meditation III which prompts these developments. I have suggested that Descartes constructs the hypothesis of Meditation III in a way that enables him to minimize the doubt it generates, that is, to treat the doubt as slight in contrast to the doubt of Meditation I. If this is a signal that Descartes did not take the doubt of Meditation III seriously at all, then we can view his introduction of that doubt as nothing but a pretext for the subsequent arguments in Meditations III and IV. This raises a question as to how Descartes could have failed to take the doubt of Meditation III seriously. We have to locate in Descartes an epistemological position that enables us to answer this question.

CARTESIAN EPISTEMOLOGY WITHOUT DIVINE VERACITY

One way to address this question is by considering an obvious objection to dissimulation hypotheses. In its most general form, the difficulty is this: if Descartes was not sincere in his appeal to Divine veracity in order to validate our cognitive faculties, what *was* his epistemological position? The following considerations generate a particularly acute form of the difficulty. The doubt raised in Meditation III extends to those "matters in which I believe myself to have the best evidence," that is, to those beliefs which are presumed to be certain even if no material objects exist. According to the dissimulation hypothesis, this doubt is a pretext for locating an apparent epistemo-

logical role for God. In Meditation I, however, Descartes has raised
a distinct doubt about the existence of material objects. In Meditation
VI, Descartes argues that material objects exist on the ground that
since he has "a very great inclination to believe . . . that [ideas] are
conveyed to him by corporeal objects" (HR I, 191; AT VII, 79–80),
God would be a deceiver if material objects did not exist. If Descartes
was not sincere in his appeals to Divine veracity, the argument for
the existence of a material world collapses, leaving Descartes with no
response to the doubt raised in Meditation 1.[29]

Proponents of dissimulation hypothesis have failed to respond
adequately to this objection. Suppose that the argument for the existence of the material world is itself dismissed as not constituting
serious Cartesian doctrine. In these circumstances, a dissimulation
theorist must embrace one of three alternative positions. The first
alternative is that Descartes was not sincere even about the doubt
raised in Meditation I.[30] This variant of the dissimulation hypothesis
cannot explain why the doubt of Meditation I is treated as based on
considerations that are powerful and mature. The second alternative
is that Descartes was serious about the doubt of Meditation I, but
failed to supply any sincere response to the doubt. This variant of
the dissimulation hypothesis has the consequence that the epistemological problem of Meditation I is left unresolved in the *Meditations*.
The third alternative is that Descartes was sincere about the doubt of
Meditation I, and does provide a response to that doubt which does
not rely on Divine veracity. I believe that, if a dissimulation hypothesis
is to receive a hearing, it will have to be coupled with this third
alternative. In this third part of my essay, I sketch one version of an
interpretation along the lines of the third alternative. The project is
to locate a Cartesian response to the doubt of Meditation I, and more
generally an overall Cartesian epistemological position, which does
not rely on the appeals to Divine veracity contained in the *Meditations*.
I believe that such a theory can be extracted from Descartes' writings.

Central to the nontheological epistemological position which I locate
in Descartes is the conception of a *hierarchy of cognitive faculties*. This
has important analogies to the conception of a hierarchy, pyramid, or
vertical structure of *beliefs* in the context of foundation theories of justification. The foundationalist defines an asymmetric relation of epistemological priority among beliefs: the belief that p is *epistemologically
prior* to the belief that q just in case one's belief that p can be justified
without appeal to the belief that q, whereas one's belief that q *cannot*
be justified without appeal to the belief that p; the belief that p is *epistemologically basic* just in case there is no belief epistemologically prior

to it. For example, in standard interpretations of Descartes, the belief "I exist" (or certain closely related beliefs) is epistemologically basic, and epistemologically prior to the belief "God exists," which is in turn epistemologically prior to the belief "there exists a material world." I believe that any such theory in Descartes is derivative from a more fundamental foundations theory of cognitive faculties. In order to generate the relevant hierarchical structure, we must define an asymmetric relation of epistemological priority among cognitive faculties.

There is an instructive passage in the *Rules:*

This furnishes us with an evident explanation of the great superiority in certitude of Arithmetic and Geometry to other sciences. The former alone deal with an object so pure and uncomplicated, that they need make no assumptions at all which experience renders uncertain, but wholly consist in the rational deduction of consequences. (HR I, 5; AT X, 364)

Descartes does not simply assert that mathematical beliefs based on reason are superior in certainty to beliefs based on sense-perception. He sketches an explanation: reason, when applied to mathematics, requires no assumptions that experience or sense-perception renders uncertain. In other words, sense-perception provides no grounds for uncertainty about mathematical beliefs based on reason. The point is generalized in Meditation III. Descartes writes of the natural light, which includes intuition or clear and distinct perception: "And I possess no other faculty whereby to distinguish truth from falsehood, which can teach me that what this light shows me to be true is not really true" (HR I, 160–161; AT VII, 38–39).[31] In other words, there is *no* cognitive faculty that can show that *any* belief based on reason is false.

In the passage about the natural light, Descartes adds that he possesses "no other faculty that is equally trustworthy" (HR I, 161; AT VII, 38). In the context, reason appears trustworthy precisely because beliefs based on reason cannot be shown to be false by any other cognitive faculty. Descartes' discussion suggests that beliefs based on any other cognitive faculty can be shown to be false by reason. This seems to be confirmed two paragraphs later with respect to the central case of sense-perception:

I find, for example, two completely diverse ideas of the sun in my mind; the one derives its origin from the senses and, should be placed in the category of adventitious ideas; according to this idea the sun seems to be extremely small; but the other is derived from astronomical reasonings, i.e. is elicited from certain notions that are innate in me, or else it is formed by me in some other manner; in accordance with it the sun appears to be several times greater than the earth. These two ideas cannot, indeed, both resemble the same sun, and reason makes me believe that the one which seems to have originated directly from the sun itself, is the one which is most dissimilar to it. (HR I, 161; AT VII, 39)

Beliefs based on sense-perception about the size of astronomical bodies can be shown to be false by reason.[32] In sum, beliefs based on sense-perception can be shown to be false by reason, but beliefs based on reason cannot be shown to be false by sense-perception, or by any other cognitive faculty.

Descartes' account of the relationship between sense-perception and reason suggests a general definition of an asymmetric relation of epistemological priority among cognitive faculties. Let us say that if a belief based on cognitive faculty f has been shown to be false by cognitive faculty g, then the belief based on f has been corrected by cognitive faculty g. Cognitive faculty f is *epistemologically prior* to cognitive faculty g just in case beliefs based on g can be corrected by f, whereas beliefs based upon f cannot be corrected by g; a cognitive faculty is *epistemologically basic* just in case there is no cognitive faculty epistemologically prior to it.

The modal force of the notion that a belief based on one cognitive faculty "can be corrected" or is "correctable" by another cognitive faculty needs to be clarified. To say, for example, that beliefs based on sense-perception can be corrected by reason does not mean that reason in fact has the resources to show that every belief based on sense-perception is false. If that were the case, reason would have the resources to show that the belief that there exists a material world is false, whereas Descartes holds that this belief is true. The idea has to be that it follows from the nature of reason and sense-perception qua cognitive faculties that reason is not precluded from correcting beliefs based on sense-perception, whereas sense-perception is precluded from correcting beliefs based on reason. Consider the example of belief in the existence of a material world. The fact that reason does not have the resources to correct this belief is not a consequence of the nature of reason and sense-perception. The belief in the existence of a material world is correct*able* in the sense that reason might have located a disproof of this belief. For example, reason *might* have produced a proof of the existence of an omnipotent deceiver; or reason might have produced a proof, in the style of Berkeley, to show that the notion of a material substance is incoherent.

Descartes' position is that reason is epistemologically prior to sense-perception, and indeed epistemologically basic, in the sense defined.

The textual evidence I have produced for this claim derives from the *Rules* (where Divine veracity plays no role),[33] and from passages in Meditation III *prior* to the proofs of the existence of a nondeceiving God.[34] This is significant. It means that Descartes' commitment to the epistemological position I have attributed to him is not grounded in the proof of the nondeceiving God. The claim that reason is epistemologically basic, and hence epistemologically prior to sense-perception in particular, is not itself deduced as a consequence of Divine veracity; it has the status of a purported necessary truth about the interconnections among various cognitive faculties. I want to emphasize that this body of doctrine is a component of Descartes' epistemology even if the dissimulation hypothesis is false.

Let us stipulate that the *output* of one's hierarchically ordered set of cognitive faculties consists in those beliefs which have withstood or survived all possible tests for correction. We can say that for Descartes a belief is maximally reasonable if it is included within the output of one's hierarchically ordered set of cognitive faculties.[35] This is the core of the nontheological epistemological theory. Since reason is an epistemologically basic cognitive faculty, such that beliefs based on reason are not correctable by any other faculty, beliefs based on reason are *ipso facto* maximally reasonable. Since sense-perception is not an epistemologically basic cognitive faculty, beliefs based on sense-perception are maximally reasonable only if they have been subjected to and withstood all possible tests for correction.

Descartes does appeal to the existence of a nondeceiving God in order to validate the output of the hierarchically ordered set of cognitive faculties. In the reply to Objections II, Descartes writes:

> . . . in the case of our clearest and most accurate judgments which, if false, could not be corrected by any that are clearer, or by any other rational faculty, I clearly affirm that we cannot be deceived. For, since God is the highest being He cannot be otherwise than the highest good and truth, and hence it is contradictory that anything should proceed from Him that positively tends toward falsity. (HR II, 40–41; AT VII, 143–144)

The mere fact that we possess a faculty that leads to false beliefs does not render God a deceiver. God is a deceiver only if we possess a faculty that leads to false beliefs which are not correctable by other faculties we possess. This is explicit in Meditation VI, where Descartes writes that it follows from "the sole ground that God is not a deceiver" that "He has not permitted any falsity to exist in my opinion which he has not likewise given me the faculty of correcting" (HR I, 191;

AT VII, 80].[36] In Meditation VI, Descartes does appeal to Divine veracity in order to guarantee the truth of those beliefs which withstand
or survive all possible tests for correction.

From the perspective of the dissimulation hypothesis, Descartes
does not take the theological validation of the hierarchically ordered
set of cognitive faculties seriously. The dissimulation hypothesis treats
the Divine validation as a cosmetic graft onto a relatively healthy
epistemological theory. The theory of hierarchically ordered cognitive
faculties embodies a nontrivial, substantive epistemological position.
Furthermore, it is a theory to which Descartes commits himself independently of any appeal to Divine veracity. Locating this theory in
Descartes enables us to meet the objection that in the absence of any
appeal to Divine veracity Descartes' epistemology virtually vanishes.

What, then, remains of the argument for the existence of the material
world in Meditation VI? The argument is embedded within a long
discussion of "the teachings of nature."[37] In Meditation III, Descartes
has already contrasted the *teachings* of nature with the *light* of nature,
identifying the former with "a certain spontaneous inclination which
impels me to believe" (HR I, 160; AT VII, 38). At the fifth paragraph
of Meditation VI, Descartes begins to discuss a particular class of
beliefs: beliefs involving "those matters which I hitherto held to be
true, as having perceived them through the senses" (HR I, 187; AT
VII, 74); beliefs held when "I had formerly made use of my senses
rather than my reason" (HR I, 188; AT VII, 75); beliefs held at a time
when "all the faith which I had rested in my senses" (HR I, 189; AT
VII, 76). These are the beliefs that had previously been based on
sense-perception alone. Descartes writes that these beliefs were taught
by nature or learned from nature (HR I, 188; AT VII, 76). At paragraph
seven, Descartes states that "nature seemed to cause me to lean towards many things from which reason repelled me" (HR I, 189; AT
VII, 77). We have already encountered an example in beliefs about
the size of astronomical bodies.

Of those beliefs which arise spontaneously on the basis of sense-
perception, which ought to be accepted, and which rejected? On the
epistemological theory I have located in Descartes, we should expect
that beliefs based on sense-perception should be accepted just in case
they have been subjected to and withstood all possible tests for correction. Some beliefs based on sense-perception would survive this process, and others would not. Descartes thus writes: "I do not in truth
think that I should rashly admit all the matters which the senses seem
to teach us, but, on the other hand, I do not think that I should doubt
them all universally" (HR I, 189–190; AT VII, 77–78). Descartes proceeds case by case.

That there exists a material world at all is proved as follows:

> But, since God is no deceiver, it is very manifest that He does not communicate to me these ideas immediately and by Himself, nor yet by the intervention of some creature in which their reality is not formally, but only eminently, contained. For since He has given me no faculty to recognise that this is the case, but, on the other hand, a very great inclination to believe [that they are sent to me or] that they are conveyed to me by corporeal objects, I do not see how He could be defended from the accusation of deceit if these ideas were produced by causes other than corporeal objects. Hence we must allow that corporeal things exist. (HR I, 191; AT VII, 79–80)

It is not simply because one has a very great inclination to believe that material objects cause sensory experiences that the Divine veracity guarantees that a material world exists. It is because one has this inclination and has no faculty to recognize that this belief is false, that is, no faculty to correct this belief. The Divine guarantee does not apply to any arbitrary belief arising from sense-perception. Such a guarantee would be much too blunt an epistemological instrument. The Divine guarantee applies only to beliefs that are resistant to correction.

It should be noted that the conclusion of Descartes' argument that *some* corporeal or material objects exist is quite weak. In the analogous passage in the *Principles,* Descartes writes: "But God cannot deceive us. . . . And hence we must conclude that there is an object, extended in length, breadth, and depth . . . " (HR I, 254–255; AT VIII–1, 41). We do not yet have an argument for any detailed conclusions about the material world; for example, that particular bodies exist, or that Descartes has a body. Descartes proceeds to accept a number of other beliefs that arise spontaneously on the basis of sense-perception. These include the beliefs: " . . . that I have a body which is adversely affected when I feel pain" (HR I, 192; AT VII, 80); "that I am not only lodged in my body as a pilot in a vessel, but that I am very closely united to it" (HR I, 192; AT VII, 81); and "that many other bodies exist around mine" (HR I, 192; AT VII, 81). Descartes does not claim that these beliefs should be accepted because they are clearly and distinctly perceived to be true. These beliefs are not based on the light of nature; they are teachings of nature, beliefs arising from sense-perception. In the case of each of these beliefs, if the argument is to parallel that for the existence of a material world, we must attribute to Descartes the implicit claim that the belief in question would withstand all possible tests for correction.[38]

By contrast, a number of other beliefs based on sense-perception "contain some error" (HR I, 193; AT VII, 82). Here Descartes lists the beliefs: that a space in which there is nothing that affects one is void;

that qualities exactly similar to sensory experiences of secondary qualities exist in bodies; and that distant bodies have the shape and size they appear to have (HR I, 193; AT VII, 82). In each case, Descartes is content to provide the briefest indication of the considerations available to reason which correct the beliefs in question (HR I, 193–194; AT VII, 82–83). A complete argument for the claim that the relevant beliefs should be rejected would have to include a fuller statement of these considerations.[39]

The important point is that the appeal to Divine veracity does not in itself enable Descartes to discriminate among the beliefs that arise spontaneously on the basis of sense-perception. The acceptability of each such belief depends crucially on whether or not the belief is resistant to correction. It is the claim that particular beliefs would, or would not, withstand all possible tests for correction which bears the argumentative weight. From the perspective of the dissimulation hypothesis, Descartes was not serious about the theological validation of the output of the hierarchically ordered set of cognitive faculties. Our discussion shows that if we jettison the appeal to Divine veracity in Meditation VI, the core of a Cartesian argument for the truth or falsity of various beliefs induced by nature is not lost. The heart of the argument would consist, in each instance, in an attempt to show that the belief in question would or would not withstand all possible tests for correction.

It will be objected that something has been lost, namely, the Divine validation of those beliefs which are resistant to correction. From the perspective of the dissimulation hypothesis, what is "lost" is something that Descartes did not believe could be won. According to this hypothesis, Descartes was aware that, in the face of doubt about the reliability of clear and distinct perception, it would be question-begging to validate beliefs based on clear and distinct perception by appeal to Divine veracity, where the proof of the existence of a nondeceiving God itself relies on clear and distinct perception. Similarly, Descartes would have realized that, in the face of doubt about the reliability of the hierarchically ordered set of cognitive faculties, it would be question-begging to validate beliefs based on this hierarchically ordered set by appeal to Divine veracity, where the proof of the existence of a nondeceiving God itself relies on the hierarchically ordered set of cognitive faculties. It is no more possible, without circularity, to validate the hierarchically ordered set of cognitive faculties by proving the existence of a nondeceiving God, than it is to validate clear and distinct perception itself by proving the existence of a nondeceiving God.[40]

I believe that attributing the nontheological epistemology to Descartes has some modest explanatory power. We have seen that in Meditation I Descartes declines to rely on the hypothesis that sense-perception is intrinsically defective. This can be explained with reference to the epistemological position I have sketched. We think of Descartes as identifying maximally reasonable belief with the output of the hierarchically ordered set of cognitive faculties. Various beliefs based on sense-perception alone do not withstand or survive all possible tests for correction; however, many beliefs based on sense-perception are resistant to correction. If sense-perception were intrinsically defective, beliefs about the material world which survive all possible tests for correction could be systematically false. This is, of course, a possibility, and Descartes never suggests otherwise. Descartes would not have invoked the hypothesis that sense-perception is intrinsically defective because in his own epistemological theory sense-perception plays an ineliminable, albeit correctable, role in generating reasonable belief. In the absence of Divine validation of our faculties, we must rely on the output of the hierarchically ordered set of cognitive faculties, and hence on the contributions of the component faculties, to include sense-perception. Descartes' refusal to challenge the reliability of sense-perception can be construed as reflecting his recognition of this point.

We have also seen that Descartes characterizes the doubts of Meditations I and III quite differently. The former is powerful and mature, the latter slight and metaphysical. I have noted two disanalogies between the hypotheses as presented by Descartes, disanalogies that might be thought to justify the difference in his assessment of the relative force of the doubts. The disanalogies are superficial, however, in the sense that Descartes could have constructed the two hypotheses in a way that would not have involved the disanalogies. What explains Descartes' preference for constructing the two hypotheses in a way that enabled him to minimize the doubt of Meditation III?

The dissimulation hypothesis provides an answer. Suppose Descartes did subscribe to the nontheological epistemological position I have attributed to him. Then the point of Meditation I is that one cannot have (maximally) reasonable belief about the material world on the basis of sense-perception alone, on the basis of beliefs that arise spontaneously from sensory experience and which have not been subjected to all possible tests for correction. Thus, in the third paragraph of Meditation I, Descartes writes: "All that up to the present time I have accepted as most true and certain I have learned either from the senses or through the senses" (HR I, 145; AT VII, 13). The hypothesis of the omnipotent deceiver is a particularly striking way of showing that beliefs about the material world, insofar as they are based on sensory experience alone, are correctable in the sense that they are susceptible to correction by reason; there is nothing in the nature of reason qua cognitive faculty which precludes it from correcting beliefs based on sensory experience by showing, for example, that there does exist an omnipotent deceiver. The function of the hypothesis of Meditation I is to suggest that sense-perception is not epistemologically basic. This is the initial stage of the argument for the hierarchical ordering of the cognitive faculties. The argument is completed in Meditation III when Descartes claims, prior to producing the proofs of the existence of God, that reason or the faculty of clear and distinct perception is epistemologically basic. In Meditation VI, against the background of the claim that the cognitive faculties are hierarchically ordered, Descartes restores or reinstates *some* of the beliefs that had previously been based on sense-perception alone, by contending that they are resistant to correction.

If this account is correct, there is a legitimate function for the hypothesis of Meditation I, but there is no comparable function for an analogous hypothesis in Meditation III. The point of the hypothesis of Meditation I is that sense-perception is susceptible to correction by reason and hence not epistemologically basic. There is no corresponding function to be served by the hypothesis about reason in Meditation III. If one thinks of sense-perception and reason as epistemologically coordinate or as coequal cognitive faculties, it will seem that equally strong doubts can be raised about both. Descartes, however, held that reason or the faculty of clear and distinct perception is epistemologically prior to sense-perception, and indeed epistemologically basic. There can be no question of this faculty's being susceptible to correction by some yet more basic cognitive faculty. This is the underlying rationale for treating the doubt about reason as slight and metaphysical, whereas the doubt about sense-perception is treated as powerful and mature. A full, direct explanation of this rationale would defeat the dissimulation by making the nontheological epistemology explicit. Descartes prefers to construct the hypothesis of Meditations I and III in a way that renders them superficially disanalogous. These disanalogies, which provide superficial reasons for the disparate characterizations of the grounds for doubt in Meditations I and III, function as proxies for the underlying rationale I have described. Attributing the nontheological epistemology to Descartes would enable us to understand why Descartes adopted such different postures toward the hypotheses of Meditations I and III.

According to the dissimulation hypothesis, Descartes nevertheless introduces the hypothesis of Meditation III as a pretext for locating a particular epistemological role for God, and it is at this juncture that dissimulation comes to dominate the developments of Meditations III and IV. In Meditation III, Descartes offers arguments for the existence of a nondeceiving God, even though he did not believe the arguments cogent. In Meditation IV, Descartes appeals to the existence of this being in support of his claim that whatever one clearly and distinctly perceives is true, even though he was aware of the circularity of his procedure.

DESCARTES' MOTIVES

Why would Descartes have engaged in such massive dissimulation? I will sketch an answer to this question. Descartes began writing his *Treatise on the Universe* in 1629. The work was ready for publication in 1633. In June of that year, Galileo was condemned by the Inquisition for his doctrine that the earth moves. This doctrine was also central to Descartes' cosmology. When Descartes heard of the condemnation, he decided not to publish his treatise. Descartes feared censure by the Church. His fear was not ill-founded, since his philosophy was condemned by Rome in 1663, sixteen years after his death.

Descartes' concerns were reinforced by his positive desire that his philosophy be taught in Church colleges.[41] Descartes went to great lengths in attempting to ensure that the Church received the *Meditations* favorably. We know that the dedication to the theology faculty at the Sorbonne, and the title page of the first edition, misrepresented the work as containing a proof of the immortality of the soul.[42] Descartes wrote to Mersenne in 1639, "To make it as good as possible, I plan to have only twenty or thirty copies printed, and send them to the twenty or thirty most learned theologians I can find, so as to have their criticisms and learn what should be changed, corrected or added before publication" (K 68; AT II, 617). He wrote to Mersenne in 1640 of his desire for "the approbation of the Sorbonne, which I want, and which seems very useful for my purposes. Because I must confess that the small *Treatise on Metaphysics* which I sent you contains all the principles of my Physics" (K 82; AT III, 233). It fell to Mersenne to solicit criticisms of the *Meditations* from theologians, though Mersenne approached others as well. It is these criticisms that constitute the various sets of Objections.

Descartes misrepresented aspects of his scientific views (insofar as they related to creation, and to the earth's motion) in print, in the *Principles of Philosophy.*[43] In light of Descartes' prudential concerns, it does seem possible that in the *Meditations* Descartes purposely misrepresented his views with respect to the role of God in epistemology. The *effect* of the misrepresentation is to suggest a specific, intimate connection between the existence of God and the possibility of human knowledge—that Divine validation of the cognitive faculties is necessary for human knowledge; the *intent* is to render other aspects of Descartes' philosophy, most especially his physics, more acceptable to the Church. I have noted that in the *Rules,* written in 1628–1629, there is no hint of skepticism about intuition or clear and distinct perception, and no epistemological role for God. Galileo was condemned in 1633. In the *Discourse on Method,* published in 1637 as a preface to treatises on light, meteors, and geometry, Descartes maintains that the certainty of clear and distinct perception is due to Divine perfection. I suggest that the apparent change in Descartes' views about the epistemological status of clear and distinct perception may have resulted from Descartes' attempt, most especially after the condemnation of Galileo, to make his philosophy more acceptable to the Church.[44] I have not attempted to establish that the dissimulation hypothesis is correct; however, I think it would be incautious to reject dissimulation hypotheses out of hand.[45]

NOTES

1. There are two contemporary proponents of the view that Descartes is engaged in extensive dissimulation in the *Meditations.* See Hiram Caton, "On the Interpretation of the *Meditations,*" *Man and World* 3, 3 (Sept. 1970):224–245; "The Problem of Descartes' Sincerity," *The Philosophical Forum* 2, 3 (Spring 1971):355–370; *The Origin of Subjectivity: An Essay on Descartes* (New Haven: Yale University Press, 1973); and "Will and Reason in Descartes' Theory of Error," *The Journal of Philosophy* 72, 4 (Feb. 27, 1975):87–104, esp. 97–100; and Kenneth Dorter, "Science and Religion in Descartes' *Meditations,*" *The Thomist* 37, 2 (April 1973):313–340. For earlier versions of dissimulation hypotheses, see Charles Adam, *Vie & Oeuvres de Descartes, Étude Historique* (Paris: Léopold Cerf, 1910), 304–307; and Maxime Leroy, *Descartes, le philosophe au masque* (Paris: Les Éditions Rieder, 1929), esp. 1:15–21, and 2:17–42.

2. This thesis is not meant to suggest that Descartes was not pious, or not a theist, or not sincere about his proof of the existence of God in Meditation V.

3. Curley treats the Cartesian circle as the principal indication of dissimulation, though Curley himself rejects the dissimulation hypothesis. See E. M. Curley, *Descartes Against the Skeptics* (Cambridge: Harvard University Press, 1978), 96–98. The problem of circularity plays a significant role in Dorter's

defense of the dissimulation hypothesis. See Dorter, "Science and Religion," 318–320, 326.

4. I use the abbreviations AT, HR, and K (explained in the General Bibliography at the beginning of this volume) for editions of Descartes' works. I also use the abbreviation CB for John Cottingham, trans. *Descartes' Conversation with Burman* (Oxford: Clarendon Press, 1976). References to specific paragraphs of the *Meditations* (e.g., "paragraph four of Meditation III") follow the paragraph divisions of the second Latin edition (1642) as edited by Adam (AT VII); this is the edition translated by Haldane and Ross (HR).

5. See Pierre Gassendi, *Metaphysical Colloquy, or Doubts and Rebuttals Concerning the Metaphysics of René Descartes, with his Replies,* Rebuttals to Med. III, Doubt One, Article One; Rebuttals to Med. IV, Doubt One, Article One, and Doubt Four, Article Two. The relevant passages are translated *in* Craig B. Bush, ed. and trans., *The Selected Works of Pierre Gassendi* (New York: Johnson Reprint Corp., 1972), 204, 231, 241–242.

6. Dorter, "Science and Religion" (esp. 326–327) also finds characteristics of the arguments for the existence of God in Meditation III suggestive of dissimulation.

7. See, for example, Norman Kemp Smith, *New Studies in the Philosophy of Descartes* (London: Macmillan, 1952), 302–303; Anthony Kenny, *Descartes: A Study of his Philosophy* (New York: Random House, 1968), 20 and 126–145; and Bernard Williams, *Descartes: The Project of Pure Enquiry* (Harmondsworth, England: Penguin Books, 1978), 142–152.

8. For criticism of the principle about causation, see A. Boyce Gibson, *The Philosophy of Descartes* (London: Methuen, 1932), 110–124; Williams, *Descartes,* 138–141, 142–143; and Margaret Wilson, *Descartes* (London: Routledge & Kegan Paul, 1978), pp. 136–138.

9. Williams (in his *Descartes*) writes of Descartes' acceptance of the principle that there must be at least as much perfection in the efficient and total cause as in its effect: "It is the question of the causation of his ideas that Descartes now pursues. And here he makes a sudden jump forward, receiving a deliverance from the 'natural light' at once more substantial and less plausible than many propositions about which he has felt qualms at earlier stages of his reflection. . . . This is a piece of scholastic metaphysics, and it is one of the most striking indications of the historical gap that exists between Descartes' thought and our own . . . that he can unblinkingly accept this unintuitive and barely comprehensible principle as self-evident in the light of reason" (p. 135).

10. The prima facie case does not directly support one component of the dissimulation hypothesis. Suppose that Descartes was sincere in proposing the ontological argument for the existence of God in Meditation V. The use of the ontological argument does not beg the question against the doubt about the existence of the material world in Meditation I. It is thus consistent with the considerations in the text that Descartes was sincere in his appeal to Divine veracity in order to prove the existence of the material world. This suggests a weakened version of the dissimulation hypothesis, according to which the dissimulation does not extend to the appeal to Divine veracity in

Meditation VI. I have more to say about the weakened version of the dissimulation hypothesis in notes 29 and 40, below.

11. See Jean Laporte, *Le Rationalisme de Descartes* (Paris: Presses Universitaires de France, 1950), 299–300, 465–466; and Caton, "On the Interpretation," 12–15.

12. See Caton, *Origin of Subjectivity*, 15–20; and Dorter, "Science and Religion," 339.

13. Descartes states in the fourth paragraph of Meditation III that the doubt he raises there can only be removed by proving the existence of a nondeceiving God. In the final paragraph of Meditation IV, Descartes appeals to the existence of a nondeceiving God in order to sustain the conclusion that whatever is clearly and distinctly perceived is true. It is therefore difficult to resist the conclusion that the doubt raised in the fourth paragraph of Meditation III is about clear and distinct perception.

14. The discrepancy has been noted, and variously explained. See: L. J. Beck, *The Method of Descartes: A Study of the* Regulae (Oxford: Oxford University Press, 1952), 38–43; L. J. Beck, *The Metaphysics of Descartes: A Study of the* Meditations (Oxford: Oxford University Press, 1965), 134–135; Caton, *Origin of Subjectivity*, 48; Curley, *Descartes Against the Skeptics*, viii, 35–38, 103; and S. V. Keeling, *Descartes* (Oxford: Oxford University Press, 1968), 15–16, 79–81, 84–85.

15. I follow Frankfurt in taking the doubt of Meditation I as extending to beliefs about mathematics only insofar as they are taken to be based on the senses. See Harry G. Frankfurt, *Demons, Dreamers, and Madmen; The Defense of Reason in Descartes'* Meditations (Indianapolis: Bobbs-Merrill, 1970), pt. 1, esp. chaps. 7–8, pp. 61–78.

16. Some commentators illicitly import the description of the ground for doubt in Meditation III into Meditation I. Beck (in *Method of Descartes*) writes: "But in the first Meditation even the truths of arithmetic are shown to be open to doubt. The doubt itself may be, as Descartes says, 'very slight': it may only be a 'metaphysical doubt which leads me to question that $2 + 2 = 4$'" (p. 40). Beck's citation (p. 40) reads "cf. *Meditationes*, I (AT VII, 36, lines 24–26)." The AT passage, of course, is found in Meditation III, not Meditation I. Also see Gerd Buchdahl, *Metaphysics and the Philosophy of Science: The Classical Origins, Descartes to Kant* (Oxford: Basil Blackwell, 1969), 157–158.

17. The issue is almost never raised explicitly. Curley (*Descartes Against the Skeptics*) is one commentator who sees that there is an interpretive problem: "the ground of doubt which Descartes here characterizes as 'valid and carefully considered' he will later . . . call 'slight and metaphysical.' This is puzzling and will require explanation . . . " (pp. 42–43). In *Knowledge and Perception* (Oxford: Oxford University Press, 1950), H. A. Prichard writes: "Though Descartes says the ground of doubt is slight, it is not really so. The ground is serious. . . . He adds that it is metaphysical. . . . To say this does not make the difficulty any less serious" (p. 85). Prichard fails to ask the obvious question: why does Descartes say that the doubt of Meditation III is slight?

18. In Meditation I, Descartes does state: "I have long had fixed in my mind the belief that an all-powerful God existed . . . " (HR I, 147; AT VII, 21). The belief in an omnipotent God is a preconceived opinion. However,

the belief in an omnipotent God *who is a deceiver* is *not* a preconceived opinion. And even if it were, this fact would not account for the difference in Descartes' description of the grounds for doubt in Meditations I and III. This is because the belief in an omnipotent God (whether or not such a being is believed to be a deceiver) would have the same status as a preconceived opinion both at the end of Meditation I and at the beginning of Meditation III, prior to the arguments for the existence of God.

19. The literature is of little help here. Wilson (in her *Descartes*) simply repeats Descartes' own inadequate explanation: "Since [Descartes] has no reason to believe there is such a [deceiving] God, the reason for doubt that depends on this idea is 'very tenuous and so to speak Metaphysical'" (p. 120; cf. p. 130). Kenny (in his *Descartes*) writes: "Descartes sometimes calls his doubt 'hyperbolical' and 'metaphysical' (AT VII, 37, 90; HR I, 159, 199). By this he means that the suppositions on which the doubt depends—that life is a dream, that there is an omnipotent deceiver—are very improbable suppositions" (pp. 23–24). Prior to the proofs of the existence of a nondeceiving God, Descartes would seem to have no resources to show that the hypotheses in question are *im*probable (except in a purely subjective sense). But the important point is that the suppositions of an omnipotent deceiver in Meditations I and II would seem to be *equi*probable, and hence Kenny cannot explain why the reasons for the former are "very powerful." Although Curley (*Descartes Against the Skeptics*) undertakes to explain the difference in the characterizations of the grounds for doubt in Meditations I and III (see n. 17, above), I do not find a satisfactory explanation in his discussion. Curley emphasizes that the hypothesis of an omnipotent deceiver is a reasonable ground for doubt prior to the end of Meditation IV (cf. pp. 106–107, 116, 119–120). It follows, as Curley admits (cf. p. 124) that it is also a reasonable ground for doubt at the beginning of Meditation III.

20. There is a difference I do not discuss. In Meditation I, Descartes initially formulates the hypothesis with reference to an omnipotent God (para. 9) and subsequently formulates the hypothesis of the evil genius (para. 12). In Meditation III, the hypothesis is formulated exclusively with reference to God. In advance of a proof of the existence of a nondeceiving God, this difference seems irrelevant to the force of the respective hypotheses. In each Meditation, the hypothesis in question is that there exists a powerful *being* who deceives Descartes in particular respects. What is more, the texts preclude assigning any epistemological significance to the difference in question. In Meditation I, the ground for doubt is described as powerful and mature on the basis of the initial formulation with reference to God, prior to the formulation with reference to a genius. Both contrasting characterizations of the grounds for doubt thus refer to hypotheses about *Divine* deception.

21. Numerous commentators agree on this point. See, for example: Beck, *Method of Descartes*, 8; Emile Bréhier, "The Creation of the Eternal Truths in Descartes' System," in Willis Doney, ed., *Descartes, A Collection of Critical Essays* (Garden City, N.Y.: Anchor Books, 1967), 193; Caton, *Origin of Subjectivity*, 68; Frankfurt, *Demons*, 7; and Harry G. Frankfurt, "Descartes and the Creation of the Eternal Truths," *The Philosophical Review* 86, 1 (Jan., 1977):37.

22. For two commentators who maintain that the doubt of Meditation III does depend upon the doctrine of the eternal truths, see Bréhier, *Creation*, and Wilson, *Descartes*, esp. 33–34, 121, 128.

23. It is frequently maintained that Descartes had prudential reasons for withholding his doctrine about the creation of the eternal truths. Cf. Bréhier, "Creation," 193; Frankfurt, *Demons*, 7; and Gibson, *Philosophy*, 53. This might be taken to defeat the expectation that Descartes would invoke the doctrine for the suggested purpose in the *Meditations*. I believe Descartes was sincere in his doctrine about the eternal truths, and that he did suppress the doctrine for reasons of prudence. I also believe, however, that since he had reasons for not taking the doubt of Meditation III seriously (see part 3, below), he would not have wanted to appeal to this doctrine in order to maintain parity between the hypotheses of Meditations I and III.

24. At the close of the ninth paragraph of Meditation I, Descartes writes of the possibility that God might have created me such that "I am always mistaken" (AT VII, 21—my translation; HR I, 147). This might be taken to suggest that in Descartes' hypothesis God creates one with a *faculty* such that one is always mistaken. The passage is at best suggestive of this interpretation, however, and does not require it. I think it reasonable to resolve the ambiguity in favor of the explicit passage in Meditation VI.

25. Cf. Frankfurt, *Demons*, 34.

26. For a different interpretation of the madness passage, see Frankfurt, *Demons*, 37–38. The interpretation of Caton, *Origin of Subjectivity*, p. 111, is congenial to my own.

27. Frankfurt (in his *Demons*) maintains that the hypothesis of Meditation I does raise "the possibility that the human mind is inherently defective" (p. 81). I have argued above that this is not the most plausible interpretation of the hypothesis of the omnipotent deceiver. As far as I can see, Frankfurt does not so much argue for his interpretation as presuppose it; he does not directly consider my alternative to it. The term *nature* does not occur in the context of the development of the hypothesis of Meditation I. It is sufficient for my purposes that the hypothesis of Meditation III, unlike the hypothesis of Meditation I, is stated in such a way as to require that the mind has an intrinsically defective faculty.

28. Why does this render the doubt of Meditation I comparatively strong? The intuitive idea is this. Suppose a skeptic generates doubt with respect to beliefs about the material world by suggesting that the faculty of sense-perception might itself be defective. Although this hypothesis does not seem illegitimate, it does seem to beg the question directly against the nonskeptic. The suggestion that our perceptual beliefs are caused by some unreliable mechanism distinct from sense-perception does not beg the question about the reliability of sense-perception itself. In this sense, the latter ground for doubt is stronger. The same points would apply to doubts relating to reason.

29. This "acute form of the difficulty" does not arise for the weakened version of the dissimulation hypothesis (see n. 10, above).

30. As Curley (*Descartes Against the Skeptics*) notes, "Dissimulation theorists

typically do not see much force in the skeptical arguments Descartes professes to reply to . . . " (p. 100).

31. " . . . *intuition* is the undoubting conception of an unclouded and attentive mind, and springs from the light of reason alone" (HR I, 7; AT X, 368); " . . . the light of nature, or the faculty of knowledge which God has given us, can never disclose to us any object which is not true, inasmuch as it . . . apprehends it clearly and distinctly" (HR I, 231; AT VIII–1, 16).

32. There is another example. Descartes maintains that the mistaken judgment, based on sight, that a stick protruding from water is bent, is corrected by reason (HR II, 252–253; AT VII, 438–439). This is true even if the stick feels straight to the touch: " . . . we need to have some reason to show why in this matter we ought to believe the tactual judgment rather than that derived from vision; and this reason . . . must be attributed not to sense but to the understanding. Hence in this instance it is the understanding solely which corrects the error of sense . . . " (HR II, 253; AT VIII, 439). Descartes concludes that "no case can ever be adduced in which error results from our trusting the operation of the mind more than sense" (HR II, 253; AT VII, 439).

33. The following passage is perhaps suggestive of the doctrine: "For the human mind has in it something that we may call divine, wherein are scattered the first germs of useful modes of thought" (HR I, 10; AT X, 373). Descartes writes more neutrally, however, of "certain primary germs of truth implanted by nature in human minds" (HR I, 12; AT X, 376).

34. I refer to the textual evidence produced in the body of my paper, not to the additional evidence in note 32, above. The latter derives from the Reply to Objections VI. Even these passages, however, make no reference to Divine veracity.

35. We can identify Cartesian knowledge with those beliefs which are both included in the output of one's hierarchically ordered set of cognitive faculties, and true. This raises an important question, which I hope to address elsewhere: In the absence of any appeal to Divine veracity, is there any Cartesian argument to show that beliefs included within the output of one's hierarchically ordered set of cognitive faculties are likely to be true?

36. Descartes writes in Meditation IV: " . . . as He could not desire to deceive me, it is clear that He has not given me a faculty that will lead me to err if I use it aright" (HR I, 172; AT VII, 54). This passage is not inconsistent with the position in Meditation VI, provided that the notion of using a faculty correctly is construed to include subjecting the faculty to correction by other faculties, as appropriate. The passage need not be interpreted to mean that the correct use of faculty, in and of itself, leads only to true beliefs.

37. The teachings of nature play a more prominent role in Descartes' epistemology than commentators generally recognize. For two notable exceptions, see: A. K. Stout, "Descartes' Proof of the Existence of Matter," *Mind*, 41, 162 (April, 1932), esp. 191–197; and Kemp Smith, *New Studies*, 247–258 and 286–293.

38. It is true that Descartes provides virtually no argument for these claims. For example, in the central case of belief in the existence of a material world,

Descartes asserts, rather than argues, that this belief is resistant to correction. This is a defect in the *Meditations* whether or not one takes seriously the appeal to divine veracity. As I have emphasized above, the Divine veracity at best guarantees the truth of those beliefs which are resistant to correction. On any interpretation, Descartes ought to have done more to show that the beliefs validated in Meditation VI satisfy this condition.

39. Such statements are forthcoming in other writings. For example, Descartes provides an extended argument against the possibility of a vacuum in the *Principles of Philosophy* II, nos. 10–18.

40. Of course, it would *not* have been question-begging to prove the existence of a nondeceiving God via an argument (whether the arguments of Meditation III, or the ontological argument of Meditation V) which relies exclusively on clear and distinct perception in order to validate sense-perception. In other words, the *Meditations* would not have been circular had it been different in two respects: first, had the doubt about clear and distinct perception itself not been introduced in Meditation III; and second, had Descartes appealed to Divine veracity solely for the purpose of validating cognitive faculties other than clear and distinct perception. It is the fact that Descartes wrote and published the *Meditations*, rather than the variant of it I have described, which leads me to think that the dissimulation hypothesis is more likely to be true than its weakened version (see n. 10, above). I suggest in part 4 that Descartes' motive for dissimulation was to render his physics more acceptable to the Church by proposing a fundamental epistemological role for God. In the variant of the *Meditations* I have described, knowledge of the existence of God is necessary for knowledge of the existence of the material world. Thus, if the weakened version of the dissimulation hypothesis were correct, Descartes could have made this epistemological offering to the Church without dissimulating at all.

41. For accounts of Descartes' various prudential concerns, see: Adam, *Vie & Oeuvres*, 165–179; Caton, "On the Interpretation," 14–19; Elizabeth S. Haldane, *Descartes, His Life and Times* (New York: E. P. Dutton, 1905), 153–157; Michael Sean Mahoney, trans., *René Descartes, Le Monde* (New York: Abaris Books, 1979, ix–xiv; and Williams, *Descartes*, 18.

42. Cf. Adam, *Vie & Oeuvres*, 304; Caton, *Origin of Subjectivity*, 101–102; Curley, *Descartes Against the Skeptics*, 99; and Dorter, "Science and Religion," 316–318.

43. For the impact of Descartes' prudential concerns on the substance of the *Principles of Philosophy*, see Adam, *Vie & Oeuvres*, esp. 361–365, 372–374, 337–383; Gibson, *Philosophy*, 26, 264–268; Haldane, *Descartes*, 289–290; and Williams, *Descartes*, 371–372.

44. Curley, in *Descartes Against the Skeptics* (pp. 35–37), advances a different explanation of the discrepancy between Descartes' treatment of clear and distinct perception in the *Rules*, on the one hand, and in the *Discourse on Method* and *Meditations*, on the other.

45. This paper benefited from discussion or correspondence with Robert Adams, Miles Burnyeat, Julie Heath, David Hills, Jaegwon Kim, Amélie Rorty, and David Velleman.

12

On the Complementarity of Meditations III and V: From the "General Rule" of Evidence to "Certain Science"

GENEVIÈVE RODIS-LEWIS

The focal point of this essay is what has always seemed to me to be a constant Cartesian "duality," namely, that of simple "persuasion" linked to the presence of evidence and "certain science" grounded in God. I first approached the matter in remarking that the whole debate is opened at the beginning of Meditation III, to close at the end of Meditation V.[1] Furthermore, this contrast may shed some historical light on the order (both chronological and philosophical) of Descartes' final writing of the *Meditations*. It seems to me that Descartes escapes the accusation of a "circle" in this context precisely because "persuasion" has a tentative validity before the grounding of science in God. This complementarity leads, secondly, to a hypothesis concerning the overall plan, if not the complete details, of Descartes' writing of Meditations III and V.

In 1629, Descartes wrote a "beginnings of metaphysics" (*commencement de métaphysique*), mention of which is made for the first time in a letter to Mersenne (15 April 1630) and repeated in December of 1630 and March (or late February) of 1637.[2] The manuscript was probably destroyed by Descartes after a first revision and, most likely, further development, as well as, surely, a final additional rewriting for the *Meditationes de prima philosophia* (1641). All of this remains forever unverifiable. No trace of the manuscript is to be found in the Inventory of Papers recovered after Descartes' death (AT X, 5–12).

Although one can only attempt to reconstruct this text on the basis of purely hypothetical suppositions, the *commencement* surely cannot

be identified, as was commonly done before F. Alquié's thesis,[3] with
the 1641 text of the *Meditations*. It does not follow, though, either that
the *commencement* was very short, as more than one commentator has
thought,[4] or that Descartes' doubt of 1629 affected only the senses.
Now, the extent of doubt is essential to determining how the problem
of a circle can be raised. In two of the letters quoted above, which
respectively precede and follow publication of the *Discourse on Method*
and in which Descartes admits having employed weakened arguments
with respect to those of the "little treatise," he repeats (in Latin) that
one must "detach the mind from the senses."[5]

Descartes does insist on "the uncertainty of all our knowledge of
material things" (AT I, 560), "amply explaining the falseness or uncertainty in all judgements depending on the senses or the imagination"
(ibid., 350). But Descartes goes on to say that "detaching the mind
from the senses" is only "in order to show afterwards what are those
[judgments] which depend only upon pure understanding, and to
what extent they are evident and certain." And, as he was writing in
French and feared troubling those who were not accustomed to metaphysical subtleties, he admits having "omitted . . . deliberately . . .
doubts and scruples which I ought to have (*qu'il m'eût fallu*) proposed"
(ibid., 350; my emphasis). For these doubts risked so striking the weak-
minded as to make it impossible for the "reasons" designed to dispel
them to get them out of the "scrape." All of this was "reasoned at
rather great length" in the *commencement* (ibid.).

The very same reasons that envisaged the grounding of certitude
regarding judgments depending on the understanding alone at the
same time risked dangerously unsettling the certainty of weaker
minds, as they went further than those of the attenuated reasons of
the *Discourse*. But, the Fourth (metaphysical) Part of the *Discourse*
already raises the question of sensory error, and the possible confusion
between waking reality and the illusion of dreams, all of which was
admitted beforehand to be on the level of "mathematical demonstrations," as "some men" err in their reasoning about the simplest
geometrical questions.

Hence, even before 1637, mathematics is no longer the model of
"science" as defined at the beginning of the second Rule in the *Rules
for the Direction of the Mind:* "certain and evident knowledge"—in the
Latin title, *certa et indubitata* (AT X, 362)—which the various French
and English translations render as "indubit*able*" (though the English
word "undoubt*ed*" does exist). Next is postulated the rule for rejecting
merely plausible opinions by deciding to give one's assent to, or admit
as true, only those objects of knowledge which are "perfectly well

known and of which there can be no doubt." The whole question lies in determining the difference between what seems to be actually shielded from doubt (*indubitata*) and what is in principle *indubitable* because it resists calling into doubt. The first precept of the *Discourse* (*Discourse* II: AT VI, 18) is a methodological rule of evidence sanctioning the following definition: " . . . what should present itself so clearly and distinctly to my mind that I would have no occasion to *call* it *into* doubt (*le mettre en doute*)" (cf. HR I, 92, who translate it simply as: "no occasion to doubt it"). The content of this rule may be identified with those of *Regulae* II, though its final formulation implies the active attitude characterizing a metaphysical enterprise—pushing doubt to its ultimate limits in order to limit the certainty that resists it. In *Discourse* IV, even when it is a question of the senses, doubt is already called "hyperbolical"; it goes very much beyond the suspicion of uncertainty that a simple suspension of judgment should evoke. Here, Descartes has just rejected the skeptical question mark of those who "only doubt for the sake of doubting" (*Discourse* III: HR I, 99; AT VI, 29). His substitute is a *negation* that rejects "as absolutely false everything as to which I could imagine the least ground of doubt" (*Discourse* IV: HR I, 101; AT VI, 31; cf. *Principles* I, 2). But, is it sufficient that "some men" (*des hommes*, *Discourse* IV: AT VI, 32; cf. *Principles* I, 5) be mistaken in elementary geometrical questions for an attentive mathematician to abandon as uncertain what was for him most typically undoubted? In the First Meditation, Descartes significantly says "others" (*alios errare*: AT VII, 21; IX, 16). The spontaneous objection to madness is the following: "What? They're madmen!" (AT VII, 19; IX, 16). He might have said here: "But they're harebrained!" The hyperbolic movement, however, does allow for calling into doubt even mathematics, as soon as the slightest error is thought possible. Among the strongest arguments that should perturb "simple people," arguments that Descartes prudently neglected to publish before 1637 and which he thus probably had in mind as early as 1629,[6] are those which deal with a deceiving God and atheism[7]—in other words, what article 30 of the *Principles* (I) calls the "supreme doubt."[8]

The absence of supreme doubt in the *Discourse* and its presence in the *Meditations* explain the slight difference between the two formulations of the "general rule" postulated after the *cogito* in the former and at the beginning of Meditation III. Seeking "what in a proposition is requisite in order to be true and certain, . . . I might assume, as a general rule . . . ," Descartes claims that what in the *cogito* makes the connection a necessary one are its clearness and distinctness (*Discourse* IV: HR I, 101–102; AT VI, 33). Likewise, in the Third Meditation, on the model of the *cogito*, he says: "I can establish as a general rule that all things which I perceive very clearly and very distinctly are true." But the following qualification is included: " . . . which would not indeed suffice to assure me that what I say is true, if it could ever happen that a thing which I conceived so clearly and distinctly could be false."[9]

In the paragraph that follows, we are reminded that several things admitted to be "very certain"[10] have later been unsettled by doubt— notably, the world perceived by our senses, along with the twofold question of its existence and essence (the things from which my ideas proceed and which they may or may not resemble).[11] Then follows the text that opens the question of the limitations of the general rule just proposed, inasmuch as supreme doubt subsists even when weakened by the encounter with the *cogito*, the evidence of which renders illusion or error *unthinkable*. This is why reason for doubt appears henceforward to be "very slight, and as it were metaphysical," as Descartes avows at the end of this passage (AT VII, 36; IX, 28). But, though it has no practical effect on our conduct (an atheist will continue to solve mathematical problems), "metaphysical" doubt still rests on the "very strong and duly considered reasons" that suddenly appear at the end of the First Meditation (AT VII, 21; IX, 17). Here, the certainty of mathematics as a model of evidence was seen to be shaken even while resisting the dream, and indeed the madness, arguments. After incidentally evoking such motives for doubt as were very common at the time—madness, dreams, sensory illusion—Plato had before assured us that even someone asleep or a madman could not confuse odd and even or seriously say that two is one (see *Theaetetus*, 157e and 190b–c). Descartes also objects: "Whether I am awake or asleep, two and three joined together make five, and a square never has more than four sides."[12] Likewise, he concludes in *Discourse* IV: "if a sleeping geometer invents a new demonstration, the fact that he is asleep will not prevent it from being true (AT VI, 39). It should be noted that this remark occurs *"after* the knowledge of God . . . has thus rendered us certain of this rule" (ibid., HR I, 105; my emphasis). This confirms the fact that the initial statement of the rule, while it does not, as in the Third Meditation, evoke the possibility of supreme doubt, does not exclude a certain subjectivity: "I came to the conclusion (*je jugeai*) that I might assume, as a general rule" (HR I, 102; AT VI, 33); "it seems to me already that I can establish as a general rule . . . " (AT VII, 35; IX, 27; HR I, 158). Despite the "deliberate omission" of the reasons that led Descartes to doubt the evidence of even those intellectual judgments appearing to be most certain, after demonstrating the existence of God,[13] he concludes that, "when a metaphysical certainty is in question," the most extravagant doubts recur as long as one is not sure that God exists. "For . . . that which I have just taken as a rule . . . is certain only because God is or exists . . . and that all that is in us issues from Him" (HR I, 104–105; AT VI, 38). The problem is really the same. Will it be said that this avowal expresses the "circle" for which Descartes is so often reproached,[14] as the rule itself was first required in order to demonstrate God's existence? The complementarity of Meditations III and V, on the progression from actually experienced persuasion to theoretical certainty, seems to me to involve something that escapes being put into logical form. To avoid going round in circles, one must change planes.

To specify the conditions of application of the general rule, the text of Meditation III currently under consideration thus first reminds us of the mathematical model, then of its unsettling, then of the (almost?) irresistible persuasion of the evidence of the *cogito,* then returns to the doubt, however slight, which finally subordinates all certainty to the demonstration of a nondeceiving God. The text progresses by oscillating between two poles—what excites my adherence (belief) and what obliges me to retract it.

(i) AT VII, 35–36 ("*Quid vero? . . . affirmarem*") is a reminder of the recognized privileged status of very simple and easy mathematical propositions, admitted to be *true* by their very clarity.

(ii) AT VII, 36 ("*Equidem . . . evidentissime intueri*") is a reminder of intervening doubt. Some God could have (the Latin *potuisse* and the French *avait pu* [AT IX, 28] both have a hypothetical sense) given me "a *nature* such that I be mistaken [*deciperer*], even regarding the things which *seem* to me most manifest."[15] This reminder is followed by the conclusion that what is still only a "preconceived opinion" about God's "sovereign power" obliges me to admit (*non possum non fateri; je suis contraint d'avouer*) that, if He so wishes, it is easy for Him to make me err (*ut errem; que je m'abuse*) even about that of which I think I have an intellectual intuition of maximal evidence.[16]

(iii) AT VII, 36 ("*Quoties vero . . . agnosco manifestam*"). Here, mention of supreme doubt is opposed to persuasion (cf. *persuadeor,* line 14, and AT IX, 28: *je suis tellement persuadé*); those things which I think I conceive[17] very clearly cannot be erroneous. This assertion, contrary to the preceding one (*vero; Et au contraire*), excites a spontaneous outburst (*ut sponte erumpam,* AT VII, 36, 14; cf. AT IX, 28: *de moi-même je me laisse emporter*) which, in spite of the possibility of an actively deceiving power (*fallat me quisque potest,* AT VII, 36, 15; cf. AT IX, 28: *Me trompe qui pourra*), expands the irresistible persuasion of the *cogito* (asserting that I think, I am, even if I am the object of deception), first to a statement in the future, then to a statement in the past; then, without discontinuity (*ou . . . ou bien* in the French; the Latin marks a progression: *vel forte etiam*, line 18), takes up the initial mathematical model (2 + 3 = 5, *et similia*, i.e., all similar propositions). I cannot deny them, because this would be a "manifest contradiction."[18]

Is there here an expansion of the rule of evidence? This is one of the fundamental questions.

(iv) AT VII, 36 (*"Et certe . . . ex ea opinione dependet"*). The French translation introduces a new paragraph here, whereas the Latin text is continuous. There having been no occasion to encounter a deceitful God, supreme doubt seems very slight and "metaphysical." The question of the existence of God, however, has not yet been examined.

(v) AT VII, 36 (*"Ut autem . . . unquam posse"*; followed by a new paragraph in the Latin). In order that supreme doubt disappear it must be considered as soon as possible[19] whether God exists and, if so, whether he may deceive. Otherwise, "I do not see that I can ever be certain of anything" (HR I, 159).

Passages (i) and (iii) follow the sense of the general rule of evidence as admitted for its persuasive power. Texts (ii) and (v) emphasize the constraint of supreme doubt as long as a deceiving God remains thinkable. He must, by demonstration, be shown to be unthinkable; this will suffice for grounding perfect certainty. Text (iv) serves as a transition by noting the relatively "slight" character of "metaphysical" doubt. It blocks, however, the spontaneous impulse of (iii), which went beyond what the general rule allowed to be affirmed. The repetition (lines 2 and 19–20 in the Latin text) of the same example as that of Meditation I (AT VII, 20—2 + 3 = 5) is not indifferently chosen. The same example is afterwards submitted to supreme doubt: it may be that God so wished it that I err (*ut fallar*) each time I add two and three (AT VII, 21).

Although the rehabilitation of this sort of second-degree evidence, thanks to a new optimism engendered by the *cogito*, has been talked about,[20] it would be abusive to extend (*vel forte etiam*) to the simplest of mathematical statements the persuasive power—apparently irresistible—of ontological axioms, transposing here the *cogito* to both the future and the past.[21]

Now, what about the axioms? Are there privileged "existential exigencies"?[22] Are the principles of causality, of the hierarchy of degrees of being, of the continuous unity of the creative act—all of which are evidentially grounded on the two a posteriori proofs of the Third Meditation—are these exempt from supreme doubt?[23] In order to throw some light on these difficult and very controversial questions, I shall make a distinction between what exactly it is that is shaken by the possibility of error even in the presence of evidence and what in any case imposes itself in virtue of the general rule.

First, a deceitful God is the most extreme hypothesis, just barely thinkable. One often passes too quickly from God-deceiver to Evil Genius[24] without stopping to consider the hypothesis of atheism, which is also mentioned in *Principles* I, 5. An atheist may very well laugh at this silly fiction, which would make me the slave of an unkind deceiver; he is no less certain of the validity of mathematics. Sartre asks how one may know whether the real is rational. How does one know, asks Descartes, whether my reason corresponds to what is real? For, the weaker the putative power of the author of my origin, "so much the more will it be probable that I am always mistaken."[25] Descartes plays on the ambivalence of the Latin *fallor*; in French, *je* and/or *on me trompe*.[26] It is hardly a question here of imagining that suddenly an all-powerful being shows me something to be an evident truth which, in truth, may be false. The theatrical illusionism of the Evil Genius only bears upon existential appearances. Much more serious is the responsibility of a deceiving God who might have created me in such a way that I always "*deceive myself*" (am mistaken). In other words, what aptitude has my reason for distinguishing between the true and the false? My *nature* is in question as long as I ignore my origins. What is in fact undoubted in mathematical knowledge when attention is closely paid to it[27] is insufficient if the appropriate "natural light," which illuminates us at the time, is fallacious because I might be the result of chance or of blind necessity.

Does the possibility of error regarding even elementary mathematical statements affect the axioms as well? We all spontaneously tend to deny this, as human thought is ruled by the principle of noncontradiction. But would this be the case without God? Undoubtedly, a little later,[28] Descartes will admit that God could have created us with a different intelligence (and thus a different logic) and mathematical truths other than those rendered intelligible by extension. In any case, the question was raised in both a preliminary and a final series of Objections to the *Meditations*. Descartes never replies that the axioms escape supreme doubt! Before sending his manuscript to Mersenne, he emphasizes the difference between persuasion and science in a letter to Regius (the latter an adherent of physiological mechanism, who did not understand the necessity of a metaphysical detour up until his violent break with Descartes in 1647). Descartes comments on his objection ("You say . . . that the truth of the axioms is . . . self-evident") by saying that "I also grant this, for as long as they are clearly and distinctly understood, because our minds are of such a nature that they cannot but admit what they distinctly conceive." But, when we only have the memory of conclusions drawn from these premises, even they are uncertain without knowledge of God. At least we may suppose so (*fingere*), "because perhaps our nature is such that we err even in the most evident things, and consequently do not have a true *science*, but a simple *persuasion*." Both terms are emphasized by Descartes himself, who continues: "science is so strong a persuasion that it can never be shaken by any stronger [persuasion]; and those who are ignorant of God never possess it."[29] Likewise, in 1648, when Burman explicitly questions the axioms used to prove God in the Third Meditation, Descartes again replies, not that they are indubitable as such, but only that one is sure of not erring while one's attention is applied to them.[30] Towards the end of the *Conversation with Burman*, this time apropos of the *Discourse on Method*, Descartes returns to the fact that, as soon as we no longer pay attention to clear and distinct ideas, we cannot assert their truth so long as we do not know that all truth has its origin in God. But even while we do not know this, we cannot as a matter of fact doubt them when we consider them attentively. "Otherwise, we could not prove that God exists."[31]

This is why, when Descartes concludes his general train of reflection on the conditions of perfect certainty threatened by supreme doubt, he comes back to the principle applying the general rule of evidence: "For the rest, whatever proof or argument I avail myself of, we must always return to the point that it is only those things which we conceive clearly and distinctly that have the power of *persuading* me entirely."[32] It could not be more clearly stated here that the problem is exactly the same for both the a posteriori and a priori proofs.[33] This also accounts for the inverted order of their presentation in, respectively, the exposition "more geometrico" of the second Replies and the *Principles*. In the latter (*Principles* I, 14), the "ontological argument" is preceded by a summary of the essential point (ibid., 13): "In what sense the knowledge of all other things depends on the knowledge of God" (HR I, 224). Here we find the same progression from persuasion to science. "Common notions," or axioms, are the starting-point of thought from which are deduced "demonstrations which are so absolutely persuasive that one is at a loss to doubt of their truth while attending to them;[34] for as long as these notions are perceived . . . their truth is very well assured." But when, at the end of a demonstration, the starting-point has been forgotten, supreme doubt may recur and affect, as has been seen, the "nature" of our thought, such that "no *certain science* may be had until one comes to know his creator."[35] The end of Meditation V develops this passage from persuasion (indispensable for advancing to the demonstration of God, but fragile so long as the demonstration is not attained) to science. The latter becomes henceforth unshakable because the very thought of supreme doubt has become impossible. After demonstration (whichever one it may be) of God's existence, "the certainty of all other things depends on it so absolutely, that without this knowledge, it is impossible ever to *know* anything perfectly."[36] Descartes then evokes, and definitely excludes, the arguments which, at the beginning of Meditation III, still awakened supreme doubt, even though weakened by the evidence of the *cogito*. Here we are reminded of a "nature" (AT IX, 51; VII, 70, line 21: *talem factum*) subject often to err, which took to be evident what was later recognized to be doubtful and even false (e.g., the existence of a world similar to my sensory representations of it). But, says Descartes, I was then ignorant of that "rule of truth" (AT VII, 70, 26: *hujus veritatis regulae ignarus*); the preceding objects of pseudo-evidence had not been clearly and distinctly perceived. The dream objection recurs here again, though it is now powerless to unsettle evidence. As was recognized at the end of *Discourse* IV, someone asleep may reason correctly and even discover new demonstrations (AT VI, 39). This is a definitive return to the initial stage preceding the supposition (recognized as fictitious) of reason doomed to error: "Whether I be awake or asleep . . . " (Meditation I: AT VII, 20; IX, 16). "But even though I should be asleep, everything which presents itself to my mind with evidence is absolutely indubitable. Thus it is that I recognize that the certainty and truth of all science depends only upon knowledge of the true God" (AT IX, 55; VII, 71).

In order to attain this "science," however, Descartes could not do without the general rule of evidence; he had to rely on the "irresistible power of persuasion" while it was *present* to his attention[37] in order to *trust* the validity of the natural light, or reason. Dealing with the three possible types of ideas, the long passage in Meditation III, which precedes the text previously commented on, assumes this. Our natural inclination to believe that certain of our ideas (*adventitiae*) come to our minds from external objects is, for the moment, insufficient; in its practical functioning, this "natural inclination" leads us equally well to what is bad as to what is good. We have no motive for trusting it with respect to knowledge (AT VII, 39, line 5; cf. the same *fidam* in line 1). On the contrary, we are presented with the distinction between true and false by the natural light, which has shown me the implication (*sequitur:* AT VII, 38) between the fact that I was doubting and my existence.[38] "And I possess no other faculty . . . which can teach me that what this light shows me to be true is not really true, and no other faculty that is equally trustworthy" (HR I, 160–161; AT VII, 38–39; IX, 30). The terms of Descartes' letter to Mersenne of 16 October 1639 are very nearly the same: "the natural light, or *intuitus mentis,* the only thing in which I hold that one must trust"; "the impulsion of nature towards the preservation of our bodies, the enjoyment of corporal pleasures, etc."; and the instinct which "is in us qua animals . . . should not always be followed."[39]

Evidence is thus sufficiently persuasive while we pay attention to it; but, as long as we are ignorant of the validity of the natural light, doubt may crop up again as soon as the evidence of present thought becomes a thing of the past. This point is emphasized in the conclusion of Meditation V: "For although I am of such a nature that as long as I understand anything very clearly and distinctly, I am naturally impelled to believe it to be true, yet . . . I am also of such a nature that I cannot have my mind constantly fixed on the same object."[40] Human thought is subjected to succession in time. This is why, in all of these impressively convergent texts,[41] Descartes associates recurring supreme doubt with memory (*souvenir*). The question has been raised whether doubt affects memory,[42] or perhaps the permanence of truths, which might have been changed in the interval of doubt by an all-powerful Being.[43] This is an ingenious hypothesis; Descartes, however, never mentions it. The question is, I think, a much simpler one. I cannot *at the same time* clearly think *both* $2 + 3 = 5$ *and* that my reasoning is perhaps mistaken. When I pay attention to the proposition, it persuades me of its truth. But the moment my attention is distracted, however little, by "motives for doubting," I must begin all over again. At the end of Meditation V, "vague and inconstant opinions" are opposed to "true and certain science" (AT VII, 69; IX, 55), the latter attained as soon as I know that my God-given rational nature cannot err when I conduct it well. *Only* the *cogito* is resistant, because only it can reassert itself in a unique and evident intuition when confronted with reiteration of doubt. This is the Archimedean "fixed point" (Meditation II: AT VII, 24; IX, 19; HR I, 149); the rule of evidence is the lever, which does not bend as long as I attend to it. Hence, it is a necessary and sufficient condition that there be a continuous chain of instances of present evidence (like those of the Third Meditation axioms, or the fact that an essence must necessarily include a property) to lead to the conclusion that God exists as a perfect Being.[44] My certainty is henceforward just as perfect. In the *Discourse on Method* Descartes is content to remark, after stating the general rule that admits as true what is evident, that "there is some difficulty in ascertaining which are those that we distinctly conceive" (*Discourse* IV: HR I, 102; AT VI, 33). After the development of supreme doubt, it had to be recognized that even if one rejects the hypothesis of a deceiving God, which goes against commonly received opinions regarding His goodness, He nevertheless permits "me to be sometimes deceived" (Meditation I: HR I, 147; AT VII, 21; IX, 16; cf. supra, note 26). This assertion suffices to ground the hyperbolic movement of doubt. If sometimes, why not always? But it also calls for justification after God's perfection has been proved. Now, in the summary of the beginnings of metaphysics (*Discourse* IV) and in the letters which mention it, no indication is made of the twofold theodicy deployed in Meditations IV and VI; nor is there mention of the new conception of judgment resting on the infinite quality of my free will.[45]

But a careful reading of the end of Meditation III and the beginning of Meditation V reveals such a close linking-up that one can readily see that an earlier writing has been resumed, the concerted movement of which corresponds to that already mentioned of the *Discourse*. After proving God by the idea of a perfect infinite in us, finite and imperfect beings, Descartes wanted to "look for . . . other truths" and fixes on the "subject matter of the geometers" (Discourse IV: AT VI, 36). Previously, he had rather quickly postulated the spirituality of God. Likewise, at the end of Meditation III, Descartes invites us to contemplate at leisure the attributes of God. But, at the beginning of the Fifth Meditation, Descartes avows that there remains much to be examined respecting the divine attributes and the nature of the soul: "I shall perhaps take up this investigation another time" (AT VII, 33; IX, 50). He then hastens to dispel preceding doubts and to discern what can be held to be certain regarding material things. It is now evident (Meditation III: AT VII, 52; IX, 41) that God cannot be a deceiver in everything that is clearly and distinctly perceived. It thus becomes necessary, first, to determine what I clearly and distinctly know concerning bodies by dissociating what appears to be in them confusedly. The "subject matter of the geometers" of the *Discourse* quickly recovers its prevailing position which, already in Meditation I, had been isolated by its simplicity with respect to the confusing complexity of sciences dealing with existing bodies (AT VII, 20; IX, 16). It was of little importance then to know whether geometrical figures are or are not in nature (ibid.). But the fiction of a deceiving God had succeeded in making me doubt (ibid.) even the description of a square as a quadrilateral figure—which was not even a complete definition. Meditation V goes much further in its revelation that the essential definition of each geometrical figure necessarily envelops certain properties. Development of the innateness issue thus directly extends Descartes' reflections on the discovery that the idea of God is innate.

The division of ideas into three types according to their (respective) origins in the Third Meditation (AT VII, 38–39; IX, 29–31) refers to a traditional distinction[46] and is shown to be powerless for going back directly from each idea to its source. This impasse is not, however, a superfluous detour. If it were, Descartes would have suppressed it. As was mentioned regarding the limitations of natural inclination, this development introduces certain suggestions, temporarily insufficient, which will intervene in the demonstration of the existence of bodies in Meditation VI. It also serves to delineate the field of innateness with respect to the other two possible types of ideas. At the start (AT VII, 38; IX, 30), it is not excluded that all my ideas may come to me from outside (*adventitiae*—integral empiricism), or that they may all be innate (as in a sort of monadology in which each event as it were germinates in advance in my nature), or that they may all be "made by *me*" (idealistic solipsism). But before explicitly developing this,[47] Descartes was able, at the end of Meditation III, to determine directly the origin of my idea of God by contrasting it with the two other types of ideas currently admitted. Either I freely fabricate my ideas, or they come to me from some other source. The idea of God is distinguished from those which I have through the organs of my senses: "*vel occurrere videntur*," "or seem to present themselves" (AT VII, 51, line 10; HR I, 170). The reality of adventitious ideas will not be proved until Meditation VI; but their possibility already plays a role in Descartes' rejection of the traditional empiricist thesis according to which nothing is in us which does not come from the senses. The rejection is here a very rapid one. In contrast with ideas that present themselves "unexpectedly" (*non expectanti*, ibid.; cf. *invito:* AT VII, 38, line 16), the idea of God requires my attention in order to conceive it. And yet I do not freely fabricate it: I can neither augment nor diminish it. It is therefore innate.[48]

It is precisely this analysis of innateness, doubly contrasted with the factitious and the adventitious, which is pursued and enriched at the beginning of Meditation V when Descartes examines mathematical essences. Their truth is "*naturae meae consentanea*" (AT VII, 63), harmonized in advance with my nature, that is, the potential development of my natural light.[49] It is of little importance, Descartes reminds us, that they have an existence outside of me. I am free to think of them or not, but their contents escape this freedom. They are imposed on my thought as true and immutable natures (AT VII, 63).

This resumption is as it were the inverted mirror image of the rapid evocation just before the end of Meditation III, which denies, first the adventitious, and then the factitious character of innate ideas. Here, the contrast with facticity comes first, and the initial reminder that they are not freely thought of dispenses with returning to what distinguishes the idea of God from those ideas which suddenly come to me against my will.[50] The whole force of Descartes' opposition to empiricism is then based on the "inestimable" wealth (*innumeras*, AT VII, 64; cf. *une infinité*, AT IX, 51; and *an infinitude*, HR I, 179) of geometrical figures with respect to the perhaps indefinite but always limited succession of what is given to us in sense-experience.[51]

The complementarity of this reflection and the first approach to innateness, expressly prolonged, seems even more striking in that it allows for the supposition that one is confronted with the first continuous nucleus of Descartes' metaphysics. The hypothesis can never be verified in detail; as Descartes himself admits, it can only concern the general drift and not the "enlightened" expression of the *Meditations*.

Leaving aside the long developments in Meditation III of the three possible sorts of ideas and the twofold aspect (formal and objective) of each idea,[52] one obtains the following schema of Meditations III and V (the correspondences in global content of each theme are apparent, as in a looking-glass):

Meditation III	*Meditation V*
(a) General rule of evidence, its insufficiency in the absence of God, its persuasive value limited to the present	(d) Evocation of the attributes of God
(b) Twofold proof of God by the idea of the infinite in us	(c) Innateness of geometrical essences, defined by contrast with factitious, then adventitious ideas
(c) Its innateness defined by contrast with adventitious, then factitious ideas	(b) Proof of God by the idea of the infinite as such
(d) Evocation of God's attributes	(a) Reminder of initial, indispensable starting-point: persuasive power of present evidence, its insufficiency in the absence of God, its certainty after God's demonstration

   The principal consequences of my hypothesis are also, for the most
part, acceptable whatever the chronology of the themes is. They are
of even greater importance, however, if they are interpreted as the
first seeds from which the whole of Cartesianism sprouts.

   1. Mathematical evidence, the perfect model of certainty in the
Regulae, is seriously shaken by the questioning of my reason's aptitude
for distinguishing the true from the false. This supreme doubt totally
opposes Descartes to the other great rationalists (Spinoza, Malebranche, Leibniz), as well as to his own most faithful disciples who
take as a starting-point his conclusion; namely, that every clear and
distinct idea is true.

   2. Only the *cogito* reinforced by reiteration of doubt is absolutely
resistant to it. A "fixed point," it is also, in the Cartesian sense of the
term, the first "principle"[53]—first, because of what is so clear and
evident that its truth cannot at all be doubted each time that it is
attentively thought of. The necessary relation between "I think" and
"I am" (*je pense, je suis*) is the only one which I must rethink each
time I try to doubt it. Second, it comes first as assured knowledge of
everything else that depends on it.

   3. The limiting of persuasion to what is at present determined by
my attentiveness, which I cannot fix for a long time on the same
point, confirms the finite and precarious character of the initial *cogito*.
"I exist . . . but for how long? . . . for as long as I am thinking" (Meditation II: AT VII, 27; IX, 21). Doubt reinforces this, but it also shows
that my knowledge has its limits. This plays a great role in my inability
to account for absolute perfection or a positive infinite. The first "principle" is in no way a "grounding" in the strong sense of the word,
and the rule of evidence has no proper validity of its own as a "criterion"[54] as long as my own reason's validity has not been assured.
The positivity of the infinite God who created me excludes falseness
qua nonbeing.

   4. The whole originality of the Cartesian project collapses if one
postulates as an initial starting-point "Thought" characterized by its
universality, indeed its impersonality, and its internal rationality as
the source of all truth.

   5. Can the ontological argument do without the *cogito*? To avoid
the new "circle" of a proof of God depending on a proof of God it
must be emphasized that, just before the statement of the "proof,"
Descartes remarks that he is going backwards: "Even if everything
which I've concluded in the preceding Meditations should prove to
be not at all true" (AT VII, 65–66; IX, 52). But is it necessary to go
back to what precedes the appearance of supreme doubt in the First
Meditation? This might be acceptable to the extent that Descartes is

here thinking especially about the mathematical atheist who rejects supreme doubt and recognizes nothing to be more certain than mathematics. At the same time, it is not sufficient that he be convinced that the notion of an all-perfect Being implies its existence the same way that the definition of a triangle implies the sum of its angles, if he persists in refusing the notion of the former. It must therefore be shown him that even when he denies God, he has an *idea* of Him. This is the starting-point of the ontological argument of *Principles* I, 14. To shake his assurance, supreme doubt must be "proposed" to him (see Replies to Objections II: AT VII, 125; IX, 111). This is why, as has been seen, the argument of the *Principles* is immediately preceded by a repetition (*Principles* I, 13) of the main point of the twofold complementary development at the end of the Third and the beginning of the Fifth Meditation. It is thus that the tentatively accepted evidence of mathematics becomes rooted in the general rule issuing from the *cogito.* This whole context should be brought out in making the ontological argument explicit. The order of invention is, however, first and foremost a probing of supreme doubt which, little by little, reveals in me the irreducible transcendence of the perfect God which thence makes doubt impossible. *Psychologically,* the ontological argument only appears when spontaneous confidence in its evidence has been strengthened. Hence the apparent subordination[55] of this new proof to the assertion that everything which I clearly and distinctly perceive in a *"res"* (here a mathematical essence) belongs to it (*revera*) (AT VII, 65; IX, 52: *en effet* = in effect) by a truth that is independent of my thought.

6. If one accepts the hypothesis that the essential points of Meditations III and V go back to the interrupted "little treatise" of 1629, the ontological proof would be a part of the latter.[56] It sprouted in Descartes' mind when he wanted to examine what we know clearly and with certainty about the essence of bodies. Only then did the twofold knowledge of God and myself, after assuring the "foundations of physics,"[57] allow Descartes to interrupt his "beginnings of a metaphysics" to concentrate on deducing from this essence the properties that must then be confirmed or disconfirmed by experiment. It will also be noted that, in the letter to Mersenne that is most directly related to mention of his first reflections on metaphysical truths, Descartes says that their demonstration is *"more* evident than the demonstrations of geometry" (AT I, 144). Now, the ontological argument is characterized by this starting-point, the certainty of which is "at least" equal to that of mathematics. Mathematical certainty is then surpassed, again by a motion of assumption, as only the true God is its foundation.[58]

7. Extending this reflection is the discovery that the truth of

mathematics, like the validity of our reason, depends entirely on God, because he created at the same time both the "laws . . . in nature" and their innate ideas in our minds (AT I, 145). The thesis of the free creation of eternal truths appears for the first time in the same letter as one of the "metaphysical questions" concerning physics on which Descartes will write "before a fortnight's time" (ibid., 146). It would not, then, seem to be a part of the treatise left in abeyance. This is probably why it is not explicitly mentioned in the _Meditations_. When Descartes resumed the interrupted manuscript for further elucidation, he retained the order of invention without modifying the progression of the argument. The thesis might have been revealed at the moment of contemplating the attributes of God (at the end of Meditation III); but, in his haste to pass on to the grounding of physics, Descartes postponed the matter until "another time." Most particularly, the thesis is linked to the _creation_ of matter, with motion as a first principle of differentiation in a homogeneous extension. Now Descartes, who never in fact doubted the existence of body (see the Synopsis of the Meditations: AT VII, 15–16; IX, 12; HR I, 143), had stopped writing the small treatise before this demonstration. It was sufficient for him to have established that the science of bodies is solely dependent on what we conceive clearly and distinctly to be in them, that is, extension. Chapter 7 of _Le Monde_ echoes the letter of 15 April 1630. The first accurate statement of the principle of inertia implies God's immutability, as well as his "continuous action," which gives a new metaphysical foundation to the "eternal truths," the model of certainty for mathematicians, henceforth inscribed in the universe as in our souls.[59]

This justifies the a priori deduction of the properties of matter from geometrical extension. The human mind is suited to discerning intelligible laws because its intelligibility is governed by the same rationality that is postulated in the unity of a creative act with no preexisting model.

When, about 1638–1639, Descartes inserted between Meditations III and V his discussion of the right use of our faculty of judging, he did not deal as such with the infinitude of divine liberty of which our freedom is the image; nor with what distinguishes the two of them.[60] One can, though, see in the conclusion to Meditation IV a discreet evocation of what again confirms the grounds of certainty: "In every clear and distinct conception there is undoubtedly [_procul-dubio_ = without _any_ doubt] something _real and positive_ which thus cannot derive its origin from nothing, but must necessarily have God for its author."[61] Though, to my knowledge, no one has noticed this, the preface to the 1647 French translation of the _Principles_ is a little more explicit. Descartes here summarizes the essential points of his metaphysics: " . . . he who would doubt all things cannot yet doubt that he exists while he doubts," that is, thinks. Thus, Descartes continues: "I have taken the being or existence of this thought as the first principle from which I have very clearly deduced the following: viz. that there is a God who is the author of all that is in the world, or who, being the source of all truth, has not created in us an understanding liable to be deceived in the judgments that it forms on matters of which it has a very clear and distinct perception" (HR I, 208; AT IX–2, 9–10).

NOTES

1. See my "Note sur le 'cercle' cartésien," Bulletin cartésien, VIII, *Archives de Philosophie* (1979), 22–26. In a long article on the Cartesian "circle," R. D. Hughes (ibid., VII [1978] 1–12) did not mention this "pair" of contrasts in his list. I shall not go into further detail here on the numerous discussions involved.

2. AT I, 144 (letter to Mersenne, 15 April 1630). The abbreviations AT and HR are explained in the General Bibliography at the beginning of this volume. In another letter to Mersenne (12 December 1630), Descartes speaks of one day finishing "a small treatise in Metaphysics, begun while I was in Friesland" (AT I, 182). And in 1637, admitting that he has weakened the arguments from doubt in the *Discourse*, Descartes says: "about eight years ago I wrote in Latin a beginnings (*commencement*) of metaphysics in which that is reasoned at rather great length" (AT I, 350).

3. Le découverte métaphysique de l'homme chez Descartes (Paris, 1950), esp. 81–83, where Alquié takes issue with C. Adam (*Vie & Oeuvres de Descartes*, AT XII, 306), who dated the whole of the writing of the *Meditations* 1629.

4. F. Alquié talks of "five or six pages written by Descartes upon arrival in Franeker" (*La découverte*, 82). But the letter to Mersenne of 13 November 1639 refers to the future *Meditations*: the "discourse in which I attempt to clarify what I have previously written on this matter . . . will only be five or six printed sheets long, but I hope that it will contain a good part of metaphysics" (AT II, 622). Printed in 16° the *Meditations* is exactly 6 × 16 = 96 pages long. This text confirms the fact that Descartes elaborated on his first metaphysical work. L. J. Beck also thought that "the small treatise on metaphysics was . . . very short" (*The Metaphysics of Descartes* [Oxford, 1965], 6). It surely must not be said that the Fourth Part of the *Discourse* "is merely the work on metaphysics which Descartes was writing in 1629" (E. Denissoff, "Les étapes de rédaction du Discours de la méthode," *Revue philosophique de Louvain* [1956], 263–264).

5. *"Ad abducendam mentem a sensibus."* Cf. letters to Mersenne, March 1637 (AT I, 349–351) and to Vatier, 22 February 1638 (AT I, 560) which repeat the formula. Alquié relies on these two letters in claiming that doubt before 1637 bears only upon the senses.

6. In July of 1629, Descartes planned to finish the little treatise; but because it contained essential points for the "grounds of physics" (letter to Mersenne, 15 April 1630 [AT I, 144]) he settled in Amsterdam and studied meteors, after receiving a description of parhelia. He then began to write *Le Monde* and, as the *Traité de l'Homme* was supposed to be a part of it, he studied anatomy. All of this, however, does not exclude the possibility that new metaphysical points were being investigated.

7. There is no textual evidence for determining whether the Evil Genius hypothesis was an early or a later one.

8. *Summa dubitatio*, "the supreme doubt" (HR I, 231). The latest translation of the *Principles*, by V. Rodger Miller and R. P. Miller (Dordrecht–Boston–London: 1983), gives "the greatest doubt." Picot's French translation of 1647 here says "hyperbolical doubt" (*doute hyperbolique*), a term that is characteristic of all methodic doubt and not just that, as in the present text, of our "faculty of knowing" or "natural light."

9. HR I, 158. Cf. AT VII, 35: *"percipio"* and the following qualification: *"si . . . quod ita clare et distinctum perciperem."* The singular number should be noted (the French text translates first *que je concevrais,* then *que nous concevons*—intellectual perception is in any case involved), as well as the *present tense* (in evoking possible error, HR translate it as "I conceived"). See my further discussion of this problem, infra, note 37.

10. Access to truth is generally put in terms of "certainty"; this is the *cogito's* first boon (see the end of the first paragraph of AT VII, 35, after the listing of the modes of thought: *sum certus*). On the primacy of this notion, see W. Doney, ed., *Descartes: A Collection of Critical Essays* (New York, 1967), Introduction, 9, and B. Williams, "The Certainty of the Cogito" (ibid., 88–107), the latter translated from a paper ("La philosophie analytique") published in French in the *Cahiers de Royaumont* (1962), 40–57.

11. AT VII, 35. Meditation VI has two distinct solutions to the twofold question. *"Ac proinde res corporeae existunt. Non tamen forte . . . tales . . . quales illas sensu comprehendi"* (AT VII, 80; no new paragraph in the Latin text). It might be supposed here that the intermediary paragraph was introduced for the first time, or rewritten, for the final presentation of the *Meditations*.

12. AT VII, 20. My translation, modified from both the French and English versions to emphasize the Latin present tenses (*sunt, habet*). The French gives *formeront* and *aura* (AT IX, 16); though HR I, 147 does translate "form five" (in the present), it adds that "the square *can* never have more than four sides."

13. It will be noted that the *Discourse* goes directly from a posteriori proofs to geometrical essences, which incite the ontological argument. The same progression will be found in Meditations III and V.

14. Cf. Arnauld, Fourth Objections (AT VII, 125, 326–328) and Descartes' Replies (ibid., 142–144, 245–246, 384). Another precise formulation of the question is given in Gassendi's *Instances* (AT VII, 405).

15. My emphases (N.B. the two conditionals in Latin). HR (I, 158) mistakenly translate using past tense: "I may have been deceived even concerning things which seemed to me most manifest."

16. The translation of *"mente oculis quam evidentissime intueri"* (AT VII, 36, lines 11–12) is accentuated here; the French translation gives simply *"connaître."*

17. Here, as in note 9, above, the Latin reads *"percipere"* meaning, however, an intellectual grasp (cf. HR I, 158 and note).

18. HR I, 159—a precise translation of the Latin here (*"repugnantiam agnosco manifestam"*); the French has a weaker sense.

19. Descartes takes things in order of reasoning rather than subject matter.

20. See L. Prenant, "Les moments du développement de la raison chez Descartes," *Europe* (1937), 315–353, esp. 332. (L. Prenant was my first professor of philosophy the very year of this article.) Cf. ibid., 325–326: "Personal judgement classed above every mark of truth implies a psychological method and criterion. . . . Descartes will try to go back to the source of his being in order to find out whether this optimism can be justified. . . . But he cannot do this without relying on the state of affairs which he intends to justify."

21. Before postulating in Meditation II that my existence qua thought resists deception (*sum si me fallit*, AT VII, 25; IX, 19, present tense), Descartes says in the past: *"certe ego eram, si quod mihi persuasi"* and then continues in the future: let him deceive me as much as he can ("will" in the French), he will never make (*efficiet*) me nothing so long as I think (*cogitabo*) that I am something. However, the connection imposes itself as "necessarily true . . . each time that I pronounce or conceive of it in my mind" (present tense). From Antiquity onwards (see Cicero's *De Fato*) it has been disputed whether the necessity of a proposition may be extended to the past (generally granted) and to the future (Aristotle and Epicurus admit only the conjunction of the two).

22. H. Gouhier, "Les exigences de l'existence dans la métaphysique de Descartes" (a 1960 article reprinted in *La pensée métaphysique de Descartes* [Paris, 1962], 265–291).

23. According to M. Gueroult (*Descartes selon l'ordre des raisons* [Paris: Vrin, 1953], t.I, 199–203), all of the Meditation III axioms are as such excluded from doubt. This claim obviates the objection of a circle and makes the two a posteriori proofs superior to the ontological argument the (fragile) evidence of which is that of mathematical truths. Gueroult always refused the "psychologistic" starting-point and the assumption of fact to principle, which seem to me to direct the Cartesian itinerary.

24. For M. Gueroult, the evil genius allows passing from psychological doubt provoked by the deceptive God to a properly metaphysical doubt. Its absence from the *Principles* would explain the fact that Descartes begins there with the ontological proof which, in the *Meditations*, is supposedly subordinate to the proofs of Meditation III. But when the evil genius is explicitly mentioned at the end of Meditation I (AT VII, 23; IX 18), it only affects the *existence* of the world and myself (at least as a body); likewise, when it is combined in a still confused thought with the All-powerful just before being definitely dispelled by the *cogito*. This may perhaps be an echo of Scholastic discussions of the power recognized in higher spirits (good or evil) to excite false appearances in us by means of real "species." Only an all-powerful God could make an

object appear to be nonexistent and, according to some disciples of Ockham, act directly on the understanding to deceive it (cf. T. Gregory, "La tromperie divine," *Studi Medievali* [Spoleto: 1982], 517–527).

25. AT VII, 21; IX 17; *Principles* I, 5.

26. The principal references with both types of translation in the *Meditations* and the *Principles* are given in my "Note sur le 'cercle' . . . " (reference supra, note 1), 23, note 49. HR I, 158–159 successively translate: "I may have been deceived," "to cause me to err," "let Who will deceive me"; cf. ibid., 220 (*Principles* I, 5): "deceived," emphasizing the idea that I am deceived by someone else, vs. "I err," i.e., I myself am responsible for my error.

27. In *Regulae* III, Descartes defines *intuitus* as "firm conception of a pure and attentive mind" (Latin in AT X, 368). Intellectual vision is not punctual or instantaneous, as it grasps a relation between two notions. This is what directs the uninterrupted flow of intuitions in deduction. The comparison with vision is pursued at the beginning of Rule 9; vision is clear when it is concentrated on one object and cloudy when it becomes too expansive. *Principles* I, 45, repeats the definition of clear and distinct knowledge as a function of the attention that determines the *presence* of its object—a condition of persuasion.

28. See my conclusion, below. In my lectures presented at the 1981 colloquium in New Orleans ("Création des vérités éternelles, doute suprême et limites de l'impossible chez Descartes," *Actes de New Orleans*, ed. Fr. L. Lawrence, Biblio 17, Papers on French Seventeenth-Century Literature [Paris–Seattle–Tübingen: 1982], 277–318), I dispute an interpretation that associates this thesis with supreme doubt; I should prefer to make the chronological order of discovery coincide with the logical order, which has been very well discussed by M. Gueroult (only the true God can furnish a ground for the immutability of created truths). I also dispute the limitations for our thought of the impossible, notably for a statement of the thought-being connection in the future or the past (ibid., 289 and notes 39–40).

29. Letter to Regius, 24 May 1640 (Latin text in AT III, 64–65). My translation here is more concise than that of the old translation in my bilingual edition of *Letters to Regius*.

30. Latin text in AT V, 148; cf. the English translation by J. Cottingham (Oxford: Clarendon Press, 1976), 61, n. 6. A strict Cartesian vocabulary would employ "persuaded" rather than *"certus,"* Descartes is not the author here.

31. Cottingham translation, 50, n. 81 (Latin text in AT V, 178).

32. HR I, 183; AT VII, 68; IX, 54. The "we" is introduced in the English translation; the Latin and French texts are in the singular. Descartes, however, does jump several times from "I" to "we" even before God's demonstration allows for postulating the existence of other persons without demonstration. Linguistic expression already suggests communication with other minds.

33. This goes against Gueroult's thesis (*Descartes* . . . , t.I, 334–346) which is criticized by H. Gouhier in "La preuve ontologique de Descartes (à propos d'un livre récent)," *Revue internationale de philosophie* (1954), 295–303. This incited Gueroult's *Nouvelles réflexions sur la preuve ontologique de Descartes* (1955).

34. *Principles* I, 13. It is regrettable that the English translations give a term other than "persuade" (even if it is an equivalent). Cf. HR I, 224: "absolutely convince us of their truth" and the Miller translation (reference in note 8, supra): "it is entirely convinced" (p. 7–8). Both translations follow the Latin at the end of this text; supreme doubt commits one to mistrusting *"de talibus"* (HR: "of such conclusions," which is already an interpretation; Miller: "doubt such things"). The French translation of 1647 seems to limit mistrust to "whatever it [*la pensée*] *does not* distinctly perceive." Of course, when this doubt recurs, the persuasive evidence of the present has become a confused memory; but it seems to me that it still affects, with their conclusions, the initial "common notions" (or axioms, cf. Second Replies, AT IX, 127). The Millers do translate the two present tenses: " . . . it was perhaps created of such a nature that it *errs* even in those things which *appear* most evident to it . . . " (p. 8).

35. "Certain knowledge" is too vague for the Latin *certam scientiam* in the two translations of the *Principles* quoted above.

36. HR I, 183. The emphasized word is weaker than the Latin *perfecte sciri* related, as is confirmed by the paragraph that follows, to *"veram et certam scientiam"* (AT VII, 69; IX, 55).

37. Clear knowledge "is present and apparent to an attentive mind" (*Principles* I, 45: HR I, 237; cf. supra note 27). But supreme doubt shakes this persuasion once it becomes, however little, a thing of the past. The past tense in the English translations is not, then, incorrect. See Meditation III (HR I, 158; notes 9 and 15 above) and *Principles* I, 30. In the latter, after concluding that God is not the cause of *our* mistakes (*Principles* I, 29), Descartes returns to the earlier stage of supreme doubt when "we did not know whether our nature had been such that we had been deceived" (HR I, 231—up to this point in accordance with the series of imperfect and various perfect tenses in the Latin and French); but then, in spite of tense agreement, Descartes writes: *"etiam in iis quae nobis evidentissime* videntur," in Picot's translation: *en toutes les choses qui nous* semblent *très claires.* If one translates: "in things that seemed most clear" (HR ibid.; in Miller: "which seemed to us to be the most evident"), the past tense weakens or even obscures Descartes' insistence on making doubt bear—*after* essentially fleeting persuasion has been effaced—on our aptitude for not confusing true and false even while they *were present.*

38. The correlation does appear in Meditation III (that of Meditation II being nearer to Augustine's formula, equally unshakable: if he deceives me, I am). It recurs in the Prefatory Letter to the French translation of the *Principles* (quoted in my conclusion, below), and is expanded particularly in Descartes' unfinished dialogue, *La Recherche de la vérité* . . . (in the part known only in its Latin version: AT X, 515, 518).

39. AT II, 599. The status of "natural impulses" will be partially restored in Meditation VI with the support of divine veracity and in a purely vital role, which will thus lead to the reality of adventitious deas. The intermediary development of Meditation III, which proposes and temporarily leaves aside arguments that will recur in Meditation VI, may suggest a contemporaneous writing of the two passages. It is in any case very close to the terms of the

letter of 16 October 1639, though the latter is more precise on the occasional ill effects of following these "inclinations."

40. HR I, 183; AT VII, 69; IX, 55. Human thought is successive because it occurs in time; the present may be more or less expanded, but also more or less clearly defined. The division of time into discontinuous instants in the second proof of Meditation III has a purely ontological significance. At whatever instant I pretend to immobilize it, *my* thought is contingent and incapable of extending its own being. But, though it is possible that I die while presently stating this proposition, it already contains two elements in the same relation. Cf. *Conversation with Burman* (Latin in AT V, 148; Cottingham translation, 6, n. 6).

41. In my next book on Descartes (Paris: Hachette, early 1984), which quotes selected fragments of Descartes and includes commentaries, I have in my section on the "circle" quoted *all* of these texts. Descartes' constantly consistent terminology on this theme becomes most apparent.

42. Memory is, of course, less certain than present intuition (see *Regulae* III, AT X, 370, where in a sense deduction derives its certainty from memory); but one can make notes—excluding the possibility that memory as such is questioned (see *Conversation with Burman*, AT V, 148). Also, contrary to the next interpretation I consider, the length of time that passes has nothing to do with present persuasion and its disappearance.

43. A passage in the *Annotationes* to the *Principles* reads thus: we would think in different ways *"si [Deus] leges naturae mutarit"* (AT XI, 654). This means that the laws of nature might have been otherwise decreed; but once so, they would remain the same forever. Descartes never suggests the possibility of unstable laws.

44. The beginning of *Principles* I, 22 emphasizes the advantage of the Cartesian proofs in showing that God is at the same time that he exists.

45. In a letter dated 27 April 1637, Descartes comments on the remark, "It is sufficient to judge well . . . " of *Discourse* III (AT VI, 28) by saying that this is a "common doctrine of the Schoolmen" according to which the clarity of intellectual representation is directed by judgment (AT I, 366). The end of *Discourse* V evokes the conclusion of the *Traité de l'Homme* (last part of *Le Monde*), as though the subject of the union between a rational soul and a bodily machine had already been treated. But what we know of *l'Homme* was interrupted just before that; Meditation VI does seem to constitute a new stage, after which Descartes will continue to investigate the mind-body union.

46. E. Gilson cites Neo-Stoic references concerning innateness which slightly antedate Descartes, in *Etudes sur le rôle de la pensée médiévale sur la formation du système cartésien* (Paris, 1930), chap. 1. For the equally numerous empiricists, there are only two sorts of ideas—those received through the senses and those which we ourselves elaborate on.

47. Cf. supra, note 4 (" . . . I attempt to clarify what I have previously written . . . ": AT II, 622). Descartes thus reworked and embellished his earlier manuscript, even regarding details. The main work one tends to date 1629.

48. Concerning use of the word *innate* in French, translations of the period

paraphrase *innatae* or *ingenitae* (Descartes goes from French into Latin when he says that truths are *"mentibus nostris ingenitae"* [AT I, 145, letter of 15 April 1630]). Curiously enough, it was Locke's *Essay* that helped to make the word *inné* a familiar term in French (see the "Extraits d'un Livre anglais qui n'est pas encore publié . . . " in *Bibliothèque universelle et historique,* t. VIII (1688), ed. J. Leclerc and J. C. de la Crose, esp. 141–142, an editorial justification of the use of new terms in French). Additional references on this score have been documented in an unpublished thesis on "Innate Ideas and Occasional Causes, from Descartes to Leibniz" (Paris, 1982) by my student, Marilynn Phillips.

49. The potential character of innate ideas was always emphasized by Descartes; Locke's criticism of a supposedly preformed idea of God is ineffectual here. Cf. in particular the *Notae in programma* (vs. Regius): AT VIII–2, 358 (innate ideas are not distinguished from the "faculty" of thinking); ibid., 361 (they are in us *"semper potentia"*); ibid., 366 (it is ridiculous to suppose that *"infantes"*—children before the age of speech, and even before birth—have an "actual" idea of God).

50. *Invito.* The passive element here will be important in the complex development of the proof of the existence of bodies.

51. This point should be related to the opposition between a limited imagination and intellection in the piece of wax passage of Meditation II (AT VII, 31: *innumerabiles*; AT IX, 24: *une infinité*, which is only an indefinite progression); see also Meditation VI, AT VII, 72–73; IX, 67–68 (polygons with a great number of sides). In the Fifth Replies (sec. 1), the important affinity between the innateness of essences and that of the idea of God is added; their "perfection" is what enables us to recognize the true triangle upon seeing the imperfect image. In various replies to empiricists (Regius, the authors of the second set of Objections, Gassendi, "Hyperaspistes") Descartes always grants that we have the power to attain the idea of God or a mathematical essence through concrete perfections gradually augmented or through a perfected image. The absolute or limiting case, however, implies a power which surpasses man and cannot come from experience.

52. I should readily grant that this solemn Scholastic vocabulary was a part of the "clarifications" added to the final writing of the *Meditations* (see supra, notes 4 and 47).

53. See the prefatory letter to the translator of the *Principles* (AT IX–2, 2). The indispensable starting-point of any "principle" (and not just the *cogito* the primacy of which is based on the fact that it is truly indubitable) is that "they should be so clear and evident that the mind of man cannot doubt their truth when it attentively applies itself to consider them" (HR I, 204). In order to proceed further, Descartes must maintain his present attention without discontinuity. The obligation revealed in Meditation III (AT VII, 35–36) is so important that it is repeated at the beginning of Meditation V. Likewise, after grounding the certainty of evidence in God, Descartes reminds us in *Principles* I, 43: "And even if this truth could not be rationally demonstrated, we are by nature so disposed to give our assent (*ei sponte assentiamur*) to things that

we clearly perceive that we cannot possibly doubt of their truth" (HR I, 236). The Miller translation reads: " . . . whenever we clearly perceive something, we spontaneously assent to it and cannot in any way doubt that it is true" (p. 20).

54. Descartes does not employ the word (which will be used later by Foucher and Leibniz). The term should be reserved for what absolutely distinguishes true from false, and not in speaking of a "psychological criterion" (supra, note 20). I expand on this point in my next book on Descartes, where I emphasize the distinction between "principle" and "grounding" (*fondement*), vs. those who along with Heidegger speak of a "twofold grounding." To be forever unshakable, clay must needs rest upon rock (*Discourse* III, AT VI, 29).

55. Descartes writes: " . . . if just because I can draw the idea of something from my thought, it follows that all which I know clearly and distinctly as pertaining to ths object does really belong to it, may I not derive from this (*inde haberi*) an argument demonstrating the existence of God?" (HR I, 180; AT VII, 65).

56. I do not accept H. Gouhier's hypothesis on this score. See his "Pour une histoire des Méditations métaphysiques," a 1951 artcle reprinted in *Études d'Histoire de la Philosophie française* (New York: Hildesheim, 1976), 18: "What the 1629 manuscript did not contain—the ontological proof and the creation of the eternal truths." (I agree, however, on the latter point; see my conclusion).

57. Letter of 15 April 1630 (AT I, 144). Descartes here says that knowledge of God comes before knowledge of the self. One might be tempted to think here that the *cogito* does not yet govern the proofs of God. But here hierarchical order is concerned (as in the title of the *Meditations*) and not the "order of reasons."

58. Cf. *Discourse* IV (AT VI, 36): "It is at least as certain that God . . . is or exists, as any demonstration in geometry could be" and ibid., 38 (quoted above, before note 14). Likewise, we find in Meditation V: "the existence of God should be held [*in my mind* = French text] to be at least as certain . . . " (AT VII, 66: *ad minimum*; IX, 52); and my analysis of the whole final development of this Meditation shows that the certainty of mathematics depends on God (no matter what the argument used).

59. See *Le Monde* VII (AT XI, 47). The French text reads: *dont la connaissance est si naturelle à nos âmes"* (the knowledge of which is so natural to our minds/ souls). There follows a justification of the a priori method, which proceeds from causes to effect. Although the existence of body is not demonstrated until the beginning of the second part of the *Principles*, *Principles* I, 24 prefigures the proof to justify the a priori method. Here contemplation of the attributes of God (which complements that of the *Meditations*) is expressed in terms of his being the "source of all goodness and truth" (*Principles* I, 22) by the unity of his understanding and will (*Principles* I, 23). The role of this thesis in Descartes' physics is precisely what made me think that it should be present in the *Principles* (see my *l'Oeuvre de Descartes* [Paris: 1971], 134–136).

60. Descartes *spontaneously* evokes divine creation of the eternal truths in the Fifth Replies (sec. 1) and expands on it in section 6 of the Sixth Replies

(though the Sixth Objection here did not call for it) and in section 8 (in reply to an Objection that was provoked by its occurrence in the Fifth Replies). In section 6 of the Sixth Replies, Descartes elaborates on what distinguishes God's freedom from man's: " . . . already seeing that the nature of goodness and truth has been established and determined by God" (AT IX, 233). This is the most explicit passage on the matter. It has not been sufficiently emphasized that Descartes spontaneously adds it to the first edition of the *Meditations*. This is probably why he only evoked it in the *Principles* without explicitly mentioning God's freedom in creating truths.

61. AT VII, 62 (for *authorem*); AT IX, 49. My emphasis in the quotation from the French text are not given in HR I, 178. Cf. the letter to Mersenne, 27 May 1630: "God is the author of all things, and . . . these truths are something, and consequently . . . he is their author" (AT I, 152).

13

The Essential Incoherence of Descartes' Definition of Divinity

JEAN-LUC MARION

Translated by Frederick P. Van de Pitte

I. THE ELABORATION OF THE QUESTION OF A DEFINITION OF GOD

In the second part of Meditation III, Descartes introduces a definition of God, in two distinct but convergent formulations. Quite apart from further considerations, such an apparition is worthy in its own right of sustained attention: In the period when Descartes wrote, to offer a definition of God (whatever its status) still amounted to taking a position on the theological terrain of the divine names. In effect, he began from a rationality not theologically assured by Christian Revelation, but metaphysically founded on the humanity of "men purely men."[1] The problematic of the divine names—originally a theological issue—is transposed *here*, perhaps for the first time, into the strictly metaphysical domain. Here we find, in its most essential roots, the foreshadowing of what will become some centuries later our modern question: What name is metaphysics qualified to give to God; what speech is metaphysics able to utter concerning God?[2]

Let us then read the two parallel definitions of God in Meditation III. To begin with: (1) " . . . *illa* [sc. idea] *per quam summum aliquem Deum, aeternum, infinitum, omniscium, omnipotentem, rerumque omnium, quae praeter ipsum sunt creatorem intelligo . . .* " (AT VII, 40); the French translation gives us: " . . . a God sovereign, eternal, infinite, immutable, all knowing, all powerful, and universal creator of all things besides himself" (AT IX–1, 32). Then follows: (2) *"Dei nomine intelligo substantiam quandam infinitam, independentem, summe intelligentem, summe potentem, et a qua tum ego ipse, tum aliud omne si quid aliud extat, quodcumque extat, est creatum"* (AT VII, 45); according to the French text: "By the name God I understand a substance infinite, eternal, immutable, all knowing, all powerful, and by which I myself and all other things (if it is true that any such exist) have been created and produced" (AT IX–1, 35, 41–36). These two formulations deploy under the name of God a series of attributes that are simply juxtaposed, without either a principle of organization, or any justification of their equivalence with such a thing as "God." Are we not required to see here only a simple nominal definition, as the repeated use of the term *intelligo* would permit us to think?[3] Such would be the case if Descartes were not so emphatic about its status: "If there is an idea of God (as it is manifest there is)" (*Si detur Dei idea* [*ut manifestum est illam dari*], AT VII, 183); "But we do possess the idea of God" (*Habemus autem ideam Dei*), AT VII, 167.[4] Even if the *idea Dei* has no categorical content, at least it is affirmed in such manner that there is nothing hypothetical about its status. Effectively, by the *idea Dei* in us, we have a hypothetical definition which is, nonetheless, categorically given. This paradox contradicts the thesis according to which the order of reason would deploy a strictly analytic rigor.

In certain privileged articulations, the *series et nexus rationum mearum* (AT VII, 9) permits the intervention of new data, which renews its vigor, as a new deal renews a game. The most significant is to be found at the midpoint of Meditation III, on the page where the definition of God first intervenes. Here, after the failure of the first attempt to rupture the solipsism of the *ego cogito* by way of resemblance, Descartes at once opens a new avenue (*alia quaedam adhuc via* [ibid., 40]). For the purely representative interpretation of ideas he substitutes their interpretation according to the principle of causality, formulated here for the first time (ibid., 40–41). The double irruption of causality and of God is completed by the first appearance of the term *substance* (ibid., 40), in which God exposes himself to causality. This new beginning of the *Meditations* provokes the first formulation of the definition of God; and it is fulfilled in the second formulation, which immediately precedes the conclusion of the proof by means of effects (ibid., 45). The double definition of God rigidly frames the proof by means of effects. It could be conceived as an ad hoc hypothesis, categorically introduced into the *ordo rationum* for the sole purpose of producing progress toward new results, although at the price of an incoherence. Descartes would categorically risk a new hypothesis concerning God, in order to emerge from a theoretical impasse, even if it would weaken the coherence of the *ordo rationum;* but this noncohesion also brings a triple suspicion to bear on the definition of God.

(a) Since this definition intervenes categorically only as an ad hoc hypothesis, is it not possible that its different terms do not compose a coherent definition at all, indeed that they contradict each other? In short, there is a suspicion concerning the internal coherence of this definition.

(b) Since this definition intervenes categorically as a disruption of the previous rational order, it is necessary to establish its provenance within the *Meditations.* In short, there is a suspicion concerning the coherence of this definition with the internal *ordo rationum* of the *Meditations.*

(c) Finally, since this definition takes in only one of the proofs for the existence of God, even within the *Meditations,* it is necessary to test its compatibility with the other definitions of God invoked by Descartes, at least in 1641. But Descartes develops at least three proofs: by means of effects in Meditation III; by the divine essence (a priori) in Meditation V; and by the principle of reason in the Replies to Objections I and IV. Corresponding to these three proofs are three metaphysical definitions of God—as *idea infiniti,* as *ens summe perfectum,* and as *causa sui*—taking the roles of three theological divine names. This triplicity gives rise to a final suspicion, regarding the compossibility of the proofs, definitions, and names of God. In short, there is a suspicion concerning the coherence of the entire rational theology of Descartes.

In view of this multiple questioning of the coherence of the Cartesian process, an attitude seems to impose itself which has been formulated in a very convincing manner by Harry G. Frankfurt:

> The value to Descartes of his proof that God exists is not that it establishes as a fact that there is a benevolent and omnipotent being to whom we owe our existence and our nature. Descartes could not purport to demonstrate that this is a fact without begging the question of whether the premises of his argument are true. But he does not need to suppose that the premises of his argument for God's existence are true, in order to achieve the aim to which the argument is devoted. He needs only to make the point that he clearly and distinctly perceives both the premises and that the proposition that God exists follows from them.[5]

This avenue leads to remarkable results which, moreover, can be complemented by other approaches.[6] But here we shall try to take another path to resolve the same difficulty. We shall attempt to mea-

sure the coherence or incoherence of Cartesian thought on God by
starting with a historical interrogation. If we succeed in reconstituting
Cartesian theses that seem incoherent by relating them to theses that
occur in this period, then the *ordo rationum* could become more coherent. The responses finally constituted by a metaphysician become
intelligible only insofar as one is able to measure them against the
questions, secret or forgotten, that he intended to resolve.[7] We therefore ask: In risking *this* definition of God (and the two others following), what difficulties was Descartes attempting to surmount?

II. THE CONSTRUCTION OF THE DEFINITION OF GOD

Let us therefore take up, step by step, the double definition of God
introduced in Meditation III: for each of the terms that are juxtaposed
without apparent order, we will attempt to reestablish the historical
implications, and therefore to disengage it from the historical situation.

A. *Quaedam (substantia)* occurs first in (2) (AT VII, 45), thus responding exactly to the initial indetermination of (1) *aliquis (Deus)* (ibid.,
40). While masked by the French translation (the indefinite article
un/une [AT IX–1, 32 and 35]), this indetermination constantly determines all the previous occurrences of God in the *Meditations*. Two
occurrences confirm it. First, at the end of Meditation I when Descartes
constructs his hyperbolic doubt, invoking indifferently the two contrary hypotheses of an omnipotent God and of a malign spirit, he yet
reunites them in the imprecision of "some God so powerful" (*tam
potentem aliquen Deum* [AT VII, 21]). Then, when at the beginning of
Meditation III the final situation of Meditation I is recalled, "some
God" (AT IX–1, 28; *aliquem Deum*, AT VII, 36) is once more called to
mind. The indetermination would not display itself so regularly unless
it had an essential function; in fact it has several of them. To begin
with, during all the moments that precede the first proof for the existence of a God, Descartes hesitates among several hypotheses: a God
who is capable of everything, and therefore permits me to deceive
myself (AT VII, 21); a *Deus fictitius* (ibid., 21), identifiable indifferently
as destiny, as chance, or as the necessary order of nature (ibid., 21), in
short, as any sort of artifice (*seu quovis alio modo* [ibid., 21]); or finally
as an undefined malign spirit (genium *aliquem malignum* [ibid., 22];
un certain mauvais génie [AT IX–1, 17]). The undefined malign spirit
can only be imagined insofar as the concept of God, while invoked,
remains fundamentally indeterminate. And moreover, all of Medita-

tion II works within the determined hypothesis of these undecided denominations: "There is *some* God, or whatever name is to be invoked" (. . . *est* aliquis *Deus, vel quocunque nomine illum vocem* [AT VII, 24]; *quelque* Dieu [AT IX–1, 19]), who can also become an "unknown deceiver" (*deceptor* nescio quis [AT VII, 25]; *je ne sais quel trompeur* [AT IX–1, 19]), therefore appropriately any deceiver (*deceptor* aliquis [AT VII, 26]; *quelqu'un qui est* . . . [AT IX–1, 21]). In fact, before the proof by means of effects, Descartes works on the determinate hypothesis of something undetermined; the only point that all of these hypotheses have in common stems from their indeterminacy itself: *aliquis*. Therefore, when the definition of Meditation III—both in (1) and in (2)—begins with an indeterminate quantifier, it does not say nothing at all. Descartes says first the only thing that he knows from experience after two and a half Meditations: By God I understand some indeterminate, *aliquis*. Here it is not the ego that would be able to say "I come forth in disguise" (*larvatus prodeo* [AT X, 212]), but rather God, who, like Voetius later, "comes to me only in disguise" (*in me non prodeat nisi personatus* [AT VIII–2, 7]). God comes to the ego only under the mask of the role (*persona*) that he has played until that point in the previous Meditations—that of an *aliquis*: negative theology.

The indeterminacy is justified, however, by a second function. The hyperbolic doubt is only able to exercise its radical *épochè* on the true science[8] by confusing two different characteristics. The "indeterminate" considered must offer sufficient omnipotence to disqualify all mathematical or logical rationality; then it must exceed the humanly unsurpassable conditions of science, therefore identifying itself in some manner or other with God. But these two characteristics can be expressed in the untenable paradox of a deceptive omnipotence, directly (a malign spirit), or indirectly (an omnipotent God who creates the objective conditions for my self-deception). This would make the initial hypothesis of the *Meditations* appear not only as hyperbolic, but as incoherent. And Descartes will not conceal it. Apart from the strict (and provisional) order of reason, an omnipotent God can neither deceive nor permit to be deceived:

And what he [Voetius] adds is inept, namely that *God is thought as a deceiver.* For although in my first Meditation some supremely powerful deceiver is spoken of, nonetheless the true God was never conceived in that context, since—as he himself says—it cannot occur that the true God be a deceiver. And if he is asked from whence he knows that such cannot occur, he must respond that he knows it from this, that it implies a contradiction in the concept, *i.e.*, that it cannot be conceived.[9]

But it is precisely this contradiction that requires provisionally the movement of the *Meditations;* in order to render it tolerable, one must weaken it, so to speak, or even disguise it. That is what the indeterminacy of an *aliquis* is intended to accomplish. Ultimately the stakes are very limited in the debate on the omnipotence of God opposed (or not) to the merely very great power of the malign spirit; the same as the distinction, in general, between these two operators of hyperbolic doubt. For the indetermination suffices to confuse them in their role, as provisional as it is unified.[10]

The indeterminacy permits us to raise another difficulty. In effect, the malign spirit, the *Deus fictitius,* the chance and necessity, only intervene in virtue of a single function: omnipotence, by which they would be able to disqualify the evidence of order and measure. Omnipotence would thus take precedence over indeterminacy itself. But, as a matter of fact, one must ask by what right it enters into the *ordo rationum:* how does it happen that, before envisaging God as such, it is deemed legitimate to bring into play the idea of an omnipotent God? Descartes' answer is steadfast. In Meditation I he says: "Nevertheless, fixed in my mind is the old opinion that there is a God who can do everything" (*Verumtamen infixa quaedam est meae menti vetus opinio, Deum est qui potest omnia* [AT VII, 21]); and Meditation III carries on with: " . . . this preconceived opinion of the supreme power of God" (*haec praeconcepta de summa Dei potentia opinio* [ibid., 36]. Omnipotence qualifies something as God, but solely on the basis of opinion. It can be established, quite apart, that such an equivalence has its origin in the nominalism of William of Ockham.[11] But here it is only important to note the manner in which a doctrine foreign to the *ordo rationum* is nonetheless able to become involved in it: it is under the aspect of *opinio,* that is, of a thought which is confused, without origin or reason; in short, indeterminate.[12] Therefore, omnipotence preceded indeterminacy only in appearance, since in fact only its indeterminacy permits it to intervene in the *ordo rationum*—on the basis of opinion, without genealogy, without status or preparation. Thus, in fact, the lexical imprecision betrays the conceptual indeterminacy in which the *ordo rationum* ends before the *"alia quaedam adhuc via"*: if one claims to come upon the determination of God on the basis of hyperbolic doubt alone, the definition would become possible only in becoming equally impossible. The aporia of such an indeterminacy can only be resolved by the introduction of a new conceptual datum.

B. *Substantia.* The appearance of the term *substance* characterizes definition (2) directly ("By the name God I understand a substance . . . "); but, indirectly, it also characterizes definition (1), which intervenes just after the first opposition between substance and accident, the hierarchy of which permits the conclusion that a certain idea of God "truly has in itself more objective reality than those [ideas] by which finite substances are manifested" (*plus profecto objectivae in se habet, quam illae per quas finitae substantiae exhibentur* [AT VII, 40]). In other words, the indeterminate idea of God becomes precise by opposing it to all accidents, but also to all finite substance. Shortly afterward, Descartes will explicitly introduce the third term, *substantia infinita*, first in definition (2) (ibid., 45), and then in what follows: " . . . however, I would not on that account have the idea of an infinite substance, since I am finite, unless it proceeded from some substance which was truly infinite" (*non tamen idcirco esset idea substantiae infinitae, cum sim finitus, nisi ab aliqua substantia, quae revera esset infinita procederet* [ibid., 45]). The same point is expressed later: " . . . I clearly see that there is more reality in an infinite than in a finite substance" (*manifeste intelligo plus realitatis esse in substantia infinita quam in finita* [ibid., 45])— a formulation that is confirmed by the Replies to Objections II: " . . . substance has more reality than accident or mode; and infinite substance has more than finite substance" (*substantia plus habet realitatis, quam accidens vel modus; et substantia infinita, quam finita* [ibid., 165]).

The introduction of the concept of substance permits certain benefits and raises a difficulty. The first benefit consists in the coherence of definitions (1) and (2). The first, (1), introduces substance into God in order to oppose it to accident, and especially to *substantia finita* (ibid., 40); the other, (2), positively determines this substance as infinite. From this flows the second benefit: Descartes surpasses the inevitable indeterminacy of his point of departure only by constructing a second definition of something as God, on the basis of new parameters imposed by the *"alia quaedam adhuc via"*: causality, the nonrepresentative status of the idea, and especially substantiality. That definitions (1) and (2) are constructed around *substantia* indicates that they share from top to bottom in the new beginning of the *ordo rationum*. In short, for Descartes, God will be defined in terms of substantiality (and causality), or not at all. But precisely what is implied by this necessary recourse to substantiality in order to define God?

In fact, Descartes here encounters an earlier debate. Theologically speaking, can one call God a substance? Undoubtedly a positive response is warranted by the formulation "a certain sea of infinite substance" (*quoddam pelagus infinitae substantiae*), which invariably translates a phrase of John Damascene: ὅιόν τι πέλαγος οὐσίας ἄπειρον καὶ ἀόριστον.[13] However, this warrant does not completely eliminate the difficulty, the origin of which is to be found in at least three authors of the first rank.

—First, St. Augustine, who holds that "clearly it is incorrect usage to call God substance" (*manifestum est Deum abusive substantiam vocari*) and he suggests his preference for *essentia* as a translation of οὐσία. The motive for this rejection is clear: substantiality presupposes the permanence of a substratum for accidental qualifications, so that "therefore, things which are changeable and not simple are properly called substances" (*res ergo mutabiles neque simplices proprie dicuntur substantiae*). In God, on the contrary, the grandeur, the goodness, and so forth, are not added like accidents to a substance that plays the role of a permanent substrate; therefore God, in order to be (*essentia*), need not be defined as a *substantia*.[14]

—Then follows St. Anselm, who also takes exception to the substantiality of God; indeed, "the term substance is primarily applied to individuals, which consist to the greatest degree in plurality. For individuals undergo, *i.e.*, are subject to accidents to the greatest degree, and thus more properly receive the name substance." Substance implies the attributes that it supports; and their plurality, in turn, inevitably implies the plurality of substances; and this contradicts the divine unicity. Therefore, "it is clear that the highest essence, which is the subject of no accidents, cannot properly be called substance, unless 'substance' serves in place of 'essence.'"[15]

—Finally, St. Thomas cannot define God as a substance for a theoretical motive of his own: God has no other ontic determination than the pure act of being (*actus purus essendi*), which takes the place of essence, and therefore *a fortiori* of substance; and, in addition, he recognizes the traditional motives of his predecessors.[16] As a matter of fact, then, *substantia* cannot be applied to God except insofar as it is equivalent to *esse* subsisting by itself.

It is not as a matter of course, therefore, that Descartes defines God as a substance. It is a question of choosing one among other possible theses. The difficulty of such a choice can easily be reconstructed when one pays attention to the echoes that occur among Descartes' contemporaries. Thus Gassendi, who, having stated that "God is commonly excluded from the category of substance" (*Deus vulgo excludatur a Categoria substantiae*), goes on to contradict this common opinion: "God is undeservedly excluded from the category of substance" (*immerito Deum a Substantiae categoria excluditur*). In fact, he treats (divine) substance exactly in the Cartesian manner, in strict parallel with (divine) causality.[17] But it is clear that, in affirming the substantiality of

God, Gassendi is fully aware that he is reversing a common opinion. Before him, other authors had at least indicated the difficulty. For example, in 1613, Goclenius (Roger Göckel) attempted to consider substance not in relation to accident—which would render it unsuited for defining God—but exclusively as perseity, as self-subsistence.[18] The same duality occurs in 1609 with Eustachius a Sancto Paulo who, in contrast to substance called *"a substando"* as *"subesse accidentibus,"* attempted to introduce a substance thinkable exclusively as "existing by itself, or not in another, which is to subsist" (*per se, seu non in alio existere, quod est subsistere*).[19] It is always in this manner that Scipion Dupleix, in 1606, attributes substantiality to God. "God is a true and very perfect substance, yet not predicamental or categorical . . . being not at all the subject or agent of any accident."[20] It seems evident that Descartes joined in this effort to define substance not as referred to accident (categorially), but as referred to itself (self-subsistence, perseity). Moreover, he will continue to maintain this attempt through many definitions: " . . . substances, *i.e.,* things subsisting by themselves" (*substantiae, hoc est res per se subsistentes* [Reply to Objections IV, AT VII, 222]); " . . . exactly this is the notion of substance: that which can exist by itself, *i.e.,* without the help of any other substance" (*haec ipsa est notio substantiae, quod per se, hoc est absque ope ullius alterius substantiae possit existere* [ibid., 226]); " . . . a true substance, or a self-subsistent thing";[21] "By substance, we are able to understand nothing other than a thing which exists in such manner that it requires no other thing in order to exist" (*Per substantiam, nihil aliud intelligere possumus quam rem quae ita existit, ut nulla alia re indigeat ad existendum* [*Principles of Philosophy* I, no. 51]). For Descartes and his immediate contemporaries, God would therefore become accessible to substantiality on the basis of his new definition—as self-sufficiency—and not as a category in relation to accidents.

This shift in the meaning of substance does not, however, explain why Descartes is able to call God by the name 'substance.' Indeed, the first precise examples of a substance "that is able to exist by itself" lead us not to God, but to a stone (AT VII, 44), or to the ego (ibid., 44, line 22 = 45, line 7: *"ego autem substantia"*). If substance *can* define God, it can also define any extended or thinking thing, as will be confirmed by the *Principles* (I, nos. 52–53), and the Reply to Objections III (AT VII, 175, 176). The new comprehension of substantiality thus opens a new means of access to God, only to run afoul of the univocity of the notion: "And so the word substance does not apply *univocally,* as is usually said in the Schools, to God and to other things [all things that are able to exist only by means of the concurrence of God]; that is, no meaning can be distinctly understood for this term which is common to both God and creatures" (*Atque ideo nomen substantiae non convenit Deo et illis univoce, ut dici solet in Scholis, hoc est, nulla ejus nominis significatio potest distincte intelligi, quae Deo et creaturis sit communis* [*Principles* I, no. 51]). As a matter of fact, "in the Schools," substance tended to become a determination applied in the same way to God and things. Thus, for Suarez, " . . . created and uncreated substance agree not only in relation to things, but also in relation to substance"; or again: "Concerning substance, it is indeed admitted that God is an uncreated substance, and thus it is possible to abstract the nature of substance commonly from created and uncreated alike." In this way, substance intrinsically accords with the creature, as well as God, in a relation that is ultimately indeterminate: not univocal, but analogous.[22] When one is aware of the univocist drift that analogy undergoes with Suarez and others, there can be no doubt that this cautious style conceals an actual univocity, which here stigmatizes Descartes. But to see a danger is not sufficient to avoid it. While taking exception to all univocity of substance, Descartes nonetheless never succeeds in conceptualizing two different meanings of this unique term. He upholds the same concept, while juxtaposing two contradictory usages:

1.   A thing is called substance that has no need of any other in order to exist; in the strict sense, this definition admits of only one consequence: "And indeed only one substance can be conceived which requires absolutely no other, namely God. We see that all other things are not able to exist except by means of the concurrence of God" (*Et quidem substantia quae nulla plane re indigeat, unica tantum potest intelligi, nempe Deus. Alias vero omnes, non nisi ope concursus Dei existere posse percipimus* [*Principles* I, no. 51]). In other words, if the earlier definition of substance debars application to God, the new debars application to anything other than God; God alone is absolutely by himself, therefore he is the only real substance. It is already a question of the solution offered by Spinoza.

2.   Descartes, however, is going to juxtapose to the first definition (with perfect inconsistency) a second definition of what he still unreasonably persists in calling substance. In the *Meditations*, it is a question of the *ratio substantiae* (common to extension and the ego [AT VII, 44]); in the *Principles* I, no. 52, it is a *communis conceptus*, in virtue of which the term *substance* is applied to "things which require only the concurrence of God in order to exist" (*res, quae solo Dei concursu egent ad existendum*). Here the divine concurrence is found to be put out of play, since it amounts to the same thing either to have no need of the concurrence of God, or to be totally in need of it. It is a question once again of the very imperfect solution of Suarez.[23]

Descartes thus does not elaborate a sufficiently articulated definition of substance to avoid an untenable alternative: either to repeat Suarez, or to anticipate Spinoza. These difficulties result from the lack of a criterion by which to conceive the divergence between the created and the uncreated. This is why Descartes will attempt to introduce a new one: the infinite. It is important to emphasize that the infinite appears in definition (2), as it were *before* his third term "*[quandam substantiam] infinitam*" is explicitly fixed. God is not defined *first* as a substance, and *then* as infinite; God could never be called substance if Descartes had not first understood substance (with respect to God) as infinite through and through. The term *substantia infinita* forms a unique syntagma, which is added without any common subset to the two preceding terms; according to the hierarchy of perfection, we are given: accident < substance (always finite) < infinite-substance. It would be necessary to venture that substance, when applied to God, becomes a simple qualification added to infinity, which alone is substantive and subject; and thus it would be necessary to speak less of an infinite substance than of a substantial infinite. Undoubtedly it seems at times that God permits himself to be called substance by simple arrangement: "The substance which we understand to be supremely perfect, and in which we conceive absolutely nothing that involves any defect or limitation of perfection, is called God" (*Substantia, quam summe perfectam esse intelligimus, et in qua nihil plane concipimus quod aliquem defectum sive perfectionis limitationem involvat,* Deus *vocatur* [Reply to Objections II, AT VII, 162]). This text is found to be counterbalanced especially by a commentary on the passage in Meditation III, which involves *substantia infinita:*

By infinite substance I understand a substance which has true and real perfections that are actually infinite and immense. This is not an accident added onto the notion of substance taken absolutely, as limited by no defects. Such defects are accidents in relation to substance, but infinity and infinitude are not.[24]

We are thus given notice, first that the perfections defining infinite substance are totally imbued with infinity, so that their reality becomes actually synonymous with infinity (which, moreover, eliminates the new definition of substantiality). Second, this substance admits of no accidents (which also eliminates the categorial definition of earlier theologians). Third, since the infinite and infinity do not constitute accidents (or defects) added to substance, they are substantially identified with it. The definition of substance is therefore articulated: the infinite. With respect to God, the infinite adds nothing to substance; rather, it is substance that results from the original infinity in God.

In the sequence of attributes of God deployed in (2), *infini* is therefore added lexically to substance because, conceptually, substance is unsuited to God, except under the primordial condition of infinity.

C. *Infinita/infinitus (Deus)/infinitum.* Therefore God is finally qualified properly as *Deus infinitus* according to (1), or *substantia infinita* according to (2). Indeed, this term dominated the rational theology of Descartes from 1630: against "the common people, who almost always imagine him as a finite thing," and against "the greater part of mankind who do not consider God as an infinite being," Descartes was establishing "that God is infinite."[25] In 1637, the infinite already counts among "all the perfections that I was able to discern in God" (*Discourse on Method*, AT VI, 35); and the preface to the *Meditations* recommended us to recall that "our minds must be considered as finite things, but God as . . . infinite" (*mentes nostras considerandas esse ut finitas, Deum autem ut . . . infinitum* [AT VII, 9]). Even in his *Conversation with Burman*, God is always defined by "*infinita perfectio.*"[26] Here we attain an absolute Cartesian invariant. As a matter of fact, with the infinite it is a question of the highest Cartesian determination of the essence (and therefore the existence) of God, which dominates all the other terms of definitions (1) and (2), but also all other conceivable definitions to follow. Infinity, as the sole proper name of God, does not express merely one of the characteristics of God, as in the *Discourse* (AT VI, 35); or indeed in (1) nor even directly the divine essence (" . . . the nature of God is . . . infinite" [*Dei naturam esse . . . infinitam* (AT VII, 55)]); it defines God as such: "But I judge God to be actually infinite" (*Deum autem ita judico esse actu infinitum* [ibid., 47]), or " . . . the perception of the infinite is in me . . . that is God" (*in me esse perceptionem infiniti . . . hoc est Dei* [ibid., 45]). In a word, God "is conceived to be infinite" (*intelligitur enim esse infinitus* [Reply to Objections V, ibid., 365]). This excellence is also attested by the priority of the infinite over the finite: " . . . the perception of the infinite is in a certain way in me *prior* prior to the finite, i.e., God is prior to myself" (*priorem quoddamodo in me esse perceptionem infiniti quam finiti, hoc est Dei quam mei ipsius* [ibid., 45]); or again, "In reality, the perfection of God is *prior* to our imperfection,"[27] Not that we reconstructed the infinite by negation, on the basis of the finite; in spite of appearances, it is the finite that results from a negation of the infinite: the sole positive reality, in title and in fact.[28] The priority of the infinite should not be understood only as a logical priority (the negation of negation), nor as an epistemological priority (the "*maxime clara et distincta*" idea [AT VII, 46]), but indeed as an a priori: the infinite precedes the finite in that it renders possible both experience and the objects of this experience; thus Descartes insists on the paradoxical fact that it is "by the same faculty" (*per eandem facultatem* [ibid., 51]), and even "at the same time" (*simul* [ibid., 51]), that the ego perceives itself and that it perceives the infite (ibid., 51), and therefore God. The idea of the infinite can claim to be prior—paradoxically, first after a difficult run— only insofar as it can be shown to be an a priori of the finite. Therefore, the infinite imposes itself as the first proper name of God; first because it alone is able to render substantiality attributable to God without univocity; then because it makes God conceivable as the a priori condition of finite experience, and of the finite objects of experience.[29] The second reason reinforces the first, and perhaps also constitutes the truth of it.

The transcendental primacy of the infinite provokes immediately two other determinations. The first is immensity, either as a direct qualification of God (*Dei immensitas* [AT VII, 231, 232]); or through the mediation of his essence (*essentia immensa* [ibid., 241]); or through the mediation of his power (*immensitas potentiae* [ibid., 237]; *immensa potentia* (ibid., 110, 119, 188); of "the immensity of his power" (AT IV, 119); *immensa potestas* (*Principles* I, no. 40); or, finally, by any one of his faculties (AT VII, 57). All that is attributed to God is found to be marked by immensity, that is, it can no longer be measured. God surpasses all measure, and therefore all subjection to the *cogitatio*, which employs the rationality of measure. But since the *Regulae*, measure—together with the order that governs it—determines the field of method, as *ordo et mensura* determines the fundamental parameters of *Mathesis Universalis*.[30] To qualify the divine properties as immense, and therefore as nonmeasurable, means that nothing concerning God depends on the domain of the application of method. Immensity is not added to the other divine properties; rather, it indicates, on the basis of the proper name "infinite," that all qualifications attributable to God will extend beyond the field of method. From this, one must conclude that nothing in the definition of God will be dependent upon science, nor consequently will it be able to be treated under the aspect of objectivity. Nothing of God can be rendered the object of a methodical science; nothing of methodical objectivity can be attributed to God.

From this follows the second determination—incomprehensibility— which Descartes deduces directly from the divine infinity: " . . . God, however, as incomprehensible and infinite" (*Deum autem, ut incomprehensibilem et infinitum* [AT VII, 9]); " . . . but the nature of God is immense, incomprehensible, infinite" (*Dei autem naturam esse immensam, incomprehensibilem, infinitam* [ibid., 55]). In fact, this deduction appears, from 1630, in the doctrine of the creation of eternal truths: " . . . God as an infinite and incomprehensible being";[31] and the coincidence of these two themes is not by chance. If the infinite surpasses method in principle (in virtue of the creation of eternal truths), then incomprehensibility will not be an irrationality in the definition of God, but the mark of its perfection and the sign of another rationality. God, as infinite, is not merely known in spite of his incomprehensibility, but even by means of it; for human reason experiences, in encountering incomprehensibility, that it transcends the finite (i.e., that it is) toward the infinite.

We have a doctrine as constant as it is paradoxical, "for one can know that God is infinite and all-powerful, in spite of the fact that our soul, being finite, cannot comprehend or conceive it" (AT I, 152); " . . . my intellect, which is finite, cannot grasp the infinite" (*intellectum meum, qui est finitus, non capere infinitum* [AT VII, 107]); " . . . the infinite, as infinite, is not at all comprehended, but it is nonetheless understood" (*infinitum, qua infinitum est, nullo quidem modo comprehendi, sed nihilominus tamen intelligi* [ibid., 112]); " . . . the idea of the infinite, granted that it be true, ought not to be comprehended by any means, since this very incomprehensibility is included in the formal nature of the infinite" (*idea infiniti, ut sit vera, nullo modo debet comprehendi, quoniam ipsa incomprehensibilitas in ratione formali infiniti continetur* [ibid., 368]); or, finally: " . . . the nature of the infinite is such that by us, who are finite, it is not comprehended" (*est de natura infiniti ut a nobis, qui summus finiti, non comprehendatur* [*Principles* I, no. 19]).[32] From the fact of the incomprehensibility of God it does not follow that we must renounce rational knowledge of God; on the contrary, it is a matter of permitting rationality to have knowledge beyond methodic objectivity, even of infinity as such, that is to say, as incomprehensible to the finite. Incomprehensibility will henceforth become the most certain indication that it is really God that is known by the *cogitatio:* in accordance with the rule that nothing divine can be known except as incomprehensible, and that nothing incomprehensible can be offered to the *cogitatio* that does not, in the end, concern God.

D. *Independens.* The attribute of independence—in (2), AT VII, 45—is deduced from the infinite, considered as an a priori, according to a fundamental Cartesian equivalence: "Independence, when distinctly conceived, includes infinity within itself."[33] The idea of God implies independence as necessarily as noncreation and the highest degree of substantiality: " . . . a clear and distinct idea of an uncreated and *independent* substance, *i.e.,* of God" (*ideam claram et distinctam substantiae cogitantis increatae et independentis, id est Dei* [*Principles* I, no. 54]). Of course, in God, substance accedes to independence only in virtue of the infinite—as opposed to the finite, which will therefore be dependent: " . . . if there be an infinite and *independent* substance, then it is more a thing than one that is finite and dependent" (*si detur substantia infinita et independens, est magis res quam finita et dependens* [Reply to Objections III, AT VII, 185]). The same opposition can be deduced from doubt, where the divine independence appears as the transcendental a priori of the experienced incompleteness of the ego (ibid., 53). Independence is directly equivalent to aseity; this is established by the French version of the passage, " . . . *si a me essem* . . . " (ibid., 48). The interpretation reads: " . . . if I were independent of every other, and were myself the author of my being . . . "[34] (AT IX–1, 38). If, therefore, independence defines divine aseity, dependence characterizes all noninfinite substance. The concept of substance breaks down, consequently, between the (substantial) infinite and (substantial) dependence; one might venture that here "substance" plays the role of a mere attribute of the infinite, or of dependence.

Dependence always characterizes the created as such: nothing is more coherent, therefore, than that Descartes should describe the eternal truths (created) as dependent.[35] Even the delicate problem of the free will of man will not modify the caesura between the divine independence and the dependence of the finite: Man, while free, remains nonetheless dependent.[36] One must therefore conclude, first, that independence is deduced directly from the infinity of God (and also, indirectly, from his substantial infinity); and then that, in virtue of this characteristic, the infinite determines *a contrario* what is not infinite. Thus definition (2), precisely because it is found to be anchored in infinity, is henceforth inclined toward the finite; or rather, the definition permits its infinity to be declined from the point of view of the finite. And, moreover, how would the infinite be able to be given in conception if not from the point of view of the finite, which the ego is? And the attributes that follow are only going to make explicit the managerial role of infinity, so to speak, the relation between infinity and infinity.

E. *Summe intelligens.* This aspect of (2) (AT VII, 45) has a corresponding element in (1), "*Deum . . . omniscium*" (ibid., 40); in the *Discourse on Method*, "the perfect being . . . all-knowing";[37] and the *ens summe intelligens* of the *Principles* (I, no. 14). In itself, this attribute calls for no particular commentary, since it seems so evident that God must be seen to assume supreme intelligence. However, not only here, but in the full range of the Cartesian texts, supreme intelligence receives no remarkable elaboration. This discretion is all the more notable, since the superlative adverb *summe* imposes a parallel with the attribute immediately following: *summe potens.* One is thus inclined to ask why supreme intelligence does not play a role comparable to that of omnipotence? Undoubtedly because the latter expresses much more than simply one attribute among others.

F. *Summe potens.* This title, stated by (2) (AT VII, 45), confirms *omnipotens,* mentioned in (1) (ibid., 40). In Meditation III, its occurrences are not sufficiently numerous to make it appear to require a particular commentary. However, omnipotence appears even before the attempt at defining the real essence of God, precisely in the notion of a "certain" God who provokes hyperbolic doubt; for Descartes clearly identifies this notion: "this preconceived opinion of the supreme power of God" (*haec preconcepta de summa Dei potentia opinio* [ibid., 36]), " . . . fixed in my mind is the old opinion that there is a God who can do everything" (*infixa quaedam est meae menti vetus opinio, Deus esse qui potest omnia* [ibid., 21]). Meditations I and III, therefore, correspond precisely: God is given to thought as all-powerful before the *ordo rationum* comes into play (*vetus/prae*), and therefore by a conception that is historically transmitted (*infixa/opinio*). Omnipotence thus anticipates the *ordo rationum* and the correct definitions of God: the omnipotence found in the earlier opinion subsequently becomes a concept; if the modality varies, the sense remains. Omnipotence, therefore, truly qualifies God, not only in (1) and (2), but even as early as Meditation I. Even before doubt was raised, the divine omnipotence that provoked this doubt had already eluded it, in short, was hyperbolically certain. The omnipotence of God is liberated, so to speak, from the *ordo rationum.*

How are we to understand this extraordinary prerogative, which is not shared by any other term of (1) or (2): the prerogative of a conceptual extraterritoriality? Actually, it is not only in 1641 that omnipotence exercises the prerogative of a polymorphous preeminence. To what does this opinion refer that has been fixed in *my* mind for so long (. . . *infixa quaedam . . . mea menti vetus opinio . . .* [ibid., 21]), and which occurs to *me* (. . . *mihi occurrit . . .* [ibid., 36])? Before investigating the probable historical origins,[38] it is necessary to recollect the early stages of the metaphysical career of Descartes himself. In 1630, he already defines God as "incomprehensible power."[39] This insight, sustained in the *Discourse on Method* in 1637 (AT VI, 35 and 36), is subsequently found as a constant factor throughout the texts of 1641; and it flourishes in the Replies to Objections, which take up once again the syntagma of 1630: " . . . and attending to the immense and incomprehensible power which is contained in his idea . . . " (*attendentesque ad immensam et incomprehensibilem potentiam, quae in ejus idea continetur* [AT VII, 110]). Indeed, this theme is not only sustained but elaborately orchestrated: *infinita potestas* (ibid., 220); *immensitas potentiae* (ibid., 111, 237); *immensa potentia* (ibid., 119, 188); *potentia exuperans* (ibid., 110); *exuperantia potestatis* (ibid., 112). This is the preferred concept, which Descartes uses from 1630 to the very end, in order to define the essence of God. For, as Descartes writes in 1648, only God is able "to grant himself, all at the same time, omnipotence, or the other divine perfections taken collectively."[40] As an invariant, omnipotence determines the divine essence, whether epistemologically (1630), or hypothetically (Meditation I), or as only one of the divine attributes (Meditation III, definitions (1) and (2); *Discourse on Method*; and *Principles of Philosophy*), or as the very essence of God: " . . . immensity of power, or essence . . . " (*immensitatem potentiae, sive essentiae* [AT VII, 237]). Permanent, invariant, indifferent to the *ordo rationum*, omnipotence resists all comparison with other limited attributes, such as supreme intelligence. In the emphasis on this attribute, Etienne Gilson saw "a new idea of God," and we discern there Descartes' most longstanding idea of God. However, are we not thereby massively contradicting ourselves? On the one hand, we offer here omnipotence (F) as the primordial definition of God; but on the other, we have already established the infinite (C) as the proper name of God. Undoubtedly the contradiction cannot be hidden here. But it remains to inquire, first, whether this contradiction could be resolved by interpreting the infinite itself (C) as the infinity of an omnipotence (F); then, whether this contradiction does not betray an inherent tension within the discourse of Descartes concerning God. In other words, does this contradiction bear on the interpretation itself, or on a characteristic inconsistency in the rational theology of Cartesian metaphysics? Since omnipotence is deployed with great indifference to the *ordo rationum*, rather than being harmoniously integrated like infinity, it might very well—by this very strangeness—be able to set us on the trail of an architectonic incoherence in Cartesian metaphysics.

G. *Et a qua tum ego ipse, tum aliud omne, si quid aliud extat, quodcumque extat, est creatum.* This formulation of (2) (AT VII, 45), confirms (1): " . . . and creator of all things which are outside of himself . . . " (*rerumque omnium, quae praeter ipsum sunt, creatorem* [ibid., 40]). The title *Deus creator omnium* (ibid., 255) does not occur with a frequency proportional to its dogmatic importance. It concerns primary two functions. First, there is a God who has created the ego such that the greatest evidence can in fact deceive it: "There is a God who can do everything, and by whom I have been created as I am" (*Deus esse qui potest omnia, et a quo talis, qualis existo, sum creatus* [ibid., 21]); " . . . so created me that I am always deceived" (*talem me creasse, ut semper fallar* [ibid., 21]); "Undoubtedly God could have created me so that I would never be deceived" (*Nec dubium est quin potuerit Deus me talem creare ut nunquam fallerer* [ibid., 55]). Second, there is a God who is creator—among all the other things—of theoretical truths. Thus, in 1630, Descartes writes:

> You ask me by what manner of causality God arranged eternal truths. I tell you that it is by the same manner of causality that he has created all things, *i.e.*, as efficient and total cause. For it is certain that he is just as much the Author of the essence as of the existence of creatures: but this essence is nothing else than these eternal truths.[41]

In 1644, the *Principles* expressly formulates this doctrine once again, always bringing into play the concept of creation (I, nos. 21 and 24).

Of these two functions of creation, one—which appears to be the first—occurs in 1641; without being able to prove it at length here, I would conjecture that the first takes on in the *Meditations* the role which in other texts is played by the second. For God (or his surrogate) would not be able to override the perfect evidence present to my consciousness unless he exceeded that evidence, and therefore exceeded truths and essences in general. But he would be able to exceed them only insofar as he created them, and distinguished himself from them. The two metaphysical functions of the attribute *creator* thus actually reduce to one.[42] But at the same time it becomes clear that Descartes adds nothing to his definition of God by mentioning that he is the creator, since creation becomes intelligible only on the basis of omnipotence being exercised as cause—"*ultima causa*" (AT VII, 50). Contrary to the nominalists, who justify the (metaphysical) omnipotence of God by reference to his (theological) role as creator, Descartes renders creation intelligible by reducing it to omnipotence, rationalized as efficient cause. The attempt at two definitions of God in Meditation III would thus have to be terminated. But such is not the case: a final name, strangely absent here, must still appear.

H. *Ens summe perfectum.* Definitions (1) and (2) are manifestly incomplete, in that they omit properties universally (or almost universally) attributed to God: unity, unicity, eternity, immutability, goodness, beauty, veracity, justice, and so on. This lack can be explained by the constraints of the *ordo rationum;* but it would then remain necessary to justify the choice permitted by the *ordo rationum.* Descartes appears to be conscious of the difficulty, which introduces—right in the middle of Meditation III—a complementary definition of God in order to bring to fruition the exoteric resumption of the proof *a posteriori.* Let us quote this definition (3): " . . . unity, simplicity, or the inseparability of all things that are in God, is one of the preeminent perfections which I conceive to be in him" (*unitas, simplicitas, sive inseparabilitas eorum omnium quae in Deo sunt, una est ex praecipuis perfectionibus quas in eo esse intelligo* [AT VII, 50]). But it must be completed by the formulations that surround it: " . . . and all those perfections that I attribute to God" (*omnesque illae perfectiones quas Deo tribuo* [ibid., 46]); " . . . all the remaining perfections of God" (*reliquas omnes Dei perfectionis* [ibid., 47]); " . . . the idea of all the perfections that I attribute to God . . . " (*omnium perfectionum, quas Deo tribuo, ideam* [ibid., 49]); " . . . all [those perfections] that I conceive to be in God" (*omnes quas in Deo esse concipio* [ibid., 50]); and, finally: " . . . I mean the very God whose idea is in me, that is, who posseses all those perfections of which I am . . . in some manner able to attain the thought" (*Deus, inquam, ille idem cujus idea in me est, hoc est, habens omnes illas perfectiones quas ego . . . quocunque modo attingere cogitatione possum* [ibid., 52]). God is therefore made accessible to thought under a new mode: his idea is not imposed directly, as was the idea of infinity before; but it can be constructed by the human mind, which reviews the perfections, reconciles them, and then attributes them to God. First the review: After unity, simplicity, and inseparability (ibid., 50), Descartes mentions goodness and truth: "For, since God is the supreme being, it is not possible that He be other than the supreme good and truth" (*Cum enim Deus sit summum ens, non potest none sse etiam summum bonum et verum* [ibid., 144]); it would even be necessary to count among these perfections *summum ens*,[43] *existentia* (ibid., 66 and 67), and so forth. Indeed, the list of perfections can never be completed, since "all the perfections that I could observe to be in God" (*Discourse* [AT VI, 35]) comprise no less than *"omnes omnino perfectiones, ut Deus,"* absolutely all the perfections: " . . . God means something such that absolutely all perfections are comprised in it."[44] Quantitatively, therefore, God accumulates perfections, the review of which will always remain in principle incomplete. But God can take on these perfections only by stamping them with the infinity that characterizes him; to the operation of review (quantitative), the human mind must add that of an amplification (qualitative). Descartes describes this operation as "the power to amplify all created perfections, *i.e.*, to conceive something as greater or more ample than they"; or again, "the power to so amplify all human perfections that they are grasped as more than human."[45] Only then can the perfections, carried to infinity, be attributed to God—conceived as "summation of perfections" (*cumulum perfectionum*) and as "comprehending all perfections" (*omnium perfectionum complementum*).[46] God not only achieves the summation of perfections but, above all, their elevation to the infinite power: from perfections infinite in number to the infinity of perfections. The highest perfection of God thus consists in the enunciation of the superlative: as Meditation III already states, " . . . the idea of the most perfect being, *i.e.,* God" (*idea entis perfectissimi, hoc est Dei* [AT VII, 51]). Later on, the syntagma reappears: " . . . God, or a supremely perfect being" (*Dei, sive entis summe perfecti* [ibid., 54]); " . . . God (*i.e.,* a supremely perfect being)" (*Deum [hoc est ens summe perfectum]* [ibid., 66]); " . . . God . . . (*i.e.,* a supremely perfect being . . .)" (*Deum . . . [hoc est ens summe perfectum]* [ibid., 67]); "The substance that we understand to be supremely perfect . . . is called God" (*Substantia,quam summe perfectam esse intelligimus . . .* Deus *vocatur* [ibid., 162]). The superlative of perfection plays the role of dominant title of God, as much by its frequency in 1641 as by its permanence in 1637 and 1644.[47] Definition (3) of God, as perfection in the superlative, supports the a priori proof for the existence of God; but, above all, it certifies this proof by its capacity to integrate into God any perfection whatever, at the mere cost of its passage to the superlative. Definition (3) furnishes more than *one* definition of the divine essence; indeed, it is the matrix of an infinity of possible definitions of the divine essence, based on any perfection carried to the infinite.

But then why is it that the attribute *ens summe perfectum* of definition (3) does not appear in either (1) or (2)? If definition (3) must govern all that follows in the *ordo rationum*—and, in particular, the a priori proof of Meditation V—how can Descartes exclude it from the new beginning that revitalizes Meditation III? We encounter here an exemplary case of inconsistency in the Cartesian process of elaborating a definition of God. And this is astonishing beyond any mere prima facie inconsistency. Indeed, here we find once again, under the aspect of omission, a difficulty that we encountered earlier under the aspect of coordination. In (1) and (2), the determination of God as infinite (C) crowned the union formed by indetermination (A) and substantiality (B), and also gave an account of independence (D). However, it was apparent that the determination of God as supremely powerful (F), and therefore also as creator (G), arose from a conceptual movement that was anterior to the determination of infinity (C), and therefore irreducible to it. This distortion indicated a primary inconsistency. There is no more audacity in adding a second inconsistency to the first, this time by omission. The omission exists between, on the one hand, the two elements of the first inconsistency—infinity (C), and omnipotence (F)—and on the other, supreme perfection, the element remarkably absent from (1) and (2). Absent? Not entirely, since, if supreme perfection consists in carrying any one perfection to the highest degree by imposing on it a superlative (*summe*, etc.), then the determinations of supreme intelligence (E), and indeed of supreme power (F), witness discretely but indisputably to the work of supreme perfection (H). Thereupon, the initial question receives a partial answer, but also a radical transformation. The response is that, to be sure, (1) and (2) are organized with coherence, but it turns out to be two partical coherences, rather than one unified coherence. The first coherence gathers (A), (B), (C), and (D) around infinity; the second coherence takes in (F) and (G) on the basis of omnipotence. Determinations (E) and (F) refer back to supreme perfection (H), formulated expressly in (3). We thus have a triple incoherence corresponding to the triple irreducibility among infinity, omnipotence, and supreme perfection. Our question no longer conduces to a testing of the internal consistency of (1) and (2), the inconsistency of which is thus established.[48] Instead we must ask, why does Descartes bring into play no less than *three* fundamental determinations of the essence of God? What are their origins and functions? To what extent can they contradict one another?

III. THE DISSOLUTION OF THE DEFINITION,
AND THE MASK OF THE INFINITE

The examination of a single one of the proofs for the existence of God makes it apparent with what difficulty the three divergent determinations achieve compatibility within it. Is it necessary to increase the plurality of the three principle proofs for the existence of God by a plurality of several fundamental determinations of the essence of God? Before conceding to such a multiplication, we must consider a more economical hypothesis: the diversity of the three determinations of the divine essence, which come to light in formulations (1) and (2), do not add to the diversity of the three proofs, but merely herald it. In other words, the three proofs of existence are perhaps not compatible among themselves,[49] since the three principle determinations of essence are divergent, beginning with their original appearance in the first proof. This interpretive hypothesis would be capable of verification only under several conditions: First, to set out again the three determinations of (1) and (2) among each of the three proofs. Then to establish that each of the three pairs thus defined (one essential determination/one proof of existence) constitutes a conceptually identifiable theoretical decision. Finally, to measure the relations of compatibility or incompatibility of each of the three proofs. The purely logical difficulties will thus be fathomed by a metaphysical questioning.

The first essential determination of God, designated hereafter as (I), apprehends him as infinity; in formulations (1) and (2), infinity (C) governs indeterminate (A) substantiality (B), but also independence (D). It renders possible the completeness of the proof by means of effects in Meditation III. Can this first pair (infinity/proof by means of effects) claim credentials from a historically identifiable metaphysical situation? Insofar as God, as infinite, proves his existence in virtue of being *causa ultima* (AT VII, 50), we would be able to consider the second *via* of St. Thomas, drawn "from the nature of efficient causality," which concludes: " . . . it is necessary to posit some first efficient cause: which everyone calls God." And, in fact, Caterus was the first to make this comparison.[50] But it is not necessary here to employ the cause as intermediary; the determination of infinity itself directly admits of an antecedent. John Duns Scotus had already attempted to conceive of God in terms of infinity, interpreted as the unconditioned a priori of all conceptualization.[51] For Duns Scotus, infinity enters in before all determinations, stamping them with indeterminacy; being the sole intrinsic aspect, it makes them all appear extrinsic. Descartes concludes from this that the divine infinity is in act: "But I judge God to be actually infinite" (*Deum autem ita judico esse actu infinitum* [AT VII, 47]). Duns Scotus, before him, had concluded in the same way: "Any infinite being exists in act."[52] In saying this, Duns Scotus takes a position, the originality of which can best be measured by confronting it with that of St. Thomas Aquinas. The latter recognized the infinity of God, but attributed it to him by deduction from his first definition, as *actus essendi*: "Since, therefore, the divine being is not a being received into anything, but is himself his own subsistent being . . . it is manifest that God himself is infinite and perfect."[53] On the contrary, Duns Scotus considers infinity as the most simple determination, and thus the first; in God, infinity precedes any other determination (including the act of being), because it is directly perceptible to us.[54] Before Descartes, we thus find explicitly stated the paradox of a negation (*in-finitum*) which, in fact, merely negates the first negation that constitutes the finite itself. Indeed, it therefore affirms absolute positivity. Here, once again, Descartes echoes his predecessors, saying: " . . . the perception of the infinite is in me in a certain way prior to the finite" (*priorem quodammodo in me esse perceptionem infiniti quam finiti* [AT VII, 45]). He thus opposes syntactical negation by means of a semantic negation: "Nor is it true that the infinite is understood through the negation of boundary or limitation, since on the contrary, all limitation contains a negation of the infinite."[55] Therefore, in determining God as infinite, Descartes assumes a perspective that is in fact a precise conceptual tradition, because it is historically identifiable. The determination of the essence of God by infinity receives the title "the principle argument for proving the existence of God" (*praecipuum argumentum ad probandum Dei existentiam* [AT VII, 14]), or the "principal grounds" for this proof (*praecipua ratio* [ibid., 101]). It holds this primacy not from the *ordo rationum*, but in virtue of its intrinsic excellence. This excellence results from its characteristic property: incomprehensibility. Indeed, incomprehensibility results directly from infinity: " . . . for the idea of the infinite, granted that it be true, ought not to be comprehended by any means, since this very incomprehensibility is included in the formal nature of the infinite."[56] The incomprehensibility of the infinite fixes the particular mode of its cognizability: the infinite is known, without, however, being understood; that is, it is not constructed according to the parameters of method, as an object of order and measure. Without taking up again an inquiry conducted elsewhere,[57] I shall recall a massive argument: the definition and the proof by infinity intervene in a sequence where (between the end of Meditation I and the ultimate conclusion of Meditation III [AT VII, 52]) the evidence of method is disqualified. If God must still be known, then it would have to be under another mode than the evidence of the objects of method. We would thus have a knowledge of God which, in virtue of hyperbolic doubt, hyperbolically exceeds the evidence (then out of play) of material simple natures—that is to say, of mathematical truths. But, one will ask, what do we really know of the infinite if it stands in such a reciprocal relationship with the incomprehensible? Descartes had already formulated the response to this question in 1630: " . . . we cannot comprehend the grandeur of God, although we know it. But our very judgment that it is incomprehensible makes us consider it to be the greater; . . . his power is incomprehensible."[58] The infinite transgresses, by its incomprehensibility, the truths commensurate with our minds, under the aspect of incomprehensible power. We thus establish a decisive consequence concerning the first determination in (I): it is incompatible with any determination of God that would maintain his essence to be on a level with the evidence of mathematical truths and the essences of finite objects. Furthermore, there is a second consequence: (I) applies the determination of cause to God, as much in 1641 (*causa ultima* [AT VII, 50]) as earlier in 1630 (" . . . a cause, the power of which surpasses the limits of the human understanding, . . . "; *efficiens et totalis causa*).[59] This causality is limited, however, to the action of God with respect to creatures, and them alone. Indeed, "cause" belongs (since the *Regulae*) among the simple natures; therefore it presents a perfectly comprehensible evidence, and produces methodical evidence. It thus renders intelligible, among other things, the relation of God to the world. But because it provides comprehensible evidence, it cannot be applied intrinsically to God. In short, comprehensible causality is an extrinsic determination of the infinite and incomprehensible God. There is, therefore, a second incompatibility: the determination (I) of God as incomprehensible infinity will be inconsistent with any determination of the essence of God based on intrinsic causality.

What I shall call determination (II) was articulated in Meditation III, as an element in formulation (3): " . . . one of the preeminent perfections which I conceive to be in him [God]" (*una ex praecipuis perfectionibus quas in eo esse intelligo* [AT VII, 50]); but it is also present in formulations (1) and (2), at least when they employ the superlative. Its real development, however, occurs only in Meditation V, where it permits the definition of the essence of God, and the proof of his existence, understood as one of his perfections. From this follows (in H) the complete determination of God as *ens summe perfectum* (ibid., 54, 66, 67, etc.). It seems possible to refer this determination tot he fourth *via* of St. Thomas, which claims to reach God on the basis of the superlative: "There is therefore something which is most true, most good, and most noble, and consequently the supreme being."[60] To be more precise about perfection, one may note that, if St. Thomas admits in principle that "all that is perfect is attributed to God," he does not consider perfection in itself; as previously with infinity, he deduces perfection from the divine *esse*, rather than clarifying the divine *ens* in terms of perfection: "God is pure act, unconditionally and universally perfect; nor does any other imperfection find place in him"; better yet: " . . . it is proper that the first being, which is God, should be most perfect, and consequently the best"; or again: "The first being must be the most perfect. But it has been shown that God is the first being; therefore, he is the most perfect."[61] Perfection here results from the more fundamental determination of God as *ens*, or rather as *ipsum esse*. Perfection plays in the Thomist enterprise a merely derived role. One must therefore consider other sources than St. Thomas.

One point, at least, is certain: Descartes was able to find confirmation of the traditional authority of the syntagma *ens perfectum* in Suarez.[62] But it remains to be determined which authors before Descartes were able to determine God as the most perfect being. It would seem evident that (to have recourse to St. Anselm), the proof by means of effects, which rests on the determination of God as *ens summe perfectum*, takes up once again the celebrated Anselmian argument. But an examination of the texts of the *Monologium* imposes some limits on the comparison. Perfection makes its appearance rarely, and always as subordinated to the ontic determination: " . . . it will be seen that [God] alone exists simply, perfectly and absolutely; all other things are almost nonexistent, and hardly exist at all"; or again: " . . . each one of them [the persons of the trinity] is the perfectly supreme being."[63] The work of the *Monologium* bears less on perfection as such than on the passage to the superlative (*summe*) of all the properties attributable to God. This involves less of perfection than of quantification:

This [being], therefore, is supreme being, supreme life, supreme reason, supreme well-being, supreme justice, supreme truth, supreme immortality, supreme incorruptibility, supreme immutability, supreme blessedness, supreme eternity, supreme power, supreme unity, which is nothing other than supremely being, supremely living, and the like.[64]

We can surely recognize here certain Cartesian determinations, drawn from (1), (2), and (3). These magnitudes, however, even carried to their maximum, remain juxtaposed here without any organization or deduction on the basis of the notion of perfection. Whereas Descartes expresses an essential determination—God as the most perfect being—Anselm uses the perfection of the superlative to attribute any qualification to God. Since, for Descartes, perfection constitutes not an operator but a determination of God, he always resisted this rapprochement.[65]

What author, other than St. Anselm, can thus confirm the second Cartesian determination of the essence of God? We hazard the opinion that the answer here (as at AT VII, 21 and 36) is William of Ockham: "God is the most perfect being; therefore, since he is in some way cognizable by us . . . he will be the most intelligibly perfect." Particular perfection here, one must note, does not precede perfection as such, but is deduced from "that perfection as such which is God."[66] This perfection as such (*simpliciter*) can be understood in two senses: either in the strict sense, in which it defines God alone; or in a less literal sense, in terms of attributive perfections, which are first applied to creatures, and then as a limit case to God. The latter cases serve as concepts common to God and creatures only insofar as they constitute merely nominal concepts, incapable of attaining the divine essence.[67] But we find that, as often happens, William of Ockham criticizes the position of Duns Scotus on this point. Scotus determined the divine essence in terms of infinity; Ockham, who defines it in terms of perfection, therefore proceeds to contest the primacy of the infinite affirmed by Scotus. He points out that the concept of an infinite being is composed of an affirmation (being) and a negation (in-finite), and

therefore admits of some imperfection. Thus, "the concept of an infinite being is not formally, in itself, the most perfect concept to have, of
all the possible concepts of God."[68] This decisive opposition between
two medieval predecessors of Descartes reveals that a choice must be
made between the infinite (I) and the most perfect (II). But Descartes
does not choose. Does he nonetheless avoid the contradiction?

Descartes successively supports the two fundamental determinations of the divine essence for a very clear reason: to construct not one,
but two proofs for the existence of God. But are these determinations
compatible? Can Descartes support two theses which oppose each
other in the works of Duns Scotus and Ockham? Several arguments
plead in favor of an inconsistency between (I) and (II).

a. A number of critics have raised the issue of the "unexpected encounter" (O. Hamelin) by which, at the threshold of Meditation V—
indeed, at the end of Meditation III—" . . . *perfect* replaces infinite"
(J.-M. Beyssade).[69]

b. This lexical rupture is redoubled by an investigation of the logical
link that unites (or fails to unite) the a posteriori and the a priori proofs.
There is no need to open once again the dossier of a famous polemic.
It will suffice to show that the two solutions result in the inconsistency
of (I) and (II). If one maintains, with F. Alquié, H. Gouhier, A. Kenny,
E. M. Curley, and others, that the proof of Meditation V does not
depend on that of Meditation III, one can only wonder about their
compatibility. If, following M. Gueroult, L. Beck, and others, one
subordinates the second proof to the first, their compatibility would
thus immediately be established. But since Descartes does not explicitly formulate this subordination, one may doubt, first, whether it is
authentically Cartesian, and, second, whether it is conceptually
possible.[70]

But the discrepancy between (I) and (II) holds, even more, in the
opposition between the incomprehensibility of the idea of the infinite,
and the quasi comprehensibility of the idea of a supremely perfect
being. We emphasize, however, that three arguments of Meditation V
reduce—to the point of almost suppressing it—the caesura between
the idea of the infinite (incomprehensible) and the ideas of finite
objects (comprehensible). First we establish that, since all innate ideas
are drawn from thought (" . . . I am able to bring forth the idea of
something from my thought . . . " [*alicujus rei ideam possim ex
cogitatione mea depromere*, AT VII, 65]), the idea of God is drawn up
from storage where, among others, it was stocked: " . . . whenever
I am pleased to think of a first and supreme being, and, as it were,
bring forth the idea of him from the storehouse of my mind . . . "

(*quoties . . . de ente primo et summo libet cogitare, atque ejus ideam tanquam ex mentis meae thesauro depromere* [ibid., 67]). Undoubtedly, in (I), the idea of the infinite was given before all experience, but arising with the very act of the *cogito* (ibid., 51), and opening the horizon of all possibility, it no longer remained stored in thought. Here, on the contrary, the idea of a supreme being remains stored in the treasury (*thesaurus mentis meae*) of ideas that the *cogito* keeps available. The idea of God, certainly innate, is properly only one innate idea among others, even though it is the primary. The difference lies not between it and innate ideas, but between innate ideas—including it—and counterfeit ideas: " . . . there is a great difference between such false suppositions and the true ideas innate in me, of which the first and principal is the idea of God" (*magna differentia est inter ejusmodi falsas positiones, et ideas veras mihi ingenitas, quarum prima et praecipua est idea Dei,* [ibid., 68]). We establish, then, a second contradiction: the idea of God is inevitably found compared to other innate ideas, which offer " . . . their true and immutable natures" (*suas . . . veras et immutabiles naturas* [ibid., 64]), and therefore attest " . . . a certain determinate nature, essence, or form, which is immutable and eternal" (*determinata quaedam ejus natura, sive essentia, sive forma, immutabilis et aeterna,* [ibid., 64]).

This recalls two previous themes. To begin with, let us consider only one: that of simple natures. The mathematical truths enumerated in Meditation I (AT VII, 20)—before they are cast in doubt—are defined by the innate ideas of Meditation V as true natures and forms. In fact, these are the *naturae simplicissimae,* the theory of which is definitively elaborated in the *Regulae,* in 1628.[71] And, actually, in this context, it is really a matter of pure and abstract *Mathesis* (ibid., 65), echoing the *Mathesis Universalis* of 1628. This is why there is an equality established between the idea of God and a simple mathematical nature: "Certainly I encounter the idea of God in myself—the idea of a supremely perfect being—no less than the idea of any figure or number" (*Certe ejus ideam, nempe entis summe perfecti, non minus apud me invenio, quam ideam cujusvis figurae aut numeri* [ibid., 65]). This is a stupefying declaration: the idea of God is found to be on the same footing, at least in me, as the idea of a triangle; therefore, God becomes an idea in the same manner as the simple natures. But simple natures can intervene only before or after hyperbolic doubt (and in fact they are invoked only at the beginning of Meditation I and Meditation V), but not during this doubt. The idea of God constructed in (II) could therefore be homogeneous with simple natures only by arising from the domain that is not (or is no longer) beset by hyperbolic doubt, that is, the realm of science, and therefore method. The fundamental determination of the essence of God present in (II) remains included within the field of method. Consequently, it cannot coincide with the fundamental definition of the essence of God given in (I), since the latter transgressed the field of method. Determinations (I) and (II) contradict each other as a thought internal to hyperbolic doubt contradicts a thought external to the same hyperbolic doubt. Even more, insofar as determination (II) shares strictly—neither more nor less—the status of the simple natures revoked by hyperbolic doubt, then it would also necessarily be revoked by the determination of God as infinity (I), if by chance (as from a strictly theoretical point of view is possible) it had been mentioned *before* hyperbolic doubt.

From this point we can enter upon the third argument: What appears there as a simple nature is also defined as a nature *vera, immutabilis et aeterna* (ibid., 64). We believe that we can recognize there the mathematical truths, the created status of which is proclaimed by Descartes in 1630. But someone will object: the idea of God is caused in me by the infinite, and therefore cannot be a *created* truth. This objection, however, holds only insofar as the idea of God considered in (II) is identified with the infinite, that is, with determination (I). But this is not the case. On the contrary, we must sustain the following paradox: If we juxtapose the topic of 1630—wherein God created the comprehensible truths of mathematics by his "incomprehensible power"—with the topic of Meditation V, determination (II) of God as supremely perfect does not become confused with divine omnipotence, but occurs among the *created* truths of mathematics. In 1630, the practitioners of simple natures "understand mathematical truths perfectly, but not that of the existence of God," because this existence is demonstrated "in a fashion which is more evident than the demonstrations of geometry," and which "makes known more certainly that God exists than . . . the truth of any proposition of geometry."[72] The fundamental determination (I) thus surpasses the created mathematical truths in evidence and certitude. In Meditation V, the existence of God is inferred from his perfect essence—according to determination (II)—with "not less" (AT VII, 65) and "not more" (ibid., 66) certitude and evidence than that the essence of a triangle implies the sum of its angles. The existence of God is neither more nor less evident than mathematical truths ("at least the same degree . . . " [ibid., 65]). But this contradicts the *greatest* evidence that it offered in 1630. Is the existence of God more evident, or merely as evident, as the truths of mathematics? To this question there are only two replies.[73] Either Descartes contradicts himself clumsily; or else, in Meditation V, it is a matter of Descartes having a different idea of God than he had in

1630. But the latter amounts to saying that determination (II) of the divine essence as the supremely perfect being remains in the domain of the creations of the incomprehensible and infinite power of God; and that, on the contrary, determination (I) of God, as infinite, surpasses methodical order and measure, and therefore even the supreme perfection that (II) applies to God.

From these three arguments, we conclude that the first two fundamental determinations of the essence of God are incompatible, as, therefore, are the two corresponding proofs of his existence. In order to prevent the incompatibility between (I) and (II) from being degraded into a pure contradiction, it remains preferable, surely, to see there merely a subordination. One might say that, just as "incomprehensible power" created the eternal truths, so determination (I) of God as incomprehensible infinity surpasses, hyperbolically, determination (II) of God as the sum of comprehensible perfections. But this hierarchy between two determinations of the divine essence marks, more than it masks, their irreducible inconsistency. Definitively, it must be admitted that (I) and (II) contradict each other according to the parameter of incomprehensibility.

There remains a final fundamental determination of the essence, and therefore of the existence, of God. This determination, that I shall indicate as (III), appears in Replies to Objections I and IV. The discussion with Caterus defines God as positively *a se*, and therefore as efficient cause of his own self (*causa efficiens sui ipsius* [AT VII, 111]); or to modify the violence of such a formulation, as exercising " . . . in a certain sense, the same regard to himself as an efficient cause does to its effect" (*quodammodo idem . . . respectu sui ipsius quod causa efficiens respectu sui effectus* [ibid., 111]). That which takes the place of a cause internal to God is nothing less than his essence interpreted as an *immensa et incomprehensibilis potentia*, so that it is the "cause in virtue of which he continues to be" (*causa cur ille esse perseveret* [ibid., 110]). This interpretation of the divine essence as power defines it, therefore, as "*ens summe potens*" (ibid., 119), and retrieves precisely the terms of (I) and (II): *omnipotens, summe potens*, designated (F). But this interpretation would not be necessary if God himself were not required to respond to a principle that is stated as a *dictat* of reason: "Now the light of reason tells us, indeed, that nothing exists about which one cannot ask why it exists, whether we inquire about its efficient cause, or, if it has none, why it requires none" (*Dictat autem profecto lumen naturae nullam rem existere, de qua non liceat petere cur existat, sive in ejus causam efficientem inquirere, aut, si non habet, cur illa non indigeat, postulare* [ibid., 108]).

The discussion with Arnauld assumes that the divine essence exercises a formal causality which "has a strong analogy with an efficient cause, and on that account may be called a sort of efficient cause" (*magnam habet analogiam cum efficiente, ideoque quasi causa efficiens vocari potest* [AT VII, 243]). Here again the *immensitas potentia sive essentia* (ibid., 237) assimilates the divine essence to a power that takes the place of a positive cause: " . . . the inexhaustible power of God is the cause or reason why he requires no cause" (*inexhausta Dei potentia sit causa sive ratio propter quam causa non indiget* [ibid., 236]). If God becomes the more or less efficient cause of himself by permitting the interpretation of his essence as power, it is because he must; and he must because "the consideration of the efficient cause is the primary and principle (if not the only) means which we have to prove the existence of God" (*considerationem causae efficientis esse primum et praecipuum medium, ne dicam unicum, quod habeamus ad existentiam Dei probandam* [ibid., 238]). The two developments are thus ordered in two parallel sequences: the absolute principle of causality (and, therefore, of reason) imposes the search in God himself—"*de ipso Deo*" (ibid., 167)—for a cause; this cause will be his own essence, which can take the place of cause, since it can be interpreted as power that is inexhaustible, immense, and incomprehensible. Therefore, God is expressed positively *a se*, that is, as *causa sui*.[74] Before considering the relation of (III) with (I) and (II), the historical context must be briefly fixed.

It is precisely because E. Gilson was correct in describing Descartes here as "without known predecessor,"[75] that we must investigate the reason for this (almost) total absence of genealogy. If we return once again at this point to the five *viae* of St. Thomas, we find in the course of the second *via* an explicit refusal of the hypothesis of a *causa (efficiens) sui*: " . . . nor is it possible that something be efficient cause of itself, because it would thus be prior to itself, which is impossible" (*nec est possibile, quod aliquis sit causa efficiens sui ipsius, quia sic esset prius seipso, quod est impossible*). This amounts to defining the efficient cause as a transitive, rather than an immanent, cause, which no being can exercise except on a being other than itself. And this confirms the other two *viae*, which were, however, able to anticipate the *causa sui*.[76] God is determined, with respect to things in motion, as prime mover, and *therefore* as not himself being in motion. With respect to contingent things, he is determined as the cause of their necessity, and *therefore* is, himself, free of external necessity. God, in himself, is determined as absolutely free of movement, of necessity, of efficiency, of perfection, and of finality (in the fourth and fifth *viae*). God exercises them only insofar as he is not dependent on them. God exercises efficiency, manifests himself by efficiency, therefore he is not efficiency. God is known by causality, but is not included in or grasped by causality. This fundamental decision does not characterize St. Thomas alone. Even the most resolute of his adversaries expressly take up the position. For example, there are Duns Scotus[77] and William of Ockham.[78] As for Suarez, if he still maintains that God is "without beginning and without cause," and that to be *a se* must be understood negatively,[79] he nonetheless already conceives the possibility of the *causa sui*, either by attributing the notion to others, or by restricting (as an afterthought) the bearing of a hypothesis that he thus concedes.[80] Why this ambivalence? It seems that the origin of this attitude must be found in the earlier interpretation of the divine essence as a cause.[81] In this way Suarez can be seen to have placed Descartes on the path of the *causa sui*, by assuming before him, and more discretely than he, the audacity of seeking to produce reasons "even in God" (see AT VII, 164, 165). In this sense, Suarez roughs in two Cartesian decisions: the essence of God is interpreted as a cause, so that then God can satisfy the *causa sive ratio* principle (ibid., 165 and 236).

From this point on, we can measure the implications of determination (III) in what we will cite as the last of the Cartesian formulations on God: (4) " . . . I certainly allow that something can exist in which there is so great, and so inexhaustible a power, that it required no assistance in order to exist, and requires none now for its preservation, and therefore it is in a sense the cause of its own existence; and I understand God to be of this kind" (*plane admitto aliquid esse posse, in quo sit tanta et tam inexhausta potentia, ut nullius unquam ope egerit ut existeret, neque etiam nunc egeat ut conservetur, atque adeo sit quodammodo sui causa; Deumque talem esse intelligo* [AT VII, 109]). God has no other cause than his essence interpreted as infinite power; therefore, God himself satisfies the *dictat* of reason, by giving reason for his existence through his own essence. Determination (III), therefore, radically contradicts the second implication of determination (I): the irreducibility of God to causality. In brief, determination (III) of God as *causa sui* contradicts determination (I) of God as *causa ultima*: here causality extends as far as God, but without including him in its domain; while in (III), causality is exercised even on the divine essence. If, as F. Alquié recognizes, Descartes "subordinates God himself to causality," it seems to us impossible to sustain, as does H. Gouhier, that "one perceives here the real unity of the new theodicy."[82] In fact, this rupture settles the matter: In determination (I), God transcends the principle of reason; in determination (III), the principle of reason transcends God. The contradiction between (I) and (II), concerning causality and the principle of reason, not only indicates a new inconsistency in Cartesian thought on God but also reveals an essential decision for the whole history of metaphysics.

Having arrived at this result, we can now compare the three Cartesian determinations of the essence of God, in view of the two consequences of determination (I): God is incomprehensible; God is outside the context of causality.

(a) Determination (I) is opposed to determination (II) by virtue of incomprehensibility, since in (II) the divine essence regresses to the status of the objects of method; but (I) is in accord with (II) on the basis of the second criterion, since the idea of the infinite neither admits or a cause, nor is explained as an effect—anymore than is the idea of a supremely perfect being.

(b) Determination (I) is opposed to determination (III) by virtue of causality and the principle of reason; but according to the criterion of incomprehensibility (I) accords with (III), which neatly determines the divine essence as incomprehensible power (AT VII, 110).

(c) Determination (II) is opposed to determination (III), first in terms of the criterion of incomprehensibility: essence methodically known contradicts essence interpreted as "incomprehensible power" (of 1630 and 1641); then in terms of the *causa sive ratio* criterion: the divine essence does not have more causality, as such, than eternal mathematical truths, whereas the *causa sui* exercises causality both on itself, and on these truths.

(d) It seems possible to compare the three fundamental determinations according to a final criterion: the creation of eternal truths. It is clear that (I) and (III) permit a God who is creator of eternal truths, while (II) prohibits it. These comparisons are summarized in the following table.

From this table, certain lessons follow. Concerning identification, it seems evident that henceforth we shall not be able to avoid the simple question of the plurality of divine names in Cartesian metaphysics. The surprising employment of the term *divine names* in metaphysics is justified by the reasons that force us to recognize a plurality of such names. Descartes employs several determinations that we can no longer confuse, once we have identified (even cursorily) the historical origins of the theological debates in which these determinations have gained an irreducible singularity. As a general rule, the Cartesian discussion depends very strictly on its predecessors, and all the more when it is a case of discourse on God. Without consideration of these genealogies, the interpretation of them would become almost impossible. For the very first time, Descartes transposes some of the divine names elaborated by medieval theology into

	Determinations	I	II	III
Identifications	Divine name	infinity	*ens summe perfectum*	*causa sui*
	Formulation	Meditation III (1) and (2)	Meditation V (3)	Replies to Objections I & IV (4)
	Antecedent	John Duns Scotus	William of Ockham	Suarez?
Incoherencies	Incomprehensibility	T	F	T
	Noncausal	T	T	F
	Nonmethodic	T	F	T

the (primarily self-regulated) field of metaphysics in the modern era. The meditation of this historical transposition constitutes today one of the marking stones of the history of philosophy applied to Descartes. We hope to have established it. Concerning the inconsistency of the three determinations, one must first note that they never fit together to satisfy even one of the three criteria (the horizontal reading of the table): Incomprehensibility is contradicted by (II), transcendence in relation to cause is undermined by (III), the creation of eternal truths is abandoned by (II). The inconsistency is therefore rooted deeply through all the strata of metaphysical discourse on the divine names. Second, one must note (by means of a vertical reading of the table) that the three determinations do not contradict equally the three criteria employed. Without minimizing the fact that I have not been able to avoid a certain inevitable arbitrariness in my choice, I must nonetheless emphasize that determination (II) of God as *ens summe perfectum* contradicts two of the three criteria; Descartes' determination (III) as *causa sui* contradicts one of the three; but on the contrary his determination (I) as infinite satisfies all three. Since, in addition, determination (I) revives the "incomprehensible power" which, in 1630, names God the creator of eternal truths, it does not seem unreasonable to recognize in it a primacy over the other two. I would suggest the idea of infinity as the first of the divine names in Cartesian metaphysics. And from this we take up a final question: What metaphysical destiny do these three determinations of the divine essence have, after their Cartesian transposition?

Descartes will never overcome the plurality of divine names that he introduces into metaphysics. This radical inconsistency will pass to his successors as a task, and perhaps also as a profound aporia, never resolved because too soon forgotten. In fact, this inconsistency prevents us from posing openly the relation of finite thought to God, because the multiplicity of the divine names, which are supposed to be compatible, masks the fact that we are actually dealing with the distance between the finite and the infinite. The determination of God as infinite is masked (in virtue of an unconscious but rigorous ruse of reason) by other determinations that submit it to incomprehensibility and/or the principle of reason. Descartes, and after him the modern metaphysics which he inaugurated, masks the idea of infinity at the very moment when he attempts to recognize the primacy of it. Before God, he advances only by hiding himself from infinity; not by the masks of the theater, but by two other divine names less divine than infinity. Before God, Descartes comes forth masked: *larvatus pro Deo.*[83]

NOTES

1. *Discourse on Method* (AT VI, 3). See ibid., 8, and Letter to Mersenne, 16 October 1639 (AT II, 599). Also see the *Conversation with Burman*, where Descartes speaks very clearly (AT V, 159; *Descartes' Conversation with Burman*, ed. J. Cottingham [Oxford: Clarendon Press, 1976], sec. 32, p. 21). Or again, ibid. (AT V, 179; Cottingham, sec. 82, 0. 50). (The abbreviation AT is explained in the General Bibliography at the beginning of this volume.)

2. We have attempted it in *L'idole et la distance* (Paris, 1977) and *Dieu sans l'etre* (Paris, 1983).

3. *Intelligo* introduces a definition of God (AT VII, 40, 45, 50, 109, etc. Formulations (1) and (2) are commented upon by, among others, E. M. Curley, *Descartes Against the Skeptics* (Cambridge: Harvard University Press, 1978), 127–128; and P. A. Schouls, *The Imposition of a Method: A Study of Descartes and Locke* (Oxford, 1980), 176 ff.

4. In this context, one obviously thinks of Spinoza: *Principia Philosophia Cartesianae* I, nos. 5 and 6, corrected by *"Habemus enim ideam veram"* in the *De Intellectus Emendatione*, sec. 33.

5. H. Frankfurt, "Descartes on the Consistency of Reason," in *Descartes: Critical and Interpretive Essays*, ed. M. Hooker (Baltimore–London, 1978), 36. See also his study on "Descartes' Validation of Reason," *American Philosophical Quarterly* 2 (1965), esp. 223–225. One might consider that Gassendi has already posed the same question, when he criticizes formulation (2) term for term, remarking that the attributes are not linked necessarily. See AT VII, 186, 188.

6. Hence our studies on "L'ambivalence de la métaphysique cartésienne," *Les Études Philosophiques* (1976), presented again in *Sur l'ontologie grise de Descartes*, 2d ed. (Paris, 1980); and "Descartes et l'onto-théologie," *Bulletin de la Société Française de Philosophie* LXXVI (1982).

7. We have attempted to proceed in this way in *Sur l'ontologie grise*, secs. 1, 30, and 31; then in *Sur la théologie blanche de Descartes* (Paris, 1981), secs. 1–2 and 19–20.

8. See F. Alquié, "Expérience ontologique et déduction systématique dans la constitution de la métaphysique de Descartes," in *Descartes: Cahiers de Royaumont* (Paris, 1957), and our work *Sur la théologie blanche*, sec. 14, pp. 323 ff.

9. Et ineptum est quod subjungit, nempe Deum ut deceptorem cogitari. Et si enim, in prima mea Meditatione, de aliquo deceptore summe potenti locutus sim, nequaquam tamen ibi verus Deus concipiebatur, quia ut ipse ait, fieri non potest ut verus Deus sit deceptor. Atque si ab eo petatur unde sciat id fieri non posse, debet respondere se scire ex eo quod implicet contradictionem in conceptu, hoc est, ex eo quod concipi non possit (Letter to Voetius, AT VIII–2, 60).

See also, *Conversation with Burman* (AT V, 147 and 150; Cottingham, sec. 3, p. 4 and sec. 10, p. 9). When the *ordo rationum* permits it, the Meditations themselves will raise this contradiction, at AT VII, 53 (see *Principles of Philosophy* I, no. 29). See also Letter to Buitendijck in 1643 (AT IV, 64). This point has been clearly noted by Frankfurt, *Demons, Dreamers and Madmen: The Defense of Reason in Descartes' Meditations* (Indianapolis: Bobbs-Merrill, 1970), 48.

10. We are considering here the debate between R. Kennington, "The Finitude of Descartes' Evil Genius," *Journal of the History of Ideas* (1971), 441–446; and H. Caton, "Kennington on Descartes' Evil Genius," ibid. (1973), 639–641; then R. Kennington, "Reply to Caton," ibid. (1973), 641–643; and H. Caton, "Rejoinder: The Cunning of the Evil Genius," ibid. (1973), 641–644. See also H. Caton, *The Origin of Subjectivity* (New Haven: Yale University Press, 1973), 115–121. In fact, *summe potens* at AT VII, 45 (2) is equivalent to *omnipotens* at ibid., 40 (I), as in *Principles* I, nos. 14 and 22.

11. For this nominalist identification, see *Sur la théologie blanche*, 330–333, but also 303–304.

12. A similar indetermination is to be found in Suarez, *Disputationes Metaphysicae* XXIX, sec. 3, nn. 4 and 5 (*Opera Omnia* [Paris: Vives Edition, 1866]), 26:35. Among many others, one thinks of Richard of St. Victor: "Legi frequenter quod non sit Deus nisi unus, quod sit aeternus, increatus, immensus, quod sit omnipotens et omnium dominus, quod ab ipso est omne quod est, quod ubique est, et ubique totus, non per partes divisus" (*De Trinitate* I, 5, in *Patrologia Latina*, vol. 196, col. 893 A).

13. *De Fide Orthodoxa* I, 9, *Patrologia Graeca*, vol. 94, col. 835 A–B.

14. *De Trinitate* VII, 5, 10. Concerning the same difficulty, see ibid. V, 2, 3; and 5, 7. See also the edition by M. Mellet and T. Camelot, *La Trinitate* (Paris, 1955) I, 584, n. 33. Augustine's rejection of the substantiality of God is therefore based partly on the inclusion of substance in the pair substance/accident, and partly on the principle that nothing is in God that is not God Himself.

15. Substantia principaliter dicitur de individiis quae maxime in pluralitate consistunt. Individua namque maxime substant, id est subjacent accidentibus et idea magis proprie substantiae nomen suscipiunt. . . . Manifestum est summam essentiam quae nullis subjacet accidentibus proprie non posse dici substantiam, nisi substantia ponatur pro essentia (*Monologium*, chap. 78).

16. *Summa Theologiae* Ia, q. 29, art. 3, obj. 4, and *resp*. This does not prevent the employment of *substantia divina* in a second sense, for example, in *Summa Theologiae* Ia, q. 17, art. 7; *Summa Contra Gentiles* I, 3 and 5; II, 53 and 55, etc.

17. Quippe ut vere Deus est causa ac propterea inter causas (et prima quidem) merito habetur, ita vere ut substantia, ut proinde inter substantias numerari valeat (et quidem tanquam prima substantia, quia scilicet Deum potiore ratione, quam Socratem, quam Bucephalum, quam hunc lapidem primam substantiam appellaveris). (*Exercitationes Paradoxicae Adversus Aristoteleos*, Lib. II, d. 3, sec. 6 [B. Rochot, ed., Paris, 1959], 325–327).

18. *Lexicon Philosophicum* (Frankfurt, 1613). See texts and references in *Sur la théologie blanche*, 116 ff.

19. *Summa Philosophica Quadripartita* (Paris, 1609), Lib. I, *Logica*, I, III, sec. 1, q. 2; Vol. I, p. 98.

20. *La Métaphysique ou science surnaturelle* (Paris, 1606), V, 2, sec. 4; Vol. I, p. 193. Also, consequently, the qualification of *"sur-substance"* (ibid., X, 7, sec. 12; Vol. III, 88).

21. " . . . *Vera substantia, sive res per se subsistens*" (Letter to Regius, January 1642; AT III, 502, line 11). Here this *vera* definition is opposed to the habitual determination of substance as substantial form, therefore in relation to matter: " . . . substantiam quandam materiae adjunctam" (ibid., 501). See *Principles* I, nos. 51, 64, and the surprising text of Replies to Objections VI, n. 7 (AT VII, 435).

22. . . . Substantia creata non convenit cum increata solumin ratione entis, sed etiam in ratione substantiae; De . . . substantia, fatemur quidem Deum esse substantiam increatam, atque ita posse abstrahi rationum substantiae in communi a creata et increata. . . . Licet aliquo modo conveniat in ratione substantiae cum aliquibus entibus creatis, non tamen univoce, sed analogice (*Disputationes* XXXII, sec. 1, respectively, n. 1, n. 6, and n. 9; Vol. XXVI, pp. 312–314).

On this whole question, we refer to the more developed analysis in *Sur la théologie blanche*, sec. 7, esp. 110–120. Even more radical than Suarez, but fulfilling his logic, Gassendi concludes: " . . . dico, ut nihil recedam ex Principiis communibus, tam nomen, quam definitionem substantiae vere ac formaliter convenire Deo et creaturis, quare et convenire ipsis substantiam, sive conceptum substantiae abstractum univoce" (*Exercitationes*, Lib. II, d. 3, sec. 9, p. 355).

23. On this point, it now seems to me necessary to correct some of my conclusions in *Sur la théologie blanche*, 113, and n. 3.

24. Per infinitam substantiam, intelligo substantiam perfectiones veras et reales actu infinitas et immensas habentem. Quod non est accidens notioni substantiae superadditum, sed ipsa essentia substantiae absolute sumptam, nullisque defectibus terminatae; qui defectus, ratione substantiae, accidentia sunt; non autem infinitas et infinitudo. (Letter to Clerselier, 23 April 1649, n. 4; AT V, 355, 356.)

Since this explication follows three others, each of which comments on a formulation of Meditation III, there is no risk in relating it to (2) (AT VII, 45, lines 11, 21, 22, and 27).

25. Letters to Mersenne, respectively, 15 April 1630 (AT I, 146); 6 May 1630 (ibid., 150); and 27 May 1630 (ibid., 152).

26. AT V, 153; Cottingham, sec. 19, p. 13.

27. "In re ipsa prior est Dei infinita perfectio, quam nostra imperfectio" (ibid).

28. See AT VII, 113; and the Letter to Hyperaspistes, August 1641, n. 6 (AT III, 426, 427).

29. See F. Alquié, *La découverte métaphysique de l'homme chez Descartes* (Paris, 1950), 236–237; N. Grimaldi, *L'expérience de la pensée dans la philosophie de Descartes* (Paris, 1978), 283; and *Sur la théologie blanche*, 402–406.

30. AT X, 377, 378. See *Sur l'ontologie grise*, secs. 10–11.

31. AT I, 150. See *Sur la théologie blanche*, 270–282; 437–439.

32. See Letter to Mersenne, 11 October 1638 (AT II, 383); and 11 November 1640 (AT III, 234). See also *Sur la théologie blanche*, 396–402.

33. Letter to Mersenne, 30 September 1640 (AT III, 191). See *Sur la théologie blanche*, 411. Dependence can, in a certain sense, be conjugated with independence, for example, when it is a case of the human free will. See Letter to Newcastle (?), 3 November 1645 (AT IV, 332, 333). E. M. Curley has seen clearly the function of independence in the proof by means of effects: *Descartes Against the Skeptics*, 130–131.

34. AT IX–1, 38, which is confirmed by " . . . if I had been alone and independent of every other . . . I would have been able to have from myself, for the same reason, all the surplus that I know myself to lack; and thus to be myself infinite, eternal, immutable, omniscient, omnipotent . . . " (*Discourse on Method*: AT VI, 34–35).

35. Respectively, Letters to Mersenne, 15 April 1630 (AT I, 145); 6 May 1630 (ibid., 149); (see also ibid., 150); Reply to Objections V, AT VII, 380; (see ibid., 370). See also Letter to Mesland, 2 May 1644 (AT IV, 119), and the *Conversation with Burman*: " . . . illa et omnia alia pendent a Deo . . . ," (AT V, 160; Cottingham, sec. 33, p. 22). See *Sur la théologie blanche*, 299 and 411–414.

36. For example, Letter to Elizabeth, January 1646 (AT IV, 352–354); or Letter to Newcastle (?), 3 November 1645 (AT IV, 332–333), of which the strange conclusion should be emphasized: " . . . the independence that we experience and feel in ourselves . . . is not incompatible with a dependence which is of another nature, according to which all things are subject to God" (ibid., 333).

37. AT VI, 35. We note that the Latin translation of Courcelles (*De Methodo*, in *Specimina Philosophiae* [Amsterdam, 1644], 32 = AT VI, 560) says *omniscius*.

38. Nominalist origins, certainly (supra, n. 11). Good indications from Margaret Wilson, *Descartes* (London: Routledge & Kegan Paul, 1978), 120–131.

39. Respectively, Letters to Mersenne, 15 April 1630 (AT I, 146); and 6 May 1630 (ibid., 150). The *Principles* will say *summe potens* (I, no. 14), and *summe potens* (I, no. 22).

40. " . . . Sibi dari omnipotentiam totam simul, aliasve perfectiones divinas collective sumptas. . . . " (Letter to Arnauld, 4 June 1648 [AT V, 194]).

41. Letter to Mersenne, 27 May 1630 (AT I, 151, 152).

42. *Sur la théologie blanche*, sec. 13.

43. *Summum ens*, AT VII, 54, line 17; 67, line 21 *ens primum et summum* = 67, lines 26–28, " . . . cum animadverto existentiam esse perfectionem, recte concludam ens primum et summum existere"; ibid., 69, line 8, *summum ens sive Deus*; ibid., 144, line 3; *Principles* I, no. 18 " . . . Dei sive entis summi ideam."

44. " . . . Deus tale quid dicat quod omnes omnino perfectiones in se comprehendit" (*Conversation with Burman* [AT V, 161]; Cottingham, sec. 35, p. 24).

45. Reply to Objections V. Respectively: " . . . facultas omnes perfectiones creatas ampliandi, hoc est aliquid ipsis majus sive amplius concipiendi" (AT VII, 365); and " . . . vis perfectiones omnes humanas eousque ampliandi ut plusquam humanae esse cognoscantur" (ibid., 370, 371). Here it is actually a case of transforming finite attributes (human perfections) into divine attributes, as a text in the Reply to Objections I very explicitly indicates (AT VII, 137, 138). See Letter to Regius, 24 May 1640 (AT III, 64); and Letter to Hyperaspistes, August 1641 (AT III, 427, 429). The divine perfections are superlative: " . . . summarum Dei perfectionum ideam . . . " (*Principles* I, no. 20); " . . . summas perfectiones . . . in Deo" (ibid., I, no. 18).

46. Respectively, *Notes Against a Certain Program*, AT VIII–2, 362 (F. Alquié translates this: *"le comble et l'accomplissement des perfections,"* in *Descartes, Oeuvres Philosophiques* [Paris, 1973], 3:812); and *Principles* I, no. 18, AT VIII–1, 11 ("a complete complement of all perfections" is the translation of V. R. and R. P. Miller, in *René Descartes, Principles of Philosophy* [Dordrecht/Boston/London, 1983], 10); the same no. 18 continues by defining God: "Archetypus aliquis, omnes ejus perfectiones reipsa continens."

47. See also Reply to Objections I (AT VII, 138); Reply to Objections II (ibid., 162); *Principles* I (nos. 14, 15, 16); *Discourse on Method* (AT VI, 36): " . . . God, who is this perfect Being." (See also ibid., 35, 36, 40.)

48. See E. M. Curley, *Descartes Against the Skeptics*, 125–135.

49. I therefore oppose, at least methodologically, the opinion of F. Alquié: *"la distinction des diverses preuves employées par Descartes ne saurait être essentielle, et leur nature se découvrira mieux à qui, au contraire, considérera leur unité"* (*La découverte métaphysique de l'homme chez Descartes*, 219).

50. " . . . Necesse est ponere aliquam causam efficientem primam: quam omnes Deum nominant" *Summa Theologiae*, Ia, q. 2, art. 3, *ad resp.* See Caterus, AT VII, 94 (and the rather weak denial of Descartes, ibid., 106). This comparison is confirmed by AT VII, 383; and F. Alquié, *Descartes, Oeuvres Philosophiques*, 2:254.

51. Conceptus perfectior simul et simplicior nobis possibilis, est conceptus entis infiniti. Iste enim est simplicior quam conceptus entis boni, entis veri, vel aliorum similium, quia 'infinitum' non est quasi attributum vel passio entis sive ejus de quo dicitur, sed *dicit modum intrinsecum illius entitatis,* ita quod cum dico 'infinitum ens,' non habeo conceptum quasi per accidens ex subjecto et passione, sed conceptum per se subjecti in certo gradu perfectionis, scilicet infinitatis (John Duns Scotus, *Ordinatio* [d. 3, p. 1, q. 1–2, n. 58], in *Opera Omnia,* ed. C. Balič [Rome, 1950], 3:40. See also *Quodlibet* V, n. 4)

Here it is very remarkable that the infinite is imposed on substance by affecting it with indetermination. Descartes reproduces the position of Scotus term for term (see elements A, B, and C of [1] and [2]). In the same sense, *Ordinatio* I, d. 8, p. 1, q. 3, n. 102: "Quidquid est in Deo perfectio essentialis, est formaliter infinitum—in creatum finitum" (*Opera Omnia,* 4:202); or: "Divinitas est formaliter infinita" (*Quodlibet* V, n. 17).

52. "Aliquod infinitum ens existit in actu" (*Ordinatio* I, d. 2, p. 1, q. 1–2, n. 147 [*Opera Omnia,* 2:214]). Infinity is indeed the proper name of God, in opposition to creatures: "Cognitio enim esse divini sub ratione infiniti est perfectior cognitione ejus sub ratione simplicitatis, quia simplicitas communicatur creaturis, infinitas autem non, secundum modum quo convenit Deo" (*Ordinatio* I, d. 3, p. 1, q. 1–2, n. 60 [*Opera Omnia,* 3:42]); this exactly anticipates the Cartesian position in Meditation III (AT VII, 47).

53. "Cum igitur esse divinum non sit esse receptum in aliquo, sed ipse sit suum esse subsistens . . . , manifestum est, quod ipse Deus sit infinitus et perfectus" (Thomas Aquinas, *Summa Theologiae,* Ia, q. 7, art. 1, *resp.*). On this text, and with respect to the opposition between Thomas and Duns Scotus concerning infinity in God, see E. Gilson, *Jean Duns Scott: Introduction à ses positions fondamentales* (Paris, 1952), 149–215, esp. 208–210.

54. Suarez will also say this (*Disputationes* XXVIII, respectively, sec. 1, n. 18, and sec. 2, n. 12 [*Opera Omnia,* 26:7 and 11]).

55. "Nec verum est intelligi infinitum per finis sive limitationis negationem, cum e contra omnis limitatio negationem infiniti contineat," Reply to Objections V (AT VII, 365). See Reply to Objections I (ibid., 113); and Meditation III (ibid., 45).

56. " . . . Idea enim infiniti, ut sit vera, nullo modo debet comprehendi quoniam ipsa incomprehensibilitas in ratione formali infiniti continetur" (Reply to Objections V [AT VII, 368]). Without reviving here the debate concerning the *"caractère ontologique et non purement représentatif de l'idée d'infini"* (F. Alquié, *La découverte métaphysique de l'homme chez Descartes,* 219); or, on the contrary, *"son caractère représentatif"* (M. Gueroult, *Descartes selon l'ordre des raison,* 2d ed. [Paris: Aubiev, 1968] 1:161 ff.), we will simply remark: (1) that noncomprehension does not signify nonawareness, but an awareness the object of which is not constructed according to the parameters of the *Mathesis Universalis;* one can (and must) know God as infinite without the clarity of a methodical object, but at the same time, with a greater evidence than such an object; and (2) that this deduction of incomprehensibility on

the basis of the infinite does not prevent Descartes from speaking—on the same page—of a representation of the infinite: " . . . repraesentare . . . totum infinitum, eo modo quo debet repraesentari per humanam ideam" (ibid., 368). See *Sur la théologie blanche*, 404–406.

57. References in *Sur la théologie blanche*, 399, n. 6.

58. Letter to Mersenne, 15 April 1630 (AT I, 145 and 146). See also, Letter to Mersenne, 6 May 1630 (AT I, 150).

59. Respectively, AT I, 150 and 152. In brief, as much in 1630 as in (I), *cause* has no further extension in God than *creator*.

60. "Est igitur aliquid quod est verissimum et optimum et nobilissimum et per consequens maxime ens" (St. Thomas, *Summa Theologiae, Ia*, q. 2, art. 3, *resp.*).

61. " . . . Omne illud quod est perfectionis, Deo sit attribuendum" (St. Thomas, *Summa Theologiae, Ia*, q. 29, art. 3, *resp.*); "Deus est actus purus, et simpliciter et universaliter perfectus neque in eo aliqua imperfectio locum habet" (ibid., q. 25, art. 1, *resp.*); " . . . oportet primum ens, quod est Deus, esse perfectissimum et per consequens optimum" (*De Potentia*, q. VII, art. 1, *resp.*); "Primum ens debet esse perfectissimum. Ostensum est autem Deum esse primum ens; ergo est perfectissimus" (*Summa Contra Gentiles*, 1:28).

62. " . . . Deus est primum ens . . . ; ergo est etiam summum et perfectissimum essentialiter; ergo de essentia ejus est, ut includat aliquo modo omnem perfectionem possibilem in tota latitudine entis" (Suarez, *Disputationes XXX*, sec. 1, n. 5 [*Opera Omnia*, 26:61]). See also, sec. 2, n. 21 (ibid., p. 71), where the perfection of the superlative (*summum*) is deduced.

63. " . . . Ille solus videbitur simpliciter et perfecte et absolute esse, alia vero omnia fere non esse et vix esse" (St. Anselm, *Monologium*, chap. 28); " . . . unius quisque illorum est perfecte summa essentia" (ibid., chap. 59).

64. "Illa igitur est summa essentia, summa vita, summa ratio, summa salus, summa justitia, summa veritas, summa immortalitas, summa incorruptibilitas, summa immutabilitas, summa beatitudo, summa aeternitas, summa potestas, summa unitas, quod non aliud est quam summe ens, summe vivens, et alia similiter" (ibid., chap. 16). See, in the same sense, chapters 4 and 6. Chapter 3 seems to give a formulation which is, at the same time, more powerful, coherent, and abstract: " . . . aliquid quod, sive essentia, sive substantia sive natura dicetur, optimum et maximum est et summum omnium quae sunt." However, it is still precisely a case of a maximum, and thus a quantification, rather than properly a perfection. One should consult here the work of Coleman Viola, "La dialectique de la grandeur. Une interprétation du 'Proslogion,'" in *Recherches de Théologie ancienne et médiévale* 37 (1970):23–55.

65. Letter to Mersenne, December 1640 (AT I, 260).

66. " . . . Deus est ens perfectissimum; igitur cum sit aliquo modo cognoscibilis a nobis . . . , erit intelligibile perfectissimum" (William of Ockham, *In Sententiarum*, I, d. 3, q. 1, in *Opera Philosophica et Theologica*, ed. S. Brown [New York, 1970], 2:390); " . . . illa perfectio simpliciter quae est Deus" (ibid., q. 2 [*Opera Philosophica*, 413]). Concerning the possibility of an indirect histor-

ical link, see G. Rodis-Lewis, "Descartes aurait-il eu un professeur nominaliste?" *Archives de Philosophie* 34 (1971):37–46.

67. William of Ockham, *In Sententiarum*, I, d. 2, q. 2 and q. 3 (*Opera Philosophica*, 62 and 98).

68. " . . . Conceptus entis infiniti non sit formaliter in se perfectior conceptus omni conceptu possibili haberi de Deo" (ibid., d. 3, q. 3 [*Opera Philosophica*, 422]). Against Duns Scotus, see *Ordinatio*, I, d. 3, p. 1, q. 1–2, n. 58, in *Opera Omnia*, 3:40 ff.

69. O. Hamelin, *Le système de Descartes* (Paris: 1911), 202, n. 1; and J.-M. Beyssade, *La philosophie première de Descartes* (Paris, 1979), 311. Here we follow H. Gouhier (*La pensée métaphysique de Descartes* [Paris, 1962], 146) who emphasizes the lexical heterogeneity between the two proofs, against M. Gueroult, who sees Descartes "*conciliant par dépassement saint Anselme et Duns Scot,*" and effecting "*la conciliation du Dieu cause efficiente et du Dieu archétype*" (*Descartes selon l'ordre des raisons* 1:204, 207). For, apart from the fact that it is not a question of Anselm, but of Ockham, and that they do not oppose efficient causality to the archetype, but perfection to infinity, the two versions are not at all found to be placed explicitly in equivalence.

70. In favor of the independence of the proofs, see: F. Alquié, *La découverte métaphysique* . . . , 212, 225, 226; H. Gouhier, "La preuve ontologique de Descartes (A propos d'un livre récent)," *Revue Internationale de Philosophie* 29 (1954):295–303; and *La pensée métaphysique de Descartes*, 117. In favor of the subordination of the second proof to the first, see: M. Gueroult, *Descartes selon l'ordre des raisons*, I, chap. 8; then *Nouvelles réflexions sur la preuve ontologique* (Paris, 1955); followed by L. J. Beck, *The Metaphysics of Descartes. A Study of the Meditations* (Oxford, 1965), 231–237. Finally, see D. Cress, "Does Descartes' 'Ontological Argument' Really Stand on Its Own?" *International Studies in Philosophy* 5 (1973):127–136.

71. In particular, *Regula XII* (AT X, 419). See *Sur la théologie blanche*, 351–356.

72. Letters to Mersenne, 6 May 1630 (AT I, 150); then, 15 April 1630 (ibid., 144); and 25 November 1630 (ibid., 182).

73. The *Discourse on Method* hesitates between the two positions: on the one hand, it follows (II): " . . . *je trouvais que l'existence qui y* [i.e., the idea that I had of a perfect being] *étais compris en même façon qu'il est compris en celle d'un triangle que ses trois angles sont égaux à deux droits* . . . " (AT VI, 36); on the other hand, it seems to want to follow (I) by correcting with " . . . *ou même encore plus évidemment.*" There is a similar hesitation in the commentary by F. Broadie, *An Approach to Descartes' Meditations* (London, 1970), 84; and that of M. Gueroult, *Descartes selon l'ordre des raisons*, 1:333–339.

74. On the entire collection of these texts and their doctrine, see *Sur la théologie blanche*, sec. 18; and B. Casper, "Der Gottesbegriff ens causa sui," *Philosophisches Jahrbuch* LXXVI (1968–1969).

75. E. Gilson, *Études sur le rôle de la pensée médiévale dans la formation du système cartésien* (Paris, 1930; 3d ed., 1967), 226.

76. " . . . Nec est possibile, quod aliquis sit causa efficiens sui ipsius, quia

sic esset prius seipso, quod est impossibile." See St. Thomas, *Summa Theologiae*, Ia, q. 2, art. 3, *resp.*

77. " . . . Penitus incausabile," Duns Scotus, *Ordinatio*, I, d. 2, p. 1, q. 1–2, n. 57 and 59 (*Opera Omnia*, 2:162–163 and 165). See also, *De primo principio*, III, 2, 3, 4, and 5.

78. William of Ockham, *In Sententiarum*, I, d. 3, q. 2 (*Opera Philosophica*, 1:405).

79. Suarez, *Disputationes*, respectively, I, sec. 1, n. 27 (*Opera Omnia*, 25:11); and XXVIII, sec. 1, n. 7 (*Opera Omnia*, 26:12).

80. "Et in hunc modum exponendi sunt aliqui Sancti, cum dicunt Deum esse sibi causam sui esse" (Suarez, *Disputatones* XXVIII, s. 1, n. 7 [*Opera Omnia*, 26:3]; " . . . neque Deus habet causam sui esse per quam a priori demonstretur, neque si haberet, ita exacte et perfecte a nobis cognoscitur Deus, ut ex propriis principiis illum assequamus" (ibid., XXIX, s. 3, n. 1 [*Opera Omnia*, 26:47]).

81. "Quamvis ergo demus ens, in quantum ens, non habere causas proprie, et in rigore sumptas priori modo, habet tamen rationem aliquam suarum proprietatum; et hoc modo etiam in Deo possunt hujusmodi rationes reperiri, nam ex Dei perfectione infinita reddimus causam, cur unus tantum sit, et sic de aliis" (Suarez, *Disputationes* I, s. 1, n. 29 [*Opera Omnia*, 25:12]).

82. F. Alquié, note in his *Descartes, Oeuvres Philosophiques* 2:682; and H. Gouhier, *La pensée métaphysique de Descartes*, 175.

83. Of course Descartes wrote *Larvatus prodeo* (AT X, 213), "I come forth masked," and not *Larvatus pro Deo*, "masked before God." This pure invention is permissible, first, because it is thought provoking. and then because others have hazarded the notion before us: J.-L. Nancy, in *Ego sum* (Paris, 1979) [tr. "Larvatus pro Deo" by D. A. Brown, in *Glyph 2* (Johns Hopkins Textual Studies, 1979)]; and L. Brunschwig, "Métaphysique et mathématiques chez Descartes," *Revue de Métaphysique et de Morale* (1927), 323.

14

Can I Be the Cause of My Idea of the World? (Descartes on the Infinite and Indefinite)

Margaret D. Wilson

. . . If the objective reality of any of my ideas is so much that I am certain that it is not in me either formally or eminently, and hence I myself cannot be the cause of this idea, it necessarily follows, that I am not alone in the world, but some other thing, which is the cause of this idea, also exists. (Meditation III, AT VII, 42; HR I, 163)

But as to the ideas of corporeal things, nothing occurs in them, which is so great that it does not seem that it could have originated from myself. (AT VII, 43; HR I, 164)

Therefore there remains only the idea of God, about which it must be considered whether it is something that could not originate from myself . . . (AT VII, 45; HR I, 165)

. . . Although a certain idea of substance is in me from the fact that I am a substance, nevertheless there would not be on that account an idea of infinite substance, since I am finite, unless it originated from some substance which really is infinite. (AT VII, 45; HR I, 166)

It is repugnant to my conception, or, what is the same, I think it implies a contradiction, that the world is finite or bounded . . . (Letter to Henry More, 15 April 1649: AT V; PL, 251)

I

In his first argument for the existence of God in Meditation III, Descartes argues that his idea of God requires a cause outside himself. As a finite substance, Descartes (considered as a mind) possesses within himself enough reality or perfection to be the cause of each of his other ideas. The implication is that all of these other ideas represent only finite substances, or their (finite) modes. "There remains only the idea of God" which, representing an infinite substance, cannot be explained by Descartes' own causal resources.

This reasoning has a strange feature, when considered in relation to other prominent Cartesian texts. In Meditation III Descartes writes as if all his ideas of the corporeal world were ideas of particular subparts of this world (like the idea of a stone). Yet many other texts reveal that *res extensa,* or the material world, is conceived of as a substance that exceeds any limits we can assign it, and may in fact be limitless. This conception is not even mentioned in the survey in Meditation III.[1] Nor are any of the nonsubstantial conceivables that Descartes also mentions elsewhere as exceeding (at least) our powers to assign limits, such as the natural number series.

It is true that Descartes—as he says in the *Principles*—reserves the term *infinite* "for God alone." The extension of the world, the divisibility of matter, the series of numbers—all apparently limitless from our point of view—are instead characterized as *indefinite.* Still, they are specifically not conceived as finite. Can *these* conceptions then be accounted for by the causal resources of a finite mind, according to Descartes' theory?

In the next sections of this paper I will try to delineate the nature and grounds of Descartes' distinction between the infinite and indefinite.[2] (Some of my remarks will particularly concern indefinite substance, or *res extensa,* but most will apply to the indefinites in general.)[3] I will show that Descartes uses two distinct considerations to ground this distinction. The first has to do with God's greater perfection: I call this the metaphysical criterion. Much more interesting and difficult is Descartes' further claim that we have different epistemological relations to God and to the indefinites. I call this the epistemological criterion. Clarification of the infinite/indefinite distinction—and particularly of problems surrounding the epistemological criterion—will then provide background for dealing with the question of how exactly conceptions of the indefinite fall within Descartes' theory about adequate causes of ideas. I will return to this question, and some of its implications, at the end of the paper.

II

The infinite/indefinite distinction, as it relates, for example, to *res extensa* and the number series, figures in most of Descartes' central works, including *The World*, *Discourse on the Method*, Replies to Objections, and *Principles of Philosophy*, as well as the *Conversation with Burman* and a number of important letters.[4] Sometimes the distinction is associated with theologico-political or other strategic concerns in a way that has suggested doubts about its theoretical genuineness. For example, the heading of *Principles* I, 26 reads:

[We] must not dispute about the infinite, but only regard as indefinite those things in which we perceive no limits [*in quibus nullos fines advertismus*], such as the extension of the world, the divisibility of the parts of matter, the number of stars, etc. (AT VIII-1, 14–15; HR I, 229)

Descartes' elaboration of the Principle continues the theme of "avoiding disputes":

We will thus never tire ourselves with disputes about the infinite. For surely, since we are finite, it would be absurd for us to determine anything about it, and thus try, as it were, to limit [*finire*] and comprehend it. We will not, therefore, bother to reply to those who ask whether, if an infinite line be given, half of it is also infinite; or whether an infinite number is even or odd and so on: because it seems that no one ought to think about these things, unless they judge their mind to be infinite. We however will not indeed affirm all those things, in which we can find no limit under any consideration, to be finite, but rather we will view them as indefinite. (AT VIII-1, 14–15; HR I, 229–230)

Considerations of piety seem to be evoked at the beginning of the next Principle:

And we shall call these things indefinite rather than infinite: first so that we may reserve the name of infinite for God alone . . . (AT VIII-1, 15; HR I, 230)

And in at least one other place—a later letter to Chanut—Descartes mentions the issue of Church censure in connection with the question of the infinity of the world. He seems to indicate that affirmation of the infinity of the world need not lead to objection, but that in any case his own position is even less problematic. Chanut had reported from Stockholm Queen Christina's concern that man's conception of his position in the world might be threatened by conceiving the world "in this vast extension" which Descartes calls indefinite (AT V, 22). Descartes does not reply directly to this interesting concern, but offers the following observation instead:

. . . I recall that the Cardinal of Cusa and several other Doctors have supposed the world to be infinite without ever being reproved by the Church on this account; on the contrary, one is thought to honor God by having his works conceived as very great. But my opinion is less difficult to accept than theirs; because I do not say that the world is *infinite*, but only *indefinite*. (6 June 1647: AT V, 51; PL, 221)

These passages show that Descartes saw his characterization of *res extensa* as indefinite, rather than infinite, as having strategic advantages. They may lead one to wonder whether the distinction really is introduced as a theoretically cogent one—or merely as a way of evading trouble. Several scholars have indeed suggested or assumed that the distinction, especially as it applies to *res extensa*, is in effect specious. In E. M. Curley's words: "Perhaps Descartes merely wishes to avoid offending the theologians; as he might, if he called any created thing infinite."[5] But whatever the advantages of the distinction from this point of view, Descartes also persistently represents it as conceptually grounded. It is the nature of this conceptual grounding that I now wish to examine. (I will return later to the issue of theoretical sincerity.)

III

Principles I, 27 is concerned specifically with "the difference between the indefinite and the infinite." Descartes writes:

And we shall call these things indefinite rather than infinite: first so that we may reserve the name of infinite for God alone, because in him alone in every respect [*omni ex parte*], not only do we recognize no limits, but also we understand positively that there are none; then too, because we do not in the same way positively understand other things in any respect [*aliqua ex parte*] to lack limits, but only negatively admit that their limits, if they have them, cannot be found by us. (AT VIII–1, 15; HR I, 230)

In this passage, I suggest, we find combined two distinct reasons for denying the designation "infinite" of "these things" and calling them "indefinite" instead. First, we "positively understand" that there are no limits in God, while with respect to other things we only "negatively admit" that we cannot discover their limits if they have them. That is surely the dominant point. But there is present, too, a more muted contrast between God's unlimitedness *in all respects*, and the fact that other things, if unlimited, are unlimited *only in some respect*. In my terminology these are the "epistemological" and the "metaphysical" criteria for the infinite/indefinite distinction.[6] I will now show that

Descartes sometimes uses each criterion in separation from the other, and critically discuss each in turn. I begin with the metaphysical criterion.

IV

A typical statement of the metaphysical criterion is found in a letter to Clerselier, written in 1649. Descartes explains:

> By infinite substance, I understand substance that has actually infinite and immense true and real perfections. This is not an accident superadded to the notion of substance, but the very essence of substance taken absolutely, and bounded by no defects; which defects, *ratio substantiae*, are accidents; but not infinity or infinitude. And it must be noted that I never use the word 'infinity' to signify only not having limit, which is negative and to which I have applied the word 'indefinite', but to signify a real thing, which is incomparably greater than all those which have some limit. (23 April 1649: AT V, 355–356; PL, 254; italics omitted)

A passage from a letter to Henry More, written about the same time, contains a somewhat similar statement:

> I say . . . that the world is indeterminate or indefinite, because I recognize no boundaries [*terminos*] in it; but I would not dare to call it infinite, because I perceive that God is greater than the world, not *ratione extensione*, which, as I have often said, I do not understand as a property in God, but *ratione perfectionis*. (15 April 1649: AT V, 344; PL, 250–251)

Descartes' point in the latter passage is that God is appropriately called infinite, and the world is not, because God exceeds the world in perfection. In the Clerselier letter Descartes similarly indicates that he uses 'infinity' to signify something "incomparably greater than all those which have some limit." The point is put still more sharply in Descartes' reply to the First Objections—a reply that clearly foreshadows some of the language of *Principles* I, 26–27:

> And here indeed I distinguish between 'indefinite' and 'infinite', and only call that properly 'infinite' in which in no respect are limits found [*in quo nulla ex parte limites inveniuntur*]: in which sense only God is infinite; those things, however, in which under some respect only [*sub aliqua tantum ratione*] I do not recognize a limit, as extension of imaginary space, the multitude of numbers, the divisibility of the parts of quantity, and the like, I indeed call 'indefinite', because they do not lack limit in all respects [*quia non omni ex parte fine carent*]. (AT VII, 113; HR II, 17)

Perhaps the main difficulty raised by the metaphysical criterion is the following: how are we to conceive the relation between that which lacks limit in all respects, and that which lacks (or may lack) limit in some respect only? For example, if *res extensa* is thought without limit in some respect, should it not follow that God is thought without limit in that respect among others? From such an interpretation of the metaphysical criterion it would seem a short step to the Spinozistic conception of *res extensa* as an infinite attribute of God—a view that Descartes explicitly rejects in the letter to More just quoted.

Descartes evidently thinks this result can be avoided on the traditional grounds that extension implies divisibility, an imperfection, and hence cannot be attributed to God.[7] Spinoza rejected this argument with the claim that Cartesian extension, which does not admit of vacuums, cannot be conceived as really divisible.[8] Whether or not this objection of Spinoza's is right, there does at least seem to be something incomplete or loose in Descartes' statement of the metaphysical criterion of the infinite/indefinite distinction. Perhaps a more precise formulation could readily be constructed, but I will not attempt to do so here.

The metaphysical criterion, at any rate, suggests one possible answer to my original question about whether Descartes would think that his finite mind is sufficient to cause his conceptions of the indefinite. The indefinite, we are told, differs from the infinite in being unlimited, at most, in some respect only. But according to Meditation IV Descartes (as mind) *is* unlimited in some respect: namely with respect to his will or power of willing.[9] One might conjecture that Descartes' possession of unlimitedness in one respect would be sufficient, in his theory, to account for the possibility of his originating ideas of indefinite things, though not of infinite things (according to the metaphysical account of this distinction). This suggestion, though, seems incompatible with Descartes' few remarks on the subject, as I will try to show later.

V

In *Principles* I, 26–27 Descartes observes that we positively know that God is limitless, but lack such positive knowledge with respect to *res extensa*, the number series, and so on. He clearly holds, however, that we are in some kind of epistemological relation to these latter things, which prevents us from construing them as finite. There is in the texts some haziness about just what this epistemological relation is. Sometimes the relation is stated weakly and nonmodally: we "notice no limits" in the things he calls indefinite. But more typically Descartes bases his characterization of something as indefinite (rather than finite) on conceptual considerations, which seem to yield (in his view) a conclusion about what is possible for us:

> Thus because we cannot imagine an extension so great, that we do not understand yet a greater to be possible, we should say that the magnitude of possible things is indefinite. And because it is not possible to divide any body into such parts, that we do not understand each of these parts still to be divisible, we will think that quantity is indefinitely divisible. And because it is not possible to conceive [*fingi*] such a number of stars, that we do not believe yet more could have been created by God, we will also suppose their number indefinite; and so of the rest. (*Principles* I, 26: AT VIII-1, 114–15; HR I, 230)

Sometimes, as we will see, Descartes even endorses the apparently stronger claim that we encounter some sort of conceptual repugnancy or contradiction in attempting to suppose that *res extensa* has limits. Although these vacillations in formulation are inconvenient to the commentator, I do not think that they reflect any significant fluctuation in Descartes' conception of the status of *res extensa* as indefinite. (I will develop this point in greater detail below.)

We have seen that Descartes' metaphysical account of the infinite/indefinite distinction, subordinated to the epistemological criterion in the *Principles*, is put at the forefront in certain other passages. The epistemological criterion is sometimes mentioned alone, however, particularly in several discussions of *res extensa*. Such passages tend to suggest that *only* our lack of positive knowledge, rather than some inherent limitation of perfection in comparison with God, precludes applying the term *infinite* to matter and so forth. The letter to Chanut cited above provides one example. Having noted the theological advantage of calling the world "indefinitely great" rather than "infinite," Descartes continues:

> There is a quite notable difference [between the two]: for in order to say that a thing is infinite, one must have some reason which makes it known as such [*la fasse connoistre telle*], which one can have concerning God alone; but to say that it is indefinite, it's enough not to have any reason by which one could prove that it has limits. Thus it seems to me that one cannot prove, nor even conceive, that there are limits in the matter of which the world is composed. (AT V, 51–52; PL, 221)

Descartes goes on to explain the latter point as follows. Where there is three-dimensional spatiality, there is, *ipso facto*, matter (according to Descartes' theory of matter). But if one tries to suppose that the world is finite, "one imagines outside its limits some spaces which have their three dimensions"; and will therefore themselves contain matter. Hence one cannot successfully imagine a limit to the world. Then,

Having therefore no reason by which to prove, and even not being able to conceive that the world has limits, I call it 'indefinite'. But for all that I can't deny that there may perhaps be some [reasons] which are known by God, although they are incomprehensible to me: that is why I do not say absolutely that the world is 'infinite'. (AT V, 52; PL, 221)

A very similar line is taken by Descartes in another letter to More (5 February 1649). More had criticized Descartes' use of the term *indefinite* with respect to *res extensa* on the grounds that the world is in itself either infinite or not. More seems to be saying that introducing a term like *indefinite*, tied to our way of conceiving the world, merely obscures the issue. He further seems not to take seriously the idea that Descartes is genuinely motivated by views about the inadequacy of our knowledge. Descartes replies:

It is not indeed from affected modesty, but, on my view, necessary caution, that I say that some things are indefinite rather than infinite. For it is only God whom I positively understand to be infinite; of the rest, such as the extension of the world, the number of parts into which matter is divisible, and similar things, I acknowledge that I do not know whether they are infinite simpliciter or not; I only know that I recognize no limit in them, and on that account with respect to me I say they are indefinite.

And although our mind is not the measure of things or of truth, it certainly should be the measure of those we affirm or deny. For what is more absurd, what more inconsidered, than to want to render judgement of those things to which we admit the perception of our mind cannot attain? (AT V, 274; PL, 242)

Descartes goes on to make again the point that matter must not be conceived as surrounded by empty space, since there can be no space without matter.

Principles I, 27, the letter to Chanut, and the letter to More, despite their differences in formulation, suggest a reasonably constant perspective on the infinite/indefinite distinction, in so far as it is to be construed epistemologically. We do not perceive that *res extensa*, for example, is limited; we have no reason to believe it is limited; indeed we cannot conceive it as limited (for to do so would require an unacceptable conceptual divorce of *res extensa* from space). Therefore, on one hand, it must not be considered finite. On the other hand, while we positively know God to be unlimited, we cannot have this positive knowledge in other cases.

To modern ears this dictum will sound particularly odd as it applies to number series and the like. In fact, some of Descartes' own remarks raise questions about the viability of the epistemological criterion: but, as it happens, these mainly concern *res extensa*. Thus, if the conceptual argument about matter and space that Descartes presents to both Chanut and More has any value in showing that we cannot conceive *res extensa* as limited, why doesn't it suffice as "reason" for affirming that *res extensa* is unlimited? Certain other passages from the More correspondence intensify the question. In the letter dated 15 April 1649, Descartes writes:

It is repugnant to my conception to attribute any boundary [*terminus*] to the world, and I have no other measure of those things which I should affirm or deny, than my own perception. I say therefore that the world is indeterminate or indefinite, because I recognize no boundaries in it . . . (AT V, 344; PL, 250–251)

It is repugnant to my conception, or, what is the same, I think it implies a contradiction, that the world is finite or bounded, because I cannot not conceive space beyond whatever limits are assumed of the world; but according to me such a space is a real body. (AT V, 345; PL, 251)

If my conception is the only measure of my affirmation, and if it is repugnant to my conception that *res extensa* is limited, then must I not affirm that *res extensa* is unlimited?

Such statements have been taken to support the view, mentioned above, that Descartes' infinite/indefinite distinction is insincere or specious (at least as it applies to the physical world). Alexandre Koyré has held that the last quoted passages are significantly more definitive than the earlier remarks to More on the subject, and show Descartes' true view slipping out. According to Koyré they commit Descartes to the positive view that the world has no limits, since "it would be contradictory to posit them."[10]

Although Descartes' language does become somewhat more forceful in the latter statements to More, I find quite doubtful Koyré's conclusion that Descartes has made a new admission. He still speaks, as he did earlier, of "not recognizing" limits to matter, of not being able to conceive a limit to matter without space (and hence without matter) beyond it. Descartes' view all along has been, I suggest, that there is *something inconceivable to us* in the idea that the world has limits, some conceptual barrier to positing limits to matter. Yet he seems to hold that this fact does *not* commit him to the view that the world lacks limits. I don't think that the mention of "repugnancy" does more than point up a problem of intelligibility that has been there all along: the problem, namely, of reconciling the claim that the limitation of matter is *inconceivable*, with the claim that we don't know matter to be limitless. Does Descartes really think this makes sense?

Recall that Descartes told Chanut that he refrained from calling the world infinite because God might know some reasons for regarding it as having limits, even though these reasons are inaccessible to Descartes. A similar remark is cited by Burman:

> As far as we are concerned, we are never able to discover any limit in these things [extension of the world, number, etc.], and so with respect to us they are indefinite. . . . But as far as God is concerned, maybe he conceives and understands certain limits in the world, number, quantity, and understands something greater than the world, number, and so on; and so for him these things may be finite. As for us, we see that the nature of these things is beyond our powers, and since we are finite, we cannot comprehend them, and so with respect to us they are indefinite or infinite. (AT V, 167; CB, 33–34)[11]

Descartes' position seems to be that our conceptual experiments don't allow us *simply to affirm* that such things are limitless, because what is inconceivable to us may still be true from God's point of view.

This alleged dichotomy between what is conceivable to us, and what may be the case for God, might suggest a tie-in between Descartes' position on the indefinite and another, more famous feature of his philosophy. For Descartes of course maintains in many places— the More correspondence among them—that our conception does not impose a limitation on God's power: he can do anything that we distinctly perceive as possible, but we can't say that he cannot do what appears to us contradictory.[12] Perhaps the conceptual repugnancy in supposing that *res extensa*, for example, is limited requires interpretation in a similar context. When we consider the limitations of our minds in relation to the limitlessness of God, we see that our sense of contradictoriness may be merely a function of the former.

The doctrine of God's superiority to our conceptual "repugnancies," however, as it is normally interpreted, implies only that God could have made, say, two plus two not equal four; it does not restrain us from rationally judging now that two plus two equals four. In fact, insofar as the latter judgment rests on clear and distinct perception, it is precisely Descartes' doctrine that our knowledge of God warrants it. So it seems that Descartes' caution about affirming the infinity of the world, or numbers, or the divisibility of matter cannot rest simply on his general views about God's power over the eternal truths.

It seems, therefore, that Descartes' refusal positively to affirm that such things are unlimited can be construed as theoretically honest only if we assume the following. Descartes must believe that the "repugnancy" or other conceptual difficulty we find in supposing them to be limited is epistemologically weaker than the repugnancy or "manifest contradiction" we encounter in trying to suppose that two plus two does not equal four. The conceptual difficulty cannot, in other words, amount to *a clear and distinct perception that matter is unlimited.*[13]

This suggestion would seem to derive emphatic support from the French version of *Principles* I, 27 (already cited in note 5, above). The relevant statement reads:

As to other things [than God] . . . , although we sometimes notice in them some properties which seem to us to have no limits, *we do not fail to know that that proceeds from the defect of our understanding, and not from their nature.* (AT IX–2, 27, italics in text)

I do not think, however, that we should regard as conclusive this reference to the "defect of our understanding" in connection with the seeming apprehension of limitlessness in things other than God. First, the passage presents the familiar problem of judging whether a deviation from the original in an "authorized" translation of Descartes is due to Descartes or the translator. Second, the French version seems inherently confused, since it indicates that the considerations just quoted are needed to show that things like *res extensa* "are not . . . absolutely perfect"—yet surely Descartes does not think that unlimitedness in some property is sufficient for absolute perfection. Finally, the passage deals with the apparent limitlessness of the indefinites only in the weakest terms ("which seem to us not to have limits"): that is, the issue raised elsewhere of "repugnancy in conception" isn't addressed.

I am thus not inclined to count the French version of the *Principles* as providing decisive textual support for the suggestion that Descartes denied the status of clear and distinct perception to the conceptual repugnancy he found in the supposition that, for example, *res extensa* has limits. Nor do I find other direct support for the suggestion. So, on balance, I can only propose that this *might* be the position that Descartes is trying to convey.

The main alternative reading—that, epistemologically interpreted, Descartes' infinite/indefinite distinction is merely a pragmatic ploy—is by no means incredible. But I do want to hold that this alternative reading is not as evidently correct as its proponents tend to indicate. Descartes' statements that the limits of matter are inconceivable—or even that it implies a contradiction to suppose that matter has limits—do not *necessarily* mean to him that (he knows that) matter is limitless.

For the statements *may* be dissociated in his thinking from an affirmation of clear and distinct perception. Certainly passages that have been taken specifically to imply knowledge of the limitlessness of matter (etc.) sometimes appear in close proximity to denials that we have such knowledge.

Now even the supposition that Descartes never means to hold that we have a clear and distinct perception of limitlessness in the things he calls indefinite will not solve all riddles about the epistemological criterion. There will remain the objection that it is not strictly true that this criterion grants "God alone" the title "infinite." For, as we've seen in passing, Descartes also thinks that the human will is *known* to be unlimited. Perhaps more important, there remain difficulties in grasping the grounds for a Cartesian claim that we do have positive knowledge of the unlimitedness of God, yet do not achieve clear and distinct perception of the limitlessness of (for example) matter. Descartes implies that our attempts at knowledge are thwarted in the case of the indefinites because such things *exceed our comprehension,* since we are finite. But this warrant for agnosticism is either incomplete or misleading. For Descartes holds that his idea of infinite God is clear and distinct to the highest degree.[14] In the next section I will examine this problem more closely.

VI

Descartes' use of the epistemological criterion requires that some things that we cannot conceive as limited are such that we do not positively know them to be unlimited. It further assumes that we do have positive knowledge of unlimitedness, at least in the case of God. But if, as finite beings, we are unqualified to judge that *res extensa* and so forth are unlimited, why are we not similarly disqualified from knowing such a fact about God?

Notice that the question I am raising here is not quite the same as the more familiar question of how Descartes reconciles his claim that we have a clear and distinct idea of God with his denial that we comprehend God.[15] What I am asking is rather: How is Descartes' claim that our finitude disqualifies us from asserting the limitlessness of things other than God (like the material world) to be reconciled with the claim that we have positive knowledge that God is infinite?

There are some passages in Descartes' writings that make this question seem very problematic indeed. For some of Descartes' statements seem to suggest that our epistemological relation to God and his attributes is after all closely similar to our epistemological relation to things called indefinite. In the Third Objections, for example, Hobbes observes:

. . . to say that God is *infinite* is the same as if we say that He is among those objects the limits of which we do not conceive. (AT VII, 187; HR II, 72)

It is difficult to see how Descartes can accept such a negative characterization of our epistemological relation to God's "limitlessness," without undermining his distinction between our knowledge of God and matter in this respect. And yet his reply to Hobbes seems more to endorse than to reject the characterization:

Who is there who does not perceive that he understands something? And hence who does not have this form or idea of understanding, which being indefinitely extended, forms the idea of the divine understanding, and so of the rest of his attributes? (AT VII, 188; HR II, 73)[16]

A remark to Regius similarly suggests that our idea of God is formed by indefinite extrapolation from the finite, while also touching on a comparison of God and quantity in this respect:

In your first [objection] you say: from the fact that there is in us a certain wisdom, power, goodness, quantity etc., that we form the idea of an infinite or at least indefinite wisdom, power, goodness, and the other perfections which we attribute to God, as also the idea of infinite quantity; all of which I freely concede, and am fully convinced that there is in us no idea of God except one that is formed in this manner. (24 May 1640: AT III, 64; PL, 73, italics omitted)

Descartes goes on to say:

But the whole point of my argument [sc. for the existence of God, Meditation III] is that I contend I cannot be of such a nature that I can by thought extend these perfections, which are minute in me to infinity, unless we have our origin in an Entity in which they are actually infinite. (Ibid.)

(Although Descartes admittedly does speak here of extending something finite *in infinitum*, it's not clear he means this in a strict sense distinct from indefinite extension.)

This is, however, by no means the only, or usual, picture that Descartes presents of our epistemological relation to God's limitlessness. Certain passages suggest that while our *idea* or *conception* of God's limitlessness is formed in the way just indicated, we still have some *additional*, positive knowledge that God is unlimited. Other texts—

including, notably, Meditation III—insist straightforwardly that our idea of God is wholly prior to our ideas of finite things.

The "additional knowledge" picture is found in such passages as these:

We do not conceive, but understand the perfections and attributes of God: or, rather, that we may conceive them, we conceive them as indefinite [*concipimus illa tanquam indefinita*]. (AT V, 154; CB, 14–15)[17]

Besides I distinguish between *rationem formalem* of the infinite or of infinity, and the thing which is infinite; for as to infinity, even if we understand it to be something maximally positive, we do not nevertheless understand it except in some negative way, that is from the fact that we notice no limit in the thing. (First Replies: AT VII, 113; HR II, 17)

These passages indicate that the negative, or indefinite, conception is not the whole story about our knowledge of the infinite. Of course they leave unexplained how the idea derived by extrapolation from the finite happens to be transcended by positive knowledge in the *one* case of God (or, perhaps, in the *two* cases of God and the will).

Sometimes, though, Descartes straightforwardly maintains that the idea of the infinite, and hence of God, must be in me prior to the ideas of myself and other finite things. According to Meditation III:

And I should not think that I do not perceive the infinite by a true idea, but only by negation of the finite, as I perceive rest and shade by negation of motion and light; for on the contrary I manifestly understand that there is more reality in an infinite substance than in a finite one, and hence in some way the perception of the infinite is prior in me to the perception of the finite, that is that of God to that of myself. (AT VII, 45; HR I, 166. Cf. letter to Clerselier, 23 April 1649: AT V, 355–356; PL, 254; also Fifth Reply: AT VII, 365; HR II, 216; also letter to Hyperaspistes, August 1641: AT III, 426–427; PL, 114)

This passage seems to contradict the concession to Regius that we "have no idea of God except" one formed by some kind of extrapolation from the finite. An even more straightforward contradiction of the statement to Regius is found in a remark that Descartes makes to Gassendi:

Whence can be the faculty of amplifying all created perfections, i.e. of conceiving something greater or more ample than they, except from the fact that the idea of something greater, or God is in us? (AT VII, 365; HR II, 216)

According to this passage the idea of God must be in us prior to that power of amplifying which, in the Regius letter, is presented as the only source of the idea of God!

It does seem, in any case, that Descartes' application of his epistemological account of the infinite/indefinite distinction requires him to hold that we have knowledge of God's infinity independently of our power of amplifying (which can yield only "negative" knowledge). Further, consistently with his use of this criterion he must hold that such positive knowledge of God's infinity cannot yield positive knowledge of the limitlessness of the extension of the world, the number series, and so forth. In fact, if "God alone," or God plus the human will, are the only things admitted as "infinite" by the epistemological criterion, we can have no source of positive knowledge of infinity in any other case. But why should this be so? Is it merely a brute fact about what clear and distinct ideas we happen to possess?

Another, perhaps more satisfying explanation might be found in the suggestion that only God is *unlimited by nature*. (See AT IX–2, 37, and the end of note 5, above.) We have clear and distinct ideas both of God's essence and of, for example, the essence of matter. God's essence, but not the essence of matter, includes or entails unlimitedness. Hence a clear and distinct perception of unlimitedness is available to us in the former case. In the case of matter (and the indefinites generally) a final determination about unlimitedness is denied us by the *combined* factors that there is no essential unlimitedness, and that our limited minds cannot take in all features of the immense entity. Again, when Descartes says there is a repugnancy in conceiving *res extensa* as limited, he would not be claiming to have grasped an essential truth about it.

Of course this suggestion merely serves to draw out the story a little. It indicates that there is more to our ignorance about the ultimate limitlessness of matter than a mere contingent fact about what sort of innate ideas we happen to possess. But, it seems, the weight of "brute fact" is merely shifted to the claim that God alone possesses unlimitedness essentially. A Spinozist who claimed that it's an essential truth that the attributes (such as extension) are unlimited (and a truth that is distinctly perceived) would still find no rationally compelling response in Descartes' position.

I conclude by returning to the question with which I began: namely, would Descartes consider a finite mind sufficient to originate conceptions of the indefinites?

VII

We have seen that in the Third Meditation Descartes includes in his survey of ideas only the ideas of finite things, and the idea of God.

He simply does not mention the ideas of things he calls indefinite, *res extensa* in particular. Gassendi, however, partially made the connection, in effect asking Descartes whether reasoning analogous to his causal argument for the existence of God could not be deployed to infer from certain philosophers' ideas of an infinite world, or an infinity of worlds, the claim that such a world, or worlds, exist (AT VII; 295, 299; HR II, 165, 168). Descartes says in reply that only the idea of God permits us to infer the *existence of that of which it is the idea* (AT VII, 369; HR II, 219). There is sound logic behind this answer: According to Descartes' principles, we only know of the causes of our ideas that they have at *least as much* reality as is contained in the idea. The idea of a being of infinite reality and perfection must have as its cause a being of infinite reality and perfection; but then the reality contained in any other idea, however great or small, could have this *same* being as its cause. Still, the question stands: Is the idea or conception of, for example, *res extensa*, as opposed to the ideas of particular bodies and their modes, sufficient from Descartes' point of view to prove the existence of *something* outside of, and greater than, himself? If so, contrary to the suggestion of Meditation III, the idea of God would not provide a *unique* bridge to external reality.

Two passages bearing on this question have already been quoted. Descartes told Regius that the perfections of wisdom, power, and goodness are so minute in him that he wouldn't be able to extend them to infinity "unless we have our origin in an Entity in which they are actually infinite." He adds the further comment (which I did not quote):

. . . and neither could I conceive an indefinite quantity by inspection of a very small quantity, or finite body, unless the magnitude of the world also was or at least could be indefinite. (24 May 1640: AT III, 64; PL, 73)

This last comment, of course, would take some reconciling with the point just made that God is sufficient to cause any idea. But this much seems clear: Descartes is saying that his finite nature is not sufficient to generate (even) indefinite conceptions. We also noted that Descartes tells Gassendi that the power of amplifying created perfections requires the existence in us of the idea of something greater. Finally, consider this statement from the Second Replies:

. . . I contend that from the fact alone that I attain in whatever way by thought or understanding any perfection which is above me, for example from the fact alone that I notice that in the course of numeration I can not arrive at the greatest of all numbers, and hence I recognize that there is

something in *ratione numerandi* which exceeds my powers, I conclude necessarily, not indeed that an infinite number exists, . . . but that this power of
conceiving that a greater number is thinkable than could ever be thought by
me, is received in me not from myself but from some other entity more perfect
than I. (AT VII, 139; HR II, 37; cf. AT V, 157; CB, 18; letter to Hyperaspistes,
August 1641: AT III, 427–428; PL, 114)

Textually speaking the answer seems clear: Descartes *does* think his
power of generating conceptions of the indefinite cannot be accounted
for by his own nature, but requires the existence of something outside
himself. The fact that he ascribes to himself an unlimited power of
willing doesn't seem to affect this judgment. Even though the number
series, for instance, differs from God in not being "unlimited in all
respects" (according to the metaphysical criterion), Descartes holds
that his power of numbering still requires an external cause. Similarly
the presumptive lack of a clear and distinct perception that the number
series, for instance, is unlimited does not seem to affect the judgment
that our conception of it requires an external cause. Thus Descartes
seems to hold that merely negative knowledge that something is such
that we cannot find its limits (if it has them) is sufficient to generate
a causal argument for *some* external existent. In this respect, then, the
idea of the infinite and conceptions of the indefinite—however otherwise distinguished by Descartes—have a similar significance in his
thought.[18]

NOTES

Abbreviations AT and HR are explained in the General Bibliography at the
beginning of this volume; in addition, I use CB for *Descartes' Conversation with
Burman*, ed. John Cottingham (Oxford: Clarendon Press, 1976), and PL for
Descartes: Philosophical Letters, trans. and ed. Anthony Kenny (Oxford: Clarendon Press, 1970).

1. See also *Discourse on the Method*, Part IV (AT VI, 33–35; HR I, 102–103).
In the *Discourse* Descartes, noting his own imperfection as a doubter, reports
raising the question where he had "learned to think of something more
perfect" than himself: " . . . and I knew evidently that this must be of such
a nature that was in effect more perfect." Here, too, only the idea of God is
recognized as that of something more perfect. In the next paragraph, however
(which concludes with an affirmation that existence is included in God's
essence), Descartes does mention "the object of the Geometers, which I conceive as a continuous body, or a space indefinitely extended in length, width
and height . . . " (AT VI, 36; HR I, 103).

In the *Meditations*, Descartes speaks repeatedly of "corporeal nature in general and its extension," "that quantity which philosophers commonly call continuous," "this corporeal nature which is the object of pure mathematics," etc., but the issue of limits or indefiniteness isn't touched on (AT VII, 20, 63, 74; HR I, 146, 179, 187).

Descartes seems to acknowledge that the idea of an angel involves more perfection than he possesses, and is itself dependent on the idea of God: AT VII, 43, 124, 138–139; HR I, 164; II, 26, 37.

2. Contrary to an odd comment in the *Conversation with Burman*, the distinction between infinite and indefinite was hardly "invented" by Descartes (AT V, 167; CB, 33). See Alexandre Koyré, *From the Closed World to the Infinite Universe* (New York: Harper, 1958), chap. 1, for discussion of a pre-Cartesian version of the distinction in Nicholas of Cusa.

3. It is sometimes said that Descartes held that the speed of light is "infinite": see, for example, Spyros Sakellariadis, "Descartes' Experimental Proof of the Infinite Velocity of Light and Huygen's Rejoinder," in *Archive for History of Exact Sciences* 26 (1982):1–12; also Gerd Buchdahl, *Metaphysics and the Philosophy of Science* (Cambridge: MIT Press, 1969), 99. And of course Descartes does speak of light as extending its rays "in an instant"—which might well *seem* to come to the same thing. (See for instance *La Dioptrique* I [AT VI, 84]; letter to Beeckman, 22 August 1634 [AT I, 307]). However I haven't so far found a case where Descartes actually uses the term *infinite* in connection with the propagation of light. Certainly Sakellariadis doesn't quote any. Buchdahl puts *infinite speed* in quotation marks, but without a supporting reference.

4. I cite relevant passages from most of these works below. See also AT XI, 32–33 (*Le Monde*); AT VIII–1, . . . (*Principles* II, 34–35). Toward the end of Meditation III Descartes speaks of himself as "a thing incomplete and dependent on another, and a thing aspiring to greater and greater or better," and of God as having in Himself "all these greater [things] not only indefinitely and potentially, but *reipsa infinite.*" (Cf. AT V, 154; CB, 14–15.)

5. E. M. Curley, *Descartes Against the Skeptics* (Cambridge: Harvard University Press, 1978), 223. Curley also mentions "paradoxes involved in the notion of infinity which might well have given Descartes a philosophical reason for avoiding use of the term outside of the theological contexts." Descartes also refers to the "paradoxes" somewhat more provocatively in an early letter to Mersenne (15 April 1630: AT I, 146–147; PL, 12).

See also Koyré, *From the Closed World*, chap. 5; and CB, 101–102.

6. Cf. Jean Laporte, *Le rationalisme de Descartes* (Presses Universitaires de France, 1945), 260–261. Laporte recognizes the appearance of two foundations of the distinction in Descartes, but considers it clear that the two "come to the same": " . . . for what positive reason can one have to think that a being has no limits, except that this being possesses in itself a perfection, a superabundance, a power of existing that repels all limitation—and which only belongs to the *Ens amplissimum?*" I think there is something to what Laporte says here: as I will suggest later, the epistemological criterion ultimately seems to require some sort of metaphysical backing. But Laporte goes

too far in saying the two foundations "come to the same." For one thing, his rhetorical question is far from unanswerable (see, e.g., note 9, below). For another, the two criteria have the potentiality for yielding different results (insofar as Descartes sometimes indicates that he would be entitled to call *res extensa* infinite if he could know that it really is of unlimited size). Incidentally, the letter to Clerselier that Laporte cites (p. 261, n. 2) doesn't really support his point, since it says nothing at all about "positive reason" for believing that something lacks limits.

As Roger Ariew has pointed out to me, the French translation of *Principles* I, 27 differs from the original Latin in clearly indicating that the appearance of unlimitedness, even in single properties, of things other than God "proceeds from the defect in our understanding, and not from their nature" (AT IX–2, 37). I suppose this declaration could be read as implying that *res extensa*, the number of stars, etc., are *not* unlimited in *any* respect, thereby rendering the metaphysical criterion nugatory. However, this implication would not hold if it could be true that something is unlimited even though unlimitedness doesn't follow from its nature. Certainly there are numerous passages besides the Latin version of I, 27 which seem to leave open the *possibility* that things other than God are in some respect unlimited.

7. *Principles* I, 23 (AT VIII–1, 13; HR I, 228); cf. Étienne Gilson, *Index Scolastico-Cartésien* (Vrin, 1979; 2d ed.), 80, 82.

8. *Ethics* I, xv, Scholium. Alan Donagan has argued that Spinoza's argument is question-begging. See "Spinoza and Descartes on Extension," *Midwest Studies in Philosophy* I, ed. Peter A. French et al. (Morris, MN: University of Minnesota Press, 1976), 31–33.

9. Descartes says he experiences his will or freedom of choice "as circumscribed by no limits": *sane nullis illam limitibus circumscribi experior* (AT VII, 56; HR I, 174). (Further, "it is the will alone, or freedom of choice, that I so experience in myself, that I apprehend the idea of none greater" [whereas he does have the ideas of greater powers of understanding and memory than his own]: AT VII, 57; HR I, 175.) It is principally the will by virtue of which he understands that he bears "a certain image and likeness of God" (ibid.).

Principles I, 35 goes further: "In fact the will can in a certain manner be called infinite [*Voluntas vero infinita quodammodo dici potest*]" (because we never notice anything that can be an object of any other will to which our will can't extend, too): AT VIII–1, 18; HR I, 233.

If *experior* signifies positive knowledge, something besides God evidently does satisfy the epistemological criterion of infinity.

10. Koyré, *From the Closed World*, 124. See also Cottingham's commentary, CB, 102. Cottingham thinks that Descartes' argument to Chanut, in particular, is intended "to demonstrate the logical impossibility of a finite universe."

11. I have omitted here a remark to the effect that we may perhaps say that the world, number, etc., are infinite, because repeated multiplication of the indefinite is the same as infinity. (For a very similar remark, see AT V, 154; CB, 14–15.) Cottingham interprets this talk of "multiplying the indefinite" in terms of the example of being able to conceive of space, and hence body,

beyond any boundary we try to assign to the world. Therefore he takes the Burman passage, too, as acknowledging the "logical impossibility" of a bounded universe. (See note 10, above.) What Cottingham does *not* note is that in this very passage Descartes distinguishes between what we can conceive on this subject, and what may be true from God's point of view. In my opinion, Cottingham (like Koyré) is over-hasty in assuming that Descartes' thought-experiments amount for him to a clear and distinct perception of logical impossibility.

12. For discussion of this doctrine, and references, see my *Descartes* (Routledge & Kegan Paul, 1978), 120 ff.

13. This seems to be Laporte's conclusion, too: cf. *Le Rationalisme*, 263. (Laporte refers to a letter to More [5 February 1649] on the indefinite divisibility of matter; Descartes claims that even though he can't number the parts of matter, he can't say that God couldn't complete the division [AT V, 273–274; PL, 241–242].)

14. See, for instance, Meditation III)AT VII, 46; HR I, 166).

15. This issue is already discussed at some length in the *Objections and Replies*: cf. e.g., AT VII, 112–114; HR II, 17–18.

16. See also AT VII, 137; HR II, 36: "I grant . . . that the idea we have, e.g., of the divine understanding, does not differ from that which we have of our understanding, except only as the idea of an infinite number differs from idea of a number of the fourth or second power . . . "

17. Cf. Cottingham's commentary (CB, 76) and, especially Jean-Marie Beyssade, "Création des vérités éternelles et doute métaphysique," *Studia Cartesiana* 2 (1981): 86–105. Beyssade shows that Descartes normally distinguishes "conceiving" and "understanding": *"on conçoit l'indefini, on entend l'infini"* (p. 91). Correspondingly, Descartes speaks of *concepts* of the indefinite, *ideas* of the infinite (although he does not always insist on this distinction: cf. AT VII, 139 11, lines 23–24; HR II, 38). We can form indefinite conceptions of certain of God's perfections (e.g., understanding) by extrapolation by the limited instances of these perfections in us. Of some other divine perfections (e.g., absolute unity) we have no representational conceptions (since we are acquainted with no instances), but only pure ideas. See also Beyssade, "RSP ou Le Monogramme de Descartes" in his edition of *L'entretien avec Burman* (Presses Universitaires de France, 1981), 171–181.

Perhaps when Descartes told Regius that we "have no idea of God" except from amplification of the finite, he meant *conception* of God. This emendation would greatly help to reconcile the letter to Regius with this and other texts.

18. I wish to thank Desmond Clarke, Daniel Garber, Amélie Rorty and, especially, Roger Ariew for comments that have resulted in revisions of this paper. The research for this paper was supported by a grant from the American Council of Learned Societies under a program funded by the National Endowment for the Humanities.

15

The Idea of the True God in Descartes

Annette Baier

Hence I have undertaken the further enquiry—*whether I could exist if God did not exist*—not for the purpose of adducing a proof distinct from the preceding one, but rather in order to give a more thorough-going explanation of it.[1]

The Third Meditation often seems to embarrass even the warmest of Descartes'·English-speaking admirers. Those who delight in exposing the errors of the great leap in willingly enough, to show the invalidity they perceive in his main arguments, but even sympathetic readers of the *Meditations* often seem to be defeated by the moves in the Third Meditation. Such defeat should not be taken lightly, given the form and title of Descartes' masterpiece. To be unable to give a sympathetic reading of the heart of that work, the point where the meditator finds his most proper object of meditation and contemplation, is tantamount to total failure. I shall give a version of the Third Meditation which I think makes its moves easier to endorse, but which also finds the subject matter of the meditation to be not quite what it is usually taken to be. I shall do some reinterpreting of what is meant by "God," and what is meant by "idea of God in me." As a result I get an explanation of the two stages of the argument, of the transition between them (AT VII, 47–48; HR I, 167), of the gradual shift in emphasis as to which divine perfections are the "principal" perfections, and an explanation of why the prolonged contemplation of "the true God," that "greatest satisfaction of which we are capable in this life" (AT VII, 52; HR I, 171) has to be delayed until after the second round of the argument is completed. I shall also have an explanation of why so few words need then to be spent on what, on the face of it, was the main question to be tackled, namely whether the God who can do anything might be using that power to deceive the meditator.

I. A DECEITFUL GOD?

The idea of an all-powerful God was introduced in the First Meditation, but there inspired no ecstatic contemplation. On the contrary, fear and doubt were the responses to the idea of a powerful God, creator, for inscrutable divine ends, of one's cognitive faculties. At the beginning of the Third Meditation this fear that a powerful creator may block one's access to truth has been lessened by the discovery, in the Second Meditation, of an indubitable idea, that of oneself as thinker, which not even a powerful God could make false, since "he can never cause me to be nothing as long as I think that I am something" (AT VII, 25; HR I, 150). But although the fear that *no* idea can ever be known as a true idea is thereby banished, there still remains great instability. The very idea of "the sovereign power of a God" (AT VII, 36; HR I, 158) brings with it the constrained admission that "it is easy for Him, if He wishes it, to cause me to err, even in matters in which I believe myself to have the best evidence" (ibid.). Is my own existence as a thinker one of these matters on which I believe myself to have the best evidence, but where divine power could deceive me? Yes and no. The idea of divine omnipotence implies that I *could* be deceived, no matter what the apparent self-evidence of the idea. Yet "on the other hand, always when I direct my attention to things which I believe myself to perceive very clearly, I am so persuaded of their truth that I let myself break out into words such as these: Let who will deceive me, He can never cause me to be nothing while I think that I am, or someday cause it to be true to say that I never have been, it being true to say now that I am, or that two and three make more or less than five, or any such thing in which I perceive a manifest contradiction" (AT VII, 36; HR I, 158–159). The inclusion of my own existence as a thinker, along with other self-evident ideas, shows that the power of God in principle *could* make that false, although I cannot *believe* this when I attend to the idea itself. So I may vacillate between "Yes, God can do *anything*," when I attend to the idea of God, and "No, God cannot make *this* false," when I attend to the idea of myself as a thinker.

One hypothetical solution to this instability of even the most evident ideas, their degeneration into "vacillating opinions" (AT VII, 69; HR I, 184), would be to avoid giving attention to that destabilizing idea of an omnipotent God, and to keep attention on the self-evident ideas. At the end of the Second Meditation, the meditator had shown that, whatever material thing he considered, that idea could make evident to him the certainty of his own existence as a thinker, so that this first truth need never be obscured, this Archimedean point need never be deserted, even temporarily. One need merely frame any thought about bodies, or numbers, with "I think that . . . ," and one's attention could then remain sufficiently directed upon that indubitable truth for its certainty never to leave one. Never, that is, unless what completes the "I think that . . . " is the idea of the existence of the "sovereign God of preconceived opinion." Then there is worse than vacillation, there is internal conflict between the certainty-engendering "I think" and the uncertainty-engendering "that there is a God who can do anything." And just as the reassuring certainty, "I think," can accompany the other ideas that are framed by "I think . . . ," so the uncertainty induced by the idea of God can contaminate other ideas, since each idea now comes with a disturbing closing frame, in the form " . . . , God willing." The hypothetical solution, namely inhibiting the idea of God, is no usable solution once every idea includes the idea of God.

So the task the meditator finds before him, after the first four paragraphs of the Third Meditation, is one in which "I must inquire whether there is a God as soon as the occasion presents itself; and if I find that there is a God, I must also inquire whether He may be a deceiver; for without a knowledge of these two truths I do not see that I can ever be certain of anything" (AT VII, 36; HR I, 159). This leads us to expect that there will indeed be two stages to the argument that follows, one settling the first question of whether there is a God, the other settling the second question of whether God may be a deceiver. But in fact what follows does not fall into those two parts, but into what may seem two arguments answering the first question, concerning God's existence, followed by a perfunctory few lines answering the second question, and announcing that it is now evident that "He cannot be a deceiver, since the light of nature teaches us that fraud and deception necessarily proceed from some defect (AT VII, 52; HR I, 171). This surprisingly brief "inquiry" into whether or not God could be a deceiver is slightly expanded in the recapitulation given in the Fourth Meditation, when we are told that "although it may appear that the power to deceive is a mark of subtlety or power [*acuminis aut potentiae*], yet the desire to deceive without doubt testifies to malice or feebleness [*malitiam vel imbecillitatem*]" (AT VII, 53; HR I, 172). What we will need to see is why the natural light could not have illuminated this truth earlier, and so cut short the worry about a deceiving God the moment that worry had arisen, namely in the First Meditation; or, if not then, at least at the beginning of the Third Meditation. Presumably something that occurred in the course of the Third Meditation sheds this "natural light," which had to remain obscured until then.

II. THE NATURAL LIGHT AND ITS SOURCES

The natural light makes its first appearance, heralded only by the preceding metaphor of "clarity," in the ninth paragraph of the Third Meditation, when the meditator distinguishes the "lessons of nature," things he is naturally inclined to believe, from things recognized by the natural light to be indubitable. "For I cannot doubt that which the natural light causes me to believe to be true, as, for example, it has shown me that I am from the fact that I doubt, or other facts of the same kind" (AT VII, 38; HR I, 160). He goes on to say that we have no other faculty that could correct this natural light, nor even compete with it for trustworthiness. What faculty had apparently challenged the certainty of clear and distinct ideas in the fourth paragraph of the Third Meditation? Whatever it was that discerned the implications of "this preconceived opinion of the sovereign power of a God," and "constrained" the meditator to confess that such a God could cause him to err even where he had the best evidence, that is, presumably, to err even where the natural light seemed to be at work. What was that faculty? It might seem to be the very same perceiver of deductive connections and detector of manifest contradictions which counts as the natural light itself. But here we should recall that the "manifest contradiction" in trying to deny "I exist as a thinker" was *not* a formal contradiction, nor was "*sum res cogitans*" the conclusion of a deductive argument. The natural light that illuminates the truth "I am a thinker" is not quite the same as whatever faculty detects a formal contradiction in the attempt to claim "God is omnipotent, but there is one thing He cannot do."

So far, then, all we know of the natural light is that it gave the meditator his first truth, "I am a thinker." The next truth it is claimed to give him is one which it seems to have withheld from most of Descartes' readers, namely, "There must be at least as much reality in the efficient and total cause as in its effect" (AT VII, 30; HR I, 162), where the effect in question is an idea, and that effect's reality is both objective and formal. In his reply to the Second Objections, Descartes speaks of "those whose natural light is so exceedingly small that they do not see this first principle, viz. *that every perfection existing objectively in an idea must exist actually in that which causes the idea*" (AT VII, 136; HR II, 35). This is a "first principle," which suggests that it has some close connection with the meditator's "first knowledge," and it is that connection I now want to discuss.

"I am certain that I am a thing that thinks; but do I not then likewise know what is requisite to render me certain of a truth. Certainly in this first knowledge there is nothing that assures me of its truth excepting the clear and distinct perception of that which I state . . . " (AT VII, 35; HR I, 158). Here, at the beginning of the Third Meditation, the meditator wants to extend his knowledge, to let his first knowledge shed light on other truths. What exactly was it that made that first truth clear and distinct, which enabled it to escape the seemingly all-encompassing doubt the meditator had induced in himself by the end of the First Meditation? What he says in the third paragraph of the Second Meditation is this: "But how can I know there is not something different from those things which I have just considered, of which I cannot have the slightest doubt? Is there not some God, or some other being by whatever name we call it, who puts these reflections in my mind? That is not necessary, *for is it not possible that I am capable of producing them?*" (AT VII, 24; HR I, 150, my emphasis). He then produces the first thought that must be a true thought: "I am, I exist, is necessarily true each time that I pronounce it or that I mentally conceive it." The self-evidence of this truth is quite explicitly linked with its being self-generated, with its independence from any external cause. It is because the meditator sees that the idea "I think" is produced by his own current act of thinking, sees that it needs no external cause, God or evil genius, that it is immune to doubt. Like a source of light, it illuminates itself. It is its self-evident causal origin that validates it as an effect which displays, in its object, a reality truly in its cause. Although the concepts of objective and formal reality, and the causal principle that uses them, are not formulated until the Third Meditation, causal locutions concerning ideas are used here in the Second. The first talisman clear and distinct idea is one whose objective reality is the effect of its own formal reality. The validating cause contains all the reality of the validated effect. Here, I suggest, is the *ground* for the causal principle itself. It is a generalization of the causal dependence of the meditator's indubitably true idea "I think" on the thinking that was sustaining cause and also validator of that idea. The only application of the causal principle which the meditator *has*, to illuminate its own generalization, is a case where the effect known to derive all its reality from its (in this case) self-evident cause is an idea, and where the reality in question is objective reality. *If the causal principle did not apply to objective reality, then it could not be known to the meditator ever to hold good.* What illuminates it, in its general form, is the very special cause-effect pair that gave the meditator his first knowledge.

This version of what lights up the causal principle, namely, its own paradigm case, the self-illuminating cause of the thought "I am a thinker," is confirmed by Descartes' explication of the concepts of objective and formal reality at the end of his reply to the second set of Objections. He defines objective reality first; then formal reality in relation to that. "To exist formally is the term applied when the same thing exists in the object of an idea in such a manner that the way it exists in the object is exactly like what we know of it when aware of it" (HR II, 53). This restricts formal existence to verifiers of ideas, and fits the case of self-awareness particularly aptly. The same thing, thought, exists in the object of the idea "I think," in such a manner that it is exactly like what we know of that thinking, through being aware of thinking "I think." In the Third Meditation as well, we get the concept of objective reality, and degrees of that, introduced first in the thirteenth paragraph, while only in the following paragraph is formal reality introduced, and introduced as what will be found in any verifying cause of ideas with a given objective reality. Margaret Wilson says that formal reality for Descartes is "reality *simplicitur*,"[2] but I suggest that reality for Descartes is never really simple and that formal reality is a *more* complex notion for him than is objective reality. Objective reality is the reality we start with, and remain with until any suspicion arises, any suggestion of "material falsity." After introducing the concept of material falsity in connection with ideas of sense "which exhibit so little reality to me" (AT VII, 44; HR I, 165), the meditator says, of his idea of God, "as this idea is very clear and distinct and contains within it more objective reality than any other, there can be none which is of itself more true, nor any in which there can be less suspicion of falsehood" (AT VII, 46; HR I, 166). Once there is any suspicion of falsehood, then we must look for a verifier, so formal reality becomes relevant. We need refer to it only when there is a question of verification, that is, a need for a response to a challenge about truth. Like a "fact," formal reality is always relational to what it confirms, to objective reality. "For just as this mode of objective reality pertains to ideas by their very nature, so does the mode of formal existence pertain to the causes of those ideas" (AT VII, 42; HR I, 163). If the causes of ideas are their verifiers (or their falsifiers), then formal existence pertains to such verifiers by their very nature, and I am suggesting that the very nature of formal reality is to play such a verificatory role.

What I have claimed about the causal principle, and about the distinction between objective and formal reality which it involves, is that the meditator trusts these ideas only because they are derivable from, exemplified in, his first certainty, "I exist as a thinker." I would extend this claim to cover those other concepts used in an apparently uncritical way in the course of the Third Meditation—the concepts of substance and mode. It is only in as far as the meditator already sees that he himself as a thinking thing includes each of his own doubtings and wishings and affirmings that he knows the distinction between relatively independent inclusive substance and dependent included modes. He generalizes from the contrast between "I doubt" and "I exist as a thinker," to get the distinction between modes and substances, and sees the greater or more inclusive reality of the latter.

If we read the Third Meditation this way, we avoid having to attribute to the meditator the use of wholly dogmatic, unexamined principles. If everything he uses is exemplified in his first self-certainty, then its clear light can be a quite legitimate natural light for him to rely on. He uses the only light he has, and, if he does diffuse its beam by risky generalization, at least that seems a procedure more in keeping with his initial aim of giving no uncritical assent than would be a reliance on old inherited dogmas. He really is trying to rely on nothing but his already found certainty to produce further certainties.

III. IDEAS AND THE FORMAL REALITY OF THE IDEA OF GOD

Having tried to explain why Descartes felt warranted in using the causal principle in the form he uses it, and so explaining how he quite correctly could accuse readers who objected to that of having a natural light which was exceedingly small, I now move to consider the idea of the idea of God, that effect whose objective and formal reality is the evidence for the existence of "the true God in whom all the treasures of science and wisdom are contained" (AT VII, 53; HR I, 172). My suggestion here is that this idea is special among ideas not merely in its objective reality, but also in its formal reality. In brief, I suggest that it is the meditator himself, insofar as he is a self-conscious thinker. This suggestion may meet with some outraged resistance from readers of Descartes who are certain that they know what he means by "idea of God," even if they are uncertain about why he thinks he can derive what he does from the existence of that idea. So I must, like Descartes, try to break down this resistance, to produce that overthrow of preconceived opinions which is the darkness that must precede the coming of light. Before considering the textual evidence for my interpretation, however, let me hold out a suitable lure, so that this dark night of the interpretative soul may seem worth risking. If the idea of God is, as I claim, the self-conscious thinker himself, then the Third Meditation has a firmer structure than it otherwise could be seen to have, since then both arguments, namely, that up until AT VII, 47–48; HR I, 167 and that coming after that break, after that realization that the object of contemplation was not yet attained, will be inferences to the only adequate explanation of the same *explanandum*—the meditator's idea of God, which is himself, qua self-conscious thinker. The inadequacy of the first round of explanation will also be easily explained, since in the first round the idea of God is not explicitly presented as the exceptional idea it is, in its formal as well as objective reality. The extra considerations brought in, during the final and more satisfactory argument, namely, those concerning actual, nonregressive infinities, and concerning unity in complexity, will also be seen to be well-timed additions, since, when the effect is seen as something *self-referential*, we then need to worry about infinite regresses, and need to find some especially tight unity-in-complexity in the cause of such an effect. At this stage these remarks of mine can serve as no more than hints, to tantalize and arouse the interest of those whose preconceived version of the structure of the Third I wish to help them overthrow, so that we can rebuild anew from the foundation, and rebuild the firmer structure which, I think, Descartes built with typical subtlety.

It may also help to prepare the way for acceptance of my wider reading of "idea" to remind the reader that, even on more usual interpretations, Descartes' use of that term departed from the traditional use, and inaugurated the "new way of ideas." My interpretation makes it an even greater departure from established usage. But we inheritors and transformers of the Cartesian way of ideas have now learned from Hegel, Heidegger, Wittgenstein, and Sellars that the vehicles of thought need not be inner episodes in the mental history of private thinkers, but can be out there in the public world. To see Descartes as using the term *idea* as widely as I am suggesting is simply to see him as the father of more of modern philosophy than he is usually held responsible for, and to see him as a father figure we need not overthrow to make room for ourselves.[3]

Now to the texts. Ideas, we are told in the Third, are, in the stricter sense, as if images of things (*tanquam rerum imagines*). In the less strict sense they are acts of will involving such image-like ideas, judgings, approvings, denyings. At the end of the Second Replies Descartes defines an idea as "the form of any thought," and thought as "anything that exists in us in such a way that we are immediately conscious of it" (AT VII, 160; HR II, 52). Presumably the form of any thought is whatever makes that thought the thought it is, makes it an affirming or a denying, makes it as it were an image of whatever it is as it were an image of. What range of things can have this sort of form, be acts of some will's affirmation, or be as it were images? It is here that I am suggesting that Descartes allows a much wider range than has usually been assumed, and that included in this range of ideas in both the wise and the stricter sense are self-conscious thinkers. The already cited definition of thought quite clearly allows the self-conscious thinker's very existence to count as thought, and so allows the thinker's "form" of existence to count as an idea. There are other passages that confirm that thinkers can count, not merely as the havers of ideas but as ideas themselves, in both the strict and the wider senses.

An idea in the strict sense is, as it were, an image of something, perhaps of something other than itself (although the meditator's first true idea, "I think," imaged itself). At the end of the Third Meditation we are explicitly told that we should understand ourselves not merely to contain but possibly to *be* representations of our sustaining cause. "And one certainly should not find it strange that God, in creating me placed this idea within me to be like the mark [*nota*] of the workman imprinted on his work; *and it is likewise not essential that the mark shall be something different from the work itself.* For from the sole fact that God created me it is most probable that in some way he has placed his image and similitude upon me [—valde credibile est me quodamodo ad imaginem & similitudinen ejus factum esse] and that I perceive this similitude (in which the idea of God is contained) by means of the same faculty by which I perceive myself . . . " (AT VII, 51; HR I, 170, my emphasis). This passage makes it quite clear that the idea of God, which is the maker's mark on the work, need not be thought to be other than the work itself, that is to say the thinker, whose "similitude" to his cause is, when recognized as such by him, the idea he has of God. So that the thinker can through this mode of self-consciousness become one of his own ideas in the narrow sense, can become aware of himself as *tanquam imaginem*. The passage also repeats what had been said in the previous paragraph; namely, that the idea of God is grasped by the same faculty as the idea of oneself.

"It is innate in me, just as the idea of myself is innate in me." The *kind* of innateness the idea of oneself has is not merely independence from sense perception, and resistance to any of one's attempts to add or subtract anything from it, but, more positively, dependence on one's own nature. "As I have the power of understanding what is called a thing, or a thought, it appears to me that I hold this power from no other source than my own nature" (AT VII, 45; HR I, 166). The idea of oneself as a thinking thing is innate in that it applies to oneself, and so can be self-derived. Of course the idea of God is not similarly self-exemplified. "Although the idea of substance is within me owing to the fact that I am a substance, nevertheless I should not have the idea of an infinite substance—since I am finite—if it had not proceeded from some substance which was veritably infinite" (ibid.). What does apply to the human thinker, I am suggesting, is the idea of *idea of God*. Just as I can have the idea of substance since I am a substance, the idea of a thinker since I am one, so I can have the meta-idea of idea of God because, since the mark of the workman is here the work itself, I am this idea, and in becoming conscious of myself I thereby become conscious of what in fact is this idea. Just as I need not be conscious of myself as a substance to be conscious of myself, who am in fact a substance, so I need not be, and indeed before the Third Meditation was not, conscious of myself as the idea of God merely by being self-conscious. The point of this Meditation was to let that self-consciousness grow, since "I do not yet know clearly enough what I am, I who am certain that I am" (AT VII, 25; HR I, 150). This was said in the Second Meditation, but the progressive advance of self-consciousness continues right to the end of the *Meditations.*[4] At the beginning of the Fifth the meditator says "Many other matters concerning the attributes of God and my own nature or mind remains for consideration" (AT VII, 63; HR I, 179), and he links those two subject matters in the way we would expect, if progress in self-understanding entails progress in understanding the precise relationship between the first true idea the meditator had achieved, that of himself, and that next true idea, that of the true God, which quickly gets promoted into "the first and principal of the true ideas born in me" (AT VII, 68; HR I, 182). Somehow the idea of self and the idea of God tie for being the first-born true idea, and this sharing of the honors would be easily understood if the ideas are related in the way I am suggesting—that idea of self is an idea of what in fact is and is soon seen as the idea of God. The Third Meditation is where this crucial joining of the two "first truths" occurs, or rather when their correlativity is realized. "In some way I have in me the notion of the infinite before that of the finite—to wit, the notion of God before that of myself. For how would it be possible that I should doubt and desire, that is to say, that something is lacking in me, and that I am not quite perfect, unless I had within me some idea of a Being more perfect than myself, in comparison with which I should recognize the deficiencies of my nature?" (AT VII, 45–46; HR I, 166). The not quite perfect desiring and striving thinker has, *in himself*, in his very defective but defect-overcoming nature, the idea of what it would be to lack those defects. Just as every desire, or every willing, or every affirming, must as it were image the satisfaction of that desire, the doing of that will, the object of that affirmation, so the thinker, aware of his imperfections and aspirations, somehow represents the perfections he so far lacks.

Before turning to the *content* of the idea of God, which I am now construing to be what is represented or meant by the self-conscious finite thinker himself, not merely what is represented by some one of his ordinary acts of thinking (his consciousness of himself as one who bears in himself the similitude of God being an extraordinary such act), I first want to show some evidence that the finite thinker might count as a Cartesian idea in the less "strict," as well as the strict sense. For to be an image, or as it were an image of something, would not make the thinker into an idea unless that image were used as such in an idea in the wide sense—in some questioning, or affirming, or desiring, or denying or other mode of willing. Acts of image-recognizing and of deliberate representing are needed to make images or representations into *ideas*, forms of thought. Just as old portraits of unknown persons and broken idols of no longer worshipped gods are evidence of *past* acts of representing, so thinking things might be images of creators who were no longer sustainers, unless they could be seen as ideas in the less strict sense, as the forms of complex will-involving acts of representation-making and representation-recognizing thought. There is no difficulty in construing Cartesian thinking things as such thought, since thinking is their essence, and their essence "must not be considered otherwise than the very substances tha: think" (*Principles* I, 63: AT VIII, 30–31; HR I, 245). There is nothing in a Cartesian thinking thing over and above its connected willed thought. For it to count as "an idea," then, the problem is not in construing it as thought, but in construing it as the "form" of *a* thought. But this would only be a problem if there were any clear principle of individuation for thoughts, and if "form" individuated them. For Descartes, however, the difference between *a* thought, with its form, and a sequence of thoughts, with their cumulative form or sequences of forms, seems of no importance, or, more accurately, of the same importance as the difference between intuition and deduction, or between "single" acts of the mind not requiring reliance on memory, and more drawn out, memory-dependent thinking. No clear line can be drawn, and none needs to be drawn. So too with the difference between seeing oneself as a sequence of ideas or forms of thought and seeing oneself as a longer-lasting, more inclusive idea or form of thinking—the difference is not important. It might become important were the identity of each thinker, his or her difference from other thinkers, connected with the "unity" of its peculiar form of thought, so that to be one idea would be to be one thinker, to be more than one would be to be a collection of thinkers, but Descartes avoids this issue by never getting to the point of meditating on his relation to other individual, finite thinkers.

IV. THE CONTENT OF THE IDEA OF GOD

That the formal reality of "the idea of God in the meditator" is all of what he is conscious of there being in him, that he can *be* this idea of his, in both the strict and the less strict sense of "idea," may be more easily accepted once we get clearer about the objective reality of this special idea, and my reconstruction of what "idea of God in me" means for Descartes requires some correlative reconstruction of what "God" means for the meditator. To some extent the plausibility of construing the human thinker as an idea for that thinker depends on what meaning that idea is claimed to have, what objective reality is found in the "thinking idea." If the human thinker signifies anything to the human thinker, it might be thought most natural to take its meaning to concern human nature, rather than the divine nature. Human potentiality and human limitations might be signified by a human thinker, but how could anything more than that be in us, even if we are *tanquam rerum imagines?* To answer this question we need to attend to the precise way in which the content of the idea of God is spelled out by the meditator in the course of the *Meditations.* I shall suggest that what occurs within the Third Meditation amounts to a switch from an orthodox Christian conception to a more heterodox version of God, and that it is this switch that explains why the idea of "a God who can do anything" changes from a threat to human power and knowledge to a source of support and reassurance for human ambitions.

Writing to Mersenne in July 1641 Descartes says, "I mean by the idea of God what all men habitually understand when they speak of Him."[5] Like so many of his claims, this one is ambiguous. It can be read to claim that by "idea of God" he means what *he* understands when he speaks of God, just as each man, by "idea of God," means what that one understands when that one speaks of God. The stronger, and surely insincere, claim would be that Descartes sees the idea of God he ends with simply to repeat in content the idea he expects all his theist readers to share. After all, as he had written in an earlier letter to Mersenne, most people "stick at the syllables of His name, and think it sufficient knowledge of Him to know that 'God' means what is meant by *deus* in Latin, and what is adored by men."[6]

What is adored by men can be either a mysterious, powerful being, wholly other, whose very mystery inspires awe and reverent worship, or, alternatively, they can adore something more like themselves, especially if that holds out prospects for their *own* eventual glorification. Traditional Christianity had, by the doctrine of the incarnation, tried to make its God both human enough for concepts like love to apply, and also nonhuman enough to inspire due awe and self-abasement. The God referrd to in the *Meditations* is throughout a God whose power is emphasized. In the First Meditation, that power limits human power, and is a threat to human prospects for knowledge. "Nevertheless I have long had fixed in my mind the belief that an all-powerful God existed, by whom I have been created such as I am. But how do I know that He has not brought it to pass that there is no earth, no heaven, no extended body, no magnitude, no place, and that nevertheless they seem to me to exist exactly as I now see them?" (AT VII, 21; HR I, 147). Divine goodness is then referred to, but a not fully comprehensible goodness, since "it would also appear to be contrary to His goodness to permit me sometimes to be deceived, and nevertheless I cannot doubt that He does permit it" (ibid.). The divine goodness, according to that old idea of God, must be construed as like the goodness of the more powerful human parent, whose deception of the powerless child may be for its own good, a good it cannot be expected to grasp while it is subject to benign parental deceit and perhaps to other apparent evils from the parental hand. The God referred to briefly in the Second Meditation, and again at the beginning of the Third, is still this "old idea" of "a" or "some" God, a mysterious, powerful creator whose ways are not our ways. "Every time that this preconceived opinion of the sovereign power of a God presents itself to my thought, I am constrained to confess that it is easy for Him, if he wishes it, to cause me to err even in matters where I believe myself to have the best evidence" (AT VII, 36; HR I, 158). The crucial thing is His wishes, but they are incomprehensible if He is wholly other. If His version of goodness is not ours, then we cannot hope for much that we will find good.

Once the meditator turns, however, not to the old preconceived inherited idea of God, but rather to his own innate idea, to an idea "from no other source than my own nature," we get a rather different conception. Its first formulations are orthodox enough: "a supreme God, eternal, infinite, omniscient, omnipotent, and Creator of all things which are outside of Himself" (AT VII, 40; HR I, 162). This formula is repeated three pages later, with a slight change concerning creative power: "and by which I myself and everything else, if anything else does exist, have been created" (AT VII, 45; HR I, 165). Then interesting claims are made about the relation of this idea to that of oneself. So far, it is clear that the relation is one of nonidentity and of creator-created. But now we are told that it is more closely correlative. "In some way I have in me the notion of the infinite earlier than the finite, to wit the notion of God before that of myself. For how would it be possible that I should know that I doubt and desire, that is to say that something is lacking in me, unless I had within myself some idea of a Being more perfect than myself, in comparison with which I should recognize the deficiencies of my nature?" (AT VII, 45–46; HR I, 166). This defines God as the being who is the way one would like to be—with desires satisfied, the Being who is in the state one would regard as the best state. Divine goodness now is quite comprehensible goodness—it is the goodness one would like to possess, the goodness of enjoyment of satisfied desire.

This relativity of the divine attributes to human conceptions of perfection does nothing to dislodge any of the traditional attributes— power, knowledge, creativity, are all human goods. But whereas with the old inherited idea of God, divine omniscience did not imply that human knowledge was a good for humans, since that omniscient God might forbid man to eat of the tree of some sorts of knowledge, with the meditator's innate idea of God, to say that God has knowledge is thereby to say that one wants knowledge. God has become the being defined by the content of human desires.

This becomes even clearer in the next move of the argument, when the meditator raises the question of whether he might derive the idea of these perfections from some aspect of himself, some potential that might yet disclose itself in actuality. Although he rejects the possibility that his idea of God might be derived from his own potential, he rejects this without altogether disclaiming "divine" ambitions and "divine" potential. "As a matter of fact I am already sensible that my knowledge increases [and perfects itself] little by little, and I see nothing which can prevent it from increasing more and more into infinitude, nor do I see, after it has thus been increased [or perfected], anything to prevent my being able to acquire by its means all the other perfections of the Divine nature" (AT VII, 47; HR I, 167). What follows is the recognition that he will never reach a point where no further advance is possible, and that however far he advances his history will doom him to imperfection since "it is an infallible sign of imperfection in my knowledge that it increases little by little" (ibid.). Hence even the best he can hope for is short of supreme perfection. God, then, is not defined as the being who is the way the meditator hopes to be, since for *logical* reasons he cannot *hope* to be in a state incompatible with hope as its predecessor state, and, for less clear reasons, he *does* not expect to be in a state where no further improvement is to be expected. So God's perfections define a limit, a necessarily unreachable limit, to his own confident ambitions. Or, to say the same thing, his own ambitions and his own confidence in fulfilling them define the direction in which divine perfection is to be found, at the limit.

This intimate union between his conception of his own progress as a thinker and his conception of God is spelled out several times in what follows. If the meditator were the author of his own being, he would have given himself the divine perfections. "Nor should I have deprived myself of any of the things contained in the idea which I form of God, because there are none of them which seem to me specially difficult to acquire . . . " (AT VII, 48; HR I, 168). Since he knows that he is not the author of his own being, these perfections define the limit of his hopes, not his achievements, the direction of his unfolding future, not the place of his fixed past. Again "when I reflect on myself I not only know that I am something [imperfect] incomplete and dependent on another, which incessantly aspires after something which is better and greater than myself, but I also know that He on whom I depend possesses in Himself all the great things to which I aspire [and the ideas of which I find within myself] and that not indefinitely or potentially alone, but really, actually and infinitely; and that thus He is God" (AT VII, 51; HR I, 170).

This idea of what it would be like to have "all the great things to which I aspire" is clear and distinct, but not adequate. It is clear and distinct because "all that I conceive clearly and distinctly of the real and true, and of what conveys some perfection, is of its entirety contained in this idea" (AT VII, 46; HR I, 166). It is, however, no more adequate than is any thinker's idea of what it will be like to have solved the problems currently confronting her—it is clear that those currently unanswered questions will be answered, but what new questions will thereby have arisen cannot yet be clear and distinct. The meditator at this point does not clearly see even the precise form of the doubts and questions to be answered in the Sixth Meditation, let alone in his physics. But in the true God all these as yet unimagined treasures of wisdom and science are contained. To aspire incessantly after something that is better and greater is of necessity not to know distinctly *all* the things to which one will aspire, and will one day know more distinctly, both as aspirations and possibly as achievements, if indeed "none of them seem to me especially difficult to acquire."

V. A DECEITFUL AUTHOR?

This idea of God, as the Being who has, actually and eternally, the perfections that the human person aspires to, and may get gradually, is not the alien, inscrutable, all-powerful creator of the First Meditation. This one *could* not be a deceiver, unless deception is something one aspires to. Does the meditator aspire to deceive? Does Descartes the author aspire to successful deception of stupider and weaker thinkers? It is hard to avoid the conclusion that the theological content of the Third Meditation is somewhat masked, if that content is what I am suggesting it to be. For there is no explicit noting of the fact that the idea of God has undergone transformation or replacement by the end of the Third. By then, we no longer have the God of the orthodox Christian tradition, the God of preconceived theological opinion. Although that tradition had included talk of the imitation of Christ, and had included a divine command to be perfect as God the father is perfect, nevertheless this command was not seriously expected to be obeyed, since at the center of the Christian teaching was a claim to *monopoly* of humanly attainable perfection. "There is one God, and one meditator between God and man, the man Christ Jesus" (St. Paul). To aspire to divine perfections, or to a finite human version of is to have impious, heretical, and radically subversive aspirations. For Christians, that "all have sinned and come short of the glory of God" is a timeless truth, and it is sin, not just doubt or error, which keeps them short of that glory. Descartes was later accused of the heresy of Pelagianism—denying original sin—but what I am pointing to seems a much more radical heresy, in effect not merely the Protestant claim of the priesthood of all believers, but an assertion of the potential *divinity* of all human thinkers, every person his or her own second person of the god-head. Like Helen Wadell's Abelard, Descartes teaches "Ye are gods." And what *counts* as God depends upon human subjective desire—God is the being who has the perfections the meditator wants to acquire, and, in as far as they are compatible with gradual acquisition, is reasonably confident he can and will eventually acquire.

Read this way, Descartes' Third Meditation is very deviously titled "Of God, that He Exists." If there is, as I am suggesting, a switch in conceptions of God, from one at least vague enough to be taken as the God of the Christian theological tradition to a very different, humanly centered conception, then it shows more subtlety than non-deceit on Descartes' part to have titled the Third Meditation as he did, and to have dedicated the *Meditations* as he did to the "most wise and illustrious dean and doctors of the sacred faculty of Theology in Paris," offering them his improved proofs of God's existence as a contribution to "the cause of God and religion to those who have always been the most worthy supports of the Catholic Church" (AT VII, 6; HR I, 137).

Indeed the whole treatment of theology by Descartes shows that the will to reveal the truth was a perfection he had either lost or not yet achieved, doubtless one which had to wait on increase in power. Rightly does he put that lack of need to deceive others, which goes with supreme power, in the being whose perfections contrasted with and complemented and completed his own. Perhaps we should read Descartes' claims about deceit and weakness as a sort of explanation of his own policy—as long as he was subject to the power of the Catholic Church, the will to deceive must be expected, in self-defense. After Galileo's condemnation by the Holy Inquisition, Descartes announced to Mersenne in April 1634 his intention to adopt the maxim of Ovid *"Bene vixit, bene qui latuit,"* and to withhold publication of his *Treatise of the World* "lest it make unwanted acquaintances."[7] His semi-transparent deceit of his readers in the *Meditations*, if that is what it is, is proportionate to his powerlessness, but not to what he takes to be his relative position as concerns subtlety, knowledge and acumen. He must, indeed, have counted on his ecclesiastical readers being not sharp enough to notice the heresies that were being introduced, perhaps not even sharp enough to wonder about the alleged superiority of the proof of God in the Third Meditation over those more usual appeals to the authority of Holy Scripture which were, as he said in the dedication, open to the accusation of "reasoning in a circle" (AT VII, 2; HR I, 133). He presents to us what has become known as "the Cartesian circle," with an official dedication which claims that *his* arguments will make God's existence more manifest to the infidel than the circular arguments of the Christian apologists.

Hiram Caton[8] has suggested that Descartes' intent is to offer only *ad hominem* arguments for God's existence, to placate the guardians of theology, and so leave free scope for the Cartesian scientific program to go ahead and ultimately rule with undisputed authority. I do not regard the Third and Fifth Meditations as wholly insincere, but I do think that their theses are presented in somewhat masked forms, and call for a bit of uncovering before their import becomes clear and distinct to attentive readers. It is not simply that a confused idea of God is clarified and made distinct in the course of the Third Meditation, it is rather that a *different* idea[9] is made distinct—not the God of preconceived Christian theological opinion, handed down by tradition, learned when one learned the catechism, but an innate idea, the converse, or reverse, of one's idea of oneself, barely separable from one's ambitions for oneself. "When I think only of God and direct my mind wholly to him [*totusque in eum me converto*] I discover [in myself] no cause of error or falsehood, yet directly afterward, when recurring to myself [*ad me reversus*] experience shows me that I am nevertheless subject to an infinitude to errors . . . " (AT VII, 54; HR I, 172). This passage from the Fourth Meditation repeats the same language used at the end of the Third; the meditator "turns" alternately from the idea of his own ambitions to the idea of the being who has the perfections to which he aspires. Since the one idea converts so readily into its converse, the meditator can say, of the true God, that "I do not think the human mind is capable of knowing anything with more evidence or certitude" (AT VII, 53; HR I, 172)—not anything with more certitude, not even one's own existence as a thinker. That one exists as an imperfect thinker is known with exactly the same certitude as one knows the correlate of this truth.

VI. THE ARGUMENT AND ITS TWO VERSIONS

Does the argument offered by Descartes to the theologians do better than their arguments? Is it a good argument, and does it avoid vicious circularity? So far I have reinterpreted "idea of God," and "God," and spoken about the warrant for the causal principle. Now I shall look at the structure of the argument, to show, as promised, how the interpretation I have given of its key terms enables us to discern a tighter structure, and to explain the incompleteness of the argument as given in the first round—that is, up until HR I, 167. There the meditator says this: "To speak the truth, I see nothing in all that I have just said which by the light of nature is not manifest to anyone who desires to think attentively on the subject; but when I slightly relax my attention, my mind, finding its vision somewhat obscured and so to speak blinded by the images of sensible objects, I do not easily recollect why the idea that I possess of a being more perfect than I must necessarily have been placed in me by a being which is really more perfect; and this is why I wish here to go on to inquire whether I, who have this idea, can exist if no such being exists" (AT VII, 47–48; HR I, 167). In the initially quoted passage, Descartes told the writers of the Second Objections that what follows is given for the sake of those whose natural light does not show them how the cause of the idea of God must contain, formally or eminently, all the perfections that idea has objectively and formally. What we now need to see is how the first round of the argument might have failed to provide that light, and what the second round does to remedy it. We shall also see why the images of sensible things might blind us to the version of the first round of the argument, which makes it clear and distinct.

The first round of the argument claims that the only adequate cause of the idea of an all-powerful, all-knowing creator is such a being. It would be perfectly natural for a reader of the first round of the argument to suppose that the "idea" of God was a passing mode of the finite thinking thing, no greater, in its formal reality, than the sense-derived idea of the sun, or that other idea of the sun acquired from astronomical reasonings. "If ideas are only taken as certain modes of thought, I recognize amongst them no difference or inequality, and all appear to proceed from me in the same manner, but when we consider them as images, one representing one thing and the other another, it is clear that they are very different from one another" (AT VII, 39; HR I, 161). This seems to allow us to take all ideas to be, in their formal reality, equal modes of thought. Indeed most readers do take this implication even after giving the *Meditations* the careful reading and rereadings Descartes believed essential.[10] But the passage does not say that all ideas *are* equal modes of thought. If one of them, the idea of God, were a mode that reflected, formally, the substance of which it is a mode, then it would be superior to other modes. I have claimed the idea of God *is* the thinker qua self-conscious. Whenever self-consciousness is achieved, as it was in the Second Meditation, the thinker's thought mode does, in its formal reality, reflect his essence. Descartes says to the writers of the Second Objections, " . . . when you say that in ourselves there is a sufficient foundation to construct the idea of God, your assertion in no way conflicts with my opinion. I myself at the end of the Third Meditation have expressly said that this idea is innate in me, or alternatively that it comes to me from no other source than myself" (AT VII, 133; HR II, 33). We can "construct" self-consciousness in the way the meditator does in the Second Meditation, and see what that self-consciousness means as far as its sustaining cause goes, in the way the meditator does in the Third. "The whole force of my argument lies in the fact that the capacity for constructing such an idea could not exist in me unless I were created by God" (ibid.).

If we suppose that the idea of God, whose cause is inferred to be God, is in fact the thinker qua self-conscious, but that the inferrer is not yet fully conscious of that, is still vague about what exactly the effect in question is, in its formal reality, then we get a possible explanation of why there is no mention in the first round of the argument of either the unity of the divine attributes or the impossibility of an infinite regress of causes. Once the effect whose cause is to be inferred is clearly seen to be the thinker, in as far as he has realized his capacity to *have* this idea of God in himself, that is, to be self-conscious and to see what self-consciousness means, then the cause required for this complex but unified effect must itself be a sustaining unity in complexity, something with a similar structure. The self-reference in the effect also poses the possibility of regress, and that possibility has to be ruled out. The finite thinker's self-referential thought, "I, who am thinking this thought, exist as a thinker," engenders no vicious regress, and there was an implicit contrast drawn early in the Second Meditation between its successful self-reference and the unsuccessful self-reference of the skeptical thought: "Perhaps nothing, except this, is certain." When the effect whose cause is sought, in the Third, is the self-conscious thinker, the thinker who has the ideas both of self and of God in himself, then and only then is the possibility of a regress of causes raised: "And it is perfectly manifest that in this there can be no regression into infinity, since what is in question is not so much the cause which formerly created me, as that which conserves me at the present time" (AT VII, 50; HR I, 169). Just as the thinking that sustains the true thought, "I exist as a thinker," is my current thinking, this current thinking, and cannot be some ever-reggressing support, since it is expressed now, in the thought I now pronounce, so what supports and is expressed in me, this current, self-conscious thinker, must be a containing cause that is present with me now, not ever retreating. Self-reference in the effect calls for self-reference in its cause, and self-reference introduces the possibility of regress. But that possibility is considered only to be dismissed when the self-reference in question is of the sort found in the meditator's first self-evident certainty, and in its self-evidencing cause.

The regress into infinity is blocked because the self-reference of the effect is self-consciousness, and the self-reference of the needed cause must have that perfection, formally or eminently. To have it is to avoid vicious regress. So it is proper at this point in the argument to emphasize this divine perfection, that which eminently contains self-consciousness, and this is what the meditator does, in the next paragraph: " . . . the unity, the simplicity or the inseparability of all things which are in God is one of the principal perfections which I conceive to be in Him. And certainly the idea of this unity of all Divine perfections cannot have been placed in me by any cause from which I have not likewise received the idea of all the other perfections; for this cause could not make me able to comprehend them as joined together in an inseparable unity without having at the same time caused me in some measure to know what they are" (AT VII, 50; HR I, 169–170). The image, or as it were image, of this inseparable unity is the finite thinker's self-consciousness uniting, as that does, will and intellect, affirmation and what is affirmed. As he cannot comprehend that unity without knowing in some measure the various levels of his self-referential thought, so also with what that complex but unified thinking signifies about its complex but unified cause. The divine power and the divine knowledge are tightly united, since all of what God knows is what God has made so, just as what the meditator knew in the Second Meditation was what he currently was doing.[11] Power, knowledge, and the unity of power and knowledge are found finitely in the meditator's self-consciousness, found eminently and infinitely in its sustaining cause.

The threat of a plurality of causes, whether a regressive plurality or simply a pair of parents, as causes of the meditator as effect, is considered and banished here in the second round of the argument. As for his parents, not only do they not now conserve him, but "nor are they the authors of my being in any sense, in so far as I am a thinking being" (AT VII, 50; HR I, 170). Self-consciousness is not explained by biological inheritance. The human person, as a living being, may indeed contain the mark of his biological ancestry, and so "signify" that, but it is only as self-conscious thinker, not as living biological reality, that the meditator so far knows himself. Still, the as yet unvalidated opinion that some of his physical characteristics derive from one parent, some from the other, might have caused him some worry about his inference from single effect to single cause earlier in the argument. Here, once the singleness of the effect is seen to be so singular a singleness, a special unity in complexity, that possible worry is banished; but why was it not raised earlier, in the first round of the argument?

I suggest that the meditator, after the First Meditation, explicitly raises only such problems as he can solve with the resources he has explicitly introduced up to that point. In the first round of the argument, where "idea of God" is the effect whose cause is sought, and where no positive clues are given us to show us just what that idea *is*, in its own formal reality, no answer could have been given had the worry then surfaced. Were the idea of God an idea like the idea of the sun, then any number of diverse causes might have contributed to its formation. The meditator is to claim, in the Sixth Meditation, that the causes of the sense-derived idea of the sun *are* multiple—the perceiver's nervous system, light, the earth's atmosphere, and the physical sun itself, all go into making this idea which, on the face of it, is an idea of *one* thing. Astronomical reasonings give us what may at first be a quite different idea of the sun, which we then use to interpret the sense-derived idea, which thereby ends up with a very large family of both true progenitors and current sustainers, for all its apparent singleness. Why should not the idea of one God turn out to be similarly diverse in its causes if it is an idea like other ideas as far as its formal reality is concerned?[12]

Now there is one sense in which I think Descartes, in the Third Meditation, *is* saying that there are two sources for "the" idea of God, namely inherited theological tradition, and meditation on one's own nature. One explanation of why the meditator says not that astronomical reasonings affect our idea of the sun, but rather that they give us a second idea, a true one in place of a false one, is that this is what is to happen also with the idea of God. As the meditator has "two completely diverse ideas of the sun in my mind," which "cannot indeed both resemble the same sun" (AT VII, 39; HR I, 161), so he has the old idea of God, from a preconceived tradition into which there were as many diverse inputs as go into the purely sense-derived idea of the sun, and, quite different and opposed to that, an idea of God derived from "certain notions innate in me." And as, by the Sixth Meditation, the meditator is able to read his true idea of the sun into the data his senses give him, has managed to construe the false idea in terms of the true, and so to correct it, so in the dedication, Descartes speaks to the custodians of the old idea of God as though that old preconceived idea could be reinterpreted, so as to serve as the transmitter of the new one, the always newly conceived one, derived not from revelation or tradition but from oneself. "Reason makes me believe that the one which seems to have originated directly from the sun itself is the one which is most dissimilar to it" (ibid.). But even the idea based on astronomical reasonings would seem to have no guarantee of the singleness of its ultimate cause. That it is, in its content, the idea of *one* thing does not show that its ultimate and sustaining cause is one thing. Even innate ideas, for all the singleness of their apparent objective reality, might have multiple causes, and so be materially false as far as oneness and plurality are concerned.

This worry, which one would think should have arisen early in the argument, is expressed and answered only in the second round, and answered by emphasis on the unique type of unity the divine perfections have. The earlier suppression of this worry could explain the form taken by the dissatisfaction expressed at the end of the first round of the argument. It is "the images of sensible objects" which distract the meditator, which obscure the manifest truth that God must exist as cause of the idea of God, and so which prevent this certainty from becoming stabilized, ready to stabilize other certainties. If the idea of God is taken to be as it were an image of God in the way even the astronomer's idea of the sun is an idea, then the argument is not manifestly sound, since the possibility of a plurality of causes is not yet ruled out. If the meditator's idea of "idea of God" is not yet distinctly recognized as a "mark," which need not be different from the work itself, then this first argument could shift from validity to invalidity as the sense of "idea" vacillates from true wider to preconceived narrower senses. If one forgets the context of the argument, namely, what is established in the Second Meditation, then both one's confidence in the causal principle and one's ability to see the sort of unity the idea of God has will falter, and one will "not easily recollect why the idea I possess of a being more perfect than I must necessarily have been placed in me by a being which really is more perfect" (AT VII, 47; HR I, 167). In what follows, in the second round of the argument, Descartes expressly takes the self-consciously imperfect thinker as the effect whose cause is inferred, and expressly addresses the peculiar unity of the idea of God, but does not expressly say that the self-conscious thinker is his own idea of God. Only at the very end does he put all the bits together, since only then are we told that the idea of God, whose special unity requires a unified cause, is a mark which need not be construed as other than the work itself, that is, the self-conscious thinker. It is not exactly that an incomplete and ambiguous argument, in the first round, is followed by a completed and nonambiguous one, in the second round. It is rather that only after both rounds are we given the hint that enables us to see how we must in each round construe the effect whose cause is inferred, for the inference to be sound. In the first round Descartes explicitly considered the idea of God; in the second, he explicitly considered "I, who have this idea in me." The last turn of the argument, the explication of the peculiar "manner" in which this idea is "in" the thinker, enables us to go back and complete "idea of God," in both rounds, with a "namely myself when I am conscious of myself as having not yet realized but confident ambitions, ambitions which as it were image what it would be for those ambitions to be realized;

and where my very self consciousness itself as it were images the instantaneous nongradual satisfaction of those ambitions." When the first argument is seen as being about *the self-conscious thinker*, qua idea of God, its faults are mainly faults of suppressing needed but available premises. When the second round of the argument is seen as about the self-conscious thinker *qua idea of God,* I think it is as faultless as we can make it. Both arguments are inferences to cause of the same effect, but each argument presents that effect obscurely, and only the last clarification presents it to us clearly and distinctly.

I shall now try to present, clearly and distinctly, the two rounds of the argument, in each case including in parentheses what earlier or later developments license us to add. That way I hope to make clear the different incompletenesses of each round of argument, the improvement of each by the later glosses, and the collapse of the two arguments into a repetition of the one argument that Descartes claimed they were.

FIRST ROUND

1. A sustaining cause must (like the only such cause I know as such, namely, myself, who thinks) contain all the reality its effect contains, formally and objectively (as my thinking in the Second Meditation both exemplified and referred to thought).

2. I have in myself an idea (namely, myself, in as far as I am conscious of myself) of a being who has the perfections to which I aspire, the perfections of independence, creative power, knowledge (and the unity of these).

3. (This effect contains nonregressive self-reference.)

4. I am not the cause of this idea, since I do not yet contain what I aspire to, and because this very history of aspiration before achievement rules out the perfection that lies at the limit of my aspirations.

5. (The cause of this idea must itself contain formally, or eminently, as well as objectively, the nonregressive self-reference of its effect.)

6. Therefore the cause of my idea of God (that is, the cause of me) is another being who has those perfections, the very being the idea of whom I have in me (that is, the idea that, when self-conscious, I am).

SECOND ROUND

1. A sustaining cause must (like the only such cause I know as such, namely, myself, who thinks), contain all the reality its effect contains formally and objectively (as my thinking in the Second Meditation both exemplified and referred to thought).

2. I, with my idea of a being who has the perfections of independence, creative power, knowledge, and the unity of these (which idea is identical with me in as far as I am conscious of not possessing these perfections to which I aspire), exist.

3. (This effect contains nonregressive self-reference.)

4. I am not my own sustaining cause (not the cause of my idea of God) since I am not yet all-knowing, but would be, if I were powerful enough to sustain myself.

5. What causally explains my existence cannot be a regress of causes, since it sustains me now (me, with my current nonregressive, self-referential self-consciousness).

6. The cause of me who has in myself (of me who am, when self-conscious) the idea of God is the very God of whom I have (am, when self-conscious) the idea.

VII. THE SUBTLETY AND POWER OF THE ARGUMENT

Is this argument, which is given twice, but with varying omissions, in the Third Meditation, a good argument? The weak point is still the causal principle. What warrant is there for generalizing from the special case of self-referential thinking, whose sustaining cause contains formally what it contains not merely formally but also objectively, to what seems the very different case of what sustains the thinker? Even granted that something sustains him, why must it contain not merely the perfections he has achieved, nor even those he expects to achieve, but those which lie at the limit, those of which he has an idea but cannot confidently aspire to? Why must the cause of necessity outdo the effect, in its formal reality, if it is to equal its objective reality? Was there a similar outdoing by the cause of the effect in the case which I am claiming sheds its light on this case, namely the cause-effect pair of the finite thinker of the Second Meditation and the thought of which he is conscious? If the move from dependent thought to thinker referred to in that thought, thinker who contains that thought, was sound, then the parallel move from dependent thinker to what that thinker's very existence refers us to, its sustaining cause, is another case of a similarly sound move from lower reality to higher, more inclusive reality. In both cases the higher reality on which the lower depends is as it were imaged in the lower reality, giving it its objective reality. But when we reach God, we have a limit to this two-step chain of effects with their formal and objective reality dependent on their more-inclusive causes. For there we have a Being who "has the power of actually possessing all the attributes of which it has the idea" (AT VII, 50; HR I, 169). God's ideas are all self-referential; they cannot point only beyond, since God is sustainer, self-expressive creator and, in a sense, *container* of whatever there is. If the relation between God and thinker is like that between thinker and the single thought, "I think," then it is a relation of whole to dependent self-expressive and microcosmic part. So the true God turns out to be other, yet not wholly other, than the imperfect thinker, since He must contain that thinker, as the thinker was other, but not wholly other, than any one of his thoughts. The meditator is not alone in the world, but not because he has shown there to be something wholly outside himself.

In the special case of the affirmation, "I exist as a thinker," there is reference to the more inclusive finite reality, the thinking thing, the affirmer,[13] but not all of that reality is manifested in the current thinking, which is, however, enough to verify that thought. What verifies that thought is *overlap* between its objective and its formal reality, containment of the latter in the former, and that overlap is similarly depended on to verify the idea of God. Its formal reality, the thinker, with his partially achieved aspirations, his confident expectation of greater achievement, is contained in what has objective reality in that idea, the being with actual possession of all the perfections of which that being has the idea and of which the finite thinker has a less adequate idea.

On this interpretation the argument *is* circular, or at least spiral, but the circular movement is its virtue, not its vice. Since the effect is a self-expressive, self-referential, and mutually involving cause-effect pair, thinker and his awareness of his essential self-conscious thought, and the inferred cause is a self-expressive, self-referential God, and the only warrant for the inference is the natural light shed by the effect's finite, self-contained microcosm of causal dependency, the inference has to be circular or spiral, to be warranted. Only if one trusts the natural light can it illuminate its more ultimate source, and one cannot fail to trust the light it shed in the Second Meditation. If one trusts nothing *but* that light, then only an argument with the same structure as that of the Second Meditation can be used in the Third, and it can be used only to infer a cause that stands to its effect in the same relation as the self-conscious thinker stood to his own idea of his thought. That means that the thought of the Third Meditation is bootstrap thinking, moving from the certainty of one's own existence by reusing the form of argument that got one there, looking for the cause of one's own causal power, the sustainer of one's own limited power to sustain the idea of oneself as thinker.

This still leaves the argument's soundness in doubt, and the doubt concerns the strength of the bootstraps, the warrant for thinking that any other cause-effect pair could be like the pair composed of the thinker and his consciousness of himself. To take that pair, and expect it itself to be related to something else as its sustaining and containing cause, as its own more derivative number is to its more independent member, is perhaps to move in the only direction open to the meditator, if he is not to remain forever wrapped up in narcissistic self-contemplation; but is it to move from truth to truth? I believe that my reconstruction not only unites the two phases of the argument, and links them more closely to the Second Meditation, but also makes the whole argument of the Third sounder than it is on other interpretations. But sounder isn't sound. Even when we do not equate all ideas with dependent modes of a finite thinking thing, it is not so easy to remember why one can only have the aspirations one has if one is sustained by a being who has everything one wants without ever having needed to aspire to it, not even if we interpret this Cartesian God as a Peircean ideal truth-attaining human community. "We must in the end acknowledge the infirmity of our nature," as the meditator says to end the Sixth Meditation, and perhaps must acknowledge the infirmity of our arguments too. At least I acknowledge that, even on my reconstruction, the argument of the Third Meditation does not make me want to pause any longer, even when the God in question is made human, "to contemplate God himself, to ponder at leisure His marvellous attributes, to consider and admire and adore the beauty of a light so resplendent . . . " (AT VII, 52; HR I, 171). The intricacies of the argument, as much as the distraction of more ordinary ideas, can dazzle and perhaps blind the mind's eyes.

One final doubt, since we seem to be ending on a penitential note. If my interpretation is right, then it is fair to ask why Descartes didn't *say* directly that the idea of God in question in the Third Meditation is this special idea, the self-conscious thinker. If this is what he meant, he certainly masked his meaning. Why? One answer, that which I have already given, is that he could not afford to offend powerful church authorities. But it is hard to resist the impression that he *enjoyed* constructing puzzle texts, that for him subtlety was a perfection higher on the hierarchy of his values than were clarity and distinctness. If I have correctly read the clues he left us, then God could be a deceiver only if deception were something we aspired to. If "deception is a mark of subtlety or power" (AT VII, 53; HR I, 172) and we value that power in ourselves more than bland veracity, then our God could be a deceiver, after all. Since the God established by the Third Meditation partially incorporates the meditator, the meditator's powers and acts of deception could coincide with, and be sustained by, the divine deception. But who then plays the role of the deceived? We other, less subtle, finite thinkers? But we too can learn to make just the moves the Cartesian meditator made. So if any meditator aspires to deceive, and his/her sustaining cause contains the aspirer's powers and those he/she aspires to, then divine deceit, if not also human deceit, becomes self-deceit. Once again, perhaps "we must in the end acknowledge the infirmity of our nature," as well as the anthropomorphism of our gods. But yet again, if Descartes' mask is as semitransparent as it must be for us to have seen the sardonic face behind that mask, then the meditator's God could also be a subtle tease, concealing only to increase the satisfaction of the eventual revelation. As human self-deceit is never entire, so divine self-deceit would become a game of delayed self-revelation, an eternal narcissistic dance of the seven veils. If we must towards the end acknowledge the anthropomorphism of our involuted gods, then we must in the very end acknowledge not so much the infirmity as the mask-loving frivolity of our nature.

NOTES

1. Descartes to Caterus (AT VII, 105–106; HR II, 2). (References AT, HR, and K are explained in the General Bibliography at the beginning of this volume.)

2. Margaret D. Wilson, *Descartes* (London: Routledge & Kegan Paul, 1978), 105.

3. I explore other neglected aspects of Descartes' philosophy of mind in "Cartesian Persons," *Philosophia*, vol. 10, no. 3–4 (Dec. 1981), and in "Intention, Practical Knowledge, and Representation," in *Action Theory*, ed., Brand and Walton (Dordrecht, Boston: Reidel, 1976).

4. Eventually, in the Sixth Meditation, the meditator finds himself to be extended in space as well as thinking. So all these earlier versions of what he is should read "I am *at least* a thinker."

5. AT III, 393; K, 106.

6. AT I, 48; K, 14.

7. AT I, 286; K, 26.

8. Hiram Caton, *The Origin of Subjectivity: An Essay on Descartes* (New Haven: Yale University Press, 1973).

9. Various readers of drafts of this paper have pointed out that there were strands in the tradition of Christian thought which anticipated what I claim to be Descartes' humanism, so that my claim that his idea of God is different from "the" Christian idea will not be true for all versions of that, but only for the official theologians' versions.

10. See his letter to Mersenne of 24 December 1640 in which he expresses his conviction that the writers of the second set of Objections could not possibly have yet absorbed the content of the *Meditations* sufficiently to be in a position to criticize it.

11. "In God, willing and knowing are a single thing in such a way that *by the very fact of willing something he knows it, and it is only for this reason that such a thing is true*" (Descartes to Mersenne, 6 May 1630 [AT I, 149; K, 13–14]).

12. My colleague Joseph Camp has, in an unpublished paper, "Meditation Three," explored the possibility of such ontological confusion.

13. The theses about will and intellect developed in the Fourth Meditation enable us to treat self-consciousness at its best as consciousness of how affirming will affirms "images" that the intellect makes distinct. For finite thinkers they are most distinct when our own will, like God's will, affirms ideas that image its own activity. However, since the human will is said to be infinite, while our intellect's power is finite, the human intellect seems doomed not to fully succeed in properly imaging the (divine?) human will, but at best to image or represent an occasional exercise of that will, when the mind turns and returns on itself and on what it takes itself, as a unity of will and intellect, to image.

16

Confused and Obscure Ideas of Sense

MARTHA BOLTON

I

At least one aim of the theory of error in the *Meditations* is to reconcile the perfection of God with the tendency in His creatures to hold false beliefs. The solution depends on a distinction between having a proposition in mind and judging or affirming that it is true; the former is a function of understanding, whereas the latter is a voluntary action of the will. Error can occur when one affirms or denies what has been only confusedly or obscurely (vs. clearly and distinctly) understood. The problems arising from the doctrine that judgment or belief is voluntary have been much discussed.[1] A different set of issues is raised by the doctrine of confused and obscure ideas. This doctrine is especially prominent in the discussions of sense perception in Meditations III and VI, for Descartes holds all sense experience to be to some degree confused and obscure perception of material things.

What is there to explain about confused and obscure ideas, in general, and in particular about the perceptions of sense? It is Descartes' contention that confusion and obscurity belong to an idea, not because of what it is, but because of what it lacks (namely clarity and distinctness). A lack cannot be explained in the same way that a positive character can; privations can only be understood through that characteristic of which they are deprived (AT VII, 374; HR II, 222). So, it would be a mistake to expect a full-blown explanation of confusion and obscurity, and how they lead to error.

There are, nevertheless, two problems about confused and obscure ideas that, I believe, received Descartes' attention. One is a metaphysical puzzle about how an idea can *be* obscure or confused; to have an idea is to apprehend a certain object, but to have a confused or obscure idea is to fail to apprehend that thing. Descartes' notion is not incoherent, but he must *account* for how an idea can represent something and also not represent it. The second, closely related problem is to explain how these ideas contribute to false judgment. Descartes has important reasons, some of them theological, to avoid saying that ideas positively mislead us. But when we make familiar perceptual mistakes about particular things, such as the size of the sun, there is a temptation to say our senses *prompt* the error. The difficulty is compounded, because Descartes regards as *erroneous* the widespread opinion " . . . that in a body which is warm there is something entirely similar to the idea of heat which is in me; that in a white or green body there is the same whiteness or greenness that I perceive . . . and similarly in other cases" (AT VII, 82; HR I, 193).

There are few places where Descartes confronts these problems directly. But they are just beneath the surface of passages in Meditations III and VI, and they are brought out in the Objections of Arnauld.[2] I want to maintain that Descartes has in mind a resolution of these two problems; and, further, that the solution governs his progress from doubt about his senses to realization of how they lead to error and how they can be instruments of truth.

II. MEDITATION III: THE POSSIBILITY OF FALSE IDEAS

Early in Meditation III, Descartes sets out to locate where error enters his activities as a thinking thing. His ideas do not provide material for error as long as they are not related to anything beyond themselves. It is only in judgments that he can be deceived: "But the principal error and the commonest which we may meet with in them consists in my judging that the ideas which are in me are similar or conformable to the things which are outside me" (AT VII, 37; HR I, 160). At this point, Descartes is unable to find reason to think either that sense ideas proceed from external objects or, if they do, that the ideas are like those objects. In fact, he has two different ideas of the sun which cannot both resemble it: according to the sense idea, the sun seems very small, whereas according to the astronomers' idea, it is much larger than the earth.[3] The sense idea, Descartes believes, is less similar to the sun (AT VII, 39; HR I, 161). So, it is a mistake to think all sensory ideas exactly resemble their objects (and their causes) and this *sort* of belief is suspected of being a main source of error.

Our two problems about confused and obscure ideas are broached a little further into the Meditation, when Descartes remarks that colors, heat, cold, and other such qualities are " . . . thought by me with so much obscurity and confusion that I do not even know if they are true or false" (AT VII, 43; HR I, 164). The immediate context is a sketch of Descartes' strategy to prove the existence of God. He intends to move from certainty about his own existence as a thinker who has various ideas to certainty about God by means of a causal maxim:

> In order that an idea should contain some one certain objective reality rather than another, it must without doubt derive it from some cause in which there is at least as much formal reality as this idea contains of objective reality. (AT VII, 41; HR I, 163)

Ideas can be considered as images representing things that have various degrees of reality or perfection (AT VII, 37; HR I, 159).[4] An idea's objective reality is a measure of the degree of reality belonging to what it represents. For example, the idea of heat, or that of a stone, has objective reality commensurate with the reality of heat, or of a stone (AT VII, 41; HR I, 163). We can infer from this that what an idea *represents* is the object of an idea, what the idea is *of*. Every idea has an object which it represents or, as Descartes sometimes says, "exhibits" to mind.[5] But it is clear that some ideas have objects that do not exist outside of thought; the paradigms of ideas include the idea of a chimera, as well as ideas of a man, an angel, and God (AT VII, 37; HR I, 159).[6] What does exist outside of thought is governed by the causal maxim: something with reality at least as great as the objective reality of a given idea must exist in the actual world, for the idea must have such a thing as cause. Descartes' argumentative strategy is to canvass his ideas in search of one whose objective reality is so great that he can be certain he himself is not the idea's cause.

Some ideas of corporeal things are clear and distinct, but represent things whose reality is no greater than what a thinker can ascribe to himself. These are ideas of magnitude, figure, situation, movement, as well as substance, duration, number. Next, thoughts of light, colors, sounds, tastes, heat, cold, and other tactile qualities are so confused and obscure that " . . . I do not even know if they are true or false, i.e. whether the ideas which I form of these qualities are actually the ideas of real objects or not." The explanation that follows raises a number of interesting questions about ideas:

For although I have before remarked that it is only in judgments that falsity, properly speaking, or formal falsity, can be met with, a certain material falsity may nevertheless be found in ideas, i.e. when these ideas represent what is nothing as though it were something. For example, the ideas which I have of cold and heat are so far from clear and distinct that by their means I cannot tell whether cold is merely a privation of heat, or heat a privation of cold, or whether both are real qualities, or are not such. And inasmuch as there cannot be any ideas which do not appear to represent some things, if it is correct to say that cold is merely a privation of heat, the idea which represents it to me as something real and positive will not be improperly termed false, and the same holds good of other similar ideas. (AT VII, 43–44; HR I, 164)

Descartes goes on to say that his own perfection suffices to account for the cause of these ideas, in either case. If these ideas are true, they "exhibit so little reality to me that I cannot even clearly distinguish the thing represented from non-being," and so he himself could be their cause. If the ideas are false, however, " . . . they issue from nought, that is to say, they are only in me so far as I am lacking in some perfection" (AT VII, 44; HR I, 165).[7]

One interesting issue about false ideas is how there can be an idea of nonentity: a false idea represents although there is nothing (possible) that it represents. Another important, but quite different issue is how an idea represents nonentity "as something positive." The first issue has little to do with our two problems about confused and obscure ideas. But the second issue draws attention to the fact that a false idea represents something (nonentity) which it also, in some way, does not represent to mind (represents it *as* something positive). A false idea thus gives a special case of our metaphysical problem about confused and obscure ideas. In Meditation III, as we just saw, Descartes identifies false ideas as those that *both* represent nonentity and represent it as something other than it is (I will continue to use the term *false idea* in that way). It is significant, however, that in the Replies he treats ideas that represent nothing as one class of false ideas. There he describes false ideas more broadly as all ideas that "provide materal for error" (AT VII, 233–234; HR II, 106–107, also 215 and 41).[8] On this broader view, all confused and obscure ideas are false (although Descartes insists ideas of heat, cold, and so forth, provide more opportunity for error than others do). It thus seems safe to say that an idea that represents nothing as if it were something is an example of a larger class of confused and obscure ideas that represent things as if they were something they are not.

On the basis of the passage from Meditation III, it is difficult to see Descartes' solution to the problem of how a false idea represents nonentity but fails to represent it. There is some basis for thinking Descartes means to say that a false idea exhibits to mind something that is *not* the object of the idea. If the idea of cold is false, its object is one thing (a nonentity such as a privation or chimerical quality), but it exhibits something else (a positive, real quality). Such a position is fraught with difficulties. But putting them aside, it does provide an explanation of error: what the idea exhibits to mind will be judged (falsely) to be true of the idea's object.

Arnauld understood Descartes to have taken this view of false ideas, and he argued acutely that it is disastrous.[9] It undermines the very notion of an idea; the idea of cold, for instance, is "cold itself in so far as it is objectively in the understanding." Thus, if cold is a privation, nothing positive existing objectively in the mind can be the idea of cold. Again, an idea is positive on account of "the objective existence which it contains and displays to the intellect" (AT VII, 206; HR II, 87). So although a positive idea may not be the idea of cold (for cold may be a privation), it cannot falsely represent what it *is* the idea of. Arnauld accuses Descartes of confusing judgments, which can be false, with ideas, which cannot.

Further, Arnauld points out that in the course of his argument, Descartes assumes that what an idea exhibits to mind *is* its object. In the case of his clear and distinct idea of God, there is no worry about material falsity, Descartes argues: "For although perhaps we can imagine that such a Being does not exist, we cannot nevertheless imagine that His idea represents nothing real to me" (AT VII, 46 and 206; HR I, 166 and II, 87). One advantage the idea of God has over the idea of cold is in the clarity with which it exhibits its object; there is no doubt about the reality of its object *because* there is none about what it displays. Arnauld does not develop the point, but it would be fatal for Descartes to hold that the cognitive content of an idea can diverge from the object of the idea, that it does so when the idea is confused or obscure. For, if an idea can exhibit one thing and have another as object, how could the clarity of its exhibition ground assurance about what its object is?

Finally, Arnauld points out another serious difficulty. He supposes that Descartes means to cite the positive cognitive content of the idea of cold to explain why we judge (perhaps wrongly) that cold is a real quality. Assuming cold is privative, Arnauld argues:

Further, what is the cause of that positive objective being, which makes you conclude that that idea is materially false? It is, you reply, myself, in so far as I participate in nonexistence. Therefore the positive objective existence of a certain idea may proceed from nothing, a conclusion which upsets the most important fundamental principles of M. Descartes. (AT VII, 207; HR II, 87)

More generally, divorcing an idea's cognitive content from its object wreaks havoc with the causal maxim. It may then turn out that the idea's cognitive content has more reality than its object has, so that the idea must have a cause with *greater* reality than its object.

Descartes accepts Arnauld's analysis of difficulties attending this account of false ideas. He replies by denying that it is his account:

> But M. Arnauld asks what that idea of cold reveals to me, that I said was materially false. For, he says, if it reveals privation, it is thereby true; if it display to him some positive entity it is not the idea of cold. Quite right; but the only reason why I call that idea materially false is because, since it is obscure and confused, I cannot decide whether it displays to me something outside my sensation or not; and this is why I have an opportunity for judging that it is something positive, although perchance it is a privation. (AT VII, 234; HR II, 106–107)

Arnauld's objection to Descartes' position on this metaphysical issue is summed up by the charge that he confused judgments and ideas. Descartes replies that his contrast between the formal falsity of judgments and the material falsity of ideas should have prevented the charge. A modern reader may misunderstand this contrast. We are likely to think Descartes intends to say that judgments, unlike ideas, have propositional form and are capable of being false and true; ideas, being more like terms, cannot be said literally to be either one. But Descartes does not hesitate to think of ideas as propositional (see Anthony Kenny, *Descartes*, 106); after all, they are representations of things. The contrast he means to make is that ideas, taken as propositional, cannot fail to be true and it is only in judgments that *falsity*, strictly taken, can occur. It may not be entirely plausible to claim, as Descartes does, that his remark about formal and material falsity makes it clear that a "materially false" idea gives opportunity for error. But in any case, Descartes fully acknowledges Arnauld's point that an idea cannot falsely *exhibit* its object.

It is not, then, Descartes' *considered* position that a false idea exhibits one thing and has another as object. What lends support to Arnauld's interpretation is Descartes' saying that a false idea "represents nothing as though it were something"; and, again, "inasmuch as there cannot be any ideas which do not appear to represent some things," if cold is a privation then "the idea which represents it to me as something real and positive" can be called false. I think we must conclude that in these rather obscure passages Descartes did *not* mean that a false idea exhibits something real and represents nonentity; he meant instead that a false idea *seems* to exhibit something positive, but *actually* exhibits nonentity. Or, extending the view more broadly, a confused and obscure idea seems to exhibit its object in a way in which it does not actually exhibit it. This is a more promising approach to our metaphysical problem, but it does not go far toward specifying a solution. Neither does it go far toward explaining error. What is it for an idea to *seem* to represent what it does not represent, over and above its being an idea about whose object we are likely to err?

The details of the doctrine pose some delicate problems. The distinction between what an idea appears to represent and what it actually does will have to be carefully drawn. What a false idea actually exhibits must be latent cognitive content, but still exhibited to mind. Objects of thought need not all be immediately accessible, but the actual object of an idea cannot be wholly veiled from recognition.[10] Moreover, what a false idea seems to exhibit threatens to become a sort of second, phantom object of thought. Do we apprehend the real quality a false idea seems to represent? There is some temptation to treat the apparent quality as an auxiliary object accompanying and obscuring the actual (non-)object of the idea. To do so is folly. If the phantom "object" is the real quality cold, there is such a (possible) quality and the idea of cold is not false. If the auxiliary object is not something real, then it is not something different from the actual object of the idea, after all. Either way, the solution to our metaphysical problem is lost. Descartes presumably did not mean that a false idea has an actual (non-)object and a phantom one.

Instead, I suggest, a false idea (or any confused, obscure idea) represents by means that are not evident from the idea itself. Descartes reminds us several times that an idea is like an image, a representation of some sort or other; and we know an idea represents truly whatever it represents. Scope for confusion and error lies in the *basis* of representation: what is it about a confused or obscure idea that (correctly) portrays its object? To someone who makes a false assumption about its representational device, a false idea seems to represent something, although really it represents nothing; more generally, to such a person, a confused and obscure idea seems to represent something it does not. Such an idea portrays its object by obscure means. A person who understands the means correctly apprehends the idea's object; one who misunderstands them is likely to make errors about its object, but still has an idea that correctly exhibits it. This resolves our two problems about false ideas and I think it is the account of false ideas Descartes intends in Meditation III.

In reply to Arnauld, Descartes does not repeat the doctrine that false ideas seem to represent something positive. He says only that he called the idea of cold materially false " . . . because, since it is obscure and confused, I cannot decide whether it displays something outside my sensation or not," and this provides opportunity for judging cold to be positive when perhaps it is not (AT VII, 234; HR II, 106–107). This is not a significant shift from his Meditation III position on how false ideas lead to error.[11] For, a false idea taken alone does not seem to represent something positive; taken alone, its representational content is merely obscure. But when the idea is viewed in the context of false assumptions about its manner of representation, it seems to exhibit what it does not. Due to its obscurity, the idea gives us opportunity to judge its object in the context of ill-considered assumptions.

This doctrine is illustrated by the discussion of sense ideas as the meditation progresses. Our initial presumption was that ideas of sense represent by exhibiting the features of material things; accordingly, it seemed that ideas of heat and cold (their representational contents) resemble physical qualities. That assumption is placed in doubt, first, by the glimpse at the end of the Second Meditation of what it is to know bodies clearly and distinctly (recalled in Meditation III [AT VII, 43; HR I, 164]). Next, no reason can be found to think these ideas resemble external objects; finally, belief in representation by exact resemblance is shown to be false for the visual idea of the sun. At this point, we can see that some sense ideas are so obscure we cannot be sure what they represent; perhaps they represent nothing. It seems they do represent something real, only because we still suppose that they *are* ideas and that ideas represent real things. If these suppositions are correct, the ideas of heat and cold are not false after all; if heat and cold are nothing, however, at least one of these basic beliefs is false. Descartes says in Meditation III that ideas of heat and cold *may* be false, but he does not declare that they are. What is at issue, besides the status of certain presentations of sense, is the truth of these background beliefs, which make it seem that felt heat and cold represent something real.

III. MEDITATION VI: THE TRUTH IN CONFUSED AND OBSCURE IDEAS

The question about presentations of heat and cold left hanging in the Third Meditation is resolved in the Sixth. I want to maintain that felt heat, cold, and so forth, turn out *not* to be false ideas. When Descartes argues that certain beliefs about sensible things are true, his reasoning presupposes that *all* ideas of sense represent material things. Doubt that ideas of heat and so forth *resemble* bodies is nevertheless raised again. Apparently these ideas are not false in that they represent nothing, but they belong to the broader class of ideas that represent obscurely. If I am right about these confused and obscure ideas, they exhibit bodies without resembling bodies in the way we initially suppose.

The foremost concerns in Meditation VI are to complete the demonstration that mind is distinct from body and to establish that corporeal substance actually exists. But Descartes goes on to examine several sorts of beliefs about objects of sense, arguing some are true and others uncertain. And, finally, he develops an account of our composite nature which reconciles our tendency to noncognitive, practical error with the perfection of our creator. My contention is that the argument for the existence of corporeal substance *presupposes* that all sorts of ideas of sense represent material things; moreover, this argument plays an essential role in distinguishing true perceptual beliefs from those that are uncertain.

To show that corporeal substance exists, Descartes first reflects that his receiving "ideas of sensible things" requires that something cause them (AT VII, 79; HR I, 191). He himself is not their cause. In the first place, the power to cause them does not presuppose a thinking nature like his own and, in the second place, he does not receive these ideas at will. The power to cause them must reside in a substance that has formally all the reality contained objectively in the ideas:

And this substance is either body, that is, a corporeal nature in which there is contained formally all that which is objectively in these ideas, or it is God Himself, or some other creature. (AT VII, 79; HR I, 191)

But he is strongly inclined to believe these ideas proceed from body, so God would deceive him if they were caused by something else. What induces the strong belief God's veracity guarantees is clearly the fact ideas of sense *exhibit* bodies (HR II, 35 and 56).

Descartes' conclusion is quite restrained. It extends to the existence of a substance of the sort we clearly and distinctly apprehend by intellect (not sense), that is, extended substance modified by figure, size, position, motion; further, this extended substance causes our "ideas of sensible things." Descartes does not go so far as to infer anything about the causes of particular sorts of ideas or the rectitude of particular perceptual beliefs. However, his only reason for thinking bodies affect our senses depends on the assumption that sense presentations exhibit material things. So, unless ideas of heat, cold, and so forth, do exhibit bodies, no *reason* for thinking they proceed from bodies has been supplied.

Descartes turns next to particular perceptual beliefs, for example, about the shape of the sun, and "things less clearly and distinctly conceived, such as light, sound, pain, and the like" (AT VII, 80; HR I, 191). He invokes two principles for examining them: that God "has not permitted any falsity to exist in my opinion which He has not likewise given me the faculty of correcting," and that "in all things which nature teaches me there is some truth contained" (AT VII, 80; HR I, 191–192). He aims to ascertain what his nature really teaches him, and to distinguish that from what may seem natural but involves detectable error.

All his spontaneous actions and unreflective beliefs are candidates for being natural. Descartes needs a way of telling which are genuinely so. His nature, taken strictly as what pertains to mind and body united, teaches him ways of acting, what to pursue and to avoid; but it does not teach him to form opinions about things outside himself without the scrutiny of pure intellect. The *opinions* taught by nature proceed from his nature taken more fully as the set of faculties that includes intellect acting alone, as well as in union with his body (see AT VII, 82; HR I, 193). What this full nature teaches, it turns out, are those habitual beliefs Descartes is able to find a *reason* to hold.

His full nature teaches him first that he has a body and that other bodies exist around his own; apparently the reason for this is the argument that shows corporeal substance to exist in accord with God's veracity. Then:

And certainly from the fact that I am sensible of different sorts of colours, sounds, scents, tastes, heat, hardness, etc., I very easily conclude that there are in the bodies from which all these diverse sense perceptions proceed certain variations which answer to them, although possibly these are not really at all similar to them. (AT VII, 81; HR I, 192)

At least part of the means of reaching this conclusion must be the same argument from God's veracity; it provides the *only reason* Descartes supplies for thinking ideas of color and the like proceed from bodies. As we have seen, that argument does not apply to these ideas unless they are taken to represent material things.

But "possibly" these ideas are not at all similar to the bodies they represent. Some things nature seems to have taught are really due only to inconsiderate judgment. Such are the beliefs that a space where there is nothing sensible is void, and:

. . . that in a body which is warm there is something entirely similar to the idea of heat which is in me; that in a white or green body there is the same whiteness or greenness that I perceive; that in a bitter or sweet body there is the same taste, and so in other instances; . . . (AT VII, 82; HR I, 193)

Descartes does not claim these opinions are false, only that he finds no reason to think them true. They are thus neither taught by nature nor guaranteed by God's truthfulness; it is an epistemic error to think ideas of heat represent by (exact) resemblance.[12]

Descartes does *not* go on to say we were wrong to think felt heat, cold, and so forth, are ideas or that they represent something real. The omission is significant because these points were at issue in Meditation III and because it is assumed in Meditation VI that (all sorts of) sense perceptions exhibit bodies. Still, Descartes proceeds cautiously. He does not affirm explicitly that felt heat and so on are ideas of material things. And he goes on to describe his former errors with regard to his senses in a way that does not commit him to treating sense presentations as representations; at this point, his account is compatible with the suggestion that they mark variations in bodies by nonrepresentational means.[13] He formerly relied on " . . . perceptions of sense . . . as though they were certain rules by which to determine immediately the essences of bodies which are outside me, concerning which they signify, in fact, nothing that is not very confused and obscure" (AT VII, 83, translation mine). I think Descartes leaves the door ajar to the view that felt heat and so on may "signify" bodies without exhibiting them; nevertheless, he *does not* close the door against the representational view.[14]

In Meditation III, doubt that ideas of heat and the like resemble bodies led to speculation that such ideas might not represent anything real. The doubt about resemblance is confirmed in Meditation VI and yet Descartes assumes all sorts of ideas of sense do exhibit bodies. What accounts for his readiness to allow that all sense ideas represent bodies, when earlier he questioned whether some do? And, further, how *can* ideas of heat and so forth exhibit bodies, if they (their representational contents) do not resemble them? I maintain the answers are that these ideas represent their objects differently from what we are likely to suppose.

When Descartes speculated earlier that ideas of heat and the like might be false, each idea was considered in isolation from other ideas of sense. In Meditation VI, sense experience is considered as a whole (see especially the quotation above from AT VII, 51 and the argument that material substance exists [AT VII, 79; HR I, 191]). When taken as elements in a more complex experience, perceptions of heat and the like have a representative character they lack when considered apart. In the context of an experience that represents bodies by other devices, striking phenomenal differences represent significant variations among bodies. But in order to play this role, ideas of heat, colors, and so on, do not need to be individual representations of bodies. It is critical to identify what the unit of representation is; it is not isolated ideas of color or heat, but a complex pattern in which these ideas are elements.[15]

Properly considered, the most obscure ideas of sense have some sort of resemblance to bodies. At least ideas of heat occur in relation to a pattern of other ideas of sense in a position analogous to the position of physical heat in relation to the bodies represented by the pattern of ideas. Obscure ideas do not resemble bodies in the respect, or to the extent, we are likely to think. But by treating sense experience as a unit within which felt heat, cold, and so forth, represent variations among bodies, Descartes preserves our deep conviction that bodies are exhibited by sense perceptions of heat, colors, sound, and the rest.[16]

Although ideas of heat, cold, and so on, offer most opportunity for error, other sense ideas are to some degree confused or obscure. The visual idea of the sun is likely to yield a false opinion about the sun's size (AT VII, 39; HR I, 161); we are reminded in Meditation VI that we can err about the shape of a distant tower and the size of a statue atop it and, further, that whatever we perceive by sense can also seem to be present in a dream (AT VII, 76–77; HR I, 189). I think Descartes' view on confusion, obscurity, and error involving these other ideas is similar to his account of the ideas of heat and so forth.[17] That is, none of these *mis*represents its object, but we misjudge its object when we have false assumptions about how it represents.

It turns out, then, that obscurity in all ideas of sense takes much the same form, as does the way to avoid false judgments. The problem is that we take one or two ideas to exhibit actual things, when in fact it is a larger segment of experience that (correctly) represents them. Near the end of the *Meditations*, Descartes finds his reflections on his senses enable him to avoid mistakes about particular objects of sense. For he knows that all his senses usually indicate truly what benefits his body:

. . . and being able almost always to avail myself of many [senses] in order to examine one particular thing, and, besides that, being able to make use of my memory in order to connect the present with the past, and of my understanding which already has discovered all the causes of my errors, I ought no longer to fear that falsity may be found in matters every day presented to me by my senses. (AT VII, 89; HR I, 198)

More over, the place of a single perception in the course of sense experienc(as a whole is crucial in assuring him that he is not dreaming:[18]

> . . . cur memory can never connect our dreams one with the other, or with the whole course of our lives, as it units events which happen to us while we are awake. . . . But when . . . I can connect the perceptions which I have of them with the whole course of my life, I am perfectly assured that these perceptions occur while I am waking and not during sleep. (AT VII, 89–90; HR I, 199)

In sum, we find that ideas of heat and the like represent physical qualities in the context of a larger pattern of ideas; a perception of an object's size or shape (correctly) represents only in connection with perceptions of the object from many senses and various circumstances; and, finally, nothing short of the whole course of one's experience represents actual things (vs. things dreamed). There is no firm rule about how large a segment of experience is the unit of representation in a particular case (although God's perfection ensures there is one). Descartes concludes the meditation acknowledging the "infirmity of our nature," because the press of affairs often forces us to judge particular things "before having leisure to examine matters carefully" (AT VII, 90; HR I, 199). Deep in this observation is a suggestion of the ineliminable element of obscurity in ideas of sense.[19]

NOTES

The abbreviations AT and HR are explained in the General Bibliography at the beginning of this volume.

1. See e.g., E. M. Curley, "Descartes, Spinoza and the Ethics of Belief" in *Spinoza: Essays in Interpretation*, ed. Maurice Mandelbaum and Eugene Freeman (La Salle, Ill.: Open Court, 1975); Bernard Williams, *Descartes: the Project of Pure Enquiry* (London: Penguin, 1978), chap. 6; Margaret D. Wilson, *Descartes* (London: Routledge & Kegan Paul, 1978), 139–150.

2. Margaret Wilson (in her *Descartes*, chap. 3) discusses these passages from Meditation III, Arnauld's Objections and Descartes' Reply. I differ on several points of interpretation and analysis. Nevertheless, I consider Wilson to have done the ground-breaking work on the topic of false ideas.

3. The exact wording is important for matters at issue in this essay: " . . . duas diversas solis ideas apud me invenio, unam tanquam a sensibus haustam, . . . per quam mihi valde parvus *apparet*, aliam verò ex rationibus Astronomiae desumptam, . . . per quam aliquoties major quàm terra *exhibetur*; utraque *profecto* similis eidem soli extra me existenti esse non potest, & ratio persuadet illam ei maxime esse dissimilem, quae quàm proxime ab ipso videtur emanasse." AT VII, 39, emphasis added.

4. Ideas are said to be like images several times: AT VII, 37 and 42; HR I, 159 and 163; in addition, in the French version: AT IX–1, 31 and 34; HR I, 162 and 164. Ideas are also called *similitudinem* (AT VII, 37), as well as *tableaux* (AT IX–1, 33).

5. See e.g., AT VII, 39, 40, 43, 44 (for this last, HR I, 165).

6. Descartes explains in his preface (AT VII, 8; HR I, 138) that *idea* is ambiguous. The word can mean an entity that exists only as an object of thought (vs. existing in the actual world); in this sense, a chimera is an idea. The word can also be used to refer to a modification of mind that represents such an entity; we have the idea of a chimera. When Descartes says in Meditation III that *ideas* can be considered either as modifications of mind or as images representing various things (AT VII, 40; HR I, 161–162), I take it he uses "idea" in the second sense and that the things ideas represent include "ideas" in the first sense, as well as things in the actual world.

7. Even if the idea of heat is merely a sensation that represents nothing, it is a modification of mind which, it seems, requires a positive cause. Wilson (*Descartes*, 111) suggests what seems to me the answer to this.

8. The term *false idea* is used in this broader way twice in the Replies: AT VII, 144 and 363; HR II, 41 and 215. There is an interesting shift in the treatment of false ideas in *Discourse on Method* and *Meditations*, but there is not space to discuss it here; cf. AT VI, 33–34; HR I, 102, and AT VI, 38; HR I, 104–105.

9. More recently, this interpretation is given by Anthony Kenny, in *Descartes: A Study of His Philosophy* (New York: Random House, 1968), 120–121.

10. On latent content of ideas, also see AT VII, 147; HR II, 43; on latent content of clear and distinct ideas, AT VII, 371; HR II, 220.

11. Compare Margaret Wilson (*Descartes*, 115–116), who urges that the account of false ideas in Meditation III is significantly different from that in the Fourth Replies. The latter is less successful in explaining error, she argues, because an idea's obscurity is cited to explain both why we cannot tell whether its object is positive and why we falsely judge that it is positive; moreover, even if that could be resolved, Descartes' saying that false ideas provide opportunity for error is a decidedly weak explanation of the fact of error. There is, I suggest, no conflict between the claim that a false idea (considered in itself) provides opportunity for error and the claim that a false idea seems (in the context of false assumptions about its manner of representation) to represent what it does not actually represent. The two claims together explain the occurrence of error.

12. Charles Larmore, in "Descartes' Empirical Epistemology" in *Descartes: Philosophy, Mathematics and Physics*, ed. Stephen Gaukroger (New Jersey: Barnes & Noble, 1980), correctly observes that Descartes' physics is required to show that it is *false* that these ideas resemble physical qualities. But he overlooks the fact that the *Meditations* argues quite independently of physical theory that it is an *epistemic* error to think sense ideas resemble bodies.

13. Descartes clearly takes this sort of view in other works. In *Le Monde*, he points out that words signify things they do not resemble, but still bring

to mind ideas of those things; in a similar way, he suggests, sensations (and corporeal impressions) are set up by nature to signify to mind material things they do not resemble (hence, do not represent) (AT XI, 3–6). A doctrine of "natural signs" clearly appears later in Meditation VI in connection with practical errors (actions harmful to the body); certain "cerebral motions" are "signs" to the mind to form certain sensations accompanied by inclinations to act (e.g., pain, thirst, but also "all the other perceptions of our senses") (AT VII, 87–88; HR I, 197). But here cerebral motions are not "signs" the reading of which involves formation of *beliefs* about external things. Several commentators seem to me much too quick to say that in the *Meditations* sensations of heat, etc., are linked to beliefs about bodies by a doctrine of "natural signs"; e.g., Martial Gueroult, *Descartes selon l'ordre des raisons* (Paris: Aubier, 1968), 2 vols, 2:91 f.; John W. Yolton, "Perceptual Cognition with Descartes," *Studia Cartesiana* 2 (1981):63–83.

Further, in *Principles*, Descartes declares outright that felt heat, etc., are "sensations" that "represent nothing outside the mind" and contrasts them to "perceptions" of size, shape and motion, which exhibit modes of external things (I, 71). Here sensations are not said to "signify" bodies; instead, the senses "stimulate" formation of clear and distinct ideas (presumably not sensory) of extended substance (II, 1).

14. Although the representational view I ascribe to the *Meditations* and a doctrine of natural signs are significantly different accounts of how sensations refer the mind to bodies, they are not mutually incompatible.

15. Descartes repeatedly says an image does not resemble its object in every detail (e.g., AT VII, 373; HR II, 221). *La Dioptrique* provides an especially lucid warning about regarding sense impressions as images (AT VI, 112–113).

16. Wilson observes (*Descartes*, 119) that Descartes' position in the *Principles* is implausible because it takes felt heat, etc., to be *presented as* sensations without representational content, while perceptions of size, figure, and motion are supposed to exhibit bodies.

17. Descartes reveals in Replies that ideas or perceptions of colors, etc., belong exclusively to sense, whereas judgments about external objects and perceptions of their sizes, shapes, and distances from the perceiver derive from the understanding in response to perceptions of sense (AT VII, 436–437; HR II, 251–252). I take it Descartes intends to hold that thoughts derived from the understanding, as well as the perceptions of sense, involve ideas that represent the objects of thought; in addition to passages already mentioned from Meditation III, see AT VII, 160–161; HR II, 52.

18. It is, of course, unclear how much assurance this provides in practice, for one could merely dream that a certain experience is connected with the course of one's life. I suspect that Descartes did not overlook this point and that it is an especially poignant part of what he means by the remark that ends the Meditation.

19. I want to express my appreciation to Amélie Rorty for very stimulating conversation about matters in this essay, and to Margaret Wilson, who supplied useful comments on an earlier version.

17

Will and the Theory of Judgment

DAVID M. ROSENTHAL

Contemporary discussions typically give somewhat sort shrift to the theory of judgment Descartes advances in the Fourth Meditation.[1] One reason for this relative neglect is presumably the prima facie implausibility of the theory. It sounds odd to say that, in believing something, one's mental affirmation is an act of free will, on a par with freely deciding what to do. In addition, Descartes advances the theory as a way to explain the possibility of human error, which doubtless strikes many as a rather esoteric undertaking. The need to explain error, moreover, arises because of the divine guarantee, and epistemic theodicy is a project unlikely to interest most contemporary readers. And because the theory of judgment postulates two mental faculties, it very probably evokes the general skepticism, and even hostility, we now have toward faculty psychologies of the sort that flourished in the nineteenth century.

Lack of interest in, and sympathy for, Descartes' theory of judgment is doubtless reinforced by the impression that the theory is relatively independent of Descartes' main position. In broad outline, the central argument of the *Meditations* consists of a vigorous challenge to all our claims to have knowledge, followed by a systematic reinstatement of much of that knowledge, newly based on solid epistemological procedures and reformulated in clear and distinct terms. Aside from Meditation IV, every Meditation after the First sets out to rehabilitate some area of knowledge that Meditation I had called into question.

Meditation IV, alone, seems to stand apart from this progressive reconstituting of knowledge. The theory of judgment can therefore come across as being relatively inessential for understanding the remaining Meditations.

My aim in this paper is to show that Descartes' theory of judgment and, in particular, his view about the role the will plays in judging, actually give us a satisfactory and penetrating account of the nature of mental acts. And I also argue that, contrary to initial appearances, that theory is an important and integral part of Descartes' overall position, and that we cannot correctly understand his views about mind and methodology without appeal to the theory of judgment.

In section I, I argue that the theory is the natural and inevitable result of conclusions Descartes has reached earlier in the *Meditations* about the nature of the mind. In section II, I address the role of the will in judging. I argue that whatever initial impression we may have that the will plays no such role is unfounded. I also show how Descartes' appeal to the will fits well with, and even helps explain, our commonsense conception of the nature of mental acts. In section III, then, I take up and rebut the most important and penetrating objections to the theory, objections that might keep one not only from accepting it but even from giving it serious consideration. In section IV, finally, I briefly indicate a few of the ways in which it can be shown that the two-faculty theory of judgment helps us understand, and even defend, a number of doctrines Descartes holds about mind and methodology. To illustrate the importance of the theory in Descartes' thought, I discuss some of the consequences the theory has concerning the relation of language to thought, the doctrine of compelled assent, the role of doubt in the *Meditations*, and the *cogito*.

I. THE TWO-FACULTY THEORY

The problem that Descartes intends the theory of judgment to solve stems from the divine guarantee of Meditation III. The infinite perfection of his creator leads Descartes to conclude that he could have no "faculty that, rightly used, could lead [him] to err" (AT VII, 53–54; HR I, 172)[2] and, indeed, no "faculty that is not perfect of its kind [*in suo genere*]" (AT VII, 55; HR I, 173). But errors do occur, and their occurrence "argue[s] that there is some imperfection in me" (AT VII, 56; HR I, 174). The problem is to square the imperfection in my mental nature that my errors indicate with the perfection that the divine guarantee confers on my faculties.

The way Descartes structures the preceding discussion makes this problem especially pressing. For one and the same set of considerations leads both to the discovery of my imperfection and to the divine guarantee. My doubting and desiring of things indicates a lack in me, thereby establishing that I am finite and imperfect. But, Descartes argues, I could not comprehend or recognize my own imperfection and finitude unless I already had, as a standard for comparison, an idea of what it is to be perfect and infinite, that is, an idea of an infinitely perfect being (AT VII, 45–46; HR I, 166). And only such a being could cause in me that idea. Descartes stresses that the conflict that Meditation IV is meant to resolve arises, in this way, from a single set of factors. For, in the opening paragraph of that Meditation, he summarizes the situation by reminding us that "when I direct my attention to . . . my being an incomplete and dependent thing, a clear and distinct idea occurs to me of an independent and complete being . . . " (AT VII, 53; HR I, 171–172).

Accounts of Descartes' solution usually emphasize the obvious analogy with traditional moral theodicy. Only if "rightly used" is it impossible for my faculty of judging to lead to errors. So a satisfactory solution must credit me with sufficient freedom of will in my making judgments to explain my errors as due to the wanton use of my faculty of judging. Difficulties for the theory then seem immediately to arise. Descartes also holds that "it is not possible for [him] not to judge something he apprehends as clearly [as the *cogito*] to be true" (AT VII, 58; HR I, 176). It seems he must therefore offer a contorted and ad hoc account of our freedom in making judgments, an account that undermines whatever little analogy does hold between judging falsely and wanton wrongdoing. And we do not, in any case, appear actually to have the kind of freedom in making judgments that the analogy requires.

Descartes himself stresses the ways in which his theory of judging relies on analogies with moral behavior (e.g., letter to Mersenne: AT IV, 173; K, 159–160). Indeed, in section II, I exploit such analogies in arguing that the theory is, despite initial appearances, intuitively natural. But the particular analogy with traditional theodicy is highly misleading as a model for understanding the problem Descartes meant his theory to deal with. What is crucial is not the way in which freedom does or does not figure in our judging, but whether the faculty of judging is a single, unified aspect of our mental nature. Descartes' formulation of the problem makes this clear.

At the outset of Meditation IV, just after reviewing his earlier conclusion that deception implies imperfection, Descartes writes that "I experienced in myself a certain faculty of judging [*judicandi facultatem*]" (AT VII, 53; HR I, 172). The past tense here presumably refers to the end of Meditation II, where he had used the same phrase, *judicandi facultas*, to talk about whatever it is in his mind (*in mente meâ*) that enables him to judge, for example, that the things moving in the street are people, and not merely hats and coats. The issue in the earlier passage is whether Descartes knows the wax "by eyesight" or "solely by an inspection of the mind" (AT VII, 32; HR I, 155–156). The faculty of judgment is mentioned there as whatever it is in his mental nature that enables him to make judgments. It is that aspect of his mental nature which makes judging possible.

There is nothing difficult or problematic about Descartes' notion of a faculty. It is just the power or capacity to do something. Nor is there anything questionable about his inference that a faculty of judging exists. He makes judgments, so he must have the capacity to do so. The reasoning is from the exercise of a capacity to its existence. As he explains to Arnauld:

> . . . we always have actual consciousness of the actions and operations of our mind; but not always of faculties or powers [*facultatum, sive potentiarum*], except potentially; so that when we turn ourselves to the exercise of any faculty, if that faculty is in the mind, we become actually aware of it. (AT VII, 246–247; HR II, 115)[3]

Although it is unproblematic in the Second Meditation, the idea of a faculty of judging leads to difficulties in the Fourth. Errors are just false judgments. So my faculty of judging is that aspect of my mental nature which is responsible for my errors. Since my errors "argue that there is some imperfection in me," that imperfection must pertain to my faculty of judging. But I can have no faculty that is not perfect of its kind. So, if my faculty of judging is a single, undifferentiated aspect of my mental nature, we have a contradiction. An aspect of my nature that, by the divine guarantee, is perfect of its kind, gives rise to errors and is thus imperfect.

Since my faculty of judging is just whatever aspect of my nature enables me to make judgments, I can hope to learn more about that faculty by examining the character of those judgments. In particular, I may be able thus to learn whether the faculty responsible for my judgments is a single aspect of my nature, as it initially appears to be (AT VII, 32; HR I, 156), or instead involves more than one factor. What it is to be a judgment may help us learn what it is in us that makes them possible. This is clearly Descartes' strategy. For it is upon "investigating the nature of my errors [*qualesnam sint errores mei*]" that he announces his view that they "depend on two concurrent causes": the faculty of understanding, and the faculty of choosing (*eligendi*) or free will (AT VII, 56; HR I, 174).

What is it about the nature of his errors that convinces Descartes that they "depend" on the interaction of two distinct faculties? Descartes says nothing about the nature of his errors in or around the passage just quoted. So it is reasonable to conclude that he regards himself as having investigated their nature earlier. And, since errors are just false judgments, he has in fact done so when, in Meditation III, he inquires what it is that truth and falsity, properly speaking, consist in.

In that passage, Descartes "divide[s] all [his] thoughts [*cogitationes*] into certain kinds." The division is twofold: ideas, properly so called, and "others," such as volitions and judgments. Ideas are somewhat like (*tanquam*) images, presumably in that they purport to represent things. The "others" share this representative character; they also are always about things. But they have an additional aspect (*alias . . . formas*), which is exemplified "when I desire, when I fear, when I affirm, when I deny." Ideas cannot properly be said to be false—nor, presumably, true; the same holds of volitions. Only judgments can be true or false (AT VII, 36–37; HR I, 159–160).

Descartes' division here is clearly based on the structure of propositional attitudes. Judgments, being true and false, must be propositional. But they also involve an aspect in addition to the representative character they share with ideas, an aspect exemplified by desiring, fearing, affirming, and denying. The additional aspect must therefore be the mental attitude that, together with propositional content, constitutes all mental acts. And, since these mental acts result from adding a mental attitude to an idea, ideas must be just propositional contents.[4] Descartes impatiently explains the passage to Hobbes by an analogy. An idea is like seeing a lion, or seeing a person run, presumably because both involve only a representing of something. Fearing a lion "at the same time," and affirming to oneself that one sees that person running, are different, since they involve also some mental attitude (AT VII, 182–183; HR II, 69). That the structure of propositional attitudes underlies Descartes' division of "all [his] thoughts" is also attested by his giving catalogues of propositional mental acts when he explains, in Meditations II and III, what it is to be a thinking thing (AT VII, 28 and 34; HR I, 153 and 157).

There is indirect textual evidence for thinking that Descartes has the division of Meditation III in mind when, in the next Meditation,

he talks of investigating the nature of his errors. In the Third Meditation passage, he begins by considering "all [his] thoughts," and asking
"in which of them truth and falsity consist." But having made his
division, he then speaks, in the next paragraph, only of judgments
being false, and not also of their being true. So that paragraph turns
out to be about just those of our judgments which are errors.

In any case, Descartes' division does explain how the nature of
errors and, more generally, of judgments, prompts his two-faculty
theory. The propositional content of any particular judgment can occur
without the mental attitude that goes into that judgment, for it can
occur with many other mental attitudes. Similarly, affirming and denying, which are the mental attitudes distinctive of judging, can occur
without the propositional content that is involved in any particular
judgment. These two aspects of judgments—their attitude and content—are therefore distinct components. In Descartes' technical terminology, they are modally distinct (*Principles* I, 61: AT VIII–1, 29;
HR I, 244). When in Meditation II Descartes takes judgments to be
undifferentiated unities, the making of judgments was sufficient to
make him aware of a faculty, or power, that makes judging possible.
His new awareness in Meditation III of the two distinct components
of judgments accordingly leads, in the Fourth Meditation, to his awareness of two corresponding faculties: a faculty whose exercise supplies
propositional content, and another whose exercise results in the holding of mental attitudes.

The two-faculty theory of judging, therefore, does not result from
any analogy with the role played by free will in traditional theodicy.
Rather, the theory is a direct response to the difficulty of conceiving
of judgments as being due to a single, undifferentiated aspect of our
mental nature. By itself, the idea that more than one cognitive capacity
plays a role in our making judgments, and that the interaction of such
capacities helps explain how some judgments end up being erroneous,
is neither novel nor in conflict with common sense. But one of the
factors common sense tends to regard as playing a role in judging is
sense perception. This Descartes' dualism does not allow. For he
holds that sensory qualities are products of the interaction between
body and mind (AT VII, 81; HR I, 192). And, as the wax passage
makes clear, he thinks of judging as a purely mental activity. So, if
judging is to involve more than one cognitive capacity, the faculties
Descartes invokes must all be purely mental.

That judging should involve understanding things is straightforward enough. The problem is about Descartes' deploying the faculty
of will as the other factor. If he does not do so because of an analogy

with the role free will plays in traditional theodicy, we must ask whether he has any satisfactory reason for claiming that it figures at all in our making judgments, and for giving the account he does of the will and of what it is for the will to be free. It has seemed to most commentators that the role he assigns free will in his theory of judging is both unmotivated and misguided. Thus Zeno Vendler, for example, suggests that Descartes assigned the task of generating mental attitudes to the will only because "nothing but the will is available in the scholastic arsenal besides the understanding to handle the higher functions of man."[5] I want now to argue that far more compelling considerations are available to explain Descartes' appeal to the will.

II. MOTIVATION AND EXPLANATORY VALUE

When Descartes divides all his thoughts in Meditation III, he mentions four mental attitudes: desiring, fearing, affirming, and denying. Affirming and denying are the two kinds of judging that involve opposing mental attitudes one can take toward a proposition. Desiring and fearing also have the structure of propositional attitudes, and again involve opposing attitudes. If we attributed the attitude of desiring to the operation of any faculty, it would be the will. So it is reasonable to regard fearing, insofar as it is a propositional attitude and not a bodily feeling, as due to an aversive act of the will. That Descartes has these considerations in mind seems clear from the parallel passage in the *Principles* (I, 32); there, the mental attitudes he lists as due to the operation of the will are desiring (*cupere*), aversion (*aversari*), affirming, denying, and doubting (AT VIII–1, 17; HR I, 232). Descartes' aim is to find some faculty whose operation explains the mental-attitude component of these and other mental acts. For it is reasonable to hold that the faculty of understanding explains the propositional content of mental acts; we cannot perform any mental act without understanding its propositional content (letter to Regius: AT VIII, 372; K, 102). The will is the obvious candidate to explain the mental attitudes of two of the most salient mental acts: desire and aversion. It is thus natural to try out the hypothesis that its operation is responsible for all other mental attitudes as well.

This hypothesis is, of course, far from initially compelling. The will's involvement with one pair of mental attitudes does not imply any connection with the other. And the traditional view of the will is that, whatever its role in conative mental acts, it plays none whatever in cognitive acts. Moreover, there seems to be no obvious reason to take conative acts as paradigms of mental acts generally, especially since they figure far from prominently in the lists of mental acts Descartes gives.

It will help here to see exactly what role the will does appear to play in the conative cases. For only then will it be clear whether parallel considerations apply to cognitive mental acts. The most compelling reason to associate the will with conative attitudes is the connection those attitudes have with action. Though this consideration is of course unavailable in Meditation IV, it is nonetheless central to the way we think about the will and the way it operates. The more intense a desire or aversion is, the stronger we expect its impact on action to be. Moreover, the strength of desires and aversions is at least in part a function of the object of desire or aversion. Highly attractive or repellent objects prompt powerful conative attitudes— powerful both in their felt intensity and in their probable effect on action. When two incompatible options have us undecided, we may feel torn, or pulled in opposite directions, and the opposing tendencies to affect action may then cancel each other, or come close to doing so.

There is a popular paradigm, according to which we can abstract from the great variety of kinds of mental attitudes we have, and explain behavior as due simply to the combined operation of systems of interrelated beliefs and desires. On this model, beliefs contribute the cognitive content required for behavior, and the impetus for action is due solely to our desires. However useful this model may be as a theory or an experimental paradigm, it is quite misleading when applied to the actual dynamics of our mental lives. Our desires always have cognitive content; they could not be formulated save in propositional or conceptual terms. And beliefs are no less necessary for causing actions than desires. It is common to note that somebody with many beliefs but no desires will presumably do nothing. But a person with desires but no beliefs would be no less inactive, and no less mentally paralyzed.

Once we correct for the distortion the belief-desire model tends to induce, it is clear that the considerations that lead us to associate the will with conative mental attitudes apply as well to mental acts such as judging, doubting, and the like. We experience beliefs, doubts, and affirmative and negative judgments as having different intensities, just as we do with desires and aversions. And the more firmly we believe, doubt, and judge, the stronger the tendency is for us to do whatever, in the context of our other mental states, that belief, doubt, or judgment inclines us to do. A strong desire coupled with a weak belief may well be no more likely to lead to action than a weak desire accompanied by a strong belief.

Do the objects of belief affect the intensity or firmness with which we believe things, in the way that attractive or repellent objects affect the intensity of our desires or aversions?[6] The answer to this question requires care. For we may slip into thinking that the objects of belief and desire are different sorts of things. What we believe is, of course, propositional; but it is tempting to think that what we desire are the objects, typically extramental objects, whose acquisition would satisfy our desires. The present context, however, plainly requires that we take the objects of desire and aversion to be propositional, just like those of belief. It is not because a particular painting, say, is so attractive that one desires it so strongly; it is because the idea of one's having it is so attractive. The more attractive the idea, the more intense our desire.

It is clear that parallel remarks apply to belief. The objects of beliefs do affect the intensity with which we believe things in the way the objects of desire do with our desiring. Indeed, this observation is pivotal to Descartes' view about the role in cognition of clear and distinct perception. When a proposition we believe is cognitively highly attractive—that is, plausible—we believe it with greater conviction than we believe only moderately plausible propositions. Of course, how attractive a proposition is, cognitively, may well be affected by lots of extrinsic factors: our other beliefs, and conative factors such as laziness, habit, or a desire to deceive ourselves. But the same is true of the objects of our desires and aversions. The overall attractiveness of the idea of getting or avoiding something is often a product of factors in addition to how intrinsically attractive that idea is.

Some propositional objects of both belief and desire are, of course, highly attractive in their own right, independent of any such extrinsic factors. Elementary mathematical propositions are cognitively very attractive, regardless of what else we believe or desire. In the conative realm, the propositions that I survive and that I not suffer are intrinsically highly attractive. These propositions, when they enter into suitable mental acts, induce in us very intensely felt beliefs and desires, which have a proportionately powerful effect in determining what we do.

Perhaps there are propositional objects of belief or desire that owe their high degree of attractiveness solely to their intrinsic character. Then, perhaps, when they entered in a clearly recognizable way into our beliefs and desires, their effect on our mental lives would be overwhelming and irresistible, no matter what else we believed and desired. Such is Descartes' view about the effect some propositional contents have, cognitively, when we distinctly and attentively apprehend them (AT VII, 58–59, 69–70, 144–145; HR I, 176, 183–184, II, 41).

But whatever our verdict about that view, it is reasonable to conclude that the propositional objects of judgments, like those of desires and aversions, do affect the intensity and conviction with which we make our judgments. If so, the principal considerations that lead us to associate the will with our conative mental acts apply equally to our cognitive mental attitudes.

Despite those considerations, however, we feel that what we desire is up to us in a way that what we believe is not (see W, 145 and C, 176–178). And it is likely to strike us that this disanalogy undermines the idea that the will plays any role in our believing things. It is only when the mental attitude we adopt is up to us, one may argue, that the will is operative. But when highly attractive objects are in question, we speak of being gripped or even overcome by desire; the more powerfully an object of desire moves us, the less it is up to us whether or not we shall desire it. The more indifferent we are about such objects, the more control we can readily exert over the relevant desires. Belief behaves similarly. We have little control over whether to believe things when they strike us as obvious or clear. But when there is nothing we understand to be obvious about a matter, one way or the other, we can choose to remain uncommitted, or to hazard a guess about which way things are. The result is not a strongly held belief. But, as noted, strongly held desires are also not readily within our control.

So far, the considerations that lead us to assign some role to the will in desiring have applied equally to believing. We have encountered no disanalogy between believing and desiring that would argue against a parallel role for the will in belief. Moreover, there are positive reasons to conclude that the will does play such a role. The firmness with which we hold some of our convictions and the passion with which we announce and argue for them suggest that the force of will is at work. And people sometimes seem willful in the way they hold onto certain cherished beliefs. We speak of changing our minds both when we change what we believe and when we change what we want. Changing one's mind in either case suggests some control over our mental lives and, accordingly, the operation of some degree of will power.

In these kinds of cases, it is natural to think of the will as having something to do with the forming of our beliefs. Moreover, our not noticing the will at work in other cases of believing is no reason to conclude that it is not operative there as well. For we typically notice the operation of the will only when we need to exert some effort. And, as noted in section I, Descartes does not hold that we are invariably aware of our "faculties, or powers"; it is only "when we turn ourselves to the exercise of any faculty . . . that we become actually aware of it" (AT VII, 246–247; HR II, 115). The will, whatever else is clear about it, has to do with effecting things in our mental lives. So we would only "turn ourselves to [its] exercise" when some notable effort is called for. Indeed, even with conative mental acts, we do not generally notice the operation of the will unless we must make some unusual effort in connection with those acts. Nonetheless, we regard the will as contributing to all our conative acts, whether or not they require particular effort. The cases just considered in which the will seems to make some contribution to cognitive mental acts—changes of mind, passionately held beliefs, and willful believing—all involve a kind of cognitive exertion usually absent in our believing. If we notice the will only when some special effort is involved, then our noticing it in these cases of believing is good reason to conclude that it is operative, albeit unnoticed, in all other cases, as well.

Part of what leads Descartes to think that the will makes an essential contribution to our judging is the role played in judging by our understanding things. Understanding is not believing. But presumably we cannot believe anything that we do not at all understand (as Descartes notes: letter to Hyperaspistes: AT III, 432; K, 118). One may claim to believe an abstruse mathematical theorem, without understanding it at all. But in such a case one is commonly claiming only imperfect understanding, and not none at all. In the absence of any understanding, one could not actually believe the theorem; one could at best believe only that whatever mathematicians mean by those words is true.

Sometimes, moreover, our understanding something seems to suffice for our believing it. Having been puzzled by something, I may finally say, with an air of achievement, "Now I understand!" We would typically take this to mean that I now also believe it, and do so as the direct result of having come to understand it. This phenomenon may seem most at home in the context of mathematical learning, but it occurs elsewhere as well. When we have strong convictions it is natural to think that others who do not share them simply do not understand. How else, we may ask, could they help but believe as we do? And in any context we can say "I don't understand" as a way of indicating that I don't believe, either because the matter seems not to make sense or simply because I do not see what would lead anybody to believe it. These idiomatic ways of speaking suggest that we take it for granted that, although understanding is not, by itself, believing, it can have a powerful effect on what we believe, perhaps sometimes sufficiently powerful to determine singlehandedly what our beliefs are.

These considerations help explain why people sometimes seem willful in believing as they do, and how passions become aroused over
beliefs. People appear to us to be willful in believing when we think
that an unclouded understanding of things would clearly incline them
to believe differently; they seem to be refusing to let their understanding of things so incline them. People become passionate in their beliefs
when others disagree with them, and they think an unclouded understanding of things would clearly incline everybody to believe similarly.
In these kinds of cases, people sometimes seem almost to be fighting
just to fuel and sustain their beliefs. This kind of phenomenon obviously occurs with ideological matters, but it can occur whatever the
issue. It occurs whenever we think that somebody's understanding
of things has less influence than it should not only on what that
person believes but on how strongly the person believes it. Such
occurrences lend additional support to the idea that the will plays a
crucial role in forming our beliefs. In these cases, it is the particular
way that our believing is affected by how well we understand things
that intuitively indicates some operation of will power. Descartes'
theory that the will and understanding collaborate in giving rise to
judgments no less than desires is thus far better motivated than most
commentators have thought. For it fits strikingly well with, and even
enables us to explain, many commonsense observations about the
ways we come by and hold onto our beliefs. I therefore turn now to
specific objections that have been raised to the theory.

III. MEETING OBJECTIONS

It is tempting to think that the idea that willing plays a role in our
believing as we do is tantamount to saying that our beliefs result from
decisions we make about what to believe (see W, 145; C, 175–178).
But we typically decide things only when they are up to us, or in any
case seem to be. And it is not generally up to us what to believe, at
least not in any obvious or straightforward way (see W, 149). This is
not Descartes' picture. Decisions are themselves mental acts in their
own right, consisting of propositional content and a suitable mental
attitude. Descartes' theory is not that to judge or believe we must
first perform some conative mental act. It is that the faculty of will
contributes the mental attitudes that enter into judging and believing,
just as it contributes the mental attitudes that go into desires, decisions, and the like. On this theory, the will cannot produce desires
or decisions on its own, but only in tandem with the understanding.

The will is simply that mental capacity by virtue of which I incline (*propendeo*), in one direction or another, with respect to various propositional contents (AT VII, 57–58; HR I, 175).

But, if the will is the faculty by virtue of which we incline with respect to propositional contents, does it also supply the special impetus and motive force that accompanies conative mental acts? If not, what faculty does so? And if so, does Descartes' theory conflate two very different tasks: that of providing mental attitudes for mental acts generally, and that of supplying the distinctive impulse to action that characterizes conative mental acts in particular? Descartes' answers to these questions are clear once we note that, on his view, the motive force that distinguishes conative mental acts is not strictly a function of the mind. It is one aspect of the causal connection between mind and body: the tendency some mental acts have to issue in bodily behavior. Descartes would thus regard no mental faculty as responsible for that motive force. The will functions solely to provide mental attitudes for mental acts of whatever sort.

The two objections just considered both rely on the idea that judging and believing are kinds of actions. In the case of ordinary, nonmental actions, such as walking, the will makes its contribution by way of our decisions to perform those actions, and by seeming somehow to provide the impetus that issues in our actually performing them. Describing judging and believing as mental acts may encourage us to regard them as kinds of actions, though it is probable that calling something a mental act originally meant no more than that it was a mental actuality. In any event, Descartes says things that seem explicitly to invite the assimilation of mental acts to ordinary actions. It is not unusual for him to describe volitions as actions (e.g., letters to Mesland: AT IV, 113; K, 148, and to Elizabeth: AT IV, 310; K, 178). And he goes along with Gassendi (AT VII, 259; HR II, 137) in counting thoughts (*cogitationes*) as kinds of actions (*actiones*) (AT VII, 352; HR II, 207).

But Descartes also distinguishes two sorts of action: "actions of the soul, which terminate in the soul itself, . . . [and] actions that terminate in our body," such as walking (*Passions* I, xviii: AT XI, 343; HR I, 340). We cannot, accordingly, simply assume that whatever holds of nonmental actions holds also of thoughts. One difference is plain. In the case of bodily actions, we may will some action without that action's actually taking place. This cannot happen with thoughts; in that context, Descartes is explicit that "we never will anything without at the same time understanding it" (letter to Regius: AT III, 372; K, 102; cf. letter to Hyperaspistes: AT III, 432; K, 118). No more is needed to have a complete thought than the joint contributions of the will and understanding. Willing, in the case of "actions of the soul," cannot occur apart from the complete action. This disanalogy suffices to undermine the two objections just raised.

In many cases, what we understand is not the sort of thing that leads ineluctably to any affirmation or denial; in others, our understanding is too confused to have that effect. Margaret Dauler Wilson raises the question of how, in such cases, Descartes can explain our making any judgment at all. Why, in these cases, would the will incline us in any direction at all (W, 144)? Of course Descartes holds that we should, in such circumstances, "abstain from offering any judgment." As an example, he professes cognitive indifference about whether a thinking nature is the same as or distinct from a corporeal nature, since at that point in Meditation IV he has not yet arrived at a clear understanding of the issue (AT VII, 59; HR I, 176). Wilson's point is that it is unclear, on Descartes' theory, why such abstention would not be automatic, since the will is indifferent to what we do not understand. In this light it seems surprising that Descartes holds instead that this indifference actually contributes to our making false judgments (AT VII, 58; HR I, 175–176). False judgments, like any others, require some mental attitude. But if the will is really indifferent, why would it—indeed, how could it—contribute any such attitude?

Wilson suggests that Descartes may have thought that "a kind of lust for knowledge leads us to affirm or deny things we are not justified in believing or disbelieving" (ibid.). And Descartes' insistence that the scope of the will's operation greatly exceeds that of the understanding does evoke a picture of the will's bounding impetuously ahead, heedless of whatever directives do or do not issue from the understanding. The tendency sometimes to regard Descartes' thought as containing a Platonic strain may reinforce this idea, by calling to mind the *Phaedrus* myth of the charioteer and horses (246 ff., esp. 253D–254E).

But Descartes actually advances a different explanation of why the will supplies a mental attitude when we understand things imperfectly. Earlier, he had noted that his "principal and most frequent error . . . consists in the circumstance that I judge ideas, which are in me, to be similar or conform to things situated outside me" (AT VII, 37; HR I, 160). In Meditation VI, he explains how such errors arise. Our bodily sensations and the sensory qualities of our perceptions are ordered so as to be most conducive to the conservation of the healthy person (AT VII, 87; HR I, 197). The will thus acts innocently enough when it provides mental attitudes for ideas based on such sensations.

Errors arise, however, when we misinterpret these perceptions. Perceptions are "given by nature for the purpose of signifying to my mind what is favorable or unfavorable to the [mind-body] composite of which my mind is a part." Errors result when I take my perceptions to indicate, instead, the character of external objects, that is, when "I use [my perceptions] somewhat like rules for immediately discerning what the essence is of bodies situated outside us." Such misinterpretation constitutes "a new difficulty," beyond those noted in Meditation IV, which induces a multitude of errors (AT VII, 83; HR I, 194).

Understanding something involves interpreting it, that is, formulating some conception of what it is. Some misinterpreting something implies that one has a faulty understanding of it. Accordingly, when we misinterpret our perceptions, by viewing them as resembling non-mental objects rather than as indicating what favors the preservation of the whole person, we fail to understand those perceptions adequately. Such misinterpreting issues in false judgments. Because misinterpreting is a species of faulty understanding, it is intuitively natural to assign responsibility for those false judgments to the faculty of understanding, rather than to that faculty which provides mental affirmation and denial.[7]

The process of thus misinterpreting our perceptions leads, on Descartes' view, to layers of unconsidered judgments—"prejudices [*praejudicii*]" (e.g., AT VII, 12, 69, 422; HR I, 140, 183; II, 241; AT IX–1, 203–205; HR II, 126–127). Prejudices, Descartes explains to Clerselier, are "all and only [*seulement . . . toutes*] those opinions which have been given credence by judgments we have previously made" (AT IX–1, 204; HR II, 126). And the power of prejudice is sufficient, Descartes holds, even to prevent some from clearly perceiving the eternal truths themselves (*Principles* I, 1: AT VIII–1, 24; HR I, 239). To counteract and overcome such layered prejudice would doubtless call for very considerable mental effort. That we must so exert ourselves in order to revise our beliefs helps bolster the intuitive appeal of the claim that the will is implicated in making judgments. It will emerge, moreover, in section IV that the need for such mental exertion is important also for understanding the role of doubting in the *Meditations*.

Descartes' theory postulates a division of labor in the producing of judgments. The faculty of understanding supplies the propositional content that the faculty of will affirms or denies. But one might question whether there is any need for the will to act, once the understanding has made its contribution. Propositions, by themselves, are affirmative or negative. So, when the mind has formulated a proposition, one might argue, it has produced an affirmation or denial and, hence, has affirmed or denied something (see C, 173–174). Descartes denies that the product of the understanding can, on its own, be either true or false. But E. M. Curley urges that we discount that contention. For we can only make sense of ideas if they are propositions, and propositions do have truth values.[8]

Several distinct questions are at issue here. For one thing, there is reason to doubt that Descartes did think of ideas quite as propositions, in the modern sense. Ideas, properly speaking, are one of the two kinds (*genera*) into which Descartes divides his thoughts (*cogitationes*). We have become accustomed to use "thought" and its cognates equivocally, to refer both to propositional mental states and to propositions themselves, conceived of as abstract objects. And, on some accounts, such abstract objects enter into our mental lives by somehow being directly apprehended by the mind. But there is little reason to think that Descartes held that view of how the understanding operates, or that he meant to divide his *cogitationes* into mental acts and abstract propositional objects. Indeed, his definition in the Geometrical Appendix to the Second Replies suggests the opposite: "By the word 'idea' I understand that form of thought [*cogitationis formam*] by the immediate apprehension of which I am conscious of that very thought" (AT VII, 160; HR II, 52). And his speaking of dividing his thoughts suggests the distinguishing of two aspects of mental acts—the attitudinal and the propositional. Ideas are aspects of actual mental acts, not independently existing abstract objects.[9]

If ideas were abstract propositions, and the understanding somehow apprehended them, it might be tempting to argue that any other faculty would be superfluous. But, if ideas are aspects of actual mental acts, then the role of the understanding is to do no more than comprehend the content of those acts—to comprehend "that form of thought by the immediate apprehension of which I am conscious of that very thought." It is then less inviting to think that another faculty would automatically be superfluous. For there is more to thinking than understanding.

A particular propositional content can figure in thinking not only as the content of a complete mental act, but also as part of the content of a compound or complex thought, for example, as the antecedent of a hypothesis one puts forth. This Fregean point suggests the involvement of more than the faculty of understanding, since the same content occurs affirmed or denied in one context, but in another not. Doubtless Descartes was aware of this consideration and doubtless it played some role in motivating his theory. But the point is hardly decisive. For Curley can respond that, in the compound or complex case, the understanding grasps a compound or complex propositional content, of which the simple content is a component. One can draw the distinctions required for the Fregean point by invoking only the understanding, without relying on help from another faculty.

There is, however, another way to meet the charge that another faculty is redundant, a way that connects more immediately with Descartes' concerns. The understanding is responsible for propositional content. Curley, Anthony Kenny, and Wilson all maintain that Descartes is mistaken when he claims that propositional contents cannot, on their own, be true or false. (See n. 8.) But if Descartes' claim can be sustained, the understanding alone could not provide bearers of truth values. For that, we would presumably need to invoke another faculty.

The issue of what the bearers of truth and falsity are is, of course, controversial. But well-known problems arise if we take them to be propositions or sentences. Sentences frequently contain token-reflexive components, including the tenses of verbs. Truth values of such sentences are notoriously unstable, altering along with changes in what their token-reflexive components refer to. If propositions can contain token-reflexive components, the same considerations apply. Two standard techniques exist for dealing with this difficulty. One can purge all token-reflexive elements from sentences or propositions, replacing them with words or concepts whose reference is independent of particular circumstances of use. Or one can retain such elements, but index each occurrence to a particular situation, thereby determining their reference.

No such adjustment is needed if particular mental acts or speech acts are the bearers of truth and falsity. Tokens of mental acts and speech acts occur in particular situations, and in connection with particular objects and events. So there is generally no problem about the referents of contained token-reflexive elements. If one regards such elements as ineliminable without loss of meaning or expressive power, one will have good reason to insist that only mental acts and speech acts are nonderivatively true and false. Propositions and sentences could be seen as derivatively true or false once they were suitably indexed or relativized; but such indexing or relativization would serve simply to mimic the characteristics of tokens of mental acts and speech acts.

Descartes' persistent first-person formulations of the *cogito* leave little doubt that he regards token-reflexive words and concepts as ineliminable without loss of expressive power. It is unlikely (*pace* Harry G. Frankfurt: F, 105–106) that Descartes would have accepted any non-token-reflexive way of putting the point he is making in the *cogito*. Accordingly, we should expect him to refer to the *cogito* not as a propositional content—that is, not as an idea—but as a mental act or speech act. This expectation is borne out; to my knowledge Descartes never speaks of the *cogito* as an idea, and in most pivotal passages it is described in terms that clearly suggest or imply a mental act or speech act. In Meditation II it is a pronouncement or statement (*pronuntiatum*) (AT VII, 25; HR I, 150); in *Principles* I, 7, it is a cognition (*cognitio*) (AT VIII–1, 7; HR I, 221); in *The Search after Truth* it is a piece of reasoning (*ratiocinium*) (AT X, 523; HR I, 324).[10]

By itself, understanding some propositional content does not typically pin down the reference of whatever token-reflexive components are involved. Understanding 'Theaetetus is sitting' does not determine the time that the present tense refers to; understanding 'He gives it to her' does not suffice to pick out any particular people or gift. To pin down reference in such cases, one typically needs more than an act of understanding; one needs a particular mental act of affirming or denying. A faculty other than the understanding is needed.

Appeal to mental faculties of whatever sort, however, may strike some as suspect. Descartes' mental faculties may be ontologically innocuous, since they are particular kinds of capacities, but perhaps they are also ineffectual when it comes to explaining anything. If faculties are no more than capacities for certain sorts of mental phenomena to occur, how can they have any explanatory value? Why would it be more fruitful or revealing to say that a mental act is due to some mental faculty than to say, for example, that the effects of opium are due to its dormative power?

Descartes' purpose in invoking mental faculties, however, is not to explain the occurrence of mental acts, but simply to have a handy way to talk about the abilities that a thinking thing must have. Prior to Meditation IV, he speaks of this ability in a wholly undifferentiated way, as the faculty of judging. Only when he needs to distinguish two components of the capacity to think things does he divide the capacity to think in a way that matches his Third Meditation division of thoughts. Descartes' appeal to faculties, therefore, is reductive in spirit.[11] A great variety of distinct mental phenomena—all the different kinds of propositional mental acts—results from the smallest number of mental faculties one can make do with. The appeal to faculties involves none of the theoretical prodigality that has given faculty psychologies a bad name.

Moreover, the reductive character of Descartes' theory does greater justice to the mental data than does the reductive account now in greatest favor, which seeks to reduce all mental acts to just belief and desire. Descartes' two faculties mark a crucial distinction between two aspects of all mental acts; any adequate theory must somehow reflect that distinction. It is hardly likely, however, that one can, by compounding beliefs and desires that have varying intensity and content, successfully reproduce the vast array of mental attitudes that actually occur.

Descartes constructs his theory of judgment expressly to explain how error can occur. And on his view the occurrence of error is hardly the esoteric epistemic issue it may now strike us as being. As Wilson has usefully emphasized (W, chap. 1), Descartes sees error as occurring in epidemic proportions, principally because we habitually take perceptions to resemble extramental reality. As noted earlier, perceptions thus misinterpreted are cases of faulty understanding.

The connection between error and the understanding is illustrated especially vividly by Descartes' answer, when Gassendi asks him to explain what it is that the will extends to "which escapes the understanding." Descartes replies: "everything in which it happens that we err" (AT VII, 376; HR II, 224). Every false judgment involves the faulty understanding of something that we think we understand satisfactorily. But this reply appears to cause a problem for Descartes, at least if we think of abstract propositions as the objects of the understanding. For, as Wilson notes, it seems natural to suppose that we can clearly and distinctly understand false propositions (W, 141).

What we understand is, of course, propositional, as is what we affirm, doubt, deny, and desire. But it does not follow that what we understand are propositions, whether true or false. What we understand is how things are, and we do so propositionally because how things are is always expressible by a propositional clause. Similarly, what we affirm, deny, doubt, and desire is that things are a certain way, and that too can always be captured by a propositional clause. Once we recast the issue in terms of understanding how things are, rather than understanding abstract propositions, Descartes' reply to Gassendi accords well with common sense. We would not regard ourselves as actually understanding how things are if our understanding of those things could be material for false judgments.[12]

The tendency to think of the objects of understanding as abstract propositions, which can be true or false on their own, obscures the way in which understanding resembles knowing. I cannot truly claim to know something if the propositional clause following "know" is false. But it is undeniable that we can understand false propositions. It is therefore tempting to conclude that, whereas 'know' is factive, 'understand' is not.

But while it is plain that we do understand false propositions, it is far less obvious exactly how such cases should be described. If I understand the proposition that 2 + 2 = 5, it hardly follows that I understand that 2 + 2 = 5. Presumably I understand something like what the false proposition amounts to, or means. Like knowing, it seems we cannot truly claim to understand something that we express by means of a false propositional clause. Descartes' insistence that the propositional contents of mental acts are concrete aspects of those mental acts and not abstract objects, and that those contents cannot be true or false independently of any mental act or speech act, help guard against thinking that we can.

Descartes formulates his two-faculty theory in terms of a view of freedom that may, on its own account, seem problematic. According to Descartes, the more strongly I incline (*propendeo*) toward one of two opposing objects of belief or desire, the greater my freedom. In the case of clear and distinct perception, such as the *cogito*, it is impossible for me "not to judge to be true that which I so clearly under[stand]." Although there is a great inclination (*propensio*) of the will in these cases, one is not subject to "the compulsion of an external force [*vi externâ*]." And freedom, on Descartes' conception, occurs in connection with believing and desiring when "we sense ourselves to be determined by no external force"—the phrase is the same: *nullâ vi externâ* (AT VII, 57–59; HR I, 175–176). But it may seem that this conception of freedom not only is unduly paradoxical but, in the context of the doctrine of compelled assent, is ad hoc as well.

But the appearance of paradox can be dispelled, and Descartes' conception seen not to be ad hoc, by turning again to some relatively commonsense observations. As noted in section II, the more strongly we believe or desire something, the less control we have over whether to do so. If we accept that the will acts when we desire things, it is natural to suppose that the more strongly we want something, the more powerfully the will acts. A puzzle therefore emerges about where, in this complex set of factors, to locate freedom. Should we say the will is most free when it acts most powerfully? Then it will turn out that the will is most free when we have the least control over our desires. Or should we say instead that we are most free when we have the greatest control over what we want, that is, when the will acts most weakly? Neither option is without its unappealing consequences, but whatever air of paradox there is here results solely from our commonsense views about these things. On Descartes' account, the puzzle applies to believing no less than desiring. But, if the argument of section II is correct, believing contributes no special problems of its own.

We tend today not to regard the concept of a faculty of will as being especially intuitive. So it may seem to us as though Descartes made the wrong choice: Better to talk about ourselves being most free when we have the most control than about the will's being most free when it acts most powerfully. But, as noted earlier, Descartes' talk of faculties is innocuous; to talk of the will is only to talk about a particular capacity. And, in any event, a good commonsense case can be made for Descartes' decision. Our voluntary actions are not necessarily those over which we can exert the most control over whether to perform them or not. They are those whose performance is not due to external factors—those which are self-determined. If we take the voluntary as paradigmatic of freedom, one will conclude with Descartes that the absence of external determination is more important than how much control we have over our mental acts. Indeed, it is doubtful that we do have very much control over our mental acts.

It is evident that Descartes had these considerations in mind: " . . . the voluntary and the free," he explains to Hobbes, "are one and the same" (AT VII, 191; HR II, 75). And it is equally clear that he regards this point as essentially a matter of common sense. Having written to Mesland that "I call free everything that is voluntary," he defends his terminological decision by saying that, "concerning names, I desire nothing more than to follow usage and precedent" (AT IV, 116; K, 150).[13]

It may, however, seem that such commonsense usage fits poorly with the rather ambitious claims Descartes makes on behalf of his freedom of will. He "experience[s] it as circumscribed by no limits"; he experiences, moreover, so much free will in himself that he "apprehend[s] an idea of none greater" than his own. Indeed, even God's freedom of will does not seem greater than ours when ours is "regarded formally and precisely in itself" (AT VII, 56–57; HR I, 174–175). The comparison with God is particularly notable given Descartes' view that the eternal truths are themselves products of God's unrestricted free will.

But these claims are rather less extravagant than they may at first sight seem. "[R]egarded formally and precisely in itself," our will is unlimited simply because it can act with respect to whatever propositional content it may encounter. Descartes' doctrine about God's having created the eternal truths is bound up with his view that, in God, the will and understanding are not distinct (AT I, 149, and IV, 118–119; K, 13–14 and 151). But, whereas God's understanding is infinite, the human understanding is "very small and very finite" (AT VII, 57; HR I, 174). Moreover, "we never will anything without at the same time understanding it" (letter to Regius: AT III, 372; K, 102). Accordingly, the divine will "extends to more objects" than does ours not because of any inherent limit on what our will can do, but because our faculty of understanding is only able to present the will with far fewer propositional objects with respect to which it can act (AT VII, 57; HR I, 174–175). Indeed, this view accords well with Descartes' conception of freedom as the sensed absence of external determinants. For on that conception, so long as the will can act with respect to any propositional content it encounters, its freedom is unrestricted. It need not also exercise control over how it acts.

IV. MIND AND METHODOLOGY[14]

As noted in section I, Descartes' explanations of what it is to be a thinking thing make it clear that he regards all thinking as the holding of a mental attitude toward some propositional content. Even sensing and feeling, insofar as they are genuinely mental, have the structure of propositional attitudes. They consist of its appearing to me that p (AT VII, 29; HR I, 153) or, even more pointedly, of my thinking that I sense (AT VII, 33; HR I, 156; cf. the three "grades" of sensing distinguished in the Sixth Replies: AT VII, 436–437; HR II, 251). Because we become aware of faculties only by being aware of their exercise, the two-faculty theory goes hand in hand with the propositional-attitude structure of thinking. And Descartes evidently holds that the two faculties are no less crucial to the nature of the mind itself than mental attitudes and content are to the nature of thinking. Thus he writes to Regius: "Understanding is properly the passive aspect of the mind, and willing its active aspect"; "they differ only as the active and passive aspects of the same substance" (AT III, 372; K, 102).

Descartes' insistence that all thinking has both an attitudinal and a propositional component has noteworthy consequences concerning the importance of language for expressing thought. Nonverbal behavior often indisputably invites interpretation in propositional terms. If thinking involved only a propositional aspect, language would be unnecessary for its expression. Propositional content can be conveyed by nonlinguistic as well as by linguistic means.

Mental attitudes fare far less well with nonlinguistic behavior. Such behavior sometimes does seem to convey some pro or con attitude: frequently desire or aversion, sometimes belief, and perhaps, occasionally, disbelief. But it is usually unclear that the desire or aversion we see in nonverbal behavior is directed at a propositional object. When nonverbal behavior seems to express belief, it is often just that it expresses some propositional content. And nonverbal behavior less obviously indicates mental affirmation or denial than it does desire and aversion. Thus such behavior seldom, if ever, seems by itself to signal mental denial or disbelief.

Moreover, it is plain that nonlinguistic behavior, however subtle, cannot capture the great variety of distinct mental attitudes, such as wondering, doubting, refusing, anticipating, surmising, suspecting, wishing, hoping, contemplating, considering, and a host of others, which differ in ways that are often difficult even to describe accurately. Language is clearly tailored for the task. As Vendler has elegantly shown (*Res Cogitans*, chap. 3), for virtually every kind of mental attitude, there is at least one distinct kind of illocutionary force, which determines a kind of speech act that can express that mental attitude. Without words for these illocutionary acts, it is doubtful that we could discriminate among so many different kinds. And without a way of readily conveying various propositional contents, which language provides, it is unlikely that such a variety of distinct illocutionary acts could have developed.[15]

In the first paragraph of Meditation III, Descartes announces that, "looking into myself more from within, I shall try to make myself gradually better known and more familiar to myself." And so, in the next paragraph, he examines whether there are things "pertaining to me that I have not yet noticed." It is there that the *cogito* suggests to him "a general rule . . . that all that I perceive exceedingly clearly and distinctly is true" (AT VII, 34–35; HR I, 157–158). The rule thus emerges as a hypothesis about our nature as thinking things: our nature is such that whatever we perceive thus clearly and distinctly is true.

That the general rule is a hypothesis about our mental nature should be no surprise, given Descartes' representative theory of ideas. Ideas are the propositional contents of mental acts and, thus, the direct objects of mental acts (AT VII, 181; HR II, 67–68); they are what we affirm, suppose, doubt, desire, and so forth. Our access to extramental reality is accordingly indirect, and we cannot establish simply by examination whether our ideas ever correspond to or resemble extramental reality. Our principal error is judging that such correspondence or resemblance obtains. So Descartes needs some way to reach the truth about extramental reality which relies on the nature of the mind. The way (*via:* AT VII, 40, line 5, 53, line 18; HR I, 161, 172) he proposes is the general rule, validated by the divine guarantee.

Reliance on solely mental factors to reach the truth about extramental objects usually involves a coherence theory of knowledge or of truth. Such theories would be anathema to Descartes; if coherence could enable us to reach the truth, why would the demon matter? Moreover, such theories are, on independent grounds, unavailable to him. Conceptual truths cannot, on Descartes' view, be self-certifying; they must at best play an oblique epistemic role. For the eternal truths are due to God's agency, and but for the relevant divine act of will they could be different. God could even have made it "not true that . . . contradictories cannot exist [be true] together" (letter to Mesland: AT IV, 118; K, 151). Coherence is presumably the conceptual possibility of a conjunction. Descartes cannot, therefore, rely on coherence in the search for truth, at least not without some independent ratification.

The two-faculty theory of mind, however, enables Descartes to formulate a mind-based procedure for reaching the truth that does not collapse into a coherence theory. Some ideas have no special effect on the will; if we affirm or deny them, it is because of extrinsic factors. But others have a powerful effect, some so much so that simply understanding them makes us affirm them. Descartes' general rule is the hypothesis that, when the understanding irresistibly impels the will, the result is a true judgment. The rule is a mind-based way to reach the truth that avoids coherence theories.[16]

Such theories would presumably be unavoidable, however, if only the understanding played a role in judging. The role of the understanding is to apprehend things; all it could do to arrive at the truth would be, at best, to determine what is and is not conceivable—that is, what is and is not capable of being understood. If judging were just a matter of understanding, some ideas or judgments could be favored over others only by reason of coherence—that is, by reason of being jointly conceivable. The power that understanding something has in making us believe things, and our seemingly automatic passage from understanding to affirming, may mislead one into thinking that only the understanding is at work. It should thus be no surprise that Spinoza, who rejects Descartes' view that the will plays a role in judging (*Ethics*, pt. 2, prop. 49), also espouses a coherence theory of knowledge.

Our inability to conceive the contradictories of eternal truths is an example of the finitude of the human understanding. For the will to be infinite means that it can act with respect to any propositional content it encounters. For the understanding to be finite means that there are things we cannot comprehend, though they are in themselves comprehensible and, thus, comprehensible by a less limited intellect. The eternal truths depend on the divine will, and the divine will and understanding are indistinguishable. So on Descartes' view

God clearly can comprehend the contradictories of all eternal truths. These contradictories are thus intrinsically comprehensible.[17]

Given either that the human understanding is limited, or that the eternal truths could have been different, our ability to gain knowledge must depend on our mental nature somehow incorporating a bias toward the truth. Without such a bias, we could not count on our unaided understanding to reveal accurately what is necessary and possible. And being wrong about that would skew our knowledge about other things as well. The converse also holds. If we must rely on some such built-in bias, our reliance will presumably affect how we understand things, thereby in effect imposing limits on how or what we can comprehend.

But there is reason for skepticism about the idea that the human understanding is restricted in respect of what it can grasp propositionally. For it is reasonable to suppose that, given time to define terms and explain theories, a certain threshold intelligence is all one needs to comprehend any proposition whatever. It is thus arguable that the human understanding is in this way unlimited—as Descartes would put it, infinite; no mental act or speech act is possible whose content could, in principle, elude us. If so, no nativist doctrine that implies limits on the human understanding can be sustained.[18]

The two-faculty theory is also important for understanding Descartes' procedure in the *Meditations*. The doubts Descartes invites us to share in Meditation I are so extraordinary that one cannot help wondering whether his invitation can have been serious and, indeed, even whether such doubting is psychologically possible. In the synopsis of the *Meditations*, moreover, Descartes notes that "nobody of sound mind has ever doubted seriously that there really is a world, and that people have bodies" (AT VII, 16; HR I, 143). And in Meditation I itself he resolves not to doubt in the way insane people do. Perhaps considerations pertaining to dreaming and the demon do provide the reasons Descartes insists on having for his doubts (AT VII, 21; HR I, 148). But it is far from obvious that such reasons suffice to make actual doubting about such matters any less insane.

Doubting is a mental act, and thus on Descartes' view involves an exercise of will. And the exercise of one's will can sometimes cost us very strenuous effort. These considerations point toward a reason for taking Descartes seriously when he enjoins us actually to try to doubt in the way he describes. Meditation I is quite brief. And, unlike the other five, it involves no special difficulty in understanding the argument. Yet at its close Descartes describes this first day's activity as laborious (*laboriosum*) (AT VII, 23; HR I, 149). Nothing about the length of, or difficulty in understanding, the Meditation makes clear what has required such laborious exertion. But if we imagine Descartes as having really doubted the things he says he has, the mental exhaustion he avows is readily understandable. Doubting those things would involve the most extreme efforts of willpower. Genuine doubting of that kind could not be merely "routine," as Frankfurt holds it is (F, 17); it would have to be, to use his term, impressively "heroic." To explain Descartes' remarks at the close of Meditation I, we must suppose that he seriously meant for us to try actually to doubt the things he asks us to.

Since the attempts to doubt in Meditation I are made in order to find out whether doubting in particular cases is really possible, success may well be easier than one might have imagined. To show that doubting something is possible, one need not sustain a doubt that actively enters into one's mental economy. Doubting for just a moment will do. In the cases Descartes describes, presumably the most strenuous efforts would still be needed to achieve even a merely momentary doubt. But it is reasonable to think that such efforts can succeed in producing a momentary, but psychologically real doubt. This observation enables us also to resolve the difficulty about sanity. Anybody who doubted the things Descartes asks us to in more than a merely momentary way would certainly be insane, reasons or no. But momentary doubting need not be a sign of madness.

The need to show the real possibility of the various doubts is not the only reason that actual doubting is important. Descartes holds, as noted above, that one is aware of a faculty only when one turns oneself to its exercise. Moreover, to be aware of one's mental faculties is to be aware of oneself. For "the faculties of willing, sensing, understanding, and so forth cannot be said to be parts of [the mind], because it is one and the same mind that wills, that senses, that understands" (AT VII, 86; HR I, 196). To be aware of those faculties is thus to be aware of that mind. The role the will plays in Descartes' theory of mental acts helps us understand both his desire that we engage in psychologically real doubting and his belief that it is possible to. And that doubting, if genuine, makes us in turn aware of the faculty of will.

Descartes' claims about mind and his views about methodology intersect most dramatically in connection with the *cogito*, and there, again, the two-faculty theory is important for understanding and defending his views.[19] Descartes asserts not only that "I am, I exist" is true whenever I say or think it, but that it is necessary as well. And, if truth attaches to mental acts and speech acts rather than to their propositional contents, presumably necessity must as well. But this conclusion may seem problematic. How, exactly, are tokens of mental acts and speech acts supposed to be necessary?

Several passages make clear that Descartes does hold that tokens of mental acts can be necessary and, indeed, that nothing else can be. Eternal truths are not strictly speaking necessary, for they could have been otherwise than they are. Rather, it is just that we have been "given such a mind that" we cannot conceive otherwise (letter to Arnauld: AT V, 224; K, 236). In addition, "All contradiction or impossibility consists in our conception [*conceptu*; French Version: *concept ou pensée*] alone." For anything "situated outside the understanding . . . [is] possible" (AT VII, 152, IX–1, 119; HR II, 46). And, if anything outside the mind is possible, nothing extramental can be necessary. Moreover, "my thinking imposes no necessity on things" (AT VII, 66; HR I, 181).

Whenever I attentively and distinctly understand something, it is impossible for me not to affirm it.[20] Every such affirmation is a mental act that it is necessary for me to perform; the necessity is hypothetical on my understanding the right way, but it is necessity nonetheless. Speech acts are then derivatively necessary if they express mental acts that are necessary in this way. There is no other way mental acts, or anything else, can be necessary, since nothing "outside the understanding" is impossible.[21] The necessity of the *cogito* is of exactly this kind; it is Descartes' most vivid and revealing case of compelled assent. For it is the *cogito* that leads to the speculation that whenever understanding something irresistibly leads us to affirm it, that affirmation is true.

Descartes' presentation of the *cogito* in Meditation II is unusual in that he does not use his celebrated rubric, *cogito, ergo sum*, which he so often relies on elsewhere. The demon hypothesis has led us at the outset of Meditation II to "set aside as though . . . altogether false" (AT VII, 24; HR I, 149) all logical and conceptual truths. So *ergo*, in *cogito, ergo sum*, could not express such a connection; nor can any reasoning that leads to Descartes' conclusion. Moreover, the necessity of my thinking or saying that I exist must, on the foregoing argument, be necessity that derives from compelled assent. Descartes' formulation of the *cogito* in the *Meditations* seems designed to reflect these very considerations.

Before Descartes gets to his existence, he rehearses the mental acts of Meditation I, noting that he cannot doubt their occurrence. He then connects his remarks about his mental acts to the certainty that he exists by writing: "having considered all these things satisfactorily, it is thereupon necessary to hold for certain that . . . " (AT VII, 25;

HR I, 150). And he then goes on to tell us that the statement "I exist" is necessarily true every time I say or think it; that is, my mental act or speech act is both true and necessitated. It is necessitated not only by my mental act of understanding the idea that I exist. It is necessitated by any mental act I perform that calls attention, as the mental acts of Meditation I do, to the question of my existence. The bearing my thinking has on my existing is that my being attentively and distinctly aware of my thinking necessitates my affirming that I exist.

NOTES

1. Conspicuous exceptions are E. M. Curley's "Descartes, Spinoza and the Ethics of Belief," in *Spinoza: Essays in Interpretation,* ed. Eugene Freeman and Maurice Mandelbaum (LaSalle, Ill.: Open Court, 1975), 159–189 (henceforth cited as C); Anthony Kenny's "Descartes on the Will," in *Cartesian Studies,* ed. R. J. Butler (Oxford: Basil Blackwell, 1972), 1–31 (henceforth cited as B); and chapter 4 of Margaret Dauler Wilson's *Descartes* (London: Routledge & Kegan Paul, 1978) (henceforth cited as W). I owe much to these discussions.

2. I use AT, HR, and K as explained in the General Bibliography at the beginning of this volume. Additional abbreviations are D for *Descartes,* ed. Willis Doney (New York: Anchor Books, 1967), and F for Harry G. Frankfurt, *Demons, Dreamers, and Madmen* (Indianapolis: Bobbs-Merrill, 1970). Translations are my own, though I provide references where possible to HR and K.

3. These considerations may help resolve puzzles about Descartes' claims concerning our knowledge of our faculties raised by David Fate Norton in "Descartes on Unknown Faculties: An Essential Inconsistency," *Journal of the History of Philosphy* 6, 3 (July 1968):244–256.

4. See the Fifth Replies: "The term 'idea' . . . I extend to whatever is thought" (AT VII, 367; HR II, 217), and the Second Replies: "I take the term 'idea' to stand for whatever the mind directly perceives" (AT VII, 181; HR II, 67–68). Descartes does say that ideas can be expressed by either terms of propositions (letter to Mersenne, AT III, 395; K, 106). Presumably terms express ideas by expressing some propositional content; thus Descartes writes earlier in the same letter that the idea of God is just "what all people habitually understand when they speak about Him" (AT III, 393; K, 106).

In *Descartes* (Brighton: Harvester and Minneapolis: University of Minnesota Press, 1985), chapter 1, and "Ideas and Judgment in the Third Meditation: An Object Lesson in Philosophical Historiography," *Independent Journal of Philosophy* (1985), Marjorie Grene forcibly advances an alternative interpretation of these matters.

5. Vendler, *Res Cogitans* (Ithaca, N.Y.: Cornell University Press, 1972), 169.

6. I use "belief" here and in what follows as a convenient term to cover both nonconative mental acts in general and dispositions for such mental acts to occur.

7. On the importance of how we interpret ideas to Descartes' conceptions of clarity and distinctness, see Alan Gewirth, "Clearness and Distinctness in Descartes," in D, 250–277.

8. Curley credits Spinoza (*Ethics* II, prop. 49) with this line of criticism. Wilson (W, 144) and Kenny ("Descartes on the Will," 96, and *Descartes* [New York: Random House, 1968], 117) also insist that, *pace* Descartes, ideas must be able to be true and false, since they are the propositional contents of mental acts.

9. Descartes' talk of true and immutable natures that "do not depend on [his] mind" (AT VII, 64; HR I, 180) may seem to suggest that he did hold that the mind grasps abstract objects. But, even if the issue of true and immutable natures does have a bearing on the ontological status of propositions, our perception of those natures, Descartes explains, is due to "the nature of [one's] mind" (AT VII, 65; HR I, 180). So it is reasonable to regard them as forms of thought over which we have no control. On Descartes' alleged Platonism with respect to abstract objects, see Gewirth, "The Cartesian Circle Reconsidered," *The Journal of Philosophy* 67, 19 (October 8, 1970):668–685; Kenny, "The Cartesian Circle and the Eternal Truths," ibid., 685–700; and Gewirth, "Descartes: Two Disputed Questions," *The Journal of Philosophy*, 68, 9 (May 6, 1971):288–296.

10. The French version of the *Meditations* has *proposition* (AT IX–1, 19), presumably explaining the HR 'proposition.' And the Latin term *proposition* occurs, e.g., in *Principles* I, 10 (AT VIII–1, 8; HR I, 222) and in the letter to Reneri for Pollot (AT II, 38; K, 52). But like their English counterpart, the French and Latin terms colloquially refer to a proposal or similar speech act.

11. I am grateful to Sidney Morgenbesser for this observation.

12. Thus, although ideas cannot strictly speaking be true or false, they can, Descartes tells us, be materially false when they "furnish the judgment [*judicio*] with material for error" (AT VII, 231; HR II, 105), by representing "something that is not a thing as if it were" (AT VII, 43; HR I, 164).

13. See his letter to Mesland of about a year later, in which he explains that "liberty regarded as in the actions of the will" coincides with what is voluntary (AT IV, 174–175; K, 160–161), and the Appendix to the Second Replies, in which "the essence of will" is identified with acting "voluntarily and freely" (AT VII, 166; HR II, 56).

14. This section summarizes some of the results I develop and argue for in my "Will, Mind, and Method in Descartes" (henceforth cited as WMMD), forthcoming.

15. These considerations help explain Descartes' insistence that, because nonhuman animals lack language, they have no mental lives (*Discourse:* AT VI, 56–59; HR I, 116–117; letter to Newcastle: AT IV, 573–576; K, 206–208; to More: AT V, 275–279; K, 243–245, and in various Replies: AT VII, 204–205, 263, 269–271, 413–414, 490; HR II, 85, 140, 145–146, 235, 290).

16. For evidence that Descartes regarded his doctrine of impelled assent as a doctrine about our mental nature, see AT VII, 65, lines 6–9 and 69, lines 16–18; HR I, 180 and 183, and *Principles* I, 43 (AT VIII–1, 21; HR I, 236). For evidence that he also explicitly saw the divine guarantee as bearing on our

mental nature, see AT VII, 36, 70, 77, and 80; HR I, 158, 184, 189, 192, and cognate passages in *Principles* I, 13 and 30 (AT VIII–1, 9–10 and 16; HR I, 224 and 231) and letter to Regius (AT III, 64–66; K, 73).

17. On the importance of the connection between Descartes' doctrine about the eternal truths and the finitude of the human understanding, see Frankfurt, "Descartes on the Creation of the Eternal Truths," *The Philosophical Review* 86, 1 (January 1977):36–57, esp. 45–46. I am indebted to Frankfurt's lucid and convincing account of these matters.

In WMMD (sec. 2) I argue that Descartes' doctrines about the eternal truths and the finitude of the human understanding are intimately connected in ways that have not generally been recognized.

18. In *Rules and Representations* (New York: Columbia University Press, 1980) Noam Chomsky explicitly recognizes the connection between nativism and the view that the human understanding is limited, and accepts that limitation as a consequence of nativism (e.g., pp. 33, 46, and 180). Because Chomsky's nativism is biologically based, and operates without benefit of any guarantee of its veracity, it faces the additional difficulty that different cognitive beings could have incommensurable cognitive capacities.

19. In WMMD (sec. 4) I develop a positive account of the *cogito* based on pragmatic incoherence of the sort encountered in Moore's paradox: 'It is raining, but I don't believe it' (G. E. Moore, "Russell's 'Theory of Descriptions,'" in *The Philosophy of Bertrand Russell*, ed. Paul Arthur Schilpp [LaSalle, Ill.: Open Court, 1944], 177–225, p. 204). The account I develop lends itself to being formulated in terms of the two-faculty theory.

20. As Descartes explains in *Principles* I, 45, perceptions cannot be distinct without being clear (AT VIII–1, 22; HR I, 237).

21. Thus in Meditation V Descartes describes as necessary, some half-dozen times, particular mental acts that we are necessarily led to perform (AT VII, 67; HR I, 182).

18

Objectum Purae Matheseos: Mathematical Construction and the Passage from Essence to Existence

DAVID R. LACHTERMAN

"Mad Mathesis alone was unconfined."
—(Pope, *The Dunciad*)

I. TEXTS AND SUBTEXTS: READING NOTES

Descartes' proclivity toward, and gift for, distancing himself from the readers of his published texts by practicing a rhetoric of subterfuge and self-concealment are amply attested both by his private remarks and by the reactions of such noteworthy contemporary readers as Hobbes, Gassendi, and Leibniz. His announced resolution regarding the writing, which was to become the anonymous *Meteors* of 1637: "I have resolved . . . to be hidden behind the canvas in order to hear what people are going to say about it," might well be extended to apply to all four of his published writings, as much as could the Ovidian motto he chose for himself, *Bene vixit, bene qui latuit*—"He lived well who hid well." In these circumstances it is little wonder that an extremely gifted seventeenth-century disciple could write "even the Cartesians did not understand what Descartes intended."[1]

If what may fairly be called the "orthodox" school of modern Cartesian interpretation, especially those of its members schooled in analytical philosophy, has largely discounted these signs of heterodox or hidden intentions behind Descartes' official teachings, its implicit rationale is not completely patent in the studied displacement of such signs to the penumbra of mere biography or in the accusation that interpreters who do take an interest in their significance are recklessly ascribing paranoia or the like to Descartes. Rather, or so I would suggest, this strategy of discounting or dismissal seems to stem from the expectation that nothing but a philosophical void would remain once Descartes' argumentative and/or confessional candor had been called into question.[2] Everything that has long since assumed pivotal standing among the recognized substantive issues in contemporary epistemology and metaphysics—for example, the argument from hyperbolical doubt, the search for unimpeachable (if circular) guarantees of our epistemic claims about the external world, psychophysical dualism—would cease to be anchored to the Cartesian texts if the latter ceased to be trustworthy historical sources, or worse, if every official Cartesian assertion had to be deciphered as masking its own contradictory.

The present study is an experiment designed to allay such disconcerting suspicions by showing some of the ways in which what is nowadays the most prominent Cartesian work, the *Meditations,* does not lose, but instead *gains,* in philosophical substance when we try to excavate or reconstruct the "subtext" it veils. Indeed, the *Meditations* offers an especially apt test case since we have Descartes' own declaration on the eve of publication: "And I will tell you, between us, that these six Meditations contain the foundations of my physics. But, please, one must not say this; for those who favor Aristotle would perhaps have more difficulty in approving them and I hope that those who read them will become accustomed to my principles unawares and will recognize their truth before noticing that they will destroy Aristotle's" (AT III, 298).

We need only remind ourselves of his equally familiar assertion, also to Mersenne: "The whole of my physics is nothing other than geometry" (AT II, 268) to be set straightaway in search of the *geometrical foundations of Cartesian physics,* foundations kept far from visible in the public text, but potentially recoverable from a subtext, or pre-text, towards which Descartes might have wanted to point some of his contemporary readers.

In the finale of the *Meditations,* the passage from essence to existence, Descartes does indeed seem to be giving such clues when he uses the phrase *objectum purae matheseos* three times in the last two parts and only in those parts. (Readers of the French translation were spared the evocations of the Latin phrase by circumlocutions such as *"l'objet des démonstrations de géométrie"* with its much more traditional ring.)[3]

Accordingly I want to try to see how the last two Meditations might look *sub specie purae matheseos*, once this has been more distinctly identified. At the end of my essay (section V) I want to compare some of the features of the sketch, which will emerge with a few prominent aspects of the published text. One intended consequence of this strategy is to show that Descartes' search for firm foundations is not to be understood as a free-floating enterprise indifferent to the technical achievements and prospects of particular bodies of knowledge; on the contrary, Cartesian foundationalism remains moored, for good or for ill, to the specific format and the warranted procedures of *physico-mathematical* explanation such as he envisioned and elaborated them.

At all events, my efforts to restore the subtext underlying Meditations V and VI will necessarily be both elliptical and hyperbolical, falling short of the whole body of relevant evidence, yet exceeding in its implications what can be readily sustained by the evidence I do present.

II. *PURA MATHESIS* AND DESCARTES' *GEOMETRY:* PRELUDE

Even a slightly more than cursory inspection of the tortuous paths of doubt laid out in the First Meditation and pursued until the end of the text will have revealed a number of ambiguous signposts and apparent culs-de-sac.[1] How are the arguments against the veracity of sensory information and inference related to the arguments against the reliability of mathematics? For example, how strongly or how faintly are the premises and prejudices uncovered in perceptual beliefs—the externality of the referent and its (putative) existence, the resemblance of the *sensum* to its "object," and the causal origin of sensation in something other than the pertinent faculty—still at work in the critique of mathematical imagination and, even, mathematical intellection?[2] What takes place in the transition from mathematical simples to imaginative complexes, that is, the reverse of the explicative movement Descartes traces in Meditation I? Are those simples themselves locatable in, or fabricated by, the same imagination which the painter uses to depict a Siren, or do they reside and originate elsewhere, perhaps in the pure intellect? And if the latter, how do we get from these "more simple and universal" items to the complex images fashioned out of them? Is this process essentially one of demonstration or deduction and hence open to doubts of its validity on each occasion or of its reliability over time? Or does Descartes envision another sort of procedure, possibly subject to another variety of doubt?[3] What does it signify that initially the mathematicians are said "not, or barely, to care whether their 'things' are in the nature of things" (*utrum eae [sc. res] sint in rerum natura necne, parum curant* [AT VII, 20]), while in the opening paragraph of the last Meditation the now indubitable existence of the object of *pura mathesis* is the bridge from essence to existence generally? What, in other words, is the relation of mathematical objects treated as *"res simplicissimae et valde generales"* (Meditation I) to the "same" items considered as *res materiales, quatenus sunt purae matheseos objectum* (Meditation VI)?

What light, if any, might Descartes' only published work in mathematics, the *Geometry* of 1637, throw on these and cognate questions? These are not questions that he treats *ex professo* in that text, although the near or exact counterparts of several of them *are* on exhibit in the *Rules,* the prelude to something quite akin to the later *Geometry.* It is rather as if the *Geometry* offered us in the mode of realized and felicitous *practice* what the *theoretical* reflections of both the *Discourse* and the *Meditations* must reckon with and account for. The temptation to allot priority or greater importance to the theoretical must, however, be checked by the recollection that, for Descartes himself, the hallmark of his *new* science is precisely that it is not unproductively speculative but apt to the making of useful results. Gauged by that explicit measure, a work embodying the products of epistemic inventiveness (e.g., the *Geometry*) cannot be simply subordinated to a text exploring the "theoretical" foundations of that inventiveness.[4]

Even granted that this is interestingly so, are we entitled to take *pura mathesis* in the *Meditations* as an analeptic allusion to the *Geometry* or, at least, to the project it actively, if partially, displays? Doubts are quickly put to rest by Descartes' own declaration, in a letter to an anonymous correspondent in 1637 setting forth the plan of the *Essays* following the *Discourse:* the *Dioptrics* treats of "a subject mixing philosophy [sc. physics] and mathematics," the *Meteors,* "a whole purely of philosophy," while the *Geometry* is "a whole purely of mathematics" (*un tout pur de Mathématique*) (AT I, 370).[5]

This documentary evidence does not, however, eliminate further corollary questions provoked by the identification of the *Geometry* as the subtext of Meditations V and VI: What does *objectum* mean here? What are the ties that bind *pura mathesis* in the style of the *Geometry* to that "other kind of geometry which takes for its questions the explication of the phenomena of nature" (AT II, 268) on which Descartes tells us his attention was trained?[6] Finally, what affiliations are detectable between the "pure mathesis" exhibited in the *Geometry* and *mathesis universalis,* the notorious phrase used only in Rule IV and, for some, the matrix of the Cartesian project in its entirety? Let me say a word about these three queries.

Objectum in Cartesian idiom refers to the subject matter of a discipline, a *field* of intellectual concentration, as it were, held in place and shaped by the sustained methodical attentions of the mind.[7] An *objectum*, far from being an entity (or class of entities) standing on its own, is just what method requires in response to its objectives (cf. Rule II: [*Arithmetica et Geometria*] *habentque objectum quale requirimus*) (AT X, 365). More determinate items (e.g., geometrical formations) belong to a specified *objectum* as so many modal versions, multiple fashions in which the general character invested in the *objectum* takes on distinctive particularity. This explains why Descartes can shift from plural nouns back to the singular *objectum* in describing *res materiales . . . quatenus sunt purae matheseos objectum* (Meditation V). The synonymous expression *natura corporea in communi* (Meditations I and V) plays the same role in designating a unified field of attention, but inevitably raises the second corollary question concerning the bearing of the *objectum* of pure mathematics on the extended body, or substance, with which physics is exercised. Not only does Descartes argue against any ontological distinction between extension and *res extensa* (of a kind that would lend support to an abstractionist view of mathematical entities); he is willing to assert the complete identity of mathematical and physical body, even while denying that, for example, impenetrability is an essentially necessary feature of the being of any body. As Descartes notes, this identification constitutes "the objection of objections" raised against his *mathematical* physics; failure to withstand that objection would entail abandoning the very science requiring a *fundamentum inconcussum*.[8]

Third, despite both the long controversy dating at least from Liard, and the recent historical clarification brought to the matter by Giovanni Crapulli, the meaning and scope of Descartes' *mathesis universalis* remain quite dark.[9] In particular, it has not been sufficiently noticed, as far as I can judge, that this rubric reappears in the titles of Descartes' mathematical successors and opponents and does so in ways clearly suggesting the most intimate affiliation between what he had actually achieved in the *Geometry* and this encompassing science, method, or mathematics *sensu latissimo*. Van Schooten, on the one hand, entitled his 1651 Latin edition of the *Geometry* together with contributions by younger Cartesian experts, *Principia Matheseos Universalis, seu Introductio ad Geometriae Methodum Renati Cartesii*. Leibniz, on the other hand, criticizes Descartes' version of *mathesis universalis* not for its ambitiousness but for its overly constricted range: "Meanwhile, Algebra is not to be confused with *mathesis universalis*. . . . In truth, whatever falls under the imagination, insofar as it is distinctly conceived, falls under *mathesis* and for this reason *mathesis* treats not only quantity [as Algebra does] but also the disposition of things."[10]

I have mentioned these three corollary questions in order to keep firmly in view the limits of the sketch to follow. Even if the *Geometry* provides the best specimen of Cartesian *pura mathesis* at work and hence furnishes indispensable clues to an understanding of what Descartes appears to presuppose in the *Meditations*, on its own the *Geometry* cannot explain to us in full *why* methodical attention should take priority over what there is (or seems to be) in the world in advance of *method*, or *how* the identity of mathematical and physical body is to be secured. It may, however, illustrate what it would mean for *order and measure* to serve as the unique and exhaustive topics of Cartesian mathematics and, thus, of Descartes' philosophy itself insofar as it aims at rigorous certainty.[11]

III. THE PRINCIPAL CHARACTERISTICS OF CARTESIAN GEOMETRY

Writing to Mersenne about his reactions to Desargues' *Projet brouillon*—the only work by a contemporary mathematician that inspired his enthusiasm—Descartes refers to what "I am in the habit of calling the metaphysics of geometry" (AT II, 490). He had specifically in mind the Ancients' use of so-called *diorismoi* to determine the limits within which the solution to a geometrical problem is possible; but the phrase can also supply a leitmotiv for Descartes' own text if we take "metaphysics" to mean here the establishment of the most general conditions that must be met by any course of fruitful and, hence, legitimate mathematical procedure. A close study of what Descartes both does and says in the *Geometry* would, I think, bring to light the following aspects of his implicit "metaphysics of geometry."[12]

1. Descartes' mathematics is devoted exclusively to problem-solving, *not* to theorem-proving. The proximate occasion for the composition of the *Geometry*, the challenge to solve the long-outstanding Pappus locus-problem for four or more straight lines, also shapes the work's systematic dimension. The latter is not a chain of theorems deduced from axioms and definitions, but a lesson evolved from the sample Pappus-problem concerning how to go about fruitfully solving problems of any sort in geometry (i.e., how one can reduce them all

to a single type of problem: "to find the value of the roots of some equation" [AT VI, 401]). Two points are in order:

a. To solve a problem is, in Descartes' vocabulary, to *construct* a problem, not, of course, in the sense of making up a problem, but as the successful process of finding and exhibiting the relevant geometrical item(s) satisfying the conditions set out in an algebraic equation. This technical usage, most likely borrowed from Viète, will later pass into the phrase "construction of an equation" in Leibniz and Wolff, whence it becomes truncated into Kant's simple word *"construction."*[13]

b. Descartes thereby shifts the center of emphasis from the *mos geometricus* to a dramatically revised conception of mathematical procedure as the production of an infinity of more and more complex solutions, always moving from a lower to the next-higher degree of the pertinent equation(s); this is the technically solid counterpart to the more "atmospheric" recommendation of rule three in the *Discourse* (*"comme par degrés"*). Correspondingly, when Descartes talks of *synthesis* in the strictly mathematical context he means the *constructions* of the required loci and/or the roots; these he is content to leave to readers who can enjoy "the pleasure of inventing them" on their own (AT VI, 413). In every sense, he wants to substitute the inventive *activity* of constructing solutions at first hand for the passivity both of traditional mathematical education via authors and of the inspection of given figures or complexes of figures in the hope of catching sight of relations already proved by theorems.[14]

2. The "metaphysics of geometry" demands a set of uniformly applicable operations so that all the "items" singled out as ingredients in any problem can be treated on a par and, hence, be subjected to manipulations (e.g., multiplication, division, etc.) guaranteed to yield a new item or group of items belonging equally to the original format of activity. The mutually discrepant labels "the arithmetization of geometry" and "the geometrization of arithmetic" capture only superficially the force of Descartes' principle of homogeneity invoked at the debut of the *Geometry* and sustained throughout. Most fundamentally, this principle cancels the seemingly natural heterogeneity between discrete multitudes and continuous magnitudes, on the one hand, and, within the latter category, between continua of different dimensions on the other. Descartes invites us to reinterpret the dimensional differences expressed by exponents (x^2, x^3, x^n) as marking positions in a *continuous ordering of ratios,* not as signifying perceptible (or, in cases where $n > 3$, imperceptible) distinctions (as, e.g., between a two-dimensional square and a three-dimensional cube). Moreover, arithmetical integrity is suppressed in favor of the arbitrary choice of

a line-segment to be the unit measure within each problem; this selection *à discrétion*, as Descartes terms it, seems to allow him to circumvent the issue of incommensurability, the crux of the Euclidean tradition.[15]

3. Along with the principle of homogeneity the metaphysics of geometry imposes another strong constraint on full-dress mathematical intelligibility. This is the principle of kinematic determinateness, as I shall call it, according to which all and only those curves are to be admitted into geometry which are producible either "by a single continuous motion or by several successive motions, the later ones being completely ruled by those which precede; for by this means one can always have an exact knowledge of their measure" (AT VI, 390). Descartes' decision to widen the class of geometrical curves to include mechanically produced curves such as the conchoid or cissoid, while barring those which cannot be described, by hand or machine, through appropriately conjoined successive moments (i.e., to restrict geometry to curves whose equations have only rational exponents), brings to sight several essential commitments.

First, the Ancients' distinction between "geometrical" and "mechanical" curves is myopic, since the instrumental origin of a curve need not compromise its intelligibility (cf. the Cartesian compasses). The Cartesian geometer can intervene with mechanical devices in the traditionally pure theoretical domain of geometry without loss of certainty or exactness.[16] Second, this exactness is owed to the *control* the geometer exercises over the production of the curves utilized in the "construction of problems"; so long as each point of the relevant curve "bear(s) a definite ratio to all the points of a straight line" the curve as a whole can be expressed by a single equation, giving its "precise and exact measure." Epistemic transparency is a function of productive control of motion, or, in other terms, by producing a curve in an exactly regulated manner one can know with certainty the origin and the determinate measure of each of its (infinite) points. Finally, the outward motions by which admissible curves can be "traced *or conceived*" (my emphasis) are so many allegories or metaphors of inward cognitive movements performed with the same or even greater attention to exactness and orderliness of execution. This inference is supported by the *Rules* in which deduction, passing in a systematic way along a continuous series of determinate ratios (cf. Rule 6), is a *cogitationis motus* (cf. Rule 7); indeed, instantaneous intuition of a whole and continuous deduction from part to part can, in the most desirable instance, appear "to coalesce" into a single operation "through a certain motion of cogitation" (Rule 11). Whatever else needs to be said about the relation of pure *mathesis* to physics, we have to keep in mind this correspondence or homology between mental and extra-mental movements.[17]

4. When he is not being said to have arithmetized geometry or to have geometrized arithmetic, Descartes is described as having alge-braized geometry or, conversely, geometrized algebra. This latter pair of descriptions also fails to reach the core of Descartes' designs. For him algebra is a *tool* for calculating the relations among the lengths and distances figuring in a problem-complex; it has no epistemic (or ontological) standing on its own, even though in its methodical role it borrows such standing from the "nature" of its "objects." Descartes thus has to be prodded into releasing to Mersenne and others an *Intro-duction à ma Geometrie*, written by an unnamed Dutchman and later found by Leibniz under the title *Calcul de Monsieur des Cartes*. (This short tract sets out more simply and plainly the rules for calculating with algebraic symbols utilized in the *Geometry* and adds several spec-imen illustrations of elementary problem-solving by calculating the *roots* of equations.)[18] More significantly, he recommends that Desar-gues employ the algebraic calculus inasmuch as most readers will grasp multiplication more readily than the method of compounding ratios. This recommendation shows us not only the primarily rhetor-ical or expository function of the algebraic calculus but also the true root of Descartes' conception of an equation, namely, the composition of ratios.

Compounding ratios is an undefined technique put importantly to use in Euclid despite its being quite illegitimate, since a ratio of magnitudes ($m : n$) must be treated as though it were itself a mag-nitude suited for manipulation in (quasi-) arithmetical settings such as multiplication.[19]

Thanks to the principle of homogeneity and the operational free-doms it licenses, Descartes is no longer embarrassed by this discrep-ancy between practice and theory. If the problem at hand is, say, the duplication of the cube (i.e., the finding of two mean proportionals between known a and b), we can form the continuous proportion $a/x = x/y = y/b$ and then multiply (i.e., compound) the pairs of ratios ($a/x, x/y; x/y, y/b$) in turn, giving us $ay = x^2$ and $bx = y^2$. Then, also, $x^2 = y^4/b^2$ and $y^4/b^2 = ay$ or, $y^3 = ab^2$, the equation for the duplicate volume of a cube when $a = 2$ and $b = 1$. Moreover, one can always recover the ingre-dient ratios and proportions from the final equation.

A Cartesian equation, however, does not only encapsulate a series of composite ratios; its equational form is decisive in fitting it for a demonstrative role in Cartesian analysis and synthesis (i.e., construc-tion). Because an equation, as its name tells us, expresses an equality, and equalities are automatically reversible, the pattern of "upward" inference in analysis ($p \rightarrow q \rightarrow r$, where r is an already-proved theorem or, more precisely, an already-established equation) can be reversed without further ado ($r \rightarrow q \rightarrow p$) to yield a demonstration, (i.e., another equality). The major "obstacle" in Ancient practice to taking analysis as demonstrative in its own right is thus removed with a single stroke (still another reason for Descartes' insouciance over failing to give the synthesis of the Pappus-problem in full; that can be done straightforwardly by reversing the analysis.)[20]

The new art of equations also reflects the cognitive stature ascribed to symbolization in the "economy" of Cartesian methodical science. Far from being merely abbreviatory marks, the symbolic letters (Viète's *species*) figuring in an equation embody and announce Descartes' key resolve, first, to treat all magnitudes alike as representable by line-segments (another consequence of the principle of homogeneity) and then, more radically still, to treat the lengths of those line-segments not as "absolute" magnitudes but as functional by-products of the roles their "names" can be seen to play in company with one another and against the backdrop of the *lignes principales,* the Cartesian axes selected *à discrétion* for each locus-problem. In other words, the Cartesian resolve to treat "magnitude in general" by means of algebraic symbolization entails the relativization of magnitude (or measure) as such, or, the same thing seen differently, it is the subordination of magnitude to the rule of ordering. The thematic complicity between the *Geometry* and its own pre-text, the *Rules,* allows us to trace this last implication to an even deeper stratum of Cartesian thinking. Just as human science remains one and the same throughout its diverse fields of attention, inasmuch as pure intellect is uniformly at work in them all (Rule I) so, too, it is the measures taken by the mind in its deliberately ordered progression from known to unknown (but always potentially knowable, since homogeneous) terms that confer unity on an equation and are, in turn, the genuine referents of the symbolic notation from which equations are forged.[21]

This, however, is not yet the whole story. Equations can and did become the focus of interest for their own sake; indeed, the development of *algebra* after Descartes (and Newton) is largely in the direction of a theory of equations and combinatorial methods of determining their roots (e.g., the theory of determinants in Leibniz). If what I have suggested in the last four paragraphs and in subsection (1) above is plausible, then this development is quite alien to Descartes' intentions, for its advocates consciously eliminate or at least demote the role of actual constructions.[22] The issue here is by no means narrowly technical; the specifically Cartesian route from *pure mathematics* to a physics of the corporeal world is at stake. Let me try to spell this out as briefly as possible.

The complete mathematical process of which a construction is the terminus consists of a *double transcription*. The algebraic equations expressing the ratios of the line-lengths in a given problem transcribe into symbolic notation the ordered sequence of the steps the mind takes in arranging the terms of that problem according to knowns and unknowns; this, in conformity with the *"praecipuum . . . artis secretum"* divulged in Rule 6 (AT X, 381, lines 7–15). The algebraized equation, in turn, not only encodes and retains that intellectual sequence, it is also the expression of a quantity whose *roots* are the actual line-segments to be drawn from points at specified distances from the chosen axes. The set of points determined by these measures *is* the locus of a curve. The transcription or inscription of the abstract equation into a visible geometrical configuration *is* the construction being sought.[23]

It is impossible not to observe the crucial significance of this double transcription: both the algebraic notation and the ensuing geometrical curve mark the passage from the order of the intellect into the domain of perception. Furthermore, the direction of the passage is essential, since it informs us that the marks or shapes accessible to perception are caused to be there by the intellect imaging its own activities. Descartes' discussion of the two sources of experience (*experientia*) in Rule 12 is salient here: "We experience . . . whatever arrives at our intellect either from elsewhere [*aliunde*] or from its reflexive contemplation of itself" (AT X, 422, line 25–423, line 1). The first source, being other than the intellect, enslaves the latter to chance and uncertainty; the second, reflexive source, being the self-identical intellect, enables it to master its own productions even when these are presented in an alien domain. Pre-Cartesian geometry is slavishness; Cartesian geometry, mastery.

Not, however, limitless mastery! The process of construction, mimicking as it does the mind-body problem in technical miniature, shares in its opacity. The limits to the power of intellect to image itself in the domain of perception are given by the very restriction on admissibility (i.e., the requirement of kinematic determinateness) that simultaneously ensures the exactness and certainty of constructions. *Only* those equations all of whose exponents are rational correspond to admissible curves (those Descartes calls "geometric" and Leibniz will call "algebraic" in distinction from "transcendental" curves). Conversely, only those curves constructed in the requisite manner succeed in transcribing algebraic equations of the appropriate form. This means that there are curves occurring in the sensible domain (e.g., the logarithmic spiral) *or* producible by instruments (e.g., the quadratrix), as well as equations expressing authentic problems (e.g., $x^x + x = 1$, the formula for cutting an angle in a given ratio), that permanently elude the grip of Cartesian technique, despite Descartes' being thoroughly acquainted with most of these formations.[24] The range of intelligibility, then, does not coincide with the domains either of perceptual accessibility or of algebraic tractability. This limitation comes out in another, striking way in the phenomenon of *imaginary roots*. Descartes' anticipation of the fundamental theorem of algebra—that an equation has as many roots as the unknown has dimensions—will not jibe exactly with his own demand that all the roots be actually constructible in a single, uniform "space." Once again technical limitations haunt Descartes' projected identification of the mathematical with the corporeal *simpliciter*.

Despite these intrinsic limitations, the Cartesian commitment to constructivism remains emphatic. Had the term not been usurped for another purpose we might have said that Descartes the geometer is an "exhibitionist" since both the procedures of the intellect in prosecuting the links among terms in a problem and the algebraic notation that symbolizes these procedures must be exhibited, must be, so to speak, bodied forth in a forum not of the mind's own making, however much it stands under the authority of mind.

IV. ESSENCE AND EXISTENCE IN CARTESIAN *PURA MATHESIS*

It is now time to reckon up the implications of these principal characteristics of Cartesian geometry for the relationship between essence and existence as that relationship shows itself in the mathematical domain.

In light of what I have been suggesting above the question of existence *sub specie matheseos* seems readily answered: To exist (geometrically) is to have been actually constructed in accordance with determinate regulations. Or, put differently, the existence of a particular geometrical item (e.g., a root = line-segment) is evidenced by its mode of coming into being, its methodical genesis. This ready answer should not, however, mask the further complication introduced by Descartes' discretionary selections of his "lignes principales" (the coordinate axes) and the unit-length suited to a given problem: the magnitude of a constructed root does not individuate that root in an absolute way since the measure of magnitude has been relativized by those two selections. Furthermore, the same equation (of degree > 1) has more than one positively or negatively valued root; hence, the existence of a single root does not yield uniqueness, but counts as typifying the infinite subclass of roots of the "same" length, relative, that is, to the initial choices. (This same point can be made, *mutatis mutandis*, of the corresponding curves.)

This last aspect of geometrical existence brings us face to face with the issue of mathematical essence. Descartes' formulation in Meditation V, speaking of the triangle, *"determinata quaedam . . . natura, sive essentia, sive forma, immutabilis et aeterna,"* is bound to suggest that the ontology of Cartesian *pura mathesis* is fundamentally the same as, or continuous with, traditional ontologies, of Platonic or Aristotelian provenience, depending on whether emphasis falls on the notion of an eternal form known prior to sensory experience or on that of an immutable essence separable in thought from sensory corporeal instances. Descartes' *practice* in the *Geometry* (together with his theoretical program in the *Rules*), gives the lie, I think, to both of these historical associations and thereby opens up a novel horizon for thinking about the mode of being peculiar to mathematical entities in respect to their essences and their existence alike.[25]

This can be seen most easily from the following considerations. Cartesian "figures" are not the geometrical shapes exhibited in Euclidean geometry (and here the example cited in Meditation V has to be reassigned to the outer *integument* of true mathematics); they are not, that is, figures with their own integrity, shapes to be captured by demonstrated theorems or by constructions always responsive to the particular, pre-given nature of each relevant shape. Nor are the figures of Cartesian geometry *defined* in advance of the problem-solving in which they are put to use, not simply because Descartes presupposes acquaintance with the antecedent tradition, but more significantly because the shift from theorems to problems also transfers his focus from the pre-given character of certain configurations (squares, circles, etc.) to their *utility* in a constructive procedure.[26]

This transfer of interest from the pre-"given" forms of Greek geometry to constructive utility has repercussions palpable throughout the corpus of Descartes' mathematics. First, the abstract symbolic equation takes precedence, at least in the *ordo cognoscendi*, over the corresponding structure into which it may be transcribed. Leibniz was acutely sensitive to the implications of this precedence when he set about designing his *characteristica geometrica* or *analysis situs:* The symbolic equation of, say, a circle gives us no direct or advance information concerning the geometrical shape resulting from it. "For algebraic characters [sc. as in Descartes] do not express all those matters which ought to be considered in space [e.g., the similarity and dissimilarity of figures] . . . nor do they directly signify the *situs* of the points. . . . "[27] In Cartesian terms, it is the equation that holds us closer to the ordering and measuring activity of pure mind, and farther from the figurate extension of the visible.

Accordingly, were we to begin from Euclidean shapes, we would have to dis-figure or de-form them to arrive at the concatenation of the better-known simples of which they intellectually consist (cf. Rule XII: AT X, 422) and, thence, at the algebraic formulation that gives the law of their intelligible and precise genesis via the appropriate ordering and compounding of such simples. In this regard, a Cartesian mathematical essence is a formula, not a (Euclidean) form.[28]

The influence of this transposition is also felt in Descartes' determination of the "nature" of curves in Book Two of the *Geometry*. Not only are these admissible in geometry just insofar as they result from suitably conjoined motions (performed by hand or with instruments), the nature or essential being of an admissible curve is to be a locus of (infinite) points each of which is, in principle, clearly and distinctly constructible. This determination of "nature" is not as innocent as it might initially sound and, when we compare Descartes' procedures with those of Apollonius, his primary source in matters of conic sections, the salient theoretical differences begin to stand in relief.

First, for Apollonius the locus-property of a conic section is not counted among its *archicha symptōmata*, "those features belonging to it primarily," nowadays called its "planimetric properties," even though the three- and four-line locus-properties do follow necessarily from the nature of each section. Descartes, however, begins from the locus-property (the ratios of known and unknown line-segments) and then reconstructs or regenerates the conic section from this. In doing so he effects two further changes: the ordinates and abscissas, which were for Apollonius intrinsic to each of the conic sections, become the "lignes principales" or axes instituted prior to the construction of any conic; they belong, that is, to the conditions of the problem, not to the figural nature of the section. Second, he eliminates any trace of what Apollonius named the *eidos*, or defining form, in the case of the ellipse and the hyperbola, as though to indicate by that name the presence of any invariantly intelligible relation *within* the configuration of curved and straight lines featured in the section. For Descartes, as already suggested, this invariance occurs at the level of the formula and is only derivatively present in the graphic shape insofar as if the latter has been artfully constructed. We are reminded of Viète's use of the phrase *species sive formae rerum* to denote the algebraic letters referring to indeterminate (or general) magnitude(s), instead of the visible *and* knowable figure somehow recurring whenever a specimen geometrical item is encountered.[29]

Descartes' radical transformation of the Ancients' stable geometrical shapes, accessible prior to demonstration and to construction, into the symbolic formulae for the potential generation of such shapes, also alters in a profound way the understanding of the connection between universality and individuality. *Grosso modo*, one could suggest that Descartes abandons an arithmetical or set-theoretical picture of their connection in favor of a geometrical conception. In the former picture, individuals of a certain type are seen as falling under or within a general class or sort which itself possesses in full the class-character displayed more or less completely by those individuals; all individual ellipses, for example, are tokens of the type *ellipse* of which true theorems are demonstrated. Each token somehow exhibits the general elliptical character or nature at which those theorems are aimed. For Descartes, individuals or particulars are evolved by progressive delimitation from an indeterminate, general formula or function that does not denote any specific type or nature. Thus, Descartes' general equation for *any* conic section, viz $Ax^2 + Bxy + Cy^2 + Dx + Ey + F = 0$, where $A \ldots F$ are integral constants, is not the equation of any *one* type of conic section, nor does it capture some *one* essence in which all types and their tokens participate in varying degrees. Instead, it presents a continuum of abstract possibilities given determinate actuality in particular cases by variations in the values of the coefficients. This extensive continuum is, as it were, punctuated by discrete acts of selection to yield individual sections of a certain type. Hence, to exist individually is, in Cartesian mathematics, to be the result of evaluating the variables bound within the general equation. To have discrete being of a certain type or kind, in the Cartesian perspective, is not to share in or exhibit some *one* "determinate nature or essence or form," as his traditional readers are likely to have interpreted these terms; it *is* to be a limited variation on a formally unlimited theme in which the uniformly pure intellect gives a continuous, virtuoso performance.[30] And yet, to come back full circle, the unlimitedness in question here is itself checked by factors apparently falling outside the ambit of mind and, indeed, of its imaginative auxiliary. Some algebraic formulae do not correspond to any constructible figures since their terms defy the requirement of kinematic continuity and control; other formulae have no real, but only "imaginary," roots, which cannot be inscribed in the space available to Cartesian geometry. Conversely, some figures inscribable in this space prove to be only illusory wholes since they cannot be generated from algebraic equations of the appropriate sort (i.e., having only rational exponents).[31] The subsequent history of the metaphysics of geometry, from Leibniz, Wallis, and Newton to Lambert, Kant, and Euler will be in large part an effort to eliminate the sources of these extrinsic checks on the constructive powers of the mind.

V. MORALS *PAR PROVISION*

Much remains to be filled out in this tentative sketch of *pura mathesis;* nonetheless, I want to end this contribution by tracing some possible lessons from what I have delineated so far.

I began in section II by pointing to some of the issues raised by the transition from doubt of the senses to doubt of mathematics in the First Meditation, as well as by the reverse path from the truth of mathematics (as a matter of essences) to the existence of *material things* in the Fifth and Sixth Meditations. The preceding attempt at excavating the subtext to which the *Meditations* seems to allude should put us in a position to gauge how differently or similarly these issues might look *sub specie matheseos.*

Let me start with the issue of resemblance or nonresemblance between a sensation, an image, or an idea, on the one hand, and their respective "objects," on the other. Even in the case of sensation, readers of the *Dioptrics* are likely to have been disconcerted by the invocation of the principle of resemblance and by the doubt occasioned by the possibility of its systematic violation, inasmuch as Descartes had already tried to show that veridical perception is possible without any strong likeness between the sensory datum and the sensed object. By what he calls in that text a "natural geometry," even a blind man is able to see, thanks to his ability to make sound inferences from sensations of touch and pressure to the shape, magnitude, and position of an external physical object. In the case of the mathematical items considered in the *Geometry* the claim that resemblance is a necessary condition for veracity is weakened to the point of vanishing altogether.[32] The relations germane here are (1) between a concatenation of purely intellectual simples and the algebraic equation into which it is transcribed; (2) between that equation and the "graph" by which it may be constructed; and (3) between that visible graph and a shape or configuration believed to belong to an independently existing material object. As far as relations (1) and (2) are concerned resemblance is out of the question, although we could say that the second term in each represents or expresses the first relation; for example, the equation expresses, in the sense of codifying, the operations of the intellect in disposing and ordering the terms of a problem, while the graph expresses one version of the equation, in the sense of constructing it under certain determinations (the "values" of the variables and the choice of coordinates). As for relation (3), it raises the most troublesome problems, at least at the start, only for someone who believes that mathematics proceeds by abstracting such shapes from the perceptual experience of external bodies, a belief Descartes seems at pains to controvert by the evidence of his own mathematical practice.

This mistaken belief works hand in hand with the second prejudice shaping our naive or native view of the origin of our knowledge of the world, namely, the principle of causality, applied in such a way that a nonmental object is assumed to be the cause of which a mental entity is the effect.[33] Descartes' distinction in the *Rules* between experience as it comes *aliunde* (from elsewhere) and experience arising from the mind's reflex knowledge of itself has already paved the way for the more extensive challenge to this application of the principle of causality in the mathematical domain. There Descartes' constructivism is potently at work to show the reader the geometer's mind in the act of producing the symbolic notation and the subsequent graphs, which it causes to function as its nonresembling representatives or deputies. The inward private motions of the intellect somehow become public in this vicarious fashion. ("Somehow" strikes the right note of unclarity, since this dual process of publication or embodiment (in symbols and in linear graphs), indispensable as it is from the evidentiary standpoint, nonetheless remains fundamentally enigmatic both with respect to its *modus operandi* and to its public works. I shall return briefly to this twin enigma in a bit.)

At all events, what comes to sight in Descartes' mathematical practice, as well as in his comments on the roots of that practice, is the essentially productive character of *ideas* themselves. A primitive Cartesian *idea*, whatever else it is or seems to be, serves as a "pâtron ou un original," an *instar archetypi*, in the language of the Third Meditation, first as generating other *ideas*, and then as a template for the derivation of other things, including *"les choses extérieures,"* from our thoughts and thus from our formative powers.[34] William Carlo, at the end of his richly detailed study of the differences between the Thomistic and the Cartesian idea of *ideas*, concludes that the item Descartes identifies as an idea " . . . was not the principle of knowledge functioning as the principle of knowledge, but the principle of artistic production." I want only to add that this shift from the cognitive to the artisanal is not a mistake but comes about by design.[35] In his Reply to the Third Objections Descartes justifies the way he has used the term *idea* by reminding his interlocutors that "it was already commonly received by the philosophers for signifying the forms of the conceptions of the divine understanding." Descartes, we might conjecture, takes over for the mind's role-model a Christianized Demiurge, not the Aristotelian *nous* whose whole actuality consists in thinking its own thinking.

If the requirements of resemblance and of causality *ab alio* are disarmed when the sources of mathematical achievement are brought retrospectively into view, all that remains as an occasion for diffidence vis-à-vis mathematics is the principle of externality or of independent, extramental existence. Needless to say, this "remnant" is more perplexing and more intractable than any of the preceding occasions for doubt. To take the measure of its power we would need to begin shuttling back and forth from the subtext of *pura mathesis* to the overt argument of the last two Meditations. Since I cannot rise to that intricate challenge in the present setting, let me end this study by calling attention to three of the manifestations of the power intrinsic to this final principle.

First, Cartesian "dualism" is already at issue in mathematics and hence is not parochially tied to the psycho-physical dualism in which my *own* body and, above all, its responses to pleasure and pain, play a selfish role. For the mind to externalize itself through its productive expression in equations and then in constructions accessible to perception it must be both independent of, and connected with, the corporeal. It is in the *Rules,* more extensively than in any other writing, that Descartes faces this conundrum and embodies it in his doctrine of the *imagination.* The latter, said to be "a true part of the body," must somehow be capable both of taking inward, incorporeal directions and of giving them outwardly perceptible shape. The exercise of this second capacity is always in jeopardy since the outward shape qua outward returns to impress the imagination and to encounter the intellect as something both alien and exempt from its autonomy. Kant will articulate this same conundrum under the rubric "The Schematism of the Pure Concepts of the Understanding."

Second, the externality required by this process of imaginative self-exhibition presents a seemingly insuperable obstacle to the complete intellectualization of phenomena set into motion by the project of Cartesian mathematical physics. As we saw in the details of Descartes' geometry, not all algebraic equations can be constructed or represented phenomenally. Those that can do not require any particular external body or discrete bodily shape to validate them; they do require, however, a receptacle or a phenomenal continuum, not of the mind's own making, in which successful constructions can make their appearances. If the "evil demon" symbolizes the seductiveness of pretheoretical nature, the seductiveness Descartes aims to resist by exposing the ways it compromises the project of Cartesian science, it remains indispensable to that very project that the appearances it sets out to master continue to appear, or, more exactly, that phenomenality in general remain as a foil to the dramatic displays of mathematical power. However far Cartesian science goes towards conquering and possessing nature, however successfully it mobilizes techniques for transforming prescientific nature into new appearances conformable to human will, this science cannot sunder its attachment to the givenness (or, perhaps, createdness) of appearance as such.[36]

Third, and finally, the very success anticipated by Cartesian mathematical science brings doubt in its wake, doubt, ultimately, over whether the mathematical laws obeyed by phenomenal nature or imposed upon it to bring about a new ordering of phenomena, are in the last analysis the uniquely necessary laws. Malebranche's compromise—to argue that our knowledge of extension and its quantifiable modes need only be similar to the world of extramental experience—would not have satisfied Descartes in his most radical or anhypothetical frame of mind.[37] As he wrote to Mersenne in 1640:

As for Physics, I would believe myself to know nothing of it if I knew only how to say how things can be, without demonstrating that they cannot be otherwise . . .

Perhaps this is the point at which the claims of *pura mathesis*, the official arguments of the *Meditations*, and his private references to the "creation of eternal truths" meet.[38]

NOTES

1. See his letter to Mersenne, 8 October 1629 (AT I, 23). (The abbreviation AT is explained in the General Bibliography at the beginning of this volume.) All translations are my own. (The disciple is Daniel Lipstorp; cf. his *Specimina philosophiae Cartesianae* [Lyon, 1653], *Praefatio ad lectorem*, 7.)

2. The two fundamental studies on this theme are R. Verneaux, "La sincérité critique chez Descartes," *Archives de philosophie* 13 (1937):15–100, and H.

Caton, "The Problem of Descartes' Sincerity," *Philosphical Forum*, n.s. 2 (1971):355–370. It might be well to recall that the same Leibniz who expressed surprise at the ease with which Descartes' artful distortions of meanings duped his readers also declared to one of his own correspondents: "Metaphysics should be written with accurate definitions and demonstrations, but nothing should be demonstrated in it that conflicts too much with received opinions." (Cf. *Discours de Metaphysique*, 2d ed., ed. H. Lestienne [Paris: Vrin, 1952], p. 14 note.)

3. See the occurrences of *objectum purae matheseos* in the Fifth Meditation (AT VII, 71) and in the Sixth Meditation (AT VII, 71 and 80).

4. I have in mind, of course, the Sixth Part of the *Discourse on Method* (AT VI, 61–62). For the thesis that the new science or philosophy must be preeminently practical, see R. Kennington, "Descartes and Mastery of Nature," in *Organism, Medicine and Metaphysics*, ed. S. F. Spicker (Dordrecht: Reidel, 1978), 202–223, and Sergio Sarti, "Considerazioni sul 'cogito' e sull' idea cartesiana di perfezione," *Giornale di Metafisica* 18 (1963):71–88.

5. More needs to be said about the exact sense of "purity" relevant here and about the inclusiveness of Descartes' own geometry. On the second issue it is imperative to consider the exchange of letters with Ciermans (AT II, 56 and 70) in which Descartes is expressly asked why he did not use the title *Mathematica pura* in place of *Geometria*. His answer points us to his unpublished work, *De solidorum elementis* (AT X, 265–276) and to his concern there for relations of order, which depend on the nonarbitrary measures of the angles of polygons and polyhedra. On this text, see P. T. Federico, *Descartes on Polyhedra* (New York: Springer, 1982), in which, however, no mention is made of the letter to Ciermans.

6. This focus was in evidence from the days of his early studies in "Physico-Mathematica" with Beeckman; cf. AT X, 67–78 and compare Stephen Gaukroger, "Descartes' Project for a Mathematical Physics," in *Descartes: Philosophy, Mathematics and Physics*, ed. Stephen Gaukroger (New York: Barnes and Noble, 1980), 97–140.

7. *Objectum*, together with the other key word in Descartes' vocabulary of method, *res*, needs more detailed study. An indispensable starting point is Johannes Lohmann, "Descartes' 'Compendium musicae' und die Entstehung des neuzeitlichen Bewusstseins," *Archiv für Musikwissenschaft* 36 (1979):81–104, in company with the medieval material studied by L. Dewan, "'Objectum': Notes on the Invention of a Word," *Archives d'histoire doctrinale et littéraire du moyen âge* 48 (1981):37–96. These linguistic results add strength to the more general interpretation offered by Pascal Marignac, "Descartes et ses concepts de la substance," *Revue de métaphysique et de morale* 85 (1980):298–314.

8. For "the objection of objections," see AT IX–1, 212, and compare Roberval's letter to Des Noyer's concerning Descartes' insistence on the identity of *corpus mathematicum* and *corpus physicum* at AT XI, 688–690.

9. See L. Liard, "La méthode et la mathesis universale de Descartes," *Revue philosophique* 10 (1880):569–600 and Giovanni Crapulli, *Mathesis Universalis: Genesi di una idea nel XVI secolo* (Roma: Edizioni dell'Ateneo, 1969). For more recent studies, see T. Mittelstrass, "Die Idee einer mathesis universalis bei

Descartes," *Perspektiven der Philosophie* 4 (1978):177–192; John A. Schuster, "Descartes' *Mathesis Universalis*, 1619–1628," in *Descartes*, ed. Stephen Gaukroger, 41–96; and F. P. Van de Pitte, "Descartes, *Mathesis Universalis*," *Archiv für Geschichte der Philosophie* 61 (1979):154–174.

10. See Leibniz, *Mathematische Schriften* (ed. Gerhardt) 7:205 and compare, ibid., 53–76, together with the Fragments *in* L. Couturat, *Opuscules et Fragments inédits de Leibniz* (Paris: Alcan, 1903), 348–351. (The relations between the Cartesian and Leibnizian versions of this project are studied in Roswitha Engelbrecht's *Der Begriff "Mathesis Universalis" bei Descartes und Leibniz* [Phil. diss., Vienna, 1970] and in J. Mittelstrass, "The Philosopher's Conception of 'Mathesis Universalis' from Descartes to Leibniz," *Annals of Science* 36 [1979]:593–610.)

11. The most excitingly plausible reconstruction of the provenance and meaning of *ordo et mensura* in the *Rules* is to be found in Jean-Luc Marion, *L'Ontologie grise de Descartes* (Paris: Vrin, 1975), esp. 71–99.

12. I have presented more of this view in a lecture, "Geometry and Knowledge in Descartes," to be published in the *Graduate Faculty Philosophy Journal*. Among the works by which my interpretation has been inspired are J. Hyppolite, "Du sens de la géométrie de Descartes dans son oeuvre," in *Figures de la pensée philosophique* (Paris: P.U.F., 1971) 1:7–19; T. Lenoir, "Descartes and the Geometrization of Thought: The Methodological Background of Descartes' *Géométrie*," *Historia Mathematica* 6 (1979):355–379; R. Mitrovitch, *La théorie des sciences chez Descartes, d'après sa "Géométrie"* (Thèse du doctorat, Paris, 1932) and J. Vuillemin, *Mathématiques et métaphysique chez Descartes* (Paris: Vrin, 1960).

13. For Viète, cf. *Opera Mathematica* (Lyon, 1646), 312: *Problematis Adrianici Constructio*. Wolff's definition of the construction of an equation is given in his *Mathematisches Lexicon* (Leipzig, 1716; Hildesheim: Olms, 1965), 421, and is followed by Kant in, e.g., his *Metaphysik der Sitten* (orig. ed.), ix: "wie man es in der Geometrie auch an der Konstruktion der Gleichungen wahrnehmen kann."

14. See, for one example, Descartes' letter to Mersenne, 20 February 1639 (AT II, 524). Descartes' reinterpretation of synthesis or demonstration as the manifest "construction of problems" assumes its full revolutionary force when it is studied together with Proclus's discussion of the Academic debates concerning the different status of theorems (to be demonstrated) and problems (to be generated or constructed); cf. *In Primum Elementorum Librum*, ed. Friedlein, 77.7–79.2.

15. See Jacob Klein, *Greek Mathematical Thought and the Origin of Algebra* (Cambridge: M.I.T., 1968), 172–178 (with notes), for the principle of homogeneity in Viète. Leibniz will later introduce his *lex homogeneorum transcendentalis* to permit further extensions of the field of algebraic operations (cf. *Mathematische Schriften* 5:377–381). As for Descartes' circumvention of the problem of incommensurability, compare the remarks on Rules XIV–XV by Costabel and Marion in their annotated translation of the *Rules* (The Hague: M. Nijhoff, 1976), 275.

16. The issue of the admissibility of "mechanical" ("transcendental") curves

into geometry will become one of the pivotal points in Leibniz's debate with Descartes. See, for example, *Mathematische Schriften* 5:278–279; 285–288, as well as Emile Turrière, "La notion de transcendence géométrique chez Descartes et Leibniz," *Isis* 2 (1914):106–124 and H. J. M. Bos, "On the Representation of Curves in Descartes' Géométrie," *Archive for History of Exact Sciences* 24 (1981):295–338.

17. In the manuscript of reflections, which Leibniz entitled *"Cartesius,"* we find the following comparison: *Intellectio est ad mentem ut motus ad corpus et voluntas ut Figura . . .* (AT XI, 647; the astronomical observation on p. 650 may date this manuscript to ca. 1642). The prevalence of the general theme—motions of the mind—in Descartes' thinking has been convincingly exhibited by J.-M. Beyssade, *La philosophie première de Descartes* (Paris: Flammarion, 1979), 129–176.

18. Cf. letter to Mersenne, 11 October 1638 (AT II, 392–393). (Earlier he had referred to "ma vieille Algèbre," presumably from his own hand [AT I, 501].) The text of the *Calcul* is printed [AT X, 659–680] and contains no axioms or theorems. Newton undertook to place analytical geometry on an axiomatic basis, but in conscious opposition to *"l'esprit de géométrie Cartésienne"*: see his *Mathematical Papers,* ed. D. Whiteside (Cambridge: Cambridge University Press, 1968) 2:450 sq.

19. Cf. Euclid, *Elements* V, def. 9 and the interpolated def. 5 in Bk. VI, together with Heath's comments *ad loc.* It is very much worth noting that the passage in Adriaan van Roomen's *Apologia pro Archimede* [1597] to which Crapulli (*Mathesis Universalis*) traces the first use of the expression *mathesis universalis* concerns a later Greek attempt to make sense of the operation of "compounding a proportion from proportions," i.e., the matrix of an equation (cf. Crapull, ibid., 209–210).

20. Compare Aristotle, *Anal. post.* II, 78a10–13 and the discussion in M. Mahoney, "Another Look at Greek Geometrical Analysis," *Archive for History of Exact Sciences* 5 (1969):318–348. The emphasis given by J. Hintikka and U. Remes (*The Method of Analysis* [Dordrecht: Reidel, 1974]) to Greek analysis as a method for discovering proofs of new theorems has, in my judgment, been effectively countered in the review by Erkka Maula, "An End of Invention," *Annals of Science* 38 (1981):109–122 and the article by A. Szabó, "Analysis and Synthesis," *Acta Classica* [*Debrecen*], 10–11 (1974–75):155–164.

21. For a closely related account of symbolic generalization and its ties to the Scholastic theory of *actus signatus,* see J. Klein, *Greek Mathematical Thought,* 197–211 (and notes).

22. For a brief but informative study of this transition see Carl Boyer, "Cartesian and Newtonian Algebra in the Mid-Eighteenth Century," *Actes du XIᵉ Congrès International d'Histoire des Sciences* (Wroclaw: Ossolineum, 1968) 3:195–202. An exemplary statement of the Cartesian's aim can be found in Van Schooten's commentary (1683 edition) 1:145.

23. In this respect Hobbes's insistence on the "exposition to sense" (*English Works* [ed. Molesworth] 1:311) as the cognitive finale of Euclidean synthesis is at one with Descartes' commitment to constructibility, quite apart from

Hobbes's rejection of algebraic symbolization as a necessary auxiliary to proofs. See William Sacksteder, "Hobbes: The Art of the Geometricians," *Journal of the History of Philosophy* 18 (1980):131–146.

24. See his communications to Mersenne concerning the quadratrix (AT I, 70–71) and the logarithmic spiral (AT II, 360–361) and to De Beaune on the logarithmic curve (AT II, 514–517). On the issue in general, see J. Vuillemin, *Mathématiques*, 9–55.

25. On the analogous treatment of number (as identical with the things numbered), see Helen Lauer, "Descartes' Concept of Number," *Studia Cartesiana* 2 (1981):137–142.

26. Cf. Descartes' letter to Princess Elisabeth (Nov. 1643) in which he proudly declares that the *Géométrie* presupposes only two theorems demonstrated by Euclid (AT IV, 38).

27. Leibniz, *Mathematische Schriften* 5:142. On the philosophical underpinnings of Leibniz's own passionately promoted *characteristica geometrica* (or analysis situs), see Gilles-Gaston Granger, "Philosophie et mathématique leibniziennes," *Revue de métaphysique et de morale* 86 (1981):1–37 (esp. 13–16) and H. P. Münzenmayer, "Der Calculus Situs und die Grundlagen der Geometrie bei Leibniz," *Studia Leibnitiana* 11 (1979):275–300.

28. I have borrowed the motif "dis-figuration" from Jean-Luc Marion, *Sur la théologie blanche de Descartes* (Paris: P.U.F., 1981), 231–263, whose analysis is detailed and exemplary.

29. For further examination of these and other salient differences between classical Greek and seventeenth-century *Begrifflichkeit*, see Jacob Klein, "The World of Physics and the 'Natural' World," translated from a Marburg lecture of 1932 by D. R. Lachterman and published in *The St. John's Review* 33 (1981): 22–34.

30. Pascal, in his Fragmentary *Traité des sections coniques*, is even more explicit in proposing this new manner of conceiving the universal in mathematics; for example, a point, two straight lines, and a right-angle all become *cases* of the notion "conic section" when the mode of generation *and* the position of the geometer's eye are taken into account. See R. Taton, "L'oeuvre de Pascal en géométrie projective" in *L'Oeuvre scientifique de Pascal* (Paris: P.U.F., 1964), 17–72.

31. On this and other pertinent matters, compare Lüder Gäbe, *Descartes' Selbstkritik* (Hamburg: Felix Meiner Verlag, 1972), 123–128.

32. Compare the treatment of the "similarity-thesis" in R. Kennington, "The 'Teaching of Nature' in Descartes' Soul Doctrine," *Review of Metaphysics* 26 (1972):86–117, and the very helpful study by Gerard Lebrun, "La notion de 'ressemblance' de Descartes à Leibniz," in *Sinnlichkeit und Verstand in der deutschen und Französischen Philosophie von Descartes bis Hegel*, ed. H. Wagner (Bonn: Bouvier Verlag, 1979), 39–57. It is surely worth considering whether a representation, for Descartes as much as for Leibniz, *deputizes*, rather than resembles.

33. See K. C. Clatterbaugh, "Descartes's Causal Likeness Principle," *Philosophical Review* 89 (1980):379–402.

34. Compare AT IX–1, 33 with AT VII, 43 and see also AT II, 36 on what it means to assert that "external things follow from our thoughts." On the phrase *instar archetypi*, see A. Doz, "Sur la signification de 'instar archetypi.' Descartes, Troisième Méditation," *Revue philosophique de la France et de l'Étranger* 93 (1968):380–387.

35. William E. Carlo, "Idea and Concept: A Key to Epistemology," in *The Quest for the Absolute*, ed. F. J. Adelmann (Chestnut Hill, Mass.: Boston College Studies in Philosophy, 1, 1966), 47–66. On the artisanal or productive paradigm in Descartes, compare Lucien Laberthonnière, *Oeuvres: Études sur Descartes* II, ed. L. Canet (Paris: Vrin, 1935), 287–315.

36. The issue here is twofold: First, that appearances are indeed "given" or "manifest" prior to intellectual construction, and, second, that they do indeed appear or *make their appearance*. Leibniz will try arduously to secure both these conditions while claiming, at least in some writings, that the mind makes the phenomena or phenomenalizes itself (cf. *Opuscules*, 528: *Nostra Mens phaenomenon facit, Divina . . . Rem [sc. Facit]*).

37. Malebranche, *Recherche de la Vérité* (ed. Bouillier) 2:118: *"Il suffit que le monde que nous concevrons être formé d'étendue, paraisse semblable à celui que nous voyons . . . "* (my emphasis). See Genette Dreyfus, "Physique et géométrie chez Descartes et chez Malebranche," in *Descartes: Cahiers de Royaumont, 1655* (Paris: Editions de Minuit, 1957), 187–207.

38. The most vigorous defense of the centrality of the doctrine of the creation of eternal truths is provided by Marion, *Sur la théologie blanche*, esp. 264–312. See also the three studies by J.-M. Beyssade, G. Rodis-Lewis, and G. Simon on "La création des vérités éternelles" published in *Studia Cartesiana* 2 (1981):85–135.

19

The Status of Necessity and Impossibility in Descartes

HIDE ISHIGURO

INTRODUCTION

This is an attempt to understand one important aspect of Descartes' claim, originally made in letters to Mersenne in 1630,[1] and assumed in the *Meditations*, that eternal truths (such as those of mathematics and logic) are dependent on God's creation, and hence on God's free decrees. To say that an eternal truth or a necessary truth—for example, that $2 + 3 = 5$—holds only because of God's free decree is to say that it was possible for $2 + 3 = 5$ not to have been a necessary truth; that is, that it was not necessary that $2 + 3 = 5$ be necessary. In other words, For Descartes, $\Box p$ does not entail $\Box\Box p$, and this is a claim about the status of modality—the status of the necessity and possibility of truths, and of impossibility.

I examine Descartes' views on the creation of eternal truths focusing on the nature of modality and God's omnipotence.[2] In doing this, I follow Leibniz, Martial Gueroult, and Jacques Bouveresse, although my views diverge strongly from theirs. (Leibniz judged Descartes to be simply wrong. Gueroult thought that Descartes had actually anticipated Leibniz's distinction of absolute and hypothetical necessity, whereas Bouveresse, on the contrary, believes that Descartes' modality is entirely epistemic.) My aim is a limited one: it is to work out the implication of what Descartes says on this problem in the *Meditations* and his Replies to the Objections, and to correct what seems to me to be a widespread mistaken interpretation of its implication. I want to argue that a view of necessity like that of Descartes, which says that a necessary truth need not necessarily have been a necessary truth, does not imply that God could have made a contradiction true. Descartes does not say, for example, that $2 + 3 = 6$ could have been a necessary truth, or that God could have made it the case that $2 + 3 = 6$. In showing this I also want to point to an interesting asymmetry between the status of necessity and that of impossibility. These problems arise out of certain things Descartes writes about: (a) our mental constitution, (b) the unchanging natures or essences of certain objects of thought, and (c) God's omnipotence.

(a) First, according to Meditation V (AG, 106; the Pléiade, 315–316),[3] we are so constituted that we cannot but believe something to be true at the time of perceiving it clearly and distinctly, even if we can conceive the possibility of being mistaken. For example, Descartes writes that when he, who is conversant with geometrical principles, considers the nature of a triangle, it is most evidently apparent to him that its three angles are equal to two right angles. So long as he attends to the proof, he cannot but believe that this is true. It is important to notice that the constitution of the mind which is at issue here is not, for example, one that enables a person to perceive correctly what exists in the world. For previously in the same Meditation V he has made clear that *even if no triangular figure were to exist outside his consciousness and never did exist* the triangle he imagines has a determinate nature, or form or essence, which is unchangeable and eternal.

(b) This nature of the triangle is no figment of his own. It does not depend on his [individual] mind, he says, and the proof of this lies in the fact that various properties can be proved of it (that its angles equal two right angles), even if he had not thought of these properties in any way when he had previously imagined a triangle. We see that this nature or essence is not an empirical property of things either, since it exists even were no figure to exist outside of our minds. And although Descartes uses the expression "eternal truth" interchangeably with "essence" in a letter to Mersenne,[4] the essence in question is *not* an Aristotelian one: it is not an essential sortal property of an existing thing. As someone who rejected the Aristotelian-Scholastic doctrine of substantial forms, Descartes would not be interested in the question of how such forms could have been created from all eternity before the creation of actual individuals. Even when he talks of the essence of material substance, it is extension or motion and its geometrical properties that concern him.[5] His example of an eternal truth that is an essence is the truth that lines drawn from the center to the circumference of a circle are equal in length. (Thus although Descartes claims that God is the total efficient cause of eternal truths as he is of other things, the way in which he causes them to exist is different.) Descartes even says to Mersenne that, if Mersenne should want to attribute the word *creavit* (created) only to that of the existence of things, Descartes would be prepared not to use the word in relation to eternal truths or essences and say that God "ordained and established them" (*Illas diposuit et fecit*). For, as he also says elsewhere, we do not take an eternal truth, such as the truth that something cannot be made out of nothing, to be a thing or a property of a thing, but something we might call a common notion or maxim, which has its site in our mind.[6]

Thesis (a) then should be understood as saying that our mind is constituted in such a way that we find ourselves assenting to these eternal truths. These truths concern the immutable forms of the internal objects of our imaginings and thinkings, and of which we can have clear and distinct ideas. They are rules and forms of the working of the mind freely created by God. Descartes says that "God like a sovereign legislator ordained and established them for all eternity" (Reply to Sixth Objections, VIII). They are obviously laid down by Him not in the form of a code, but in the constitution of our mind. In creating our mind, he creates the eternal truths. One should thus not say that eternal truths depend on human understanding or on the existence of things but say that they depend on God's will (ibid.). Our mathematics and geometry, for Descartes, would be the way they are because of God's creation of our minds—*even if there were no external physical world to which we would apply them*. They are not special capacities that enable us to enter into a privileged relation with physical things in the external world also created by him, as a good pair of eyes would be. They are there, in the language Kant was to use, as a priori forms of thinking.

(c) The third point is not the one (which Descartes argues at greater length) about God's existence and his benevolence on which our constitution seems to depend. What we are concerned with is rather Descartes' point that even if God's creation is to be accepted we can further wonder whether God could have made different sets of truths necessary from the ones that we have. Descartes' answer, as we know, was Yes. We will see that (a), (b), and (c) together lead to unexpected tensions.

THE DISTINCTION BETWEEN ETERNAL TRUTHS AND
TRUTHS OF PHYSICS

If logical and mathematical truths depend in Descartes' philosophy on the free decrees of God, would the status of logical and mathematical truths not resemble that of truths of physics? Anachronistically using Leibnizian terminology, Bouveresse has recently suggested that for Descartes no eternal truths are true in all possible worlds.[7] Yet, in Descartes' system, the status of logic or mathematics remains quite distinct from that of physics. Laws of Nature or what Descartes also called "principles" of physics, such as the inertial laws and conservation laws, are "the rules following which changes in nature take place."[8] And although Descartes proceeds to try to justify them in terms of the immutable nature of God, he also acknowledges elsewhere that truths about the world can only be discovered by reasoning on what we perceive through our senses (*Principles of Philosophy* I, 28). Specific conservation laws cannot be discovered just by a priori reasoning based on the nature of God. He is indeed right since we know, for example, that through an inadequate formulation of what he observed and measured Descartes wrongly asserted that the quantity of motion (rather than energy) is what is conserved. (Descartes' injunction is a negative one of urging people *not* to invoke God's purpose but only his nature in our explanation of the world. He does not deny the role the senses play, insufficient as it obviously is, in our obtaining the notion of matter and motion.) General conservation principles and the immutable nature of laws may be explained by reference to the immutability of God, but the identity of what is conserved cannot be.

How Descartes conceived the status of laws of nature is not a simple problem since he did claim that had God created many worlds the very same laws of nature would be observed in all of them (*Discourse on Method*, 5). This was because in order to avoid controversies of the kind Galileo was involved in, he wanted to base his physics not on any particular facts about this world, but only on the basic properties of matter and motion encapsulated in the laws of nature. These are nevertheless rules governing changes in the created world and are not eternal truths. In his explanation of physics, Descartes invokes both his three basic laws of nature *and* the eternal truths of mathematics, but the status of the two are kept apart.[9] Truths about the world are truths of a temporal nature even if they be unchanging. God willed them to be true in creating the world; whereas God not only willed logical and mathematical truths to be true, he also willed that they be necessarily true (Response to sixth set of Objections, VI: HR II, 248; Pléiade 535). We will therefore have to understand what this "decreeing that they be necessarily true" amounts to.

To decree that a truth be necessarily true is to decree it to be a necessary truth. When Descartes wrote "It is one thing to will that truths be necessary, quite another thing to necessarily will that they should be so,"[10] Descartes was denying only the latter to God; not the former. What then is the distinction for Descartes between truths that are necessary and those that are not, if both kinds of truths depend on God's free creation and are not "necessarily willed"? For one thing, we can imagine a physical state of affairs different from the ones that actually obtain or those which change following different laws from the ones that operate in the actual world. But we cannot imagine two plus three not adding up to five, nor (Descartes mistakenly thought) can we imagine the angles of a triangle not to add up to two right angles. Why would this be if Descartes could not say that the contradictory of a necessary truth is impossible, as Leibniz was to do? Surely, as it has often been pointed out, Descartes wrote of the possibility of it not being the case that $2 + 3 = 5$ in the Third Meditation?

The reason why when we add two and three we cannot but get the sum of five is because eternal truths, according to Descartes, have their seat in the mind[11] (*Principles of Philosophy* I, 49). They do not, it is true, depend on how particular individual minds are made—for example, to be cleverer or to perceive better. We should therefore not call the Cartesian notion of modality "epistemic." Descartes' modality does not depend on historical states of our knowledge, nor on the development of our concepts. It does not depend on any *individual's* state of knowledge either.[12] In fact, what Descartes means by eternal truths having their seat in the mind seems closer to Kant's view on the a priori than it does to epistemic views like that of Hume. What is at issue is the universal validity of these eternal truths in our mental constitution—and this is something that Descartes discovers by the inspection of forms of our clear and distinct thoughts and not by an empirical investigation of psychological dispositions.

To see Descartes' concept of modality as being a priori is to challenge an interesting view of the influential French historian of philosophy, Gueroult, who saw in Descartes the beginning of the distinction Leibniz was to make between absolute necessity and hypothetical necessity (which are both metaphysical necessities).[13] Physical necessity, like the necessity of the truth of the way the tide ebbs and rises, is hypothetical for Leibniz, since it is only necessary given the way the world was created with its gravitational laws and the earth and the moon.

In contrast to this, the laws of logic and conceptual truths, such as the truth that a part cannot be bigger than the whole, were absolute for Leibniz. They did not depend on how the world was created, but they logically preceded creation. To claim, as Gueroult did, that in Descartes one could already find the distinction between absolute and hypothetical necessity is controversial, since at first glance the doctrine of the creation of eternal truths seems to make all truths hypothetical in Leibniz's sense; that is, it seems to make all truths depend on how God created the world. To say that, despite appearances to the contrary, there is in Descartes an anticipation of the Leibnizian distinction is based on Gueroult's conviction that there are limits even to what Descartes' God could do. Descartes cannot ascribe to God acts that limit his omnipotence: we can no more conceive God to be a deceiver than we can conceive him not to exist. Nor can Descartes conceive God as creating beings that are independent of him. And what God cannot help but do would correspond to Leibniz's absolute necessity.

Descartes' position, which is extremely subtle and is worthy of a sympathetic reading, is not quite captured even by Gueroult or Bouveresse. It is true that in Descartes we already have a distinction somewhat similar to that between absolute and hypothetical necessity; but the line is not drawn exactly where Leibniz was to draw it. There is, I suggest, both absolute and hypothetical modality for Descartes within the realm of logical or conceptual truths. Moreover, the need to demarcate absolute from hypothetical truths does not arise out of the inappropriateness of ascribing to God an act that limits his omnipotence—if by this we mean that we coherently describe a situation that God could have created, and then refrain from ascribing to God the ability to create it, because we judge that if we do so we would portray God as less than omnipotent. Descartes' clearly stated position to make all truths dependent on God's creation does not lead one to adopt such a confused account of withdrawing the possibility of certain acts from God on the grounds that they limit His omnipotence. The distinction between absolute and hypothetical necessity within logic arises from the way Descartes understands negation and from the fact that we are bound by our thought and the expressive powers of our language (from which Descartes can no more escape than we can).

ABSOLUTE IMPOSSIBILITY

On the one hand, there is absolute nonepistemic modality even in Descartes: the impossibility of actualizing something that falls under a contradictory concept is *absolute*. It is not true that Descartes' God could have made it true (let alone necessary) that two times four be seven or two plus two be five. Nor should one think that once God has freely created the impossibility of two plus two being five, it is for that reason beyond him to make it possible that two plus two be five. It is not only the necessity of $2 + 2 = 4$ and the other arithmetical truths that depend on God's creation of our mind. The very concepts of natural number and of addition or multiplication depend on God's having made our minds in the way He did. God could not have created minds to have the very same concepts of two, four, five, + or ×, and *at the same time made it true* that $2 + 2 = 5$, or that $2 \times 4 = 7$. It is thus absolutely impossible for God to have made $2 + 2 = 5$ true, or to have made a contradiction true.

For example, in his reponse to the Second Objections to the *Meditations* compiled by Mersennes, Descartes insists that in describing God's nature he has not supposed anything that is repugnant to thought or to the human concept; if not, he writes, "you pretend to conjure up (*feignez*) some other possibility from the side of the object, but such a possibility can never be known by the human understanding if it does not agree with the preceding kind [i.e., the kind that accords with thought and human concepts]."[14] A better way to put Descartes' point might be to say that he has not purported to ascribe to God something that is contradictory within the human concept. We do not ascribe anything at all to anything if we contradict ourselves. We cannot ascribe to God the power of creating that $2 + 3 = 6$ or that $2 > 3$, because we have not succeeded in describing a possible state of affairs that a creator could bring about. In using our language, we cannot describe what our language does not allow us to describe. We may confusedly think that we are imagining or describing a possible state of affairs, but we are not. We are describing nothing. To admit that we cannot ascribe to God the possibility of actualizing a nothing is *not* to set a limit to his omnipotence. As Descartes writes elsewhere, someone's not being able to do what we cannot conceive to be possible is no mark of impotence.[15] There are no contradictory states of affairs but only contradictory ideas. In the second response quoted above, Descartes says, "For all impossibility, or if it is permitted to use the scholastic terminology, all 'implicantia' consists only in our concept or thought which cannot conjoin ideas which contradict one another."[16] (This quotation continues: "It cannot reside in anything external to the mind, because by the very fact that a thing is outside the mind it is clear that it is not contradictory, but is possible.")

It is obvious that what Descartes means by thought not being able to conjoin ideas that contradict one another is not that human beings as a matter of fact do not entertain inconsistent thoughts. They obviously do. What he is saying is that no thoughts which contain ideas that are contradictories of one another can be instantiated—that they are not thoughts of anything, they are impossibilities. It is absolutely impossible that a contradiction be instantiated, and so the ideas made up of contradictory elements are not coherent ideas.

Thus in his Replies to the sixth set of Objections (Sixth Replies, VIII: HR II, 251; Pléiade, 538) when Descartes gives an example of a possibility we must be willing to think is available to God though incomprehensible to us, it is not the possibility of two times four being seven that he gives, but the possibility of *two times four not being eight*. Of course there are possibilities other than ones that we can understand or describe, but we cannot say which possibilities these are. Not only is there no passage in the *Meditations* or in the Replies to Objections where Descartes gives a positive contradiction (as distinct from a negation of a necessary truth) as something God could make true, I am as yet unaware of any example in his other works either. The one difficult example, which we will discuss later, is in the letter to Mesland quoted above. He ascribes to God the possibility of making *not true* the *impossibility* of contradictories holding together. By ordinary assumptions about double negations canceling themselves out, this might suggest that Descartes is ascribing to God the ability to make true what is a specific positive contradiction. That this is not so will be seen later when we discuss negation.

CONDITIONAL NECESSITY

On the other hand, the necessity of a truth like $1 + 2 = 3$ is conditional (or if we borrow the expression Leibniz was to use, it is hypothetical) because it is necessary only given that God freely chose to make our minds in a certain way. Thus, far from saying that it could have been possible for God to have made $1 + 2 = 4$, Descartes says in a letter to Arnauld, "I do not even dare say that God could not make it the case that a mountain be without a valley or that one and two not make three. I say only that God gave me a mind such that I cannot conceive a mountain without a valley or a sum of one and two which should not be three (je n'oserais même pas dire que Dieu ne peut pas faire qu'une montagne soit san vallée, ou qu'un et deux ne fassent pas trois: je dis seulement qu'il m'a donne un esprit de telle nature que je ne saurais concevoir un montagne sans vallée ou une somme d'un et deux qui ne serait pas trois)."[17]

Here Descartes is saying that different facts could have been a priori for us, but we cannot conceive of them nor describe what they might be. If there had been created no minds that counted or did arithmetic then there would have been no judgment that $1 + 2 = 3$. Descartes thus clearly departs from traditional theological views, as well as from the view that Leibniz was to articulate, that such truths of reason are independent of and logically precede God's creation, governing *God's* thought of possibles. If mathematical truths can be identified only with reference to a system of mathematical judgments and calculations, then in a created world that lacks minds with such a system one cannot meaningfully identify a mathematical truth. It is thus possible that it not be the case that $1 + 2 = 3$. But this is not the same as claiming, for example, that it is possible for it to have been true that $1 + 2 = 4$. Descartes says that he does not even dare to say that God could not have made one plus two *not be* three. We cannot conceive of the particular state of affairs that makes true the negation of an eternal truth, or the negation of any truth that is conditional on how our mind is constituted. Descartes makes this very clear in his Reply to the sixth set of Objections. In his point VIII he says "It is also useless to ask why God could make it the case from all eternity that two times four not to have been eight, for I confess that we cannot understand this. But because on the other hand I understand very well . . . that it was very easy for God to order certain things in such a way that men would not understand that things could have been otherwise than the way they are—so that it would be completely against reason to doubt things that we understand very well—because of some other things which we don't understand and which we do not see at all that we should understand. . . . "[18] The point Descartes is making here is nothing else than what we earlier referred to; namely, that what is necessary is not necessarily necessary. The world need not have been as we understand it to be. Even the eternal truths could have been different. We can conceive of this fact perfectly well, while accepting that even our description of counterfactual situations are bound by our understanding. We can conceive that God made us incapable of understanding other possibilities. It is this that makes all Cartesian necessity in some respect resemble Leibniz's hypothetical necessity, that is to say, dependent on God's choice—on the facts of creation. Necessity is then a conditional modality.

One of the examples that Descartes uses in the 2 May 1644 letter to Mesland is especially interesting for us here. It is the limitation of our own intelligence, Descartes writes, that makes it difficult for us to conceive that it was open to God to make the three angles of a triangle *not* add up to two right angles.

We know today that the concept of a triangle is not limited to Euclidean geometry and that, depending on the geometry, the angles of a triangle could add up to more or less than two right angles. Indeed we can see how the above proposition would be true in a Euclidean geometry and false in general in Riemannian geometry. Thus, as Descartes writes, God could instantiate two apparent contradictories (e.g., when each belongs to a different geometry). We learn that each of the apparent contradictories were conditional truths, dependent on distinct, different antecedent conditions, and not contradictories. We cannot conjoin, as Descartes says, ideas that really contradict one another, and expect anything to instantiate it. If we can often come to see that what we take to be necessary truths are only necessary conditional on how our mind was created, it is easy to comprehend that all necessities be conditional.

NEGATION

We are used to defining possibility in terms of necessity and negation and vice versa (viz. $\Box p$ as $-\Diamond -p$ and $\Diamond p$ as $-\Box -p$.) Thus the asymmetry that I have suggested between the absolute character of impossibility and the hypothetical character of necessity may appear counterintuitive. If p is contradictory and the impossibiliity of p is absolute, wouldn't the necessity of not-p be absolute also? What would this amount to in Descartes' terms?

It may be dangerous to make general claims on behalf of Descartes based on conjecture when he himself does not develop a general theory. But the view I have suggested is based on being able to treat negation not as a content of a proposition but as an operation carried out on it. Descartes' view in the Fourth Meditation where he treats negating as on a par with affirming—as well as the examples carefully chosen by him in the various passages quoted above from his responses to the Objections and elsewhere, in which the negation of a necessary truth is never confused with the affirmation of a contradiction—seems to indicate the way Descartes thinks of negation. The identity of a negation or a denial depends on what is denied, just as the identity of an affirmation depends on what is affirmed. But, as we know, in the case of a denial of a contradiction, what is denied is not a possible state of affairs. What is it then that is being denied? The only way to specify it seems to be to treat it as an attempted construction of a state of affairs out of recognizable constituents and operations. We specify these, and then, by negating the purported end result, we indicate that nothing was actually constructed.

That is the reason why, when we deny that a certain state of affairs is possible and we go on to wonder whether God necessarily ordained that this be so, we get into an apparent puzzle. When Descartes concluded that God freely ordained that two times four be necessarily eight, we saw that this was because the identity of *this truth* could not be given independently of the system of mathematics, which depends on the constitution of our mind which God created. When we deny, say, that 2 > 3, what we deny is an impossibility, but we want to distinguish what we are denying from other impossibilities; for example, that three is even or that π is a rational number. Such a distinction cannot be made without referring to our system of numbers with its eternal truths which, according to Descartes, depends on the constitution of the mind. The identity of this particular denial also depends on how our minds are constituted—something freely decided by God. The necessity of the denial of 2 > 3 therefore remains conditional. We cannot have this particular denial without the system of natural numbers: a system in virtue of which there are truths about the numbers two and three as well.

In one of the most difficult passages describing what is possible for God, in the letter to Mesland mentioned earlier, Descartes claims that God was at liberty to have made it not be true—in general—that contradictories are incompatible. We have to understand why Descartes allows God the ability of making untrue, for example, the incompatibility of 2 > 3 and 3 > 2, rather than that of making true that 2 > 3. If the impossibility of 2 > 3 depends on the system of natural numbers with their eternal truths that God ordained in creating the kind of mind we have, then by not creating our mind in this way and not establishing the system of natural numbers, he could have made it not true that there are any contradictions governing numbers either. What we are ascribing to him is not the ability to produce something we express by a contradiction. We are simply saying that he is not bound by the conditions that bind us in making denials of contradictions.

To conclude, then, I have tried to indicate that, although modal concepts in Descartes are not epistemic and do not concern the degree of certitude or states of knowledge, the site of the necessary eternal truths (of logic and mathematics) is said to be the mind, and depends on how God created the human mind. We can, nevertheless, see in Descartes a distinction between hypothetical and absolute necessity, as Gueroult suggests. The reason for the distinction is not, however, the one offered by Leibniz nor the one that Gueroult gives of Descartes' needing to deny to God anything that limits his omnipotence. The distinction is rather a reflection of the expressive powers of our language or the forms of our thoughts. The impossibility of a positive contradiction is absolute even for Descartes since when we assert a contradiction we do not succeed in describing a possible state of affairs which we then can imagine God to have been able to create in a different world. As Descartes says, no possibility can ever be known by us if it does not fall under human concepts. In contrast to the absoluteness of the impossibility of a positive contradiction, the necessity of an eternal truth is not itself necessary for Descartes.[19] We can conceive that it would be possible for God not to have constituted our minds in the way he has, and hence we can conceive what it would be for us not to have this system of thoughts within the framework of which alone an eternal truth has its identity. We can thus meaningfully ascribe to Him the ability of making true the denial of a necessary truth.

NOTES

1. Letters to Mersenne 15 April 1630, 6 May 1630, 27 May 1630, *Philosophical Letters*, ed. A. Kenny (Oxford University Press, 1970), 13–14; Pléiade, 933, 936–938.

2. I was made to think of these problems when I was asked to reply to a most interesting paper, "La Theorie de Possible chez Descartes" by Jacques Bouveresse of the University of Paris and University of Geneva at the conference on Descartes at the Institut Français of London, April 1979. Both papers were published in *Revue Internationale de Philosophie* (no. 46) in 1983. I also profited from pertinent questions raised by Willis Doney of Dartmouth College and Charles Larmore of Columbia University on this matter. I have developed many of my arguments in an attempt to answer their questions. I hope that I have made clear why I disagree with some of their views. Mary Mothersill, Amélie Rorty, and Peter Winch helped me make the paper considerably clearer than it was.

The problem of the creation of eternal truths was already taken up by some of Descartes' contemporaries who wrote the Objections to the *Meditations* and also by several recent philosophers who are also distinguished scholars of Descartes. For example, Emile Brehier, "Creation of Eternal Truths in Descartes' System" in *Descartes: A Collection of Critical Essays*, ed. W. Doney (Garden City, N.Y.: Doubleday, 1967), 192–208, originally published in *Revue Philosophique de la France et de l'Etranger*, May–Aug. 1937; Martial Gueroult, *Descartes selon l'ordre de raisons* (Paris: Vrin, 1953); Harry G. Frankfurt, "Descartes on the Creation of Eternal Truth" in *Philosophical Review* 76 (Jan. 1977); Margaret Wilson, *Descartes* (Routledge & Kegan Paul, 1978), chap. 3, sec. 3, pp. 120–138. Jean-Luc Marion's *Sur la Théologie blanche de Descartes*, a work I regret I had not read when I wrote this paper, published in 1981 also discusses this problem.

3. The reference AG refers to *Descartes: Philosophical Writings*, E. Anscombe and P. T. Geach, eds. and trans. (London, 1969).

4. This was pointed out by Brehier in the article cited in note 2, above. Letter to Mersenne, 27 May 1630 (Pléiade, 937).

5. Descartes' problem seems remote from Suarez's question "What is the essence of a creature prior to its production by God?" Cf. J. Cronin in "Eternal Truths in the Thought of Descartes and Suarez," *The Modern Schoolmen*, May 1961.

6. *Principles of Philosophy* I, 49 (Pléiade, 593).

7. "La Theorie de Possible chez Descartes"; see n. 1, above.

8. *Le Monde ou le Traité de la Lumière*, in *René Descartes, Oeuvres*, ed. Adam and Tannery, Vol. XI, 37.

9. Ibid., 47.

10. Letter to Mesland, 2 May 1644 (Pléiade, 1167).

11. Pointed out by Bouveresse in work cited.

12. Bouveresse rightly draws our attention to the historical atemporal feature of Cartesian modality, but still chooses to characterize it as "epistemic," which I believe is misleading.

13. Martial Gueroult, *Descartes selon l'ordre des raisons* II, 39.

14. Pléiade, 383–384, my translation. There is also a translation in HR II, 45. (The abbreviation HR is explained in the General Bibliography at the beginning of this volume.)

15. Letter to Morus, 5 February 1649 (Pléiade, 1316).

16. Pléiade, 385; HR II, 46.

17. Letter to Arnauld, 29 July 1648 (Pléiade, 1309–1310).

18. Sixth Reply, VIII (Pléiade, 538; HR II, 251).

19. It may be asked what is the status of truth "Given the way our mind was created, it is necessary that $2 + 3 = 5$." Is this not an absolute necessary truth? Would this not be a counterexample to my thesis that the necessity of eternal truths is hypothetical for Descartes? Obviously this truth, or any hypothetical truth, which has a proposition stating how God created our mind as its antecedent, and an eternal truth as a consequent, cannot in its turn depend on another condition, i.e., how our mind was created. Now such theological meta-truths are not the created eternal truths with which Descartes was concerned, and they do have a special status in Descartes' thinking. It may be true to say that propositions of this form are both absolute and necessary.

20

Descartes: "All Things Which I Conceive Clearly and Distinctly in Corporeal Objects Are in Them"

RUTH MATTERN

In the Sixth Meditation, Descartes adds to his proof of the existence of corporeal things a qualifying remark about what is certainly in them:

Hence we must allow that corporeal things exist. However, they are perhaps not exactly what we perceive by the senses, since this comprehension by the senses is in many instances very obscure and confused; but we must at least admit that all things which I conceive clearly and distinctly, that is to say, all things which, speaking generally, are comprehended in the object of pure mathematics, are truly to be recognized as in them.[1]

What can be attributed for certain to corporeal things? How does the *Meditations* lead up to this claim, and what is the Cartesian justification for it?

"I FURTHER FIND IN MYSELF FACULTIES . . . "

After concluding that he is a thinking and unextended thing distinct from his body, Descartes surveys the faculties which he finds in himself.[2] He states that some of these faculties (imagination and feeling) are modes of himself (modes of mind). Other faculties, such as the "change of position" and the "assumption of different figures," are modes of corporeal substance. This passage relies on concepts of substance and mode which Descartes discusses more fully elsewhere in his writings.

Aristotle wrote that it is "a distinctive mark of substance, that, while remaining numerically one and the same, it is capable of admitting contrary qualities."[3] Though he does not have a concept of mode, his conception of substance may be a starting point for Descartes' thinking about the distinction between modes and substances.[4] In Descartes' view, one mode may be substituted for another in the same substance, whereas substances cannot be substituted for another in the substance-mode complexes in which they occur. Descartes writes in one of his letters:

. . . shape and motion are modes, in the strict sense, of corporeal substance; because the same body can exist at one time with one shape and at another with another, now in motion and now at rest; whereas, on the other hand, neither this shape nor this motion can be without this body.[5]

The existence of a mode seems to depend on its substance, whereas the substance does not depend for its existence on the mode. The claim appears to be that

(1) m is a mode of a substance s only if m cannot exist without s, and s can exist without m.

Attributes are also predicated of substances; but whereas the modes of a substance can vary or change, its attributes cannot. In the *Principles*, Descartes classifies existence and duration as attributes, and claims that justice and mercy are also attributes of God (since God can never lack those qualities).[6]

Modes are conceptually as well as existentially dependent on substances:

. . . we can clearly conceive substance without the mode which we say differs from it, while we cannot reciprocally have a perception of this mode without perceiving the substance.[7]

There are two possible readings of this sort of asymmetric dependence:

(2) m is a mode of a substance s only if m existing without s cannot be conceived clearly and distinctly, and s existing without m can be conceived clearly and distinctly.[8]

(3) m is a mode of a substance s only if m cannot be conceived clearly and distinctly without conceiving s, and s can be conceived clearly and distinctly without conceiving m.

Version (2) refers to the attempt to conceive certain states of affairs, m existing without s or s existing without m; version (3) concerns what is included in the concept of m and the concept of s.

As interpretations of Descartes, there is something to be said for each version. Formulation (2) has the advantage that it would explain why Descartes shifts back and forth between (1) and (2), since they are linked by the "Conceivability-Possibility Principle," the claim that whatever can be conceived clearly and distinctly is possible, and whatever is possible can be conceived clearly and distinctly. There is some evidence that Descartes accepts this principle, which would explain his acceptance of (2) along with (1).[9] Since many of his formulations of the conceptual dependence of mode on substance seem to imply claim (3) more than (2), he may well slide from (2) to (3). For example, in the *Notes against a Programme*, he writes:

It belongs to the theory of modes that, though we can easily comprehend a substance apart from a mode, we cannot, conversely, clearly comprehend a mode unless at the same time we conceive the substance of which it is a mode . . . [10]

. . . the nature of a mode consists in this, that it can by no means be comprehended, except it involve in its own concept the concept of the thing of which it is a mode . . . [11]

This sense of "clear," or "clear and distinct," conception in formulation (3) is the "formal concept" of the Sixth Meditation.[12] The defining concept of a mode, the concept revealing its nature, involves the concept of the substance on which it depends; yet the defining concept of a substance does not include the concepts of any modes.

If the defining concept reveals the essence, the asymmetric dependence of mode on substance can also be formulated in terms of a dependence of the mode on the *essence* of its substance. Descartes does refer to the dependence of modes on *essences*; in the *Principles*, he writes:

. . . there is always one principal property of substance which constitutes its nature and essence, and on which all the others depend. Thus extension in length, breadth, and depth, constitutes the nature of corporeal substance; and thought constitutes the nature of thinking substance. For all else that may be attributed to body presupposes extension, and is but a mode of this extended thing; as everything that we find in mind is but so many diverse forms of thinking.[13]

Descartes' shift from substance to essence reflects his view of their close interconnection.[14] The interpretation of modes becomes:

    (4) *m* is a mode of substance *s* only if *m* presupposes the essence of *s*, and *s* does not presuppose the essence of *m*.

The claim that a mode "presupposes" a substance is left rather vague. Is presupposition dependence with respect to existence, so that the dependence is like that expressed in formulation (1), or is it a conceptual dependence, so that the dependence is like that expressed in (2) or (3)?

Because the important concepts of essences of mind and body are concepts of *general* essences, there is an important shift between the first and later formulations. Formulation (1) is implicit in those discussions that center on particular individuals, Aristotelian substances, as examples of substances; the corporeal modes are determinate tokens. One example is a particular stone;[15] a particular shape is a mode of this stone. The move to formulations (3) and (4) is a move from the level of substances as particulars to the level of general essences, thought, and extension. Those formulations, too, allow room for modes as determinables (e.g., *shape* is a mode because it presupposes the essence *extension*). Although Descartes starts out with a substance/mode distinction that owes much to the Aristotelian conception of substance and accident, he gives the traditional idea of asymmetric dependence a creative new interpretation.

The Sixth Meditation survey of faculties presupposes this Cartesian conception of modes of mind as conceptually dependent on thought, and of modes of corporeal substance as presupposing extension.[16] The faculties of imagination and feeling are modes of mind precisely because their "formal concepts" include intellection. The clear and distinct ideas of other faculties include extension and not thought; Descartes classifies these powers as modes of corporeal substance.

What does Descartes want to locate in the world independent of minds? Are the items existing there substance, mode, essence, or attribute? Earlier in the *Meditations,* Descartes analyzed his clear and distinct idea of corporeal things:

And in regard to the ideas of corporeal objects . . . I find that there is very little in them which I perceive clearly and distinctly. Magnitude or extension in length, breadth, or depth, I do so perceive; also figure which results from a termination of this extension, the situation which bodies of different figure preserve in relation to one another, and movement or change of situation; to which we may also add substance, duration and number.[17]

Extension, of course, is the essence of corporeal things; figure and motion are paradigm examples of modes; and duration and number are attributes. Situation (*situs*) may count as a mode.[18] Magnitude (size) provides an illustration of the distinction among some of the different formulations of the concept of modes. Size would count as a mode if formulation (3) or (4) were taken as a sufficient condition for being a mode; size presupposes extension, and the concept of extension is contained in the concept of size (but not vice versa). In his correspondence, however, Descartes classifies size as an attribute rather than a mode.[19] His implicit reasoning may rely on formulation (1) of the concept of a mode. A particular corporeal thing is individuated as an entity with a particular volume; if its dimensions change, it is no longer the same thing.[20] Since size is a quality essential to body, it cannot count as a mode. The conception of a substance as an individual thing rather than a general essence is necessary to this reasoning.[21]

"HENCE WE MUST ALLOW THAT CORPOREAL THINGS EXIST"

Descartes employs at least two different strategies for restoring the credibility of claims undermined by the doubt developed in the First Meditation. One method is the application to specific cases of the principle that any proposition conceived clearly and distinctly is true. This is his most straightforward strategy for showing that a given proposition is true.

The Sixth Meditation, however, does not take the straightforward route to showing that corporeal things exist. Perhaps Descartes does not attempt to use this strategy because he cannot give good grounds for construing "there are corporeal objects" as a proposition conceived clearly and distinctly. The argument to which he resorts has a more complicated structure. First, continuing the survey of faculties in himself, he asserts the existence of a passive faculty of perception, a power of receiving ideas of sensible things. There must be a correlative active faculty that produces these "passively" received ideas. Three exhaustive alternatives must be examined: the active faculty resides in corporeal objects; or it resides in himself; or it resides in something other than himself which is not corporeal. Two of these alternatives are eliminated in order to establish that the active faculty is in corporeal things. The general form of the argument is:

(i) Either p, or q, or r.

(ii) I have a very great inclination to believe p.

(iii) I have no faculty to determine that q or r is the case rather than p.

(iv) God would be allowing deception to occur if q or r were true instead of p, given that (ii) and (iii).

(v) God is not a deceiver.

(vi) God would be a deceiver if he allowed deception of the sort specified in (iv).

(vii) Therefore, p.

This argument is not a simple application of the principle "Whatever

I conceive clearly and distinctly is true." Conspicuously absent from the premises is the claim that I understand clearly and distinctly that bodies exist. The proof is a clever one precisely because it uses the *lack* of the usual mark of truth as a means of bringing the proposition in question within the scope of credible claims; the argument hinges on the *absence* of a faculty in us to decide which alternative is the correct one. To admire Descartes' strategy as clever is not, of course, equivalent to endorsing the argument; the proof has problems.[22] But it is hard to think of a better example of the resourceful use of limitations.

The substance/mode conceptual scheme plays a powerful role in the argument for the existence of corporeal things. Descartes' reason for ruling out the possibility of the active faculty residing in himself is partly that this faculty "does not presuppose thought." He relies not only on his earlier contention that his essence is thought but also on the claim that, for something to be *in* a thinking thing, it must presuppose the essence *thought*. It is formulation (4) of the substance/mode distinction that is at work here.

The assumption that the three alternatives are exhaustive also presupposes the substance/mode scheme. After concluding that the active faculty is not in himself but exists independently of his mind, the problem is to characterize the being that has the faculty. He does not consider the possibility that the active faculty is neither a substance nor a mode.

But Descartes' handling of the substance/mode scheme has problems. Though he is quick to reject the possibility that the active faculty presupposes thought, he devotes no time to showing that it presupposes extension. Yet there is as little plausibility in saying that it presupposes one as that it implies the other. If he is to conclude that the power to cause sensible ideas is truly a mode of corporeal objects, then he owes the reader an argument to the effect that it fulfills the conditions for being a mode, under some interpretation of the concept of mode. It seems unlikely that he could succeed in this task using either formulation (3) or (4) of the dependence of a mode on a substance.

"ALL THINGS WHICH I CONCEIVE CLEARLY AND DISTINCTLY . . . "

A cursory reading of Descartes might lead to the interpretation that *anything* conceived clearly and distinctly is attributable to corporeal things. But surely those modes of *mind* which are conceived clearly and distinctly are not attributed to corporeal objects. The French version of the *Meditations* is a little more careful than the Latin in its formulation of Descartes' qualifying remark about what is independent of minds. The Latin refers to those things which I conceive clearly and distinctly [*quae clare et distincte intelligo*], whereas the French translation refers to those things which I conceive clearly and distinctly *there*, that is, in corporeal things [*toutes les choses que j'y conçois clairement et distinctement*].[23] The relevant concept is the latter one, the idea of conceiving something clearly and distinctly in corporeal objects or (to use an alternative formulation) the idea of conceiving corporeal objects clearly and distinctly as having such and such properties.

The *Meditations* introduces two versions of clear and distinct conception of an object as such and such. (For brevity, I will use O for the object and Ø instead of "such and such" for what is predicated of the object.) (1) One type of clear and distinct conception warrants inferring the *possibility* of what is conceived. That is, if I conceive clearly and distinctly O as Ø, then I am entitled to conclude the possibility of O existing as Ø. For example, Descartes infers from the clear and distinct conception of mind as existing apart from body the *possibility* of mind existing apart from body.[24] The principle correlating the clear and distinct conception of O as Ø with the *possibility* of O as Ø rests on the existence of an omnipotent being, a being who "can carry into effect all that of which we have a distinct idea."[25] (2) A second, and stronger, type of clear and distinct conception of O as Ø warrants inferring that O is Ø on the grounds that a predicate Ø is "drawn from the thought" of O: " . . . just because I can draw the idea of something from my thought, it follows that all which I know clearly and distinctly as pertaining to this object does really belong to it.[26] This rule is used in the Fifth Meditation proof of the existence of God, where "eternal existence" is claimed to belong to the nature of God. The principle of inference " . . . if I clearly and distinctly conceive O as Ø, then O is Ø" rests on the nondeceiving nature of God.

Descartes claims that the things conceived clearly and distinctly in corporeal things really *are* there, and not merely that they could be there. But in the Sixth Meditation passage he is only willing to certify claims that attribute general qualities to corporeal things. Particular claims, "as, for example, that the sun is of such and such a figure," only merit the more limited confidence that one *could* arrive at the truth about them."[27]

Descartes has good reason to be cautious about particular claims, limiting conclusions of the form O is Ø to claims about determinable rather than determinate qualities. The problem that can be solved by this maneuver can be formulated by using the distinction between two sorts of clear and distinct conception of O as $\emptyset$. To make a claim that O is $\emptyset$ on the basis of clear and distinct conception, Descartes needs to use the second sort of conception; the first type is too weak, for it only warrants belief in the *possibility* of O existing as $\emptyset$. But there is a natural connection between conceiving a body as having a certain mode and conceiving O as $\emptyset$ in the *first* way. For example, if we clearly and distinctly conceive the sun as a spherical body, it is reasonable to interpret this as the first sort of clear and distinct conception and to infer the *possibility* that the sun is a spherical body. It is much less plausible to invoke the second principle of inference from clear and distinct conception, saying that sphericity is known to be in the sun because the idea of sphericity can be "drawn from the thought" of the sun. In the second principle about clear and distinct conception, quality-entailment is the relevant relation between the essence of O and the quality $\emptyset$: the presence of that essence is a sufficient condition for the presence of $\emptyset$. But in the relation between mode and essence, the entailment goes the other way; the presence of the mode implies the presence of the essence of the substance, but not vice versa.

Earlier in the *Meditations*, Descartes only claimed the *possibility* of the existence of corporeal things with various qualities.[28] In the Sixth Meditation, things conceived clearly and distinctly in corporeal objects are really in them. The stronger claim rests on the idea that some qualities can, at least in their general form, be "drawn from the thought" of corporeal things.

There are some indications that Descartes thinks the determinable qualities of shape (figure) and motion *can* be "drawn from the thought" of extension. Though his usual discussions of the relations among extension, shape, and motion merely affirm the modal dependence of the latter two on the former, he says in a letter to Elizabeth that the ideas of shape and motion are entailed by [*suivent de*] the idea of extension.[29] This relation does not sound like modal dependence; the claim is that the idea of extension is *sufficient* for the other concepts, not that it is *necessary* for them. And Descartes refers to figure as following from the termination of extension, in describing the clear and distinct idea of corporeal objects in the Third Meditation.[30]

If the idea of shape can be drawn from some thought, it seems that the relevant thought is the idea of corporeal things and not the abstract idea of extension. Suppose that we conceive a universe with infinite extension in the x, y, and z dimensions: what grounds would there be for saying that figure is a quality really instantiated in such a universe? Or suppose that we conceive a universe with infinite extension in the x, y, and z dimensions, and with two corporeal objects;

the x-z plane is the boundary between them, and one of the bodies includes all of the points such that y is greater than zero, while the other includes all of the points such that y is less than or equal to zero. Shape does not seem to be necessary for describing this universe. But if one thinks of a universe with bounded corporeal things, where "bounded" implies "enclosing a finite volume," then one thinks of a universe of figured entities.[31]

Does Descartes believe that situation can be "drawn from the thought" of corporeal things? I am inclined to think that he holds that objects must be spatially located, if they are corporeal objects and there is more than one of them. Descartes interprets situation as relative: if there are two corporeal things, their location is relationally defined.[32]

Motion is a translation of body from one situation to another.[33] Of course, it is possible for bodies to be at rest; does this imply that motion is only modally dependent on corporeal objects, rather than being entailed by their existence? Descartes could evade this problem by looking at rest as one determinate of the determinable *motion*. Both Galileo and Boyle treat the primary quality motion as motion-or-rest.[34] Some evidence that Descartes treats rest in this way too is found in the following passage:

> . . . shape and motion are modes, in the strict sense, of corporeal substance; because the same body can exist at one time with one shape and at another with another, now in motion and now at rest . . . [35]

In this letter, Descartes assumes that the same substance can have a succession of different determinate modes of the same determinable; the change from motion to rest is treated as an example of change analogous to the change from one shape to another. If "motion" is understood as the determinable "motion-or-rest," the concept of motion is implied by the concept of a universe with at least two corporeal things.

In this reading, the ideas of shape, situation, and motion are drawn from the thought of corporeal things and not simply from the idea of extension. It is significant that Descartes formulates the conclusion of the proof of a world independent of minds as the claim that corporeal *things* exist; the plural term is important in the use of the claim as a step in the argument that corporeal qualities exist independent of the mind.

My reconstruction of Descartes' motivation for the claim that the primary qualities really exist independent of the mind poses a problem: does it conflict with his view that extension has a special priority as the essence of body? I think that Descartes can retain some version of both views. First, situation and motion need not be essential to body qua body. They are relational characteristics: a body would not have them if it were the sole body in the universe. Second, for qualities that are essential to body qua determinables (e.g., shape), Descartes can still say that extension is prior in the sense of being the quality on which the other essential features are modally dependent. Retaining this asymmetry might seem to require an unmotivated comparison of extension as determin*able* with the mode as determin*ate*. This objection, however, would not pertain to formulations (3) and (4) of the contrast between substance and mode. The idea of shape includes the idea of extension, but not vice versa.[36]

Descartes' strategy in the *Meditations* for showing that the qualities conceived clearly and distinctly in bodies are really there differs in an interesting way from his version of the argument in the *Principles*. If my interpretation of the *Meditations* passage is correct, then Descartes' rationale for holding that some real objects are extended is quite different from his rationale for holding that other clearly and distinctly conceived qualities are really in those objects. Extension is shown to be in objects independent of the mind by the circuitous route appealing to reason's inability to choose among alternative hypotheses about the cause of ideas of sensible objects. But the corporeal modes are known to be in objects independent of the mind because of their necessary connection with the existence of corporeal objects. If the ideas of determinable modes can be "drawn from the thought" of corporeal things, then the same strategy *cannot* be used to establish both the external existence of extension and the external existence of the corporeal modes. The circuitous route is ruled out if the route appealing to clear and distinct conception of the second sort is even *possible*.

Though Descartes uses different strategies concerning extension and the corporeal modes in the *Meditations,* in the *Principles* he uses the same strategy for showing that both are in objects independent of the mind. Both extension and the modes of body have their existence certified by appeal to the clearness of ideas in the *Principles*.[37] But since Descartes does not explain exactly how the appeal to clearness is supposed to establish the existence of extension, the *Principles* version cannot be considered an improvement over the *Meditations* argument.

The distinction between determinate and determinable qualities has an interesting implication for the claim in the Sixth Meditation about the existence of corporeal modes. As we saw earlier, Descartes suggests such a distinction later in the passage, and it is necessary for making his position coherent. But it does affect the interpretation of the principle which entitles Descartes to say that the corporeal modes exist, the principle that "just because I can draw the idea of something from my thought, it follows that all which I know clearly and distinctly as pertaining to this object really does belong to it."[38] It might seem to follow that the quality drawn from the idea of an object would be exactly the same quality that is concluded to be in the object. But modal qualities drawn from the thought of corporeal things are determinable features, whereas the qualities of corporeal things are determinate modes. Descartes is committed to the view that the qualities in objects are determinates rather than determinables, and exist as tokens rather than as types.[39] When Descartes says that "all which I know clearly and distinctly as pertaining to this object really does belong to it," he must be interpreted to mean that all which he knows clearly and distinctly as pertaining to an object has some determinate tokens that really belong to the object as it exists outside the mind.

THE STATUS OF ATTRIBUTES

Since some attributes (size or magnitude, number, and duration) are part of the clear and distinct idea of corporeal things, it seems that they should be included within the scope of Descartes' claim about the qualities known to be in such things. But some of his claims seem not to allow attributes in bodies. In the *Principles*, he writes that "extension . . . constitutes the nature of corporeal substance . . . all else that may be attributed to body presupposes extension, and is but a mode."[40] Attributes are not modes. If something that is *in* corporeal things *inheres* in them, and if inherence is modal dependence, then attributes cannot be in corporeal things. Might attributes be part of the clear and distinct idea of corporeal things, yet not be known to be in corporeal objects? The suspicion that the attributes depend on thought is strengthened by the fact that Descartes labels them "modes of thought" in contrast to true modes,[41] and says that they are "only the modes under which we consider" things.[42]

The passages that suggest the dependence of the attributes on thought are nevertheless accompanied by other passages affirming their real existence in objects independent of mind. In the letter that refers to the attributes as "modes of thought," Descartes writes that "the thing itself cannot be outside our thought without its existence, nor without its duration or size and so on."[43] In the *Principles*, he states "that there are attributes which pertain to things and others to thought; . . . some of the attributes are in things themselves and others are only in thoughts."[44] The attributes included in the clear and distinct idea of corporeal objects in the *Meditations* are counted in the *Principles* as pertaining to things. Duration (in contrast with time) is classified as an attribute pertaining to things. Though Descartes says that "number and all universals are simply modes of thought,"[45] closer inspection shows that he only takes number "considered abstractly" to be a mode of thinking. This allows the possibility that number "in created things" has an independent status analogous to that of duration.[46] Apparently he also includes size or magnitude among the attributes that are independent of mind.[47] But is Descartes simply inconsistent in his views about the independent existence of attributes? How can he say that they exist independently of the mind if he denies real universals and denies that attributes inhere in bodies as modes do?

Apparently Descartes holds that, as they exist independently of minds, attributes are not really distinct from the objects which they characterize. In the world independent of thought, there is no difference between a piece of wax and its existence, or the man Peter and his duration, and so forth.[48] Attributes are distinct from the objects and from each other only insofar as thought imposes a distinction on them.[49] They are "modes of thought" only in a weak sense, for thought does not create them but only distinguishes them.

Descartes' position about the attributes is an interesting one, but it raises other problems. How is the identity of attribute with object to be interpreted? Is the distinction among attributes entirely a creation of thought? If so, in what sense is it thought-dependent? Apparently not in a way that makes the attributes arbitrary creations of mind, for in Descartes' view there are obvious necessary connections between corporeal things and the attributes they exhibit.[50] Descartes thinks he has a clear and distinct conception, in the second sense of "clear and distinct conception of O as Ø," that corporeal things have duration, size, and number. Regrettably, he does not analyze these necessary connections. Perhaps he means that an existing corporeal thing must have duration, understanding duration as the succession of states of itself. It must also have size; a corporeal thing has a determinate extension, and magnitude is the determinate extension of a body.[51] It is more difficult to see why a clear and distinct conception of corporeal things includes number. Descartes may actually have two different ideas of number as an attribute. In one sense, number ranges "through all the classes of real things," including mental substances.[52] This remark apparently refers to number as the quantity of things; each thing, mental or corporeal, is one thing. But number also applies to corporeal objects in an additional sense, since each of these objects has a definite quantity of extension by virtue of having a determinate magnitude.[53]

CONCLUSION

Descartes' concept of modes applies to some of the things that are clearly and distinctly conceived to be in bodies. Figure and motion are paradigm examples of modes of body. But though his idea of the relation between modes and substances provides an interpretation of what it is for something to be *in* bodies, not all of the things in the real corporeal world fall within the scope of this idea. (1) Extension, the essence of corporeal things, is certainly not in these objects as a mode is in a substance. The Sixth Meditation is not open to Berkeley's critique of the view of extension as a mode of a propertyless substratum.[54] (2) The determinable qualities and universals, as well as number qua "abstract idea," are thought-dependent (though determinate tokens of these determinables are independent of thought). (3) Attributes are instantiated in corporeal things, but they are not modally dependent on them. They are not qualities inherent in such things; the distinction between the attributes and the essence of corporeal objects is only a distinction of reason.

Descartes uses two strategies in the *Meditations* to restore the credibility of beliefs; one appeals to clear and distinct conception, while the other appeals to a strong inclination to believe, in the absence of a faculty to decide among competing alternatives. In the *Meditations*, belief in the independent existence of extension is achieved by the second route. But once this step is taken, the modes and attributes of bodies can be located in bodies without further appeal to inclinations to believe. The justification for making modes and attributes independent of thought is the clear and distinct conception of bodies as having those modes and attributes. But caution is needed, for one type of clear and distinct conception of corporeal things with modes serves only to establish the *possibility* of bodies having those qualities. The relevant sort of clear and distinct conception must reveal extension in corporeal objects as a *sufficient* condition of the presence of the other qualities.

Essence, modes, and attributes each present a special challenge in Descartes' attempt in the *Meditations* to establish and characterize corporeal objects independently of the mind. To show that extension exists independently of thought, Descartes must overcome the lack of clear and distinct propositions proving that our sensible ideas are caused by corporeal objects. To show that modes exist independently of mind, the determinable forms of the modes must be shown to follow from the essence of body, and the mind-dependence of determinable qualities must be shown to allow the mind-independent char-

acter of determinate qualities. Finally, the mind's role in distinguishing
the attributes from one another and from extension cannot be so great
as to undermine the independence from thought of corporeal things
and their attributes.

NOTES

The abbreviations AT, HR, and K are explained in the General Bibliography
at the beginning of this volume.

1. The Latin text reads:

Ac proinde res corporeae existunt. Non tamen forte omnes tales omnino existunt,
quales illas sensu comprehendo, quoniam ista sensu comprehendo, quoniam ista
sensum comprehensio in multis valde obscura est et confusa; sed saltem illa omnia
in iis sunt, quae clare et distincte intelligo, id est omnia generaliter spectata, quae in
purae Matheseos objeto comprehenduntur. (AT VII, 80)

The French text reads:

Et partant il faut confesser qu'il y a des choses corporelles qui existent. Toutefois
elles ne sont peut-être pas entièrement telles que nous les apercevons par les sens,
car cette perception des sens est fort obscure et confuse en plusieurs choses; mais
au moins faut-il avouer que toutes les choses que j'y conçois clairement et distinctement, c'est-à-dire toutes les choses, généralement parlant, qui sont comprises
dans l'objet de la géométrie spéculative, s'y retrouvent véritablement. (*Descartes:
Oeuvres et Lettres,* textes presentes par André Bridoux [Bibliothèque de la Pléiade,
1953], 325)

2. HR I, 190; AT VII, 78–79.
3. Aristotle, *Categories* 17–18, in R. McKeon, ed., *The Basic Works of Aristotle*
(New York: Random House, 1941), 14.
4. Aristotle does, of course, have a concept of accidents and this might be
considered an ancestor of the Cartesian concept of modes; but I will not pause
here to develop this issue.
5. K, 186–187; AT IV, 348.
6. HR I, 242; AT VIII, 26.
7. HR I, 244; AT VIII, 29.
8. In this paper, I do not distinguish "clear" from "clear and distinct," since
it does not seem to me that Descartes observes such a distinction in the
relevant passages. For a brief discussion of Descartes' inconsistent use of
these terms, see Laurence J. Lafleur, "Introduction concerning the Translation," in *Descartes: Meditations* (Indianapolis: Bobbs-Merrill, 1960), xii–xiii.
9. Descartes says that "All things which I apprehend clearly and distinctly
can be created by God as I apprehend them" (HR I, 190; AT VII, 78); I take
it that Descartes holds that what is conceivable clearly and distinctly is possible. The *impossibility* of some faculties existing apart from their substance is

inferred from the *inconceivability* of their existence apart; this inference in the Sixth Meditation suggests that Descartes holds that what is possible is conceivable (HR I, 190; AT VII, 78).

10. HR I, 436.

11. HR I, 440.

12. HR I, 190; AT VII, 78.

13. HR I, 240; AT VIII, 25.

14. Descartes identifies substance and essence when he writes that thought and extension "must not be considered otherwise than as the very substances that think and are extended, i.e., as mind and body" (*Principles* I, 63, HR I, 245–246; AT VIII, 30–31).

15. HR I, 244; AT VIII, 29.

16. HR I, 190; AT VI, 78.

17. HR I, 164; AT VII, 43.

18. "The situation of parts" is listed among the modes of body at *Principles* I, 65, HR I, 246; AT VIIII, 32. Also, "situation" is listed among the items "pertaining to extended substance" at Principle 48 in Part I (HR I, 238; AT VIII, 23). However, it seems that Descartes should say that minds can also have situation (though not parts with situation), which would make situation count as an attribute along with the other matters that "range through all the classes of real things" (HR I, 238; AT VIII, 23). It is interesting that Descartes sometimes includes situation or position among the features of bodies cited in scientific explanation (e.g., K, 43), while at other points he does not include situation in the list (e.g., K, 41).

19. K, 187; AT IV, 348; AT VI, 345.

20. HR I, 257; AT VIII, 44.

21. For other discussions of the concepts of substance and mode relevant to this section, see David S. Scarrow, "Descartes on His Substance and His Essence," *American Philosophical Quarterly* 9 (1972):18–28; Norman J. Wells, "Descartes and the Modeal Distinction," *Modern Schoolman* 43 (1965–1966): 1–22; and Alan Donagan, "Descartes's 'Synthetic' Treatment of the Real Distinction between Mind and Body," *in* Michael Hooker, ed., *Descartes: Critical and Interpretive Essays* (Baltimore: Johns Hopkins, 1978), 186–196.

22. Among the many questions that the proof raises are the following: It is not obvious what a "very great inclination to believe" amounts to; is it merely a strong psychological inclination, or a tendency that must be interpreted in epistemic terms (something that confers upon p a reason for believing it, though not a reason as strong as that relevant to clear and distinct understanding)? How are we to be sure of the negative existential claim made in premise (iii), that a faculty of discovery is completely absent? And, is the missing faculty to be read as a capacity to apprehend q or r clearly and distinctly?

23. For references to the Latin and French, see note 1.

24. HR I, 190; AT VII, 78.

25. HR I, 190; AT VII, 78.

26. HR I, 180; AT VII, 65.

27. HR I, 191; AT VII, 80.

28. HR I, 185; AT VII, 71.

29. K, 138; AT III, 664.

30. HR I, 164; AT VII, 43.

31. Descartes writes that shape "arises from the boundary of the extension" (HR I, 164; AT VII, 43).

32. Descartes treats situation as relative when he writes: "if we say that a thing is in a particular place, we simply mean that it is situated in a certain manner in reference to certain other things" (HR I, 261; AT VIII, 48; HR I, 260, AT VIII, 47).

33. HR I, 266; AT VIII, 53.

34. Robert Boyle, "Origin of Forms and Qualities" (first published in 1666), *in* M. A. Stewart, ed., *Selected Philosophical Papers of Robert Boyle* (New York: Barnes and Noble, 1979), 20. Galileo, "The Assayer" (first publshed in 1623), *in* Stillman Drake, ed., *Discoveries and Opinions of Galileo* (Garden City, N.Y.: Doubleday, 1957), 274.

35. K, 186–187; AT IV, 348.

36. HR I, 255–256; AT VIII, 42.

37. HR I, 254–255; AT VIII, 40–41.

38. HR I, 180.

39. HR I, 242–243; AT VIII, 27–28.

40. HR I, 240; AT VIII, 240.

41. K, 187; AT IV, 348.

42. HR I, 241; AT VIII, 26.

43. K, 187; AT IV, 348–349.

44. HR I, 242; AT VIII, 26–27.

45. HR 242; AT VIII, 26–27.

46. HR 242; AT VIII, 26–27.

47. HR 246; AT VIII, 31.

48. K, 187; AT IV, 348–349.

49. HR 245; AT VIII, 30.

50. Descartes states, in a passage cited earlier (K, 187) that "the thing itself cannot be outside our thought without its existence, nor without its duration or size and so on." He also says that substance, duration, order, number and other such things "range through all the classes of real things" (HR I, 238); and he writes that the most general "primitive notions" apply to "everything we can conceive" (K, 138; AT III, 664). These remarks indicate Descartes' belief that being a corporeal substance implies having the attributes.

51. In the Third Meditation list of qualities included in the clear and distinct idea of body, magnitude is not even listed as a quality separate from extension, but as equivalent to a (determinate) extension (HR I, 164).

52. HR I, 238; AT VIII, 22.

53. HR I, 258; AT VIII, 44–45. It is possible that the two ideas of number derive from two different uses of the idea of substance, one a conception of a thing (so that the relevant notion of quantity is the number of things), and the other a conception of substance as stuff (so that the amount of stuff is the relevant conception of quantity).

54. George Berkeley, *Principles of Human Knowledge, in* Colin Murray Turbayne, ed., *Berkeley: Principles, Dialogues, and Philosophical Correspondence* (Indianapolis: Bobbs-Merrill, 1965), 28–29; first published in 1710.

An earlier version of this essay was read to the Seventeenth Century Study Group, meeting at the Institute for Advanced Study in Princeton, N.J. The members of this group, and other individuals, have provided comments, questions, criticisms, and moral support at various stages of the essay's development. I am especially grateful to E. M. Curley, Willis Doney, Mark Kulstad, Susan Murphy, R. C. Sleigh, Jr., and Margaret Wilson.

21

Why Was Descartes a Foundationalist?

Frederick F. Schmitt

According to the standard interpretation, Descartes is taken to hold that all knowledge is either intuited or deduced from what is intuited.[1] He is thought to have held this belief on the ground that intuition and deduction alone offer the indubitable foundational premises and secure inferences necessary for answering the queries of the skeptic.

My aim in this essay is not the absurd one of denying what everyone knows, that Descartes is a foundationalist.[2] Rather, I wish to question the depth of his commitment to foundationalism, by distinguishing two versions of foundationalism to which he subscribes.[3] Descartes needs, and is aware that he needs, nonfoundational reasoning to do what he wants in metaphysics and science. But only one of the versions of foundationalism stands in his way here, and this one need play no role at all in his answer to skepticism. The other version is central in answering skepticism, but much more defensible than one might suppose.

THE STANDARD ACCOUNT AND ITS DIFFICULTIES

Let us begin with a brief outline of the standard account of Descartes' motives for foundationalism in the *Meditations*. Though in some instances recent interpreters have moved quite far from this account, its major features still find expression in many well-known interpretations of Descartes' epistemology.[4]

The standard account traces Descartes' foundationalism to his insistence that knowledge requires the removal of skeptical doubt. The removal of doubt requires basic propositions, whose own dubitability is removed without appeal to further propositions. Any appeal to further propositions would only push back the problem of removing the dubitability of those propositions. Rather, basic propositions remove their own dubitability. The process by which they do so is called *intuition*. *Deduction* removes doubt from all other knowable propositions by a process of appeal to intuition, in which the indubitability of the former is secured, given the indubitability of the latter. Only judgments in the form of intuited or deduced propositions—or, as we might say, judgments sanctioned by intuition and deduction—count as knowledge.[5]

The basic, or first, propositions concern the existence and nature of one's own mind.[6] These are intuited. From these, propositions concerning the existence and nature of God and, finally, of bodies are deduced. Descartes exhibits the first propositions as intuited so as to remove doubts. As these doubts are allowed to be hyperbolic, and thus include the doubt that he is deceived by a demon, removing them takes some doing and eventually requires deducing propositions concerning the existence and nature of God. If God is no deceiver, clearly and distinctly perceived (that is, intuited or deduced) propositions are invariably true. This removes the hyperbolic doubt.

This, in outline, is the standard account of Descartes' motivation for foundationalism in the *Meditations*. It is undeniable that there is considerable truth in this presentation. I am prepared to concede that the program of removing doubt motivates a version of foundationalism in the *Meditations*.

But there are reasons to resist the standard account. If that account is right, Descartes' view of knowledge admits at best a modest amount of knowledge. To require that knowledge be either intuited or deduced is to require too much if much knowledge is desired. Let us suppose that Descartes is successful in his arguments and can remove doubt from propositions concerning the existence and nature of his own mind and that of God, the nature of bodies conceived as objects of geometrical demonstration, the existence of body, the three laws of motion, and the seven subsidiary rules of motion. Still, in the standard account, he can never get further than this. For he can never deduce from any of these the more specific laws governing the types of bodies to be found on earth—fire, the magnet, the rainbow, and the like—nor propositions concerning the origin and constitution of the earth. Still less can he hope to deduce propositions concerning the existence and nature of particular bodies in his environment, even of his own body. In the standard account, Descartes is a skeptic about all these matters.

This attribution of skepticism might not by itself open the standard account to significant criticism. What is significant is the ground on which it would attribute such skepticism. It would trace this skepticism to a sort of epistemic prudery on Descartes' part.[7] By attributing an insistence on removing doubt, the standard account depicts Descartes as driven by a prudish aversion to false propositions. There is no obvious reason to insist on avoiding false judgments at the expense of the correlative and equally important goal of making true judgments (or the less important goal of relieving agnosticism). The significant objection to the standard account, then, is not merely that it attributes skepticism, but that it traces this skepticism to the motive of minimizing false judgments at the expense of making true judgments.

Now it is not my intention to defend in full this attack on the standard account. Indeed I will argue at the end of this essay that there is a respect in which an extreme aversion to falsity is entirely reasonable. The point here, however, is that the standard account can supply no reason why a policy of minimizing false judgments will also further making true judgments. The resources of the standard theory seem too limited to afford any way around the prudery of minimizing false judgments.

The standard account and its imputation of skepticism and prudery might stick were there not abundant textual evidence that Descartes is neither a skeptic nor a prude. He believes that we can attain truth and knowledge in the very propositions excluded on the standard account. Meditation VI is the locus of evidence for this view. There Descartes does not restrict himself to judgments sanctioned only by intuition and deduction, but accumulates judgments sanctioned by a quite different principle of reasoning, hypothetico-deduction. He offers this argument for the existence of body: "I easily understand, I say, that the imagination could be thus constituted if it is true that body exists; and because I can discover no other convenient mode of explaining it, I conjecture with probability that body does exist" (AT VII, 73; HR I, 186–187). More schematically: if body exists, then imagination is constituted thus; there is no equally good explanation of the constitution of imagination; therefore body exists. The existence of body is a hypothesis from which the phenomena of imagination may be deduced. As it is the best hypothesis, we are to assent to the existence of body. This is a hypothetico-deductive argument. And it is clear that Descartes offers this argument to secure our assent to the proposition that body exists. Why else would he have offered the argument?

Descartes does go on to back the argument with an apparently deductive argument for the existence of body. Referring to his ideas of sensation, which are passively received and so not produced by him, he says: " . . . since God is no deceiver, it is very manifest that He does not communicate to me these ideas immediately and by Himself. . . . For since He has given me no faculty to recognize that this is the case, but, on the other hand, a very great inclination to believe [*magnum propensionem ad credendum*] that they are conveyed to me by corporeal objects, I do not see how He could be defended from the accusation of deceit if these ideas were produced by causes other than corporeal objects" (AT VII, 79–80; HR I, 191). But it is hard not to detect some hesitation in this passage. If Descartes' argument for body is to be deductive, assent to the existence of body must be compelled.[8] For only if God compels assent can He be convicted of deception when the judgment turns out false. But Descartes attributes to himself only a very great inclination to believe that the causes of sensation are corporeal. I do not think that he can quite bring himself to rule out the alternative that something noncorporeal causes his ideas. His assent is not compelled, and the argument is not deductive. Even this argument, then, may rest on the tentative hypothesis that he has canvassed all the options for explaining his ideas, and may in this sense be a hypothetico-deductive argument. Note finally, in support of this interpretation, that it would explain why Descartes feels the need to supplement the present argument for body with the preceding argument from sensation—a fact not easily explained if the present argument is intended to be deductive, since deductive arguments are conclusive and need no supplementation.[9]

Descartes also offers only a hypothetico-deductive argument against the dream hypothesis of Meditation I. In the closing paragraph of the *Meditations*, he says:

I ought to set aside . . . that very common uncertainty respecting sleep, which I could not distinguish from the waking state; for at present I find a very notable difference between the two, inasmuch as our memory can never connect our dreams one with the other, or with the whole course of our lives, as it unites events which happen to us while we are awake. And, as a matter of fact, if someone, while I was awake, quite suddenly appeared to me and disappeared as fast as do the images which I see in sleep, so that I could not know [*scilicet*] from whence the form came nor whither it went, it would not be without reason that I should deem it a spectre or a phantom formed by my brain rather than a real man. But when I perceive things as to which I know distinctly both the place from which they proceed, and that in which they are, and the time at which they appeared to me; and when, without any interruption, I can connect the perception which I have of them with the whole course of my life, I am perfectly assured that these perceptions occur while I am waking and not during sleep. (AT VII, 89–90; HR I, 198–199)

Here Descartes takes the whole course of his apparent waking experience as the phenomenon to be explained, and he considers which hypothesis better explains this phenomenon, the dream hypothesis or what we may call the body hypothesis, that the objects of apparent waking experience are currently perceived bodies. And he argues that the body hypothesis is preferable on the ground that it better explains the course of apparent waking experience.

If we consider any sufficiently small episode of apparent waking experience, then, according to Descartes, the dream hypothesis will explain this episode just as well as the body hypothesis does. The virtue of the body hypothesis emerges only when we consider larger portions of experience. We can of course string two dream hypotheses together to account for two episodes of experience. But the body hypothesis concerning these episodes is superior to the dream hypothesis in its power to explain an additional fact. The body hypothesis explains not just the two episodes, but also that the episodes bear a relation of continuity. The body hypothesis explains this fact because it has a component that remains constant across episodes, the component according to which particular bodies are perceived. The dream hypothesis, however, leaves the episodes unrelated and cannot explain the fact of continuity.

Perhaps this interpretation will be resisted. Perhaps it will be denied that the body hypothesis explains an additional fact, on the ground that the dream hypothesis may also explain continuity: we dream continuous dreams. But then we may offer the alternative interpretation that the body hypothesis has the different advantage of explaining continuity more parsimoniously than the dream hypothesis. The body hypothesis has a component that remains constant across episodes, while the dream hypothesis must hypothesize different causes of experience in the two episodes. In this interpretation, the body hypothesis is preferable to the dream hypothesis, not because it explains more phenomena, but because it explains the same phenomena more parsimoniously. Descartes then assumes that a hypothesis is better the more parsimonious its explanation of the phenomena. He proposes that when confronted with competing hypotheses that explain the same phenomena, we are to assent to the more parsimonious hypothesis.

Descartes' argument against the dream hypothesis on this latter interpretation is strikingly like his hypothetico-deductive argument for corpuscularean hypotheses in the *Principles*. A brief aside on the role of hypothesis in Descartes' science is therefore in order. In his early scientific work—the *Discourse* and the essays it introduces—Descartes announces his intention to argue from hypotheses (AT VI, 76–

77; HR I, 129)—about the nature of light in the *Optics,* about corpuscles in the *Meteorology*—without presenting deductions of these hypotheses from intuited principles of physics. He is somewhat evasive in accounting for his use of hypothesis in these works. On the one hand, he claims to be able to supply deductions wherever he has introduced hypotheses, and he offers expository reasons for his use of hypothesis: in the *Optics,* to avoid appeal to principles that artisans might not understand (AT VI, 82–83; O, 66); elsewhere to avoid appeal to principles that might invite misinterpretation of his physics. On the other hand, he shows a keen appreciation of how difficult it is to supply deductions, and he seems to allow that he cannot actually deduce all his hypotheses. To deduce a hypothesis from general principles, it is necessary to rule out alternative hypotheses from which the observational and experimental results may be equally well deduced, and this can only be done by performing further experiments (AT VI, 63–64; HR I, 120–121). But Descartes admits that he is far from having performed such experiments (AT VI, 65; HR I, 121–122; AT VI, 75; HR I, 128). This admission entails that the resort to hypotheses is not merely an expository convenience but a necessity. I see no way to reconcile these opposing remarks, and I believe we must content ourselves with a reading in which Descartes' claims to be able to supply deductions are an expression of hope for the future.

By the time of the *Princples,* however, Descartes has abandoned any such hope and allows hypothetical arguments to stand on their own. In *Principles* I, II, and III, he does present his metaphysics, general mechanics, and kinematic astronomy as deductive. But at *Principles* III, 44, he announces a switch to hypotheses (AT VIII–1, 99; AG, 224). In the remainder of *Principles* III and *Principles* IV, he presents corpuscularean accounts of the ether, the formation of the stars, the composition of light, the communication of motion through the vortex, and a host of terrestrial phenomena. At the end of the *Principles* he expresses his satisfaction with this style of argument: "I believe that I have done all that is required of me if the causes I have assigned are such that they correspond [*accurate respondeant*] to all the phenomena manifested by nature" (AT VIII–1, 327; HR I, 301). Hypotheses are morally certain in virtue of corresponding to the phenomena, which is enough for prediction and so for science insofar as it contributes to the conduct of life. But hypotheses do not attain absolute certainty, which is secured only by deduction. Moral certainty is a weaker status consistent with falsity, since contending hypotheses may equally well correspond to the phenomena, even though at least one must be false.

Descartes' remarks here invite the interpretation that he is abandoning the project of a true science in favor of one that is merely useful for the conduct of life, and this is the way he is usually read.[10] As this would be an abandonment of his most cherished hope, charity calls for an alternative interpretation. We must appreciate first that, from the outset, Descartes intends hypothetical arguments to persuade the reader that the hypothesis is true, and not merely to exhibit the hypothesis as corresponding to the phenomena and hence useful (AT VI, 76; HR I, 128. AT I, 563; K, 48). But a hypothetical argument is to persuade, not when the hypothesis merely corresponds to the phenomena, but when it effects parsimony of explanation, depending on fewer hypotheses (AT VI, 239; O, 268; AT VI, 334; O, 338; AT II, 199-200; K, 58–59). By the time of the *Principles*, Descartes not only uses and advocates this form of argument but offers a rationale: parsimonious hypotheses are better than contending hypotheses in being very much more likely to be *true*.[11] He should not, then, be interpreted as abandoning the project of a true science in favor of one useful for the conduct of life.

It remains to ask why Descartes comes to view parsimonious hypotheses as likely to be true. It is tempting to look to his metaphysics for an answer, to look for a commitment to the view that the world really is simple, so that parsimonious hypotheses are more likely to be true than contenders. But I know of no evidence that he holds such a view. The alternative is to look for an answer in his epistemology. Our earlier remarks about his rejection of the dream hypothesis indicate that he must have arrived at his favorable attitude toward parsimonious hypotheses by the time of the *Meditations*. This suggests looking for the ground of this favorable attitude in the epistemology of the *Meditations*, and this is what I propose to do.

By the end of Meditation V, Descartes has established against skeptical doubts that all clearly and distinctly perceived propositions are true—intuition and deduction are perfectly reliable. He has, however, offered no comparable argument for (parsimonious) hypothetico-deduction. Without such an argument, his hypothetico-deductive argument against the dream hypothesis has only traded one skeptical question for another larger question, the reliabilty of hypothetico-deduction. We must ask then, whether, despite the absence of an explicit argument, Descartes has the resources to answer skepticism about hypothetico-deduction, as his metaphysical and scientific reasoning requires if it is to lead to more than conjecture.

Perhaps it will be suggested that Descartes has already removed skeptical doubt by the end of Meditation V, and so need offer no argument that hypothetico-deduction is reliable. But while Descartes may have once and for all removed the doubt raised about clear and distinct perception in Meditation III, it does not follow that he has removed comparable doubts that may be raised about hypothetico-deduction. Even if all clearly and distinctly perceived propositions are true, it may be that all hypotheses are false.[12] Nor can Descartes just shrug off such a doubt. There is as much motivation for worrying about the reliability of hypothetico-deduction as there is for worrying about the reliability of clear and distinct perception. Nor is there any evident motivation for exempting hypothetical judgments from skepticism on the ground that our aim in hypothetical judgments is not what it is in judgments sanctioned by clear and distinct perception. There is no evident motivation for setting aside the aim of truth in hypothetical judgments. There is no evident peculiarity either of subject matter or of logical form which could distinguish hypothetical judgments enough to justify laying aside the aim of truth. (Indeed, corpuscularean hypotheses have a subject matter very close to that of the laws of motion, and are equally general.) On all counts, it would seem that Descartes needs to remove doubts about the reliability of hypothetico-deduction just as badly as he needs to remove doubts about clear and distinct perception.

I believe that Descartes offers the glimmer of an argument to remove doubt in the concluding sentences of the *Meditations,* immediately after the argument against the dream hypothesis: "I ought in no wise to doubt the truth of such matters if, after having called up all my senses, my memory, and my understanding, to examine them, nothing is brought to evidence by any one of them which is repugnant to what is set forth by the others. For because God is in no wise a deceiver, it follows that I am not deceived in this" (AT VII, 90; HR I, 199).[13]

It is tempting to read the passage as arguing that judgment in accordance with all faculties, hence properly cautious hypothetico-deduction, is always true. But such a reading would make the argument unpersuasive, as well as too strong for the purposes at hand. To convict God of deception, we must catch him compelling our assent to a false proposition. But judgment in accordance with all our faculties is not necessarily compelled. If that were so, it would never have been possible for Descartes to paralyze his sensory judgment by entertaining doubts about sensation. These are the very doubts to which Descartes is attempting to respond here, so he cannot assume that they have been dissolved, leaving a will compelled to make sensory judgments. Descartes cannot mean to show that judgment in accordance with all our faculties is always true. Nor should he want to: hypothetico-deduction is not perfectly reliable.

I believe what Descartes must have in mind is a more modest and correspondingly more defensible argument. God inclines our assent to judgment in accordance with all our faculties. For, so long as memory and clear and distinct perception say nothing to contradict sensation, the doubts that infect sensory judgment in Meditation I are no longer sufficient to prevent the will from assenting, once we see that clearly and distinctly perceived propositions are true. The will is not compelled to assent, but neither is there any force sufficient to prevent it from assenting. And our will is inclined to assent. Consequently, judgments in accordance with all our faculties are generally true.

In the remainder of this essay, I wish to explain exactly what argument Descartes must have in mind here, and what sort of framework the argument must belong to, if Descartes is to succeed in claiming knowledge of hypotheses—nonfoundational knowledge.

THE ORDERS OF KNOWLEDGE

The standard account of Descartes' foundationalism prohibits nonfoundational knowledge and denies Descartes' express reliance on hypothesis. For doubt cannot be removed from nonfoundational knowledge. Only intuition and deduction remove doubt, and only what is indubitable qualifies as knowledge.

I wish to propose another view. Descartes can maintain that only what is intuited or deduced removes doubt, while denying that only what removes doubt qualifies as knowledge. In this view, knowledge requires only that doubt *be* removed, and the doubt attaching to a judgment can be removed by *other* judgments. Intuition and deduction can remove doubt from nonfoundational judgments. Descartes' aim in his brief argument might be to claim as knowledge judgments that cannot remove doubt, by appeal to judgments that can.

This aim requires picturing knowledge as encompassing two orders. We cannot assign nonfoundational knowledge to the same system of knowledge to which the indubitable judgments that remove doubt belong. For to do so would be to treat nonfoundational judgments as *derived,* if not deduced, from intuited and deduced judgments, and thus founded on them—contrary to hypothesis. What is needed here is a distinction between an order of knowledge that contains nonfoundational judgments (as well as intuition and deduction, though not in their capacity as removers of doubt), and an order that contains foundational judgments in their capacity as removers of doubt. The distinction concerns the function of reasoning, not the intrinsic (psychological) nature of reasoning or the nature of the judgments that result from reasoning. The first of these two orders is the order at which the hypotheses in the *Meditations, Optics, Meteorology,* and *Principles* count as knowledge. The second is the order at which the doubts that can be raised about hypotheses are answered. The first order may admit nonfoundational judgments, even if the second order excludes them.

There is textual evidence against the standard account in favor of this two-ordered interpretation. There is first of all evidence against interpreting Descartes as engaged in constructing knowledge by intuition and deduction. The most forthright rejection of this strategy comes in a letter to Clerselier (June or July 1646):

> One should not require the first principle to be such that all other propositions can be reduced [*reduire*] to it and proved by it. It is enough if it is useful for the discovery [*trouver*] of many, and if there is no other proposition on which it depends, and none which is easier to discover. It may be that there is no principle at all to which alone all things can be reduced. They do indeed reduce other propositions to the principle that *the same thing cannot both be and not be at the same time,* but their procedure is superfluous and useless. On the other hand it is very useful indeed to convince oneself first of the existence of God, and then of the existence of all creatures, through the consideration of one's own existence. (AT IV, 444–445; K, 197)[14]

Descartes uses the term *first principle* here in the same manner in which he uses it elsewhere, to refer to the proposition that he exists. He explicitly denies that all knowledge must be reduced to this doubt remover. "Reduce to" apparently means "deduce from," as the Scholastic practice he excoriates is one of trying to deduce many propositions from metaphysical principles. His point, then, is that the first proposition does not serve as a premise for the deduction of the remaining propositions—presumably, those which qualify as knowledge. Rather, it serves in a different way, by enabling us to *discover* the remaining propositions.

Descartes must have in mind here his method of discovery, or analytic method. The method of discovery is not to be contrasted with the method of proof or justification; as Descartes says, "*the method of proof* [*demonstrandum*] *is two-fold, one being analytic . . .* " (AT VII, 155; HR II, 48). Nowadays we tend to follow Reichenbach in distinguishing the context of discovery from the context of justification. But Descartes made no such distinction. Analysis is supposed to prove by removing doubt. In analysis, a principle that removes doubt is discovered by extrapolation from the discovery of the first proposition. This principle is the principle of assent to all clearly and distinctly perceived propositions.[15] The principle is then applied to discover many further judgments.[16] The principle is indeed identical with the principle of intuition and deduction, and in the *Meditations* Descartes officially restricts judgment to what is intuited and deduced, thereby excluding nonfoundational judgments. This restriction is forced so long as it is assumed that the principle of judgment must be discovered by extrapolation from the discovery of the first proposition; for the first proposition must be intuited if it is to remove doubt from itself. Even so, the method of discovery opens the possibility of discovering a nonfoundational principle of judgment,[17] for it may be denied that principles must be discovered by extrapolation from the discovery of the first proposition. It would seem quite enough if the first proposition and other discovering judgments could remove doubt from the principle by supplying a reliable argument. The two stages of the method, the one involving the discovering of the principle, the other the application of the principle to form judgments, would seem to make room for the discovery of a nonfoundational principle, even though the discovering judgments must be intuited or deduced.[18]

Inasmuch as Descartes' method of discovery is also a method of proof, it seems fair to say that it yields knowledge. The two stages of the method thus become two orders of knowledge. There is the stage at which the discovering judgments are themselves discovered and applied to discover the principle, and the stage at which many judgments are discovered through the application of the principle. I will refer to the latter judgments as attaining first-order knowledge. The judgments by which we discover the principle I will refer to as attaining second-order knowledge. By extension we may label as second-order knowledge all those judgments which result from the application of the principle when the principle has been discovered in accordance with the method of analysis.[19]

The two orders of knowledge are reflected in Descartes' distinction between *cognitio* and *scientia*. *Cognitio* is what I am calling first-order knowledge, while *scientia* best fits second-order knowledge in the extended sense. *Cognitio* is what results from clear and distinct perception, and *scientia* is *cognitio* from which doubt has been removed by the discovering judgments (excluding, perhaps, the discovering judgments themselves). At the end of Meditation V, Descartes reiterates that all knowledge [*omnis scientiae*] depends on the knowledge [*cognitione*] of God. And in the famous atheist passage in the Second Replies, he says: "*That an atheist can know [cognoscere] clearly that the three angles of a triangle are equal to two right angles*, I do not deny, I merely affirm that, on the other hand, such knowledge [*cognitionem*] on his part cannot constitute true science [*scientiam*], because no knowledge [*cognitio*] that can be rendered doubtful should be called science [*scientia*]" (AT VII, 141; HR II, 39). Here Descartes allows that the atheist's judgment (in a deductive matter, it should be noted) can attain *cognitio*, apparently on the ground that the atheist can clearly and distinctly perceive propositions. He goes on to deny that the atheist has *scientia*, on the ground that the atheist cannot discover the principle of clear and distinct perception. The atheist can attain first- but not second-order knowledge.

Not only does Descartes distinguish orders of knowledge, but it appears from the passage in his letter to Clerselier that his reason for doing so is to admit many judgments as known—to admit plenty of first-order knowledge. He recognizes that the judgments capable of removing doubt are too few in number to yield much knowledge by deduction. He therefore chooses to have them remove doubt from an entire principle, the principle of clear and distinct perception.

The distinction between the two orders of knowledge is just what Descartes needs to accommodate nonfoundational knowledge. He may maintain that only what is intuited or deduced removes doubt. And he may continue to hold that only what removes doubt qualifies as second-order knowledge, since only the judgments that serve to enable him to discover the principle of judgment remove doubt. Such a view does not, however, commit him to the view that only what removes doubt qualifies as *first-order* knowledge. On the contrary, since the judgments that discover the principle function to remove doubt, there is no need to insist that other judgments remove doubt as well. There is no need to require that first-order knowledge remove doubt, so no need to require that it consist of intuition and deduction. First-order knowledge may admit nonfoundational judgments as well.

THE PLAUSIBILITY OF FIRST-ORDER
NONFOUNDATIONALISM

To say that first-order knowledge may admit nonfoundational judgments is not yet to reach nonfoundational knowledge. To determine whether there is nonfoundational first-order knowledge, we need to determine whether second-order knowledge can discover any nonfoundational principle in the manner in which it discovers the principle of clear and distinct perception. The question is whether there are judgments that remove their own doubt which are also capable of removing the doubt that attaches to nonfoundational judgments. The answer will be affirmative if Descartes can supply judgments that discover some nonfoundational principle so similar to the judgments that actually discover the principle of clear and distinct perception that there can be no question they equally well remove doubt, both from themselves and from the nonfoundational principle.

To supply judgments that discover a nonfoundational principle, Descartes need only produce judgments from which he can argue that the principle is reliable. To arrive at such judgments, Descartes need only make minor modifications in his argument that all clearly and distinctly perceived propositions are true. To see this, just recall his argument. God produces in us the faculty of clear and distinct perception and this faculty compels the will's assent. But God would be a deceiver if ever he were to produce in us a faculty that compels assent to false propositions. God being no deceiver, all clearly and distinctly perceived propositions are true.[20]

The key premise of Descartes' argument is that God would be a deceiver if he were to produce in us a faculty that compels assent to a false proposition. The underlying claim that makes this premise plausible is that to avoid deception God must supply true judgments to the extent that he directs us toward the judgments. Yet for God to direct us toward a judgment it is not necessary that he compel assent. It is necessary only that he incline assent. When God implants in our nature a principle that does not compel but still inclines assent, he must supply us with truths to the extent that he inclines us. A principle belonging to our nature must therefore yield true beliefs with a frequency proportional to the degree to which it inclines assent.[21]

This generalized argument establishes a proportion between the reliability and the inclination to assent of principles belonging to our nature.[22] The generalized premise, furthermore, seems as capable of removing its own doubt as the original premise it underwrites. All the discovering judgments that serve as premises of the generalized argument therefore remove doubt as effectively as the premises of the original argument. Though clear and distinct perception alone compels assent, there is another principle with an equal claim to belong to our nature, and this principle inclines assent. I have in mind parsimonious hypothetico-deduction. As Descartes reiterates, any alternative to the hypothesis that makes the most phenomena cohere seems inconceivable.[23] By the generalized argument, the principle of parsimonious hypothetico-deduction is reliable. The generalized argument therefore removes doubt from this nonfoundational principle.

Something like the generalized argument must be what Descartes has in mind in the closing sentences of the *Meditations*. Referring to the results of parsimonious hypothetico-deduction, he says: "I ought in no wise to doubt the truth of such matters if, after having called up my senses, my memory, and my understanding, to examine them, nothing is brought to evidence by any one of them which is repugnant to what is set by the others. For because God is in no wise a deceiver, it follows that I am not deceived in this" (AT VII, 90; HR I, 199).[24] Assent in these matters is not compelled, but parsimonious hypothetico-deduction inclines assent so long as memory and clear and distinct perception say nothing to contradict it. While the principle only inclines assent, the doubts that countervail it are not enough to prevent assent, and Descartes thinks he ought to go ahead and assent even in the face of such doubts. For God being no deceiver, the principle must be generally reliable to the extent that it inclines.

WHY WAS DESCARTES A FIRST-ORDER FOUNDATIONALIST?

If what I have so far argued is correct, Descartes makes generous use of hypothetico-deduction in his metaphysics and science and has all the resources needed to vindicate such a nonfoundational principle. Furthermore, in the account I have sketched, the need for intuition and deduction in removing doubt does not entail that first-order knowledge must be foundational, and Descartes is deprived of the chief motive for foundationalism attributed to him by the standard account. Yet these conclusions threaten to leave mysterious Descartes' obvious attachment to first-order foundationalism. Why does he feel the need to stand ready with deductive arguments to replace hypothetico-deduction? Any account of Descartes' foundationalism must explain his nominal commitment to first-order foundationalism.

I would like to suggest an explanation. From early on Descartes expects that intuition and deduction will offer a *complete* principle of judgment in the range of topics on which we can hope to judge (AT VI, 19; HR I, 92).[25] That is, he assumes that intuition and deduction will answer all questions in this range. If they are indeed complete, then there is no room for the application of any other principle. Being perfectly reliable, they will supply the truth on all issues; where any other principle disagrees, that principle must be wrong. It is easy to appreciate how an appetite whetted by such an expectation might be dissatisfied with any other principle, even after it had become clear that the expectation would not be fulfilled.[26]

But why does Descartes expect intuition and deduction to be complete? Here I can offer only a conjecture. A century before the *Medi-*

tations it was a common view that God conceals nothing from us, and it may well be that Descartes' hope for completeness is fueled by such a view.[27] From the assumption that God is no concealer, completeness does indeed follow, though not quite the completeness of intuition and deduction. If God is no concealer, he must ensure that for each true proposition there is one principle that sanctions that proposition and is more inclining than any that sanctions its contrary. In this way, for each true proposition, some one of the principles that sanction it is *maximally inclining* with respect to that proposition. The view that God is no concealer thus implies the completeness of the set of maximally inclining principles. To be sure, this argument does not establish the completeness of any particular principle, or even any set of assent-compelling principles. So far as the argument goes, every principle may fail to compel assent, and so be less than perfectly reliable. The completeness established by the argument may therefore pertain to intuition-deduction and hypothetico-deduction together. But it is easy to appreciate how Descartes might overlook this subtlety and treat the conclusion as establishing the completeness of a single assent-compelling principle. The suggestion is that Descartes' reluctance to let nonfoundational judgments stand alone may derive from his faith that God is no concealer; and his chagrin in being unable to back these judgments with deductions may derive from nothing less than a feeling that God has let him down. Descartes' commitment to first-order foundationalism, in this view, is not the fruit of a prudish and unreasonable aversion to doubt and falsity, to less than perfect reliability, as the standard account would have it.

WHY WAS DESCARTES A SECOND-ORDER FOUNDATIONALIST?

I have so far argued only that Descartes' method of discovery distinguishes first- and second-order knowledge and yields nonfoundational first-order knowledge. The question remains whether Descartes' method permits nonfoundational second-order knowledge. Does the removal of doubt require a foundational argument for the reliability of the foundational or nonfoundational principles? I am prepared to allow that it does, that Descartes is essentially committed to second-order foundationalism. But I would argue once again that Descartes' commitment to foundationalism is not prudery. Descartes has the most sensible and modest of reasons for his commitment to second-order foundationalism.

To appreciate why this is so, we need only reflect on the purpose of second-order knowledge. Descartes' method of discovery has two stages, the first of which is the discovery of principles of judgment, the second, the discovery of judgments through the application of these principles. The ultimate aim of the method is to make true judgments and avoid making false judgments in pursuing metaphysics and science. The first stage of the method is therefore designed to discover principles that sanction true judgments and avoid sanctioning false judgments. Strictly speaking, the ultimate aim of the method (in making judgments) would not be satisfied if some false judgments were made. It would not be satisfied, that is, if some of the discovered principles were less than perfectly reliable. Yet, so long as these judgments are relatively few in number, so long as these principles are reliable, the ultimate aim of the method is clearly approximated. From the standpoint of the ultimate aim, making some false judgments is an unhappy but relatively trifling consequence. When Descartes embraces nonfoundational principles, he must tolerate this unhappy consequence. Nonfoundational principles do not compel assent and so are not perfectly reliable.

The same nonchalance about falsehood would be intolerable in the first stage of the method of discovery, where the stakes are much higher. An error in discovery at this stage would not amount merely to acquiring falsehood. It would amount to future reliance on an unreliable principle, hence the future acquisition of many falsehoods, perhaps mostly falsehoods, even an entire system of false judgments. It is impossible to exaggerate, therefore, the crucial role played by the judgments that discover the principle. The most extreme care must be taken to ensure that the discovered principle really is reliable. The discovered principle is ensured reliable only to the extent that the discovering judgments are ensured true. Extreme care in discovering the principle therefore calls for extreme caution in selecting the discovering judgments. To ensure that the discovering judgments are true, Descartes should select them by a principle of judgment that is perfectly reliable. By his own forthcoming argument for the reliability of clear and distinct perception, only an assent-compelling principle is perfectly reliable. And only intuition and deduction are assent-compelling. It follows that the discovering judgments must be foundational, sanctioned by intuition and deduction. As there are no judgments made in the method of discovery prior to making the discovering judgments, Descartes must begin with intuited judgments and continue on to deduced judgments to complete the argument for the reliability of the discovered principles. Since second-order knowledge and the discovering judgments are one and the same, to qualify as second-order knowledge a judgment must be foundational. Descartes is essentially committed to second-order foundationalism.[28]

From these reflections, we can see that it is not prudery that drives Descartes to second-order foundationalism, but ordinary prudence, as Descartes himself several times insists (AT VII, 548; HR II, 335). To one whose aim is to acquire true judgments by application of a principle, prudence dictates the most extreme caution in the discovery of the principle, lest a very unreliable principle be chosen. Caution in turn requires true discovering judgments. And true discovering judgments are ensured only when the principle that sanctions them is perfectly reliable. Prudence dictates using a perfectly reliable principle in discovering the discovering judgments, which must therefore be foundational.

The arguments of this essay, then, converge on the conclusion that most contemporary criticisms of Cartesian foundationalism are misplaced and the remainder are peculiarly insensitive to the demands of the Cartesian project. Most recent criticisms try to make points against Cartesian foundationalism by denying that there is enough intuition to support any significant superstructure of deductive knowledge, or by denying that deduction is sufficiently powerful to amplify intuition into a significant superstructure of knowledge. While these protests are no doubt correct, they undermine Cartesian foundationalism only as it is understood in the standard account. In the standard account, Descartes is indeed bound to deduce all knowledge from intuited propositions. But in the two-ordered account I am proposing, he is by no means required to do so. He need not deduce all first-order knowledge from intuited propositions. On the contrary, he need not deduce *any* first-order knowledge from intuited propositions. There is nothing to prevent first-order knowledge from being entirely hypothetical.

If the argument of this section is correct, there must, of course, be a small number of intuited propositions if there is to be second-order knowledge of the sort Descartes needs to discover first-order knowledge. The Cartesian project is therefore vulnerable to the objection that there are no intuited propositions at all. If this objection is correct, Cartesian foundationalism must fail in its objective of removing doubt from hypothetical judgments. The crucial point for understanding Descartes' project, however, is that the search for intuition is made entirely reasonable by the demands of second-order knowledge and is not the product of prudery or hubris it is so often made out to be. No matter how modestly one formulates the project of removing doubt, it will be reasonable to seek intuition. And certainly the project is a reasonable one, formulated with suitable modesty. Though there is little hope that there will ever turn out to be any intuition in the sense needed for Descartes' project, one cannot help but sympathize with the spirit that finds it necessary to seek it out.

NOTES

Abbreviations AT, HR, and K are explained in the General Bibliography at the beginning of this volume. In addition, I use CB to refer to *Descartes' Conversation with Burman*, trans. John Cottingham (Oxford, Clarendon Press, 1976).

1. I would like to thank William Alston, Hugh Chandler, Lois Frankel, John Heil, William Lycan, George Pappas, Amélie Rorty, Michael Smith, and Steven Wagner for helpful comments. This paper profited from presentations at Ohio State University (October 1982) and the University of Illinois at Urbana-Champaign (October 1982). Research for the paper was supported by an Ohio State University Postdoctoral Fellowship (1982).

2. It isn't quite uncontroversial that Descartes is a foundationalist. I read Harry G. Frankfurt as denying this in *Demons, Dreamers, and Madmen* (Indianapolis: Bobbs-Merrill, 1970).

3. I warn the reader that this is a paper about the *Meditations*. I will have only a word to say about Descartes' foundationalism in the *Discourse* and *Principles*, and nothing at all to say about the *Regulae*. I view his foundationalism in the *Regulae* as substantially different from that in the *Meditations*. For example, the metaphysics of simple and complex natures which underwrites his account of intuition and deduction in the *Regulae* plays at best a subsidiary role elsewhere. The reason for this, I conjecture, is that Descartes' aim in the *Regulae* is to characterize what our cognition must be like if it is to be error free in virtue solely of its representational relation to its objects. In later works, however, he abandons this insistence on a representational argument against error in favor of a theological argument.

4. The standard account is assumed, for example, in Bernard Williams' article on Descartes in *The Encyclopedia of Philosophy*, ed. Paul Edwards (New York: Macmillan, 1967), 344–354. Despite a general flight from the account, elements of it remain in Frankfurt; E. M. Curley, *Descartes Against the Skeptics* (Cambridge: Harvard University Press, 1978); and Williams, *Descartes: The Project of Pure Enquiry* (New York: Penguin, 1978). James van Cleve has perhaps moved furthest from the account in "Foundationalism, Epistemic Principles, and the Cartesian Circle," *Philosophical Review* 88:55–91. I do not, however, endorse all aspects of his view.

5. I choose the term *sanctioned by* to remain neutral on the question of whether knowledge is to be conceived as judgment that *conforms to* intuition and deduction, in the manner of conformity to a rule, or as judgment *caused*

by intuition and deduction, in the manner of causation by a perceptual process. Margaret Wilson argues persuasively for the latter interpretation in *Descartes* (London: Routledge & Kegan Paul, 1978), but the issue has no bearing on the concerns of this paper.

6. For doubts as to whether this component of the standard account is correct, see Curley, 171–193. Actually, Curley omits the most striking counterevidence, CB, 15, where Descartes explains how there is room for error in judgments about ideas even if they are not referred to any external object.

7. The term *epistemic prudery* is William Lycan's.

8. I assume that a very strong inclination differs from compelled assent. The will can withhold assent from a proposition, even in the presence of a very strong inclination, provided that it has some sufficiently strong reason to doubt the proposition. The consideration of doubts is just what enables Descartes to withhold assent in Meditation I. These doubts are still operative at this point in Meditation VI and are indeed the very doubts to be removed here. The presence of a very strong inclination is therefore not enough to compel assent to the existence of body.

9. It is true that Descartes intends to back his hypothetical arguments in the *Optics* and *Meteorology* with deductive arguments for the same conclusions. But his professed reason for using hypothesis in that context is that he has no room to present the deductions, whereas this cannot be his reason in Meditation VI, since he actually does present the allegedly deductive argument. Of course, Descartes does sometimes present more than one deductive argument for a conclusion, as with his arguments for the existence of God. But it is not clear that he really conceives of the cosmological arguments in Meditation III as distinct arguments, and the ontological argument in Meditation V would seem worth adding because of the very different epistemological status of its premises.

10. See, for example, Daniel Garber, "Science and Certainty in Descartes," *in* Michael Hooker, *Descartes: Critical and Interpretive Essays* (Baltimore: Johns Hopkins University Press, 1978), 114–151. I take the alternative line sketched below in "Hypothesis in Descartes' Science" (manuscript).

11. In the *Principles*, Descartes says: "They who observe how many things regarding the magnet, fire, and the fabric of the whole world are deduced [*deducta*] from so few principles even if they thought my assumption [*assumpta*] of those principles groundless would admit that so many things could hardly cohere [*cohaerent*] if they were false" (AT VIII–1, 328; HR I, 301). I observe that Descartes in fact recognizes the coherence of his science from early on (AT I, 140–141, 285, 423–424; K, 10, 25–26, 40), but he does not attempt to account for its significance until after the *Discourse*.

12. It is unclear whether all doubt must be removed in a single sitting, so that in removing doubt from any principle we would need to appeal only to premises that remove doubt from themselves. Or whether instead doubt may first be removed from one principle, and this principle may then be applied to generate judgments that remove doubt about other principles.

13. Perhaps it will be suggested that after having advanced the argument

for body, Descartes offers an argument to vindicate sensation. For he seeks a way to avoid error in sensory judgment by asking what the function of sensory judgment might be. His chief observation is that our senses are so constituted as to apprise us of the presence of helpful and harmful bodies in our environment, and it is mainly (though not exclusively) when we go beyond judging their presence that we end in error. The trouble with reading this argument as a vindication of sensation is that it assumes propositions of the very sort doubted here. It assumes propositions about particular bodies— e.g., the existence of one's own body, of the senses, and of surrounding bodies. Now Descartes does ascribe judgments of this sort to nature when he says "there is nothing which this nature teaches me more expressly than that I have a body," and again "nature teaches me that many other bodies exist around mine, of which some are to be avoided and others sought after" (AT VII, 80–81; HR I, 192). But by "nature" here he refers only to "the complex of all the things which God has given me," and not to what pertains to his own nature. His argument for the reliability of sensory judgment is therefore not designed to remove skeptical doubt, but rather to discover the principle of sensory judgment from which doubt may be removed by a theological argument.

14. A similar remark to Clerselier appears at AT IX–2, 206; HR II, 127: "For it is certain that in order to discover the truth we should always start with particular notions, in order to arrive at general conceptions subsequently, though we may also in the reverse way, after having discovered the universals, deduce other particulars from them."

15. Descartes refers to the *principle* of clear and distinct perception in the *Discourse* (AT VI, 41; HR I, 106). The significance of principles is exemplified in this passage from the *Discourse:* " . . . I am convinced that if in my youth I had been taught all the truths for which I have since sought the demonstrations, and if I had had no difficulty in learning them I might never have known any others" (AT VI, 72; HR I, 126).

16. There is additional evidence that discovery has two stages. In the *Discourse*, Descartes warns the reader that not everyone has the temperament for the method of doubt (AT VI, 15; HR I, 90). Descartes is not saying here that such people ought not to engage in cognition, so there must be a stage of discovery distinct from the stage in which the method of doubt is applied.

17. Perhaps it will be objected that the two stages of discovery collapse because clear and distinct perception requires the removal of doubt. But even if clear and distinct perception does require the removal of doubt there is still a distinction between the use to which clear and distinct perception is put in removing doubt and the use to which it is put in discovering particular judgments. It is this distinction of use that is crucial here.

18. It may be that only some intuitions and deductions are capable of removing doubt. If so, then Descartes must already treat the remainder as having doubt removed in virtue of the discovery of a *principle*. He may well need to distinguish two stages of discovery quite independently of the need to interpolate nonfoundational judgments.

19. The distinction between orders of knowledge here resembles William Alston's levels of knowledge in "Two Types of Foundationalism," *Journal of Philosophy* 73 (1976):165–185, and elaborated in "Level-Confusions in Epistemology," in Peter French et al., *Midwest Studies in Philosophy V: Studies in Epistemology* (Minneapolis: University of Minnesota Press, 1980), 135–150. Alston's levels, however, iterate a single knowledge-operator, while mine distinguish two knowledge-operators. Furthermore, Alston tries to defend the plausibility of combining first-level foundationalism and second-level nonfoundationalism, while I will attribute to Descartes the reverse combination. My distinction bears a closer resemblance to Alvin Goldman's level distinction in "The Internalist Conception of Justification," in French's *Midwest Studies,* 27–51. But Goldman, like Alston, suggests combining first-level foundationalism and second-level nonfoundationalism.

20. There is a problem with Descartes' argument for reliability that seems to have gone unnoticed. Even if God must treat us to truths to the extent that he compels our assent, it follows that clear and distinct perception is reliable only if we are compelled by God to assent to clearly and distinctly perceived propositions. But from the mere fact that clear and distinct perception compels assent when used, it does not follow that we are compelled by God to assent to clearly and distinctly perceived propositions. For it may well be that we could avoid ever clearly and distinctly perceiving any proposition, and so never have our assent compelled. To skirt this problem, Descartes must assume not only that God is no deceiver but also that he is no concealer, that he supplies us with a faculty whose exercise will eventually yield some truths.

21. It is worth noting that the generalized argument establishes that most of the judgments we actually make in accordance with the discovered principles are true, and not merely that in the long run most of the judgments we would make would be true. For God would be a deceiver were he to supply us with actual false judgments; he cannot avoid deception by supplying us with principles that would eventually sanction mostly true judgments, even though we never get to the point where we make these true judgments. Of course, the argument leaves quite unanswered the question of how we are to tell whether a given principle is really one of the discovered principles. To answer this, we would have to say how we can tell whether a given principle belongs to our nature and compels assent, by no means an easy task.

22. It may be noted that Descartes' argument does not establish that most of *his* judgments are true. It may establish only that most judgments that result from hypothetico-deduction are true. It might well be that his judgments are unlucky enough to fall into the false output of hypothetico-deduction. But the community as a whole must make mostly true judgments. This sort of communication is not, however, as alien to Descartes as one might think. Descartes' individualism has been overemphasized. His remarks sometimes indicate that he conceives of science as a communal enterprise, to which any individual can make only a limited contribution (e.g., AT VI, 63, 65; HR I, 120, 122).

23. AT VIII–1, 329; HR I, 302.

24. Descartes does go on to say that only precipitation in judgment need issue in falsity. But it is obvious that he cannot mean this quite literally. He has already recognized that error can result from stimulation of the nerves by objects other than the intentional object of perception. No amount of caution can save us from mistakes of this sort if the false stimulation is sufficiently global. Descartes' argument at best shows that cautious judgment is generally reliable.

25. Descartes relegates theological matters to the realm of faith (AT I, 143–144, 146, 153; K, 10, 12, 15; AT III, 274; K, 91; CB, 32).

26. Descartes does make exceptionally strong claims about the need to avoid falsehood (AT II, 501; AT III, 544; K, 132). But in his more considered moments he relents: "For he really gives battle who attempts to conquer all difficulties and errors which prevent him from arriving at a knowledge of the truth, and it is to lose a battle to admit a false opinion touching a matter of any generality and importance" (AT VI, 67; HR I, 123). He does not object here to false opinion per se, but to false opinion touching a matter of generality and importance. He may mean to object, not to false opinion at all, but to *principles* that sanction much false judgment.

27. See, for example, Paracelsus, *Die 9 Bücher der Natura Rerum, Sämte Werke*, ed. Karl Suhdorff (Munich: Otto Wilhelm Barth Verlag, 1925), 11:393.

28. Note, however, in the extended sense in which second-order knowledge is merely first-order knowledge that results from a principle actually discovered by second-order knowledge, the second-order knowledge need not be foundational.

22

Cartesian Passions and the Union of Mind and Body

AMÉLIE OKSENBERG RORTY

"It is on these," Descartes says of the passions, "that the good and ill of this life depends" (AT XI, 488; HR I, 427). This line of thought had already been announced, in some detail, in Meditation VI: " . . . when we need to drink, the throat becomes dry in such a way as to move the nerves, and thus the inner parts of the brain. That movement produces the feeling of thirst in the mind because on such an occasion nothing would serve us better than to know that we need to drink, in order to preserve our health."[1] This seems a strange remark for Descartes, of all people, to make, having characterized the ego as "a *thinking* thing, a mind which doubts, conceives, affirms, negates, wills, refuses; which also imagines and senses."[2] If it is *thinking* that is essential to the mind, and if the passions are not necessary to the mind's identity as a thinking thing, how can the good or ill of this life depend on the passions?

Who is this creature who is so well served by the passions? How is it related to the ego whose existence is demonstrated by the *cogito*? Or to the ego of Meditation VI, which is *conjunctum* with its body; which is *quasi permixtum* with its own body; and which composes a single whole with its particular body [*adeo ut unum quid cum illo componam*] (AT VII, 81; HR I, 192)?

Descartes' description of the functions of the passions in *Les Passions de L'Âme* (PA) does not by itself help answer these questions. After having distinguished the functions of the soul from those of the body, the soul's actions from its passions, and having defined the general class of passions as ideas predicated of the soul, caused by the body acting through the mediation of the pineal gland, Descartes distinguishes the varieties of passions (perceptual sensations, bodily sensations, and the passion-emotions). With his usual confident and engaging obscurity, he says: "The function of all the passions [passions narrowly speaking, passion-emotions] consists in this alone, that they dispose the soul to will those things which nature teaches us are useful to ourselves, and to persist in this volition, and also that the same agitation of the spirits which usually causes them disposes the body to those movements which serve to bring about those things [i.e., those things which are useful to us]."[3] He then proceeds to give an account of the function of each of the basic passions as it affects the body, as it affects the soul, and as it affects the compound individual.

But this quotation really introduces three characters—the soul, the body, and then the third character, the *we*. But *we* might ask: Who is served by the passions? And how are we served? Descartes presents at least two quite different accounts of the mind and of the mind-embodied ego, each with a corresponding picture of the proper function of the passions. He thinks that he has a theory that unites these two accounts, a theory that shows how, despite having diverse and sometimes apparently conflicting ideas and functions, the mind is nevertheless strongly unified. Initially no friend of the passions, Descartes comes to find in them a clue to the unity of the mind as well as the unity of the individual, as compounded of mind and body.

I

Let's first see what kind of mind this kind of mind is, that has passions and is benefited by them. Then we shall look at the functions of the three kinds of passions—perceptual sensations, bodily sensations, and emotion-passions. Finally we shall try to determine what the passions tell us about the various relations between the mind and the body, and their union.

Because it is more familiar, a sketch of the first account of the mind will suffice. It is the account presented in the early, cathartic sections of the *Meditations*, when Descartes is laundering our conceptions of the essential identity of the mind or soul from the Aristotelian debris of occult powers, entelechies, and final causes in order to reveal the true ground for the immortality of the soul (Dedication: AT VII, 1 ff.; HR I, 133). He wrote the *Meditations*, he says, in order to demonstrate that rational belief in the existence of God and in the immortality of the soul (or at least its substantial distinction from the body) need not rest on superstition, faith, or authority.[4]

This "I" of the first section of the *Meditations*, this mind which, as he says to Gassendi, "is not part of the soul but the whole of the soul which thinks" (HR II, 210) is any rational mind whatever, without distinctions of persons. The true and strict story of the mind's essence as a thinking thing establishes immortality by the mind's separability from the body and by the indestructibility that is supposed to be guaranteed by indivisibility. In this strict view the ego would remain unaffected if it had no passions, perceptions, or bodily sensations.[5] After all, passions, by definition, are not actions of the mind; they are ways in which it is affected or modified. They are confused; they are contingently caused by the body.[6]

But these arguments for the immortality of the mind have dark consequences. In the first place, the argument from the distinctness and separability of the mind is incomplete: since the mind might have its own forms of dissolution, its distinctness from the body would not be sufficient to establish its immortality. It is also necessary to establish that indivisiblity assures indestructibility and indestructibility assures immortality. Even if immortality could be assured by indivisibility, an additional argument is required: since compound unities are divisible and destructible, the mind is immortal only if it is a simple and indivisible unity. If the mind is not a simple, indivisible unity (if, for instance, some of its ideas or functions could be removed without changing its essential identity), only that part of the mind which forms a simple, indivisible unity can be immortal. But the sort of immortality that is assured by indivisible indestructibility is not very interesting: any mathematical point can have it.

Even more serious complications arise from Descartes' doctrine that, although the world forms a completely self-explicating system, it is not a self-sustaining, self-creating substance. The world continues to exist only because God continually chooses to re-create it, and to re-create it in such a way as to preserve the same laws through each creation. He has chosen not only to create minds that are immortal, remaining numerically identical in all re-created worlds, but also to create individual minds that are distinct from one another. While an infinite God is not comprehensible to finite minds, he has structured the world according to comprehensible principles. There should therefore be an account of the individuation and distinctness, as well as of the immortality, of mind. (1) What, other than God's choice, is the principle that assures the numerical identity of a mind through re-created worlds? (2) What assures the distinctness of individual minds? (3) Are immortal minds individuated and distinct?

1. The identity of an individual mind through God's re-creations is assured by its essence, its thinking (the same) necessary ideas. But since there are plenty of necessary ideas to go around, it might in principle be possible for a mind to have one set of necessary ideas at one time and another set at another. It might seem as if the identity of the mind depended on the fact that necessary ideas form a unified system: a mind that has any set of necessary ideas implicitly has the whole set. In this interpretive defense, the continuing identity of mind follows from the indivisible unity of the pure understanding. But that, in turn, rests on Descartes' account of the unity of science.

2. But the argument that could secure the identity of a mind through re-created worlds seems to threaten the distinguishability of individual minds. For if a mind retains its identity by virtue of the indivisible, systematic unity of its necessary ideas, then any mind that has just that set of ideas is indistinguishable from any other. What assures the identity of a mind through time might assure the identity of any minds. It is not clear that Descartes accepts the principle of the identity of indiscernibles. But even if he does not, he is committed to a rational reconstruction of the principles of God's creating distinct, individual minds. Descartes certainly thinks that God created individual minds as distinct. But what principle—other than divine fiat—distinguishes individual minds?

a. Minds might be individuated by their passions, by those ideas which they receive from body (perceptions, bodily sensations, passion-emotions). But any mind can be divested of its contingent passions without losing its identity. If passions are not necessary to the mind's essential identity, they are not part of the mind's indivisible unity. (And, as we shall see, while perceptions and bodily sensations can in principle be absorbed into strict science, the passion-emotions cannot be absorbed into the unified system of necessary ideas.) But if the passions are not integral parts of the mind's indivisible unity, they have no part in its immortality.

b. Minds might be individuated by the history of their thoughts, the sequences of their ideas, affirmations (denials and suspended judgments). But the history of a mind's ideas and propositional attitudes includes confused ideas and judgments of confused ideas. Minds individuated by their distinct histories would be only contingently individuated, because those histories are only contingently distinct.

c. Individual minds might be distinguished by the nature and structure of their wills. But the will—and presumably if there are distinct wills, each individual will—is infinite, that is, unconditioned and unlimited in its capacity to assert, deny, or refrain from judging. If individual minds were distinguished by their respective wills, they would be differentiated by the vicissitudes of the history of their respective affirmations and denials. But such a history would be contingent, particularly as it would include the will's judgment of confused ideas. So if individual minds were distinguished by the history of their willings they would be distinguished by features contingent to each of them.

3. The principles that rationalize the identity of an immortal mind undermine the distinguishability of individuated minds. Furthermore, the principles that individuate and distinguish minds do not follow from the mind's essential definition: the ideas that distinguish and individuate minds are contingent on their identity. While God chose to create distinct, individuated immortal minds, there is no rational principle—and certainly none that follows from the essence of mind— that necessarily preserves the individuality and distinctness of immortal mind(s).

Presumably Descartes had good reasons for not explicating these consequences of his arguments for immortality in the *Meditations*. After all, he is there primarily interested in establishing the immortality of The Mind. But while this strict and severe story of the ego is the true story, it is not the whole of the story of the ego, not the story of the *we* who might be served by the passions. What is the status of all those contingent ideas, the confused perceptual sensations, bodily sensations, and passions that the mind found necessary to doubt? What is their relation to the mind? And what can they reveal about its character?

II

The second story of the mind—developed in Meditation VI—is intended to answer these questions. It takes confused ideas—perceptions, bodily sensations, and passions—seriously.[7] While these are not part of the mind's essence as a thinking thing, are neither necessary to it nor affirmed by it as true, they do have adequate explanations. However confused, they reveal something about their causes. What is as important is that they also reveal something about the body's relation to the mind.

Taken together as a class, the passions are all caused in the soul by the body, through the intermission of the nerves bringing animal spirits to act on the pineal gland (PA, 27: AT XI, 349; HR I, 334). But in fact the three types of passions are quite different from one another, each revealing something distinctive about the mind's relation to extension (AT XI, 344–349; HR I, 341–343; PA, 21–25).

1. Perceptions are confused representations of their causes, the real properties of Extension. That the mind has perceptual ideas shows it is the sort of entity that can be conjoined with Body in such a way that it can be affected or modified by the properties of Extension.

2. Bodily sensations reveal that the mind is actually *quasi-permixtum* with a section of Extension. It is not only causally conjoined with Body at some point, but is in fact pervasively blended through and through with a section of Extension so that it feels the states of that section as its own proper body.

3. The passions proper, the emotion-passions, reveal that the entity formed by the mind's pervading its own body can form a single whole, a unity whose distinctive benefits and harms are not reducible to those of its contributing constitutive substances.[8] The passions show that the mind is not only permixed with the body but that, taken together, mind and body form a whole with interlocked functions, directed to the well-being of that whole. The *we* who is served by the passions is not only the machine-organism, but the combined mind-and-body, taken as a composite whole.

But there is at least initially some question about how to characterize the unity of a mind that performs some functions by virtue of its contingent union with the body, and yet performs other functions by virtue of its being essentially a purely intellectual substance. Can these two apparently quite different sorts of functions be brought together in a substance that is supposed to be an indivisibly unified whole?

Before turning to that question, we need to examine the intellectual functions of the distinctive varieties of the passions. Because this is relatively well trod ground, we can be short about perceptions. What is the relation between the Extension we perceive confusedly and the Extension whose properties we conceive intellectually, clearly, and distinctly? After all, in principle there might be two distinct sorts of Extension: the Extension whose properties are exhaustively analyzed and demonstrated in mathematical physics on the one hand, and the Extension whose properties are the causes of our confused ideas on the other. The veracity of God underwrites the teaching of the light of nature. The Extension of mathematical, scientific knowledge, the Extension whose properties might be known, deductively demonstrated, even if we had no body (Meditation VI: AT VII, 82–83), also exists formally as the cause of our perceptual ideas. It is this that legitimizes our using the confusions and apparent contradictions of perceptual ideas as the occasions for scientific inquiry. And of course it is also for this reason that a deductive, mathematical science can in principle explain the systematic structure of our perceptions: optics is the science of sense perception. But perceptual sensations also tell us something about the mind. Even though perceptions are caused by the independent substance they confusedly represent, they can be systematically connected with the mind's system of clear and distinct ideas. Once perceptual ideas are clarified, they have a place in the science of optics, and once they have a place in the science of optics they have a place in physics. They are not therefore in themselves a threat to the unity of mind, because they are absorbed in the unified system of scientific knowledge.[9]

The two other sorts of passions—bodily sensations and emotion-passions—reveal the complexity of the relations between mind and body. The mind is (as a matter of fact) so connected to a section of Extension—its own body—that it senses the condition of that body. Bodily sensations—thirst, hunger, pain—are standardly distinguishable from the mind's perceptual ideas of those bodily conditions (Meditation VI: AT VII, 87–88). Like perceptions, bodily sensations are attributed to, and confusedly represent, their bodily causes. Though not reliable at face value, they are, when properly understood, genuinely informative indices of the body's condition. The limits of bodily sensations indicate the limits and domain of the mind's own body, as a distinguishable section of Extension. Perceptual ideas are standardly transmitted with, or through, bodily sensations: we perceive the heat of a hot stove by its affecting the heat of our body. We can nevertheless distinguish the perceptual idea of the warmth of a stove from the sensation of the warmth of our hands as they come close to the stove, just as we can distinguish the sensations of being feverish from perceptual sensations of the temperature of the air.

If perceptions were the only passions of the mind, we might conclude that the mind is conjoined with only one section of Extension, the pineal gland, and that the mind is "lodged in the body as a pilot in a ship." But the pineal gland that transmits perceptions turns out to be a functional part of a larger section of Extension, a part of the body which is, as we discover from the passions proper, a functionally organized whole. The boundaries of our bodily sensations delimit the boundaries of the mind's own body. Even though we can, as amputees sometimes do, draw mistaken inferences about the boundaries of our proper bodies, standardly bodily sensations not only define the area of the mind's own body but also inform us of its condition.

We do not yet know what sort of body this is. Taken simply as a section of Extension, a human body is divisible; and its parts do not remain identical through what we commonsensically and confusedly think of as the individual's lifetime. Descartes sketches his position on bodily identity in a letter to Mesland (9 February 1645): "When we speak of the body of a man, we do not mean a determinate part of matter with a determinate size. For though the matter change, we still believe that it is numerically the same provided it remains joined in substantial union with the same soul. And we think the body is whole and entire provided it has in itself all the dispositions required to preserve that union."[10]

But it seems circular to identify a numerically identical body by the soul of the man to which it is joined and yet to individuate particular minds by their sensations and passions. If this seems circular, it is because it is circular. Although the idea of an individual ego formed and compounded of two substances is a confused idea, still the confused idea of such an entity, a mind-suffused section of Extension, is the idea of an entity identified by the *coordination* of a section of Extension, with a particular set of passion-ideas. Neither of these would, without their coordination, be sufficient to identify a continuing, numerically identical individual. Bootstrap operations are indeed circular, but they are not unilluminating on that account.

Briefly the sequence goes roughly like this: A set of perceptions and sensations "carve out" the area of a particular body, a particular section of Extension, at-a-time. This body-at-a-time is numerically identical over time, by virtue of its relation to the mind's perceptual and bodily ideas, including perceptual and sensory memories. The mind's perceptions and bodily sensations are referred and formally attributed to a body as their cause. But that body is itself numerically identical by virtue of its continuing functional relation to the association of ideas in the mind. The mind would not have had just those perceptions and sensations without just that body; but the body's continuing numerical identity is fixed by its continuous coordination with a set of bodily sensations that demarcate it.

But our main interest is, after all, the passions proper, and it is to these we now should turn. Bodily sensations demarcate the body: systematically taken together with perceptions, they assure us of the numerical identity of the individual. But they tell us nothing about the organization, let alone the unity, of that mind-suffused body, the individual. If we had only perceptions and bodily sensations, the mind might be merely mixed with the body: a mixture rather than a properly unified compound. passions proper, passion-emotions, reveal that the mind, when quasi-permixed with the body, forms a unified whole that can function well or ill as that whole, and not merely as a continuing, individuated mixture of two substances, mind and body. Like animal bodies, human bodies form a self-contained, self-regulating homeostatic system whose parts are functionally identified by their roles in the maintenance of that machine. The only benefits and harms that can come to that body, so identified, are the benefits and harms to its continuing to function as just that machine.[11] But when Descartes maintains that the passions benefit us in this life, and that they cause us to think and to persist in thinking about what is beneficial and important to us, he is not only referring to the functions of the passions in maintaining organized homeostatic *bodies* (PA, 52). This emerges dramatically when it becomes evident that at least some of the passions must be assigned distinctive and apparently conflicting functions and priorities in maintaining the body simply as an animal machine, or in maintaining the individual, mind-suffused section of Extension.[12] To see how this conflict in the priorities among the passions might present a problem, and to see Descartes' attempt to solve this problem, we need to look at the passions in some greater detail.

The passions proper are functions of functions. When our bodies interact with other parts of Extension, they undergo further modifications that enhance or diminish normal functioning. Something impinges on us—we see a lion rushing directly towards us. The nerves and animal spirits are agitated in such a way that, besides the perception of a bounding, tawny, sinuous creature, and certain bodily sensations (dry throat, trembling hands), we also register fear. Insofar as the passions come through or with sensations, they are *sentimens*, feelings; insofar as they interrupt or change the course of thought, they are *émotions* (PA, 28; AT XI, 350; HR I, 344). Since fear does not represent its cause, even in a confused way, we cannot even begin to transform it into a clear and distinct idea, though we can be quite clear, on reflection, that we *are* afraid. Nevertheless, fear concentrates the mind quite wonderfully. Instead of allowing us to pursue our thoughts in random associations, the passions direct them to what is useful. They cause us to think, and to persist in thinking, about the dangers that confront us: we remember remedies for such dangers; we associate and elicit reinforcing emotions and images; we form and are inclined to follow appropriate volitions. As a result of this concentrated, fortified, directed association of ideas, the will can resolve either to flee from what is dangerous or to overcome and disarm it. In either case, the action of the mind in willing to flee or to combat danger causes just that movement of the pineal gland which, by exciting the animal spirits and eventually the muscles, standardly produces the sort of appropriate, useful motion that the body, acting as a self-regulating machine, would produce on its own behalf. When the will affects the body, it does so materially.[13] And so it is for every passion: when it appears in the mind, standardly in combination with perceptions and bodily sensations, it produces a set of associated ideas, directed by desire—itself a passion—to promote a particular condition of well-being.

But again we are forced to ask: Whose well-being? In principle the body can maintain itself quite efficiently all by itself. The animals do, after all, manage quite well, having been designed by God to regulate themselves as self-sustaining machines. And even if the mind intervenes, it does so by producing just that motion of the pineal gland which is in any case the same as that produced by the body on its own, in its self-regulatory activity (PA, 52). The very motion of the pineal gland which produces the passion is already producing the beginning of the regulatory motion.

But the body's self-regulatory system operates without a long-range memory: its responses are relatively immediate, directed by and to its present condition. The mind initiates the retrieval of relevant perceptual memories: it sifts and evaluates information, introducing long-range considerations that modulate and correct purely machine-like reactions (PA, 41–45; AT XI, 359–363; HR I, 350–352). An animal licks and scratches its wounds; when it is depleted it is set to begin eating and drinking. But even though it is set to scratch an itch, a *minded* body might refrain from scratching, reflecting that such scratches tend to become infected sores. Similarly, a minded body suffering from the flu might drink even though it wasn't thirsty, believing that fluids are beneficial. It might decide to do this by making itself thirsty, choosing to eat salty food. The mind actively cooperates in the body's functioning by initiating, regulating, or checking those motions which the body itself employs in its own maintenance. The mind's functions—its associating ideas, its focusing on certain sorts of ideas—are continuously interlocked with those of the body, forming one whole system directed to the long-range maintenance of the body defined by its interlocked functioning with the mind rather than merely by its immediate, present condition. The mind does not just receive passions: once they are in the mind, they become active emotions, directing the association of ideas and inclining (though of course not determining) the will to form volitions that are useful to the compound individual, and to the body as part of that compound.

It might seem as if this argument only entitles Descartes to conclude that the mind and the body interact to form a mutually beneficial consortium. Why then does he draw the much stronger conclusion that mind and body form a substantial union? Benefits that accrue to a consortium accrue to each member, identified independently of its membership in the consortium. But the benefits of the interlocked interaction of mind and body accrue to each substance only as it is identified as part of the union. The long-term considerations that the mind brings to the body's welfare do not benefit the body *as such*, for the human body regarded as body-simpliciter only has the benefits that accrue to a piece of Extension regarded as a machine. But these are such short-lived benefits that it is questionable whether they should be regarded as benefits at all. After all, the identity of a piece of Extension regarded *as such* is changed when a particle of its matter changes. "When we speak in general of body, we mean a determinate part of matter. . . . If any particle of the matter were changed we would at once think the body was no longer quite the same, no longer numerically the same."[14] The long-term benefits that accrue to the body are *benefits* only to a minded-body, that is, to an entity whose numerical identity is defined by its contributions to the substantial union of mind and body. Similarly, the benefits that accrue to the mind from its union with the body are not essential to its nature as a thinking thing: they accrue to the mind from its union with the body in a compounded substance.

III

But we are by no means ready to define the *we* who is benefited by the passions. True, we now see that the passions incite the mind to think, and to persist in thinking, a train of thought that is useful to the compound individual and to the body as a member of that union. But it turns out that some passions that are extremely useful to the body-as-a-member-of-the-compound are disruptive to the mind, while other passions that are highly functional for the mindful individual are only of minor utility to the body (PA, 137; AT XI, 429–432; HR I, 391–393). The utility and priority of a passion vary with the respective weighting of mind and body in their compound union. Hate, for instance, fear and anger are extremely useful to the body because they generate protective motions: for sheer survival these passions are more useful than the pleasant motions assured us by love and joy. But of course if the body is sitting on a hot stove while the mind is thinking deep mathematical thoughts, hate, fear, and grief are distractions from what is most useful to the mind as *mind*, and to the individual who thinks himself primarily as mind. For mind as scientific inquirer, wonder, joy, and self-esteem are far more useful. Only if the mind is already conceived as attached to the body and needing that body's well-being in order to get on with thinking are the negative passions useful to the mind; and only if the body is already conceived as attached to and identified by its connection with the mind are wonder and self-esteem and *generosité* useful to it. But this again forces the questions: "Who is the *we* so well served by the passions? How unified is that entity?" Because apparently conflicting perceptual ideas can be systematically integrated into the system of scientific ideas, their conflicts do not jeopardize the mind. But no such guarantee can be given for conflicting volitions engendered by apparently conflicting passions. "Flee the lion" counsels a train of thought generated by fear—the thought of a body-dominated individual. "Outwit and lure it away from the village" counsels a train of thought generated by self-esteem and *generosité*—the thought of a mind-dominated citizen-individual. Since passions are not representational ideas, and since they are cross-substantially predicated, caused by one substance and yet predicated of another, there can be no science of the passions, not even of the reductive kind available for perceptions. Because passions are only contingently associated with perceptions, their functional interconnections—their associations with perceptions—remain contingent. (And this is highly beneficial to us. Because passions are only contingently connected with their associated perceptions, it is possible to correct idiosyncratic and dysfunctional emotions originally formed by atypical experiences. It is possible to form new and stronger associations to replace the old, inappropriate ones.) Passions cannot secure a place for themselves in *proper* science by riding on the coattails of their contingent associations with perceptions. They are useful to the individual, but they are an embarrassment to the completeness of science, and possibly a threat to the unity of the mind.

Descartes was, of course, himself concerned about how conflicting passions that generate conflicting volitions might jeopardize the unity of the mind. And in fact it is precisely in the context of trying to explain the phenomena of *akrasia* that he affirms the unity of the soul (PA, 47–50; AT XI, 364–370; HR I, 353). His first move is quite simple: he denies that a conflict of passions in producing an appropriate volition is a conflict between the "upper" and the "lower" parts of the soul, between the will and the passion of desire (PA, 46–47). He proposes the solution that such conflicts involve a time lag between long-term and short-term judgments. The body's own automatic responses begin a set of motions that can conflict with the motions resulting from the chain of causes which also includes the contributions of the mind. Such counterbalancing motions produce the phenomenon of vacillation. But Descartes clearly recognizes that this solution—the standard Stoic solution to the problem of *akrasia*, which subsumes conflict under vacillation—is inadequate for cases of conflict between the priorities of joy and love and those of hate and anger, or between the counsels of fear and those of *generosité*, conflicts that arise from different weightings given to the body and to the mind in determining the welfare of the compound individual (PA, 137 and 139; AT XI, 429–432). After all, it is not enough to be assured that the individual is a compound union of mind and body: we need the formula for the compound, the weighting of the two contributors.

Interestingly enough, it is again in the passions that Descartes finds a clue to the solution of his problem. In Part III of the *Treatise on Passions of the Soul*, Descartes introduces a new set of passions: self-esteem, pride, self-satisfaction and, most significantly, *generosité*, respect for others grounded in proper self-esteem.[15] Although the immediate origins of these attitudes are intellectual, they function in the same way that passions and emotions do: they direct the association of ideas, providing the guiding principles that incline the will. Also called *habitudes*—stable dispositions to apply specific principles guiding the association of ideas—these attitudes have physical origins and physical effects.

Self-esteem has only one proper object and one proper ground: the mind's free will and its absolute power over its volitions. Like other passions, self-esteem incites the mind to persist in thinking certain useful thoughts. It focuses attention on what is essential to ourselves, the will's capacity to elicit ideas and to affirm or deny them. In concentrating attention on our essential properties, self-esteem promotes and incites the will's activity: its power to avoid errors by refraining from judging, to redirect disturbing passions by redirecting the mind's thoughts and, as we now see, its power to resolve apparent conflicts between passions by determining the respective weights of intellectual and bodily functions in the individual.

The power of the will over the passions is the same as its power over other confused ideas. While it cannot, solely by deciding, obliterate fear—any more than it can, by deciding, eradicate a particular perception or sensation (or, for that matter, an inclination to belief)—it can avoid the consequences of fear as it avoids making erroneous perceptual judgments. It can avoid affirming false judgments on the basis of passions, and it can elicit counterbalancing ideas. In an exuberant passage, Descartes says that there is no mind so weak that it

cannot avoid error, or so weak that it cannot strive to counterbalance
the turbulent passions when they are not useful to the mind by attending to ideas that redirect desires (PA, 50). If a mind is terrified at a
charging lion, and finds itself poised in a powerful desire to flee,
self-esteem can remind the will that it is not limited to affirming reflex
motions, that it has the power to countermand the fearful desire for
flight by calling forth a variety of ideas to countervail the passions it
receives from the body. So reminded, it is free to be a generous citizen
rather than a fearful fleer: the will can elicit ideas to fortify the *passion-
habitude* of courage. More to the point, the will, prompted by a *generosité* that opposes fear, can elicit safe stratagems to lure the lion
from the village.

All the passions generate a train of thought; all save wonder and
joy incline the will to form some sort of particular volition. Of course
the will is autonomous: it cannot be externally determined. But occasions—and particularly occasions of conflict—are useful incliners. As
conflicting priorities among the passions can generate an intellectual
inquiry by producing the passion of *admiration,* so conflicting priorities
among the passions can, with the help of self-esteem, awaken the
will to exercise its proper powers.

But of course this only gives us a rule or a formal solution to the
problem. What *should* the will will when fear counsels fleeing and
generosité counsels otherwise? It is unfortunately not true that the
welfare of the bodily weighted individual will always be served by
the welfare of the enlarged, or intellectually weighted, individual.
Citizens who die saving the village from a lion do not thrive, at any
rate not as citizen-individuals. There is an embarrassing slide in Descartes' account: the notion of functional self-maintenance is initially
rooted in the notion of the body as a self-regulating system. When
this notion is applied to the individual whose well-being is not wholly
defined by the well-being of the body, it is extended without clear
criteria for its application. Descartes allows that a pure-minded individual might indeed choose—and even properly choose—to follow
the counsel of *generosité* even at the risk of her bodily life. After all,
the mind can retreat to its immortality even if the individual cannot.
That the choice between the continuity of the embodied person and
the immortality of a mind-once-citizen is left to the power and centrality of the will is another instance of Descartes using the will as a *deus
ex machina factotum.* From this point of view, the unity of the mind
lies in the power and the unity of the will. It not only ensures the
mind's capacity for reflective correction of all kinds of error: it is also
crucial in affirming the unity of the mind and the body by its power

to elicit ideas, which then incline it to form volitions to serve the compound individual's long-term interests rather than the short-term interests of the body. Crucially, it also has the power to determine the weightings and priorities of the respective claims of mind and body in defining the welfare of their substantial union.

Descartes gives us at least one interesting example of how the will forms a compound entity, joining two individuals in a complex union. In his all too brief discussion of the distinctions between the passion of love, the *émotion interieure* of love, and intellectual love, he characterizes love as a heightened sense of well-being that incites the will to join itself freely to the objects it judges to be the cause of that well-being (PA, 79–83). The explanatory cause of the *émotion*, love, is not, as it is for primary passions, a present condition of the body, but a set of ideas about an object associated with heightened well-being. Although its origins lie in memory and the imagination, the emotion of love has the same consequences as the passion of love: it incites the will to join itself freely to form a compound with the objects that produce that sense of well-being. Intellectual love arises from a judgment rather than a fortuitous association of ideas, but it has the same effect: as a result of judging that an object is beneficial or good, the will decides to "affirm a new entity, a unity formed by previously distinct individuals." The usual range of the consequences of love—the associated passions of joy and desire, as well as an enlarged susceptibility to fear and grief—attach themselves to the emotion of love and to intellectual love as they do to the passion of love.[16]

Certainly Descartes' account of the will's power to form a new entity on the basis of a judgment of the benefits of such a union has its clearest application as an account of marriage and the formation of a political community. But the account can be generalized and, when generalized, it can serve as the model for the role of the will in determining the character of the compound individual, composed of two independent entities.

Why should the will affirm the unity of mind and body in the individual? What would be the grounds for such a judgment? The three varieties of passions help answer that question. Perceptions provide the soul with occasions for scientific inquiry; although they are not veridical, they help evaluate the scope of competing hypotheses. Bodily sensations provide information necessary for the passions to protect the individual's survival and to promote his health. The passions, especially wonder and joy, provide the impetus and the direction for thought. Without the passions to direct the principles of association, the mind would not be motivated to think one thing rather than another: it might just reproduce the *cogito* or some mathematical proof over and over. The passions introduce *value, utility*, and *importance*, as well as the criteria for benefit and harm.[17] Although they are not essential to the mind's thinking, they do indeed provide the life of the mind, and the benefits and harms that can affect it.

Of course the will does not create the compound individual, the union of mind and body, as it does, in a sense, create a new entity in affirming a marriage or a polity. Nevertheless, whenever the will must choose between a course of action that favors mind-oriented passions and one that favors bodily-oriented passions, it is implicitly choosing the weighted proportion of the contributions of the two substances in the compound. Furthermore, it must be possible for the will to form an *habitude*, a principle by which it determines its affirmations. And indeed, it is this that constitutes virtue: the will has affirmed a principle that forms a set of specific *habitudes*, settled habits of choice and action, that are capable of according the appropriate priority to mind-oriented or to bodily-oriented passions.[18]

We are now in a better position to see the central role that the will plays in Descartes' account of the powers and unity of the mind, and of its union with the body. Having initially introduced the will to affirm, deny, or suspend judgment, Descartes expands its functions: it has access to all the ideas of the understanding, including passions and bodily sensations; it combines ideas to form compound ideas; it selects ideas for focused attention; it initiates the process that retrieves memories; it initiates the measures that correct inappropriate passions by eliciting just the ideas which can produce an *émotion intérieure* capable of overcoming an inappropriate or harmful passion; its choices determine the weighting of mind and body in the compound individual. This heterogeneous list of functions is arbitrarily formed, extended in an ad hoc manner, as the exigencies of system construction seem to require.

Descartes glosses over a number of difficulties. The will requires a criterion for weighting the respective contributions and priorities of the mind and the body: it cannot itself provide that criterion. On the one hand, the will seems to require the understanding to determine appropriate volitions. Even though it functions independently, it is dependent on the understanding for its proper functioning. On the other hand, the will is both infinite and free, not determined in direction by any other power.

Descartes also ignores the difficulties of giving a unified account of the various functions of the will. In the first place, he suggests that the power of the will to correct inappropriate passion-ideas is on a par with its power to correct erroneous perceptions. But the suspension of action is not analogous to the suspension of belief; willing *not* to act involves performing some *other* action, or at least assenting to what would normally occur in the absence of intervention.

More seriously, however, the heterogeneity of the functions of the will raises further questions about the simple unity of the mind. Descartes assures us that the multiplicity of the mind's faculties does not affect its unity. We saw that if the immortality of the mind rests on the unity of its ideas—that is, on the systematic structure of necessary truths in a unified science—then Descartes' argument for immortality of the soul does not by itself secure the immortality of minds contingently individuated and distinguished by their passions. If the unity of the mind is assured by the unity of science, passions do not form part of that system: they are not absorbed into a strict science because they are only contingently connected with the mind's clear and distinct ideas.

It seems more reasonable to suppose that the unity of the will is an important guarantee of the unity of the mind. For one thing, such a view supports the orthodox doctrine that the character of a person's immortality is a function of the character and the purity of his will. For another, the will is infinite in scope, capable of affirming or denying every idea, including passions. Presumably passions are (contingently) part of the unified system of the mind because they are associated with perceptual ideas and because the will can affirm or deny them, modify or redirect them. But the functions of the will in controlling the passions go far beyond its functions in suspending judgment. When does a distinction between functions become a distinction between faculties? What would establish that the will is a simple unity, if its functions can be performed independently of one another? If the immortality of the mind rests on its unity, and its unity rests on the power and the unity of the will, Descartes' argument for immortality is incomplete until he accounts for the unification of the apparently heterogeneous functions of the will. While the unity of the will is not threatened by its assuring the power of judgment, and while that power is presupposed by its other functions, it is by no means clear that the strict unity of the will is preserved by such a heterogeneous extension of its powers.

Descartes might be forgiven for failing to give specific regulative directions to the will in unifying its theoretical and its practical functions. His enterprise attempts to reconcile and fuse two traditions, each with distinctive and conflicting attractions. There is, first, the tempting Platonism that his mathematical discoveries suggest: *Nous* contains the Formulae of Extension; individual minds have these formulae as their innate ideas; they can return to *Nous* and thus their proper immortality by scientific inquiry. Developing this view would move Descartes to construe the relation of mind to body as that of formal model to its instantiation.[19] The form is, of course, no longer infused with a teleological pull: it has become the mathematical formalism of Cartesian theoretical physics. In this view, ideas are representations of their formal causes. Following this line mutes the role of the will: it simply asserts, denies and, above all, reflexively refrains from judgment. The individual is a mind-embodied entity that can transcend its particularity. The lure of this view for Descartes is that it provides a powerful ontology for a unified, deductive, mathematical physics. That it also assures the immortality of the soul is no incidental benefit.

A second tradition pulls Descartes to the Enlightenment rationalism that emphasizes the independence and autonomy of the individual inquiring mind. Descartes' critique of authoritarian and dogmatic establishments attracts him to those aspects of Augustinian theory which centralize the autonomy of the will. But developing these strands of his thought leads him to attempt to make the will materially efficacious by integrating its activities into his mechanistic physiology. Following this line pulls him towards the beginning of a functionalist account of at least some thoughts: those which are characterized by their causal roles in the associational sequence. This strand in Descartes' thought clearly has its own internal tensions, tensions between an account of the will that emphasizes its autonomy, and those which emphasize it as the effective active mediator between the mind and the body, the link that unites the two in a single functional system. Even if we have reservations about Descartes' solutions, we can at least admire the bold ambition of his enterprise. Far from being a dogmatic dualist, Descartes suffers from an unexpected *generosité* in his respect for the conflicting traditions that his system attempts to reconcile.[20]

NOTES

1. Meditation VI:

Eodem modo, cum potu indigemus, quaedam inde oritur siccitas in guttere, nervos ejus movens & illorum ope cerebi interiora; hicque motus mentem afficit sensu sitis, quia nihil in toto hoc negotio nobis utilitus est scire, quam quod potu ad conservationem valetudinis egeamus. (AT VII, 88; HR I, 198)

2. "Nempe dubitans, intelligens, affirmans, negans, volens, nolens, imaginans quoque et sentiens" (AT VII, 28; HR I, 153).

3. L'usage de toutes les passions consiste en cela seul, qu'elles disposent l'âme a vouloir les choses que la nature dicte nous estre utile, et a persister en cette volonté comme aussi la mêsme agitation des ésprits, qui a coustume de les causer, dispose le corps aux movements qui serve a l'exécution de ces choses. (AT XI, 372; HR I, 358)

4. Descartes' criterion for the real, substantial distinction between mind and body echoes Suarez, *Disputationes Metaphysicae:* Disputatio VII (*de variis distinctionum generibus*), trans. C. V. Marquette (Milwaukee: University of Wisconsin Press, 1947) 16–36.

5. *Principles* I, 53: " . . . nous pouvons concevoir la chose qui pense sans imagination ou sans sentiment." Cf. also Meditation VI: AT VII, 73: "Ad haec considero istam vim imaginandi quae in me est, prout differt a vi intelligendi, ad mei ipsius, hoc est ad mentis meae essentiam non requiri; nam quamvis illa a me abesset, procul dubio manerem nihilominus ille idem qui nunc sum; unde sequi videtur illam ab aliqua re a me diversa pendere."

6. Descartes has at least two quite different reasons for wanting to assure the distinctness of individual minds. For once, the requirements of Christian orthodoxy coincide with his antiestablishment, antiauthoritarian views that any and every individual can initiate and validate inquiry.

7. Descartes uses *idea* in both a general and a narrow, or specific, sense. Generally, all thoughts (*cogitationes*), including volitions and passions as well as clear and distinct ideas, are called *ideae*. But sometimes the ideas of the pure intellect are contrasted with volitions, imagination, and passions. I shall use the term in its general sense. Similarly, *perceptiones* has a general and a more specific signification. Generally, all ideas are perceptions when they are objects of reflection: but, more specifically, they are perceptual sensations, as distinguished from both bodily sensations and from clear and distinct ideas. I shall use the term in its narrower signification. The class of *passions* includes all ideas caused in the mind by the action of the body: in this sense, perceptions and bodily sensations are passions. But I shall use the term in its narrower, or more specific, sense, as referring to the class of *émotion-passions* or *sentimens*.

8. In Meditation VI, Descartes classifies hunger, thirst, and pain together with those physiological conditions which involve avoiding harm and pursuing what is beneficial. This class includes some (but not all) bodily sensations and some (but not all) passion-emotions. It is contrasted with the class of intellectual ideas which includes both perceptual sensations and clear and distinct ideas (AT VII, 64–70; HR I, 192–198). In *Principles* IV, 190, however, Descartes distinguishes sensation (*sensum perceptiones, sensus*: the five external senses); appetites (*appetitus*) such as hunger and thirst; and passions (*affectus*). The passions are caused by the actions of the body, are felt as certain sorts of sentiments (*sensus*) as, for instance, a sense of joy. And they also produce *commotiones* specific to each passion. In the *Treatise on the Passions of the Soul,* the general class of passions (all ideas that are caused in the mind by the action of the body) is subdivided into perceptual sensations, bodily sensations,

and passions proper (PA, 23–25; AT XI, 346–347; HR I, 342–343). The differences in these classificatory schemes do not represent any major change in Descartes' views, save that he has become interested in dropping the Scholastic term *appetitus*, which carries connotations of a natural movement for species preservation incompatible with his mechanistic physiology. The differences in classification can be explained by the differences in contexts. In the *Meditations*, Descartes is primarily concerned with reestablishing the rough reliability of what nature and experience teach us. While the legitimation of sense perception is ensured by its absorption into pure science, the reinstatement of the promptings of thirst and fear must take another route. For this purpose, the differences between such bodily sensations as thirst and such passions as fear are irrelevant. In *Principles* IV, however, Descartes is presenting an account of human physiology: for these purposes, the distinctions between bodily sensations and passions are of no interest. It is only in the *Passions of the Soul* that Descartes turns his attention to the psychological distinctions between passions and bodily sensations; it is only there that it is important for him to distinguish their functional roles.

9. See the essays by Nancy Maull, John Schuster, and Stephen Gaukroger in *Descartes: Philosophy, Mathematics and Physics,* ed. S. Gaukroger (New York: Harvester Press: 1980). And also the articles by Harry Frankfurt, Daniel Garber, and Arthur Danto in *Descartes,* ed. Michael Hooker (Baltimore: Johns Hopkins University Press, 1978).

10. . . . quand nous parlons du corps d'un homme, nous . . . entendons toute la matière qui est ensemble unie avec l'âme de cet homme; en sorte que, bien que cette matière change . . . nous croyons que c'est le même corps . . . [et] . . . que ce corps est tout entier, pendants qu'il a en soi toutes les dispositions requises pour conserver cette union. (Letter to Mesland, 9 February 1645: AT IV, 166–167; Alquié III, 547; K, 156–157)

11. There seems to be a problem about Descartes' introducing a discussion of the *functions* of the passions, especially as he speaks of the passions as serving the preservation and health of the body, and the union of the mind and body. How can this be reconciled with his rejection of teleological explanation? (1) One possibility is that Descartes might have thought that a treatise on medicine, an essay on moral and psychological therapy, is exempt from the strictures set for pure science. But this solution undermines the unity of science: it raises problems about whether biology—which must, after all, be continuous with medicine—can be absorbed into physics. (2) The best solution would be to show that Cartesian functionalism is innocent of teleology, in much the same way that Spinozistic *conatus* is free of final causality. Cartesian functionalism only requires that there be some sections of Extension that, as it happens, are so organized that their parts are interrelated in such a way that they (happen to) preserve and maintain the continuity of that section of Extension over some period of time. Such a "thing" can be considered as a machine-organism: its parts do not maintain the functioning of the whole *for the sake of doing so;* rather their happening to do so is a by-product of the ways that the laws of motion operate in that region of Extension. In such cases, it

is possible to speak of a *whole* and to trace the functional roles of its parts in preserving and maintaining the machine-organism without violating the anti-teleological dictum.

12. There are, of course, problems about tracing the numerical identity of the machine-body of animals who are not supposed to have souls. Having initially identified the parts of human-machine-bodies by their functional contributions to the survival of the individual, Descartes would then identify those of animals by analogy. Such identifications are in any case quite rough: we are here working with confused ideas of common sense, without the hope of a strict science.

13. Cf. J. J. MacIntosh, "Perception and Imagination in Descartes, Boyle and Hooke." (Unpublished manuscript.)

14. . . . quand nous parlons d'un corps en général nous entendons une partie déterminée de la matière, . . . en sorte qu'on ne saurait . . . changer aucune particule de cette matière, que nous ne pensions pas après que le corps n'est plus totalement le même, ou *idem numero*. (Letter to Mesland, 9 February 1645: AT IV, 166–167; Alquié III, 547; K, 156–157)

15. The ancestor of *generosité* is *megalopsucheia;* its descendant is Kant's respect for the moral law and rational beings; the principle of charity is one of its contemporary forms.

16. This highly condensed and cryptic discussion raises many problems. There is, first, the apparent incoherence of the description: how can an individual love and choose to be committed to the welfare of a new entity of which "it" has become only a functional part? Furthermore, if there is an intellectual form of love, arising from a judgment, are there not intellectual forms of all the passions—not only intellectual joy but also intellectual desire and intellectual grief, all generated by judgments? Descartes seems to have opened the way to triplication: passions and their analogue emotions and intellectual emotions. Of course following this line of thought leads directly to Spinoza.

Descartes' distinction between the passions, the emotions, and the intellectual emotions reveals his Stoic inheritance: it is emotions rather than passions that are the "harm of this life." Because an *émotion* is not, as such, psychologically distinguishable from a passion, it may generate inappropriate volitions. An attentive mind, alert to the sources of its passions, can avoid acting on inappropriate *émotions*, generated by fictions. Yet it is the *émotions* that can constitute the good and ill of this life. For while acting from an emotion rather than from a passion can be inappropriate and even dangerous, it is through the evocation of *émotions* that the will can counteract the effects of passions it does not affirm. When the citizen wills to lure the lion away from the village, the will evokes a passion strong enough to countervail the effects of fear. But such passions (self-esteem, *generosité*, the thought of a possible shame or grief) are, strictly speaking, *émotions* or *habitudes:* their sources are ideas or general principles rather than immediate conditions of the body.

17. . . . les objets qui meuvent les sens n'excitent pas en nous diverses passions à raison de toutes les diversités qui sont en eux, mais seulement à raison des di-

verses façons qu'ils nous peuvent nuire ou profiter, or bien en général être impor-
tants; et que l'usage de toutes les passions consiste en cela seul qu'elles disposent
l'âme a vouloir les choses que la nature dicte nous être utiles. (PA, 52; Alquié, III
998; AT XI, 372)

18. Just as passions are identified by their characteristic bodily causes and
effects, as well as by the ideas with which they are characteristically associated,
so *habitudes* are identified and distinguished from several perspectives, by a
variety of functional roles. Because their immediate origins are intellectual,
and because they can be formed and strengthened by the will, they are
intellectual passions. Unlike intellectual love or intellectual joy, however,
they do not have corresponding bodily passions, and they are not characterized by any particular physical condition. Such *habitudes* as *generosité* and
estime de soi même can be both stronger and more general than individual
passions: they are dispositions to generate characteristic ideas, passions, and
associations of ideas. A person of *generosité* is directly inclined to apply the
principle of charity in interpreting the thoughts and actions of others, without
having to will to do so on each occasion. Because the cognitive component
of *habitudes* are general maxims or principles rather than particular ideas,
Descartes refers to virtues as *habitudes*. Yet despite the fact that *habitudes* are,
as their name suggests, dispositions, they can function in just the same way
that passions do, to produce associations of ideas that form and incline specific
volontés. It is not clear that Descartes can unite the various functional characterizations of *habitudes* as neatly as he manages to unite the physical and the
cognitive characterizations of the passions. But it would take an extended
study to determine whether Descartes has made an important discovery about
the relations between *habitudes, passions,* and principles or whether he is
glossing over a devastating difficulty.

19. Cf. my "Formal Traces in Cartesian Functional Explanation," *Canadian
Journal of Philosophy*, December 1984.

20. I am grateful to John Etchemendy and Martha Bolton for their comments
on earlier drafts of this essay. I also benefited from discussions at colloquia
at Brandeis, the University of Illinois at Chicago Circle, and at the University
of Wisconsin.

Contributors

Amélie Oksenberg Rorty is a professor of philosophy at Rutgers University

L. Aryeh Kosman is a professor of philosophy at Haverford College

Gary Hatfield is an assistant professor of philosophy at Johns Hopkins University

Daniel Garber is an associate professor of philosophy at the University of Chicago

Michael Williams is an associate professor of philosophy at Northwestern University

Gareth B. Matthews is a professor of philosophy at the University of Massachusetts

E. M. Curley is a professor of philosophy at the University of Illinois at Chicago Circle

Vere Chappell is a professor of philosophy at the University of Massachusetts

John P. Carriero is an assistant professor at the Massachusetts Institute of Technology

Calvin Normore is an associate professor of philosophy at the University of Toronto

Louis E. Loeb is an associate professor of philosophy at the University of Michigan

Geneviève Rodis-Lewis is a professor of philosophy at the University of Paris-Sorbonne

Jean-Luc Marion is a professor of philosophy at the University of Poitiers

Margaret D. Wilson is an associate professor of philosophy at Princeton University

Annette Baier is a professor of philosophy at the University of Pittsburgh

Martha Bolton is an associate professor of philosophy at Rutgers University

David M. Rosenthal is a professor of philosophy at the City University of New York

David R. Lachterman is an associate professor of philosophy at Vassar College

Hide Ishiguro is a professor of philosophy at Barnard College

Ruth Mattern is an associate professor at Rice University, currently studying medicine at Harvard University

Frederick F. Schmitt is an assistant professor of philosophy at the University of Illinois

Printed in the United Kingdom
by Lightning Source UK Ltd.
132649UK00001B/144/A